MICROECONOMICS

MICROECONOMICS

NINTH CANADIAN EDITION

Richard G. Lipsey
Simon Fraser University

Christopher T. S. Ragan
McGill University

Paul N. Courant
The University of Michigan

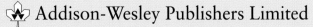 Addison-Wesley Publishers Limited

Don Mills, Ontario • Reading, Massachusetts
Menlo Park, California • New York • Wokingham, England
Amsterdam • Bonn • Sydney • Singapore • Tokyo • Madrid
San Juan • Paris • Seoul • Milan • Mexico City • Taipei

Senior Editor: Brian Henderson
Developmental Editor: Shirley Tessier
Project Coordination and Compositor: York Production Services
Text Designer: A Good Thing, Inc.
Cover Designer: Wycliff Smith Design
Cover Photo: © David Starrett
Art Studio: A Good Thing, Inc.
Senior Manufacturing Manager: Willie Lane
Printer and Binder: R. R. Donnelley & Sons Company
Cover Printer: The Lehigh Press, Inc.

MICROECONOMICS, Ninth Canadian Edition
Copyright © 1997 by Richard G. Lipsey, Christopher T. S. Ragan, and Paul N. Courant
Portions of this work were first published in the United Kingdom as
An Introduction to Positive Economics, © 1989 by Richard G. Lipsey.

ISBN 0-673-98359-5

Canadian Cataloguing in Publication Data

Lipsey, Richard G., 1928-
  Microeconomics

9th Canadian ed.
Includes index.

ISBN 0-673-98359-5

1. Microeconomics.   I. Ragan, Christopher.   II. Courant, Paul N.   III. Title.

HB172.L727   1997   338.5   C96-931262-8

345678910—DOW—0099

BRIEF CONTENTS

TO THE INSTRUCTOR

Economics is a living discipline, changing and evolving in response to developments in the world economy and in response to the research of many thousands of economists throughout the world. Through nine editions, *Economics* has evolved with the discipline. Our purpose in this edition, as in the previous eight, is to provide students with an introduction to the major issues facing the world's economies, to the methods that economists use to study those issues, and to the policy problems that those issues create. Our treatment is everywhere guided by three important principles:

1. Economics is *scientific,* in the sense that it progresses through the systematic confrontation of theory by evidence. Neither theory nor data alone can tell us much about the world, but combined they tell us a great deal.

2. Economics is *useful* and it should be seen by students to be so. An understanding of economic theory combined with knowledge about the economy produces many important insights about economic policy. Although we stress these insights, we are also careful to point out cases where too little is known to support strong statements about public policy. Appreciating what is not known is as important as learning what is known.

3. We strive always to be *honest* with our readers. Although we know that economics is not always easy, we do not approve of glossing over difficult bits of analysis without letting readers see what is happening and what has been assumed. We always take whatever space is needed to explain why economists draw their conclusions, rather than just asserting the conclusions. We also take pains to avoid simplifying matters so much that students would have to unlearn what they have been taught if they continue their study beyond the introductory course. In short, we have tried to follow Albert Einstein's advice: *Everything should be made as simple as possible, but not simpler.*

THE ECONOMIC ISSUES OF THE 1990S

In writing the ninth edition, we have tried to reflect the major economic issues of the last decade of the twentieth century.

GLOBALIZATION AND GROWTH

Enormous changes have occurred throughout the world over the last few decades. Flows of trade and investment between countries have risen so dramatically that it is now common to speak of the "globalization" of the world economy. Today it is no longer possible to study any economy without taking into account developments in the rest of the world.

What is true for most countries is also true for Canada. Economic relations between Canada and the rest of the world have a significant impact on most of the major "domestic" issues in the news. Here are three examples that we discuss, along with many others, in the ninth edition of *Economics.*

1. Throughout most of this century, Canadians, Americans, and Europeans have each regarded the policies that they adopted to support their farmers as strictly their own concern. Now, with the globalization of agricultural markets, what one country does to support its own agricultural sector impacts greatly on farmers in other countries. No longer is any one nation an island unto itself. Each nation's agricultural policies affect agricultural producers throughout the world and therefore concern all countries.

2. Throughout most of the twentieth century, successive generations of Canadians have found themselves, on average, substantially better off than their parents as a result of the nation's economic growth. Over the last two decades, however, this generation-by-generation advance has applied to only the top income levels; for the rest, average incomes are little higher, and sometimes lower, compared with the previous generation. Although some of the causes may be peculiar to the Canadian economy, many have to do with worldwide changes in technology and in patterns of international trade.

3. Over the past fifteen years, Canadians have worried about large government budget deficits. They wonder if the failure to balance the budget will lead to higher taxes in the future. Canadian firms worry about how the budget deficits affect domestic interest rates and the external value of the Canadian dollar, and about how their competitive positions in world markets will be affected.

THE TRIUMPH OF MARKET CAPITALISM

Since the 1980s, the century-long ideological conflict between capitalism and communism has virtually ended. The most powerful communist economy in the world, the Soviet Union, has disappeared, both as a nation and as a planned economy. Mixed capitalism, the system of economic organization that has long prevailed in much of the industrialized world, now prevails in virtually all of it. Many of the less-developed economies are also moving in this direction. The reasons for the failure of the planned economies of Eastern Europe are discussed in Chapter 1 as a contrast to the reasons for the relative success of mixed capitalism. The difficulties of transition to mixed capitalism are also discussed in Chapter 3.

DECLINING GROWTH IN MARKET ECONOMIES

At the same time that the once communist world of Eastern Europe has begun to establish free markets, the economies of western Europe, the United States, Japan, and Canada have experienced a marked reduction in economic growth.

In Canada, average real wages, which rose steadily from 1900 to 1970, have remained nearly constant since the mid 1970s. Over the lifetimes of you who are now using this book, in contrast to readers of our first edition, steadily rising personal incomes have been the exception rather than the rule. Issues raised by the changing growth performance in most advanced industrial countries are discussed frequently in this book.

A GLOBALIZED ECONOMICS TEXTBOOK

Economic growth and the implications of globalization are pressing issues of the day. Much of our study of economic principles and the Canadian economy has been shaped by these issues.

In Chapter 6, foreign trade provides an example of demand and supply in action. Our discussion of agricultural policy in Chapter 6 also has an international dimension. Foreign direct investment and transnational corporations are introduced along with imperfect competition in Chapter 12, and they receive detailed attention in many subsequent chapters, including Chapter 14 on the organization of firms. The newer method of "lean production" or "flexible manufacturing," first developed in Japan and now displacing the older mass-production techniques developed by Henry Ford, is discussed in Chapters 8, 12, and 14.

We treat international trade theory and trade policy in two chapters. Chapter 35 examines the basic theory of international trade. Chapter 36 provides a detailed discussion of policies that interfere with the free flow of international trade, and of trade-liberalizing arrangements such as the GATT and the North American Free Trade Agreement (NAFTA).

In addition to specific coverage of growth and internationally oriented topics, growth and globalization appear naturally throughout the book in the treatment of many topics once thought to be entirely "domestic."

MICROECONOMICS: STRUCTURE AND COVERAGE

Beginning Part 1, Chapter 1 introduces the issues of scarcity and choice and then briefly discusses alternative economic systems. The problems of converting command economies to market economies will be with us for some time, and comparisons with command economies help to establish what a market economy is *by showing what it is not*. We then survey a number of national and international trends to introduce students to many of the issues studied in detail later in the book. We end Chapter 1 with a discussion of the importance and role of economic policy. Chapter 2 makes the important distinction between positive and normative inquiries and goes on to an introductory discussion of the construction and testing of economic theories. Chapter 3 provides an overview of market economies, including a discussion of the important distinction between microeconomics and macroeconomics.

Part 2 deals with demand and supply. After introducing price determination and elasticity in Chapters 4 and 5, we apply these tools in Chapter 6. The case studies are designed to provide practice in applying the tools rather than a full coverage of each case.

Part 3 presents the foundations of demand and supply. The theory of consumer behaviour is developed via marginal utility theory in Chapter 7, which also provides an introduction to consumer surplus and an intuitive discussion of income and substitution effects. The Appendix to Chapter 7 covers indifference curves, budget lines, and the derivation of demand curves using indifference theory. Instructors' tastes differ greatly on how much demand theory is desirable in an introductory course, and the approach that we have taken in Chapter 7 allows the instructor to choose whether or not to use indifference curves without running into problems later in the book. (Further use of indifference curves is presented in appendices and optional boxes throughout the book.)

Chapter 8 introduces the firm as an institution and develops short-run costs. Chapter 9 covers long-run costs, the principle of substitution, and goes on to consider shifts in cost curves due to technological change. The latter topic is seldom if ever covered in the micro part of elementary textbooks, yet applied work on firms' responses to changing economic signals shows it to be extremely important. Although firms' short- and long-run responses matter, the response of their innovative activity is also highly significant. For example, a change in the wage rate, in capital costs, or in the exchange rate may cause firms to alter prices, outputs, and plans for capital expansion, but they will also cause firms to redirect their R&D expenditures. How firms choose to innovate their way out of unprofitable situations has come to be understood as a critical part of the microeconomic response to changes in market signals.

The first two chapters of Part 4, Chapters 10 and 11, present the standard theories of perfect competition and monopoly with some discussion of international cartels. Chapter 12 deals with monopolistic competition and oligopoly, which are the market structures most commonly found in Canadian industries. Strategic behaviour plays a central part in the analysis of this chapter.

The first half of Chapter 13 deals with the efficiency of competition and the inefficiency of monopoly. The last half of the chapter is largely concerned with competition policy. Part 5 begins in Chapter 15 by discussing the general principles of factor pricing and how factor prices are influenced by factor mobility. Chapter 16 then examines the operation of labour markets while Chapter 17 discusses capital and nonrenewable resources.

The first chapter of Part 6 (Chapter 18) provides a general discussion of market success and market failure, introduces social choice theory, and outlines the arguments for and against government intervention in a market economy. Chapter 19 deals with environmental and health and safety regulation. In addition to providing current applications of microeconomic theory to policy-making, it contains a boxed discussion of the U.S. experience with tradable emissions permits for sulphur dioxide. Chapter 20 analyzes taxes, public expenditure, and the main pillars of Canadian social policy. These three chapters expand on the basics of microeconomic analysis by providing current illustrations of the relevance of economic theory to contemporary policy situations.

The final part of *Microeconomics* focuses primarily on international economics. Chapter 35 gives the basic treatment of international trade, developing both the traditional theory of static comparative advantage and newer theories based on imperfect competition and dynamic comparative advantage. Chapter 36 discusses both the positive and normative aspects of trade policy, as well as the GATT and prospects for regional free-trade areas. There is also a detailed discussion of NAFTA and a box on Canada-U.S. trade disputes.

Strategic Behaviour

One of the most important advances in microeconomic analysis in recent years is the increased focus on strategic behaviour, including game theory and principal-agent analysis. In Chapter 12 we use elementary game theory in our discussion of competition among oligopolies. In Chapter 14 we introduce the principal-agent problem in the context of the market for corporate control. In Chapter 18 we discuss asymmetric information as a source of market failure.

Chapter 14 deals with the market for corporate control. A discussion of takeovers and mergers leads naturally to a brief consideration of why firms may and may not maximize their profits, since the possibility that existing management is not maximizing profits is widely viewed as an important motive for takeovers.

In all of these cases our approach is to introduce strategic behaviour when it is appropriate to the topic under discussion.

Economic Policy

Most chapters of the book contain some discussion of economic policy. We have two main goals in mind in these discussions:

1. We aim to give students practice in using economic theory, because applying theory is both a wonderfully effective teaching method and a reliable test of students' grasp of theory.

2. We want to introduce students to the major policy issues of the day.

Both goals reflect our view that students should see economics as useful in helping us to understand and deal with the world around us.

We hope you find this menu both attractive and challenging; and we hope students find the material stimulating and enlightening. Many of the messages of economics are complex—if economic understanding were only a matter of common sense and simple observation, there would be no need for professional economists and no need for textbooks like this one. To understand economics, one must work hard. Working at this book should help readers gain a better understanding of the world around them and of the policy problems faced by all levels of government. Furthermore, in today's globalized world, the return to education is large. We like to think that we have contributed in some small part to the understanding that increased investment in human capital by the next generation is necessary to restore incomes to the rapid growth paths that so benefited our parents and our peers. Perhaps we may even contribute to some income-enhancing accumulation of human capital by some of our readers.

CHANGES TO THIS EDITION

We have done a major revision and update of the entire text with guidance from an extensive series of reviews and feedback from both users and nonusers of the previous editions of this book. As always, we have strived very hard to improve the teachability and readability of the book. Toward this goal, the revised text has been "test read" by a person *who is not an economics instructor* to locate difficult passages and confusing explanations and examples. This process led to the rewriting or considerable revision of many passages in the text; we are confident that students will have fewer difficulties with this edition.

OVERALL FORMAT

In addition to the usual tasks of rewriting and updating for the new edition, there are some changes to what might be called the "format" of the book. Here are some of the highlights.

Part Openers.   Each part of the book (eleven in all) now begins with a brief description of what topics are covered in the part. There are a number of questions which we pose, not only to kindle the students' interest, but also to give them some indication of the type of questions they will be able to answer after successfully working through the material. In some cases, the questions are quite general; but in many cases the questions relate to specific examples that are covered within the following chapters.

Use of Colour Passages.   We have reduced the use of colour passages in the text. Our view was that in order for these passages to have the most impact on the student, we had to be more selective in their use. We also thought that having fewer colour passages would improve the flow of the argument.

Footnotes.   Wherever possible, we have tried to shorten or eliminate footnotes, while at the same time making sure that we are not glossing over important details. We hope this makes the presentation of the central ideas less choppy.

Boxes.   In this edition, we have added many new boxes and dropped many old ones (there are 24 new boxes). We have also differentiated the ways in which we use boxes in the text. All boxes are optional, and thus the student is able to skip all boxes without losing any *central economic principles*. The student's understanding of economics, however, will naturally be deeper if the material in the boxes is not skipped. In this edition, boxes are coded as one of two types.

1. *Applications* are meant to show economics in action, providing examples of how theoretical material relates to issues of current interest.

2. *Extensions* are designed to provide a deeper and more detailed treatment of a topic that is discussed in the text.

Chapter Summaries.   In this edition, we have introduced a new format for our chapter summaries. The main section headings from the chapter now appear in the summaries, with the summary points organized appropriately. Making this change revealed to us that in previous editions we had not covered all parts of the chapter in the summary, and thus we have added many new summary points to fill these gaps. These revised and expanded summaries should be a very useful study tool for students.

End-of-Chapter Questions.   We have updated and added to the list of questions at the end of each chapter. The answers to these questions are found in the Instructor's Manual (which is available for free to all adopters).

Mathematical Notes.   Mathematical notes are collected in a separate section at the end of the book. Since mathematical notation and derivation is not necessary to understand the principles of economics but is helpful in more advanced work, this seems to be a sensible arrangement. Mathematical notes provide clues to the uses of mathematics for the increasing number of students who have some background in math, without loading the text with notes that are unnecessary and are a put-off to other readers.

Glossary.   The glossary at the end of the book offers definitions of the terms that are used in boldface in the text. In addition, the glossary includes some commonly used terms that are not printed in boldface in the text because they are not, strictly speaking, technical terms.

Time Line of Great Economists.   New to this edition, we have constructed a time line which runs from the mid 1700s to the middle of this century. Along this time line we have placed brief descriptions of the life and works of some great economists, most of whom the students encounter in the textbook. So that the students have a better appreciation of *when* these economists did their work, the time line also lists some major world events. We hope this will improve the students' sense of history and their sense of who these great economists are. The time line is located at the back of the book, immediately following the glossary.

CHANGES IN MICROECONOMICS

Here is a brief description of the major changes to *Microeconomics*.

Part 1 The Nature of Economics

- Chapter 1 has a new discussion of why opportunity cost changes along the production possibility boundary and there is a new box on the opportunity cost of a university education. There is a new final section in the chapter discussing the importance of economic policy.

- Chapter 2 has a new section on economic models, discussing the various ways in which economists use the term "model," and connecting model building to the process of developing and testing theories. In the appendix there is a clarified discussion of the difference between cross-sectional and time-series data.

- In Chapter 3, the box on comparative advantage has been completely rewritten. It now shows what happens when specialization occurs in the "wrong direction." There is also a new box on the difficulties involved in converting from command economies to market economies.

Part 2 An Introduction to Demand and Supply

- Chapter 4, which introduces the concepts of demand and supply, has a reworked discussion of what causes shifts in demand and supply curves. The existing box on "what really happens" has new examples of weather-generated demand and supply shocks. (The old appendix on foreign trade has been moved to Chapter 6.)

- In Chapter 5, the old box on the use of averages for computing elasticities has now been integrated into the text. In an effort to reduce the dryness of this chapter, we have added a new final section that presents "two examples where elasticity matters." This section examines the issue of tax incidence and the distinction between short-run and long-run elasticities.

- Chapter 6 has been substantially redesigned. It begins with a general discussion of government-controlled prices. It then goes on to examine the case of rent controls (this discussion has been extensively rewritten), agricultural policy, and foreign trade and tariffs. Each of these three applications can be covered independently. The chapter then ends with a section on "four lessons about resource allocation" which generalizes the specific lessons learned throughout the chapter.

Part 3 Consumption, Production, and Cost

- Chapter 7 has been completely rewritten. We now lay out the basic theory of consumer demand using marginal utility theory. This has proved to be the most accessible to students. Indifference curve analysis is now presented in the appendix. The more formal approach is thus still available to those instructors who prefer it. Consumer surplus, income and substitution effects, and the total-marginal distinction, all of which we view as key concepts, are developed in the text of Chapter 7.

- Chapter 8 is now the first chapter in the theory of the firm. It combines definitional material (economic profit, opportunity cost) with the analysis of cost and production in the short run. We have added a new box which presents a glossary of the different short-run cost concepts.

- Chapter 9 examines the firm in the long run and the very-long run. We have rewritten the discussion of the profit-maximizing factor mix. There is also a new box on Jacob Viner's famous error. The appendix develops the long-run cost model via the use of isoquants and isocost curves.

Part 4 Pricing and Market Structure

- Chapter 10, which examines perfect competition, is unchanged in its basic structure. The box which contrasts the firm's and the industry's demand elasticity has been rewritten. We have also rewritten the discussion of entry and exit and the conditions required for long-run equilibrium.

- In the discussion of monopoly in Chapter 11, there is a new box on "fashion knockoffs" as an example of how technilogical change has lowered entry barriers.

- Chapter 12 has been retitled to reflect its added emphasis on strategic behaviour. The first section has been completely rewritten and now better motivates both the discussion of monopolistic competition and oligopoly. There is a new box on the prisoner's dilemma, and the discussion of strategic behaviour has been recast to emphasize game theory.

- In Chapter 13, we have tried to emphasize that allocative efficiency is a property of an *economy* rather than just a single industry. We have also made some clarifying changes in the discussion of marginal-cost and average-cost pricing. There is a new box on the pricing policies of the provincial hydro authorities.

- Chapter 14 combines institutional material from Chapter 9 of the previous edition with a streamlined discussion of the market for corporate control and the behaviour of foreign direct investment. We have added some data on the flows of inward- and outward-bound foreign investment since 1960.

Part 5 The Markets for Factors of Production

- In Chapter 15, the section on "the demand for factors" has been substantially reworked, emphasizing the distinction between the physical and revenue aspects of marginal revenue product. The section on "policy issues" now concludes with an examination of data on Canadian interprovincial labour mobility. This should emphasize the importance of the chapter's main theme of factor mobility.

- Chapter 16 now begins with a discussion of the conditions required to have a single wage in the labour market. The chapter then examines violations of these conditions. The discussion of wage differentials now leads to a new box on the puzzle of interindustry wage differentials in Canada. The section on labour unions has been substantially reworked, and a discussion of the union wage premium has been added. The final section presents the "good jobs—bad jobs" debate.

- Chapter 17 discusses the pricing of capital and non-renewable resources. The discussion on present value has been clarified. A new box has been added on inflation and the distinction between nominal and real interest rates. The section of the equilibrium interest rate has been substantially reworked.

Part 6 Government Policy in the Market Economy

- In Chapter 18 we now make a very clear distinction between what we call the "formal" and the "informal" defences of free markets. The section on externalities has been completely rewritten and now ends with a new example of the Coase theorem. There is a new box on the Atlantic fishery illustrating the Tragedy of the Commons. The existing box on the "lemons problem" has been moved to this chapter to complement the discussion on information asymmetries.

- Chapter 19 examines environmental and safety regulation. The discussion on pollution regulation is now complemented with a new box on the U.S. experience with tradable emissions permits for sulphur dioxide.

- Chapter 20 examines government taxation and expenditure, and is the merger of Chapters 22 and 23 from the previous edition. It has also been extensively rewritten. The discussion on equity and efficiency of the tax system now leads to a new box on the negative income tax. There are considerable changes in the discussion of fiscal federalism. The final section of the chapter examines what we call the five pillars of Canadian social policy—education, health care, income support, unemployment insurance, and retirement support.

Part 11 International Economics

- Chapter 35 examines the theory of international trade. The section on the sources of comparative advantage now contains a discussion of acquired comparative advantage. The box on the gains from trade has been changed to apply to an economy with a concave production possibilities boundary. In the final section, we have added data on Canada's terms of trade.

- Chapter 36, which discusses trade policy, has been substantially rewritten. In addition to thorough discussions of the theoretical arguments for and against free trade, there is an extensive discussion of the GATT, the formation of the WTO and the creation of NAFTA. There is a new discussion of trade creation and trade diversion. There is also a new box on Canada-U.S. trade disputes which discusses the cases of softwood lumber, supply-managed agricultural products, and cultural industries.

SUPPLEMENTS TO THE TEXTBOOK

There are several products to accompany *Micro-economics,* either for the student or for the instructor.

Study Guide. Our book is accompanied by a Study Guide, written by Kenneth Grant and William Furlong. The Study Guide can be used either in the classroom or by the students on their own. It offers additional study support and essential reinforcement for each text chapter, including chapter overviews, objectives, multiple-choice questions, exercises, short problems, and answers. It is available in one- or two-volume editions.

Instructor's Manual. Prepared by us, the Instructor's Manual includes an explanation of the approach used in each text chapter, along with a chapter overview, answers to all end-of-chapter questions, and additional teaching suggestions.

Test Bank. The Test Bank to accompany *Micro-economics* has been completely overhauled by Ingrid Kristjanson-Ragan and Christopher Ragan. Approximately one-third of the questions in each chapter have been replaced by new questions. Many others have been revised or corrected. The questions are now organized within each chapter according to topic, which should make it easier for the instructor to select questions. We have also added two new levels of difficulty for questions. Each question was previously coded as either Difficulty 1, 2, or 3. These categories still exist (though we have in many cases reclassified the difficulty of the question). Difficulty 4 now pertains *only* to questions that are based on material found in the appendices. Difficulty 5 now pertains *only* to material found in the boxes. This is in keeping with our general approach that boxes and appendices are optional.

The Test Bank is free to adopters. It is now available in a new computerized version utilizing Brownstone's Diploma software, and in an updated version (Version 2.1) of TestGen-EQ.

Transparencies. For this edition, over 100 illustrations from 18 key theory chapters are reproduced as four-colour transparency acetates. These are available free to adopters.

Software. Also available with this text is a student software package. It contains an interactive tutorial with multi-coloured graphs and exercises to help your students learn key material from 15 chapters. Interactive learning can make it much easier to absorb graphically presented concepts. The student software also offers a self-test program which asks questions about any text chapter, and scores results.

ACKNOWLEDGMENTS

The starting point for this book was *Economics,* Eleventh Edition, by Richard G. Lipsey and Paul N. Courant. It would be impossible to acknowledge here all the teachers, colleagues, and students who contributed to that book. Hundreds of users have written to us with specific suggested improvements, and much of the credit for the fact that the book does become more and more teachable belongs to them. We can no longer list them individually but we thank them all most sincerely.

Ian Christensen provided research assistance for which we are thankful. A number of individuals provided reviews of the eighth Canadian edition that were most helpful in preparing the present edition. At a later stage, we were also aided by the comments from several reviewers of the revised manuscript. These people are:

Steve Ambler
(*Université du Québec à Montréal*)

David Andolfatto
(*University of Waterloo*)

Robert Cherneff
(*University of Victoria*)

David Cox
(*University of Waterloo*)

Kieran Furlong
(*University of Toronto*)

Irwin Gillespie
(*Carleton University*)

David Gray
(*University of Ottawa*)

Michael Hare
(*University of Toronto*)

Ibrahim Hayani
(*Seneca College*)

Cheryl Jenkins
(*John Abbott College*)

David Johnson
(*Wilfrid Laurier University*)

Colin Jones
(*University of Victoria*)

Marion Jones
(*University of Regina*)

Ian King
(*University of Victoria*)

George Kondor
(*Lakehead University*)

Irwin Lipnowski
(*University of Manitoba*)

Bill Morrison
(*Wilfrid Laurier University*)

A. Gyasi Nimarko
(*Vanier College*)

Sonja Novkovic
(*Saint Mary's University*)

Arnold Paus-Jenssen
(*University of Saskatchewan*)

Balbir S. Sahni
(*Concordia University*)

Brian Scarfe
(*University of Regina*)

George Slasor
(*University of Toronto*)

Brenda Spotton
(*York University*)

Weiqiu Yu
(*University of New Brunswick*).

We thank them all for their contribution to improving this textbook.

In addition, the following people reviewed the supplements that accompany this book: Study Guide—Peter Tsigaris (University College of the Cariboo), David Gray (University of Ottawa), Keith MacKinnon (York University), Eva Lau (University of Waterloo), Suki Badh (Doublas University College); Test Bank—Peter Kantrowitz (Douglas University College).

Our special thanks goes to Ingrid Kristjanson-Ragan, who closely read the entire manuscript and provided excellent comments and suggestions for improving some of the most difficult passages. She also helped tremendously with the biographical sketches of the economists for the timeline at the back of the book. For her diligence and hard work we are especially grateful.

Richard G. Lipsey
Christopher T. S. Ragan
Paul N. Courant

TO THE STUDENT

A good course in economics will give you insight into how an economy functions and into some currently debated policy issues. Like all rewarding subjects, economics will not be mastered without effort. A book on economics must be worked at. It cannot be read like a novel.

Each of you must develop an individual technique for studying, but the following suggestions may prove helpful. It is usually a good idea to read a chapter quickly in order to get the general run of the argument. At this first reading, you may want to skip the boxes and any footnotes. Then, after reading the Chapter Summary and the Key Concepts (both at the end of each chapter), reread the chapter more slowly, making sure that you understand each step of the argument.

With respect to the figures and tables, be sure you understand how the conclusions that are stated in the brief tag lines with each table or figure have been reached. You must not skip the captions. They provide the core of economic reasoning. You should be prepared to spend time on difficult sections; occasionally, you may spend an hour on only a few pages. Paper and pencil are indispensable equipment in your reading. It is best to follow a difficult argument by building your own diagram while the argument unfolds rather than by relying on the finished diagram as it appears in the book. It is often helpful to invent numerical examples to illustrate general propositions.

The end-of-chapter questions require you to apply what you have studied. We advise you to outline answers to some of the questions. In short, you should seek to understand economics, not to memorize it.

We call your attention to the glossary at the end of the book, beginning on page G-1. Any time that you encounter a concept that seems vaguely familiar but is not clear to you, check the glossary. Chances are that it will be there and that its definition will remind you of what you once understood. If you are still in doubt, check the index entry to find where the concept is discussed more fully. Incidentally, the glossary, along with the captions that accompany figures and tables and the end-of-chapter summaries, may prove to be very helpful when you are reviewing for examinations.

The bracketed boldface numbers in the text itself refer to a series of mathematical notes that are found starting on page M-1 at the end of the book. For those of you who like mathematics or prefer mathematical argument to verbal or geometric exposition, these may prove useful. Others may ignore them.

There is also a time line of great economists, located at the back of the book, immediately following the Glossary. While reading the textbook, you will encounter the names of many great economists that have shaped the way modern-day economists think. But in the text we usually do not have the space to say more than a few words about these economists. The time line at the back of the book offers a more complete (but still brief) description of the life and works of many of these great economists. They are placed on a time line that begins in the mid 1700s and continues through the middle of this century. On this time line are also placed major world events, so that you will be better able to appreciate the world in which these economists lived when they were developing their thoughts. Our hope is that your sense of history and your sense of the origins of economics will be enhanced by glancing through this time line. Do so at your leisure!

We strongly suggest you make use of the excellent Study Guide written expressly for this text: It will test and reinforce your understanding of the concepts and analytical techniques stressed in each chapter of the text and will help prepare you for your examinations. The ability to solve problems and to communicate and interpret your results are important goals in an introductory course in economics. The Study Guide can play an important role in your acquisition of these skills.

We hope you will find the book rewarding and stimulating. Students who used earlier editions made some of the most helpful suggestions for revision, and we hope that you will carry on the tradition. If you are moved to write to us (and we hope that you will be!), please do. You can send any comments or questions regarding the text (or any of the supplementary material, such as the Study Guide) to:

Christopher Ragan
Department of Economics
McGill University
855 Sherbrooke St. West
Montreal, Quebec
H3A 2T7

Or, if you prefer to communicate through E-mail, send your comments to:

ragan@leacock.lan.mcgill.ca

PART ONE

THE NATURE OF ECONOMICS

What is economics all about? How will the study of economics help you to understand how modern economies function, and how modern economies differ from the economies of the past? Why does it appear that economists seldom agree on anything among themselves, or is this only an illusion? What makes some economic theories more sensible than others? What is the difference between microeconomics and macroeconomics, and is one more important than the other? These are questions that you will be able to answer after reading the following three chapters.

Chapter 1 introduces you to the concepts of *scarcity, choice, and opportunity cost;* each is central to understanding any economic system. You will then learn about various types of economic systems, ranging from the primarily *command economies* of the former Soviet Union to the primarily *market economies* of Canada, the United States, or Japan. This chapter also discusses the importance of *economic policy,* and emphasizes that *trade offs* between various policy goals are inevitable, and are often the source of disagreements about what constitutes the "best" policy.

Chapter 2 discusses the study of economics itself. You are introduced to the distinction between *positive statements* and *normative statements,* a distinction upon which the progress of economics as a social science is based. We then examine the role of *theory* in economics, and we explain why economists—like physicists or chemists—build *models* to help them think about the complex world they are trying to understand. Finally, you will learn about the way economists *test* their theories by confronting the *predictions* of their theories with the *evidence* drawn from the real world.

Chapter 3 presents a broad outline of the way market economies function. You are first shown how economies developed from ones in which all individuals were largely self sufficient to modern economies in which *specialization* and *trade* play a crucial role. You then meet the economy's main cast of characters—*households, firms, and governments.* Like characters in a play need the props and the lighting, you will see that a modern economy needs *markets* and *institutions* in order to operate smoothly. Finally, we examine the two separate but complementary ways of viewing the economy—*microeconomics* and *macroeconomics.* The questions and the emphasis differ markedly between the two, but we need both to understand the whole economy.

CHAPTER 1

THE ECONOMIC PROBLEM

Turn on the TV news, read your local newspaper or *The Globe and Mail*, glance at *Maclean's* or *The Economist* magazines and you will see for yourself that many of the world's most pressing problems are economic.

Why did communism fail to deliver acceptable living standards to the citizens of the countries of Eastern Europe and the republics of the former USSR? Why is the transition from communism to markets proving so difficult for many of these countries? Are the developed nations right in making the adoption of more market-oriented economic policies a precondition of increased foreign aid to the less-developed countries of the world? What is the impact of the growth of vast transnational corporations that conduct business over much of the world? Will the growth of mouths to feed outrun the growth of food to feed those mouths? Are economists right in arguing that environmental protection is often best accomplished using market incentives rather than direct government intervention?

Your media survey of press, radio, and TV will also show the importance of economic issues in the problems facing Canada today.

How is it that when the average Canadian citizen enjoys one of the highest living standards the world has ever seen, a standard vastly higher than has been achieved by most of the people who have ever lived on the earth, many Canadians are living below the so-called "poverty line" and worrying about how to feed their children? Should Canada feel threatened by Japanese economic power, or by the emerging economic power of the countries known as the "Asian Tigers"? Has the North American Free Trade Agreement (NAFTA) been a good or bad thing for the average Canadian? Why are so many large and established companies engaged in re-engineering (often a euphemism for downsizing, which in turn is a euphemism for laying workers off), and what does this imply for people's job prospects?

Does the size of the Federal government's budget deficit affect the average Canadian's living standards? Is the Bank of Canada right in believing that a low inflation rate is good for the country? Why has labour productivity in Canada and most other developed countries grown more slowly in the past two decades than through most of this century? Does it pay you to go on to higher education? Does it pay the nation to subsidize you to do so?

Of course, not all the world's problems are primarily economic. Political, biological, social, cultural, and philosophical issues often predominate. However, as the following examples suggest, no matter how noneconomic a particular problem may seem, it will almost always have a significant economic dimension.

1. The crises that lead to wars often have economic roots. Nations often fight for oil and rice and land to live on, even when the rhetoric of their leaders evokes God, glory, and nation.

2. It took 100,000 years, from the time *Homo sapiens* first appeared on earth until the year 1800, for the human population to reach 1 billion. In the next 100 years, a second billion was added. Three billion more came in the next 80 years. The world's population is predicted to reach 10 billion by the middle of the twenty-first century. The economic consequences are steady pressures on the environment and the food supply. Unless the human race can find ways to deal with these pressures, increasing millions of people face starvation, and increasing billions face rising levels of environmental degradation.

3. *Global warming* describes the possibility of a gradual warming of the earth's climate due to a cumulative buildup of carbon dioxide (CO_2) in the atmosphere. If the possibility proves a reality, the warming will have significant economic consequences, changing both production possibilities and consumption patterns.

WHAT IS ECONOMICS?

We have mentioned a handful of important current issues on which economics can shed some light. One way to define *economics* is to say that it is the social science that deals with such problems. A better known definition comes from the great economist Alfred Marshall (1842–1924), whom we will encounter at several points in this book: "Economics is a study of mankind in the ordinary business of life." A more penetrating definition is the following:

Economics is the study of the use of scarce resources to satisfy unlimited human wants.

Scarcity is inevitable and is central to economic problems. What are society's resources? Why is scarcity inevitable? What are the consequences of scarcity?

RESOURCES AND PRODUCTS

A society's resources consist of natural endowments such as land, forests, and minerals; human resources, both mental and physical; and manufactured aids to production such as tools, machinery, and buildings. Economists call such resources **factors of production**[1] because they are used to produce the outputs that people desire. We divide these outputs into goods and services. **Goods** are tangible (e.g., cars and shoes), and **services** are intangible (e.g., haircuts and education). Notice the implication of positive value contained in the terms *goods* and *services*. (Compare the terms *bads* and *disservices*.)

People use goods and services to satisfy many of their wants. The act of making them is called **production,** and the act of using them to satisfy wants is called **consumption.** Goods are valued for the services they provide. An automobile, for example, helps to satisfy its owner's desires for transportation, mobility, and possibly status.

SCARCITY

For most of the world's 6 billion people, scarcity is real and ever present. In relation to desires (for more and better food, clothing, housing, schooling, entertainment, and so forth), existing resources are woefully inadequate; there are enough to produce only a small fraction of the goods and services that are wanted.

But are not the advanced industrialized nations rich enough that scarcity is nearly banished? After all, they have been characterized as affluent societies. Whatever affluence may mean, it does not mean the end of the problem of scarcity. Most households that earn $80,000 per year (a princely amount by world standards) have no trouble spending it on things that seem useful to them. Yet it would take nearly twice the present output of the Canadian economy to produce enough to allow all Canadian households to earn that amount.

CHOICE

Because resources are scarce, all societies face the problem of deciding what to produce and how much each person will consume. Societies differ in who makes the choices and how they are made, but the need to choose is common to all. Just as scarcity implies the need for choice, so choice implies the existence of cost. A decision to have more of something requires a decision to have less of something else. The less of "something else" can be thought of as the cost of having the more of "something."

Scarcity implies that choices must be made, and making choices implies the existence of costs.

Opportunity Cost

To see how choice implies cost, we look first at a trivial example and then at one that vitally affects all of us; both examples involve precisely the same fundamental principles.

Consider the choice that must be made by a young girl who has 50 cents to spend and who is determined to spend it all on candy. For the child, there are only two kinds of candy in the world: gumdrops, which sell for 5 cents each, and chocolates, which sell for 10 cents each. The child would like to buy 10 gumdrops and 10 chocolates but soon discovers that this is not possible: It is not an *attainable combination* given the scarce resources available. However, several combinations are attainable: 8 gumdrops and 1 chocolate, 4 gumdrops and 3 chocolates, 2 gumdrops and 4 chocolates, and so on. Some of these combinations leave money unspent, and the child is not interested in them. Only six combinations, as shown in Figure 1-1, are both attainable and use the entire 50 cents.

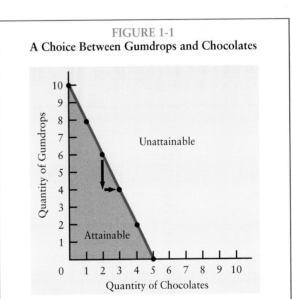

FIGURE 1-1
A Choice Between Gumdrops and Chocolates

A limited amount of money forces a choice among alternatives. Six combinations of gumdrops and chocolates are attainable and use all of the child's money. The negatively sloped line provides a boundary between attainable and unattainable combinations. The arrows show that the opportunity cost of 1 more chocolate is 2 gumdrops.

---

[1]Definitions of the terms in boldface can be found in the glossary at the back of the book.

| APPLICATION 1-1 |

THE OPPORTUNITY COST OF YOUR UNIVERSITY DEGREE

As discussed in the text, the opportunity cost of choosing one thing is what must be given up as *the best alternative*. Computing the opportunity cost of a college or university education is a good example to illustrate which factors are included (and which are excluded) from the computation of opportunity cost. You may also be surprised to learn how expensive your university degree really is!*

Suppose that a Bachelor's degree requires four years of study and that each year you spend $2,500 for tuition fees—approximately the average at Canadian universities in 1996—and a further $1,000 per year for books and materials. Does this mean that the cost of a university education is only $14,000? Unfortunately not; the true cost of a university degree is much higher.

The key point is that the opportunity cost of a university education does not just include the out-of-

pocket expenses on tuition and books. You must also take into consideration *what you are forced to give up* by choosing to attend university. Of course, if you were not studying you could have been doing any one of a number of things, but the relevant one is *the one you would have chosen instead*—your best alternative to attending university.

Suppose that your best alternative to attending university was to get a job. In this case, the opportunity cost of your university degree must include the earnings that you would have received had you taken that job. Suppose that your (after-tax) annual earnings would have been $18,000 per year, for a total of $72,000 if you stayed at that job for four years. To the direct expenses of $14,000, we must therefore add $72,000 for the earnings that you gave up by not taking a job. This brings the true cost of your university degree—the opportunity cost—up to $86,000!

Notice that the cost of food, lodging, clothing, and other living expenses did not enter the calculation of the opportunity cost in this example. This is because living expenses must be incurred in either case—whether you attend university or get a job. Of course, it is possible that your total living ex-

---

* This box considers only the cost *to the student* of a university degree. For reasons that will be discussed in detail in Part 6 of this book, the government heavily subsidizes post-secondary education in Canada. Because of this subsidy, the cost *to society* of a university degree may be quite different from the cost to an individual student.

After careful thought, the child has almost decided to buy 6 gumdrops and 2 chocolates, but at the last moment she decides that she simply must have 3 chocolates. What will it cost to get this extra chocolate? One answer is 2 gumdrops. As seen in the figure, this is the number of gumdrops the child must forgo to get the extra chocolate. Economists describe the 2 gumdrops as the *opportunity cost* of the third chocolate.

Another answer is that the cost of the third chocolate is 10 cents. However, given the child's budget and her intentions, this answer is less revealing than the first one. Though the real choice is between more of this and more of that, the cost of "this" is usefully viewed in terms of what one cannot have of "that."

The idea of opportunity cost is one of the central insights of economics. Here is a precise definition. The **opportunity cost** of using resources for a certain purpose is defined to be *the benefit given up by not using them in the best alternative way*. That is, it is the cost measured in terms of other goods and services that could have been obtained instead. If, for example, resources that could have produced 20 miles of road are used instead to produce two small hospitals, the opportunity cost of a hospital is 10 miles of road; looked at the other way round, the opportunity cost of 1 mile of road is one-tenth of a hospital.

Every time a choice is made, opportunity costs are incurred.

penses as a student are different from what they would have been had you taken the job. In this case, the calculation of opportunity cost would need to be adjusted. For example, perhaps the job you would have taken *required* you to spend $3,000 for clothes so that you could look presentable to customers. In contrast, you find that your university classmates and professors are pretty relaxed about fashion and that your old jeans are perfectly adequate. In this case, the opportunity cost of your university degree would be only $83,000 because by attending university you "saved" $3,000 that you otherwise would have had to spend on clothes.

Notice also that the higher is your earning potential in a job, the higher is the opportunity cost of attending university. For example, if your best alternative to attending university was to get a job that paid $25,000 per year (instead of $18,000), the opportunity cost of your degree rises from $86,000 to $114,000. When your earning potential is high, the opportunity cost of getting a degree is high because you are giving up a lot to go to university. The reverse is also true; when high school graduates can only expect low-

paying jobs, or when the prospects of getting any job is poor (when the unemployment rate is high), the opportunity cost of attending university is lower. This suggests that university enrollments should be higher during periods of high unemployment, and this is indeed the case in Canada.

If the opportunity cost of a university degree is so high, why do students choose to go to university? The simple answer is that they believe that they are better off by going to university than by not going (otherwise they would not go!). Maybe the students simply enjoy learning, and thus are prepared to incur the high cost to be in the university environment. Or maybe they believe that a university degree will significantly increase their future earning potential. In this case, they are giving up four years of earnings at one salary so that they can invest in their own skills in the hopes of enjoying many more years in the future at a considerably higher salary.

Whatever the case, the recognition that a university degree is very expensive should convince students to make the best use of their time while they are there. Read on!

See Application 1-1 for an example of opportunity cost which should seem quite familiar to you—the opportunity cost of getting a university degree.

Production Possibilities

Although the choice between gumdrops and chocolates is a minor consumption decision, the essential nature of the decision is the same whatever the choice being made. Consider, for example, the important choice between producing military and civilian goods.

If resources are fully employed, it is not possible to have more of both. However, as the govern-

ment cuts defence production, resources needed to produce civilian goods will be freed up. The opportunity cost of increased civilian goods is therefore the forgone military output. (Or, if we were considering an increase in military output, the opportunity cost of military output would be the foregone civilian goods.)

The choice is illustrated in Figure 1-2. Because resources are limited, some combinations—those that would require more than the total available supply of resources for their production—cannot be attained. The negatively sloped curve on the graph divides the combinations that can be attained from those that cannot. Points above and to the right of this curve cannot be attained because there are not enough resources; points below and to the left of the curve can be attained without using all of the available resources; and points on the curve can just be attained if all the available resources are used. The curve is called the **production possibility boundary** or **production possibility curve**. It has a negative slope because when all resources are being used, producing more of one kind of good requires producing less of the other kind.

A production possibility boundary illustrates three concepts: scarcity, choice, and opportunity cost. Scarcity is indicated by the unattainable combinations above the boundary; choice, by the need to choose among the alternative attainable points along the boundary; and opportunity cost, by the negative slope of the boundary.

The shape of the production possibility boundary in Figure 1-2 implies that an increasing amount of civilian production must be given up to achieve equal successive increases in military production. This shape, referred to as *concave* to the origin, indicates that the opportunity cost of either good grows larger and larger

as we increase the amount of it that is produced. A straight-line boundary, as in Figure 1-1, indicates that the opportunity cost of one good in terms of the other stays constant, no matter how much of it is produced.

The concave shape in Figure 1-2 occurs because each factor of production is not equally useful in producing all goods. To see why differences among factors of production are so important, consider beginning at a point where all resources are devoted to the production of military goods, and then consider gradually shifting more and more resources toward the production of civilian goods. The first resources you shift might be, just to take an example, nutrient-rich land that is particularly well-suited to growing wheat. This land may not be very useful for making military equipment, but it is very useful for making certain civilian goods (like bread). This shift of resources will therefore lead to a very small reduction in military ouptut, but a substantial increase in civilian output. Thus the opportunity cost of producing the first unit of civilian goods, which is equal to the foregone military output, is very small. But as we shift more and more resources toward the production of civilian goods, we must shift more and more resources that are actually quite well suited to the production of military output, like airplane mechanics or the minerals needed to make gunpowder. This implies that as we produce more and more civilian goods (by having more and more resources devoted to producing them), the amount of military output that must be foregone to produce one *extra* unit of civilian goods rises. That is, the opportunity cost of producing one good rises as more of that good is produced.

FOUR KEY ECONOMIC PROBLEMS

Modern economies involve thousands of complex production and consumption activities. While this complexity is important, many of the basic kinds of decisions that must be made are not very different from those made in primitive economies in which people work with few tools and barter with their neighbours. Whatever the economic system, most problems studied by economists can be grouped under four main headings.

What Is Produced and How?

The allocation of scarce resources among alternative uses, called **resource allocation**, determines the quan-

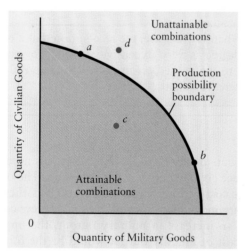

FIGURE 1-2
A Production Possibility Boundary

The negatively sloped boundary shows the combinations that are just attainable when all of the society's resources are efficiently employed. The production possibility boundary separates the attainable combinations of goods, such as *a*, *b*, and *c*, from unattainable combinations, such as *d*. Points *a* and *b* represent full and efficient use of society's resources. Point *c* represents either inefficient use of resources or failure to use all the available resources.

tities of various goods that are produced. What determines which goods get produced? Choosing to produce a particular combination of goods means choosing a particular allocation of resources among the industries or regions producing the goods.

Further, because resources are scarce, it is desirable that they be used efficiently. Hence it matters which of the available methods of production is used to produce each of the goods. What determines which methods of production get used and which ones do not?

In terms of Figure 1-2, these questions relate to where the economy will produce. Will the economy be inside the production possibility boundary because resources are used inefficiently? If resources are used efficiently, then at which point on the boundary will production take place?

What Is Consumed and by Whom?

What is the relationship between an economy's production of goods and the consumption enjoyed by its citizens? Economists seek to understand what determines the distribution of a nation's total output among its people. Who gets a lot, who gets a little, and why?

If production takes place on the production possibility boundary, then how about consumption? Will the economy consume exactly the same goods as it produces? Or will the country's ability to trade with other countries permit the economy to consume a different combination of goods?

Questions relating to what is produced and how, and what is consumed and by whom, fall within the realm of microeconomics. Microeconomics is the study of the allocation of resources as it is affected by the workings of the price system and government policies that seek to influence it.

Why are Resources Sometimes Idle?

When an economy is in a recession, many workers who would like to have jobs are unable to find employers to hire them. At the same time, the managers and owners of offices and factories would like to operate at a higher level of activity—that is, they would like to produce more goods and services. Similarly, during recessions raw materials are typically available in abundance. For some reason, however, these resources—labour, factories and equipment, and raw materials—are idle. In terms of Figure 1-2, this means that the economy is operating within its production possibility boundary.

Why are resources sometimes idle? Should governments worry about such idle resources, or is there some reason to believe that such occasional idleness is appropriate in a well-functioning economy? Is there anything that the government could do to reduce such idleness?

Is Productive Capacity Growing?

The capacity to produce goods and services grows rapidly in some countries, expands slowly in others, and actually declines in others. Growth in productive capacity can be represented by an outward shift of the production possibility boundary, as shown in Figure 1-3. If an economy's capacity to produce goods and services is growing, combinations that are unattainable today will become attainable tomorrow. Growth makes it possible to have more of all goods. What are the determinants of growth? Can governments do anything to increase economic growth?

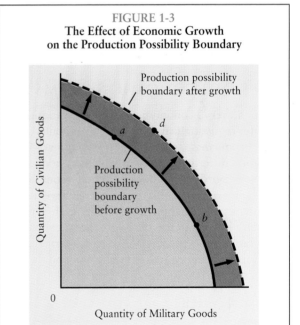

FIGURE 1-3
The Effect of Economic Growth on the Production Possibility Boundary

Economic growth shifts the boundary outward and makes it possible to produce more of all products. Before growth in productive capacity, points *a* and *b* were on the production possibility boundary and point *d* was an unattainable combination. After growth, as shown by the dark shaded band, point *d* and many other previously unattainable combinations are attainable.

Questions relating to the idleness of resources during recessions, and the growth of productive capacity, fall within the realm of macroeconomics. Macroeconomics is the study of the determination of economic aggregates such as total output, total employment, the price level, and the rate of economic growth.

ALTERNATIVE ECONOMIC SYSTEMS

An economic system is a distinctive method of providing answers to the basic economic questions just discussed. All such systems are complex. They include producers of every sort—public and private, domestic and foreign. They include consumers of every sort—young and old, rich and poor, working and nonworking. They include laws—such as those relating to property rights—rules, regulations, taxes, subsidies, and everything else that governments use to influence what is produced, how it is produced, and who gets it. They also include customs of every conceivable kind and the entire range of contemporary mores and values.

TYPES OF ECONOMIC SYSTEMS

Although every economy is in some ways unique, it is helpful to distinguish three pure types, called *traditional, command,* and *market* economies. These economies differ in the way in which economic decisions are coordinated. But no actual economy fits neatly into one of these three categories—all real economies contain some elements of each type. Of particular interest in the 1990s are the so-called *transition economies,* notably those of Eastern Europe, which are moving away from the command form toward a market orientation.

Traditional Systems

A traditional economic system is one in which behaviour is based primarily on tradition, custom, and habit. Young men follow their fathers' occupations. Women do what their mothers did. There is little change in the pattern of goods produced from year to year, other than those imposed by the vagaries of nature. The techniques of production also follow traditional patterns, except when the effects of an occasional new invention are felt. Finally, production is allocated among the members according to long-established traditions. In short, the answers to the economic questions of what to produce, how to produce, and how to distribute are determined by traditions.

Such a system works best in an unchanging environment. Under static conditions, a system that does not continually require people to make choices can prove effective in meeting economic and social needs.

Traditional systems were common in earlier times. The feudal system, under which most people in medieval Europe lived, was a largely traditional society. Peasants, artisans, and most others living in villages inherited their positions in that society. They also usually inherited their specific jobs, which they handled in traditional ways. For example, the blacksmith made customary charges for dealing with horses brought to him, and it would have been unthinkable for him to decline his services to any villager who requested them.

Today, only a few small, isolated, self-sufficient communities still retain mainly traditional systems. Examples can be found in the Canadian Arctic and in Patagonia. Also, in many less-developed countries, significant aspects of economic behaviour are still governed by traditional patterns.

Command Systems

In command systems, economic behaviour is determined by some central authority, usually the government, which makes most of the necessary decisions on what to produce, how to produce it, and who gets it. Such economies are characterized by the *centralization* of decision making. Because centralized decision makers usually lay down elaborate and complex plans for the behaviour that they wish to impose, the terms **command economy** and **centrally planned economy** are usually used synonymously.

The sheer quantity of data required for central planning of an entire economy is enormous, and the task of analyzing it to produce a fully integrated plan can hardly be exaggerated. Moreover, the plan must be continually changing to take account not only of current data but also of future trends in labour supplies, technological developments, and people's tastes for various goods and services. Doing so involves the planners in *forecasting.* This is a notoriously difficult exercise, not least because of the unavailability of all essential, accurate, and up-to-date information.

A decade ago, more than one third of the world's population lived in countries that relied heavily on central planning to deal with the basic economic questions. Today, the number of such countries is small. Even in countries where planning is the proclaimed system, as in China or Cuba, increasing amounts of market determination are being quietly permitted.

Market Systems

In the third type of economic system, the decisions about resource allocation are made without any central direction. Instead, they result from innumerable independent decisions made by individual producers and consumers. Such a system is known as a **free-market economy** or, more simply, a **market economy.** In such an economy, decisions relating to the basic economic issues are *decentralized*. Despite the absence of a central plan, these many decentralized decisions are nonetheless coordinated. The main coordinating device is the set of market-determined prices—which is why free-market systems are often called *price systems*. Because much of this book is devoted to studying how market systems work, little more needs to be said about them at this point.

Mixed Systems

Economies that are fully traditional or fully centrally controlled or wholly free-market are pure types that are useful for studying basic principles. When we look in detail at any real economy, however, we discover that its economic behaviour is the result of some mixture of central control and market determination, with a certain amount of traditional behaviour as well. In practice, every economy is a **mixed economy** in the sense that it combines significant elements of all three systems in determining economic behaviour.[2] Furthermore, within any economy, the degree of the mix will vary from sector to sector. For example, in some planned economies, the command principle was used more often to determine behaviour in heavy-goods industries, such as steel, than in agriculture. Farmers were often given substantial freedom to produce and sell what they wished in response to varying market prices.

When we speak of a particular economy as being centrally planned, we mean only that the degree of the mix is weighted heavily toward the command principle. When we speak of one as being a market economy, we mean only that the degree of the mix is weighted heavily toward decentralized decision making in response to market signals. It is important to

realize that such distinctions are always matters of degree and that almost every conceivable mix can be found across the spectrum of the world's economies.

Although no country offers an example of either system working alone, some economies, such as those of Canada, the United States, France, and Singapore, rely much more heavily on market decisions than others, such as the economies of China, North Korea, and Cuba. Yet even in Canada, the command principle has some sway. Crown corporations, legislated minimum wages, rules and regulations for environmental protection, quotas on some agricultural outputs, and restrictions on the import of items such as textiles and shoes are the obvious examples.

OWNERSHIP OF RESOURCES

We have seen that economies differ as to the principle used for coordinating their economic decisions. They also differ as to *who owns* their productive resources. Who owns a nation's farms and factories, its coal mines and forests? Who owns its railways, streams, and golf courses? Who owns its houses and hotels?

In a private-ownership economy, the basic raw materials, the productive assets of the society, and the goods produced in the economy are predominantly privately owned. By this standard, Canada has primarily a private-ownership economy. However, even in Canada, public ownership extends beyond the usual basic services such as schools and local transportation systems to include such other activities as housing projects, forest and range land, and electric power utilities.

In contrast, a public-ownership economy is one in which the productive assets are predominantly publicly owned. This was true of the former USSR, and it is true to a significant extent in present-day China. In China, however, private ownership exists in many sectors, including the rapidly-growing part of the manufacturing sector that is foreign owned, mainly by Japanese and by Chinese from Taiwan, Hong Kong, and Singapore.

The Coordination-Ownership Mix

Leaving aside tradition because it is not the predominant coordinating method in any modern market economy, there are four possible combinations of coordination and ownership principles. Of the two most common combinations, the first is the private-ownership market economy, in which the market principle is the main coordinating mechanism and most productive assets are privately owned. The second most common combination during the twen-

---

[2]Although tradition influences behaviour in all societies, we shall have little to say about it in the rest of this chapter because we are primarily interested in the consequences of making economic decisions through the market and command principles.

APPLICATION 1-2

THE FAILURE OF CENTRAL PLANNING

In 1989, communism collapsed throughout Central and Eastern Europe, and the economic systems of formerly communist countries began the transition from centrally planned to market economies. (See Application 3-3 in Chapter 3 for further discussion of these transitions.) Although political issues surely played a role in these events, the economic changes generally confirmed the superiority of a market-oriented price system over central planning as a method of organizing economic activity. The failure of central planning had many causes, but four were particularly significant.

THE FAILURE OF COORDINATION

In centrally planned economies, a body of planners tries to coordinate all the economic decisions about production, investment, trade, and consumption that are likely to be made by producers and consumers throughout the country. Without the use of prices to signal relative scarcity and abundance, central planning generally proved impossible to do with any reasonable degree of success. Bottlenecks in production, shortages of some goods, and gluts of others plagued the Soviet economy for decades. For example, for years there was an ample supply of black-and-white television sets but severe shortages of toilet paper and soap. In 1989, much of a bumper harvest rotted due to shortages of storage and transportation facilities.

FAILURE OF QUALITY CONTROL

Central planners can monitor the number of units produced by any factory and reward plants that exceed their production targets and punish ones that fall short. Factory managers operating under these conditions will meet their quotas by whatever means are available, and once the goods pass out of their factory, what happens to them is someone else's headache.

In market economies, poor quality is punished by low sales, and retailers soon give a signal to factory managers by shifting their purchases to other suppliers. The incentives that obviously flow from such private-sector purchasing discretion are generally absent from command economies, where purchases and sales are planned centrally and prices and profits are not used to signal customer satisfaction or dissatisfaction.

Not surprisingly, very few Eastern European manufactured products were able to stand up to the newly permitted competition from superior goods produced in the advanced market societies.

MISPLACED INCENTIVES

In market economies, relative wages and salaries provide incentives for labour to move from place to place, and the possibility of losing one's job provides an incentive to work diligently. This is a harsh mechanism that punishes losers with loss of income (although social programs provide floors to the amount of economic punishment that can be suffered). In planned economies, workers usually have complete job secu-

tieth century has been the public-ownership planned economy, in which central planning is the primary means of coordinating economic decisions and property is primarily publicly owned.

The two other possible combinations are a market economy in which the resources are publicly owned, and a command economy in which the resources are privately owned. No modern economy has operated under either hybrid type. Nazi Germany from 1932 to 1945 went some way toward combining private own-

ership with the command principle. The United Kingdom from 1945 to 1980 went quite a way toward a public-ownership market economy in that many industries and much housing were publicly owned. On balance, however, Germany and the United Kingdom were still best described as private-ownership market economies. (The United Kingdom's privatization program in the 1980s returned most publicly-owned assets to private ownership, firmly placing that country back in the ranks of private-ownership market economies.)

rity. Industrial unemployment is rare, and even when it does occur, new jobs are usually found for all who lose theirs. Although the high level of security is attractive to many people, it proved impossible to provide sufficient incentives for reasonably hard and efficient work under such conditions. In the words of Oxford historian Timothy Garton Ash, who wrote eyewitness chronicles of the developments in Eastern Europe from 1980 to 1990, the social contract between the workers and the government in the Eastern countries was "We pretend to work, and you pretend to pay us."

Because of the absence of a work-oriented incentive system, income inequalities do not provide the normal free-market incentives. Income inequalities were used instead to provide incentives for party members to toe the line. The major gap in income standards was between party members (in positions of power) on the one hand and non-members on the other. The former had access to such privileges as special stores where imported goods were available, special hospitals providing sanitary and efficient medical care, and special resorts where good vacations could be enjoyed. Non-members had none of these things.

ENVIRONMENTAL DEGRADATION

Fulfilling production plans became the all-embracing goal in planned economies, to the exclusion of most other considerations, including the environment. As a result, environmental degradation occurred in all the countries of Eastern Europe on a scale unknown in ad-

vanced Western nations. A particularly disturbing example occurred in central Asia where high quotas for cotton output led to indiscriminate use of pesticides and irrigation. Birth defects are now found in nearly one child in three, and the vast Aral Sea has been half drained, causing major environmental effects.

This failure to protect the environment stemmed from the pressure to fulfill production plans and the absence of a "political marketplace" where citizens could express their preferences for the environment versus economic gain. Imperfect though the system may be in democratic market economies—and in some particular cases it has been quite poor—their record of environmental protection has been vastly better than that of the command economies.

THE PRICE SYSTEM

In contrast to the failures of command economies, the performance of the free-market price system is impressive. One theme of this book is *market success:* how the price system works to coordinate with relative efficiency the decentralized decisions made by private consumers and producers, providing the right quantities of relatively high-quality outputs and incentives for efficient work. It is important, however, not to conclude that doing things better means doing things perfectly. Another theme of this book is *market failure:* how and why the unaided price system sometimes fails to produce efficient results and fails to take account of social values that cannot be expressed through the marketplace.

COMMAND VERSUS MARKET DETERMINATION

For over a century, a great debate raged on the relative merits of the command principle versus the market principle for coordinating economic decisions in practice. The former Soviet Union, the countries of Eastern Europe, and China were command economies for much of this century. Canada, the United States, and most of the countries of Western Europe were, and still are, primarily market economies. The successes of the

Soviet Union and China in the early stages of industrialization suggested to many observers that the command principle was at least as good for organizing economic behaviour as the market principle, if not better. Over the long run, however, planned economies proved a failure of such disastrous proportions that they seriously depressed the living standards of their citizens.

Rarely in human history has such a decisive verdict been delivered on two competing systems. Application 1-2 gives some of the reasons why central planning was a failure in Eastern Europe and the former Soviet Union. The discussion is of more than purely historical interest because the reasons for the failure of central planning give insight into the reasons for the relative success of market economies. The current and recent problems of the Eastern European economies also show that markets do not simply happen—rather, they need to be supported by a complex set of institutions, customs, and rules, all of which are currently being developed in Eastern Europe. We discuss the progress of these Eastern European *transition economies* in some detail in Chapter 3.

Still Room for Disagreement

The failure of centrally planned economies suggests the superiority of decentralized markets over centrally planned ones as mechanisms for allocating an economy's scarce resources. Put another way, it demonstrates the superiority of mixed economies with substantial elements of market determination over fully planned command economies. However, it does *not* demonstrate, as some observers have asserted, the superiority of completely free-market economies over mixed economies.

There is no guarantee that completely free markets will, on their own, handle such urgent matters as controlling pollution or providing public goods (like national defence). Indeed, as we shall see in later chapters, much economic theory is devoted to explaining why free markets often fail to do these things. Mixed economies, with significant elements of government intervention, are needed to do these jobs.

Furthermore, acceptance of the free market over central planning does not provide an excuse to ignore a country's pressing social issues. Acceptance of the benefits of the free market still leaves plenty of scope to debate the kinds, amounts, and directions of government interventions into the workings of our market-based economy that will help to achieve social goals.

It follows that there is still considerable room for disagreement about the degree of the mix of market and government determination in any modern mixed economy—room enough to accommodate such divergent views as could be expressed by conservative, liberal, and modern social democratic parties. People can accept the free market as an efficient way of organizing economic affairs and still disagree about

many things. A partial list includes the optimal amount and types of government regulation of various parts of the economy; the types of measures needed to protect the environment; whether health care should be provided by the public or the private sector; and the optimal amount and design of social services and other policies intended to redistribute income from more to less fortunate citizens.

ASPECTS OF A MODERN ECONOMY

Throughout this book, we study the functioning of a modern, market-based, mixed economy such as is found in Canada today. By way of introduction, this section introduces a few salient aspects that should be kept in mind from the outset.

ORIGINS

The modern market economies that we know today first arose in Europe out of the ashes of the feudal system. As we have already mentioned, the feudal system was a traditional one in which people did jobs based on heredity (the miller's son became the next generation's miller) and received shares of their village's total output based on custom. Peasants were tied to the land. Much land was owned by the crown and granted to the lord of the manor in return for military services. Some of it was made available for the common use of all villagers. Property such as the village mill and blacksmith's shop never belonged to the people who worked there and therefore could never be bought and sold by them.

In contrast, modern economies are based on market transactions between people who voluntarily decide whether or not to engage in them. They have the right to buy and sell what they wish, to accept or refuse offered work, and to move where they want when they want. Key institutions are *private property* and *freedom of contract*, both of which must be maintained by active government policies. The government creates laws of ownership and contract and then provides courts to enforce these laws. It is precisely these sorts of institutions that the transition economies of Eastern Europe did not have when their command systems broke down in the late

1980s. Successful transition to fully developed market economies depends on the development of such institutions, which has so far proved more difficult than many economists had anticipated.

LIVING STANDARDS

The material living standards of any society depend on how much it can consume of various goods and services. What is available to consume, however, depends on what is produced. If the productive capacity of a society is small, the living standards of its typical citizen will be low. Only by raising that productive capacity can average living standards be raised. No society can generate increased real consumption merely by voting its citizens higher money incomes.

How much a society can produce depends on how many of that society's factors of production are employed to produce things and on the productivity of those factors. Labour is perhaps the single most important factor of production. How well has the Canadian economy performed with respect to the employment and the productivity of its labour?

Employment

In spite of some short-term ups and downs, the trend of total employment has been upward over most of modern Canadian history. For example, in 1975 there were just over 9.5 million Canadians employed, whereas in 1995 the figure was almost 13.5 million. This is a net creation of almost 4 million new jobs, a 42 percent increase over that 20-year period.

These new jobs provided employment for a rising labour force. The number of people over the age of 15 who were in the labour force (either working or looking for work) increased from about 10.2 million in 1975 to just over 15 million in 1995. This 47 percent increase in the labour force reflects not only an increase in the population, but also a five percentage point increase in the labour-force participation rate (the fraction of the population in the labour force).

This overall increase in both the level of employment and the size of the labour force, however, does not reveal some important changes in the *composition* of the labour force. In particular, the share of women in the labour force (and in total employment) has increased markedly over the past 20 years. Women accounted for 37 percent of the labour force in 1975; by 1995, women made up 45 percent of the Canadian labour force.

Labour Productivity

Labour productivity refers to the amount produced per hour of work. Rising living standards are closely linked to the rising productivity of the typical worker. If each worker produces more, then (other things being equal) there will be more production in total and hence more for each person to consume on average.

From 1750 to 1900, the market economies in Europe and North America became industrial economies. With industrialization, modern market economies have raised ordinary people out of poverty by raising productivity at rates that appear slow from year to year but have dramatic effects on living standards when sustained over long periods of time.

> Over a year, or even over a decade, the economic gains [of the late eighteenth and the nineteenth centuries], after allowing for the growth of population, were so little noticeable that it was widely believed that the gains were experienced only by the rich, and not by the poor. Only as the West's compounded growth continued through the twentieth century did its breadth become clear. It became obvious that Western working classes were increasingly well off and that the Western middle classes were prospering and growing as a proportion of the whole population. Not that poverty disappeared. The West's achievement was not the abolition of poverty but the reduction of its incidence from 90 percent of the population to 30 percent, 20 percent, or less, depending on the country and one's definition of poverty.[3]

Figure 1-4 shows the rise in the productivity of Canadian labour from 1946 to 1995. In spite of many short-term variations, the general trend is unmistakably upward. Every hour worked has produced more and more total output during the entire course of this half century. Over the period shown in the figure, labour productivity doubled and then doubled again. As a result, each person produces four times as much now as he or she did in 1946. The basis of our rising living standards is our ability to produce more and more as time passes. This comes not only from technological im-

---

[3]N. Rosenberg and L. E. Birdzell Jr., *How the West Grew Rich* (New York: Basic Books, 1986).

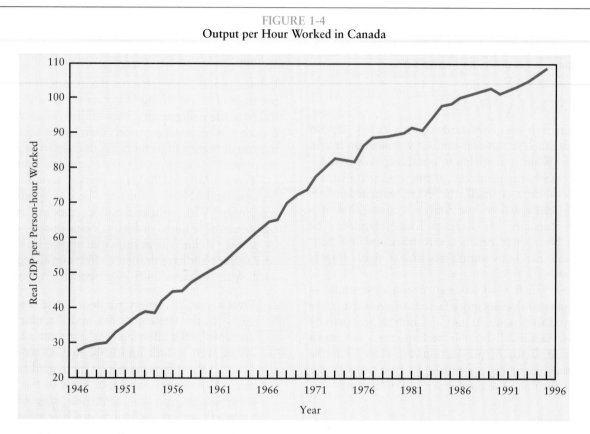

FIGURE 1-4
Output per Hour Worked in Canada

Output per hour worked in Canada has increased four-fold since 1946. The graph is based on a measure of total output in Canada (the GDP) divided by the total number of hours worked by the Canadian labour force. The data are expressed as a percentage of the value of the output per hour worked in 1986 (1986 is therefore shown as 100). The steady rise in outout per hour, which is the basis for rising living standards, is quite apparent. So also is the slowdown in the growth rate of output per hour that began in the mid 1970s.

Source: Statistics Canada, 15-204.

provements, but also from increases in the average skill of the labour force.

These are potent sources of increases in living standards. Over the long period of rising productivity, Canadian citizens (as well as the citizens of most industrial countries) got used to each generation being substantially better off than each preceding generation. In the period from 1938 to 1974, individuals whose income relative to their contemporaries was the same as their parents' could expect to earn about *twice the real income* their parents had enjoyed.

In the mid 1970s, this productivity growth slowed substantially. By the mid 1990s, the typical individual 25 years younger than his or her parents could expect to be *no more than 30 percent better off* than his or her parents were at the same age. This is a remarkable reduction in the rate that each gener-

ation is becoming wealthier. Over long periods of time, however, even 1 percent productivity growth is still a potent force for change, because it doubles real output per worker about every 72 years, or about one human lifetime. (A helpful device is the *rule of 72:* Divide 72 by the annual growth rate, and the result is approximately the number of years required for income to double.) [1][4]

Distribution of Income

Not only has the rate of increase in aggregate income slowed dramatically in recent years, but the way in

_____

[4]Notes giving mathematical demonstrations of the concepts presented in the text are designated by reference numbers. These notes can be found at the back of the book, beginning on page M-1.

which that income is distributed among the various income groups has also altered.

Some of the most dramatic shifts have occurred in the United States. Incomes became progressively more equally distributed up through the 1960s. In the 1970s, the trend reversed, and ever since the distribution of income has slowly become more unequal. For example, the share of income received by the lowest 20 percent in the U.S. income distribution rose from 5.0 percent in 1947 to 5.7 percent in 1968, then fell to 4.4 percent in 1992. That is a 20 percent decrease in the share of total income going to the poorest group over a 25-year period. At the other end of the U.S. income distribution, the share of income going to the richest 20 percent fell from 43.0 percent in 1947 to 40.5 percent in 1968, then rose to 44.6 percent by 1992. That is close to a 10 percent increase in the share of total income going to the richest group in the society.

Though similar changes have been observed in several advanced industrial economies, it is interesting that Canadian data do not show this turnaround. Instead, inequalities in income have continued to narrow right up to the middle of the 1990s. For example, the poorest 20 percent of families received only 2.8 percent of total income in 1967; by 1993 the same group earned 6.7 percent of total income. While they are still poor by our standards, they did more than double their share of an increasing total of the nation's income. In contrast, the richest 20 percent of families received 46.3 percent of the nation's total income in 1967; by 1993, their share had fallen to 39.9 percent.

The difference between Canada and the United States appears to be largely due to the different effectiveness of the tax-and-transfer systems in the two countries—that is, the systems whereby resources are transfered from high-income to low-income families. The *pre-tax* distribution of income over the past several years has been very similar in the two countries, but the stronger presence of taxes and transfers in Canada has resulted in reduced *after-tax* income inequality over the same period in which (after-tax) income inequality has been increasing in the United States.

ONGOING CHANGE

The growth in incomes over the centuries since market economies first arose has been accompanied by continual technological change. Our technologies are our ways of doing things. New ways of making old things, and new things to make, are continually being invented and brought into use. These technological changes make labour more productive, and they are constantly changing the nature of our economy. Old jobs are destroyed and new jobs are created as the technological structure slowly evolves.

Job Structure

Figure 1-5 shows the change in industrial structure of Canadian employment since the end of the last century. The most dramatic changes are associated with the decline of jobs in agriculture and the rise of jobs in the service sector (including government). The share of total employment in the manufacturing sector rises for the early part of the century, peaks during the Second World War, and then declines continually to the current day. This decline in the relative importance of manufacturing has been the focus of much attention; indeed, many observers lament the "deindustrialization" of the Canadian economy. If that term applies to the Canadian economy, it also applies to the economies of the United States and most Western European countries, where similar changes have been observed.

Services in Manufacturing. The enormous growth in what are recorded as service jobs overstates the decline in the importance of the manufacturing of goods in our economy. This is because many of the jobs recorded as service jobs in fact are an integral part of the production of manufactured goods.

First, some of the growth has occurred because many services that used to be produced within manufacturing firms have now been "out-sourced" to specialist firms. These often include design, quality control, accounting, legal services, and marketing. Indeed, one of the most significant of the new developments in production is the breakdown of the old hierarchical organization of firms and the development of the production unit as a loosely knit grouping of organizations, each responsible for part of the total activities; some units are owned by the firms, but many are under contract to it.

Second, as a result of the rapid growth of international trade, production and sales have required growing quantities of service inputs for such things as transportation, insurance, banking, and marketing.

Third, as more and more products become high-tech, increasing amounts are spent on product design

FIGURE 1-5
One Hundred Years of Change in the Composition of Canadian Employment

Over the past century, major shifts in employment have taken place between sectors of the economy. In 1891, over 45 percent of Canadian employment was in agriculture, and only 9 percent in services (including government). One hundred years later, agriculture accounted for only 3 percent of employment, while services had increased to 41 percent. The share of employment in manufacturing and construction increased from 26 percent in 1891 to 32 percent just after the Second World War, and then declined back to 20 percent by 1991.

Source: Canadian Census, various years, authors' calculations.

at one end and customer liaison at the other end. These activities, which are all related to the production and sale of goods, are often recorded as service activities.

Services for Final Consumption. As households' incomes have risen over the decades, households have spent a rising proportion of their incomes on services rather than goods. Today, for example, eating out is common; for our grandparents, it was a luxury. This does not mean, however, that we spend more on food. The extra expenditure goes to pay for the services of the people who prepare and serve in restaurants the same ingredients that our grandparents prepared for themselves at home. Young people spend far more on attending live concerts than they used to, and all of us spend vastly more on travel. In 1890, the salesman in a small town was likely to be

the best-traveled citizen because he had gone 600 kilometres by train to the provincial capital. Today, such a person would be regarded by many as an unworldly stay-at-home.

New Products

When we talk of each generation having more real income than previous generations, we must not think of just having more and more money to spend on the same set of products that our parents or grandparents consumed. In fact, we consume very few of the products that were the mainstays of expenditure for our great-grandparents.

One of the most important aspects of the change that permeates market economies is the continual introduction of new products. It was not until well into this century that electricity was brought to rural areas. Most of the myriad instruments and tools in a modern dentist's office, doctor's office, and hospital did not exist 50 years ago. Penicillin, painkillers, bypass operations, movies, stereos, videocassettes and recorders, pocket calculators, computers, ballpoint pens, compact discs, and everyday travel on aircraft have all been introduced within living memory. So also have the products that have eliminated much of the drudgery formerly associated with housework. Dishwashers, detergents, disposable diapers, washing machines, vacuum cleaners, refrigerators, frozen foods, and their complement, the supermarket, were not there to help your great-grandparents when they first set up house.

Globalization

A relatively new aspect of the constant change that occurs in evolving market economies is the *globalization* that has been occurring at an accelerating rate over the past two decades. At the heart of globalization lies the rapid reduction in transportation costs and the revolution in information technology. The cost of moving products around the world has fallen greatly in recent decades. More dramatically, our ability to transmit and to analyze data has been increasing dramatically, while the cost of doing so has been decreasing equally dramatically.

Many *markets* are globalizing; for example, as some tastes become universal to young people, we can see the same designer jeans and leather jackets in virtually all big cities. Many *corporations* are globalizing, as they increasingly become what are called *transnationals*. These are massive firms with a physical presence in many countries and an increasingly decentralized management structure. Many *product markets* are globalizing, as the revolutions in communications and transportation allow the various components of any one product to be produced all over the world. A typical compact-disc player or automobile contains components made in literally dozens of different countries. We still know where a product is assembled, but it is becoming increasingly difficult to say where it is *made*.

One result of this globalization of production is that components that can be produced by unskilled labour can now be produced in any low-wage country around the world, where previously they were usually produced in the country that did the assembly. This has proved valuable for developing countries. They

have a better chance of becoming competitive in a small range of components than in the integrated production of whole products. However, unskilled labour in developed countries is losing (relatively, and possibly absolutely for a while), as their labour becomes less scarce relative to the need for it. In short, the market for unskilled labour is globalizing, throwing unskilled labour in advanced countries into direct competition with unskilled labour in poorer countries.

Globalization has greatly increased the amount of international trade. This has risen roughly twice as fast as total production over the decades since the end of the Second World War in 1945. Canada has always depended greatly on foreign trade. Most of its exports went to the United Kingdom up until 1945. Today, however, the United States is Canada's most important market, in most years taking over 70 percent of all Canadian exports.

Globalization has also increased U.S. dependence on foreign markets. In 1959, exports amounted to only 4.1 percent of total U.S. production (as measured by its gross domestic product, or GDP). The rest was used domestically. In 1994, the figure was 10.6 percent. The proportion of total U.S. production of *goods* that is exported is much larger than 10 percent. Without the export market, many of the existing sources of U.S. employment and income would not exist.

On the investment side, the most important result of globalization is that large firms are seeking a physical presence in many major countries. In the 1950s and 1960s, most foreign investment was made by U.S. firms investing abroad to establish a presence in foreign markets. Today, most developed countries see major flows of investment in both directions, inward as foreign firms invest in their markets and outward as their own firms invest abroad.

In 1967, fully 50 percent of all outward-bound foreign investment came from the United States and went to many foreign countries. In 1989, according to United Nations figures, the United States accounted for less than 30 percent of all outward-bound foreign investment. At the same time, the United Kingdom accounted for 16 percent, Japan and Germany accounted for just under 10 percent each, and Canada for 2.1 percent.

On the inward-bound side, the change is more dramatic. In 1967, the United States attracted only 9 percent of all foreign investment made in that year. In 1989, however, it attracted 27 percent. Not only do U.S. firms hold massive foreign investments in foreign countries, but foreign firms now hold massive investments in the United States. In 1990, Canada, a much smaller country, received 3.2 percent of all inward-bound foreign investment.

Being a small country with enormous resources beyond the power of domestic capital to develop fully, Canada has always relied heavily on foreign investment for much of its growth. As the Canadian economy matured and Canadian firms grew in size, however, Canadian firms began to finance their own investment and also began to look outward, making Canada a growing source of outward-bound investment. Foreign ownership of Canadian industry peaked in the early 1970s and has been declining ever since—with a small upsurge around 1990 when Canada's Free Trade Agreement with the United States increased Canada's attractiveness to foreign firms seeking to locate in the North American market.

The world is truly globalizing in both its trade and investment flows. Today, no country can take an isolationist economic stance and hope to take part in the global economy, where an increasing share of jobs and incomes are created. Not only do a large number of Canadians work for foreign-owned companies operating in Canada, but a growing number of foreigners work for Canadian-owned companies operating abroad.

CONCLUSION

In this section, we have briefly discussed how people's living standards are affected by the availability of jobs, the productivity of labour in those jobs, and the distribution of the income produced by those jobs. We have seen how the economy is characterized by ongoing change in the structure of jobs, in the production techniques used by the workers, and in the kinds of goods and services produced. We have also seen that these changes exist in the context of a rapidly globalizing economy, one in which events occuring in any one country have major consequences in many other countries.

These issues will arise at many places throughout this book. We will study what is happening in more detail and will use economic theory to explain why it is happening. Because most of the issues are interrelated, it helps to know the basic outlines of all of them before studying any one in more depth.

ECONOMIC ANALYSIS AND ECONOMIC POLICY

So far in this chapter, very little has been said about economic policy, but the analysis of economic policy plays a large role in many parts of this book. This chapter concludes by making some general points about some issues related to the analysis and evaluation of economic policies.

THE PERVASIVENESS OF POLICY DECISIONS

Governments derive their authority to form and carry out policy from their police power—indeed, the words "policy" and "police" come from the Greek word for state, *politeia*.

Some governments lean toward a policy of not intervening with the workings of the free market. Such a policy is often referred to as a *laissez-faire* policy. Other governments lean toward a policy of attempting strict control over every facet of the economy. Note that both of these extreme cases involve a choice of particular economic policies.

All governments have economic policies. Even the decision not to act but to let nature take its course is a policy decision.

Every year thousands of economic policy decisions are made by municipal, provincial, and federal governments. Most of them are never seriously debated. Nor is every facet of existing policy debated anew each year; indeed, many policy decisions now in force (such as giving unions the right to organize) were made decades ago. Only a few policy issues attract attention and become the subject of earnest and heated argument in any particular year.

Debates Over Means and Ends

To understand the debate associated with any given issue of economic policy, it is important to distinguish between the goals of our actions and the methods that we use to achieve those goals. Our goals are called **ends**; they are the things that we strive for. The things that we use to achieve our ends are our **means**; they are the methods of achieving our goals.

The debate over the "right" degree of government involvement in the economy is often really a debate about the alleged potency of *alternative means to achieve agreed ends.* For example, command and free-market economies were both seen (by different people) as means to higher living standards and better control over the environment. Starting in 1989, the countries of Eastern Europe made the choice to move toward a free-market system, in part because their citizens came to believe that it was a superior means to the end of higher living standards.

Other examples are the debates over government intervention in the markets for rental housing and farm production. Supporters of such intervention do not value intervention for its own sake. Rather, they hope that such intervention will be a means toward higher incomes for producers or lower prices to consumers, which in turn means a rise in the living standards of the people concerned. Opponents agree that a rise in living standards is desirable but argue that these means are an inappropriate way of achieving this end.

Economic debates also arise when various groups who are *pursuing different ends* come into conflict. For example, everyone may agree that a particular agricultural policy makes farmers better off, but only at the expense of consumers who must pay higher prices for their products. In this case, there is a real conflict between groups. The issue then becomes deciding between competing ends—improving the lot of farmers or of consumers—rather than judging between alternative means to agreed ends.

Conflicts can also emerge over ends because different groups put *different values on alternative ends.* When environmental groups oppose the establishment of a local pulp mill while potential employees support it, the two groups are applying different values to two competing ends: more local job creation and more environmental protection.

FOUR COMMON QUESTIONS ABOUT ECONOMIC POLICIES

Though each issue typically has its own special characteristics, most issues of economic policy share some common elements. Here are four main questions which can be asked about every proposed economic policy.

1. What are the policy goals?

2. Does the proposed policy achieve those goals?

3. Does the proposed policy have adverse side effects?

4. Are there alternative means of achieving the goals?

As an illustration of how these four questions may be applied in practice, consider the position of a team of economists asked to examine the case for and against the government enacting a policy to control the rents of apartments and houses. How should the economists go about evaluating this policy proposal?

First, the economists would ask what goals such "rent control" is meant to achieve. They might find that it is primarily intended to redistribute income from rich to poor.

Second, the economists would ask if rent control does in fact help to realize this policy goal. Rent control means that tenants pay less rent than they otherwise would and landlords receive less income than they otherwise would; thus rent control redistributes income from landlords to tenants. But do landlords tend to be richer than their tenants? If a survey shows that most tenants are, in fact, richer than their landlords, the economists can conclude that rent control does not achieve the redistributive goal for which it was being used. Then the case against rent control is clear, and that is the end of the story. If, however, the survey indicates that most tenants have lower incomes than their landlords, the economists will conclude that rent control is a means of obtaining the desired goal of income redistribution. Further study is then needed.

Third, the economists would ask if rent control has effects that conflict with other policy objectives. Rent controls may, for example, lead to the deterioration into slums of some areas where landlords do not find it economically worthwhile to maintain their property. It may also lead to a decrease in the total amount of rental housing as some owners shift their property out of rental uses and potential new investors do not find it worthwhile to construct apartment buildings and other rental units. When a policy action helps to achieve one goal but hinders the attainment of another, it is necessary to establish a trade off between goals. Usually there will be some rate at which people will trade a loss in one direction for a gain in another.

Fourth, the economists need to consider alternatives to see if there are other measures that will achieve the goals at a lower sacrifice in terms of setbacks to other policy objectives. It is probable, for example, that the progressive income tax redistributes income from rich to poor with more certainty and precision and with fewer undesired side effects than does rent control.

At any one of the four stages of their investigation, the economists may conclude that rent control is not a very effective means of achieving the policymakers' objectives. (In fact many economists *have* reached that conclusion about rent controls. We discuss rent controls in detail in Chapter 6.) But suppose that the team of economists concludes that rent control *does* achieve the desired goals, that the undesirable effects in other directions are judged (by the policymakers) to be less important than the desirable effects in achieving the stated policy goals, and that there are no other practicable measures that would better achieve the goals? The team will then conclude that there is a strong case in favour of rent controls.

Do not the views—and prejudices—of the investigators have a great deal to do with the outcome of their investigation? A particular group of economists may have strong views on the particular measure it is attempting to assess. If the economists do not like the measure, they are likely to be relentless in searching out possible unwanted effects and somewhat less than thorough in discovering effects that help to achieve the desired goals. It is therefore important (though often difficult) to guard against an unconscious bias of this sort. Fortunately there are likely to be others with different biases. One advantage of publishing evaluations and submitting them to review and discussion is that it provides opportunities for those with different biases to discover arguments and evidence originally overlooked.

CONFLICTS OF POLICY

Governments have many policy goals. A particular policy that serves one goal may hinder another and have no effect on yet a third. Unemployment insurance, for example, may protect unemployed families from debilitating hardship; at the same time it may hinder the quickness with which labour moves from labour-surplus to labour-scarce occupations, thereby increasing total unemployment in the country. Moreover, it will almost certainly have no effect one way or the other on the levels of air pollution.

The significance of this point is too frequently overlooked. It is never enough to show that a proposed policy advances one of society's objectives. What must be shown about the policy is that it advances certain objectives sufficiently to overcome the cost in terms of the amount that it retards other objectives. In order to do this, it is necessary to determine how much of one must be given up to get how much more of the others. This involves the question of opportunity cost, on which the studies of economists can shed light. It is also necessary to decide whether the opportunity cost is worth incurring, and this is a matter of social valuation.

Economic and Political Objectives

Actual policymaking is more complicated than the previous discussion suggests, and a few of the many reasons policy issues get settled in a less systematic fashion deserve mention.

Decisions on interrelated issues of policy are made by many different bodies. Federal and provincial parliaments pass laws, the courts interpret laws, and the governments decide which laws to enforce with vigor and which to soft-pedal. The Department of Finance and the Bank of Canada, both agents of the federal government, influence financial markets through their actions. And a host of other agencies and semi-independent bodies determine actions in respect to different aspects of policy goals. Because of the multiplicity of decision makers it would be truly amazing if fully consistent behaviour resulted.

Furthermore, in a system such as ours, inconsistent decisions may result from political compromises between two or more interested groups, factions, or agencies. Compromises are frequently necessary to reconcile conflicting interests among the provinces or between the federal government and the provinces.

Another problem arises because legislators in a democracy have their own and their party's reelection as one of their important goals. This means, for example, that any measure that imposes large costs and few benefits obvious to the electorate over the next few years is unlikely to find favour, no matter how large the long-term benefits are. There is a strong bias toward myopia in an elective system.

Although much of this bias stems from shortsightedness and selfishness, another part reflects genuine uncertainty about the future. The further into the future the economist is calculating, the wider is the margin of possible error in his or her statements. Thus it is not surprising that politicians who must worry about the next election often tend to worry less about the long-term effects of their actions.

SUMMARY

A. WHAT IS ECONOMICS?

- Most of the world's pressing problems have an economic aspect, and many are primarily economic. A common feature of such problems is that they concern the use of limited resources to satisfy virtually unlimited human wants.
- Scarcity is a fundamental problem faced by all economies. Not enough resources are available to produce all the goods and services that people would like to consume. Scarcity makes it necessary to choose. All societies must have a mechanism for choosing what goods and services will be produced and in what quantities.
- The concept of opportunity cost emphasizes the problem of scarcity and choice by measuring the cost of obtaining a unit of one product in terms of the number of units of other products that could have been obtained instead.
- Four basic questions must be answered in all economies: What is produced and how? What is consumed and by whom? Why are resources sometimes idle? Is productive capacity growing?

B. ALTERNATIVE ECONOMIC SYSTEMS

- Different economies resolve these four basic questions in different ways and with varying degrees of efficacy. Economists study how these problems are addressed in various societies and the consequences of using one method rather than another to provide solutions.
- We can distinguish three pure types of economies: traditional, command, and free-market. In practice, all economies are mixed economies in that their economic behaviour responds to mixes of tradition, government command, and price incentives.
- In the late 1980s, events in Eastern Europe and the USSR led to the general acceptance that the system of fully centrally planned economies had failed to produce minimally acceptable living standards for its citizens. All of these countries are now moving toward greater market determination and less state command in their economies.

C. ASPECTS OF A MODERN ECONOMY

- Market economies are based on private property and freedom of contract. They have generated sustained growth, which, over long periods, has raised material living standards greatly.
- Market economies are characterized by constant change in such things as the structure of jobs, the structure of production, the technologies in use, and the types of products produced.
- Driven by the revolution in transportation and communications, the world economy is rapidly globalizing. National and regional boundaries are becoming less important as transnational corporations locate the production of each component part of a product in the country that can produce it at the best quality and the least cost.
- As part of this globalization, most countries are much more heavily involved in foreign trade than in the past. Most advanced countries have become both host countries for investment by foreign firms and source countries for investment located in foreign countries.

D. ECONOMIC ANALYSIS AND ECONOMIC POLICY

- All governments have economic policies. Even the decision not to interfere with the workings of the free market is a policy decision. Understanding debates about economic policy requires that a distinction be made between the ends and means of policy actions.
- There are four basic questions which should be asked about any proposed policy. What are the policy goals? Does the proposed policy achieve those goals? Does the proposed policy have adverse side effects? Are there alternative means of achieving the goals?
- It is not sufficient to show that a proposed policy advances one of society's objectives. What must be shown is that the policy advances certain objectives enough to offset the amount that it retards others. Policy trade offs are therefore pervasive.

KEY CONCEPTS

Scarcity and the need for choice
Choice and opportunity cost
Production possibility boundary
Resource allocation

Growth in productive capacity
Traditional economies
Command economies

Market economies
Globalization
Policy means and ends

DISCUSSION QUESTIONS

1. What does each of the following questions tell you about the policy conflicts perceived by the person making the statement and about how that person has resolved them?

   a. "It is an industry worth several hundred jobs to our province; we cannot afford to forgo it." A provincial premier explaining the decision to organize a killing of wolves in his province so that more game animals could grow up to be shot by hunters.

   b. "The annual seal hunt must be stopped, even if it destroys the livelihood of the seal hunters." An animal-rights advocate opposing the seal hunt in Canada.

   c. "Considering our limited energy resources and the growing demand for electricity, Canada really has no choice but to use all of its possible domestic energy sources, including nuclear energy. Despite possible environmental and safety hazards, nuclear power is a necessity." A provincial hydro authority replying to critics.

   d. "The proposed pulp mills must be opposed because of the pollution they cause, even though they bring new and diversified jobs and even though they are based on the most advanced, pollution-minimizing technologies." An opponent of the proposal to construct new pulp and paper mills in the Peace River District of northern Canada during the 1990s.

   e. "Damn the pollution—we want the jobs!" A labour leader in Brazil advocating permission to build new pulp mills in his area.

2. What is the difference between scarcity and poverty? If everyone in the world had enough to eat, could we say that food was no longer scarce?

3. Consider the right to free speech in political campaigns. Suppose that the Flat Earth Society, the Communists, the Reform Party, the Conservatives, the Liberals, the Bloc Quebecois, and the NDP all demand equal time on network television in an election campaign. What economic questions are involved? Can there be freedom of speech without free access to the scarce resources needed to make one's speech heard?

4. Evidence accumulates that the use of chemical fertilizers, which increases agricultural production greatly, damages water quality. Analyze the choice between more food and cleaner water involved in using such fertilizers. Use a production possibility curve with agricultural output on the vertical axis and water quality on the horizontal axis. In what ways does this production possibility curve reflect scarcity, choice, and opportunity cost? How would an improved fertilizer that increased agricultural output without further worsening water quality affect the curve? Suppose that a pollution-free fertilizer were developed; would this mean that there would no longer be any opportunity cost in using it?

5. Pick one of the major socialist countries that have recently introduced market-oriented reforms and discuss the start-up problems that the reforms encounter. Explain why you think these problems will or will not persist over the next few years.

6. Many opponents of Canada's participation in the North American Free Trade Agreement (NAFTA) predicted that many Canadian jobs would flow south to Mexico. Proponents of this view based their arguments on the substantially lower wages of Mexican workers compared to Canadian workers and on the perception that Mexican workers are somehow willing to accept lower standards of living, *ceteris paribus*. Evaluate the strength of these arguments. What is one factor that might account for the differences in real wages between the two countries? How might this affect the conclusion that Canadian jobs must necessarily flow to lower-priced labour?

7. Discuss the following statement by a leading U.S. economist: "One of the mysteries of semantics is

why the government-managed economies ever came to be called planned and the market economies unplanned. It is the former that are in chronic chaos, in which buyers stand in line hoping to buy some toilet paper or soap. It is the latter that are in reasonable equilibrium—where if you want a cake of soap or a steak or a shirt or a car, you can go to the store and find that the item is magically there for you to buy. It is the liberal economies that reflect a highly sophisticated planning system, and the government-managed economies that are primitive and unplanned."

CHAPTER **2**

ECONOMICS AS A SOCIAL SCIENCE

Economics is regarded as a social science. But unlike many sciences such as chemistry or physics, many economists would say that a training in economics provides the student more with a "way of thinking" than with a collection of facts. This does not mean that facts are unimportant to the economist—quite the contrary. It means only that facts are typically harder to establish in economics than in the "hard" sciences and often economists do not know which facts are important without first having a way to organize their thinking.

    Central to the economist's way of thinking is the distinction between *positive statements* and *normative statements*. Also of crucial importance to the economist is the role of *theory* and, in particular, the use of economic *models* to provide a framework for thinking about complex issues. Such models can be used to generate *testable hypotheses*.

    In this chapter, we explore what it means to be "scientific" in the study of human behaviour and to establish criteria for evaluating how well economics succeeds in meeting that goal.

THE DISTINCTION BETWEEN POSITIVE AND NORMATIVE

The success of modern science rests partly on the ability of scientists to separate their views on what *does* happen from their views on what *they would like* to happen.

Positive statements concern what is, was, or will be. Positive statements, assertions, or theories may be simple or complex, but they are basically about matters of fact. Positive statements assert things about the world. If it is possible for a positive statement to be proved wrong by empirical evidence, we call it a *testable statement.*

Normative statements concern what one believes ought to be. They state, or are based on, judgments about what is good and what is bad. They are thus bound up with philosophical, cultural, and religious systems. Normative statements are not testable. Disagreements over such normative statements as "It is wrong to steal" or "It is immoral to have sexual relations out of wedlock" cannot be settled by an appeal to empirical observations.

Many positive statements are testable, and disagreements over such statements are appropriately handled by an appeal to the facts. Different techniques are needed for studying normative and positive questions.

It is therefore useful to separate normative and positive inquiries. We do this not because we think one is less important than the other but merely because they must be handled in different ways.

Here is a simple example. The statement "It is impossible to break up atoms" is a positive statement that can be (and of course has been) refuted by empirical observations. In contrast, the statement "Scientists ought not to break up atoms" is a normative statement that involves ethical judgments. The questions "What government policies will reduce unemployment?" and "What policies will prevent inflation?" are positive ones, whereas the question "Should we be more concerned about unemployment than about inflation?" is a normative one.

As we said above, disagreements over positive statements are appropriately handled by an appeal to the facts, whereas disagreements over normative statements involve competing value judgments.

Economists are often maligned for their apparent inability to agree on anything, including the facts. Extension 2-1 examines why this may be so.

THE IMPORTANCE OF THE DISTINCTION

As an example of the importance of this distinction, consider the question "Has the payment of unemployment benefits increased the amount of unemployment?" This positive question can be turned into a testable hypothesis such as "The higher the benefits paid to the unemployed, the higher will be the total amount of unemployment." If we are not careful, however, attitudes and value judgments may get in the way of the study of this hypothesis. Some people are opposed to all welfare measures and believe in an individualistic self-help ethic. They may hope that the hypothesis is correct because its truth could then be used as an argument against welfare measures in general. Others feel that welfare measures are desirable, reducing misery and contributing to human dignity. They may hope that the hypothesis is wrong because they do not want any welfare measures to come under attack. In spite of different value judgments and social attitudes, however, evidence is accumulating on this particular hypothesis. As a result, we have more knowledge than we had 20 years ago of why and to what extent unemployment benefits increase unemployment. This evidence could never have been accumulated or accepted if investigators had not been able to differentiate their feelings about how they wanted the answer to turn out from their assessment of evidence on how people actually behaved.[1]

The distinction between positive and normative statements allows us to keep our views on how we would like the world to work separate from our views on how the world actually does work. We may

---

[1]Of course, economists, like all scientists, are not immune from the possibility that what they find will be influenced by what they want to find. For a study of this problem in a different context, see Stephen Jay Gould, *The Mismeasure of Man* (New York: Norton, 1981). The more likely it is that value judgments will affect our judgments of positive issues, the more important it is that the test of consistency with facts be accepted as an important criterion for the acceptance of theories.

WHY ECONOMISTS DISAGREE

If you listen to a discussion among economists on *The National* or *Morningside* or read about their debates in the daily press or weekly magazines, you will find that economists frequently disagree among themselves. Why do economists disagree, and what should we make of this fact?

In a *Newsweek* column, Charles Wolf Jr. suggested four reasons:

1. Different economists use different benchmarks (e.g., inflation is down compared with last year but up compared with the 1950s).

2. Economists fail to make it clear to their listeners whether they are talking about short-term or long-term consequences (e.g., tax cuts will stimulate consumption in the short run and investment in the long run).

3. Economists often fail to acknowledge the full extent of their ignorance.

4. Different economists have different values, and these normative views play a large part in most public discussions of policy.

There is surely some truth in each of these assessments, but there is also a fifth reason: the public's *demand for disagreement*. For example, suppose that most economists were in fact agreed on some proposition, such as "Unions are not a major cause of inflation." This view would be unpalatable to some individuals. Those who are hostile to unions, for instance, would like to blame inflation on them and would be looking for an intellectual champion. Fame and fortune would await the economist who espoused their cause, and a champion would soon be found.

Notice also that any disagreement that does exist will be exaggerated, possibly unintentionally, by the media. When the media cover an issue, they naturally wish to give both sides of it. Normally, the public will hear one or two economists on each side of a debate, regardless of whether the profession is divided right down the middle or is nearly unanimous in its support of one side. Thus the public will not know that in one case a reporter could have chosen from dozens of economists to present each side, whereas in another case the reporter had to spend three days finding someone willing to take a particular side because nearly all the economists contacted thought it was wrong. In their desire to show both sides of all cases, however, the media present the public with the appearance of a profession equally split over all matters.

Thus anyone seeking to discredit some particular economist's advice by showing that there is disagreement among economists will have no trouble finding evidence of some disagreement. But those who wish to know if there is a majority view or even a strong consensus will find one on a surprisingly large number of issues. For example, a survey published in the *American Economic Review* showed strong agreement among economists on many propositions such as "Rent control leads to a housing shortage" (85 percent yes).

These results illustrate that economists do agree on many issues—where the balance of evidence seems strongly to support certain predictions that follow from economic theories.

be interested in both. It can only obscure the truth, however, if we let our views on what we would like bias our investigations of what actually is. For this reason, the separation of positive from normative statements is one of the foundations of science. It is also for this reason that scientific inquiry, as it is normally understood, is usually confined to positive questions. Some important limitations on the distinc-

tion between positive and normative are discussed in Extension 2-2.

POSITIVE AND NORMATIVE STATEMENTS IN ECONOMICS

We have seen that normative questions cannot be settled by a mere appeal to facts. In democracies,

---

LIMITS ON THE POSITIVE-NORMATIVE DISTINCTION

Although the distinction between positive and normative statements is useful, it has a number of limitations.

The Classification Is Not Exhaustive. The positive and normative classifications do not cover all statements that can be made. For example, there is an important class, called *analytic statements,* whose validity depends only on the rules of logic. Thus the sentence "If all humans are immortal and if you are a human, then you are immortal" is a valid analytic statement. It tells us that if two things are true, then a third thing must also be true. The validity of this statement is not dependent on whether or not its individual parts are in fact true. Indeed, the sentence "All humans are immortal" is a positive statement that has been decisively refuted. Yet no amount of empirical evidence on the mortality of humans can upset the truth of the if-then sentence quoted. Analytic statements—which proceed by logical analysis—play an important role in scientific work and form the basis of much of our ability to theorize.

Not All Positive Statements Are Testable. A positive statement asserts something about some aspect of the universe in which we live. It may be empirically true or false in the sense that what it asserts may or may not be true of the world. If it is true, it adds to our knowledge of what can and cannot happen. Many positive statements are refutable: If they are wrong, this can be ascertained (within a margin for error of observation) by checking them against data. For example, the positive statement that the earth is less than 5,000 years old was tested and refuted by a mass of evidence accumulated in the eighteenth and nineteenth centuries.

The statement "Extraterrestrials exist and frequently visit the earth in visible form" is also a positive statement. It asserts something about the universe, but we could never refute this statement with evidence because no matter how hard we searched, believers could argue that we did not look in the right places or in the right way, that extraterrestrials do not reveal themselves to nonbelievers, or a host of other reasons. Thus some positive statements are irrefutable.

The Distinction Is Not Unerringly Applied. The fact that the positive-normative distinction aids the advancement of knowledge does not necessarily mean that all scientists automatically and unerringly apply it. Scientists are human beings. Many have strongly-held values, and they may let their value judgments get in the way of their assessment of evidence. Nonetheless, the desire to separate what is from what we would like to be is a guiding light, an ideal of all science. The ability to do so, albeit imperfectly, is attested to by the acceptance, first by scientists and then by the general public, of many ideas that were initially extremely unpalatable—ideas such as the close relationship between humans and other primates.

---

normative questions relating to government policies are often settled by voting. So on the one hand, we look to observations to shed light on the issue of the extent to which unemployment insurance deters people from working. On the other hand, we use the political process to decide whether or not, when all the pros and cons are considered, we should have such insurance.

Economists need not confine their discussions to positive, testable statements. Economists can usefully hold and discuss value judgments. Indeed, the pursuit of what appears to be a normative statement, such as "Unemployment insurance ought to be abol-

ished," will often lead to positive hypotheses that underlie the normative judgment. In this case, there are probably relatively few people who believe that government provision of unemployment insurance is in itself good or bad. Their advocacy or opposition will be based on beliefs that can be stated as positive rather than normative hypotheses—for example, "Unemployment insurance causes people to remain unemployed when they would otherwise take a job" or "Unemployment insurance increases the chance that workers will locate the jobs for which they are best suited by supporting them while they search for the right job."

THE SCIENTIFIC APPROACH IN ECONOMICS

An important aspect of the scientific approach consists of relating questions to evidence. When presented with a controversial issue, investigators, whether in the natural or the social sciences, will look for relevant evidence.

In some fields, scientists are able to generate observations that provide evidence for use in testing their hypotheses. Experimental sciences such as chemistry and some branches of psychology have an advantage because it is possible for them to produce relevant evidence through controlled laboratory experiments.

Other sciences, such as astronomy, cannot do this. They must wait for natural events to produce observations that can be used as evidence in testing their theories. The evidence that then arises does not come from controlled laboratory conditions. Instead, it arises from situations in which many things are changing at the same time, and great care is therefore needed in drawing conclusions from what is observed.

Not long ago, economics would have been put wholly in the group of nonexperimental sciences. It is still true that the majority of evidence that economists use is generated by observing what happens in the economy from day to day. However, a significant and growing amount of evidence is now being generated under controlled laboratory conditions. In this book, we concentrate on the nonlaboratory aspect of economic evidence both because it is still the predominant aspect and because the significance of laboratory-generated evidence in economics remains controversial.

Later in this chapter, we will consider some of the problems that arise when analyzing evidence generated by observing day-to-day behaviour that does not take place under controlled laboratory conditions. For the moment, however, we shall consider some general problems that are common to most sciences and are particularly important in the social sciences.

IS HUMAN BEHAVIOUR PREDICTABLE?

Social scientists seek to understand and to predict human behaviour. A scientific prediction is based on discovering stable response patterns, but are such patterns possible with anything so complex as human beings?

Does human behaviour show sufficiently stable responses to factors influencing it to be predictable within some stated margin of error? This positive question can be settled only by an appeal to evidence and not by armchair speculation. The question itself might concern either the behaviour of groups or that of isolated individuals.

Group Behaviour Versus Individual Behaviour

There are many situations in which group behaviour can be predicted accurately without certain knowledge of individual behaviour. The warmer the weather, for example, the more people visit the beach and the higher the sales of ice cream. It may be hard to say if or when one individual will buy an ice cream cone, but a stable response pattern can be seen among a large group of individuals. Although social scientists cannot predict which particular individuals will be involved in auto accidents during the next holiday weekend, they can come very close to knowing the total number who will. The more objectively measurable data they have (e.g., the state of the weather on the days in question and the trend in gasoline prices), the more closely they will be able to predict total accidents.

Economists can also predict with considerable accuracy what employees as a group will do when their take-home pay rises. Although some individuals may do surprising and unpredictable things, the overall response of workers in spending more when their take-home pay rises is predictable within a quite narrow margin of error. This relatively stable response is the basis of economists' ability to predict successfully the outcome of major changes in income-tax rates that permanently alter people's take-home pay.

Nothing we have said implies that people never change their minds or that future events can be foretold simply by projecting past trends. For example, we cannot safely predict that people will increase their spending next year just because they increased their spending this year. The stability we are discussing relates to a cause-effect response. For example, the next time take-home pay rises significantly (cause), spending by employees will rise (effect).

The Law of Large Numbers

Successfully predicting the behaviour of large groups of people is made possible by the statistical "law" of large numbers. Broadly speaking, this law asserts that random movements of many individual items tend to offset one another.

What is implied by this law? Ask any one person to measure the length of a room, and it will be almost impossible to predict in advance what sort of error of measurement will be made. Dozens of things will affect the accuracy of the measurement; furthermore, the person may make one error today and a quite different one tomorrow. But ask 1,000 people to measure the length of the same room, and we can predict within a small margin just how this *group* will make its errors. We can assert with confidence that more people will make small errors than will make large errors; that the larger the error, the fewer will be the number making it; that roughly the same number of people will overstate as will understate the distance; and that the larger the number of people making the measurement, the smaller the average of their errors will tend to be.

If a common cause acts on each member of the group, the average behaviour of the group can be predicted even though any one member may act in a surprising fashion. For example, let each of the 1,000 individuals be given a tape measure that understates actual distances. On average, the group will now understate the length of the room. It is, of course, quite possible that one member who had in the past been reading her tape measure correctly will now read more than it measures as a result of developing an eye defect. However, something else may have happened to another individual that causes him to underread his tape measure where before he was reading it correctly. Individuals may alter their behaviour for many different reasons, but the group's behaviour, when the inaccurate tape is substituted for the accurate one, is predictable precisely because the odd things that one individual does tend to cancel out the odd things that some other individual does.

Irregularities in individual behaviour tend to cancel each other out, and the regularities tend to show up in repeated observations.

THE IMPORTANCE OF THEORIES

When some regularity between two or more things is observed, curious people ask why. A *theory* provides an explanation, and by doing so, it enables us to predict as yet unobserved events.

For example, the simple theory of market behaviour that we will study in Part 2 shows how the output of a product affects the price at which it sells and hence affects the incomes of the people who produce it. As we will see in Chapter 6, this theory allows us to predict that a partial failure of the potato crop will *increase* the income of the average potato farmer.

Theories are used in explaining existing observations. A successful theory enables us to predict things that we have not yet seen.

Any explanation whatsoever of how given observations are linked together is a theoretical construction. Theories are used to impose order on our observations, to explain how what we see is linked together. Without theories, there would be only a shapeless mass of observations.

To illustrate this point, think about the common observation that something is "true in theory but not in practice." The next time you hear someone say this, you might reply, "All right, then, tell me what does happen in practice." Usually you will not be told mere facts, but you will be given an alternative theory—a different explanation of the facts. The speaker should have said, "The theory in question provides a poor explanation of the facts in question or is contradicted by some other facts. I have a different theory that does a much better job."

The choice is not between theory and observation but between better or worse theories to explain observations.

THE STRUCTURE OF THEORIES

A theory consists of:

1. a set of definitions that clearly define the variables to be used,

2. a set of assumptions about the behaviour of the variables, and

3. predictions (often called hypotheses) that are deduced from the assumptions of the theory and can be tested against actual empirical observations.

We shall consider these constituents one by one.

Variables

A **variable** is a magnitude that can take on different possible values. Variables are the basic elements of theories, and each one needs to be carefully defined.

Price is an example of an important economic variable. The price of a product is the amount of money that must be given up to purchase one unit of that product. To define a price, we must first define the product to which it is attached. Such a product might be one dozen Grade A large eggs. The price of such eggs sold in, say, supermarkets in Gimli, Manitoba, defines a variable. The particular values taken on by that variable might be $1.79 on July 1, 1997; $1.84 on July 8, 1998; and $1.95 on July 15, 1999.

In understanding any theory, it is crucial to distinguish between endogenous variables and exogenous variables. An **endogenous variable** is a variable that is explained within a theory. An **exogenous variable** influences endogenous variables but is itself determined by factors outside the theory.

Consider the theory that the price of apples in Calgary on a particular day depends on several things, one of which is the weather in the Okanagan Valley during the previous apple-growing season. We can safely assume that the state of the weather is not determined by economic conditions. The price of apples in this case is an endogenous variable—something determined within the framework of the theory. The state of the weather in the Okanagan Valley is an exogenous variable; changes in it influence prices because the changes affect the output of apples, but the state of the weather is not influenced by apple prices.

Other words are sometimes used for the same distinction. One frequently used pair is *induced* for endogenous and *autonomous* for exogenous; another is *dependent* for endogenous and *independent* for exogenous. Thus, economists use the words "exogenous," "independent," and "autonomous" interchangably; they also use the words "endogenous," "dependent," and "induced" interchangably.

Assumptions

A key element of any theory is a set of assumptions about the behaviour of the variables in which we are interested. Usually these state how the behaviour of two or more variables relate to each other.

In some cases, these linkages are provided by physical or biological laws. One example is the relation between the resources each firm uses, which economists call *inputs,* and that firm's *output.* In the case of the egg farmer, the output of eggs is related to inputs of chicken feed, farm labour, and all the other things the farmer uses.

In other cases, these linkages are provided by human behaviour. For example, economists make two basic assumptions about consumers. The first concerns how each consumer's satisfaction, or *utility,* is related to the quantities of all the goods and services consumed by that person. The second is that in making their choices on how much to consume, people seek to maximize the satisfaction they gain from that consumption.

Although assumptions are an essential part of all theories, students are often concerned about those that seem unrealistic. An example will illustrate some of the issues involved. Much of the theory that we are going to study in this book uses the assumption that the sole motive of the owners of firms is to maximize their profits. The assumption of profit maximization allows economists to make predictions about the behaviour of firms. They study how firms' profits are affected by the choices firms make. They then predict that the alternative that produces the most profits will be the one selected.

Profit maximization may seem like a rather crude assumption. Surely, for example, the managers of firms sometimes choose to protect the environment rather than pursue certain highly polluting but profitable opportunities. Does this not discredit the assumption of profit maximization by showing it to be unrealistic?

The answer is no; to make successful predictions, the theory does not require that managers be solely and unwaveringly motivated by the desire to maximize profits. All that is required is that profits be a sufficiently important consideration that a theory based on the assumption of profit maximization will lead to explanations and predictions that are substantially correct.

This illustration shows that it is not always appropriate to criticize a theory because its assumptions seem unrealistic. All theory is an abstraction from reality. If it were not, it would merely duplicate the world in all its complexity and would add nothing to our understanding of it. A good theory abstracts in a useful way; a poor theory does not. If a theory has ignored some genuinely important factors, its predictions will be contradicted by the evidence—at least where an ignored factor exerts an important influence on the outcome.

Predictions

A theory's predictions are the propositions that can be deduced from that theory; they are often called *hypotheses*. An example of a prediction concerning profit maximizing firms is: *if* the going wage for labour increases, *then* the amount of labour employed will fall.

A scientific prediction is a conditional statement that takes the following form: *If* this occurs, *then* such and such will follow.

For example, if a city government forces down the rents on residential accommodation (through a policy of *rent controls*), then a housing shortage will develop.

It is important to realize that this prediction is different from the statement "I predict that in two years' time, there will be a housing shortage in my city because I believe its municipal government will decide to impose rent controls." The government's decision to introduce rent controls in two years' time will be the outcome of many influences, both economic and political. If the economist's prophecy about a housing shortage turns out to be wrong because in two years' time the government does not impose rent controls, then all that has been learned is that the economist is not a good guesser about the behaviour of the government. However, if the government does impose rent controls and a housing shortage does not then develop, a conditional (if-then) prediction based on economic theory will have been contradicted.

Expressing Relations Among Variables

Economists deal with many relations among variables. A **function**, also known as a *functional relation*, is a formal expression of a relationship between two or more variables. When two variables are related in such a way that an increase in one is associated with an increase in the other, they are said to be positively related. When two variables are related in such a way that an increase in one is associated with a decrease in the other, they are said to be negatively related.

The prediction that the quantity of eggs people want to buy is negatively related to the price of eggs is an example of a functional relation in economics. In its most general form, it merely says that quantity demanded is related to price. The more specific hypothesis is that as the price of eggs rises, the quantity of desired purchases falls.

In many relations of this kind, economists can be even more specific about the nature of the functional relation. On the basis of detailed studies, economists often have a pretty good idea of by how much the quantity demanded will change as a result of specified changes in price; that is, they can predict magnitude as well as direction.

ECONOMIC MODELS

Economists often proceed by way of constructing what are referred to as *economic models*. Because the term *model* is used in several contexts, it is important to understand the range of meanings.

First, model is sometimes used merely as a synonym for a theory or a particular subset of theories, such as the Keynesian model of national income determination or the Neoclassical model of price determination in competitive markets.

Second, model is sometimes applied to a specific quantitative formulation of a theory. In this case, specific numbers are attached to the mathematical relationships implied by the theory, the numbers often being based on empirical evidence. The theory in its specific form can then be used to make precise predictions about, say, the behaviour of prices in the potato market or the course of national income and total employment. Forecasting models used by the Bank of Canada and the federal Department of Finance are of this type.

Third, a model is often an application of a general theory in a specific context. The successful model may then explain behaviour that previously seemed inexplicable or even perverse. An example is provided by a branch of economics known as *principal-agent theory*. The principal is the person who wants something done, and the agent is the person hired by the principal to do it. For example, managers of firms may be thought of as agents, while the owners are principals. Both principal and agent are assumed to wish to maximize their own well-being, and the principal's problem is to design a set of incentives that give the agent a self-interest in doing what the principal requires.

Specific principal-agent models have been applied successfully to many problems and have provided a rational explanation of what at first sight seemed to be perverse behaviour. For example, people put in positions of trust are often paid much more than is needed to induce people to take these jobs. Why should principals pay their agents more than they need to pay to fill the jobs? The explanation is that if the agent is paid more than she could earn in another job, she has an incentive not to violate the trust placed in her. If she does violate the trust and is caught, she loses the extra pay attached to the job.

Finally, a model may be just an illustrative abstraction which helps to organize our thoughts about a particular issue. For example, we may wish to gain insight into the consequences of the observation that the amount of research that goes into developing a new product often depends on the product's current sales (because profits to finance research and development are generated by sales). To do this, we may build a very simple model in which the amount of current research is positively related to the amount of current sales. This creates what is called *positive feedback:* The higher current sales are, the more research is done; the more research is done, the more rapidly the product improves; the more rapidly the product improves, the more current sales rise. If extended to allow several competing products, this model will reveal one key tendency of positive-feedback systems: Initial advantages tend to be reinforced, making it more and more difficult for competitors to keep up. No one believes that this simple model catches everything about the complex interactions when various new products compete in the early stages of their development. But it does alert us to certain forces to watch for when we build more complex models or create more general theories of the competition among new products and new technologies. Interestingly, these self-reenforcing characteristics have been observed in many circumstances such as the competition to be the power source of the first automobiles early in the twentieth century, the competition among alternative technologies to produce nuclear power after the Second World War, and the recent competition to produce the operating system of personal computers.

TESTING THEORIES

A theory is tested by confronting its predictions with evidence. It is necessary to discover if certain events are followed by the outcomes predicted by the theory. For example, is an increase in the wage rate followed by a decline in the amount of labour employed? Theories are sometimes tested in conscious attempts to do just that. They are also tested every time an economist uses one to predict the outcome of

some specific event. If economists continued to be mistaken every time they used some theory to make predictions, the theory would eventually be called into question.

Theories tend to be abandoned when they are no longer useful, and theories cease to be useful when they cannot predict the outcomes of actions better than the next best alternative. When a theory consistently fails to predict better than the available alternatives, it is either modified or replaced. Figure 2-1 summarizes the discussion of theories and their testing.

REFUTATION VERSUS CONFIRMATION

An important part of a scientific approach to any issue consists of setting up a theory that will explain it and then seeing if that theory can be refuted by evidence.

The alternative to this approach is to set up a theory and then look for confirming evidence. Such an approach is hazardous because the world is sufficiently complex that some confirming evidence can be found for any theory, no matter how unlikely the theory may be. For example, flying saucers, the Loch Ness monster, fortune-telling, and astrology all have their devotees who can quote confirming evidence in spite of the failure of attempts to discover systematic, objective evidence for these things.

An example of the unfruitful approach of seeking confirmation is frequently seen when a national leader is surrounded by followers who provide only evidence that confirms the leader's existing views. This approach is usually a road to disaster because the leader becomes more and more out of touch with reality.

A wise leader adopts a scientific approach instinctively, constantly checking the accuracy of accepted views by encouraging criticism from subordinates. This tests how far the leader's existing views correspond to all available evidence and encourages adjustments in the light of conflicting evidence.

STATISTICAL ANALYSIS

Statistical analysis is used to test the hypothesis that two or more things are related and to estimate the numerical values of the function that describes the relationship. In practice, the same data can be used simultaneously to test whether a relationship exists and, if it does exist, to provide a measure of it.

FIGURE 2-1
The Interaction of Deduction and Measurement in Theorizing

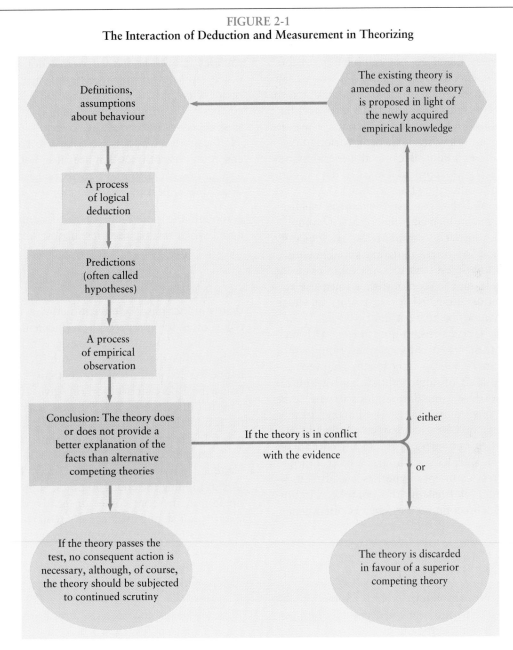

Theory and observation are in continuous interaction. Starting (at the top left) with the assumptions of a theory and the definitions of relevant terms, the theorist deduces by logical analysis everything that is implied by the assumptions. These implications are the predictions or the hypotheses of the theory. The theory is then tested by confronting its predictions with evidence. If the theory is in conflict with facts, it will usually be amended to make it consistent with those facts (thereby making it a better theory); in extreme cases, it will be discarded, to be replaced by a superior alternative. The process then begins again: The new or amended theory is subjected first to logical analysis and then to empirical testing.

Because economics is primarily a nonlaboratory science, it lacks the controlled experiments that are central to sciences like physics and chemistry. Economics must therefore use millions of uncontrolled experiments that are going on every day. Households are deciding what to purchase given changing prices and incomes, firms are deciding what to produce and how, and governments are involved in the economy through their various taxes, subsidies, and regulations. Because all these activities can be observed and recorded, a mass of data is continually being produced by the economy.

The variables that interest economists, such as the level of unemployment, the price of compact discs, and the output of automobiles, are generally influenced by many forces that vary simultaneously. If economists are to test their theories about relations among variables in the economy, they must use statistical techniques designed for situations in which other things *cannot* be held constant.

Fortunately, such techniques exist, although their application is usually neither simple nor straightforward. The appendix to this chapter provides a discussion of some tabular and graphical techniques for describing data and displaying some of the more obvious relationships. Further examination of data involves techniques studied in elementary statistics courses. More advanced courses in econometrics deal with the array of techniques designed to test economic hypotheses and to measure economic relations in the complex circumstances in which economic evidence is often generated.

THE DECISION TO ACCEPT OR REJECT

Nothing is ever absolutely certain. Some of the things we now think are true will eventually turn out to be false, and some of the things we currently think are false will eventually turn out to be true. Yet even though we can never be certain, we can assess the balance of available evidence. Some hypotheses are so unlikely to be true in the light of current evidence that for all practical purposes we may regard them as false. Other hypotheses are so unlikely to be false, given current evidence, that for all practical purposes we may regard them as true. This kind of practical decision must always be regarded as tentative. Every once in a while, we will find that we have to change our mind. Something that looked right will begin to look doubtful, or something that looked wrong will begin to look possible.

Making such decisions requires accepting some theories (to act as if they were true) and rejecting others (to act as if they were false). Just as a jury can make two kinds of errors (finding an innocent person guilty or letting a guilty person go free), so statistical decision makers can make two kinds of errors. They can reject hypotheses that are true, and they can accept hypotheses that are false. Fortunately, like a jury, they can also make correct decisions—and indeed, they expect to do so most of the time.

Although the possibility of error cannot be eliminated when testing theories against observations, it can be controlled.

The method of control is to decide in advance how large a risk to take in accepting a hypothesis that is in fact false.[2] Conventionally in statistics, this risk is often set at 5 percent or 1 percent. When the 5 percent cutoff point is used, we accept the hypothesis if the results that appear to establish it could have happened by chance no more than 1 time in 20. Using the 1 percent decision rule gives the hypothesis a more difficult test. A hypothesis is accepted only if the results that appear to establish it could have happened by chance no more than 1 time in 100.

Consider the hypothesis that a certain coin is "loaded," favouring heads over tails. The test consists of flipping the coin 100 times. Suppose that on a single test, the coin comes up heads 53 times. This result is not strong evidence in favour of the hypothesis because such an unbalanced result could happen by chance in more than 22 percent of such tests. Thus the hypothesis of a head-biased coin would not be accepted on the basis of this evidence using either a 1 percent or a 5 percent cutoff. Had the test produced 65 heads and 35 tails, a result that would occur by chance in less than 1 percent of such tests, we would (given either a 1 percent or a 5 percent cutoff) accept the hypothesis of the coin being loaded.[3]

---

[2]Return to the jury analogy: Our notion of a person's being innocent unless the jury is persuaded of guilt "beyond a reasonable doubt" rests on our wish to take only a small risk of accepting the hypothesis of guilt if the person tried is in fact innocent.

[3]The actual statistical testing process is more complex than this example suggests but must be left to a course in statistics.

When action must be taken, some rule of thumb is necessary, but it is important to understand, first, that no one can ever be certain about being right in rejecting any hypothesis and, second, that there is nothing magical about arbitrary cutoff points. Some cutoff point must be used whenever decisions have to be made.

Finally, recall that the rejection of a hypothesis is seldom the end of inquiry. Decisions can be reversed if new evidence comes to light. Often the result of a statistical test of a theory suggests a new hypothesis that "fits the facts" better than the old one.

CAN ECONOMICS BE MADE VALUE-FREE?

We have made two key statements about the positive-normative distinction. First, the ability to distinguish positive from normative questions is a key part of the foundation of science. Second, economists, in common with all scientists, seek to answer positive questions.

Some people who have accepted these points have gone on to argue that there can be a completely value-free inquiry into any branch of science, including economics. After long debate over this issue, the conclusion that most people seem to accept is that a *completely* value-free inquiry is impossible.

Our values become involved at all stages of any inquiry. For example, we must allocate our scarce time. This means that we choose to study some problems rather than other problems. This choice is often influenced by our value judgments about the relative importance of various problems. Also evidence is never conclusive and so is always open to more than one interpretation. It is difficult to assess such imperfect evidence without giving some play to our values. Further, when reporting the results of our studies, we must use words that we know will arouse various emotions in the people who read them. So the words we choose and the emphasis we give to the available evidence (and to the uncertainties surrounding it) will influence the impact that the study has.

For these and many other reasons, most people who have discussed this issue believe that there can be no totally value-free study of economics.

This does not mean that economists and other scientists should conclude that *everything* is a matter of subjective value judgments. The very real advancements of knowledge in all sciences, natural and social, show that science is not just a matter of opinion or of debating competing value judgments.

Science has been successful in spite of the fact that individual scientists have not always been totally objective. Individual scientists have sometimes passionately resisted the apparent implications of evidence. The rules of the scientific game—that facts cannot be ignored and must somehow be fitted into the accepted theoretical structure—tend to produce scientific advance in spite of what might be thought of as unscientific, emotional attitudes on the part of some scientists.

But if people engaged in scientific debate, in economics or any other science, ever succeed in changing the rules of the game to allow inconvenient facts to be ignored or defined out of existence, a major blow would be dealt to the power of scientific inquiry.

SUMMARY

A. THE DISTINCTION BETWEEN POSITIVE AND NORMATIVE

- It is useful to distinguish between positive and normative statements. Positive statements concern what is, was, or will be, whereas normative statements concern what ought to be. Disagreements over positive, testable statements are appropriately settled by an appeal to the facts. Disagreements over normative statements cannot be settled in this way.

B. THE SCIENTIFIC APPROACH IN ECONOMICS

- Successful scientific inquiry requires separating positive questions about the way the world works from normative questions about how one would like the world to work, formulating positive questions precisely enough so that they can be settled by an appeal to evidence, and then finding means of gathering the necessary evidence.

- Social scientists have observed many stable human behaviour patterns. These form the basis for successful predictions of how people will behave under certain conditions.
- The fact that people sometimes act strangely, even capriciously, does not destroy the possibility of scientific study of group behaviour. The odd and inexplicable things that one person does will tend to cancel out the odd and inexplicable things that another person does. The law of large numbers thus means that group behaviour is often easier to predict than individual behaviour.
- Theories are designed to give meaning and coherence to observed sequences of events. A theory consists of a set of definitions of the variables to be employed and a set of assumptions about how things behave. Any theory has certain logical implications that must be true if the theory is true. These are the theory's predictions or hypotheses.
- Economists use models to help them think about the complex interactions of different economic phenomena. Such models often generate testable predictions.

C. TESTING THEORIES

- A theory is conditional in the sense that it provides predictions of the type "if one event occurs, then another event will also occur." An important method of testing theories is to confront their predictions with evidence.

- The progress of any science lies in finding better explanations of events than are now available. Thus in any developing science, one must expect to discard some existing theories and replace them with demonstrably superior alternatives.
- Theories are tested by checking their predictions against evidence. In some sciences, these tests can be conducted under laboratory conditions in which only one thing changes at a time. In other sciences, testing must be done using the data produced by the world of ordinary events. (The appendix to this chapter provides a brief discussion of some of the elementary statistical techniques used to test hypotheses when many variables are changing at once.)

D. CAN ECONOMICS BE MADE VALUE-FREE?

- Although distinguishing positive from normative questions and seeking to answer positive questions are important aspects of science, it does not follow that economic inquiry can be totally value-free. Although values intrude at almost all stages of scientific inquiry, the rule that theories should be judged against evidence wherever possible tends to produce advances of positive knowledge over time.

KEY CONCEPTS

Positive and normative statements
Testable statements
The law of large numbers and the predictability of human behaviour

Variables, assumptions, and predictions in theorizing
Uses of models
Functional relations

Conditional prediction versus prophecy

DISCUSSION QUESTIONS

1. What are some of the positive and normative issues that lie behind the disagreements in the following cases?
   a. Economists disagree on whether the Government of Canada should try to stimulate the economy in the next six months.
   b. European and North American negotiators disagree over the desirability of reducing European farm subsidies.

   c. Economists argue about the merits of a voucher system that allows parents to choose the schools their children will attend.
   d. Economists debate the use of a two-tier medical system in Canada (whereby health care continues to be publicly provided, but individuals are permitted to be treated by doctors who bill the patient directly—"extra billing").

2. Much recent public debate has centred on the pros and cons of permitting continued unrestricted sale of cigarettes. Proposals for the control of cigarettes range from increasing excise taxes to the mandatory use of plain packaging to an outright ban on their sale. Identify the positive and normative assumptions that underlie the national mood to reduce the consumption of tobacco products.

3. A baby doesn't know about the theory of gravity, yet in learning to walk and eat, the child makes use of the principles of gravity. Distinguish between behaviour and the explanation of behaviour. Does a business executive or a farmer have to understand economic theory to behave in a pattern consistent with it?

4. "If human behaviour were completely capricious and unpredictable, life insurance could not be a profitable business." Explain. Can you think of any businesses that do not depend on predictable human behaviour?

5. Write five statements about unemployment. Classify each statement as positive or normative. If your list contains only one type of statement, try to add a sixth statement of the other type.

6. Each of the following unrealistic assumptions is sometimes made when economists construct models. See if you can imagine some situations in which each of these assumptions might be a useful simplification in order to think about some aspect of the real world.

   a. The earth is flat.
   b. There are no differences between men and women.
   c. There is no tomorrow.
   d. There are only two periods—this year and next year.
   e. A country produces only two types of goods.
   f. People are wholly selfish.

7. What may at first appear to be untestable statements can often be reworded so that they can be tested by an appeal to evidence. How might you do that with respect to each of the following assertions?

   a. Free-market economic systems are the best in the world.
   b. Unemployment insurance is eroding the work ethic and encouraging people to become wards of the state rather than productive workers.
   c. Robotics ought to be outlawed because it will destroy the future of working people.
   d. Laws requiring equal pay for work of equal value will make women better off.
   e. Free trade improves the welfare of a country's citizens.

8. "The simplest way to see that capital punishment is a strong deterrent to murder is to ask yourself whether you might be more inclined to commit murder if you knew in advance that you ran no risk of ending up in the electric chair, in the gas chamber, or on the gallows." Comment on the methodology of social investigation implied by this statement. What alternative approach would you suggest?

9. There are hundreds of eyewitnesses to the existence of flying saucers and other UFOs. There are films and eyewitness accounts of Nessie, the Loch Ness monster. Are you convinced of their existence? If not, what would it take to persuade you? If so, what would it take to make you change your mind?

APPENDIX TO CHAPTER 2

Graphing Relations Among Variables

The popular saying "The facts speak for themselves" is almost always wrong when there are many facts. Theories are needed to explain how facts are linked together, and summary measures are needed to assist in sorting out what facts show in relation to theories. The simplest means of providing compact summaries of a large number of observations is the use of tables and graphs. Graphs play an important role in economics by representing geometrically both observed data and the relations among variables that are the subject of economic theory.

Because the surface of a piece of paper is two-dimensional, a graph may readily be used to represent pictorially any relation between two variables. Flip through this book and you will see dozens of examples. Figure 2A-1 shows generally how a coordinate graph can be used to represent any two variables.[1]

UNDERSTANDING GRAPHS

Figure 2A-2 shows a simple two-variable graph, which will be analyzed in detail in Chapter 4. For now it is sufficient to notice that the graph permits us to show the relationship between two variables, the price of carrots on the vertical axis and the quantity of carrots (per month) on the horizontal axis.[2] The downward-sloping curve, labeled D for a *demand curve,* shows the relationship between the price of carrots and the quantity of carrots that buyers wish to purchase.

---

[1]Economics is often concerned only with the positive values of variables, and the graph is then confined to the upper right-hand (or "positive") quadrant. Whenever a variable has a negative value, one or more of the other quadrants must be included.

[2]The choice of which variable to put on which axis is discussed in math note 9 at the back of the book.

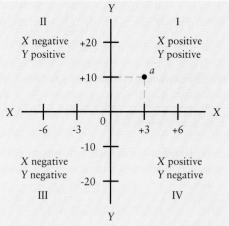

FIGURE 2A-1
A Coordinate Graph

The axes divide the total space into four quadrants according to the signs of the variables. In the upper right-hand quadrant, both X and Y are greater than zero; this is usually called the *positive quadrant.* Point a has *coordinates* $X = 3$ and $Y = 10$ in the coordinate graph. These coordinates define point a.

Figure 2A-3 is very much like Figure 2A-2, with one difference. It generalizes from the specific example of carrots to an unspecified product and focuses on the slope of the demand curve rather than on specific numerical values. Note that the quantity labeled q_0 is associated with the price p_0, and the quantity q_1 is associated with the price p_1.

STRAIGHT LINES
AND THEIR SLOPES

Figure 2A-4 illustrates a variety of straight lines. They differ according to their slopes. **Slope** is defined as the

FIGURE 2A-2
The Relationship Between the Price of Carrots and the Quantity of Carrots That Purchasers Wish to Buy: A Numerical Example

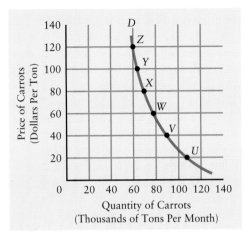

A two-dimensional graph can show how two variables are related. The two variables, the price of carrots and the quantity that people wish to purchase, are shown by the downward-sloping curve labeled *D*. Particular points on the curve are labeled *U* through *Z*. For example, point *Z* shows that at a price of $120 per ton, the demand to purchase carrots is 60,000 tons per month.

FIGURE 2A-3
The Relationship Between the Price of a Product and the Quantity of the Product That Purchasers Wish to Buy

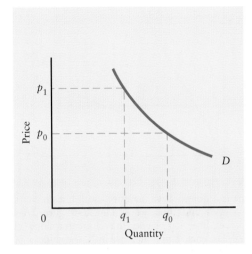

Graphs can illustrate general or specific relationships between variables. Here, in contrast to Figure 2A-2, price and quantity are shown as general variables. The demand curve illustrates a quantitatively unspecified negative relationship between price and quantity. For example, at the price p_0, the quantity that purchasers demand is q_0, whereas at the higher price of p_1, purchasers demand the lower quantity q_1.

FIGURE 2A-4
Four Straight Lines with Different Slopes

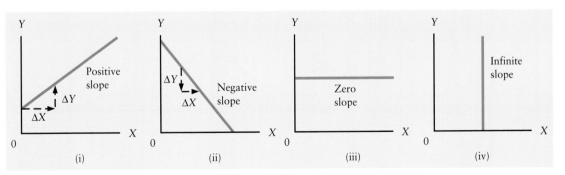

The slope of a straight line is constant but can vary from one line to another. The direction of slope of a straight line is characterized by the signs of the ratio $\Delta Y/\Delta X$. In part (i), that ratio is positive because *X* and *Y* vary in the same direction; in part (ii), the ratio is negative because *X* and *Y* vary in opposite directions; in part (iii), it is zero because *Y* does not change as *X* changes; in part (iv), it is infinite.

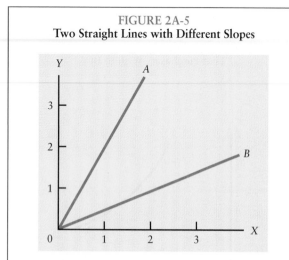

FIGURE 2A-5
Two Straight Lines with Different Slopes

Slope is a quantitative measure. Both lines have positive slopes and thus are similar to Figure 2A-4(i). However, line *A* is steeper (has a greater slope) than line *B*. For each 1-unit increase in *X*, the value of *Y* increases by 2 units along line *A* but only one-half unit along line *B*. The ratio $\Delta Y/\Delta X$ is 2 for line *A* and one-half for *B*.

ratio of the vertical change to the corresponding horizontal change as one moves along a straight line.

The symbol Δ (which is the Greek upper-case delta) is used to indicate a change in any variable. Thus ΔX means "the change in *X*," and ΔY means "the change in *Y*." The ratio $\Delta Y/\Delta X$ is the slope of a straight line. When ΔX and ΔY have the same signs, the ratio is positive and the line is positively sloped, as in part (i) of Figure 2A-4. When ΔY and ΔX have opposite signs, that is, when one increases while the other decreases, the ratio is negative and the line is negatively sloped, as in part (ii). When ΔY is zero (as *X* changes), the line is horizontal, as in part (iii), and the slope is zero. When ΔX is zero (as *Y* changes), the line is vertical, as in part (iv), and the slope is often said to be infinite, although the ratio $\Delta Y/\Delta X$ is undefined. [2]

Slope is a quantitative measure, not merely a qualitative one. For example, in Figure 2A-5, two upward-sloping straight lines have different slopes. Line *A* has a slope of 2 ($\Delta Y/\Delta X = 2$); line *B* has a slope of ½ ($\Delta Y/\Delta X = 0.5$).

CURVED LINES AND THEIR SLOPES

Figure 2A-6 shows four curved lines. The line in part (i) is plainly upward sloping; the line in part (ii) is downward sloping. The other two change from one to the other, as the labels indicate. Unlike a straight line, which has the same slope at every point on the line, the slope of a curve changes. The slope of a curve must be measured at a particular point and is defined as *the slope of a straight line that just touches (is tangent to) the curve at that point*. This is illustrated in Figure 2A-7. The slope at point *A* is

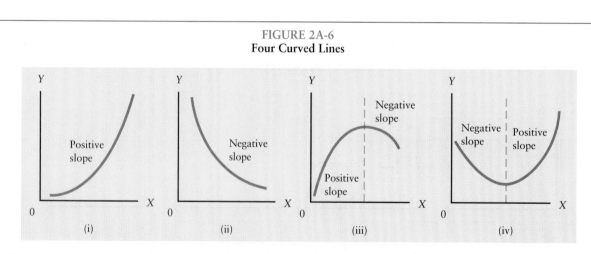

FIGURE 2A-6
Four Curved Lines

The slope of a curved line is not constant and may change direction. The slopes of the curves in parts (i) and (ii) change in size but not in direction, whereas those in parts (iii) and (iv) change in both size and direction. Unlike that of a straight line, the slope of a curved line cannot be represented by a single number because it changes as the value of *X* changes.

FIGURE 2A-7
Defining the Slope of a Curved Line

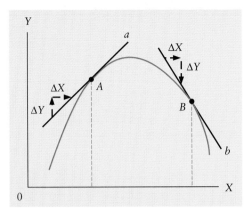

The slope of a curve at any point on the curve is defined by the slope of the straight line that is tangent to the curve at that point. The slope of the curve at point A is defined by the slope of the line a, which is tangent to the curve at point A. The slope of the curve at point B is defined by the slope of the tangent line b.

measured by the slope of the tangent line a. The slope at point B is measured by the slope of the tangent line b.

GRAPHING DATA

A coordinate graph such as that shown in Figure 2A-1 can be used to show the observed values of two variables as well as the theoretical relationships between them. For example, curve D in Figure 2A-2 might have arisen as a freehand line drawn to generalize actual observations of the points labeled U, V, W, X, Y, and Z.

CROSS-SECTIONAL DATA

Although Figure 2A-2 was not constructed from actual observations, many graphs are. To illustrate, we examine the very simple hypothesis that the income taxes paid by families increase as their incomes increase.

To test this hypothesis about the relationship between incomes and income taxes, we have chosen a random sample of 212 families from data collected by the Survey Research Center of the University of

FIGURE 2A-8
A Scatter Diagram Relating Taxes Paid to Family Income

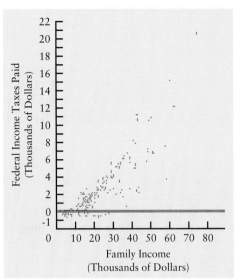

The scatter pattern shows a clear tendency for taxes paid to rise with family income. Family income is measured along the horizontal axis, and federal income taxes paid are measured along the vertical axis. Each dot represents a single family in the sample and is located on the graph according to the family's income and taxes paid. The dots fall mainly within a narrow rising band, suggesting the existence of a systematic relationship between income and taxes paid, but they do not fall along a single line, which suggests that things other than family income affect taxes paid.

Michigan. We have recorded each family's income and the federal income tax it paid in 1979. (1979 was a long time ago, but the principles illustrated in this discussion apply equally to any year.) This data is called **cross-sectional data** because data is collected *across space for the same time period*; the incomes and taxes paid by different households are compared for a single year.

One way in which the data may be used to evaluate the hypothesis is to draw what is called a **scatter diagram,** which plots paired values of two variables. Figure 2A-8 is a scatter diagram that relates family income to federal income tax payments. Income is measured on the horizontal axis and taxes paid on the vertical axis. Any point in the diagram represents a particular family's income combined with the tax payment of that family. Thus each family for which there is an observation is represented on the diagram by a dot, the coordinates of which indicate the family's income and the amount of taxes paid.

The scatter diagram is useful because if there is a simple relationship between the two variables, it will be apparent to the eye once the data are plotted. For example, Figure 2A-8 makes it apparent that more taxes tend to be paid as income rises. It also makes it apparent that the relationship between taxes and income is approximately linear. An upward sloping straight line fits the data reasonably well between about $10,000 and $40,000 of income. Above $40,000 and below $10,000 the line does not fit the data as well, but because more than two-thirds of the families sampled had incomes in the $10,000-to-$40,000 range, we may conclude that the straight line provides a fairly good description of the basic relationship for middle-income families in 1979.

The graph also gives some idea of the strength of the relationship. If income were the only determinant of taxes paid, all the dots would cluster closely around a line or a smooth curve. As it is, the points are somewhat scattered, and several households with the same income show different amounts of taxes paid.

There is some scattering of the dots because the relationship is not perfect; in other words, there is some variation in tax payments that cannot be associated with variations in family income. These variations in tax payments occur mainly for two reasons. First, factors other than income influence tax payments, and some of these other factors will undoubtedly have varied among the families in the sample. Second, there will inevitably be some errors in measurement. For example, a family might have incorrectly reported its tax payments to the person who collected the data.

TIME-SERIES DATA

The data used in the example of Figure 2A-8 are cross-sectional data because several observations are available (one for each family) at the same point in time. Scatter diagrams may also be drawn for a number of observations taken on two variables at successive periods of time.

For example, if we wanted to know whether there was any simple relationship between personal

TABLE 2A-1
Personal Income and Consumption in Canada, 1970–1994 (1986 dollars)

Year	Disposable Personal Income Per Capita	Personal Consumption Expenditures Per Capita
1970	$ 8424	$ 7854
1971	8703	8009
1972	9385	8467
1973	10065	8874
1974	10562	9229
1975	11047	9511
1976	11480	9981
1977	11581	10121
1978	11868	10228
1979	12145	10358
1980	12323	10433
1981	12643	10436
1982	12461	9980
1983	12252	10274
1984	12647	10596
1985	12903	11022
1986	12902	11352
1987	13040	11645
1988	13498	11981
1989	13845	12141
1990	13610	12024
1991	13130	11609
1992	13078	11556
1993	12943	11567
1994	13011	11847

Real disposable income per capita and real personal consumption expenditures have both grown since 1970. The former has increased from $8,424 to just over $13,000 over the period, while the latter grew from $7,854 to just under $12,000.

Source: Statistics Canada, 11-210.

income and personal consumption in Canada between 1970 and 1994, data would be collected for the levels of personal income and expenditure per capita in each year from 1970 to 1994, as is done in Table 2A-1. This information could be plotted on a scatter diagram, with consumption on the *X* axis and income on the *Y* axis. The data are plotted in Figure 2A-9, and they do indeed suggest a systematic, almost linear relationship.

Figure 2A-9 is a scatter diagram of observations taken repeatedly over successive periods of time.

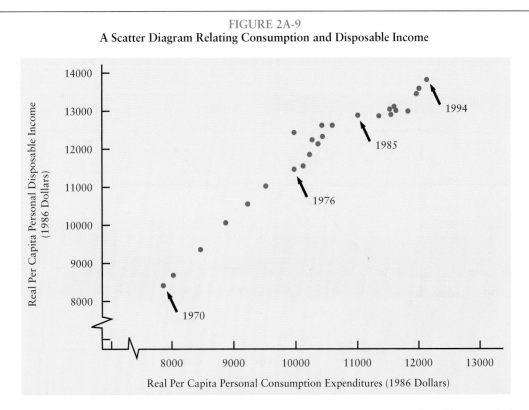

FIGURE 2A-9
A Scatter Diagram Relating Consumption and Disposable Income

This scatter diagram shows paired values of two variables. The data of Table 2A-1 are plotted here. Each dot shows the values of per capita personal consumption expenditures and per capita disposable income for a given year. A close positive linear relationship between the two variables is obvious. Note that in this diagram, the axes are shown with a break in them to indicate that not all the values of the variables between $8,000 and zero are given. Because no observations occurred in those ranges, it is unnecessary to provide space for them.

Such data are called **time-series data,** and plotting them on a scatter diagram involves no new techniques. When cross-sectional data are plotted, each point gives the values of two variables for a particular unit (say, a family); when time-series data are plotted, each point tells the values of two variables for a particular period (say, a year).

Rather than studying the relationship between income and consumption, we might instead be interested in the pattern taken in either *one* of these variables over time. Figure 2A-10 shows this information for personal consumption expenditures per capita. Time is one variable, and consumption expenditure is the other. However, time is a special variable; the order in which successive events happen is important. The year 1994 followed 1993; they were not two independent and unrelated years.

In contrast, two randomly selected households are independent and unrelated. For this reason, it is customary to draw in the line segments connecting the successive points, as has been done in Figure 2A-10.

Such a figure is called a *time-series graph,* or simply a time series. This kind of graph makes it easy to see if the variable being considered has changed in a systematic way over the years or if its behaviour has been more or less erratic.

RATIO (LOGARITHMIC) SCALES

All the foregoing graphs use axes that plot numbers on a natural arithmetic scale, with distances between two values shown by the size of the nu-

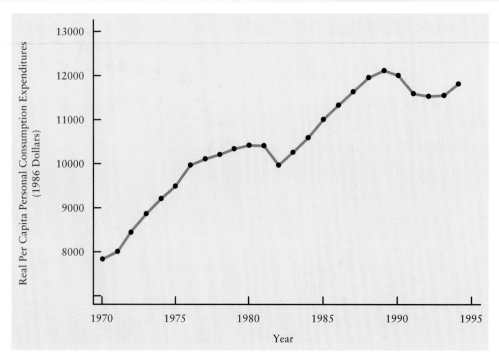

A time series plots values of a single variable in chronological order. This graph shows that with only minor interruptions, consumption measured in 1986 dollars rose from 1970 to 1994. The data are given in Table 2A-1.

merical difference. If *proportionate* rather than *absolute* changes in variables are important, it is more revealing to use a ratio scale than a natural scale. On a **natural scale,** the distance between numbers is proportionate to the absolute difference between those numbers. Thus 200 is placed halfway between 100 and 300. On a **ratio or logarithmic scale,** the distance between numbers is proportionate to the percentage difference between the two numbers (which can also be measured as the absolute difference between their logarithms). Equal distances anywhere on a ratio scale represent equal percentage changes rather than equal absolute changes. On a ratio scale, the distance between 100 and 200 is the same as the distance between 200 and 400, between 1,000 and 2,000, and between any two numbers that stand in the ratio 1:2.

TABLE 2A-2		
Two Series		
Time Period	Series A	Series B
0	$10	$10
1	18	20
2	26	40
3	34	80
4	42	160

Series A shows constant absolute growth ($8 per period) but declining percentage growth. Series B shows constant percentage growth (100 percent per period) but rising absolute growth.

Table 2A-2 shows two series, one growing at a constant absolute amount of 8 units (dollars) per period and the other growing at a constant rate of 100 percent per period. In Figure 2A-11, the series

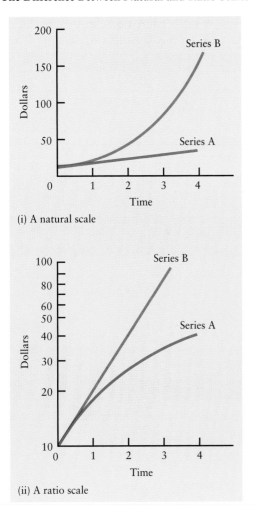

FIGURE 2A-11
The Difference Between Natural and Ratio Scales

(i) A natural scale

(ii) A ratio scale

On a natural scale, equal distances represent equal amounts; on a ratio scale, equal distances represent equal percentage changes. The two series in Table 2A-2 are plotted in each chart. Series A, which grows at a constant absolute amount, is shown by a straight line on a natural scale but by a curve of diminishing slope on a ratio scale because the same absolute growth represents a decreasing percentage growth. Series B, which grows at a rising absolute rate but a constant percentage rate, is shown by a curve of increasing slope on a natural scale but by a straight line on a ratio scale.

makes it easy for the eye to judge proportionate variations.[3]

GRAPHING THREE VARIABLES IN TWO DIMENSIONS

Often we want to show graphically more than two dimensions. For example, a topographic map shows latitude, longitude, and altitude on a two-dimensional page. This is done by using contour lines, as in Figure 2A-12.

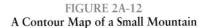

FIGURE 2A-12
A Contour Map of a Small Mountain

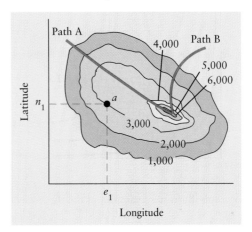

A contour map shows three variables in two-dimensional space. This familiar kind of three-variable graph shows latitude and longitude on the axes and altitude on the contour lines. The contour line labeled 1,000 connects all locations with an altitude of 1,000 metres, the contour line labeled 2,000 connects those with an altitude of 2,000 metres, and so forth. Point a, for example, has latitude n_1, longitude e_1, and an altitude of 3,000 metres. Where the lines are closely bunched, they represent a steep ascent; where they are far apart, a gradual one. Clearly, path A is a gentler climb from 3,000 to 4,000 metres on this mountain than path B.

are plotted first on a natural scale and then on a ratio scale. The natural scale makes it easy for the eye to judge absolute variations, and the ratio scale

---

[3] Graphs with a ratio scale on one axis and a natural scale on the other are frequently encountered in economics. In the case just illustrated, there is a ratio scale on the vertical axis and a natural scale on the horizontal (or time) axis. Such graphs are often called semilog graphs. In scientific work, graphs with ratio scales on both axes are frequently encountered. Such graphs are often referred to as double-log graphs.

Though topographic maps are rarely used in economics, there are many cases where economists wish to show three variables in two dimensions. The information usually takes the following general form. Consider the function $XY = a$, where X, Y, and a are variables. Figure 2A-13 plots this function for three different values of a. The variables X and Y are represented on the two axes. The variable a is represented by the labels on the curves. Several examples of this procedure occur throughout this book (for example, in the Appendix to Chapter 7 and the Appendix to Chapter 9).

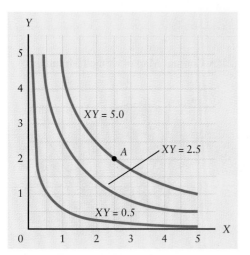

FIGURE 2A-13
Three Variables Shown in Two Dimensions

This graph illustrates examples of the three-variable function $XY = a$. The function $XY = a$ is called a *rectangular hyperbola*. The figure shows three members of the family. For example, point A represents $Y = 2.0$, $X = 2.5$, and $a = 5.0$.

AN OVERVIEW OF THE MARKET ECONOMY

All market economies have certain elements in common, although no two are exactly alike. In this chapter, we explore the main features of market economies, the details of which will occupy us for the rest of the book.

THE DEVELOPMENT OF MARKET ECONOMIES

Until about 10,000 years ago, all human beings were hunter-gatherers, providing for their wants and needs with foods that were freely provided in nature. The Neolithic agricultural revolution changed all that. People gradually abandoned their nomadic life of hunting and food gathering and settled down to tend crops and domesticated animals.

EXTENSION 3-1

THE GAINS FROM SPECIALIZATION

A simple case will illustrate the principles involved in the gains from specialization. A crucial point—and a major source of confusion in the popular press and elsewhere—is that the gains from specialization depend on *comparative advantage* but *not* on *absolute advantage*.

ABSOLUTE AND COMPARATIVE ADVANTAGE

Suppose that we consider two individuals, Jacob and Maria, and two products, sweaters and potatoes. Working full time on his own, Jacob can produce *either* 100 kilograms of potatoes *or* 50 sweaters per year. Maria can produce *either* 400 kilograms of potatoes *or* 100 sweaters per year. In this example, Maria is said to have an **absolute advantage** in the production of both goods because she can make more of each good than Jacob (for equal amount of work effort). It is immaterial *why* Maria has the absolute advantage; the key point is simply that she is better at producing both goods than Jacob.

Note that the pattern of absolute advantage is determined simply by how much of a certain product each individual can make with given inputs (in this case, one year's work). In contrast, the pattern of *comparative advantage* is determined by how much of one product must be given up in order to produce one unit of the other product. Thus *the pattern of comparative advantage depends crucially on opportunity costs.*

To see Jacob's opportunity costs in this example, suppose that he is initially devoting all of his time to producing potatoes with an output of 100 kg. He now considers switching to producing only sweaters. The opportunity cost of the 50 sweaters that he can produce is the 100 kg of potatoes that he no longer produces. It therefore *costs* him 2 kg of potatoes for every sweater he produces; or, expressing it the other way around, Jacob's cost of producing 1 kilogram of potatoes is one-half of a sweater. Using a similar argument for Maria, we see that Maria's opportunity cost of producing 100 sweaters is the 400 kilograms of potatoes that she must forego. Thus, Maria's cost per sweater is 4 kilograms of potatoes; her cost per kilogram of potatoes is one-quarter of a sweater.

Maria is said to have a **comparative advantage** in the production of potatoes because she produces them at a lower opportunity cost than Jacob. Similarly, Jacob has a comparative advantage in sweaters because his opportunity cost for producing sweaters is lower than Maria's.

Note that although Maria is better at producing both goods than Jacob—and thus has an absolute advantage in both goods—she is relatively better *only* in the production of potatoes—and thus Maria has a comparative advantage only in potato production. In this example and more generally, the pattern of absolute advantage tells us very little about the pattern of comparative advantage.

THE GAINS FROM SPECIALIZATION

Table 1 shows the output of each good per person, and the total output, in the situation where both Maria and Jacob divide their time equally between the production of the two goods.

To see the connection between comparative advantage and the gains from specialization, consider what happens when Jacob and Maria specialize

SPECIALIZATION, SURPLUS, AND TRADE

Along with permanent settlement, the agricultural revolution brought surplus production. Farmers could produce substantially more than they needed for survival. The agricultural surplus allowed the creation of new occupations. Freed from having to grow their own food, people formed new classes—artisans, soldiers, priests, government officials—as they turned their talents to performing specialized services and producing goods other than food. They also produced more than they themselves needed and traded the excess to obtain other goods.

TABLE 1
Production of Potatoes and Sweaters with Each Person's Time Divided Equally Between the Two Commodities

	Potatoes (kg)	Sweaters
Jacob	50	25
Maria	200	50
Total	250	75

along the lines suggested by the pattern of comparative advantage. Specifically, suppose that Jacob decides to specialize in the production of sweaters (he therefore produces no potatoes) and that Maria decides to spend 70 percent of her time producing potatoes (and 30 percent of her time producing sweaters). Table 2 shows the results in this case. The reason why production of both goods is higher in Table 2 than in Table 1 is that Jacob and Maria have each specialized toward the production of the good for which they have the lowest opportunity cost—that is, toward the good in which they have the comparative advantage.

Now consider what happens if Jacob and Maria specialize in the "wrong" direction. The numbers in parentheses in Table 2 show what happens if Jacob produces only potatoes and Maria spends 70 percent

TABLE 2
Production of Potatoes and Sweaters with Partial Specialization

	Potatoes (kg)		Sweaters	
Jacob	0	(100)	50	(0)
Maria	280	(120)	30	(70)
Total	280	(220)	80	(70)
Change from Table 1	+30	(−30)	+5	(−5)

of her time making sweaters and 30 percent making potatoes.

By specializing along the lines of comparative advantage, Jacob gives up only 2 kg of potatoes for each new sweater produced; Maria gives up only one-quarter of a sweater for each new kg of potatoes produced. By specializing in the opposite direction—against the pattern of comparative advantage—the cost of each new sweater is 4 kg of potatoes and the cost of each new kg of potatoes is one-half of a sweater. Comparing these opportunity costs, it is no wonder that total output is increased *only when specialization takes place along the pattern of comparative advantage!*

This example is obviously quite special, but the principles involved are very general. These principles can be generalized as follows:

- The pattern of absolute advantage is often very different from the pattern of comparative advantage.

- Total production can be increased when each person specializes in the production of the product in which he or she has a comparative advantage.

A more detailed study of the important concept of comparative advantage and its many applications to international trade and specialization must await the chapter on international trade (which is sometimes studied in courses on microeconomics and sometimes in courses on macroeconomics). In the meantime, it is worth noting that the comparative advantage of individuals and of whole nations may change. Maria may learn new skills and develop a comparative advantage in sweaters that she does not currently have. Similarly, whole nations may develop new abilities and know-how that will change their pattern of comparative advantage.

The allocation of different jobs to different people is called **specialization of labour.** Specialization has proved extraordinarily efficient compared with self-sufficiency, for two important reasons.

First, individual talents and abilities differ, and specialization allows each person to do the job he or she can do best while leaving everything else to be done by others. That production is greater with specialization than with self-sufficiency is one of the most fundamental principles in economics, known as the principle of *comparative advantage.* An example is given in Extension 3-1, and a much fuller discussion is found in Chapter 35.

Second, a person who concentrates on one activity becomes better at it than a jack-of-all-trades could. This is called "learning by doing," and was a factor much stressed by early economists. Modern research into what are called learning curves shows that learning by doing is important in many industries.

The exchange of goods and services in early societies commonly took place by simple mutual agreement among neighbours. In the course of time, however, trading became centred in particular gathering places called markets. Today we use the term *market economy* to refer to a society in which people specialize in productive activities and satisfy most of their material wants through exchanges.

Specialization must be accompanied by trade. People who produce only one thing must trade much of their production to obtain all the other things they require.

The earliest market economies depended to some considerable extent on **barter,** the trading of goods directly for other goods.[1] But barter can be a costly process in terms of the time spent searching out satisfactory exchanges. The evolution of money has made trading easier. Money eliminates the inconvenience of barter by allowing the two sides of the barter transaction to be separated. Farmers who have wheat and want hammers do not have to search for individuals who have hammers and want wheat. They take money in exchange, then find people who wish to trade hammers, and offer money for the hammers.

By eliminating the need for barter, money greatly facilitates trade and specialization.

THE DIVISION OF LABOUR

Market transactions in early economies involved mainly consumption goods. Producers specialized in making a product and then traded it for the other products they needed. Over the past several hundred years, many technical advances in methods of production have made it efficient to organize agriculture and industry on a large scale. These technical developments have made use of what is called the **division**

---

[1]Barter was common in the earliest societies that flourished before the invention of money and in medieval villages and it survived in isolated cases into more recent times. For example, much of the early North American fur trade was barter, with trinkets, gems, cloths, and firearms being traded directly for furs.

of labour, a further step in the specialization of labour involving specialization within the production process of a particular good or service. The labour involved is divided into a series of repetitive tasks, and each individual performs a single task that may be just one of hundreds of tasks necessary to produce the product.

To gain the advantages of the division of labour, it became necessary to organize production in large factories. Typical workers no longer earned their incomes by selling goods and services they had personally produced; rather, they sold their labour services to firms and received money wages in return. With this development, most urban workers lost their status as artisans and became dependent on their ability to sell their labour. Adam Smith (1723–1790), the great eighteenth-century Scottish political economist, was the first to study the division of labour in detail, as discussed in Extension 3-2.

Interestingly, recent changes have led to an increasing number of self-employed workers who are more like the artisans of old than like factory workers. Even within the factory, a new organizational principle called *lean production* or *flexible manufacturing*, pioneered by Japanese automobile manufacturers, has led to a more craft-based form of organization within the factory. In this technique, employees work as a team; each employee is able to do every team member's job rather than one very specialized task at one point on the assembly line. These important developments are discussed further in Chapter 9.

MARKETS AND RESOURCE ALLOCATION

As explained in Chapter 1, *resource allocation* refers to the distribution of the available factors of production among their various uses. There are not enough resources to produce all the goods and services that could be consumed. It is therefore necessary to allocate the available resources among their various possible uses and in so doing to choose what to produce and what not to produce. In a market economy, millions of consumers decide what goods and services to buy and in what quantities; a vast number of firms produce these goods and services and buy the factor services (labour and capital) that are needed to produce them; and millions of factor owners decide to whom they will

THE DIVISION OF LABOUR

Adam Smith begins his classic *The Wealth of Nations* (1776) with a long study on the division of labour.

> The greatest improvements in the productive powers of labour . . . have been the effects of the division of labour.
>
> To take an example . . . the trade of the pin-maker, a workman not educated to this business (which the division of labour has rendered a distinct trade), nor acquainted with the use of the machinery employed in it could scarce, perhaps, with his utmost industry, make one pin in a day, and certainly could not make twenty. But in the way in which this business is now carried on . . . it is divided into a number of branches . . . One man draws out the wire, another straightens it, a third cuts it, a fourth points it, a fifth grinds it at the top for receiving the head; to make the head requires two or three distinct operations; to put it on is a peculiar business, to whiten the pins is another; it is even a trade by itself to put them into the paper; and the important business of making a pin is, in this manner, divided into about eighteen distinct operations, which, in some manufactories, are all performed by distinct hands, though in others the same man will sometimes perform two or three of them.

Smith observes that even in smallish factories, where the division of labour is exploited only in part, output is as high as 4,800 pins per person per day!

Later, Smith discusses the general importance of the division of labour and the forces that limit its application:

> Each animal is still obliged to support and defend itself, separately and independently, and derives no sort of advantage from that variety of talents with which nature has distinguished its fellows. Among men, on the contrary, the most dissimilar geniuses are of use to one another; the different produces of their respective talents, by the general disposition of truck, barter, and exchange, being brought, as it were, into a common stock, where every man may purchase whatever part of the produce of other men's talents he has occasion for.
>
> As it is the power of exchanging that gives occasion to the division of labour, so the extent of this division must always be limited by the extent of that power, or, in other words, by the extent of the market. When the market is very small, no person can have any encouragement to dedicate himself entirely to one employment for want [i.e., lack] of the power to exchange all that surplus part of the produce of his own labour, which is over and above his own consumption, for such parts of the produce of other men's labour as he has occasion for.

Smith notes that there is no point in specializing to produce a large quantity of pins, or anything else, unless there are enough persons making other goods and services to provide a market for all the pins that are produced. Thus the larger the market, the greater is the scope for the division of labour and the higher are the resulting opportunities for efficient production.

sell these services. These individual decisions collectively determine the economy's allocation of resources.

In a market economy, the allocation of resources is the outcome of countless independent decisions made by consumers and producers, all acting through the medium of markets.

This chapter provides an overview of the market mechanism.

THE DECISION MAKERS

Economics is about the behaviour of people. Much that we observe in the world and that economists assume in their theories can be traced back to decisions made by individuals. There are millions of individuals in most economies. To make a systematic study of their behaviour more manageable, economists categorize them into three important groups: households, firms, and government, collectively known as **agents**.[2] Members of these groups are economic theory's cast of characters.

HOUSEHOLDS

A **household** is defined as all the people who live under one roof and who make joint financial decisions or are subject to others who make such decisions for them. The members of households are often referred to as *consumers* because they buy and consume most of the consumption goods and services. Economic theory gives households a number of attributes.

First, economists assume that each household makes consistent decisions, as though it were composed of a single individual. Thus economists typically ignore many interesting problems of how each household reaches its decisions, including family conflicts and the moral and legal problems concerning parental control over minors.[3]

Second, economists assume that when buying goods and services and selling factor services, households are the principal owners of factors of production. They sell the services of these factors to firms and receive their incomes in return.

Finally, economists assume that each household seeks maximum *satisfaction* or what economists call *utility*. The household tries to do this within the limits set by its available resources.

FIRMS

A **firm** is defined as the unit that employs factors of production to produce goods and services that it sells to other firms, to households, or to government. For obvious reasons, a firm is often called a *producer*. Economic theory gives firms several attributes.

First, each firm is assumed to make consistent decisions, as though it were composed of a single individual. This strand of theory ignores the internal problems of how particular decisions are reached by assuming that the firm's internal organization is irrelevant to its decisions. This allows the firm to be treated, at least in elementary theory, as the unit of behaviour on the production or supply side of product markets, just as the household is treated as the unit of behaviour on the consumption or demand side.[4]

Second, economists assume that in their role as producers, firms are the principal users of the services of factors of production. In *factor markets,* where factor services are bought and sold, the roles of firms and households are thus reversed from what they are in product markets: In factor markets, firms do the buying and households do the selling.

Finally, economists assume that most firms make their decisions with a single goal in mind: to make as much profit as possible. This goal of *profit maximization* is analogous to the household's goal of utility maximization.

GOVERNMENT

The term **government** is used in economics in a broad sense to include all public officials, agencies, government bodies, and other organizations belonging to or under the direct control of federal, provincial, and local governments. For example, in Canada, the term government includes, among others, the prime minister, the Bank of Canada, city councils, commissions and regulatory bodies, legislative bodies, and police forces. It is not important to draw up a comprehensive list, but one should have in mind a general idea of the organizations that have legal and political power to exert control over individual decision makers and over markets.

It is *not* a basic assumption of economics that government always acts in a consistent fashion. Two important reasons for this may be mentioned here.

First, what we call "government" has many levels and many branches. For example, the mayor of Toronto, an MLA from Alberta, and a senator from Nova Scotia represent different constituencies.

---

[2]Although we can get away with just three sets of decision makers, it is worth noting that there are others. Probably the most important of those omitted are nonprofit organizations such as private universities and hospitals, charities, and research organizations such as the C. D. Howe Institute and the Institute for Research on Public Policy. These bodies have a significant influence on the allocation of the economy's resources.

[3]Some economists have studied resource allocation within households. This field of study, pioneered by University of Chicago economist and Nobel laureate Gary Becker, is often treated in advanced courses in labour economics.

---

[4]At the more advanced level, many studies look within the firm to ask questions such as "Does the firm's internal organization affect its behaviour?" We briefly consider such questions in Chapter 14.

Similarly, the federal departments of Finance, Human Resources, and International Trade represent different interests, each with its own goals. Therefore, different and conflicting views and objectives are typically found within "government."

Second, decisions on interrelated issues of policy are made by many different bodies. Federal and provincial legislatures pass laws, the courts interpret laws, governments decide which laws to enforce with vigour and which not to enforce, the Department of Finance and the Bank of Canada influence monetary conditions, and a host of other agencies and semiautonomous bodies determine actions in respect to different aspects of policy goals. Because of the multiplicity of decision makers, it would be amazing if fully consistent behaviour resulted.

Individual public servants, whether elected or appointed, have personal objectives (such as staying in office, promotion, power, and prestige) as well as public service objectives. Although the balance of importance given to the two kinds of objectives will vary among persons and among types of office, both will almost always have some influence. For example, in a free vote in Parliament, most MPs would vote in favour of a popular measure—even if they believed it was detrimental to the public good—if voting against it meant likely defeat in the next election.

As this discussion reveals, an important goal of legislators and political officials is electoral success—their own and that of their political party. As a result, governments often fail to adopt measures that impose large costs and yield few obvious benefits over the short run, even if the long-term benefits may be large. In other words, there tends to be a bias toward shortsightedness in an elective system. At the same time, in a democratic system, government actions cannot get too far away from what a majority of the electorate will approve. These and other issues of government motivation are discussed further in Chapter 18.

Markets and economies

If households, firms, and government are the main actors in the economy, markets are the stage on which their drama takes place.

MARKETS

Originally, *markets* were places where goods were bought and sold. The Granville Island Market in Vancouver is a modern example of a market in the everyday sense, and many cities and towns have their own "farmers' markets." Much early economic theory explained price behaviour in just such markets. Why, for example, can you get great bargains at the end of some days, but at the end of other days you buy at prices that appear exorbitant compared to the prices quoted only a few hours earlier?

As theories of market behaviour were developed, they were extended to cover commodities such as wheat. Wheat produced anywhere in the world can be purchased almost anywhere else in the world, and the price of a given grade of wheat tends to be nearly uniform. When we talk about the wheat market, the concept of a market has been extended well beyond the idea of a single place where the producer and consumer meet to sell and buy.

Similarly, the foreign exchange market has no specific location. Instead, it operates through international telephone and computer networks whereby dealers buy and sell dollars, sterling, francs, yen, and other national currencies. Markets may indeed use all conceivable means of communication, including the press, as in the case of the markets for many second-hand goods such as automobiles. If you have a car to sell or want to buy one, you will discover that "the market" comprises the local newspapers and bulletin boards, specialized magazines, and used-car dealers.

In the modern sense, a **market** refers to any situation in which buyers and sellers can negotiate the exchange of some product. In the past, high transportation costs and perishability made many markets quite local. Fresh fruits and vegetables, for example, would only be sold close to their points of production. Today, advances in preservation, the falling cost of transportation, and the development of worldwide communications networks have led to the globalization of many markets. A visit to the supermarket will confirm that food products such as Bulgarian jam, Chilean apples, and Indian rice are no longer confined to markets within their country of origin.

ECONOMIES

An **economy** is rather loosely defined as a set of interrelated production and consumption activities. It may refer to this activity in a region of one country (e.g., the economy of the Maritimes), in a country (the Canadian economy), or in a group of countries (the North American economy). In any economy, the allocation of resources is determined by the production, sales, and purchase decisions made by firms, households, and governments.

In Chapter 1, we learned three important things about economies. First, a *free-market economy* is one in which the decisions of individual households and firms (as distinct from the government) exert the major influence over the allocation of resources. Second, the opposite of a free-market economy is a *command economy,* in which the major decisions about the allocation of resources are made by the government and in which firms produce and households consume only as directed. Third, in practice, all economies are *mixed economies* in that some decisions are made by firms, households, and the government acting through markets while other decisions are made by the government using the command principle.

The past decade has brought a fourth type of economy into prominence—the *transition economy.* The countries of Eastern and Central Europe, along with the countries of the former Soviet Union, began the difficult transition from centrally planned economies toward free-market economies in the early 1990s. These economies displayed many unique characteristics, many of which related to the absence of certain *institutions.* This is discussed in Application 3-1.

THE SECTORS OF AN ECONOMY

Parts of an economy are usually referred to as **sectors** of that economy. For example, the agricultural sector is the part of the economy that produces agricultural commodities, and the manufacturing sector produces finished goods, such as automobiles and electric shavers.

The Market and Nonmarket Sectors

Producers make goods and provide services. Consumers use them. Goods and services may pass from one group to the other in two ways. They may be sold by producers and bought by consumers through markets, or they may be given away.

When goods and services are bought and sold, producers expect to cover their costs with the revenue they obtain from selling the product. We call this *marketed production,* and we refer to this part of the economy's activity as belonging to the **market sector.** When the product is given away, the costs of production must be covered from some source other than sales revenue. We call this *nonmarketed production,* and we refer to this part of the economy's activity as belonging to the **nonmarket sector.**

In the case of private charities, the money required to pay for factor services may be raised from the public by voluntary contributions. In the case of production by government—which accounts for the bulk of nonmarketed production—the money is provided from government revenue, which in turn comes mainly from taxes.

Whenever a government enterprise *sells* its output, its production is in the market sector. Most of government's output, however, is in the nonmarket sector, often by the very nature of the product provided. For example, one could hardly expect the criminal to pay the judge for providing the service of criminal justice. Other products are in the nonmarket sector because governments have decided that there are advantages to removing them from the market sector. This is the case, for example, with public school education and medical and hospital services in Canada. Public policy places it in the nonmarket sector even though much of it could be provided by the market sector.

The economic significance of this distinction lies in the "bottom line." (In accounting, the bottom line refers to profits.) In the market sector, firms face the bottom-line test of profitability. If a product cannot be sold for a price that will cover its costs and provide sufficient profit for its makers, the product will not be made. Production in the nonmarket sector faces no such profitability test. Because the product is provided free and its costs are met by contributions, the decision to produce it depends on the willingness of government and private bodies to pay its costs and not on its ability to be sold at a cost-covering price.

The Private and Public Sectors

An alternative division of an economy's productive activity is between the private and public sectors. The private sector refers to all production that is in private hands, and the public sector refers to all production that is in public hands—that is, owned by government. The distinction between the two sectors depends on the legal distinction of ownership. In the **private sector,** the organization that does the producing is owned by households or other firms; in the **public sector,** it is owned and controlled by government. The public sector includes all production of goods and services by government plus all production of all publicly owned companies and other government-operated industries that is sold to consumers through markets.

The distinction between the market and nonmarket sectors is economic; it depends on whether or not producers cover their costs from revenue earned by selling output to users. The distinction between the private and public sectors is legal; it depends on whether the producing organizations are privately or publicly owned.

Some examples will illustrate these important distinctions. The Aluminum Company of Canada (ALCAN) is in the private and market sectors; a Salvation Army soup kitchen is in the private and nonmarket sectors. The provincial hydro authorities are in the public and market sectors. The Canadian Coast Guard is in the public and nonmarket sectors.

INSTITUTIONS

In discussions about markets, economies, and sectors, it is easy to forget about the importance of *institutions* in the operation of a market economy. In developed countries like Canada, these institutions have been operating for so many years that they are now taken for granted.

The most important example is the legal system. The existence of laws to facilitate the writing and enforcement of contracts between buyers and sellers clearly aids in the operation of a market economy. Imagine your reluctance to purchase a new car if there did not exist a civil court system which would enforce your claim to ownership, or the difficulty of operating a restaurant if your food suppliers did not honour their contractual obligations to supply your meat or fresh produce.

Laws which define and protect *property rights* and the *enforcement of contracts* are crucial to the smooth operation of market economies. In the absence of private property rights, there would be little incentive to improve land or to build plant and equipment (which could be arbitrarily confiscated at some later date). Without enforceable contracts, there would be no incentive to train workers who could not be tied by a contractual agreement to a specific period of work. Nor would there be anything like insurance or *forward markets*—there would be no

payment in advance for goods and services to be delivered at some point in the future.

The experiences of Eastern and Central Europe in recent years have brought to our attention the fact that for mixed economies to function effectively, their markets must be supported by a complicated set of governmental and private institutions. The special problems and lessons of these transition economies are discussed in Application 3-1.

MICROECONOMICS AND MACROECONOMICS

As we saw in Chapter 1, there are two different but complementary ways of viewing the economy. The first, **microeconomics,** studies the detailed workings of individual markets and interrelationships among markets. The second, **macroeconomics,** suppresses much of the detail and concentrates on the behaviour of broad aggregates.[5]

Microeconomics and macroeconomics differ in the questions each asks and in the level of aggregation each uses. Microeconomics deals with the determination of prices and quantities in individual markets and with the relationships among these markets. Thus it looks at the details of the market economy. It asks, for example, how much labour is employed in the fast-food industry and why the amount is increasing. It asks about the determinants of the output of broccoli, pocket calculators, automobiles, and hamburgers. It asks, too, about the prices of these goods—why some prices go up and others down. For example, economists interested in microeconomics analyze how a new invention, a government subsidy, or a drought will affect the price and output of wheat and the employment of farmworkers.

In contrast, macroeconomics focuses on much broader aggregates. It looks at such things as the total number of people employed and unemployed, the average level of all prices, national output, and aggregate consumption. Macroeconomics asks what determines these aggregates and how they respond to changing conditions. Whereas microeconomics looks at demand and supply with regard to particular goods and services, macroeconomics looks at aggregate demand and aggregate supply.

---

[5]The prefixes "micro" and "macro" derive from the Greek words *mikros,* for small and *makros,* for large.

| APPLICATION 3-1 |

THE TRANSITION ECONOMIES OF CENTRAL AND EASTERN EUROPE AND THE FORMER SOVIET UNION*

The countries of the former Soviet Union became a command economy after the Russian Revolution of 1917. The other countries of Eastern Europe became command economies when they fell under Soviet domination after the end of the Second World War in 1945. After the fall of the Berlin Wall in 1989, the Central and Eastern European countries then began the long process of transition from command economy to market economy. The republics of the former Soviet Union began this process in earnest in 1991. Because command economies and market economies are fundamentally different in both their essentials and their details, the transition process is proving to be lengthy and difficult. As of 1996, none of the affected economies can be considered fully command economies, but many are still far from functioning well as market economies.

The period of transition between command and market economy is generally characterized by the enactment of various economic reforms. As the transition began, most of the transition economies saw sharp drops in output followed by large decreases in employment. Many citizens experienced a fall in their living standards, and inflation greatly eroded the incomes of pensioners and others with fixed incomes. Although the difficulties of transition have been taken by some observers to signal the failure of the market system, economists generally see these hardships as a reflection of the extreme difficulty of transition from one system to the other.

Transition requires changes in institutions, custom, and the relationships between economy and government. These changes simply cannot be accomplished overnight. Several issues highlight the complexity of reform and help explain why transition takes a long time and is so painful.

THE CREDIBILITY OF REFORMS

The motivations of agents in a command economy are very different from those that operate in a market economy. To transform an economic system, agents in the economy must change their economic behaviour and learn to respond to prices, taking seriously the relationship between profit-seeking behaviour and their own economic well-being. Many people are reluctant to change their behaviour until they are certain that the reforms will indeed carry through. That is why, for transition to proceed, it is crucial that the reforms be credible—that the agents believe that the government will not reverse them.

The most obvious credibility problem in the formerly communist countries of Central and Eastern Europe and the former Soviet Union is the general disbelief that the government will allow bankrupt firms to shut down. In the days of central planning and command, the government bailed out firms that experienced financial losses. Now governments have announced that bankruptcy is possible and therefore firms need to earn profits if they want to remain in business. However, during the transition, especially in the early period of high inflation and unemployment, many firms were losing money. Governments were unwilling to allow a large proportion of productive capacity to shut down but could not easily determine which firms had the potential to become profitable in the long run. Where governments refrained from closing down firms, they made the bankruptcy reforms incredible. Firms came to believe that they would be bailed out in spite of the announced reforms, and therefore the incentive to minimize costs and maximize profits was weakened.

---

*For a very interesting discussion of the early progress made in the Eastern European transition economies, see O. J. Blanchard et al., *Reform in Eastern Europe* (MIT Press 1991); see also the subsequent progress report, O. J. Blanchard et al., *Post-Communist Reform* (MIT Press 1993).

THE RULE OF LAW

Although we often think of market economies as being governed only by the forces of demand and supply, they have a myriad of laws that help to govern economic behaviour and allow markets to run smoothly. For example, there are laws that facilitate the writing and enforcement of contracts between buyers and suppliers and between firms and workers, laws that dictate bankruptcy conditions and procedures, and laws that control the operation of stock markets and guarantee stockholders' rights as owners. Generally, these laws define and protect *property rights* in economic enterprises.

The command economies did not have such laws or the legal apparatus to support them, such as an extensive civil court system. To function effectively as market economies, each of these countries must enact laws that fit its desired political and economic structure and that establish property rights in economic activities. Often the procedure of passing the new legislation is even more time-consuming than the initial process of devising the policies and writing the legislation. Establishing institutions for enforcement takes longer still. Until the laws and institutions are in place, legal uncertainty hinders exchanges between economic agents.

One example of a crucial commercial law that is missing or nascent in transition economies is company law. Company law regulates the governance of firms; it stipulates what rights certain agents, such as stockholders and investors, have in firms' decision making. Without company law to protect these rights, agents are reluctant to invest in firms. Consequently, many firms in transition economies have been unable to attract desperately needed investment from either foreign or domestic investors.

SECTORAL ADJUSTMENT

Transition in the formerly communist countries entails two major sectoral adjustments. The first is the transfer of production from the public sector to the private sector. Such *privatization* of the economy involves both the transfer of existing physical assets from state ownership to private ownership and the entry of new private firms into the economy. Whereas facilitating new entry is relatively easy, the privatization of existing assets is very complicated, and there are many political and economic debates about how it should be done. The success of privatization to date has varied widely from one country to another.

The second necessary sectoral adjustment is a change in the proportions of economic activity accounted for by the military sector and the consumer goods sector. Central planning allowed the countries of the Soviet bloc to invest heavily in the production of military and industrial goods like weapons and machinery while skimping on the production of consumer goods like televisions and clothing. Under the market system, although the government will still be one of the economy's consumers, households will a count for the majority of the demand for goods. Households want firms to produce far more consumer goods and fewer military goods. Unfortunately, it is not easy for a firm to change its production. The machines used to make missiles cannot be used to sew clothing. Thus the sectoral shift requires large-scale retooling and in many cases the rebuilding of factories. It also requires the retraining of many employees.

THE GOOD NEWS

Most of the economies in transition are making good progress. Different countries have succeeded in different areas so far, but most have passed the point of no return. In many Central and Eastern European countries, output has begun to increase and inflation has stabilized.

AN OVERVIEW OF MICROECONOMICS

Early economists observed the market economy with wonder. They saw that even though goods and services were made by many independent producers, the amounts of goods and services produced approximately equaled the amounts that people wanted to purchase. Natural disasters aside, there were neither vast surpluses nor severe shortages of products. They also saw that in spite of the ever-changing geographical, industrial, and occupational patterns of demand for labour services, most workers were able to sell their services to employers most of the time. Visitors from highly regulated economies often have a similar reaction. How, they ask, can there be such an abundance of the right things, produced at the right time, and delivered to the right place—something that planned economies have conspicuously failed to do?

The Price System as a Coordination Mechanism

How does the market produce this order in the absence of conscious coordination? It is one thing to have the same good produced year in and year out when people's wants and incomes do not change; it is quite another thing to have production adjusting continually to changing wants, incomes, and techniques of production. Yet this adjustment is accomplished relatively smoothly by markets—albeit with occasional, and sometimes serious, interruptions.

Markets work without conscious central control because individual agents make their private decisions in response to publicly known signals such as prices, wages, and profits, and these signals, in turn, respond to the collective actions entailed by the sum of all individual decisions. In short:

The great discovery of eighteenth-century economists was that the price system is a mechanism that coordinates decentralized decision making.

In *The Wealth of Nations,* Adam Smith (1723–1790) spoke of the price system as "the invisible hand." The system allows decision making to be decentralized to millions of individual producers and consumers but nonetheless to be coordinated. A simple example may help to illustrate how this coordination occurs; Part 2 of this book develops these ideas more formally.

An Example

Suppose that under prevailing conditions, farmers find it equally profitable to produce either of two crops, carrots or broccoli. As a result, they are willing to produce some of both commodities, thereby satisfying the demands of households to consume both. Now suppose that consumers develop a greatly increased desire for broccoli and a diminished desire for carrots. This change might have occurred because of the discovery of hitherto unsuspected nutritive or curative powers of broccoli.

When consumers buy more broccoli and fewer carrots, a shortage of broccoli and a surplus of carrots develop. To unload their surplus stocks of carrots, merchants reduce the price of carrots because it is better to sell them at a reduced price than not to sell them at all. Merchants find, however, that they are unable to satisfy all their customers' demands for broccoli. Broccoli has become more scarce, so merchants charge more for it. As the price rises, fewer people are willing and able to purchase broccoli. Thus the rise in its price limits the quantity demanded to the available supply.

Farmers see that broccoli production has become more profitable than in the past because the costs of producing broccoli remain unchanged while its market price has risen. Similarly, they see that carrot production has become less profitable than in the past because costs are unchanged while the price has fallen. Attracted by high profits in broccoli and deterred by low profits or potential losses in carrots, farmers expand the production of broccoli and reduce the production of carrots. Thus the change in consumers' tastes, working through the price system, causes a reallocation of resources—land and labour—out of carrot production and into broccoli production.

The reaction of the market to a change in demand leads to a reallocation of resources. Carrot producers reduce their production; they will therefore be laying off workers and generally demanding fewer factors of production. Broccoli producers expand production; they will therefore be hiring workers and generally increasing their demand for factors of production.

Labour can probably switch from carrot to broccoli production without much difficulty. Certain types of land, however, may be better suited for growing one crop than the other. When farmers increase their broccoli production, their demands for the factors especially suited to growing broccoli also increase—and this creates a shortage of these resources and a consequent rise in their prices. Meanwhile, with carrot production falling, the demand for land and other factors of production especially suited to growing carrots is reduced. A surplus results, and the prices of these factors decline.

Thus factors particularly suited to broccoli production will earn more and will obtain a higher share of total national income than before. Factors particularly suited to carrot production, however, will earn less and will obtain a smaller share of total national income than before.

All of the changes illustrated in this example will be studied more fully in subsequent parts of this book; the important thing to notice now is how changes in demand cause reallocations of resources in the directions required to cater to the new pattern of demand.

This example illustrates the point made earlier: *The price system is a mechanism that coordinates individual, decentralized decisions.*

AN OVERVIEW OF MACROECONOMICS

We can group together all the buyers of the nation's output and call their total desired purchases *aggregate demand*. We can also group together all the producers of the nation's output and call their total desired sales *aggregate supply*.

Sudden changes in aggregate demand are called *demand shocks*, and sudden changes in aggregate supply are called *supply shocks*. Shocks cause important changes in the broad averages and aggregates that are the concern of macroeconomics, including total output, total employment, and average levels of prices and wages. Government actions sometimes cause demand or supply shocks; at other times, governments are reacting to the shocks. In the latter case, the government may attempt to cushion or change the effects of a particular shock.

The Circular Flow of Income

One way to gain insight into aggregate demand and aggregate supply is to view the economy as a giant set of flows. We build up a picture of such flows in stages.

In Figure 3-1, all producers of goods and services are grouped together in the lower coloured

area. All consumers of goods and services are grouped together in the upper coloured area.[6]

The interactions between producers and consumers take place through two kinds of markets. Goods and services that are produced by firms are sold in markets that are usually referred to as *goods markets*. The services of factors of production (land, labour, and capital) are sold in markets called *factor markets*. The interactions involve flows going in two directions. Flows of goods and services, called *real flows*, are shown flowing counterclockwise in part (i) of the figure. Flows of payments for these goods and services, called *money flows*, are shown flowing clockwise in part (ii) of the figure.

We may now look in a little more detail at the relations just outlined.

Goods Markets.   The outputs of goods and services flow from producers to consumers through what are usually known as **goods markets** (or product markets), which includes both goods and services. Note the use of the plural *markets*: Just as firms produce many products, so there are many markets in which products are sold. Households constitute one major group of consumers—indeed, the largest, by amount consumed. They buy, for their own use, goods and services such as food, clothing, train journeys, legal services, and cars. Other consumers include firms that purchase capital goods produced by yet other firms, and foreigners who purchase exports.

Factor Markets.   Most people earn their incomes by selling factor services to producers. (Exceptions are people receiving payments from such schemes as pension plans and unemployment insurance; they receive an income, but not in return for providing their factor services to help in current production.) Most of those who do sell factor services are employees. They sell their labour services to firms in return for wages. Some others own capital and receive interest or profits for providing it. Others own land and derive rents from it. The buying and selling of these factor services takes place in **factor**

---

[6]Most individuals and firms have a double role. As buyers of goods and services, they play a part in consuming that output; as sellers of factor services and other inputs, they play a part in producing that output.

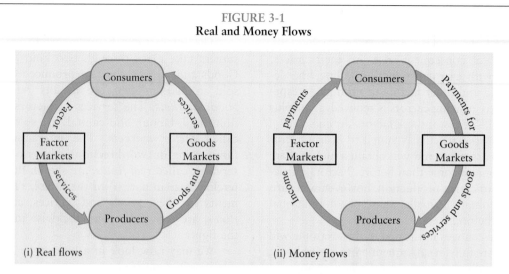

FIGURE 3-1
Real and Money Flows

(i) Real flows

(ii) Money flows

Real flows of goods and services go in one direction between producers and consumers, whereas money flows of payments go in the opposite direction. The blue arrows in part (i) show real flows. Goods and services made by producers are sold to the people who consume them, and factor services owned by consumers are sold to producers. The red arrows in part (ii) show money flows. Income payments go to consumers in return for the factor services they sell. Expenditures flow from consumers to producers in return for the goods and services they buy.

markets. The buyers are producers. They use the services that they purchase as inputs for the production of goods and services that are sold to consumers.

The Circular Flow of Income.   What we have just described involves two circular *flows*. This concept of circularity in economic relations is a crucial one. It helps us to understand how the separate parts of the economy are related in a system of mutual interaction. For example, the activities of producers directly affect household incomes because the wages that producers pay make up the largest part of people's incomes. The activities of households directly affect firms because the goods and services that households buy account for the largest part of the sales revenues of firms.

The two parts of Figure 3-1 provide alternative ways of looking at the same transactions. Every market transaction is a two-sided exchange in the sense that for every sale there is a purchase and for every seller there is a buyer. The buyer receives goods or services and parts with money; the seller receives money and parts with goods or services.

The blue arrows in part (i) of the figure show the flows of goods and services through markets. They are shown flowing counterclockwise, from consumers to producers and from producers to consumers. The red arrows in part (ii) of the figure show the corresponding flows of money payments. Flows of payments are going in the opposite direction—clockwise. Payments flow from producers to consumers to pay for factor services, and they flow from consumers to producers to pay for goods and services.[7]

To distinguish these two sets of flows, each of which is the counterpart of the other, the blue flows in part (i) are called real flows, and the red flows in part (ii) are called money flows.

Both of these ways of looking at the flows of economic transactions carry an important message. When firms produce goods and services, they create through factor payments the incomes needed to purchase their outputs; when users buy the outputs of firms, their payments create the revenues that firms need to pay for the factors of production that they employ. The main circular flow is shown passing from domestic producers to domestic households

---

[7]The direction (clockwise or counterclockwise) is of no significance. What is significant is that the real and the money flows are in opposite directions. Any real flow is matched by a corresponding money flow going in the other direction.

FIGURE 3-2
The Circular Flow Elaborated

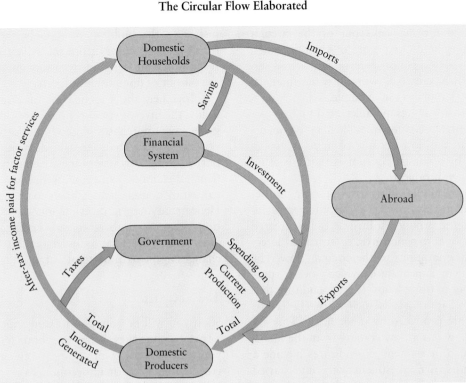

Taxes, savings, and imports withdraw expenditures from the circular flow; government purchases, investment, and exports inject expenditures into the circular flow. Some of the total income created by domestic producers leaks out of the circular flow because of government taxes on incomes. Some household income leaks out of the circular flow because of saving and imports; the rest is spent on purchasing the output of domestic firms. The injections of investment, government expenditure, and exports plus household expenditure on domestic output account for the total purchases of domestic output.

and back again. On the way, however, there are several leakages from and injections into this flow around the main circuit.

Other Flows

Figure 3-2 elaborates on the money flows shown in part (ii) of Figure 3-1. It does so by allowing for private-sector saving and investment, government taxing and spending, and foreign trade. Because we are going to allow for foreign trade, the bottom box is labeled "Domestic Producers" to distinguish them from foreign producers. In addition, because we are going to allow for several classes of consumers of output, the top box is now labeled "Domestic Households" to distinguish that group from the

other purchasers of domestic output: foreigners, government, and firms that purchase capital goods.

Leakages.   As shown in Figure 3-2, payments flow from domestic producers to domestic households by way of payments for factor services. On the way, however, there is a **leakage** of some payments out of the circular flow because of government taxes, which reduce the flow of income payments that would otherwise go to households.[8]

---

[8]Government transfers to households, such as unemployment insurance and Social Security pensions, act as injections into the flow. The taxes shown in Figure 3-2 are the net leakage—total taxes minus total government transfers to households.

Payments pass from domestic households to domestic producers when households spend their incomes to buy goods and services made by producers. Some household income leaks out of the circular flow when households save part of their incomes. The part that is saved is not spent on goods and services. Instead it is shown flowing into the financial system, which happens, for example, when households deposit their savings in banks, credit unions, or with investment trust companies. Money payments also leak out of the flow because of imports, which are purchases by domestic consumers that create incomes for *foreign* producers.

Injections.   The spending of domestic households on domestically produced output creates income for domestic producers. Income is also created by three additional expenditures, often called **injections,** that cause additions to the circular flow. The first is investment expenditure, which goes to purchase the output of other firms. It is expenditure that firms make on capital goods such as machinery or factories that are produced by other firms. This expenditure is shown as a flow coming from the financial system. Such investment expenditures include a firm financing its own investment with funds raised by selling stocks or bonds to households, which is done through intermediary agents, or directly borrowing money from a bank or other financial institu-

tion. The second injection is the funds that the government spends on a whole range of goods and services, from national defense through the provision of justice to the building of schools and roads. The third injection comes from the selling of exports in response to the demand from foreign consumers for the output of domestic producers.

Together, the expenditure of domestic households, the investment expenditure of domestic firms, government purchases of goods and services, and exports constitute the aggregate demand for domestic output. When any one of these elements of aggregate demand changes, aggregate output and total income earned by households are likely to change as a result. Hence studying the determinants of total consumption, investment, government spending, and imports and exports is crucial to understanding the causes of changes in the nation's total output.

The Next Step

Soon you will be going on to study microeconomics or macroeconomics. Whichever branch of the subject you study next, it is important to remember that microeconomics and macroeconomics are complementary, not competing, views of the economy. Both are needed for a full understanding of the functioning of a modern economy.

SUMMARY

A. THE DEVELOPMENT OF MARKET ECONOMIES

- Modern market economies are based on the specialization and division of labour, which necessitate the exchange of goods and services. Exchange takes place in markets and is facilitated by the use of money. Much of economics is devoted to the study of how markets work to coordinate millions of individual, decentralized decisions.

B. THE DECISION MAKERS

- Three groups of agents make the relevant decisions. Households, firms, and government all interact in markets. Households are assumed to maximize their satis-

faction and firms to maximize their profits. Government may have multiple objectives.

C. MARKETS AND ECONOMIES

- A free-market economy is one in which the allocation of resources is determined by production, sales, and purchase decisions made by firms and households acting in response to such market signals as prices and profits.
- Economies are commonly divided into the market and nonmarket sectors and into the public and private sectors. These divisions cut across each other; the former is based on the economic distinction of how costs are covered, and the latter is based on a legal distinction of ownership.

- Many institutions are crucial for the operation of a market economy. Most important among these is probably the legal system which is necessary for the enforcement of private contracts and for the establishment of private property rights.

D. MICROECONOMICS AND MACROECONOMICS

- The key difference between microeconomics and macroeconomics is in the level of aggregation. Microeconomics looks at prices and quantities in individual markets and how they respond to various shocks that impinge on those markets. Macroeconomics looks at broader aggregates such as aggregate production, employment, and the price level.

- The questions asked in microeconomics and macroeconomics differ, but they are complementary parts of economic analysis. They study different aspects of a single economic system, and both are needed for a complete understanding of the whole.

- Microeconomics deals with the determination of prices and quantities in individual markets and the relationships among those markets. It shows how the price system provides signals that reflect changes in demand and supply and to which producers and consumers react in a decentralized but nonetheless coordinated manner.

- The macroeconomic interactions between households and firms through markets may be illustrated in a circular flow diagram that traces real and money flows between producers and consumers. These flows are the starting point for studying the circular flow of aggregate income that is the key element of macroeconomics.

KEY CONCEPTS

Specialization and division of labour
Economic decision makers
Markets and market economies
Transition economies

Market and nonmarket sectors
Private and public sectors
The importance of institutions

Microeconomics and macroeconomics
The price system as a coordination mechanism
Circular flow of income

DISCUSSION QUESTIONS

1. In recent years, many productive activities in Canada have been moved out of the public and nonmarket sector. Can you give examples of some that have gone to the public and market sector and others that have gone to the private and market sector? What activities currently in the public and nonmarket sector could be moved into the private and market sector? Do you think such a move would be desirable?

2. Describe the tasks you performed in a job you held over the summer and discuss your duties, and those of your co-workers, in relation to the principle of the division of labour. If you were in charge, would you have divided up tasks and responsibilities differently? Why?

3. Consider the market for physicians' services. In what way has this market taken advantage of the specialization of labour?

4. Define the household of which you are a member. Consider your household's income last year. What proportion of it came from the sale of factor services? Identify other sources of income. Approximately what proportion of the expenditures by your household became income for firms?

5. "It is not from the benevolence of the butcher, the brewer, or the baker that we expect our dinner, but from their regard to their self-interest. We address ourselves, not to their humanity, but to their self-love, and never talk to them of our necessities, but of their advantages." Do you agree with this quotation from *The Wealth of Nations*? How are "our dinner" and "their self-interest" related to the price system? What are assumed to be the motives of firms and of households?

6. Discuss the effect of a sharp change in consumer demand away from fatty red meat and toward skinless

poultry as a result of continuing reports that too much fat in the diet is unhealthy.

7. Discuss some significant microeconomic and macroeconomic effects of an aging population, such as is predicted for many industrialized countries in the twenty-first century.

8. Which, if any, of the arrows in Figure 3-2 does each of the following affect initially?

a. Households increase their consumption expenditures by reducing saving.

b. The government lowers income tax rates.

c. Because of a recession, firms decide to postpone production of some new products.

d. Consumers like the new-model cars and borrow money from the banking system to buy them in record numbers. (Hint: Borrowing may be thought of as negative saving.)

PART TWO

AN INTRODUCTION TO DEMAND AND SUPPLY

In August of 1992, Hurricane Andrew struck the Florida coast, causing considerable damage to businesses and homes. Did this event cause the dramatic increase in the price of plywood that occurred in subsequent weeks, or was this just a coincidence? In the summer of 1994, Brazil experienced two frosts which severely damaged that country's coffee crop. Did this cause the large increase in the price of coffee that occurred almost immediately, or was that also a coincidence? Was Toronto's housing shortage in the 1980s related to the Ontario government's policy of *rent controls,* and if so, what is the connection? What determines the prices of specific products? What determines whether there will be a lot produced or only a little? What are the effects of government policies that seek to "administer" prices? These are the types of questions that you will be able to answer after reading the next three chapters.*

Chapter 4 introduces you to the basic concepts of *demand* and *supply.* You will see that the prices of goods in *free markets* are determined by the interaction of demand and supply. You will learn the meaning of *equilibrium,* and how equilibrium changes in response to changes to either demand or supply. With this apparatus in place, you will be returned briefly to Hurricane Andrew and to Brazil's damaged coffee crop (the price increases were *not* coincidences!).

Chapter 5 then introduces the important idea of *elasticity*—the sensitivity of one variable to a change in some other variable. This concept is central to our understanding of whether a change in the demand or supply of some commodity primarily affects *quantity* or *price.* As an application of the concept of elasticity, you will then examine the important policy issue of who bears the *burden* of commodity taxes. Do firms pay such taxes, or do consumers, or do both? How does elasticity affect the answer?

In Chapter 6 you get some practice in using what you learned in Chapters 4 and 5. We start with a general discussion of *government-controlled prices,* and then consider two examples. The first is *rent controls*—you will see that the government policy probably contributed to Toronto's housing shortage in the 1980s. The second is *agricultural price-support policies*—you will see what effects such policies have, both on farmers' incomes and on the allocation of resources. Finally, the chapter discusses the markets for internationally traded goods. You will see why Canada exports some goods and imports others, and how this pattern of trade depends on the *world prices* of the various products.

---

*Chapter 6 does not appear in *Macroeconomics.*

DEMAND, SUPPLY, AND PRICE

Some people believe that economics begins and ends with the "laws" of supply and demand. "Economics in one lesson", however, is too much to hope for. (An unkind critic of a book with that title remarked that the author needed a second lesson.) Still, the so-called laws of supply and demand are an important part of our understanding of the market system.

As a first step, we need to understand what determines the demand for and the supply of particular products. Then we can see how demand and supply together determine the prices of products and the quantities that are bought and sold. Finally, we examine how the price system allows the economy to respond to the many changes that impinge on it. Demand and supply help us to understand the price system's successes and failures. They also help us to understand the consequences of such government policies as price controls, minimum-wage laws, and sales taxes.

DEMAND

What determines the demand for any given product? Why did the fraction of total consumer expenditure on food in Canada decline from more than 33 percent in 1910 to less than 13 percent in 1996? Why has the proportion of income spent on services increased significantly over the same period? How did Canadian consumers react to the large increases in fuel prices in the 1970s, followed by the large decreases in the 1980s? We seek to understand how much of each product consumers will buy. We start by developing a theory that is designed to explain consumption of some typical product.

WHAT IS "QUANTITY DEMANDED"?

The total amount of any particular good or service that an economy's consumers wish to purchase in some time period is called the **quantity demanded** of that product.[1] It is important to notice three things about this concept.

First, quantity demanded is a *desired* quantity. It is the amount that consumers wish to purchase, given the price of the product, other prices, their incomes, their tastes, and everything else that might matter.[2] It may be different from the amount that consumers actually succeed in purchasing. If sufficient quantities are not available, the amount that consumers wish to purchase may exceed the amount that they actually purchase. To distinguish these two concepts, the term *quantity demanded* is used to refer to desired purchases, and a phrase such as *quantity actually bought* or *quantity exchanged* is used to refer to actual purchases.

Second, *desired* does not refer to idle dreams but to *effective* demands, the amounts that people are actually willing to buy, given the price they must pay for the product.

Third, quantity demanded refers to a continuous *flow* of purchases. It must therefore be expressed as so much per period of time: 1 million units per day, 7 million per week, or 365 million per year. For example, being told that the quantity of new television sets demanded (at current prices) in Canada is 50,000 means nothing unless you are also told the period of time involved. Fifty thousand TVs demanded per day would be an enormous rate of demand; 50,000 per year would be a very small rate. The important distinction between stocks and flows is discussed in Extension 4-1.

The amount of some product that consumers wish to buy in a given time period is influenced by the following important variables: [3]

- Product's own price
- Average household income
- Prices of related products
- Tastes
- Distribution of income
- Population

It is difficult to determine the separate influence of each of these variables if we consider what happens when everything changes at once. Instead, we consider the influence of the variables one at a time. To do this, we hold all but one of them constant. Then we let the selected variable vary and study how it affects quantity demanded. We can do the same for each of the other variables in turn, and in this way we can come to understand the importance of each.[3] Once this is done, we can combine the separate influences of the variables to discover what happens when several things change at the same time—as they often do.

Holding all other influencing variables constant is often described by the expressions "other things being equal," "other things given," or the equivalent Latin phrase, *ceteris paribus*. When economists speak of the influence of the price of wheat on the quantity of wheat demanded, *ceteris paribus*, they refer to what a change in the price of wheat would do to the quantity of wheat demanded *if all other forces that influence the demand for wheat did not change.*

---

[1]In this chapter, we concentrate on the demand of all consumers, added together, for products. Of course, what all households do is only the sum of what each individual household does. In Chapter 7, we study the behaviour of individual consumers in more detail.
[2]When economists say that something is "given," they mean that it is held constant. The expression "given the price of the product" therefore means that the price of the product is assumed not to change during the period under discussion.

---

[3]A relationship in which many variables (in this case, average income, population, tastes, and many prices) influence a single variable (in this case, quantity demanded) is called a *multivariate* relationship. The technique of studying the effect of each of the influencing variables one at a time, while holding the others constant, is common in mathematics, and there is a specific concept, the *partial derivative,* designed to measure such effects.

THE DISTINCTION BETWEEN STOCKS AND FLOWS

One important conceptual issue that arises frequently in economics is the distinction between stock and flow variables. Economic theories use both, and it takes a little practice to keep them straight.

As noted in the text, a flow variable has a time dimension—it is so much *per unit of time*. For example, the quantity of Grade A large eggs purchased in Edmonton is a flow variable. No useful information is conveyed if we are told that the number purchased was 2,000 dozen eggs unless we are also told the period of time over which these purchases occurred. Two thousand dozen eggs per hour would indicate a much more active market in eggs than would 2,000 dozen eggs per month.

In contrast, a stock variable is a variable whose value has meaning *at a point in time*. Thus the number of eggs in the egg producer's warehouse on a particular day—for example, 20,000 dozen eggs on September 3, 1997—is a stock variable. All those eggs are there at one time, and they remain there until something happens to change the stock held in the warehouse. The stock variable is just a number at a point in time, not a rate of flow of so much per unit of time.

The terminology of stocks and flows can be understood in terms of an analogy to a bathtub. At any moment, the tub holds so much water. This is the *stock*, and it can be measured in terms of the volume of water, say, 100 litres. There might also be water flowing into the tub from the tap; this *flow* is measured as so much water per unit time, say, 500 litres per hour.

The distinction between stocks and flows is important. Failure to keep them straight is a common source of confusion and even error. Note, for example, that because they have different dimensions, a stock variable and a flow variable cannot be added together without specifying some time period for which the flow persists. One cannot add the stock of 100 litres of water in the tub to the flow of 500 litres per hour to get 600 litres. The new stock of water will depend on how long the flow persists; if it lasts for half an hour, the new stock will be 350 litres; if the flow persists for two hours, the new stock will be 2,100 litres (or the tub will overflow!).

In economics, the amount of income earned is a flow; there is so much per year or per month or per hour. The amount of a consumer's expenditure is also a flow—so much spent per week or per month or per year. The amount of money in a bank account or a miser's hoard (earned, perhaps, in the past but unspent) is a stock—just so many thousands of dollars. The key test is always whether a time dimension is required to give the variable meaning.

QUANTITY DEMANDED AND PRICE

We are interested in developing a theory of how prices are determined. To do this, we need to study the relationship between the quantity demanded of each product and that product's price. This requires that we hold all other influences constant and ask, "How will the quantity of a product demanded change as its price changes?"

A basic economic hypothesis is that the price of a product and the quantity demanded are related negatively, other things being equal. That is, the lower the price, the higher the quantity demanded; and the higher the price, the lower the quantity demanded.[4]

Why might this be so? Products are used to satisfy desires and needs, and there is almost always more than one product that will satisfy any desire or need. Hunger may be alleviated by meat or vegetables; a desire for green vegetables can be satisfied by

---

[4]The British economist Alfred Marshall (1842–1924) called this fundamental relation the "law of demand." In Chapter 7, we derive the law of demand as a prediction that follows from more basic assumptions about consumer behaviour.

broccoli or spinach. The desire for a vacation may be satisfied by a trip to the seashore or to the mountains; the need to get there may be satisfied by different airlines, a bus, a car, or a train. For any general desire or need, there are many different products that will satisfy it.

Now consider what happens if income, tastes, population, and the prices of all other products remain constant and the price of only one product changes. As the price goes up, that product becomes an increasingly expensive way to satisfy a desire. Some consumers will stop buying it altogether; others will buy smaller amounts; still others may continue to buy the same quantity. Because many consumers will switch wholly or partly to other products to satisfy the same desire, less will be bought of the product whose price has risen. As meat becomes more expensive, for example, consumers may to some extent switch to meat substitutes; they may also forgo meat at some meals and eat less meat at others.

Conversely, as the price goes down, the product becomes a cheaper method of satisfying a desire. Households will buy more of it. Consequently, they will buy less of similar products whose prices have not fallen and as a result have become expensive *relative* to the product in question. When a bumper tomato harvest drives prices down, shoppers switch to tomatoes and cut their purchases of many other vegetables that now look relatively more expensive.

THE DEMAND SCHEDULE AND THE DEMAND CURVE

A **demand schedule** is one way of showing the relationship between quantity demanded and the price of a product, other things being equal. It is a numerical tabulation showing the quantity that is demanded at certain prices.

Table 4-1 is a hypothetical demand schedule for carrots. It lists the quantity of carrots that would be demanded at various prices on the assumption that all other influences on quantity demanded are held constant. We note in particular that average household income is fixed at $30,000 because later we will want to see what happens when income changes. The table gives the quantities demanded for six selected prices, but in fact a separate quantity would be demanded at each possible price from 1 cent to several hundreds of dollars.

TABLE 4-1
A Demand Schedule for Carrots

	Price Per Ton ($)	Quantity Demanded When Average Household Income Is $30,000 Per Year (thousands of tons per month)
U	20	110.0
V	40	90.0
W	60	77.5
X	80	67.5
Y	100	62.5
Z	120	60.0

The table shows the quantity of carrots that would be demanded at various prices, *ceteris paribus*. For example, row W indicates that if the price of carrots were $60 per ton, consumers would desire to purchase 77,500 tons of carrots per month, given the values of the other variables that affect quantity demanded.

A second method of showing the relationship between quantity demanded and price is to draw a graph. The six price-quantity combinations shown in Table 4-1 are plotted on the graph shown in Figure 4-1. Price is plotted on the vertical axis, and quantity is plotted on the horizontal axis.

The smooth curve drawn through these points is called a **demand curve.** It shows the quantity that purchasers would like to buy at each price. The negative slope of the curve indicates that the quantity demanded increases as the price falls. Each point on the demand curve indicates a single price-quantity combination. The demand curve as a whole shows something more.

The demand curve represents the relationship between quantity demanded and price, other things being equal.

When economists speak of the demand in a particular market as being given or known, they are referring not just to the particular quantity being demanded at the moment (i.e., not just to one point on the demand curve) but to the entire demand curve— to the relationship between desired purchases and all the possible prices of the product.

Thus the term **demand** refers to the entire relationship between the quantity demanded of a product and the price of that product (as shown, for example, by the demand schedule in Table 4-1 or the

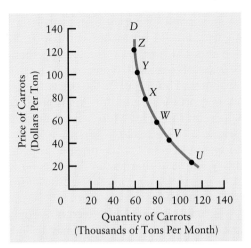

FIGURE 4-1
A Demand Curve for Carrots

This demand curve, labeled *D*, relates quantity of carrots demanded to the price of carrots; its downward slope indicates that quantity demanded increases as price falls. The six points correspond to the price-quantity combinations shown in Table 4-1. The smooth curve drawn through all of the points and labeled *D* is the demand curve.

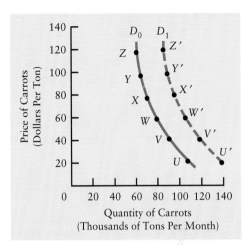

FIGURE 4-2
Two Demand Curves for Carrots

The rightward shift in the demand curve from D_0 to D_1 indicates an increase in the quantity demanded at each price. The lettered points correspond to those in Table 4-2.

demand curve in Figure 4-1). In contrast, a single point on a demand schedule or curve is the *quantity demanded* at that point. This distinction between "demand" and "quantity demanded" is an extremely important one and will be examined more closely later in this chapter.

Shifts in the Demand Curve

The demand schedule is drawn under the assumption that everything except the product's own price is being held constant. But what if other things change, as surely they do? For example, consider an increase in household income while price remains constant. If households increase their purchases of the product, the new quantity demanded cannot be represented by a point on the original demand curve. It must be represented on a new demand curve which is to the right of the old curve. Thus the rise in consumer income shifts the demand curve to the right, as shown in Figure 4-2. This illustrates the operation of an important general rule.

A demand curve is drawn under the assumption that everything except the product's own price is held

constant. A change in any of the variables previously held constant will shift the demand curve to a new position.

A demand curve can shift in many ways; two of them are particularly important. In the first case, more is bought at each price—the demand curve shifts rightward so that each price corresponds to a higher quantity than it did before. In the second case, less is bought at each price—the demand curve shifts leftward so that each price corresponds to a lower quantity than it did before.

The influence of changes in variables other than price may be studied by determining how changes in each variable shift the demand curve. Any change will shift the demand curve to the right if it increases the amount that households wish to buy, other things remaining equal. It will shift the demand curve to the left if it decreases the amount that households wish to buy, other things remaining equal. Note that changes in people's *expectations about future values* of variables such as income and prices can also influence current demand; however, for simplicity, we consider only the influence of changes in the current values of these variables.

Average Household Income. If consumers receive more income on average, they can be expected

TABLE 4-2
Two Alternative Demand Schedules for Carrots

Price Per Ton ($) P	Quantity Demanded When Average Consumer Income Is $30,000 Per Year (thousands of tons per month) D_0		Quantity Demanded When Average Consumer Income Is $36,000 Per Year (thousands of tons per month) D_1	
20	110.0	U	140.0	U'
40	90.0	V	116.0	V'
60	77.5	W	100.8	W'
80	67.5	X	87.5	X'
100	62.5	Y	81.3	Y'
120	60.0	Z	78.0	Z'

An increase in average consumer income increases the quantity demanded at each price. When average income rises from $30,000 to $36,000 per year, quantity demanded at a price of $60 per ton rises from 77,500 tons per month to 100,800 tons per month. A similar rise occurs at every other price. Thus the demand schedule relating columns P and D_0 is replaced by one relating columns P and D_1. The graphical representations of these two functions are labeled D_0 and D_1 in Figure 4-2.

to purchase more of most products even though product prices remain the same.[5] We therefore expect that a rise in average consumer income shifts the demand curve for most products to the right, indicating that more will be demanded at any given price. This is illustrated in Table 4-2 and Figure 4-2.

Prices of Related Goods. We saw that the negative slope of a product's demand curve occurs because the lower its price, the cheaper the product becomes relative to other products that can satisfy the same needs or desires. These other products are called **substitutes.** Another way for the same change to come about is for the price of the substitute product to rise. For example, carrots can become cheap relative to cabbage either because the price of carrots falls or because the price of cabbage rises. Either change will increase the amount of carrots that consumers wish to buy as consumers substitute away from cabbage and toward carrots. Thus a rise in the price of a substitute for a product shifts the demand curve for the product to the right. More will be demanded at each price.

Complements are products that tend to be used jointly. Cars and gasoline are complements; so are CD players and speakers, golf clubs and golf balls, electric stoves and electricity, and airplane flights to Calgary and ski-lift tickets in Banff. Because complements tend to be consumed together, a fall in the price of one will increase the demand for *both* products. Thus a fall in the price of a complement for a product will shift that product's demand curve to the right. More will be demanded at each price.

For example, a fall in the price of airplane trips to Calgary will lead to a rise in the demand for ski-lift tickets in Banff, even though the price of those lift tickets is unchanged.

Tastes. Tastes have an effect on people's desired purchases. A change in tastes may be long-lasting, such as the shift from fountain pens to ballpoint pens or from typewriters to computers; or it may be a short-lived fad such as hula hoops, CB radios, or Pogs. In either case, a change in tastes in favour of a product shifts the demand curve to the right. More will be demanded at each price.

Distribution of Income. If a constant total of income is redistributed among the population, demands may change. If, for example, the government increases the deductions that may be taken for children on income-tax returns and compensates by raising basic tax rates, income will be transferred from childless persons to households with large families. Demands for products more heavily bought by childless persons will decline, while demands for products more heavily bought by households with large families will increase. A change in the distribution of income will therefore cause an increase in the demand for products bought most by households whose incomes increase and a decrease in the demand for products bought most by households whose incomes decrease.

Population. Population growth does not create new demand unless the additional people have the means to purchase goods—that is, unless they have purchasing power. If there is an increase in population with purchasing power—for example, the immigration of wealthy foreigners—the demands for all the products purchased by the new people will rise. Thus we expect that an increase in population will shift the demand curves for most products to the right, indicating that more will be demanded at each price.

The reasons that demand curves shift are summarized in Figure 4-3.

---

[5]Such products are called *normal goods*. Products for which the quantity demanded falls as income rises are called *inferior goods*. These concepts are defined and discussed in Chapter 5.

FIGURE 4-3
Shifts in the Demand Curve

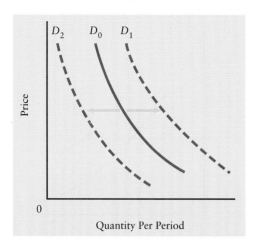

A rightward shift in the demand curve from D_0 to D_1 indicates an increase in demand; a leftward shift from D_0 to D_2 indicates a decrease in demand. An increase in demand means that more is demanded at each price. Such a rightward shift can be caused by a rise in income, a rise in the price of a substitute, a fall in the price of a complement, a change in tastes that favours that product, an increase in population, or a redistribution of income toward groups that favour the product.

A decrease in demand means that less is demanded at each price. Such a leftward shift can be caused by a fall in income, a fall in the price of a substitute, a rise in the price of a complement, a change in tastes that disfavours the product, a decrease in population, or a redistribution of income away from groups that favour the product.

Movements Along the Curve Versus Shifts of the Whole Curve

Suppose that you read in today's newspaper that the soaring price of carrots has been caused by a greatly increased demand for carrots. Then tomorrow you read that the rising price of carrots is greatly reducing the typical consumer's purchases of carrots, as shoppers switch to potatoes, yams, and peas. The two stories appear to contradict each other. The first associates a rising price with a rising demand; the second associates a rising price with a declining demand. Can both statements be true? The answer is yes—because they refer to different things. The first describes a shift in the demand curve; the second describes a movement along a demand curve in response to a change in price.

Consider first the statement that the increase in the price of carrots has been caused by an increased demand for carrots. This statement refers to a shift in the demand curve for carrots. In this case, the demand curve must have shifted to the right, indicating more carrots demanded at each price. This shift, as we will see later in this chapter, will increase the price of carrots.

Now consider the statement that fewer carrots are being bought because carrots have become more expensive. This refers to a movement along a given demand curve and reflects a change between two specific quantities being bought, one before the price rose and one afterward.

Possible explanations for the two stories are given in the following:

1. A rise in the population is shifting the demand curve for carrots to the right as more carrots are demanded at each price. This in turn raises the price of carrots (for reasons we will soon study in detail). This was the first newspaper story.

2. The rising price of carrots is causing each individual household to cut back on its purchase of carrots. This causes an upward movement to the left along any particular demand curve for carrots. This was the second newspaper story.

To prevent the type of confusion caused by our two newspaper stories, economists use a specialized vocabulary to distinguish between shifts of curves and movements along curves.

We have seen that demand refers to the *whole* demand curve, whereas quantity demanded refers to a specific quantity that is demanded at a specified price, as indicated by a particular *point* on the demand curve. In Figure 4-1, for example, demand is given by the curve D; at a price of $40, the quantity demanded is 90 tons, as indicated by the point V.

Economists reserve the term **change in demand** to describe a change in the quantity demanded at *every* price. That is, a change in demand refers to a shift of the entire demand curve. The term **change in quantity demanded** refers to a movement from one point on a demand curve to another point on the same demand curve.

A change in demand refers to a shift in the entire demand curve; a change in quantity demanded refers to a movement along a demand curve.

We consider each of these possibilities in turn.

An increase in demand means that the whole demand curve shifts to the right; a decrease in demand means that the whole demand curve shifts to the left. At a given price, an increase in demand causes an increase in quantity demanded, whereas a decrease in demand causes a decrease in quantity demanded. For example, in Figure 4-2, the shift in the demand curve from D_0 to D_1 represents an increase in demand, and at a price of $40, quantity demanded increases from 90,000 tons to 116,000 tons, as indicated by the move from V to V'.

A movement down and to the right along a demand curve causes an increase in quantity demanded; a movement up and to the left along a demand curve causes a decrease in quantity demanded. For example, in Figure 4-2, with demand given by the curve D_1, an increase in price from $40 to $60 causes a movement along D_1 from V' to W', and quantity demanded decreases from 116,000 tons to 100,800 tons.

When there is a change in demand *and* a change in the price, the overall change in quantity demanded is the net effect of the shift in the demand curve and the movement along the new demand curve. Figure 4-4 shows the combined effect of an increase in demand, shown by a rightward shift in the whole demand curve, and an upward movement to the left along the new demand curve due to an increase in price. The rise in demand causes an increase in quantity demanded at the initial price, whereas the movement along the demand curve causes a decrease in the quantity demanded. Whether quantity demanded rises or falls overall depends on the relative magnitudes of these two changes.

SUPPLY

The Canadian economy produced goods and services worth about $800 billion in 1996. Economists have as many questions to ask about production and its changing composition as they do about consumption. What determines the amount produced? What determines its composition? Why does the quantity of goods and services produced change? Why has manufacturing output fallen from almost 30 percent of total private-sector production in the early 1950s to about 20 percent in 1996? Why have agriculture, forestry, and fisheries, as a group, fallen

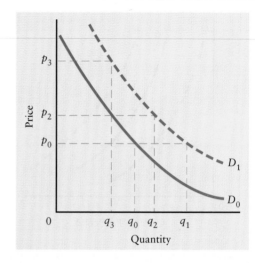

FIGURE 4-4
Shifts of and Movements Along the Demand Curve

An increase in demand means that the demand curve shifts to the right, and hence quantity demanded will be higher at each price. A rise in price causes an upward movement to the left along the demand curve, and hence quantity demanded will fall. The demand curve is originally D_0 and price is p_0, which means that quantity demanded is q_0. Suppose that demand increases to D_1, which means that at any particular price, there is a larger quantity demanded; for example, at p_0, quantity demanded is now q_1. Now suppose that the price rises above p_0. This causes a movement up and to the left along D_1, and quantity demanded falls below q_1.

The net effect of these two changes can be either an increase or a decrease in the quantity demanded. In this figure, a rise in price to p_2 means that the quantity demanded q_2 is still in excess of the original quantity demanded q_{01}; a rise in price to p_3 means that the final quantity demanded q_3 is below the original quantity demanded q_0.

from almost 7 percent in the 1950s to approximately 3 percent in 1996?

Dramatic changes have occurred within each of these market categories. Why, for example, did the aluminum industry grow much faster than the steel industry? Even within any single industry, some firms prosper and grow while others decline. A large fraction of the firms in a typical industry at the beginning of any decade are no longer present at the end of that decade. Why and how do new jobs, new firms, and new industries come into being while other jobs, firms, and industries shrink or disappear altogether?

All of these questions and many others are aspects of a single question: *What determines the quantities of products that will be produced and offered for sale?*

A full discussion of these questions of supply will come later (in Part 4). For now, it suffices to examine the basic relationship between the price of a product and the quantity produced and offered for sale and to understand what forces lead to shifts in this relationship.

WHAT IS "QUANTITY SUPPLIED"?

The amount of a product that firms wish to sell in some time period is called the **quantity supplied** of that product. Quantity supplied is a flow; it is so much per unit of time. Note also that quantity supplied is the amount that firms are willing to offer for sale; it is not necessarily the amount that they succeed in selling, which is expressed by *quantity actually sold* or *quantity exchanged*. Although households may desire to purchase an amount that differs from what firms desire to sell, they obviously cannot succeed in buying what someone else does not sell. A purchase and a sale are merely two sides of the same transaction. Viewed from the buyer's side, there is a purchase; viewed from the seller's side, there is a sale.

Because desired purchases do not have to equal desired sales, quantity demanded does not have to equal quantity supplied. However, the quantity actually purchased must equal the quantity actually sold because whatever someone buys, someone else must sell.

The amount of a product that firms are willing to produce and offer for sale is influenced by the following important variables: [5]

- Product's own price
- Prices of inputs
- Technology
- Number of suppliers

The situation with supply is the same as with demand: There are several influencing variables, and we will not get far if we try to discover what happens when they all change at the same time. So, again, we use the convenient *ceteris paribus* assumption to study the influence of the variables one at a time.

QUANTITY SUPPLIED AND PRICE

We begin by holding all other influences constant and ask, "How do we expect the quantity of a product supplied to vary with its own price?"

A basic hypothesis of economics is that for many products, the price of the product and the quantity supplied are related *positively,* other things being equal. That is to say, the higher the product's own price, the more its producers will supply; and the lower the price, the less its producers will supply.[6]

Why might this be so? It is true because the profits that can be earned from producing a product will increase if the price of that product rises while the costs of inputs used to produce it remain unchanged. This will make firms, which are in business to earn profits, wish to produce more of the product whose price has risen.

THE SUPPLY SCHEDULE AND THE SUPPLY CURVE

The general relationship just discussed can be illustrated by a **supply schedule,** which shows the relationship between quantity supplied of a product and the price of the product, other things being equal. A supply schedule is analogous to a demand schedule; the former shows what producers would be willing to sell, whereas the latter shows what households would be willing to buy, at alternative prices of the product. Table 4-3 presents a hypothetical supply schedule for carrots.

A **supply curve,** the graphical representation of the supply schedule, is illustrated in Figure 4-5. Each point on the supply curve represents a specific price-quantity combination; however, the whole curve shows something more.

The supply curve represents the relationship between quantity supplied and price, other things being equal; its positive slope indicates that quantity supplied varies in the same direction as does price.

When economists make statements about the conditions of supply, they are not referring just to the particular quantity being supplied at the moment—

---

[6]In this chapter, we introduce this key relation as a hypothesis. In later chapters, we will derive it as a prediction from more basic assumptions about the behaviour of firms.

TABLE 4-3
A Supply Schedule for Carrots

	Price Per Ton ($)	Quantity Supplied (thousands of tons per month)
u	20	5.0
v	40	46.0
w	60	77.5
x	80	100.0
y	100	115.0
z	120	122.5

The table shows the quantities that producers wish to sell at various prices, *ceteris paribus*.

that is, not to just one point on the supply curve. Instead, they are referring to the entire supply curve, to the complete relationship between desired sales and all possible prices of the product.

Supply refers to the entire relationship between the quantity supplied of a product and the price of that product, other things being equal. A single point on the supply curve refers to the *quantity supplied* at that price.

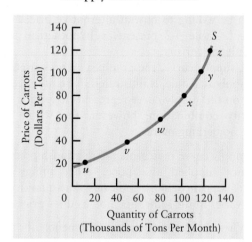

FIGURE 4-5
A Supply Curve for Carrots

This supply curve, labeled *S*, relates quantity of carrots supplied to the price of carrots; its upward slope indicates that quantity supplied increases as price increases. The six points correspond to the price-quantity combinations shown in Table 4-3.

Shifts in the Supply Curve

A shift in the supply curve means that at each price, a different quantity will be supplied than previously. An increase in the quantity supplied at each price is shown in Table 4-4 and is graphed in Figure 4-6. This change appears as a rightward shift in the supply curve. In contrast, a decrease in the quantity supplied at each price appears as a leftward shift. A shift in the supply curve must be the result of a change in one of the factors that influence the quantity supplied other than the product's own price. We now briefly consider the major possible causes of such shifts.

For supply, as for demand, there is an important general rule:

A change in any of the variables (other than the product's own price) that affects the amount of a product that firms are willing to produce and sell will shift the supply curve to a new position.

Consider the effect of changes in the following variables:

Price of Inputs.   All things that a firm uses to produce its outputs, such as materials, labour, and machines, are called the firm's *inputs*. Other things being equal, the higher the price of any input used to make a product, the less will be the profit from making that product. We expect, therefore, that the higher the price of any input used by a firm, the lower will be the amount that the firm will produce and offer for sale at any given price of the product. A rise in the price of inputs therefore shifts the supply curve to the left, indicating that less will be supplied at any given price; a fall in the cost of inputs shifts the supply curve to the right.

Technology.   At any time, what is produced and how it is produced depends on what is known. Over time, knowledge changes; so do the quantities of individual products supplied. The enormous increase in production per worker that has been going on in industrial societies for about 200 years is due largely to improved methods of production. The Industrial Revolution is more than a historical event; it is a present reality. Discoveries in chemistry have led to lower costs of production for well-established products, such as paints, and to a large variety of new products made of plastics and synthetic fibers. Such inventions as silicon chips have radically changed products such as computers, televisions, and tele-

TABLE 4-4
Two Alternative Supply Schedules for Carrots

Price Per Ton ($) P	Quantity Supplied Before Cost-Saving Innovation (thousands of tons per month) S_0		Quantity Supplied After Innovation (thousands of tons per month) S_1	
20	5.0	u	28.0	u'
40	46.0	v	76.0	v'
60	77.5	w	102.0	w'
80	100.0	x	120.0	x'
100	115.0	y	132.0	y'
120	122.5	z	140.0	z'

A cost-saving innovation increases the quantity supplied at each price. As a result of a cost-saving innovation, the quantity that is supplied at $100 per ton rises from 115,000 to 132,000 tons per month. A similar rise occurs at every price.

phones, and the consequent development of smaller computers has revolutionized the production of countless other nonelectronic products.

Any technological innovation that decreases production costs will increase the profits that can be earned at any given price of the product. Because in-

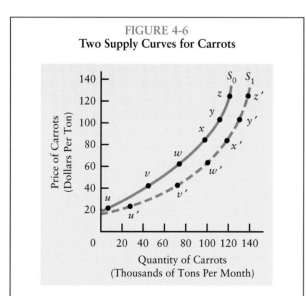

FIGURE 4-6
Two Supply Curves for Carrots

Quantity of Carrots
(Thousands of Tons Per Month)

The rightward shift in the supply curve from S_0 to S_1 indicates an increase in the quantity supplied at each price. The lettered points correspond to those in Table 4-4. A rightward shift in the supply curve indicates an increase in supply such that more carrots are supplied at each price.

creased profitability leads to increased production, this change shifts the supply curve to the right, indicating an increased willingness to produce the product and offer it for sale at each possible price.

Number of Suppliers. For given prices and technology, the total amount of any product supplied depends on the number of firms producing that product and offering it for sale. For example, in Chapter 10 we will examine the situation where profits made by existing firms producing a particular good attract other firms to enter the industry in pursuit of those profits. The effect of this increase in the number of suppliers is to shift the supply curve to the right. Similarly, if the existing firms are losing money, then they will eventually leave the industry; this reduction in the number of suppliers shifts the supply curve to the left.

Movements Along the Curve Versus Shifts of the Whole Curve

As with demand, it is important to distinguish movements along supply curves from shifts of the whole curve. Economists reserve the term **change in supply** to describe a shift of the whole supply curve—that is, a change in the quantity that will be supplied at every price. The term **change in quantity supplied** refers to a movement from one point on a supply curve to another point on the same supply curve. In other words, an increase in supply means that the whole supply curve has shifted to the right, so that the quantity supplied at any given price has increased; a movement up and to the right along a supply curve indicates an *increase in the quantity supplied* in response to an increase in the price of the product.

A change in quantity supplied can result from a change in supply, with the price constant; from a movement along a given supply curve due to a change in the price; or from a combination of the two.

THE DETERMINATION OF PRICE BY DEMAND AND SUPPLY

So far, demand and supply have been considered separately. What we really want to know, however, is how these two forces *interact* to determine price in a

TABLE 4-5
Demand and Supply Schedules for Carrots and Equilibrium Price

(1) Price Per Ton ($) p	(2) Quantity Demanded (thousands of tons per month) D	(3) Quantity Supplied (thousands of tons per month) S	(4) Excess Demand (+) or Excess Supply (−) (thousands of tons per month) D − S
20	110.0	5.0	+105.0
40	90.0	46.0	+44.0
60	77.5	77.5	0.0
80	67.5	100.0	−32.5
100	62.5	115.0	−52.5
120	60.0	122.5	−62.5

Equilibrium occurs where quantity demanded equals quantity supplied—when there is neither excess demand nor excess supply. These schedules are those from Tables 4-1 and 4-3. The equilibrium price is $60.

competitive market.[7] Table 4-5 brings together the demand and supply schedules from Tables 4-1 and 4-3. The quantities of carrots demanded and supplied at each price may now be compared.

There is only one price, $60 per ton, at which the quantity of carrots demanded equals the quantity supplied. At prices less than $60 per ton, there is a shortage of carrots because the quantity demanded exceeds the quantity supplied. This is a situation of **excess demand.** At prices greater than $60 per ton, there is a surplus of carrots because the quantity supplied exceeds the quantity demanded. This is a situation of **excess supply.**

To examine the determination of market price, suppose first that the price is $100 per ton. At this price, 115,000 tons are offered for sale, but only 62,500 tons are demanded. There is an excess supply of 52,500 tons per month. We assume that sellers will then cut their prices to get rid of this surplus and that purchasers, observing the stock of unsold carrots, will pay less for what they are prepared to buy. Thus *excess supply causes downward pressure on price.*

Next consider the price of $20 per ton. At this price, there is excess demand. The 5,000 tons produced each month are snapped up quickly, and

105,000 tons of desired purchases cannot be made. Rivalry between would-be purchasers may lead them to offer more than the prevailing price to outbid other purchasers. Also, perceiving that they could sell their available supplies many times over, sellers may begin to ask a higher price for the quantities that they do have to sell. Thus *excess demand causes upward pressure on price.*

Finally, consider the price of $60. At this price, producers wish to sell 77,500 tons per month, and purchasers wish to buy that same quantity. There is neither a shortage nor a surplus of carrots. There are no unsatisfied buyers to bid the price up, nor are there unsatisfied sellers to force the price down. Once the price of $60 has been reached, therefore, there will be no tendency for it to change.

Equilibrium implies a state of rest, or balance, between opposing forces. The **equilibrium price** is the one toward which the actual market price will tend. It will persist, once established, unless it is disturbed by some change in market conditions which shifts the demand curve, the supply curve, or both. A condition that must be fulfilled if equilibrium is to be obtained in some market is called an **equilibrium condition.** The equality of quantity demanded and quantity supplied is an equilibrium condition. [6]

The price at which the quantity demanded equals the quantity supplied is called the equilibrium price, or the market-clearing price.

---

[7]Roughly speaking, a competitive market is one that has a large number of firms and a large number of consumers, each small relative to the size of the market. The concept of a competitive market is defined more precisely in Chapter 10.

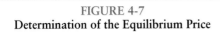

FIGURE 4-7
Determination of the Equilibrium Price

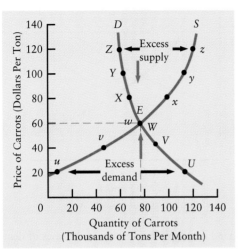

The equilibrium price corresponds to the intersection of the demand and supply curves. Equilibrium is indicated by *E,* which is point *W* on the demand curve and point *w* on the supply curve. At a price of $60, quantity demanded equals quantity supplied. At prices above equilibrium, there is excess supply and downward pressure on price. At prices below equilibrium, there is excess demand and upward pressure on price. The pressures on price are represented by the vertical arrows.

Any price at which the market does not clear—that is, quantity demanded does not equal quantity supplied—is called a **disequilibrium price.** Whenever there is either excess demand or excess supply in a market, that market is said to be in a state of **disequilibrium,** and the market price will be changing.

This same story is told in graphical terms in Figure 4-7. The quantities demanded and supplied at any price can be read off the two curves; the excess supply or excess demand is shown by the horizontal distance between the curves at each price. The figure makes it clear that the equilibrium price occurs where the demand and supply curves intersect. Below that price, there is excess demand and hence upward pressure on the existing price. Above that price, there is excess supply and hence downward pressure on the existing price. These pressures are represented by the vertical arrows in the figure.

THE LAWS OF DEMAND AND SUPPLY

Changes in any of the variables, other than price, that influence quantity demanded or supplied will cause a shift in the supply curve, the demand curve, or both. There are four possible shifts: a rise in demand (a rightward shift in the demand curve), a fall in demand (a leftward shift in the demand curve), a rise in supply (a rightward shift in the supply curve), and a fall in supply (a leftward shift in the supply curve).

To discover the effects of each of the possible curve shifts, we use the method known as **comparative statics,** short for *comparative static equilibrium analysis.*[8] Using this method, we derive predictions by analyzing the effect on the equilibrium position of some change in which we are interested. We start from a position of equilibrium and then introduce the change to be studied. The new equilibrium position is determined and compared with the original one. The difference between the two positions of equilibrium must result from the change that was introduced because everything else has been held constant.

Each of the four possible curve shifts causes changes that are described by one of the four so-called "laws" of demand and supply. Each of the laws summarizes what happens when an initial position of equilibrium is disturbed by a shift in either the demand curve or the supply curve. By using the term "law" to describe what happens, economists do not mean that they are absolutely certain of the outcome. The term "law" in science is used to describe a theory that has stood up to substantial testing. The laws of demand and supply are thus hypotheses that predict certain kinds of behaviour in certain situations, and the predicted behaviour occurs sufficiently often that economists continue to have confidence in the underlying theory.

The four laws of demand and supply are derived in Figure 4-8, which generalizes our specific discussion about carrots. Study the figure carefully. Previously, we had given the axes specific la-

---

[8]The term *static* is used because we are not concerned with the actual path by which the market goes from the first equilibrium position to the second or with the time taken to reach the second equilibrium. Analysis of these movements would be described as *dynamic analysis.*

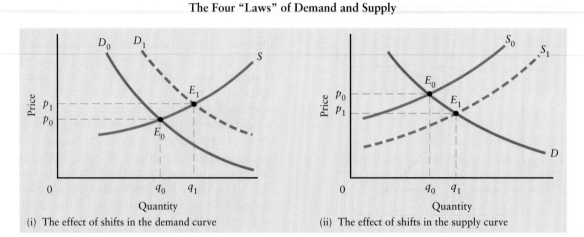

FIGURE 4-8
The Four "Laws" of Demand and Supply

(i) The effect of shifts in the demand curve

(ii) The effect of shifts in the supply curve

The effects on equilibrium price and quantity of shifts in either demand or supply are known as the laws of demand and supply.
  A rise in demand. In part (i), assume that the original demand and supply curves are D_0 and S, which intersect to produce equilibrium at E_0, with a price of p_0 and a quantity of q_0. An increase in demand shifts the demand curve to D_1, taking the new equilibrium to E_1. Price rises to p_1 and quantity to q_1.
  A fall in demand. In part (i), the original demand and supply curves are D_1 and S, which intersect to produce equilibrium at E_1, with a price of p_1 and a quantity of q_1. A decrease in demand shifts the demand curve to D_0, taking the new equilibrium to E_0. Price falls to p_0, and quantity falls to q_0.
  A rise in supply. In part (ii), the original demand and supply curves are D and S_0, which intersect to produce equilibrium at E_0, with a price of p_0 and a quantity of q_0. An increase in supply shifts the supply curve to S_1, taking the new equilibrium to E_1. Price falls to p_1, and quantity rises to q_1.
  A fall in supply. In part (ii), the original demand and supply curves are D and S_1, which intersect to produce equilibrium at E_1, with a price of p_1 and a quantity of q_1. A decrease in supply shifts the supply curve to S_0, taking the new equilibrium to E_0. Price rises to p_0, and quantity falls to q_0.

bels, but from here on we will simplify. Because it is intended to apply to any product, the horizontal axis is simply labeled "Quantity." This should be understood to mean quantity per period in whatever units output is measured. "Price," the vertical axis, should be understood to mean the price measured as dollars per unit of quantity for the same product.

The four laws of demand and supply are as follows:

1. A rise in demand causes an increase in both the equilibrium price and the equilibrium quantity exchanged.

2. A fall in demand causes a decrease in both the equilibrium price and the equilibrium quantity exchanged.

3. A rise in supply causes a decrease in the equilibrium price and an increase in the equilibrium quantity exchanged.

4. A fall in supply causes an increase in the equilibrium price and a decrease in the equilibrium quantity exchanged.

Demonstrations of these laws are given in the caption to Figure 4-8. The intuitive reasoning behind each is as follows:

1. A rise in demand creates a shortage at the initial equilibrium price, and the unsatisfied buyers bid up the price. This causes a larger quantity to be produced, with the result that at the new equilibrium, more is bought and sold at a higher price.

2. A fall in demand creates a glut at the initial equilibrium price, and the unsuccessful sellers bid the price down. As a result, less of the product is produced and offered for sale. At the new equilibrium, both price and quantity bought and sold are lower than they were originally.

3. An increase in supply creates a glut at the initial equilibrium price, and the unsuccessful suppliers force the price down. This increases the quantity demanded, and the new equilibrium is at a lower price and a higher quantity bought and sold.

4. A reduction in supply creates a shortage at the initial equilibrium price that causes the price to be bid up. This reduces the quantity demanded, and the new equilibrium is at a higher price and a lower quantity bought and sold.

In this chapter, we have studied many forces that can cause demand or supply curves to shift. By combining this analysis with the four laws of demand and supply, we can link many real-world events that cause demand or supply curves to shift with changes in market prices and quantities. Application 4-1 shows how demand-and-supply analysis can be used to examine two real-world shocks; the effects of Florida's 1992 Hurricane Andrew, and Brazil's 1994 coffee-crop failure.

The theory of the determination of price by demand and supply is beautiful in its simplicity. Yet as we shall see throughout this book, it is powerful in its wide range of applications.

PRICES AND INFLATION

The theory we have developed explains how individual prices are determined by the forces of demand and supply. To facilitate matters, we have made *ceteris paribus* assumptions. Specifically, we have assumed the constancy of all prices except the one we are studying (and occasionally one other price, when we wish to see how a change in that price affects the market being studied). Does this mean that our theory is inapplicable to an inflationary world in which all prices are rising at the same time? Fortunately, the answer is no.

The price of a product is the amount of money that must be spent to acquire one unit of that product. This is called the **absolute price** or **money price**. A **relative price** is the ratio of two absolute prices; it expresses the price of one good in terms of (relative to) another.

We have mentioned several times that what matters for demand and supply is the price of the product in question relative to the prices of other products; that is, what matters is the *relative price*.

In an inflationary world, we are often interested in the price of a given product as it relates to the average price of all other products. If, during a period when all prices are increasing by an average of 40 percent, the price of oranges rose by 60 percent, then the price of oranges rose relative to the prices of other goods as a whole. Oranges became *relatively* expensive. However, if oranges had risen in price by only 30 percent when other prices increased by 40 percent, then the relative price of oranges would have fallen. Although the money price of oranges rose substantially, oranges became *relatively* cheap.

In Lewis Carroll's famous story, *Through the Looking Glass*, Alice finds a country where one has to run in order to stay still. So it is with inflation. A product's price must rise as fast as the general level of prices just to keep its relative price constant.

It has been convenient in this chapter to analyze changes in particular prices in the context of a constant price level. The analysis is easily extended to an inflationary period by remembering that any force that raises the price of one product when other prices remain constant will, given general inflation, raise the price of that product faster than the price level is rising. For example, a change in tastes in favour of carrots that would raise their price by 20 percent when other prices were constant would raise their price by 32 percent if, at the same time, the general price level rises by 10 percent.[9] In each case, the price of carrots rises 20 percent *relative to the average of all prices*.

In price theory, whenever we refer to a change in the price of one product, we mean a change in that product's relative price. That is, a change in the price of that product relative to the prices of all other goods.

If the price level is constant, this change requires only a rise in the money price of the product in question. If the price level is itself rising, this change requires that the money price of the product in question rise faster than the price level.

---

[9]Let the price level be 100 in the first case and 110 in the second. Let the price of carrots be 120 in the first case and x in the second. To preserve the same relative price, we need x such that $120/100 = x/110$, which makes $x = 132$.

APPLICATION 4-1

DEMAND AND SUPPLY: WHAT REALLY HAPPENS

"The theory of supply and demand is neat enough," said the sceptic, "but tell me what really happens."

"What really happens," said the economist, "is that demand curves have a negative slope; supply curves have a positive slope. Prices rise in response to excess demand; prices fall in response to excess supply."

"But that's theory," insisted the sceptic. "What about reality?"

"That is reality as well," said the economist. "Changes in the prices you pay when you go to the grocery story, the hardware store, or the mall are all responses to excess supply or excess demand."

"Explaining why prices change is a pretty impressive claim," replied the sceptic. "For this to make sense, you have to convince me that these situations of excess supply and excess demand ever occur. Prices change every time I go to the grocery store, but the only time I can remember seeing excess demand was when I tried to get tickets to see the Rolling Stones."

"Shifts in the demand curve or the supply curve for some product cause excess supply and excess de-mand to occur. These shifts may be caused by a whole range of factors, but the key is that they reflect information and events that have not already been incorporated in the model. The reason why you rarely observe excess demand or excess supply is that prices usually change rapidly to eliminate these gaps," lectured the economist.

"Still too abstract," replied the sceptic.

"Let me show you a couple of examples of how the weather—something that varies in unpredictable ways—helps to illustrate this whole theoretical apparatus."

THE WEATHER AND A DEMAND SHOCK

On August 24, 1992, Hurricane Andrew struck the Florida coast, causing considerable damage to homes and business. Immediately after the storm, people needed plywood to patch roofs and cover windows.

This immediate need for plywood meant that the demand curve for plywood shifted out—upward and

---

SUMMARY

A. DEMAND

- The amount of a product that consumers wish to purchase is called the *quantity demanded*. It is a flow expressed as so much per period of time. It is determined by tastes, average household income, the product's own price, the prices of related products, the size of the population, and the distribution of income among consumers.
- The relationship between quantity demanded and price is represented graphically by a demand curve that shows how much will be demanded at each market price. Quantity demanded is assumed to increase as the price of the product falls, other things held constant. Thus demand curves are downward sloping.
- It is important to make the distinction between a movement along a demand curve and a shift of a demand

curve. A change in the product's price will cause a movement along the demand curve. This is called a *change in quantity demanded*.
- A shift in a demand curve represents a change in the quantity demanded at each price and is referred to as a *change in demand*. The demand curve shifts to the right (an increase in demand) if average income rises, if population rises, if the price of a substitute rises, if the price of a complement falls, or if there is a change in tastes in favour of the product. The opposite changes shift the demand curve to the left (a decrease in demand).

B. SUPPLY

- The amount of a product that firms wish to sell is called the *quantity supplied*. It is a flow expressed as so much to the right. At the prehurricane price, there would have been excess demand. As expected, the price of plywood rose to remove the excess demand. In Florida, there were reports that the price of plywood had doubled. The events in Florida affected the price of plywood nationwide, with prices jumping 18 percent in the two weeks after the storm.

THE WEATHER AND A SUPPLY SHOCK

In 1994, Brazil, which produces one-third of the world's coffee, experienced unusually severe weather. Two killing frosts in June and July and a period of drought thereafter severely damaged the next year's crop. Some experts estimated that the frosts had destroyed as much as 45 percent of Brazil's 1995 harvest.

This crop damage meant that the supply curve of coffee shifted in—upward and to the left. Without a change in price, there would have been excess demand for coffee, with more people wanting to buy than wanting to sell. Predictably, the market forces reacted swiftly, and coffee prices soared by nearly 100 percent on the wholesale commodity market on July 14. Consumers also felt the impact of the supply shock, with retail prices climbing by about $5 per kilogram.

BACK TO THE SCEPTIC

"Hey, that's kind of neat," said the sceptic, "I think I'm starting to get the hang of this. But I have just one problem. You said that prices usually change to eliminate the excess demands or supplies, but that doesn't explain the huge lineups I saw when I was trying to buy the Rolling Stones tickets."

"You're right," replied the economist, "but that situation can also be explained with the demand-and-supply apparatus. The situation with the Rolling Stones concert was that there was a fixed supply of tickets and a large demand for them, suggesting a high equilibrium price. But for various reasons, the concert promoters set the ticket prices below the market-clearing price and the result was exactly as predicted—excess demand leading to large lineups and ticket resales ("scalping") well above the official price."

per period of time. It depends on the product's own price, the costs of inputs, the number of suppliers, and the state of technology.

- The relationship between quantity supplied and price is represented graphically by a supply curve that shows how much will be supplied at each market price. Quantity supplied is assumed to increase as the price of the product increases, other things held constant. Thus, supply curves are upward sloping.

- It is important to make the distinction between a movement along a supply curve and a shift of a supply curve. A change in the product's price will cause a movement along the supply curve. This is called a *change in quantity supplied.*

- A shift in the supply curve indicates a change in the quantity supplied at each price and is referred to as a *change in supply.* The supply curve shifts to the right (an increase in supply) if the costs of producing the product fall or if, for any reason, producers become more willing to produce the product. The opposite changes shift the supply curve to the left (a decrease in supply).

C. THE DETERMINATION OF PRICE BY DEMAND AND SUPPLY

- The *equilibrium price* is the price at which the quantity demanded equals the quantity supplied. At any price below equilibrium, there will be excess demand; at any price above equilibrium, there will be excess supply. Graphically, equilibrium occurs where the demand and supply curves intersect.

- Price rises when there is excess demand and falls when there is excess supply. Thus the actual market price will be pushed toward the equilibrium price. When it is reached, there will be neither excess demand nor excess supply, and the price will not change until either the supply curve or the demand curve shifts.

- Using the method of *comparative statics,* the effects of a shift in either demand or supply can be determined. A rise in demand raises both equilibrium price and equilibrium quantity; a fall in demand lowers both. A rise in supply raises equilibrium quantity but lowers equilibrium price; a fall in supply lowers equilibrium quantity but raises equilibrium price. These are called the laws of demand and supply.

- Price theory is most simply developed in the context of a constant price level. Price changes discussed in the theory are changes relative to the average level of all prices. The absolute price of a product is its price in terms of money; its relative price is its price in relation to other products. In an inflationary period, a rise in the *relative price* of one product means that its absolute price rises by more than the price level; a fall in its relative price means that its absolute price rises by less than the price level.

KEY CONCEPTS

"Ceteris paribus" or "other things being equal"
Quantity demanded and quantity actually bought
Demand schedule and demand curve
Change in quantity demanded versus change in demand

Quantity supplied and quantity actually sold
Supply schedule and supply curve
Change in quantity supplied versus change in supply

Equilibrium, equilibrium price, and disequilibrium
Comparative statics
Laws of supply and demand
Relative price

DISCUSSION QUESTIONS

1. What shifts in demand or supply curves would produce the following results? (Assume in each case that only one of the two curves has shifted.)

   a. The price of pocket calculators has fallen over the past few years, and the quantity exchanged has risen greatly.
   b. Summer sublets in Kingston, Ontario, are at rents well below the regular rentals.
   c. Sales of designer jeans first rose, then declined.
   d. "Gourmet coffee market grows as affluent shoppers indulge."
   e. Du Pont increased the price of synthetic fibers, although it acknowledged that demand was weak.
   f. The Edsel was a lemon when it was produced in 1958–1960 but is now a best-seller among cars of its vintage.

2. Recently, a government economist predicted that this spring's excellent weather would result in larger crops of wheat and canola than farmers had expected. But the economist warned consumers not to expect prices to decrease because the cost of production was rising and foreign demand for Canadian crops was increasing. "The classic pattern of supply and demand won't work this time," the economist said. Discuss his observation.

3. What would be the effect on the equilibrium price and quantity of marijuana if its sale and consumption were legalized?

4. The relative price of personal computers has dropped drastically over the past 15 years. Would you explain this falling price in terms of demand or supply changes? What factors are likely to have caused the demand or supply shifts that did occur?

5. Classify the effect of each of the following as (i) a decrease in the demand for fish, (ii) a decrease in the quantity of fish demanded, or (iii) other. Illustrate each diagrammatically.

   a. The government of Canada closes the Atlantic Cod fishery.
   b. People buy less fish because of a rise in fish prices.
   c. The Catholic Church relaxed its ban on eating meat on Fridays.
   d. The price of beef falls, and as a result, consumers buy more beef and less fish.
   e. Fears of mercury pollution lead locals to shun fish caught in nearby lakes.
   f. It is generally alleged that eating fish is better for one's health than eating meat.

6. Predict the effect on the price of at least one product of each of the following:

   a. Winter snowfall is at a record high in the interior of British Columbia, but drought continues in Quebec ski areas.
   b. A recession decreases employment in Oshawa automobile factories.
   c. The French grape harvest is the smallest in 20 years.
   d. The province of Ontario cancels permission for citizens to cut firewood in provincial camp grounds.

7. Are the following two observations inconsistent? (a) Rising demand for housing causes prices of new homes to soar. (b) Many families refuse to buy homes as prices become prohibitive for them.

ELASTICITY

The laws of demand and supply predict the *direction* of changes in price and quantity in response to various shifts in demand and supply. However, it usually is not enough to know merely whether price and quantity each rise or fall; it is also important to know by *how much* each changes.

When flood damage led to major destruction of the U.S. onion crop in the 1990s, onion prices rose sharply. Not surprisingly, overall consumption of onions fell. The press reported that many consumers stopped using onions altogether and substituted onion salt, sauerkraut, cabbage, and other products. Other consumers still bought onions but in reduced quantities. Was the dollar value (price times quantity) higher or lower? The answer is important. A government concerned with the effect of a bad crop on farm income (because it has policies aimed at stabilizing farm income) will not be satisfied with being told that food prices will rise and quantities consumed will fall; it will need to know by approximately how much each will change if it is to assess the effects on farmers.

Measuring and describing the extent of the responsiveness of quantities to changes in prices and other variables is often essential if we are to understand the significance of these changes. This is what the concept of *elasticity* does.

PRICE ELASTICITY
OF DEMAND

Suppose that there is an increase in the supply of some farm crop, that is, a rightward shift in the supply curve. We saw in Figure 4-8 when we examined the laws of supply and demand that such an increase in supply will cause the equilibrium price to fall and the equilibrium quantity to rise. By how much will each change? The answer depends on what is called the *elasticity of demand*.

This is illustrated in the two parts of Figure 5-1, each of which reproduces the analysis of Figure 4-8 but using two different demand curves. The two parts of Figure 5-1 have the same initial equilibrium, and

that equilibrium is disturbed by the same rightward shift in the supply curve. But because the demand curves are different in the two parts of the figure, the new equilibrium position is different, and hence the magnitude of the effects of the increase in supply on equilibrium price and quantity are different.

A shift in supply will have different quantitative effects, depending on the shape of the demand curve. The difference may be significant for government policy. Consider what would happen if the rightward shift of the supply curve shown in Figure 5-1 occurs because the government has persuaded farmers to produce more of a certain crop. (For example, it might have paid a subsidy to farmers for producing that crop.)

Part (i) of Figure 5-1 illustrates a case in which the quantity that consumers demand is relatively responsive to price changes. The rise in production brings down the price, but because the quantity demanded is quite responsive, only a small change in price is necessary to restore equilibrium. The effect of the government's policy, therefore, is to achieve a large increase in the production and sales of this product and only a small decrease in price.

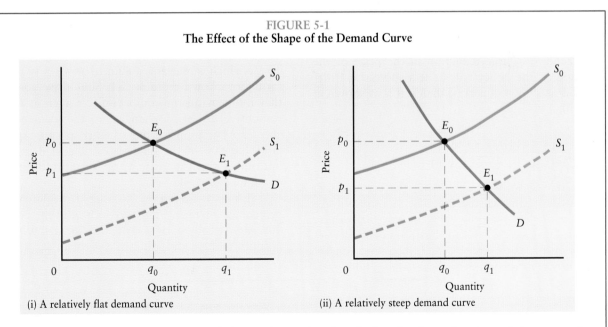

FIGURE 5-1
The Effect of the Shape of the Demand Curve

(i) A relatively flat demand curve

(ii) A relatively steep demand curve

The more responsive the quantity demanded is to changes in price, the less the change in price and the greater the change in quantity resulting from any given shift in the supply curve. Both parts of the figure are drawn to the same scale. They show the same initial equilibrium and the same shift in the supply curve. In each part, initial equilibrium is at price p_0 and output q_0 and the new equilibrium is at p_1 and q_1. In part (i), the effect of the shift in supply from S_0 to S_1 is a slight fall in the price and a large increase in quantity. In part (ii), the effect of the identical shift in the supply curve from S_0 to S_1 is a large fall in the price and a relatively small increase in quantity.

Part (ii) of Figure 5-1 shows a case in which the quantity demanded is relatively unresponsive to price changes. As before, the increase in supply at the original price causes a surplus that brings the price down. However, this time the quantity demanded by consumers does not increase much in response to the fall in price. The result is that equilibrium price falls more, and equilibrium quantity rises less, than in the first case. The effect of the government's policy is to achieve a large decrease in the price of this product and only a small increase in the quantity produced and sold.

In both of the cases shown in Figure 5-1, the government's policy has exactly the same effectiveness as far as the farmers' willingness to supply the commodity is concerned—the shifts of the supply curve are identical. The magnitude of the effects on the *equilibrium* price and quantity, however, are different because of the different degrees to which the quantity demanded by consumers responds to price changes.

If the purpose of the government's policy is to increase the quantity of this commodity produced and consumed, the policy will be more successful if the demand curve is similar to the one shown in part (i) of Figure 5-1 than if it is similar to the one shown in part (ii). If, however, the goal of the policy is to achieve a large reduction in the price of the commodity, the policy will be less successful if demand is as shown in part (i) than if it is as shown in part (ii).

THE MEASUREMENT OF PRICE ELASTICITY

In Figure 5-1, we were able to say that the curve in part (i) showed a demand that was more responsive to price changes than the curve in part (ii) because two conditions were fulfilled. First, both curves were drawn on the same scale. Second, the initial equilibrium prices and quantities were the same in both parts of the figure. Let us see why these conditions matter.

First, by drawing both figures on the same scale, the curve that looked steeper actually did have the larger absolute slope. (The slope of a demand curve tells us the number of dollars by which price must change to cause a unit change in quantity demanded.) If we had drawn the two curves on different scales, we could have concluded nothing about the relative price changes needed to get a unit change

TABLE 5-1
Price Reductions and Corresponding Increases in Quantity Demanded

Commodity	Reduction in Price (cents)	Increase in Quantity Demanded (per month)
Cheese	40 per kilogram	7,500 kilograms
T-shirts	40 per shirt	5,000 shirts
CD players	40 per CD player	100 CD players

The data show, for each of the three products, the change in quantity demanded in response to the same absolute fall in price. The data are fairly uninformative about the responsiveness of demand to price because they do not tell us either the original price or the original quantity demanded.

in quantity demanded by comparing their appearances on the graph.[1]

Second, because we started from the same price-quantity equilibrium in both parts of the figure, we did not need to distinguish between percentage changes and absolute changes. If the initial prices and quantities are the same in both cases, the larger absolute change is also the larger percentage change. However, when we wish to deal with different initial price-quantity equilibria, we need to decide whether we are interested in absolute or percentage changes. To see which is relevant, assume that we have the information shown in Table 5-1. Should we conclude that the demand for compact-disc players is not as responsive to price changes as the demand for cheese? After all, price cuts of 40 cents cause quite a large increase in the quantity of cheese demanded but only a small increase in the quantity demanded of compact-disc players.

This discussion raises the issue of absolute versus percentage changes. First, a reduction in the price of 40 cents will be a large price cut for a low-priced product and an insignificant price cut for a high-

---

[1] It is misleading to infer anything about the responsiveness of quantity to a price change by inspecting the apparent steepness of a graph of a demand curve. By the same token, it can be misleading to infer anything about the relative responsiveness of two different demands by comparing the appearance of their two curves. The reason is that you can make any curve appear as steep or as flat as you wish by changing the scales on the graph. For example, a curve that looks steep when the horizontal scale is 1 cm = 100 units will look much flatter when it is drawn on a graph with the same vertical scale but a horizontal scale of 1 cm = 1 unit.

TABLE 5-2
Price and Quantity Information Underlying Data of Table 5-1

Product	Unit	Original Price ($)	New Price ($)	Average Price ($)	Original Quantity	New Quantity	Average Quantity
Cheese	kg	3.40	3.00	3.20	116,250	123,750	120,000
T-shirts	shirt	16.20	15.80	16.00	197,500	202,500	200,000
CD players	player	80.20	79.80	80.00	9,950	10,050	10,000

These data provide the appropriate context for the data given in **Table 5-1.** The table relates the 40-cent-per-unit price reduction of each product to the actual prices and quantities demanded.

priced product. The price reductions listed in Table 5-1 represent different proportions of the total prices. It is usually more revealing to know the percentage change in the prices of the various products. Second, by an analogous argument, knowing the quantity by which demand changes is not very revealing unless the initial level of demand is also known. An increase of 7,500 kilograms is quite a significant reaction to demand if the quantity formerly bought was 15,000 kg, but it is insignificant if the quantity formerly bought was 10 million kg.

Table 5-2 shows the original and new levels of price and quantity. Changes in price and quantity expressed as percentages of the *average* prices and quantities are shown in the first two columns of Table 5-3. The **price elasticity of demand,** the measure of responsiveness of quantity of a product demanded to a change in that product's price, is symbolized by the Greek letter eta, η. It is defined as follows:

$$\eta = \frac{\text{percentage change in quantity demanded}}{\text{percentage change in price}}$$

TABLE 5-3
Calculation of Demand Elasticities

Product	(1) Percentage Decrease in Price	(2) Percentage Increase in Quantity	(3) Elasticity of Demand (2) ÷ (1)
Cheese	12.5	6.25	0.5
T-shirts	2.5	2.50	1.0
CD players	0.5	1.00	2.0

Elasticity of demand is the percentage change in quantity demanded divided by the percentage change in price. The percentage changes are based on average prices and quantities shown in Table 5-2. For example, the 40-cent-per-kilogram decrease in the price of cheese is 12.5 percent of $3.20. A 40-cent change in the price of CD players is only 0.5 percent of the average price per CD player of $80.00.

This measure is called the **elasticity of demand,** or simply *demand elasticity.* Because the variable causing the change in quantity demanded is the product's own price, the term *own-price elasticity of demand* is also used.

The Use of Average Price and Quantity in Computing Elasticity

The caption in Table 5-3 stresses that the demand elasticities are computed using changes in price and quantity measured in terms of the *average* values of each. Averages are used to avoid the ambiguity caused by the fact that when a price or quantity changes, the change is a different percentage of the original value than it is of the new value. For example, the 40-cent change in the price of cheese shown in Table 5-2 is a different percentage of the original price, $3.40, than it is of the new price, $3.00 (11.8 percent versus 13.3 percent).

Using average values for price and quantity also means that the measured elasticity of demand between any two points on the demand curve, call them A and B, is independent of whether the movement is from A to B or from B to A. In the example of cheese in Tables 5-2 and 5-3, the 40-cent change in the price of cheese is unambiguously 12.5 percent of the average price of $3.20, and that percentage applies to a price increase from $3.00 to $3.40 as well as to the decrease discussed in the text.

The implications of using average values for price and quantity for calculating elasticity can be seen as follows. Consider a change from an initial price of p_0 and quantity of q_0 to a new price of p_1 and quantity of q_1. The formula for elasticity is then

$$\eta = \frac{(q_1 - q_0)/q}{(p_1 - p_0)/p} \qquad [1]$$

where p and q are the average price and average quantity, respectively. (Thus $p = (p_1 + p_0)/2$ and $q = (q_1 + q_0)/2$.) These expressions can be substituted for p and q in Equation 1 and, after canceling the 2s, we get

$$\eta = \frac{(q_1 - q_0)/(q_1 + q_0)}{(p_1 - p_0)/(p_1 + p_0)} \qquad [2]$$

which provides a very convenient formula for calculating demand elasticity. For example, for the case of cheese in Tables 5-2 and 5-3, we have

$$\eta = \frac{7{,}500/240{,}000}{.40/6.40} = \frac{0.03125}{0.0625} = 0.5$$

which is as in Table 5-3. Further discussion of the use of averages to calculate elasticity and of alternative methods is found in the appendix to this chapter. [7]

Interpreting Numerical Elasticities

Because demand curves have negative slopes, an increase in price is associated with a decrease in quantity demanded, and vice versa. Because the percentage changes in price and quantity have opposite signs, demand elasticity is a negative number. However, we will follow the usual practice of ignoring the negative sign and speak of the measure as a positive number, as we have done in the illustrative calculations in Table 5-3. Thus the more responsive the quantity demanded (for example, CD players relative to cheese), the greater the elasticity of demand and the higher the measure (e.g., 2.0 compared with 0.5).

The numerical value of demand elasticity can vary from zero to infinity. Elasticity is zero when quantity demanded does not respond at all to a price change. As long as the percentage change in quantity is less than the percentage change in price, the elasticity of demand has a value of less than one (economists sometimes say less than *unity*). When the two percentage changes are equal, elasticity is equal to one. When the percentage change in quantity exceeds the percentage change in price, the elasticity of demand is greater than one (greater than unity).

When the percentage change in quantity is less than the percentage change in price (elasticity less than 1), there is said to be **inelastic demand**. When the percentage change in quantity is greater than the percentage change in price (elasticity greater than 1), there is said to be **elastic demand**. This terminology is important, and you should become familiar with it. It is summarized in part A of Extension 5-1.

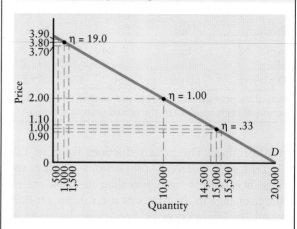

FIGURE 5-2
Elasticity Along a Straight-Line Demand Curve

Moving down a straight-line demand curve, elasticity falls continuously. On this straight-line demand curve, a reduction in price of $0.20 always leads to the same increase (1,000 units) in quantity demanded.

Near the upper end of the curve, where price is $3.80 and quantity demanded is 1,000 units, a reduction in price of $0.20 (from $3.90 to $3.70) is just slightly more than a 5 percent reduction, but the 1,000-unit increase in quantity demanded is a 100 percent increase. Here, elasticity (η) is 19.

Near the lower end, at a price of $1.00 and a quantity of 15,000 units, a price reduction of $0.20 (from $1.10 to $0.90) leads to the same 1,000-unit increase in quantity demanded. However, the $0.20 price reduction represents a 20 percent fall, whereas the 1,000-unit increase in quantity demanded represents only a 6.67 percent increase. Here, elasticity is 0.33.

A demand curve need not, and usually does not, have the same elasticity over every part of the curve. Figure 5-2 shows that a negatively sloped straight-line demand curve does not have a constant elasticity. A straight line has constant elasticity only when it is vertical or horizontal. Figure 5-3 illustrates these two cases, plus a third case of a particular *nonlinear* demand curve that also has a constant elasticity.

WHAT DETERMINES ELASTICITY OF DEMAND?

Table 5-4 shows some estimated price elasticities of demand. Evidently, elasticity varies considerably across different goods. The main determinant of demand elasticity is the availability of substitutes.

EXTENSION 5-1

THE TERMINOLOGY OF ELASTICITY

Term	Symbol	Numerical Measure of Elasticity	Verbal Description
A. Price elasticity of demand (supply)	η (η_S)		
Perfectly or completely inelastic		Zero	Quantity demanded (supplied) does not change as price changes.
Inelastic		Between zero and one	Quantity demanded (supplied) changes by a smaller percentage than does price.
Unit elastic		One	Quantity demanded (supplied) changes by exactly the same percentage as does price.
Elastic		Greater than one but less than infinity	Quantity demanded (supplied) changes by a larger percentage than does price
Perfectly, completely, or infinitely elastic		Infinity	Purchasers (sellers) are prepared to buy (sell) all they can at some price and none at all at an even higher (lower) price.
B. Income elasticity of demand	η_Y		
Inferior good		Negative	Quantity demanded decreases as income increases.
Normal good		Positive	Quantity demanded increases as income increases:
Income-inelastic		Less than one	Less than in proportion to income increase
Income-elastic		Greater than one	More than in proportion to income increase
C. Cross elasticity of demand	η_{XY}		
Substitute		Positive	Price increase of a substitute leads to an increase in quantity demanded of this good.
Complement		Negative	Price increase of a complement leads to a decrease in quantity demanded of this good.

Some products, such as margarine, cabbage, lamb, and Fords, have quite close substitutes—butter, other green vegetables, beef, and Chevrolets. A change in the prices of these products, *with the prices of the substitutes remaining constant,* can be expected to cause much substitution. A fall in price

leads consumers to buy more of the product and less of the substitutes, and a rise in price leads consumers to buy less of the product and more of the substitutes. Products defined more broadly, such as *all* foods and *all* clothing, have few, if any, satisfactory substitutes. A rise in their prices can be ex-

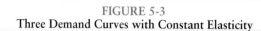

FIGURE 5-3
Three Demand Curves with Constant Elasticity

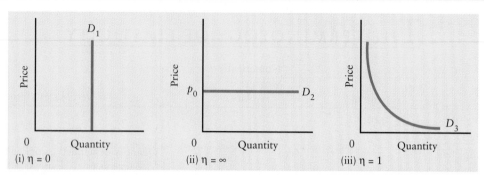

(i) $\eta = 0$ (ii) $\eta = \infty$ (iii) $\eta = 1$

Each of these demand curves has a constant elasticity. D_1 has zero elasticity: The quantity demanded does not change at all when price changes. D_2 has infinite elasticity at the price p_0: A small price increase from p_0 decreases quantity demanded from an indefinitely large amount to zero. D_3 has unit elasticity: A given percentage increase in price brings an equal percentage decrease in quantity demanded at all points on the curve; it is a rectangular hyperbola for which price times quantity is a constant.

TABLE 5-4
Estimated Price Elasticities of Demand[a]

(selected products)

Demand significantly inelastic (η less than 0.9)	
Potatoes	0.3
Sugar	0.3
Public transportation	0.4
All foods	0.4
Cigarettes	0.5
Gasoline	0.6
All clothing	0.6
Consumer durables	0.8
Demand approximately unit elastic (η between 0.9 and 1.1)	
Beef	
Beer	
Marijuana	
Demand significantly elastic (η more than 1.1)	
Furniture	1.2
Electricity	1.3
Lamb and mutton (U.K.)	1.5
Automobiles	2.1

[a]For the United States except where noted.

The wide range of price elasticities is illustrated by these selected measures. These elasticities, from various studies, are representative of literally hundreds of existing estimates. Some of the differences are discussed in the text.

pected to cause a smaller fall in quantities demanded than would be the case if close substitutes were available.

A product with close substitutes tends to have an elastic demand; a product with no close substitutes tends to have an inelastic demand.

Availability of substitutes—and hence measured demand elasticity—depends on both how the product is defined and the time period being considered. This is explored next.

Definition of the Product

For food taken as a whole, demand is inelastic over a large price range. It does not follow, however, that any one food, such as white bread or corned beef, is a necessity in the same sense. Individual foods can have quite elastic demands, and they frequently do.

Clothing provides a similar example. Clothing as a whole is less elastic than individual kinds of clothes. For example, when the price of wool sweaters rises, many households may buy cotton sweaters or down vests instead of buying an additional wool sweater. Thus, although purchases of wool sweaters fall, total purchases of clothing do not.

Any one of a group of related products will have a more elastic demand than the group taken as a whole.

Long-Run and Short-Run Elasticity of Demand

Because it takes time to develop satisfactory substitutes, a demand that is inelastic in the short run may prove to be elastic when enough time has passed. For example, at the time when cheap electric power was first brought to rural areas (long after it had come to cities), few farm households were wired for electricity. The initial measurements showed rural demand for electricity to be very inelastic; this is because many farmers did not rush to get hooked up to the electricity distribution system. Some commentators even argued that it was foolish to invest so much money in bringing cheap electricity to farmers because they would not buy it, even at low prices. Gradually, though, farm households became electrified, and as they purchased more and more electric appliances, measured elasticity increased considerably.

Petroleum provides a more recent example. In the early 1970s, the Organization of Petroleum Exporting Countries (OPEC) cartel shocked the world with its first sudden and large increase in the price of oil. At that time, the short-run demand for oil proved to be highly inelastic. Large price increases were met in the short run by very small reductions in quantity demanded. In this case, the short run lasted for several years. Gradually, however, the high price of petroleum products led to such adjustments as the development of smaller, more fuel-efficient cars, economizing on heating oil by installing more efficient insulation, and replacement of fuel oil in many industrial processes with such other power sources as coal and hydroelectricity. The long-run elasticity of demand, relating the change in price to the change in quantity demanded after all adjustments were made, turned out to have an elasticity of well over 1, although the long-run adjustments took as much as a decade to work out.

The degree of response to a price change, and thus the measured price elasticity of demand, will tend to be greater the longer the time span considered.

Because the elasticity of demand for a product changes over time as consumers adjust their habits and substitutes are developed, the demand curve also changes; hence a distinction can be made between short-run and long-run demand curves. Every demand curve shows the response of consumer demand to a change in price. For such products as cornflakes and pillowcases, the full response occurs quickly, and there is little reason to worry about longer-term effects. But other products are typically used in connection with highly durable appliances or machines. A change in the price of, say, electricity and gasoline may not have its major effect until the stock of appliances and machines using these products has been adjusted. This adjustment may take a long time to occur.

For products for which substitutes are developed over a period of time, it is helpful to identify two kinds of demand curves. A *short-run demand curve* shows the response of quantity demanded to a change in price for a given structure of the durable goods that use the product and for the existing sets of substitute products. A different short-run demand curve will exist for each such structure.

The *long-run demand curve* shows the response of quantity demanded to a change in price after enough time has passed to ensure that all adjustments to the changed price have occurred. The relationship between long-run and short-run demand curves is shown in Figure 5-4. The principal conclusion, already suggested in our discussion of elasticity, is this:

The long-run demand curve for a product will tend to have a substantially higher elasticity than the short-run demand curve for that product.

PRICE ELASTICITY AND CHANGES IN TOTAL EXPENDITURE

In the absence of sales taxes, the total amount spent by purchasers is also the total revenue received by the sellers, so we can use the terms *total expenditure* and *total revenue* interchangeably.[2] How does total expenditure react when the price of a product is changed? It turns out that the response of total expenditure depends on the price elasticity of demand.

To see the relationship between the price elasticity of demand and changes in total expenditure, we begin by noting that total expenditure is equal to price times quantity:

$$\text{Total Expenditure} = \text{price} \times \text{quantity}$$

Because price and quantity move in opposite directions along a demand curve, one falling when the other rises, the change in total expenditure appears

---

[2]Allowing for sales taxes complicates the analysis substantially but does not change the central results regarding the relationship between price, elasticity, and total expenditure. We examine sales taxes in detail in the final section of this chapter.

to be ambiguous. It is easily shown, however, that the direction of change in total expenditure depends on the percentage change in the two variables, price and quantity. If the percentage change in price exceeds the percentage change in quantity, the price change will dominate, and total expenditure will change in the same direction as the price changes; this is, of course, the case of elasticity less than unity. If the percentage change in the price is less than the percentage change in the quantity demanded (elasticity exceeds unity), the quantity change will dominate, and total expenditure will change in the same direction as quantity changes (that is, in the opposite direction to the change in price). If the two percentage changes are equal, total expenditure is unchanged—this is the case of unit elasticity.

The general relationship between demand elasticity, changes in price, and changes in total expenditure can be summarized as follows:

1. If demand is elastic, price and total expenditure are negatively related. A fall in price increases total expenditure, and a rise in price reduces it.

2. If demand is inelastic, price and total expenditure are positively related. A fall in price reduces total expenditure, and a rise in price increases it.

3. If elasticity of demand is unity, total expenditure is constant and therefore unrelated to price. A rise or a fall in price leaves total expenditure unaffected.

Table 5-5 and Figure 5-5 illustrate the relationship between elasticity of demand and total expenditure; both are based on the straight-line demand curve in Figure 5-2. Total expenditure at each of a number of points on the demand curve is calculated in Table 5-5, and the general relationship between total expenditure and quantity demanded is shown in Figure 5-5; there we see that expenditure reaches its maximum when elasticity is equal to 1. [8]

For example, when a bumper potato crop recently sent prices down 50 percent (a rightward shift in the supply curve), quantity sold increased by only 15 percent. Demand was clearly inelastic, and the result of the bumper crop was that potato farmers experienced a sharp *fall* in revenues.

Other examples are easily constructed from the information in Table 5-2. The reader can compute

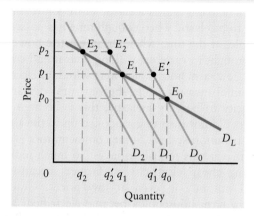

FIGURE 5-4
Short-Run and Long-Run Demand Curves

The long-run demand curve is more elastic than the short-run demand curve. D_L is a long-run demand curve. Suppose that consumers are fully adjusted to price p_0. Equilibrium is then at E_0, with quantity demanded q_0. Now suppose that price rises to p_1. In the short run, consumers will react along the short-run demand curve D_0 and adjust consumption to q_1'. Once time has permitted the full range of adjustments to price p_1, however, a new equilibrium E_1 will be reached with quantity q_1. At E_1 there is a new short-run demand curve D_1. A further rise to price p_2 would lead first to a short-run equilibrium at E_2' but eventually to a new long-run equilibrium at E_2. The long-run demand curve D_L is more elastic than any of the short-run curves.

TABLE 5-5
Changes in Total Expenditure for the Demand Curve of Figure 5-2

Price	Quantity	Expenditure
3.80	1,000	3,800
3.00	5,000	15,000
2.50	7,500	18,750
2.00	10,000	20,000
1.50	12,500	18,750
1.00	15,000	15,000

As price falls along a linear demand curve, total expenditure first rises and then falls. Along the range where price is greater than 2.00, elasticity is greater than one. As a result, the percentage fall in price is smaller than the resulting percentage increase in quantity, and total expenditure rises.

Along the range where price is less than 2.00, elasticity is less than one. As a result, the percentage fall in price is greater than the resulting percentage increase in quantity, and total expenditure falls.

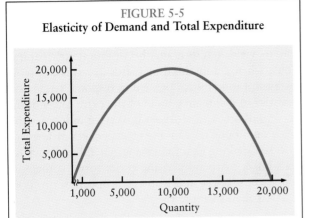

FIGURE 5-5
Elasticity of Demand and Total Expenditure

The change in total expenditure on a product in response to a change in price depends on the elasticity of demand. The total expenditure for each possible quantity demanded is plotted for the demand curve in Figure 5-2. For quantities demanded that are less than 10,000, elasticity of demand is greater than one, and hence any increase in quantity demanded will be proportionately larger than the fall in price that caused it. In that range, total expenditure is increasing. For quantities greater than 10,000, elasticity of demand is less than one, and hence any increase in quantity demanded will be proportionately smaller than the fall in price that caused it. In that range, total expenditure is decreasing. The maximum of total expenditure occurs where the elasticity of demand equals one.

total expenditure for cheese, T-shirts, and CD players both before and after the 40-cent price reduction to confirm the relationship between price, elasticity, and total expenditure.

OTHER DEMAND ELASTICITIES

The price of the product is not the only important variable determining demand for that product. Income and other prices also matter, and elasticity is a useful concept in measuring their effects.

INCOME ELASTICITY OF DEMAND

One of the most important determinants of demand is the income of the potential customers. When the Food and Agriculture Organization (FAO) of the United Nations wants to estimate the future demand for some crop, it needs to know by how much world income will grow and how much of that additional income will be spent on that particular foodstuff. As nations get richer, their consumption patterns typically change, with relatively more spent, for example, on meat and relatively less spent on staples such as rice and potatoes.

The responsiveness of demand to changes in income is termed the **income elasticity of demand** and is symbolized η_Y.

$$\eta_Y = \frac{\text{percentage change in quantity demanded}}{\text{percentage change in income}}$$

For most goods, increases in income lead to increases in demand—their income elasticity is positive. These are called **normal goods.** Goods for which demand decreases in response to a rise in income have negative income elasticities and are called **inferior goods.**

The income elasticity of normal goods may be greater than unity (elastic) or less than unity (inelastic), depending on whether the percentage change in the quantity demanded is greater or less than the percentage change in income that brought it about. It is also common to use the terms *income-elastic* and *income-inelastic* to refer to income elasticities of greater or less than unity. (See Extension 5-1 for a summary of the different elasticity concepts.)

The reaction of demand to changes in income is extremely important. We know that in most Western countries, economic growth caused the level of income to double every 20 to 30 years over a sustained period of at least a century. This rise in income has been shared to some extent by most citizens. As they found their incomes increasing, they increased their demands for most products, but the demands for some products, such as food and basic clothing, did not increase as much as the demands for other products. In developing countries, such as Ireland and Mexico, the demand for durable goods is increasing most rapidly as household incomes rise, while in North America and Western Europe, the demand for services has risen most rapidly. The uneven impact of the growth of income on the demands for different products has important economic effects, which are studied at several points in this book.

TABLE 5-6
Estimated Income Elasticities of Demand[a]

(selected products)

Inferior goods (η_Y less than zero)	
Whole milk	−0.5
Pig products	−0.2
Starchy roots	−0.2
Inelastic normal goods (η_Y between zero and one)	
Wine (France)	0.1
All food	0.2
Poultry	0.3
Cheese	0.4
Elastic normal goods (η_Y greater than one)	
Gasoline	1.1
Wine	1.4
Cream (U.K.)	1.7
Consumer durables	1.8
Poultry (Sri Lanka)	2.0
Restaurant meals (U.K.)	2.4

[a]For the United States except where noted.

Income elasticities vary widely across commodities and sometimes across countries. The basic source of food estimates by country is the Food and Agriculture Organization of the United Nations, but many individual studies have been made. Some of the differences are discussed in the text.

What Determines Income Elasticity of Demand?

The variations in income elasticities shown in Table 5-6 suggest that the more basic or staple a product, the lower its income elasticity. Food as a whole has an income elasticity of 0.2, consumer durables of 1.8. In Canada, starchy roots such as potatoes are inferior goods; their quantity demanded falls as income rises.

Does the distinction between luxuries and necessities help to explain differences in income elasticities? The table suggests that it does. The case of meals eaten away from home is one example. Such meals are almost always more expensive, calorie for calorie, than meals prepared at home. It would thus be expected that at lower ranges of income, restaurant meals would be regarded as an expensive luxury but that the demand for them would expand substantially as consumers became richer. This is in fact what happens.

Does this mean that the market demand for the foodstuffs that appear on restaurant menus will also have high income elasticities? Generally, the answer is no. When a household eats out rather than preparing meals at home, the main change is not in what is eaten but in who prepares it. The additional expenditure on "food" goes mainly to pay cooks and waiters and to yield a return on the restaurateur's capital. Thus, when a household increases its expenditure on restaurant food by 2.4 percent in response to a 1 percent rise in its income, most of the extra expenditure on "food" goes to workers in service industries; little, if any, finds its way into the pockets of farmers. This is a striking example of the general tendency for consumers to spend a rising proportion of their incomes on services and a lower proportion on foodstuffs as their incomes rise.

The more basic an item is in the consumption pattern of consumers, the lower is its income elasticity.

So far we have focused on differences in income elasticities among products. However, income elasticities for any one product also vary with the level of a consumer's income. When incomes are low, consumers may eat almost no green vegetables and consume lots of starchy foods such as bread and potatoes; when incomes are higher, they may eat cheap cuts of meat and more green vegetables along with their bread and potatoes; when incomes are higher still, they are likely to substitute frozen vegetables for canned and to eat a greater variety of foods.

What is true of individual consumers is also true of countries. Empirical studies show that for different countries at comparable stages of economic development, income elasticities are similar. However, the countries of the world are at various stages of economic development and so have widely different income elasticities for the same products. Notice in Table 5-6 the different income elasticity of poultry in the United States, where it is a standard item of consumption, and in Sri Lanka, where it is a luxury good.

Graphical Representation of Income Elasticity

Increases in income shift the demand curve to the right for a normal good and to the left for an inferior good. Figure 5-6 shows a different kind of graph, an *income-consumption curve*. The curve resembles an ordinary demand curve in one respect: It shows the relationship of quantity demanded to one other variable, *ceteris paribus*. The other variable is not price, however, but consumer income. (An in-

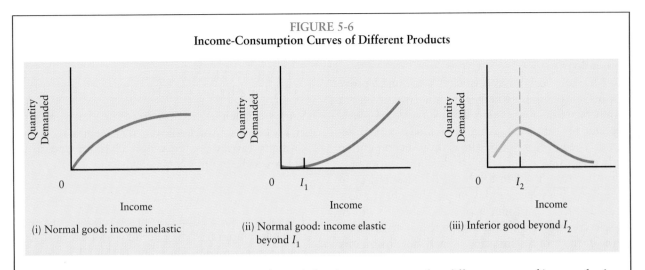

FIGURE 5-6
Income-Consumption Curves of Different Products

(i) Normal good: income inelastic

(ii) Normal good: income elastic beyond I_1

(iii) Inferior good beyond I_2

Different shapes of the curve relating quantity demanded to income correspond to different ranges of income elasticity. Normal goods have upward-sloping curves; inferior goods have downward-sloping curves. The good in part (i) is a typical normal good that is a necessity. The good in part (ii) is a luxury good that is income elastic beyond income I_1. The good in part (iii) is a necessity (normal) at low incomes but becomes an inferior good at incomes beyond I_2.

crease in the price of the product, holding income constant, would shift the curves shown in Figure 5-6 downward.)[3]

The figure shows three different patterns of income elasticity. Goods that consumers regard as necessities will generally have low income elasticities beyond some level of income. The obvious reason is that as incomes rise, it becomes possible for consumers to devote a smaller proportion of their incomes to meeting basic needs and a larger proportion to buying things that they have always wanted but could not afford. Some of the necessities may even become inferior goods. So-called luxury goods will not tend to be purchased at low levels of income but will have high income elasticities once incomes rise enough to permit consumers to sample the better things of life available to them.

CROSS ELASTICITY OF DEMAND

The responsiveness of demand to changes in the price of another product is called the **cross elasticity of demand**. It is often denoted η_{XY} and defined as follows:[4]

$$\eta_{XY} = \frac{\text{percentage change in quantity demanded of good X}}{\text{percentage change in price of good Y}}$$

Cross elasticity can vary from minus infinity to plus infinity. Complementary products, such as cars and gasoline, have negative cross elasticities. A large rise in the price of gasoline will lead (as it did in Canada in the 1970s) to a decline in the demand for cars, as some people decide to do without a car and others decide not to buy an additional car. Substitute products, such as cars and public transport, have positive cross elasticities. A large rise in the price of cars (relative to public transport)

---

[3]In Figure 5-6, in contrast to the ordinary demand curve, quantity demanded is on the vertical axis. This follows the usual practice of putting the variable to be explained (called the dependent variable) on the vertical axis and the explanatory variable (called the independent variable) on the horizontal axis. It is the ordinary demand curve that has the axes "backward". The explanation is buried in the history of economics and dates to Alfred Marshall's *Principles of Economics* (1890), the classic that is one of the foundations of modern price theory. [9] For better or worse, Marshall's scheme is now used by everybody, although mathematicians never fail to wonder at this example of the odd ways of economists.

[4]The change in the price of good Y causes the *demand curve* for good X to shift. Holding the price of good X constant allows us to measure the shift in the demand curve in terms of the change in quantity demanded of good X at the given price of good X.

would lead to a rise in the demand for public transport as some people shift from cars to public transport. (See Extension 5-1 for a summary of elasticity terminology.)

Measures of cross elasticity sometimes prove helpful in defining whether producers of similar products are in competition. For example, glass bottles and tin cans have a high cross elasticity of demand. The producer of bottles is thus in competition with the producer of cans. If the bottle company raises its price, it will lose substantial sales to the can producer. Men's shoes and women's shoes have a low cross elasticity. A producer of men's shoes is not in close competition with a producer of women's shoes. If the former raises its price, it will not lose many sales to the latter. Knowledge of cross elasticities can be important in anticombines investigations in which the issue is whether a firm in one industry is or is not competing with firms in another industry. Whether waxed paper and plastic wrap or aluminum cable and copper cable are or are not substitutes may determine questions of monopoly under the law.

The positive or negative sign of cross elasticities tell us whether or not goods are substitutes.

ELASTICITY OF SUPPLY

The concept of elasticity can be applied to supply as well as to demand. **Elasticity of supply** measures the responsiveness of the quantity supplied to a change in the product's price. It is denoted η_S and defined as follows:

$$\eta_S = \frac{\text{percentage change in quantity supplied}}{\text{percentage change in price}}$$

This is often called *supply elasticity*. The supply curves considered in this chapter all have positive slopes: An increase in price causes an increase in quantity supplied. Such supply curves all have positive elasticities because price and quantity change in the same direction.

There are important special cases. If the supply curve is vertical—the quantity supplied does not change as price changes—then elasticity of supply is zero. A horizontal supply curve has an infinite elasticity of supply: A small drop in price would reduce the quantity that producers are willing to supply from an indefinitely large amount to zero. Between these two extremes, elasticity of supply varies with the shape of the supply curve.[5]

DETERMINANTS OF SUPPLY ELASTICITY

Supply elasticities are important for many problems in economics. Much of the treatment of demand elasticity carries over to supply elasticity and so we can cover the main points quickly.

Substitution and Production Costs

The ease of substitution can vary in production as well as in consumption. If the price of a product rises, how much more can be produced profitably? This depends in part on how easy it is for producers to shift from the production of other products to the one whose price has risen. If agricultural land and labour can be readily shifted from one crop to another, the supply of any one crop will be more elastic than if they cannot.

Supply elasticity depends to a great extent on how costs behave as output is varied, an issue that will be treated at length in Part 3 of this book. If the costs of producing a unit of output rise rapidly as output rises, then the stimulus to expand production in response to a rise in price will quickly be choked off by increases in costs. In this case, supply will tend to be rather inelastic. If, however, the costs of producing a unit of output rise only slowly as production increases, a rise in price that raises profits will elicit a large increase in quantity supplied before the rise in costs puts a halt to the expansion in output. In this case, supply will tend to be rather elastic.

Long-Run and Short-Run Elasticity of Supply

As with demand, length of time for response is important. It may be difficult to change quantities supplied in response to a price increase in a matter of weeks or months but easy to do so over a period of years. An obvious example is the planting cycle of crops. Also, new oil fields can be discovered, wells drilled, and pipelines built over a period of years but

---

[5]Steepness, which is related to absolute rather than percentage changes, is not always a reliable guide. For example, as is shown in the appendix to this chapter, *any* upward-sloping straight line passing through the origin has an elasticity equal to 1 over its entire range.

not in a few months. Thus the elasticity of oil supply is much greater over five years than over one year. We explore some of the implications of the distinction between short-run and long-run elasticity in the next section.

TWO EXAMPLES WHERE PRICE ELASTICITY MATTERS

We have examined the meaning of price elasticity and the determinants of it, and we have shown how shifts in demand or supply have different effects on equilibrium price and quantity depending on the degree of price elasticity. In this chapter's final section, we examine two important situations where the elasticity of demand and supply take the centre stage.

SHORT-RUN AND LONG-RUN MARKET ADJUSTMENT

We have discussed the distinction between short-run and long-run demand curves and hence between short-run and long-run demand elasticity. Similarly, we noted the distinction between short-run and long-run supply curves and hence between short-run and long-run supply elasticity. These distinctions have important implications for the market response to shifts in either demand or supply.

Shifts in Supply

In the short run, when demand is relatively inelastic, a shift in supply leads to a sharp change in the equilibrium price but only a small change in the equilibrium quantity. However, as we saw earlier in this chapter, demand will be more elastic in the long run than in the short run. This responsiveness of demand means that in the long run, the shift in supply results in a smaller change in the equilibrium price and a larger change in quantity.

Figure 5-7 shows the effects of an increase in supply. In the short run, the supply increase leads to a movement down the relatively inelastic short-run demand curve; it thus causes a large fall in price but only a small increase in quantity. In the long run, demand is more elastic, so long-run equilibrium has

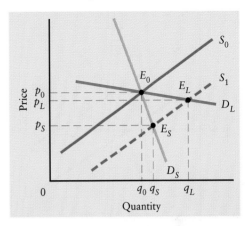

FIGURE 5-7
Short-Run and Long-Run Equilibrium Following an Increase in Supply

The magnitude of the changes in the equilibrium price and quantity following a shift in supply depends on the time allowed for demand to adjust. The change in the price is greater and the change in quantity is less in the short run than in the long run. The initial equilibrium is at E_0, with price p_0 and quantity q_0. Supply then increases such that the supply curve shifts from S_0 to S_1.

On impact, the relevant demand curve is the short-run curve D_S, and the new equilibrium immediately following the supply shock is E_S. Price falls sharply to p_S, and quantity rises only to q_S. In the long run, the demand curve is the more elastic one given by D_L, and equilibrium is at E_L. The long-run equilibrium price is p_L (greater than p_S), and quantity is q_L (greater than q_S).

price and quantity above those that prevailed in short-run equilibrium.

This pattern is often referred to as *overshooting* of the price. The overshooting of price that is evident in the figure is the way in which markets clear when demand is less elastic in the short run than in the long run. Note also that there is *undershooting* of quantity—that is, the equilibrium quantity rises by less in the short run than in the long run.

Shifts in Demand

In the short run, when supply is relatively inelastic, a shift in demand leads to a sharp change in the equilibrium price but only a small change in the equilibrium quantity exchanged. However, in the

FIGURE 5-8
Short-Run and Long-Run Equilibrium Following an Increase in Demand

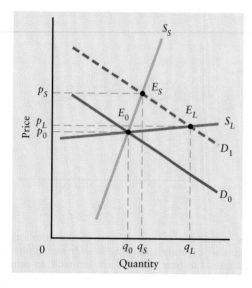

The magnitude of the changes in the equilibrium price and quantity following a shift in demand depends on the time frame of the analysis. In the short run, the change in the price is greater and the change in quantity is less than in the long run. The initial equilibrium is at E_0, with price p_0 and quantity q_0. Demand then increases such that the demand curve shifts from D_0 to D_1.

On impact, the relevant supply curve is the short-run curve S_S, so that the new equilibrium immediately following the demand shock is at E_S. Price rises sharply to p_S, and quantity rises only to q_S. In the long run, the supply curve is the more elastic one given by S_L. The long-run equilibrium is at E_L; price is p_L (less than p_S), and quantity is q_L (greater than q_S).

long run, when supply is more elastic than in the short run, the shift in demand leads to a smaller change in the equilibrium price and a larger change in quantity.

Figure 5-8 illustrates the effects of an increase in demand. The short-run overshooting of price, and the undershooting of quantity, that is evident in the figure is analogous to that shown in Figure 5-7 in response to a shift in supply. Here it arises following a shift in demand and is the market-clearing response when supply is less elastic in the short run than in the long run.

THE INCIDENCE OF SALES TAXES

The federal and provincial governments levy sales taxes on many goods. The Goods and Services Tax (GST) introduced in 1991 is a tax that applies to most goods and services at a uniform rate across the country. Special taxes (called **excise taxes**) also apply to goods such as cigarettes, alcohol, and gasoline. All such *commodity taxes* work in the following way. At the point of sale of the product, the sellers collect the tax on behalf of the government and then periodically remit the tax collections.

When the sellers write their cheques to the government, these firms feel—with some justification—that they are the ones paying the tax. Consumers, however, argue—again, with some justification—that *they* are the ones who are shouldering the burden of the tax because the tax causes the price of the product to rise.

The question of who *bears the burden* of a tax is called the question of **tax incidence**. A straightforward application of demand-and-supply analysis will show that tax incidence has nothing to do with whether the government collects the tax directly from consumers or from firms.

The burden of a sales tax is distributed between consumers and sellers in a manner that depends on the relative elasticities of supply and demand.

Consider the market for gasoline, as illustrated in Figure 5-9. To simplify the problem, we analyze the case where there is initially no sales tax. The equilibrium without taxes is illustrated by the solid supply and demand curves. What happens when a sales tax of t per litre of gasoline is introduced? A sales tax means that the price paid by the consumer, called the *consumer price,* and the price received by the seller, called the *seller price,* must now differ by the amount of the tax, t.

In terms of the figure, the effect of the sales tax can be analyzed by considering a new supply curve S' that is above the original supply curve S by the amount of the tax per litre of gasoline, t. To understand this new curve, consider the firm's situation at the original equilibrium quantity q_0. To supply that quantity, producers must receive p_0 per litre of gas sold. However, for producers to receive p_0 when there is a sales tax on gasoline, the consumer must

FIGURE 5-9
The Incidence of a Sales Tax

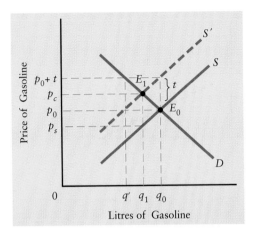

The burden of a sales tax is shared by consumers and producers. The original supply and demand curves for gasoline are given by the solid lines S and D; equilibrium is at E_0 with price p_0 and quantity q_0. When a sales tax of t per litre is imposed, the supply curve shifts up to the dashed line S', which lies above the original supply curve by the amount of the tax t.

pay a total price of $p_0 + t$. This is true whether the consumer "pays the tax directly" by giving p_0 to the firm and t to the government or whether the consumer pays the total $p_0 + t$ to the firm and the firm then remits the tax t to the government. Either way, the total amount that consumers must pay to obtain a given quantity from firms has increased by the amount of the tax t.

This upward shift in the supply curve for gasoline is depicted in Figure 5-9 as the dashed curve, S'. This shift in the supply curve, caused by the tax, will generally also cause a movement *along* the demand curve, reducing the equilibrium quantity exchanged.

Consider the situation at the consumer price of $p_0 + t$. Firms will still be willing to sell the original quantity, but households will demand less because the price has risen; there is excess supply and hence pressure for the consumer price to fall.

The new equilibrium after the imposition of the sales tax occurs at the intersection of the origi-

nal demand curve D with the tax-shifted supply curve S'. At this new equilibrium, E_1, the consumer price rises to p_c (greater than p_0), the seller price falls to p_s (less than p_0), and the equilibrium quantity falls to q_1.

Note that the quantity demanded *at the consumer price* is equal to the quantity supplied *at the seller price*, which is required for equilibrium. As shown in the figure, compared to the original equilibrium, the consumer price is higher and the seller price is lower, although in each case the change in price is less than the full extent of the sales tax.

After the imposition of a sales tax, the difference between the consumer and seller prices is equal to the tax, and hence the sum of the increase in the consumer price and the decrease in the seller price is equal to the tax. In the new equilibrium, the quantity exchanged is less than that exchanged prior to the imposition of the tax.

The role of the relative elasticities of supply and demand in determining the incidence of the sales tax is illustrated in Figure 5-10. In part (i), demand is inelastic relative to supply; as a result, the fall in quantity is quite small, whereas the price paid by consumers rises by almost the full extent of the tax. Because neither the price received by sellers nor the quantity sold changes very much, sellers bear little of the burden of the tax. In part (ii), supply is inelastic relative to demand; in this case, consumers continue to purchase almost the same quantity with little change in the price, and hence they bear little of the burden of the tax, which falls mostly on suppliers. Notice in Figure 5-10 that the size of the upward shift in supply is the same in the two cases, indicating the same tax increase in both cases.

Now we can examine who really pays for cigarette and gasoline tax increases. The demand for cigarettes is inelastic both overall and relative to supply, suggesting that a cigarette-tax increase would be borne more by consumers than by producers. Thus, the large *reductions* in cigarette taxes which took place in the summer of 1994 in Ontario and Quebec benefited consumers more than producers. The demand for gasoline is also inelastic, but much more so in the short run than in the long run. In the long run, drivers can change

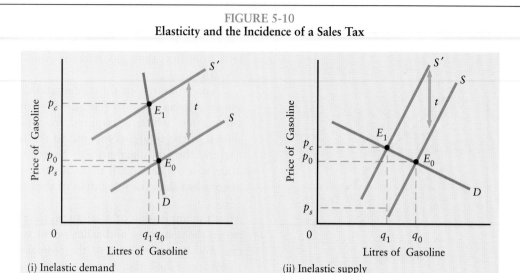

FIGURE 5-10
Elasticity and the Incidence of a Sales Tax

(i) Inelastic demand   (ii) Inelastic supply

The distribution of the burden of a sales tax between consumers and producers depends on the relative elasticities of supply and demand. In both parts of the figure, the initial supply and demand curves are given by S and D; the initial equilibrium is at E_0 with equilibrium price p_0 and quantity q_0. A sales tax of t per litre is imposed, causing the supply curve to shift up by the amount of the tax to S'. The new equilibrium is at E_1. The consumer price rises to p_c, the seller price falls to p_s, and the quantity falls to q_1. Sellers bear little of the burden of the tax in the first case (and consumers bear a lot), whereas consumers bear little of the burden in the second case (and sellers bear a lot).

their driving routines and improve the efficiency of their vehicles. In the short run, changes of both types are more costly. The supply of gasoline, given world trade in petroleum and petroleum products, is elastic relative to demand, implying that most of the tax falls on consumers.

SUMMARY

A. PRICE ELASTICITY OF DEMAND

- *Price elasticity of demand*, also called *elasticity of demand*, is a measure of the extent to which the quantity demanded of a product responds to a change in its price. Represented by the symbol η, it is defined as

$$\eta = \frac{\text{percentage change in quantity demanded}}{\text{percentage change in price}}$$

The percentage changes are usually calculated as the change divided by the *average* value. Elasticity is defined to be a positive number, and it can vary from zero to infinity.

- When the numerical measure of elasticity is less than unity, demand is *inelastic*. This means that the percentage change in quantity demanded is less than the percentage change in price that brought it about. When the numerical measure exceeds unity, demand is *elastic*. This means that the percentage change in quantity demanded is greater than the percentage change in price that brought it about.
- The main determinant of the price elasticity of demand is the availability of substitutes for the product. Any one of a group of close substitutes will have a more elastic demand than the group as a whole. Elasticity of demand tends to be greater the longer the

time over which adjustment occurs. Items that have few substitutes in the short run may develop many substitutes when consumers and producers have time to adapt.

- Elasticity and total expenditure (or revenue) are related in the following way: If elasticity is less than unity, total expenditure is positively related with price; if elasticity is greater than unity, total expenditure is negatively related with price; and if elasticity is unity, total revenue does not change as price changes.

B. OTHER DEMAND ELASTICITIES

- *Income elasticity of demand* is a measure of the extent to which the quantity demanded of some product changes as income changes. Represented by the symbol η_Y, it is defined as

$$\eta_Y = \frac{\text{percentage change in quantity demanded}}{\text{percentage change in income}}$$

The income elasticity of demand for a product will usually change as income varies. For example, a product that has a high income elasticity at a low income (because increases in income bring it within reach of the typical household) may have a low or negative income elasticity at higher incomes (because with further rises in incomes, it is gradually replaced by a superior substitute).

- *Cross elasticity of demand* is a measure of the extent to which the quantity demanded of one product changes when the price of a different product changes. Represented by the symbol η_{XY}, it is defined as

$$\eta_{XY} = \frac{\text{percentage change in quantity demanded of good X}}{\text{percentage change in price of good Y}}$$

It is used to define products that are substitutes for one another (positive cross elasticity) and products that complement one another (negative cross elasticity).

C. ELASTICITY OF SUPPLY

- *Elasticity of supply* is an important concept in economics. It measures the extent to which the quantity supplied of some product changes when the price of that product changes. Represented by the symbol η_S, it is defined as

$$\eta_S = \frac{\text{percentage change in quantity supplied}}{\text{percentage change in price}}$$

It is the analogue on the supply side to the elasticity of demand. Supply tends to be more elastic in the long run than in the short run.

D. TWO EXAMPLES WHERE PRICE ELASTICITY MATTERS

- Since price elasticities are larger in the long run than in the short run, a shift in supply (or demand) will lead to a larger change in price and a smaller change in quantity in the short run than in the long run.
- The distribution of the burden of a sales tax between consumers and producers is independent of who actually remits the tax to the government. Rather, it depends on the relative elasticities of the supply and the demand for the product.

KEY CONCEPTS

Price elasticity of demand
Inelastic and perfectly inelastic demand
Elastic and infinitely elastic demand
Relationship between demand elasticity and total expenditure
Income elasticity of demand

Income-elastic and income-inelastic demands
Normal goods and inferior goods
Cross elasticity of demand
Substitutes and complements
Elasticity of supply

Short-run and long-run responses to shifts in demand and supply
Consumer price and seller price
Tax incidence

DISCUSSION QUESTIONS

1. From the following quotations, what, if anything, can you conclude about elasticity of demand?

   a. "Good weather resulted in record wheat harvests and sent wheat prices tumbling. The result has been disastrous for many wheat farmers."

   b. "Ridership always went up when bus fares came down, but the increased patronage never was enough to prevent a decrease in overall revenue."

   c. "As the price of compact-disc players fell, producers found their revenues soaring."

   d. "Coffee to me is an essential good—I've just gotta have it no matter what the price."

   e. "The soaring price of condominiums does little to curb the strong demand in Vancouver."

2. A provincial MLA proposes legislation that would privatize all primary and secondary education. The MLA argues that the province should, in return, provide each family a subsidy of $4,000 per child—the current per student expenditure. As a result, he argues, families will actually consume more education. Is this possible? What would be required for this argument to be correct?

3. What would you predict about the relative price elasticity of demand of (a) food, (b) vegetables, (c) artichokes, and (d) artichokes sold at the local supermarket? What would you predict about their relative income elasticities?

4. "Avocados have a limited market not greatly affected by price until the price falls to less than 80 cents per kilogram wholesale. Then they are much demanded by manufacturers of dog food." Interpret this statement in terms of price elasticity.

5. Home computers were a leader in sales appeal through much of the 1980s. But per capita sales are much lower in Mexico than in Canada, and lower in Newfoundland than in Alberta. Manufacturers are puzzled by the big differences. Can you offer an explanation in terms of elasticity?

6. What elasticity measure or measures would be useful in answering the following questions?

   a. Will cheaper transport into the central city help to keep downtown shopping centres profitable?

   b. Will raising the bulk postage rate increase or decrease the revenues for Canada Post?

   c. Are producers of toothpaste and mouthwash in competition with each other?

   d. What effect will rising gasoline prices have on the sale of cars that use propane gas?

7. Interpret the following statements in terms of the relevant elasticity concept.

   a. "As fuel for tractors has become more expensive, many farmers have shifted from plowing their fields to no-till farming. No-till acreage increased dramatically in the past 20 years."

   b. "Fertilizer makers brace for dismal year as fertilizer prices soar."

   c. "When farmers are hurting, small towns feel the pain."

   d. "The development of the Hibernia oil field may bring temporary prosperity to Newfoundland merchants."

8. Suggest products that you think might have the following patterns of elasticity of demand.

   a. High income elasticity, high price elasticity

   b. High income elasticity, low price elasticity

   c. Low income elasticity, low price elasticity

   d. Low income elasticity, high price elasticity

9. Assume a stamp collector buys the only two copies of a stamp at an auction. After the purchase, the collector goes to the front of the room and burns one of the stamps in front of the shocked audience. What must the collector believe for this to be a rational, wealth-maximizing action?

10. When the New York City Opera faced a growing deficit, it cut its ticket prices by 20 percent, hoping to attract more customers. At the same time, the New York Transit Authority raised subway fares to reduce its growing deficit. Was one of these two opposite approaches to reducing a deficit necessarily wrong?

11. When an MLA proposed an increase in the provincial sales-tax rate, one critic responded that this

would hurt both producers and consumers. Discuss the sense in which this is true. From the data in Table 5-4, how would you expect the distribution of the costs between the two groups to vary between, say, the market for automobiles and the market for clothing? Would you expect the distribution in each market to be different in the short run than in the long run?

APPENDIX TO CHAPTER 5

A Formal Analysis of Elasticity

The definition of elasticity used in the text may be written symbolically in the following form:[1]

$$\eta = \frac{\Delta q}{\text{average } q} \div \frac{\Delta p}{\text{average } p}$$

where the averages are over the range, or arc, of the demand curve being considered. Rearranging terms, we can write

$$\eta = \frac{\Delta q}{\Delta p} \times \frac{\text{average } p}{\text{average } q}.$$

This is called **arc elasticity,** and it measures the average responsiveness of quantity to price over an interval of the demand curve.

Most theoretical treatments use a different but related concept called **point elasticity.** This is the measure of responsiveness of quantity to price *at a particular point* on the demand curve. The precise definition of point elasticity uses the concept of a derivative, which is drawn from differential calculus.

In this appendix, we first study arc elasticity, which may be regarded as an approximation of point elasticity. Then we study point elasticity.

Before proceeding, we should note one further change. In the text of Chapter 5, we reported our price elasticities as positive values and thus implicitly multiplied all our calculations by −1. In theoretical work, it is more convenient to retain the concept's

natural sign. Hence normal demand elasticities will have negative signs, and statements about "more" or "less" elasticity must be understood to refer to the absolute, not the algebraic, value of demand elasticity.

ARC ELASTICITY AS AN APPROXIMATION OF POINT ELASTICITY

Point elasticity measures elasticity at some price-quantity point. In the approximate definition, however, the responsiveness is measured over a small range starting from that point. For example, in Figure 5A-1, the elasticity at point 1 can be measured by the responsiveness of quantity demanded to a change in price that

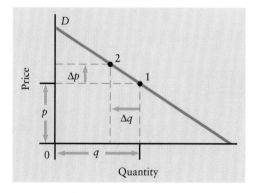

FIGURE 5A-1
A Straight-Line Demand Curve

Because p/q varies with $\Delta q/\Delta p$ constant, the elasticity varies along this demand curve; it is high at the left and low at the right.

---

[1]The following notation is used throughout this appendix.
$\eta \equiv$ elasticity of demand
$\eta_S \equiv$ elasticity of supply
$q \equiv$ initial quantity
$\Delta q \equiv$ change in quantity
$p \equiv$ initial price
$\Delta p \equiv$ change in price

takes price and quantity from point 1 to point 2. The algebraic formula for this elasticity concept is

$$\eta = \frac{\Delta q}{\Delta p} \times \frac{p}{q} \qquad \text{[A1]}$$

This is similar to the definition of arc elasticity above except that because elasticity is being measured at a point, p and q corresponding to that point are used (rather than the average p and q over an arc of the curve).

Equation A1 splits elasticity into two parts: $\Delta q/\Delta p$ (the ratio of the change in quantity to the change in price), which is related to the *slope* of the demand curve, and p/q, which is related to the *point* on the curve at which the measurement is made.

Figure 5A-1 shows a straight-line demand curve. To measure the elasticity at point 1, take p and q at that point and then consider a price change, say, to point 2, and measure Δp and Δq as indicated. The slope of the straight line joining points 1 and 2 is $\Delta p/\Delta q$. Therefore, the first term in the elasticity formula is the *reciprocal* of the slope of the straight line joining the two price-quantity positions under consideration.

Although point elasticity of demand refers to a price-quantity point on the demand curve, the first term in Equation A1 still refers to changes over an arc of the curve. This is the part of the formula that involves approximation, and, as we shall see, it has some unsatisfactory results. Nonetheless, some interesting theorems can be derived by using this formula as long as we confine ourselves to straight-line demand and supply curves.

1. *The elasticity of a downward-sloping straight-line demand curve varies from zero at the quantity axis to infinity at the price axis.* First notice that a straight line has a constant slope, so the ratio $\Delta p/\Delta q$ is the same everywhere on the line. Therefore, its reciprocal, $\Delta q/\Delta p$, must also be constant. The changes in η can now be inferred by inspecting the ratio p/q. Where the line cuts the quantity axis, price is zero, so the ratio p/q is zero; thus $\eta = 0$. Moving up the line, p rises and q falls, so the ratio p/q rises; thus elasticity rises. Approaching the top of the line, q approaches zero, so the ratio becomes very large. Thus elasticity increases without limit as the price axis is approached.

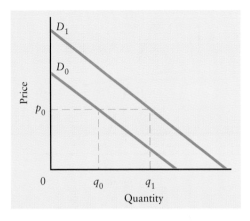

FIGURE 5A-2
Two Parallel Straight-Line Demand Curves

For any given price, the quantities are different on these two parallel curves; thus the elasticities are different, being higher on D_0 than on D_1.

2. *Where there are two straight-line demand curves of the same slope, the one farther from the origin is less elastic at each price than the one closer to the origin.* Figure 5A-2 shows two parallel straight-line demand curves. Compare the elasticities of the two curves at any price, say, p_0. Because the curves are parallel, the ratio $\Delta q/\Delta p$ is the same on both curves. Because elasticities at the same price are being compared on both curves, p is the same, and the only factor left to vary is q. On the curve farther from the origin, quantity is larger (i.e., $q_1 > q_0$) and hence p_0/q_1 is smaller than p_0/q_0; thus η is smaller. It follows that parallel shifts of a straight-line demand curve lower elasticity (at each price) when the line shifts outward and raise elasticity when the line shifts inward.

3. *The elasticities of two intersecting straight-line demand curves can be compared at the point of intersection merely by comparing slopes, the steeper curve being the less elastic.* In Figure 5A-3, there are two intersecting curves. At the point of intersection, p and q are common to both curves, and hence the ratio p/q is the same. Therefore, η varies only with $\Delta q/\Delta p$. On the steeper curve, $\Delta q/\Delta p$ is smaller than on the flatter curve, so elasticity is lower.

4. *If the slope of a straight-line demand curve changes while the price intercept remains con-*

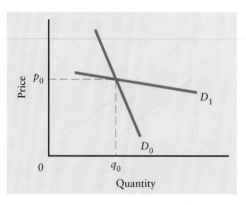

FIGURE 5A-3
Two Intersecting Straight-Line Demand Curves

Elasticities are different at the point of intersection of these demand curves because the slopes are different, being higher on D_0 than on D_1. Therefore, D_1 is more elastic than D_0 at p_0.

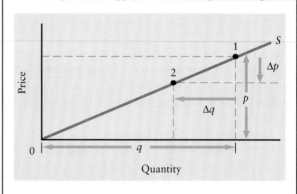

FIGURE 5A-5
A Straight-Line Supply Curve Through the Origin

At every point on the curve, p/q equals $\Delta p/\Delta q$; hence elasticity equals unity at every point.

stant, elasticity at any given price is unchanged. This is an interesting case for at least two reasons. First, when more customers having similar tastes to those already in the market enter the market, the demand curve pivots outward in this way. Second, when more firms enter a market that is

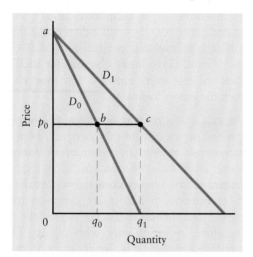

FIGURE 5A-4
Two Straight-Line Demand Curves from the Same Price Intercept

The elasticity is the same on D_0 and D_1 at any given price. This situation occurs because the steeper slope of D_0 is exactly offset by the smaller quantity demanded at any price.

shared proportionally among all firms, each firm's demand curve shifts inward in this way.

Consider in Figure 5A-4 the elasticities at point b on demand curve D_0 and at point c on demand curve D_1. We shall focus on the two triangles abp_0 on D_0 and acp_0 on D_1 formed by the two straight-line demand curves emanating from point a and by the price p_0. The price p_0 is the line segment $0p_0$. The quantities q_0 and q_1 are the line segments p_0b and p_0c, respectively. The slope of D_0 is $\Delta p/\Delta q = ap_0/p_0b$, and the slope of D_1 is $\Delta p/\Delta q = ap_0/p_0c$. From Equation A1 we can represent the elasticities of D_0 and D_1 at the points b and c, respectively, as

η at point $b = (p_0b/ap_0) \times (0p_0/p_0b) = (0p_0/ap_0)$

η at point $c = (p_0c/ap_0) \times (0p_0/p_0c) = (0p_0/ap_0)$

The two values of the elasticity are the same. The reason is that the distance corresponding to the quantity demanded at p_0 appears in both the numerator and the denominator and thus cancels out. Put differently, if the straight-line demand curve D_0 is twice as steep as D_1, it has half the quantity demanded at p_0. Therefore, in Equation A1 the steeper slope (a smaller Δq for the same Δp) is exactly offset by the smaller quantity demanded (a smaller q for the same p).

5. *Any straight-line supply curve through the origin has an elasticity of one.* Such a supply curve is shown in Figure 5A-5. Consider the two triangles with the sides p, q, and the S curve and

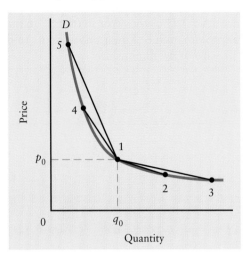

FIGURE 5A-6
Point Elasticity of Demand Measured
by the Approximate Formula

When the approximation of $\eta = (\Delta q / \Delta p) \times (p/q)$ is used, many elasticities are measured from point 1 because the slope of the chord between point 1 and every other point on the curve varies.

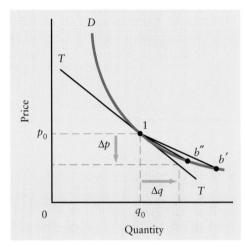

FIGURE 5A-7
Point Elasticity of Demand Measured
by the Exact Formula

When the exact definition $\eta = (dq/dp) \times (p/q)$ is used, only one elasticity is measured from point 1 because there is only one tangent to the demand curve at that point.

Δp, Δq, and the S curve. Clearly, these are similar triangles. Therefore, the ratios of their sides are equal; that is,

$$\frac{p}{q} = \frac{\Delta p}{\Delta q} \qquad \text{[A2]}$$

Elasticity of supply is defined as

$$\eta_S = \frac{\Delta q}{\Delta p} \times \frac{p}{q}$$

which, by substitution from Equation A2, gives

$$\eta_S = \frac{q}{p} \times \frac{p}{q} = 1$$

6. *The demand elasticity measured from any point* (p,q), *according to Equation A1, depends on the direction and magnitude of the change in price and quantity.* Except for a straight line (for which the slope does not change), the ratio $\Delta q / \Delta p$ will not be the same over different ranges of a curve. Figure 5A-6 shows a demand curve that is not a straight line. To measure the elasticity from point 1, the ratio $\Delta q / \Delta p$—and thus η—will vary according to the size and the direction of the price change. This result is very inconvenient

and is avoided by using the concept of point elasticity in its exact form.

THE PRECISE DEFINITION OF POINT ELASTICITY

To measure the point elasticity *exactly,* it is necessary to know the reaction of quantity to a change in price *at that point,* not over a range of the curve.

The reaction of quantity to price change at a point is called *dq/dp,* and this is defined as the reciprocal of the slope of the straight line tangent to the demand curve at the point in question. In Figure 5A-7, the elasticity of demand at point 1 is the ratio p/q (as it has been in all previous measures), now multiplied by the ratio of $\Delta q / \Delta p$ measured along the straight line T, tangent to the curve at point 1, that is, by dq/dp. Thus the exact definition of point elasticity is

$$\eta = \frac{dq}{dp} \times \frac{p}{q} \qquad \text{[A3]}$$

The ratio dq/dp, as defined, is in fact the differential calculus concept of the *derivative* of quantity with respect to price.

This definition of point elasticity is the one normally used in economic theory. Equation A1 is mathematically only an approximation of this expression. In Figure 5A-7, the measure of arc elasticity will come closer to the measure of point elasticity as a smaller price change is used to calculate the arc elasticity. The $\Delta q / \Delta p$ in Equation A1 is the reciprocal of the slope of the chord connecting the two points being compared. As the chord becomes shorter, its slope gets closer to that of the tangent T. (Compare the chords connecting point 1 to b' and b'' in Figure 5A-7.) Thus the error in using Equation A1 as an approximation of Equation A3 tends to diminish as the size of Δp diminishes.

CHAPTER 6

DEMAND AND SUPPLY IN ACTION

Now that you have mastered the theory of how prices are determined by demand and supply, you have a very powerful tool at your command. However, a full understanding of any theory comes only with practice. This chapter is designed to give you that practice by examining some cases drawn from real-world experience. These include the effects of government-administered prices (a special case of which is rent controls), the pattern of a country's imports and exports, an examination of who actually "pays" for tariffs, and the effectiveness of agricultural income-support policies. Although we hope that these illustrations are interesting in themselves, the most important reason for studying them is to practice using the theory so that you can use it to understand the many other cases where the theory applies.

GOVERNMENT-CONTROLLED PRICES

In a number of important cases, governments fix the price at which a product must be bought and sold in the domestic market. Here we examine the consequences of such policies. Later, we look at rent controls and agricultural price supports, which are examples of government-controlled prices.

The equilibrium price in a free market occurs at the price at which quantity demanded equals quantity supplied. Government *price controls* are policies that attempt to hold the price at some disequilibrium value that could not be maintained in the absence of the government's intervention. Some controls hold the market price below its equilibrium value; this creates a shortage, with quantity demanded exceeding quantity supplied at the controlled price. Other controls hold price above the equilibrium price; this creates a surplus, with quantity supplied exceeding quantity demanded at the controlled price.

DISEQUILIBRIUM PRICES

As we discussed in Chapter 4, market price generally changes whenever quantity supplied does not equal quantity demanded. Price then moves toward its equilibrium value, at which point there are neither unsatisfied suppliers nor unsatisfied demanders.

When controls hold price at some disequilibrium value, what determines the quantity *actually traded*

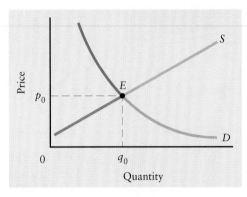

FIGURE 6-1
The Determination of Quantity Exchanged in Disequilibrium

In disequilibrium, quantity exchanged is determined by the lesser of quantity demanded and quantity supplied. At p_0, the market is in equilibrium, with quantity demanded equal to quantity supplied. For prices below p_0, the quantity exchanged will be determined by the supply curve. For prices above p_0, the quantity exchanged will be determined by the demand curve. Thus the darker portions of the S and D curves show the actual quantities exchanged at different prices.

on the market? The key to the answer is the fact that any voluntary market transaction requires both a willing buyer and a willing seller. This implies that if quantity demanded is less than quantity supplied, demand will determine the amount actually exchanged, while the rest of the quantity supplied will remain in the hands of the unsuccessful sellers. Conversely, if quantity demanded exceeds quantity supplied, supply will determine the amount actually exchanged, while the rest of the quantity demanded will represent desired purchases of unsuccessful buyers. This argument is spelled out in more detail in Figure 6-1, which establishes the following general conclusion:

At any disequilibrium price, quantity exchanged is determined by the *lesser* of quantity demanded or quantity supplied.

PRICE FLOORS

Governments sometimes establish a *price floor*, which is the minimum permissible price that can be charged for a particular good or service. A price floor that is set at or below the equilibrium price has no effect because equilibrium remains attainable. If,

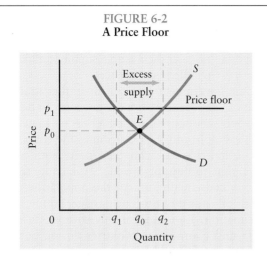

FIGURE 6-2
A Price Floor

If a price floor is above the equilibrium price, quantity supplied will exceed quantity demanded. The free-market equilibrium is at E, with price p_0 and quantity q_0. The government now establishes an effective price floor at p_1. Quantity supplied exceeds quantity demanded by q_1q_2.

however, the price floor is set above the equilibrium, it will raise the price, in which case it is said to be *binding* or *effective*.

Price floors may be established by rules that make it illegal to sell the product below the prescribed price, as in the case of the minimum wage (examined in Chapter 16). Further, the government may establish a price floor by announcing that it will guarantee a certain price by buying any excess supply of the product that emerges at that price. Such guarantees are a feature of many agricultural support policies (examined later in this chapter).

The effects of binding price floors are illustrated in Figure 6-2, which establishes the following key result:

Effective price floors lead to excess supply. Either an unsold surplus will exist, or someone must enter the market and buy the excess supply.

The consequences of excess supply will, of course, differ from product to product. If the product is labour, subject to a minimum wage, excess supply translates into people without jobs. If the product is wheat, and more is produced than can be sold to consumers, the surplus wheat will accumulate in grain elevators or government warehouses. These consequences may or may not be worthwhile in

terms of the other goals achieved. Whether they are worthwhile or not, these consequences are inevitable whenever a price floor is set above the market-clearing equilibrium price.

Why might the government wish to incur these consequences? One reason is that the people who succeed in selling their products at the price floor are better off than if they had to accept the lower equilibrium price. Workers and farmers are among the politically active, organized groups who have gained much by persuading the government to establish price floors that enable them to sell their goods or services at prices above free-market levels. The losses are spread across the large and diverse set of purchasers, each of whom suffers only a small loss (although the *total* loss may be considerable).

PRICE CEILINGS

Governments sometimes establish a *price ceiling,* which is the maximum price at which certain goods and services may be exchanged. Price controls on oil, natural gas, and rental housing have been frequently imposed by federal and provincial governments.

Although sometimes referred to as *fixed* or *frozen* prices, these price controls actually specify a maximum price that producers may legally charge, and are thus price ceilings. If the price ceiling is set above the equilibrium price, it has no effect because the equilibrium remains attainable. If, however, the price ceiling is set below the equilibrium price, the price ceiling lowers the price and is said to be *binding* or *effective*. The effects of price ceilings are shown in Figure 6-3, which establishes the following conclusion:

Effective price ceilings lead to excess demand, with the quantity exchanged being less than its equilibrium amount.

Allocating a Product in Excess Demand

The free market eliminates excess demand by allowing prices to rise, thereby allocating the available supply among would-be purchasers. Because this cannot happen with price ceilings, some other method of allocation must be adopted. Experience suggests what we can expect.

If stores sell their available supplies on a *first-come, first-served* basis, then people will rush to

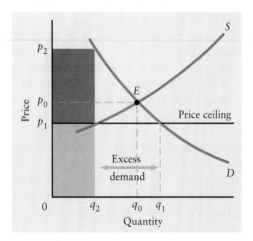

FIGURE 6-3
A Price Ceiling and Black-Market Pricing

An effective price ceiling causes excess demand and invites a black market. Equilibrium price is at p_0. If a price ceiling is set at p_1, the quantity demanded will rise to q_1 and the quantity supplied will fall to q_2. Quantity actually exchanged will be q_2. Price is not legally permitted to restore equilibrium. If all the available supply of q_2 were sold on a black market, the price to consumers would rise to p_2, with black marketeers earning receipts shown by the two shaded areas. Because they buy at the ceiling price of p_1 and sell at the black-market price of p_2, their profits are represented by the dark shaded area.

stores that are said to have stocks of the product. In some developing countries (and until recently, under communist regimes in many Eastern European countries), prices of essentials are subject to effective price ceilings, and even the rumour that a shop is selling supplies of a scarce product can cause a local stampede. Buyers may wait hours to get into the store, only to find that supplies are exhausted before they can be served. This is why standing in lines has been a way of life in command economies.

In market economies, "first-come, first-served" is often the basis for allocating tickets to concerts and sporting events when promoters set a price at which demand exceeds the supply of available seats. In these cases, a secondary market often develops, in which ticket scalpers resell tickets at market-clearing prices. Storekeepers (and some ticket sellers) often respond to excess demand by keeping goods "under the counter" and selling only to customers of their own choosing. For example, in 1979, when the U.S.

government imposed price controls and rationing of gasoline, many gas station operators sold only to regular customers. When sellers decide to whom they will and will not sell their scarce supplies, allocation is said to be by **sellers' preferences.**

If the government dislikes these allocation systems, it can choose to ration the product. To do so, it prints only enough ration coupons to match the available supply and then distributes the coupons to would-be purchasers, who then need both money and coupons to buy the product. The coupons may be distributed equally among the population or on the basis of some criterion such as age, family status, or occupation. Rationing of this sort was used by Canada and many other countries during both the First and Second World Wars.

Black Markets

Price ceilings usually give rise to black markets. A *black market* is any market in which goods are sold illegally at prices that violate a legal price control.

Many manufactured products are produced by only a few firms but are sold by many retailers. Thus although it may be easy to police the few producers, it is often impossible to enforce the price at which the many retailers sell to the general public. If the government is able to control the price received by producers but not by retailers, production remains at a level consistent with the price ceiling because the producers receive only the controlled price. At the retail level, however, the opportunity for a black market arises because consumers are willing to pay more than the price ceiling for the limited amounts of the product that are available.

Effective price ceilings create the potential for a black market because a profit can be made by buying at the controlled price and selling at the black-market price.

Figure 6-3 illustrates the extreme case in which all the available supply is sold on a black market.[1]

Does the existence of a black market mean that the goals sought by imposing price ceilings have been

---

[1]This case is extreme because there are law-abiding people in every society and because governments ordinarily have considerable power to enforce their price ceilings. Although some of a product subject to an effective price ceiling will be sold on the black market, it is unlikely that all of that product will be.

thwarted? The answer depends on what the goals are. A government might have three main goals.

1. To restrict production (perhaps to release resources for war production)

2. To keep prices down

3. To satisfy notions of equity in the consumption of a product that is temporarily in short supply

When price ceilings are accompanied by a black market, only the first objective is achieved. Black markets frustrate the second objective. Effective price ceilings on manufacturers plus an extensive black market at the retail level may produce the opposite of the third goal. There will be less to go around than if there were no controls, and the available quantities will tend to go to the people with the most money or the least social conscience.

RENT CONTROLS: A CASE STUDY OF PRICE CEILINGS

For long periods over this century, rent controls have existed in London, Paris, New York, and many other large cities. In Sweden and Britain, where rent controls on unfurnished apartments existed for decades, shortages of rental accommodations were chronic. When British controls were extended to furnished apartments in 1973, the supply of such accommodations dried up, at least until loopholes were found in the law. When rent controls were initiated in Ontario in 1975 and Rome in 1978, severe housing shortages developed, especially in those areas where demand was rising.

Rent controls are perhaps the most extensively studied form of price ceilings and provide a vivid illustration of the short- and long-term effects of this type of market intervention. Note, however, that the specifics of rent-control laws vary greatly and have changed significantly since they were first imposed many decades ago. In particular, current laws often permit exemptions for new buildings and allowances for maintenance costs and inflation. Moreover, in many countries rent controls have evolved into a "second generation" where they focus more on *regulating* the rental housing market rather than simply *controlling the price* of rental accomodation.

In this section, we confine ourselves to an analysis of rent controls which are aimed primarily at holding the price of rental housing below the free-market equilibrium value. It is this "first generation" of rent controls which produced serious results in cities like London, Paris, New York and, at times, Toronto.

THE PREDICTED EFFECTS OF RENT CONTROLS

Binding rent controls are a specific case of price ceilings and therefore Figure 6-3 can be used to predict some of their effects:

1. There will be a housing shortage in the sense that quantity demanded will exceed quantity supplied. Since rents are held below their free-market levels, the available quantity of rental housing will be less than if free-market rents had been charged.

2. The shortage will lead to alternative allocation schemes. Landlords may allocate by sellers' preferences, or the government may intervene, often through security-of-tenure laws, which protect tenants from eviction and thereby give them priority over prospective new tenants.

3. Black markets will appear. For example, landlords may require large "entrance fees" from new tenants, which reflect the difference in value between the free-market and the controlled rents. In the absence of security-of-tenure laws, landlords may force tenants out when their leases expire in order to extract a large entrance fee from new tenants.

The unique feature of rent control, however, as compared to price controls in general, is that they are applied to a highly *durable good* that provides services to consumers for a long period of time. Once built, an apartment can be used for decades. As a result, the immediate effects of rent control are typically quite different from the long-term effects.

The short-run supply response to the imposition of rent controls is quite limited. Some conversions of apartment units to condominiums and cooperatives may occur but the quantity of apartments does not change much. This implies that the short-run supply curve is quite *inelastic*.

In the long run, however, the supply response to rent controls can be quite dramatic. If the expected

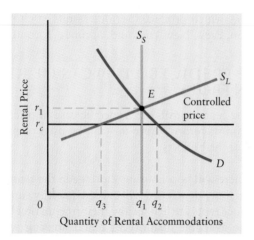

FIGURE 6-4
The Effects of Rent Control in the Short Run and the Long Run

Rent control causes housing shortages that worsen as time passes. The controlled rent of r_c forces rents below their free-market equilibrium value of r_1. The short-run supply of housing is shown by the perfectly inelastic curve S_S. Thus quantity supplied remains at q_1 in the short run, and the housing shortage is q_1q_2. Over time, the quantity supplied shrinks, as shown by the long-run supply curve S_L. In the long run, there are only q_3 units of rental accommodations, fewer than when controls were instituted. The housing shortage of q_3q_2, which occurs after supply has fully adjusted, is larger than the initial shortage of q_1q_2.

return from investing in new rental housing falls significantly below what can be earned on comparable investments, funds will go elsewhere. New construction will be halted, and old buildings will be converted to other uses, or will simply be left to deteriorate. This implies that the long-run supply curve of rental accommodations (which refers to the quantity supplied after all adjustments have been made) is highly *elastic*.

Figure 6-4 illustrates the housing shortage that worsens as time passes under rent control. Because the short-run supply of housing is inelastic, the controlled rent causes only a moderate housing shortage in the short run. Indeed, most of the shortage comes from an increase in the quantity demanded rather than from a reduction in quantity supplied. As time passes, however, fewer new apartments are built, more conversions take place, and older buildings are not replaced as they wear out. As a result, the quantity supplied shrinks steadily. At the same time there

will be an incentive for landlords to allow the existing stock of rental housing to deteriorate. Since investment in maintenance may not be profitable, general maintenance and repair are no longer worthwhile.

Along with the growing housing shortage comes an increasingly inefficient use of rental accommodation space. Existing tenants will have an incentive to stay where they are even though their family size, location of employment, or economic circumstances may change. Since they cannot move without giving up their low-rent accommodation, some may take lower-paying jobs or even become unemployed to avoid the necessity for moving. Thus a situation will arise in which existing tenants will hang on to accommodation even if it is poorly suited to their needs while new individuals and families will be unable to find any rental accommodation except at black-market prices.

The province of Ontario instituted rent controls in 1975 and tightened them on at least two subsequent occasions. The controls permitted significant increases in rents only where these were needed to pass on cost increases. As a result, the restrictive effects of rent controls were felt mainly in areas where demand was increasing rapidly (as opposed to areas where only costs were increasing rapidly). In areas that were not growing, however, and in most areas during the severe recession of the early 1990s including Toronto, the demand for housing was not rising. As a result, many of the controls did not bind because the free-market rents were at or below the controlled ceilings on rents. Application 6-1 discusses the experience with rent controls in Toronto in the 1980s.

TEMPORARY VERSUS PERMANENT INCREASES IN DEMAND

We have seen that the effects of binding rent controls are more serious in the long run than in the short run. This suggests that a policy of rent controls *imposed only for a short time* may have few costs (and may actually be beneficial). Here we consider the distinction between temporary and permanent increases in housing demand, and the effects of rent controls in each case.

When Rent Controls May Work: Short-Term Shortages

Pressure for rent controls is strongest when prices are rising most rapidly. The case for stemming the rapid

RENT CONTROLS IN TORONTO IN THE 1980S

Throughout the 1980s, Toronto was expanding rapidly. As a result, the demand for rental accommodations grew while the Ontario government's rent controls held rents down. The housing shortage at the controlled rents grew, as did the difference between the controlled rents and the rents that would have existed on the free market. This difference created a valuable asset to those tenants lucky enough to live in a rent-controlled apartment. For example, if you only have to pay $400 per month for an apartment that would rent on the free market for $700 per month, you have $300 of value per month that you do not pay for.

Naturally, people scrambled to appropriate such values. *Key money*—the price charged by landlords to gain access to a rent-controlled flat—became prevalent, and the press reported payments running into many thousands of dollars. (Such lump-sum payments are most burdensome on the low-income people that the rent-control policy is supposed to be aiding.) Subletting became common: A tenant pays the landlord the controlled rent and then sublets to someone else at the free-market rent. This is the worst of both worlds: The supplier gets the controlled price and hence supplies only a small quantity, while the occupier pays the market price, which, because of the control-induced shortage, is higher than the uncontrolled free-market price would have been. The gain goes to the tenant who is subletting. It serves no allocative purpose since that person is responsible neither

for maintaining the existing building nor for erecting new ones.

Another way of side-stepping the controlled rents—and to take advantage of the excess demand for housing—was for landlords to convert their rental apartments into condominiums which they then sold. Because the condominiums were put up for *sale*, rather than for *rent*, they were not subject to rent controls. This occurred on a significant scale until the provincial government passed legislation which effectively removed the owners' right to use their own property as they saw fit.

The Toronto housing shortage led to frantic searches for available space. A feature article in the *Toronto Star* told of searches involving bribing caretakers, hunting through obituary columns, and finding elderly tenants in the hope of being first on the scene when death made a flat available. Younger people, particularly those in less skilled jobs, told of landlord preferences for middle-aged, middle-class tenants holding white-collar jobs and earning higher incomes—a predictable allocation by sellers' preferences that tended to discriminate against some of the very groups the policy was supposed to help.

The experience of Toronto in the 1980s is no surprise to anyone who has studied the effects of rent controls elsewhere in the world. They are the all-too-predictable consequences of the system. City and provincial politicians and many other rent control advocates, however, expressed surprise at these events—being understandably unwilling to accept the responsibility for the situation.

---

rise of rents is strongest when the shortages causing the increasing rents are temporary. For example, construction of a pipeline gave rise to an enormous increase in demand for rental accommodations in Anchorage, Alaska, but it was anticipated that few of the influx of workers would remain behind once the job was done. When a temporary population floods in, market rents will rise. New construction of

apartments will not occur, however, because investors recognize that the rise in demand for rental accomodation is only temporary. In such a situation, rent controls may stop existing owners from making large profits and may result in few harmful supply effects because a long-run supply response is not expected in any case. After the boom is over, demand will fall, and free-market equilibrium rents will fall.

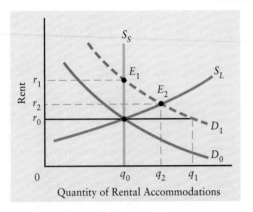

FIGURE 6-5
Rent Controls in Response to Increasing Demand

Quantity of Rental Accommodations

Rent controls prevent a temporary skyrocketing of rents when demand rises but also prevent the long-term supply adjustment where it is required.

Temporary demand fluctuations. The short-run supply curve S_S applies. In the free market, a temporary shift in demand from D_0 to D_1 and then back to D_0 will change rents from r_0 to r_1 and back to r_0. Rent control would hold rents at r_0 throughout. There would be a housing shortage of q_0q_1 because of excess demand, as long as demand was D_1, but rent control would not affect the quantity of housing supplied.

Permanent changes in demand. The long-run supply curve S_L applies. A permanent rise in demand from D_0 to D_1 will cause free-market rents to rise temporarily from r_0 to r_1 and then to fall to r_2 as the quantity of accommodations supplied grows from q_0 to q_2. Controlling the rent at r_0 then produces a *permanent* housing shortage of q_0q_1.

Rent controls may then be removed with little further effect. This is illustrated in Figure 6-5.

Although the rent controls have no long-run adverse effect under these circumstances, they will still have some disadvantages. At controlled rents, there will be a severe housing shortage but no *price incentive* for existing tenants to economize on housing or for potential suppliers to find ways to convert existing space into short-run accommodations, as would occur if rents were allowed to rise. Even though the supply of permanent apartments does not change, the supply of temporary accommodations can increase (mobile homes, and the subletting of bedrooms, for example). Such reactions are encouraged by the signal of rising rents but are inhibited by rent controls.

When Rent Controls Fail: Long-Term Shortages

Consider what happens when there is a long-term increase in the demand for rental accommodations. This has occurred most recently in Vancouver, and other cities of the lower mainland of British Columbia, where a rapidly increasing population has created local housing shortages and has forced rents to increase. Such increases in rents give the signal that apartments are highly profitable investments. A consequent building boom will lead to increases in the quantity supplied, and it will continue as long as high profits can be earned on rental housing.

If rent controls are imposed in the face of such long-term increases in demand, they will prevent landlords from earning high profits, but they will also prevent the needed long-run construction boom from occurring. Thus binding controls will convert a temporary shortage into a permanent one. This is also shown in Figure 6-5.

WHO GAINS AND WHO LOSES?

Existing tenants in rent-controlled accommodations are the principal gainers from a policy of rent control. As the gap between the controlled and the equilibrium rents grows, those who are lucky enough to be tenants gain more and more.

Landlords suffer because they do not get the return that they had expected on their investments. Some landlords are large companies, and others are wealthy individuals. Neither one of these groups attracts great public sympathy, even though the rental companies' stockholders are not all rich. Some landlords are people of modest means who have put their retirement savings into a small apartment or a house or two. They find that the value of their savings is diminished, and sometimes they find themselves in the ironic position of subsidizing tenants who are far better off than they are.

The other important group of people who suffer from rent controls are *potential future* tenants. The housing shortage hurts them because the rental housing they will require will not be there in the future. These people, who wind up living elsewhere, farther from their places of employment and study, are invisible in debates over rent control because they cannot obtain housing in the rent-controlled jurisdiction. Because of this, rent control is often stable politically even when it causes a long-run housing shortage. The current tenants benefit, and the potential tenants, who are harmed, are nowhere to be seen or heard.

POLICY ALTERNATIVES

Most rent controls today are meant to protect lower-income tenants, not only against "profiteering" by landlords in the face of severe local shortages but also against the steadily rising cost of housing. The market solution is to let rents rise sufficiently to cover the rising costs. If people decide that they cannot afford the market price of apartments and will not rent them, construction will cease. Given what we know about consumer behaviour, however, it is more likely that people will make agonizing choices, both to economize on housing and to spend a higher proportion of total income on it, which means consuming less housing and less of other things as well.

If governments do not wish to accept this market solution, there are many things they can do, but they cannot avoid the fundamental fact that the opportunity cost of good housing is high. Rent controls, as we have seen, create housing shortages. The shortages can be removed only if the government, at taxpayer expense, either subsidizes housing production or produces public housing directly.

Alternatively, the government can make housing more affordable to lower-income households by providing income-assistance to these households, allowing them access to higher-quality housing than they could otherwise afford. Whatever policy is adopted, it is important to recognize that providing rental accommodations has a resource cost. The costs of providing additional housing cannot be voted out of existence; all that can be done is to transfer the costs from one set of persons to another.

The final section of this chapter provides four general lessons concerning resource allocation and government attempts to control prices—lessons that apply to all parts of the economy, including the housing market, which we have just studied, and the agricultural sector, which we discuss next.

AGRICULTURE AND THE FARM PROBLEM

For over 80 years, policymakers in many western countries, including Canada, have been challenged and frustrated by what is often called the "farm problem." There are actually two separate farm problems, and supply-and-demand analysis can help to make it clear why they are so difficult to deal with.

LONG-TERM AND SHORT-TERM PROBLEMS

The first problem is that there is a long-run tendency for farm incomes to fall below urban incomes. The second problem is that agricultural prices fluctuate substantially from year to year, causing a great deal of variability in farm incomes. The farm policies implemented by most western countries are nominally directed at *stabilizing* farm incomes. However, the underlying trend of declining farm incomes also puts pressure on governments to implement polices which *raise* farm incomes.

Long-Term Trends

Agriculture's long-term problems arise from both the demand and the supply sides of agricultural markets.

Increasing Domestic Supply. Since 1900, the output per worker in Canadian agriculture has increased tenfold, roughly twice as fast as manufacturing productivity has increased. In 1900, one farm worker could produce enough food to feed about $2^1/_2$ people. By the year 2000, the figure will be approximately 65 people! Such growth of farm productivity means that the supply curves of farm products have been shifting rapidly to the right in Canada and most of the rest of the world.

Lagging Domestic Demand. The overall growth of output throughout the entire Canadian economy has resulted in a rising trend for the real income of the average Canadian family during the last 150 years. However, at the levels of income existing in Canada and in other advanced industrial nations, most foodstuffs have low income elasticities of demand because most people are already well fed. Thus increases in incomes are often spent mostly on consumer durables, entertainment, and travel. Thus as Canadian incomes grow, the Canadian demand for agricultural goods also grows, but less rapidly.

Export Demand. The contribution of export markets to demand for domestic production has been variable over recent decades. Explosive growth of world population in the past half century has provided an expanding demand for foodstuffs, which, over much of the period, translated into a growing export market for North American produce. This tended to alleviate somewhat the domestic pressures just discussed. Throughout the 1970s, however, many less developed countries succeeded in dramatically increasing their own food production.

Furthermore, large European agricultural subsidies turned the countries of western Europe into exporters of agricultural products rather than importers. By the beginning of the 1980s, therefore, international developments tended to exacerbate the domestic problem of agricultural surpluses instead of alleviating it.

For example, the world price of wheat fell from its peak of $6 per bushel in 1981 to about $2 in 1993. In real terms, this is the lowest price of wheat in Canadian history, including the prices at the depth of the Great Depression of the 1930s.

Excess Supply.   Both the demand and the supply curves in typical agricultural markets have been shifting to the right over the whole of this century, with the demand curve shifting more slowly than the supply curve. As a result, there is a continuing tendency for an excess supply of agricultural produce to develop at existing market prices. This naturally tends to depress world prices

for agricultural products. And since most agricultural products tend to have price elasticities of demand that are significantly less than one, it follows that the fall in the price tends to depress agricultural incomes.

Resource   Reallocation.   Depressed prices, wages, and farm incomes signal the need for resources to move out of agriculture and into other sectors. However necessary they may be, adjustments of this kind prove to be painful to those who live and work on farms, especially when resources move slowly in response to depressed incomes. It is one thing for farmers' sons and daughters to move to the city; it is quite another for existing farmers and their parents to be displaced.

The magnitude of the required supply response has been enormous. In 1900, over 45 percent of the Canadian labour force worked in agriculture; by 1930 it was down to 29 percent, and by 1995 it had fallen to approximately 3 percent.

FIGURE 6-6
The Effect on Price of Unplanned Variations in Output

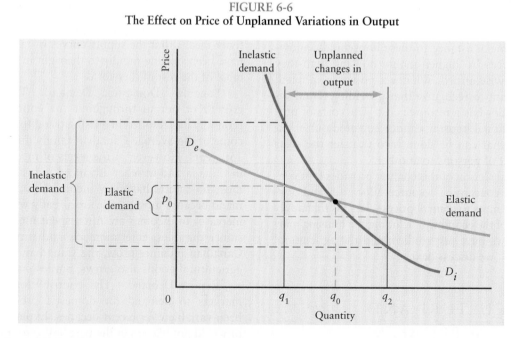

An unplanned fluctuation in output of a given size leads to a much sharper fluctuation in price when demand is inelastic than when it is elastic. Suppose that the expected price is p_0 and the planned output is q_0. The two curves D_i and D_e are *alternative* demand curves. If actual production always equaled planned production, the equilibrium price and quantity would be p_0 and q_0 with either demand curve. Unplanned variation in output, however, causes quantity to fluctuate year by year between q_1 (a bad harvest) and q_2 (a good harvest). When demand is inelastic (shown by the green curve), prices will show large fluctuations. When demand is elastic (shown by the light blue curve), price flucuations will be much smaller.

Short-Term Fluctuations

The second part of the farm problem is the short-term price volatility which is typical of many agricultural markets. It occurs mainly because of factors beyond farmers' control. For example, pests, floods, and drought can reduce farm output drastically, whereas exceptionally favourable weather can cause production to exceed expectations. By now you should not be surprised to hear that such unplanned fluctuations in supply cause fluctuations in farm prices and in farm incomes.

Fluctuating Supply with Inelastic Demand. The basic situation is shown in Figure 6-6. Variations in farm output cause price fluctuations in the direction opposite to crop size. A bumper crop sends prices down; a small crop sends them up. The less elastic the demand curve, the bigger the fluctuations in price arising from given variations in output.

What are the effects on farmers' revenues? In typical cases where demand is inelastic, increases in supply cause *decreases* in farmers' revenues.

Because demands for farm products are typically inelastic, unplanned fluctuations in production tend to cause relatively large fluctuations in price. Therefore, good harvests bring reductions in total farm receipts, and bad harvests bring increases in total farm receipts.

Thus the inelasticity of demand for most farm products explains the apparently paradoxical experience that when nature is bountiful and produces a bumper crop, farmers' receipts dwindle, whereas when nature is moderately unkind and output falls unexpectedly, farmers' receipts rise. The interests of the farmer and the consumer are exactly opposed in such cases.

Fluctuating Demand with Inelastic Supply. As the tide of business activity ebbs and flows, demand curves for all products fluctuate. The magnitude of the effects on prices and outputs depends on the elasticity of *supply*.

Agricultural products typically have rather inelastic supply curves because land, labour, and machinery devoted to agricultural uses are neither quickly transferred to nonagricultural uses when demand falls nor quickly returned to agriculture when demand rises.

Given an inelastic supply curve for most agricultural products, farm prices and farm income will be sensitive to demand shifts.

This is illustrated in Figure 6-7. As shown, a reduction in demand will cause hardship among people whose incomes depend on farm crops.

THE THEORY OF AGRICULTURAL POLICY

Governments throughout the world intervene in agricultural markets in attempts both to *stabilize* agricultural incomes and to *raise* average farm incomes. We deal with three cases that are relevant to much of Canadian agriculture. The first two cases deal purely with the stabilization of farm income—first, the production of commodities mainly for export and, second, the production of commodities mainly for domestic consumption. The third case deals with price supports above the free-market equilibrium price. In what follows, we assume that all supply curves refer to planned production per year but that actual production fluctuates around that level for reasons beyond the control of farmers.

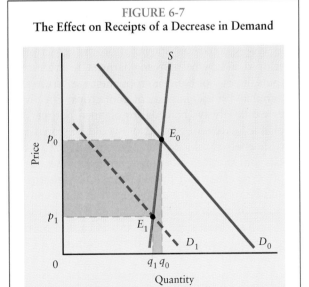

FIGURE 6-7
The Effect on Receipts of a Decrease in Demand

Inelastic supply can lead to sharp decreases in prices in response to decreases in demand. When demand decreases from D_0 to D_1, price and quantity decrease to p_1 and q_1, and total receipts decline by the shaded area. The fall in total receipts is mainly due to the sharp decrease in price. Output and employment remain high, but the drastic fall in price will reduce profits. This is typical in the agricultural sector.

Exports at World Market Prices

When Canadian production is sold on world markets, the prices are largely independent of the amount sold by Canadian producers because they contribute only a small proportion of total world supply. Thus domestic producers face a perfectly elastic demand curve, indicating that they can sell all that they wish at the given world price. A government stabilization policy then faces two key problems: first, how to cope with short-term supply fluctuations at home and second, how to react to fluctuations in world prices.

Output Fluctuations at Given World Prices. Figure 6-8 illustrates sales at a given world price when domestic output fluctuates. In years of bumper crops, sales will rise and so incomes will rise. In years of poor crops, sales will fall and so incomes will fall. In neither case do the fluctuations in domestic output affect the world price.

When domestic farmers sell at a given world price that is unaffected by their own volume of sales, their incomes fluctuate in the same direction as their short-term fluctuations in output.

The incomes of farmers who produce nonperishable crops could be stabilized if the government developed a scheme allowing farmers to store their outputs in years of bumper crops and to sell from their accumulated stocks in years of poor crops. Effectively, sales would always be equal to planned output. Any unplanned excess of production would be stored, and any shortfall would be made up out of sales from stocks. But storage costs money and postpones the receipt of revenue until the sales occur. An alternative would be to sell all the crop each year and then save the extra money received in good years to spend in bad years. This is something that farmers can do on their own without assistance from the government.

Fluctuations in World Prices. When world prices fluctuate, it may pay to hold stocks. When the government judges that this year's price is unusually low, it can store some of the output in the hope of selling it later at a better price. When the government judges that this year's price is unusually high, it can sell some of the stocks that it put aside in years when the price was low.

In a world in which future prices were known with certainty, the government would merely calculate the extra revenue that could be obtained by selling at some future price higher than the present one and subtract the costs of storage to see if the crop

should be sold now or held. In practice, the future is not known, and the government must use its knowledge of market conditions to guess its best policy. The government will be inclined to store a larger amount this year the more it expects prices to rise in future years and to sell more from stocks if it expects prices to fall in future years. If the government is good at predicting the future state of the market, it will increase farmers' revenues by selling less when prices are low and more when prices are high, as compared with a policy of selling the whole crop each year. If the government's market predictions are wrong, however, the scheme can bring losses.

Sales on the Domestic Market Only

Quite a few Canadian agricultural goods are sold mainly on the domestic market. The difference between this case and the one just considered is that the demand curve facing domestic producers is now negatively sloped and typically inelastic. The analysis of Figure 6-6 now applies, so farm income will fluctuate in the direction opposite to output. Can farm income be stabilized in this case?

Price Stabilization. Suppose that the government enters the market, buying and thereby adding to its own stocks when there is a surplus, and selling and thereby reducing its stocks when there is a shortage. If it had enough grain elevators and warehouses, and if its support price were set at a realistic level, the government could stabilize *prices* indefinitely. But this would not stabilize farmers' revenues, which would be high with bumper crops and low with poor crops.

In effect, the government policy imposes a demand curve that is perfectly elastic at the support price. The situation is then analogous to the one analysed in Figure 6-8: The product can be sold at a given price, and income fluctuates in the same direction as output.

A policy which stabilizes prices received by farmers will not stabilize farm revenues. Such a policy would, however, reverse the pattern of revenue fluctuation.

Revenue Stabilization. When the government does not intervene at all in domestic agricultural markets, farm income fluctuates in the *opposite* direction as farm output. If the government intervenes to stabilize price, then farm income fluctuates in the *same* direction as farm output. This suggests that there must exist *some* government buying-and-selling policy that is able to stabilize farmers' incomes. What are the characteristics of such a policy? As has

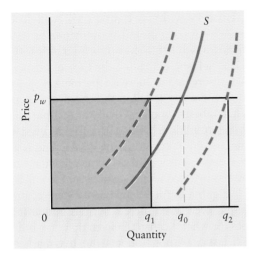

FIGURE 6-8
Exports at a Given World Price

A country that exports only a small portion of the world's supply of some product faces a perfectly elastic demand because the world price is not affected by its own sales. The given world price is p_w. The domestic supply curve shows that intended output is q_0 at that price. Unintended fluctuations cause output between q_1 and q_2. When output is q_1 (a partial crop failure), farm income is given by the dark shaded area. When output is q_2 (a bumper crop), farm income is given by the total of the bordered areas.

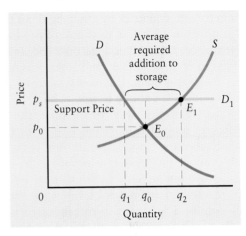

FIGURE 6-9
Price Supports Above the Equilibrium Price

The price support becomes a price floor, and the government must purchase the excess supply at that price. Average annual demand and supply are D and S, respectively. The free-market equilibrium is at E_0. If the government will buy any quantity at p_s, the demand curve becomes the light blue curve D_1 and equilibrium changes to E_1. The *average* addition to storage is the quantity q_1q_2. The government's purchases, financed by the taxpayer, add to farmers' incomes.

been seen, too much price stability causes receipts to vary directly with production, and too little price stability causes receipts to vary inversely with production. Thus it appears that the government should aim at some intermediate degree of price stability. If the government allows prices to vary in inverse proportion to variations in production, receipts will be stabilized. A 10 percent rise in production should be met by a 10 percent fall in price, and a 10 percent fall in production by a 10 percent rise in price.

To stabilize farmers' receipts, the government must make the effective demand curve unit elastic. It must buy in periods of high output and sell in periods of low output, but only enough to let prices change in inverse proportion to farmers' output.

Prices Above Equilibrium

Actual stabilization plans, whether they seek to fix prices completely or merely to dampen free-market fluctuations, often seek to maintain an average price above the average free-market equilibrium level. This is because stabilization is not the only goal; governments aim to *raise* farm incomes as well as stabilize them.

The government buys in periods of high output and sells in periods of low output, but as shown in Figure 6-9, it buys much more on average than it sells, with the result that unsold surpluses accumulate. Taxpayers will generally be paying farmers for producing goods that no one is willing to purchase, at least at prices that come near to covering costs.

Subsidies.   This is the route taken by the countries in the European Union (EU) with its Common Agricultural Policy (CAP). This policy has supported the existing farm population of Europe by guaranteeing both stable and high prices. It has also meant that Western Europe has changed from being a net importer of agricultural products—which it had been for over a century and would still be under free markets—into a net exporter. As a result of the CAP, the EU is now faced with mounting stockpiles of many agricultural products.[2] Periodically, it seeks to sell

---

[2]Some attempts are made to restrict supply, but these are insufficient to prevent an excess of quantity supplied over quantity demanded at the support price.

some of the surpluses to outside countries, charging prices well below the costs of production. The net result is that taxpayers in the EU are subsidizing consumers in foreign countries by allowing them to buy goods at prices much below their cost of production. Payments under the CAP now account for well over half of the EU's entire budget, and concern is mounting that the ever-growing payments to farmers may soon outrun the EU's ability to pay.

Quotas.   Another way of holding the price above its free-market equilibrium level is to reduce the supply through quotas. Under this system, no one can produce the product without having a government-issued quota. Sufficient quotas are issued to hold production at any desired level below the free-market output. This drives prices above their free-market level. This quota system, which is analysed in Figure 6-10, has the advantage of not causing the accumulation of massive unsold surpluses. It is widely used in Canada.

The quota system, which is called *supply management* in Canada, affects both the short-term and the long-term behaviour of agricultural markets. Consider short-term fluctuations first. There will still be good crops and poor crops and other natural disturbances, such as outbreaks of crop disease, that will cause short-term fluctuations in output. A shortfall of output below the quota will drive price upward. Farmers with no crop to sell will lose, but farmers whose outputs fall proportionally less than the price rise will gain. Since most agricultural products have inelastic demands, the typical farmer must gain—the percentage increase in market price will exceed the percentage fall in the aggregate crop.

What about unplanned extra output due to favourable conditions? The farmer is allowed to sell only the amount covered by the quota. The rest must be either destroyed or sold on some secondary market not covered by the quota system. Farm income is stabilized. The quota output is sold at the market price for that output even when there is surplus output (and the rest goes for what it can get). Given that demand is typically inelastic, without quotas the free-market price would fall by a larger percentage than output would rise, and producers' incomes would shrink drastically.

A quota system guarantees that farmers will get the free-market price of the total quota output when output equals or exceeds the quota and more when output falls short of the quota and demand is inelastic.

Thus, the quota system is superior to the subsidy system in that it really does remove the down-side risks caused by unexpected increases in output, and unlike the CAP, it does not lead to accumulating stockpiles of unsold output. The main cost is met by consumers, who on average pay a price that is higher, and consume an output that is lower, than would occur under free-market conditions.

Now consider the long term. We have seen that the quota drives price above its free-market level by restricting output. For purposes of illustration, let us suppose that the quota is for eggs. Those who are producing eggs when the quota system is first instituted must gain. Since production falls, total costs must fall; since demand is inelastic, total revenue must rise. Therefore, egg producers find their profits rising, since they spend less to earn more revenue. No wonder quotas are popular among the original producers!

But do quotas really increase farm income in the long run? Because people leave the industry for such reasons as death and retirement and new people must enter to replace them, existing holders are allowed to transfer their quotas to new would-be egg producers. But the quota is valuable, since it confers the right to produce eggs that earn a large profit as a

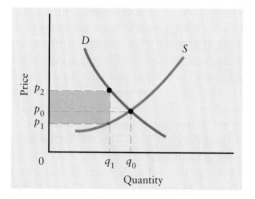

FIGURE 6-10
Price Support Through the Use of Quotas

The quota below the free-market equilibrium quantity maintains the price above the free-market equilibrium level without generating surpluses. If the total quota of q_1 is enforced, the price will rise to p_2. Since the supply curve indicates that in a free market producers would be willing to sell the quantity q_1 at the price p_1, the effect of the quota is to increase the revenues (by the shaded area) to those producers who hold quota.

result of the supply restriction. Therefore, the quota commands a price which naturally reflects the current value of the extra future profits that ownership of the quota allows.

The free-market price of a quota to produce any good will be such that the profitability of that good's production will, after deducting the cost of the quota, be no more than the profitability of other lines of activity carrying similar risks.

In other words, the whole extra profitability created by the quota system becomes embodied in the price of the quota. The extra profits created by the quota will just provide an acceptable return on the money invested in buying the quota—if it provided more, the price of the quota would be bid up; if it provided less, the price of the quota would fall.

For this reason, *new entrants* to the industry will earn no more than the return available in other lines of production. Since that would also be the case under market-determined prices and outputs, the quota does not raise the profitability of producing eggs. What it does do is reduce some of the uncertainty due to unexpected short-term fluctuations of output. Farming becomes a somewhat less risky operation than before.

AGRICULTURAL POLICY IN CANADA

The main tools of agricultural stabilization in Canada are marketing boards and income supplement programs. Sales through marketing boards account for about half of all farm cash receipts.

Marketing Boards

There are essentially two types of government marketing boards. The first seeks to influence prices by controlling supply. The second takes prices as given and acts as a selling agency for producers.

Supply Management. The supply-management schemes typically are provincially administered systems that restrict output of commodities sold in the Canadian market through quotas issued by provincial marketing boards. They vary from province to province but often cover milk, eggs, cheese, butter, and poultry. The farm profits created by these schemes are enormous and are reflected by the high prices farmers must pay to purchase quotas.

Schemes of this type, analyzed in Figure 6-10, are successful in reducing short-term fluctuations.

However, they also greatly increase the cost of becoming a producer, because a quota must be purchased in addition to the physical capital needed for production. The schemes are popular among farmers because they reduce risk in the short term and because the value of the quotas often rises over the long term. The gains to farmers and food importers are paid for by consumers in the form of higher prices.

Recently, two other important effects of supply management systems have become apparent. First, they harm Canadian manufacturers of food products. Canadian firms producing frozen and canned foods must pay high prices for Canadian produce, whereas their foreign competitors can buy their raw foodstuffs at the lower world prices. Second, they reduce competition among users of agricultural products. For example, to allocate scarce supplies of milk, the Fraser Valley Milk Marketing Board channels supplies to selected users of raw milk. These milk processors have no incentive to compete for market share or to introduce new products, because a successful competitor could not get the larger supplies of raw milk needed to increase sales.

The high domestic prices caused by supply management would normally lead to a flood of imports. To prevent this, the federal government used to impose fixed and small quotas on imports of goods subject to supply management. Under the Uruguay Round of the General Agreement on Tariffs and Trade (the GATT), Canada agreed to replace these quotas in 1994–1995 with tariffs which had an equivalent effect. In some cases the tariff rates exceeded 300 percent! The slow speed at which these tariff rates are to be reduced under the GATT will allow supply management to persist for many years. Consumers will have to wait for future tariff reductions before they get real relief from the high-price effects of Canadian marketing boards.

Orderly Marketing Schemes. The prime example of an orderly marketing scheme is the Canadian Wheat Board, which markets Canadian wheat at prices set on the world wheat market. Each year, the Wheat Board estimates the average price at which it expects the wheat crop to be sold. Seventy-five percent of that price is then paid to each farmer on delivery of the wheat. After the board sells the wheat, any proceeds in excess of the initial payments are distributed to the producers in proportion to the amount of wheat supplied by each.

The goal of the Wheat Board is not to influence world prices. Instead, by paying farmers 75 percent of the estimated average selling price over the year, the Board provides farmers with a secure cash flow early in the selling period. The Board also serves to secure farmers' incomes against intrayear fluctuations in wheat prices. It does this by pooling all of its receipts and paying them out to farmers according to the amount of wheat delivered by each farmer but irrespective of the date within the year of that delivery. So the farmer is relieved of worry about what the spot price of wheat may be on the day of delivery.

Income Supplements

The system of providing financial assistance to farmers was reorganized with the passage in 1991 of the Farm Income Protection Act (FIPA). The first programs to be established under this new legislation were the Net Income Stabilization Account (NISA) and the Gross Revenue Insurance Plan (GRIP). These two programs, combined with a system of crop insurance (and other companion programs) make up what might be called the "safety net programs" for Canadian farmers.

NISA is a voluntary program designed to help producers set aside money in good years to be used in bad years; producers' contributions of up to 2 percent of their net sales are matched by contributions from the federal and relevant provincial governments. Thus, although part of this program involves the individual producers saving their own financial resources, there is also a considerable portion of government money being used to supplement farmers' incomes.

GRIP offers producers protection from revenue loss due to output or price changes beyond their control. It provides producers with a guaranteed target revenue. Though GRIP is essentially just an insurance program, it also has an income support component. This comes from the fact that two-thirds of the insurance premiums are paid by the federal and relevant provincial governments.

All in all, the level of direct financial assistance to farmers is quite considerable, especially when seen relative to total farm income. In 1994 (an apporoximately typical year in the 1990s for Canadian farming), net cash income to Canadia farmers totalled $5.9 billion. In that same yeat, direct cash payments to farmers equalled $1.7 billion; thus direct financial assistance to farmers represented roughly 30 percent of their net cash income.

The Future of Agricultural Policy

Is there a better way to make farming an occupation in which people can invest and work without being disadvantaged relative to other citizens and without needing large payments of funds raised from the nation's taxpayers? Most economists believe that a more efficient system would assist farm workers to change occupations and farm producers to change products rather than subsidize them to stay where they are not needed and to produce products that cannot be marketed profitably. Such assistance would require significant outlays—as do the present schemes—but would allow the market to do the job of allocating resources to agriculture.

There is no doubt that a policy of allowing agricultural prices and outputs to be determined on free markets would avoid surplus production, but the human and political costs of this policy have been judged to be unacceptable. The challenge has been to respond to the real hardships of the farm population without intensifying the long-term problems. Canadian farm policy has not always succeeded in doing so; the economic analysis in the previous sections helps us to understand why.

THE DETERMINATION OF IMPORTS AND EXPORTS

In the previous chapter we examined the determination of price by demand and supply. So far in this chapter, however, we have examined situations in which the price of some commodity is determined by forces *other than* demand and supply—in particular, prices set by government as either a price floor or a price ceiling. We discovered that in such situations some mechanism other than price must be used to allocate scarce resources for the simple reason that prices are not permitted to adjust to excess demands or excess supplies. In the case of government-administered rent controls, which is a case of a price ceiling, we examined the problems associated with having the price held below the equilibrium price. In the case of agricultural subsidies or quotas, we examined the problems associated with having the price held above the equilibrium price.

We now examine a situation in which price *appears* to be determined by forces other than demand and supply. But a more accurate description of what follows is a situation where price is determined by forces other than *domestic* demand and supply. This is the situation where Canada produces some commodity where the price is determined by demand and supply *for the world as a whole* rather than by demand and supply *just in Canada*. We will see that the world price will play a key role in determining whether

Canada is an exporter or an importer of any particular product. Though international trade and trade policy are studied in detail in Chapters 35 and 36, we can use the basic tools of demand-and-supply analysis to provide some insights into a country's pattern of trade.

There are some products, such as coffee and bananas, that Canada does not produce (and will probably never produce). Any domestic consumption of these products must therefore be satisfied by imports from other countries. At the other extreme, there are some products, such as nickel or potash, where Canada is one of the world's major suppliers, and thus demand in the rest of the world must be satisfied partly by exports from Canada. There are also some products, such as housing, that are so expensive to transport that every country produces approximately what it consumes.

Our interest here is in the many intermediate cases in which Canada is only one of many producers of an internationally traded product, as with beef, oil, automobiles, wheat, and lumber. Will Canada be an exporter or an importer of such products, or will it just produce exactly enough to satisfy its domestic demand?

THE LAW OF ONE PRICE

Whether Canada imports or exports a product for which it is only one of many producers depends to a great extent on the product's price. This brings us to the so-called *law of one price.*

The law of one price states that when a product which can be cheaply transported is traded throughout the entire world, it will tend to have a single worldwide price—the world price.

Many basic products, such as copper wire, steel pipe, iron ore, and computer RAM chips, fall within this category. The world price for each good is the price that equates the quantity demanded worldwide with the quantity supplied worldwide.

The world price of an internationally traded product may be influenced greatly, or only slightly, by the demand and supply coming from any one country. The extent of one country's influence will depend on how important its demands and supplies are in relation to the worldwide totals.

The simplest case for us to study arises when the country, which we will take to be Canada, accounts for only a small part of the total worldwide demand and supply. In this case, Canada does not itself produce enough to influence the world price significantly. Similarly, Canadian purchases are too small a proportion of worldwide demand to affect the world price in any significant way. Producers and consumers in Canada thus face a world price that they cannot influence by their own actions.

Notice that in this case, the price that rules in the Canadian market must be the world price (adjusted for the exchange rate between the Canadian dollar and the foreign currency). The law of one price says that this must be so. What would happen if the Canadian domestic price diverged from the world price? If the Canadian price were below the world price, no supplier would sell in the Canadian market because more money could be made by selling abroad. Thus from the perspective of Canadian consumers, this world price is a supply curve—consumers can buy whatever amount of the product they choose at that price, but they cannot buy anything at a lower price.

Conversely, if the Canadian domestic price were above the worldwide price, no buyers would buy from a Canadian seller because money could be saved by buying abroad. Thus from the perspective of Canadian producers, the world price is a demand curve—producers can sell all of their output on the world market at the world price, but they cannot sell at a higher price.

THE PATTERN OF FOREIGN TRADE

Now let us see what determines the pattern of Canadian-foreign trade in such circumstances.

An Exported Product

To determine the pattern of Canadian trade, we first show the Canadian domestic demand and supply curves for some product, say, lumber. The intersection of these two curves tells us what the price and quantity would be *if there were no foreign trade.* Now compare this no-trade price with the world price of that product.[3] If the world price is higher, the actual price in Canada will exceed the no-trade price, there will be an excess of Canadian supply over Canadian demand, and the surplus production will be exported for sale abroad.

Countries export products whose world price exceeds the price that would rule domestically if there were no foreign trade.

---

[3]If the world price is stated in terms of some foreign currency (as it often is), then the price must be converted into Canadian dollars using the current exchange rate between the foreign currency and Canadian dollars.

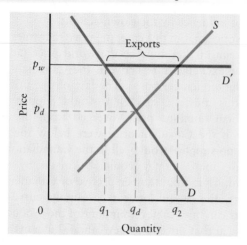

FIGURE 6-11
The Determination of Exports

Exports occur whenever there is excess supply domestically at the world price. The domestic demand and supply curves are D and S, respectively. The domestic price in the absence of foreign trade is p_d, with q_d produced and consumed domestically. The world price of p_w is higher than p_d. At p_w, q_1 is demanded while q_2 is supplied domestically. The excess of the domestic supply over the domestic demand is exported.

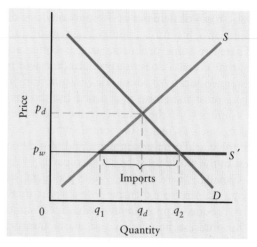

FIGURE 6-12
The Determination of Imports

Imports occur whenever there is excess demand domestically at the world price. The domestic demand and supply curves are D and S, respectively. The domestic price in the absence of foreign trade is p_d, with q_d produced and consumed domestically. The world price of p_w is less than p_d. At p_w, q_2 is demanded, whereas q_1 is supplied domestically. The excess of domestic demand over domestic supply is satisfied through imports.

This result is demonstrated in Figure 6-11.

An Imported Product

Now consider some other product—for example, oil. Once again, look first at the domestic demand and supply curves, shown this time in Figure 6-12. The intersection of these curves determines the no-trade price that would rule *if there were no foreign trade.* The world price of oil is below the Canadian no-trade price so that at the price ruling in Canada, domestic demand is larger and domestic supply is smaller than if the no-trade price had ruled. The excess of domestic demand over domestic supply is met by imports.

Countries import products whose world price is less than the price that would rule domestically if there were no foreign trade.

WHO PAYS FOR TARIFFS?

We have now developed the basic theory of how imports and exports are determined in competitive markets. In Chapters 35 and 36, this theory will be used to study a number of issues relating to Canadian trade and trade policy. Here we briefly examine an issue of recurrent interest in Canada, the use of tariffs to protect domestic industries from foreign competition.

An import tariff is simply a tax on imports, imposed at the border, when the product is imported. A tariff at rate t would raise the price of an imported product by the amount of the tariff, as shown in Figure 6-13, which is based on the analysis in Figure 6-12. Note that the tariff acts exactly like a sales tax of the same amount. It shifts the supply curve, in this case the world price, upward by the amount of the tariff. As shown in Figure 6-13, domestic consumers, facing a tariff of t, will pay $p_w + t$. Tariffs clearly make domestic consumers worse off.

Figure 6-13 also shows that the tariff has beneficial effects for domestic producers of that good. The price that they receive rises to $p_w + t$, and the quantity that they produce also rises. With the tariff in place, domestic output rises to the point where the domestic supply curve reaches the price $p_w + t$. This explains why producers of imported products often

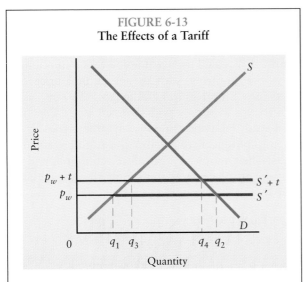

FIGURE 6-13
The Effects of a Tariff

A tariff increases the price faced by domestic consumers above the world price. Before the tariff, things are exactly as in Figure 6-12, with domestic production of q_1 and imports of $q_2 - q_1$. A tariff of t raises the domestic price to $p_w + t$, increasing domestic production to q_3 and reducing domestic consumption to q_4.

favour the imposition of tariffs. The tariffs are effective protection, increasing the portion of the domestic supply curve on which it is profitable for the domestic producers to operate.

A tariff causes conflict between domestic producers, who are benefited by it, and domestic consumers, who are made worse off due to the higher prices they pay.

In Chapter 36, we will show that the producers' well-being generally improves by less than the amount that consumers are hurt, so that the tariff makes the country as a whole worse off. But that analysis is considerably more complicated and will need more than simple demand and supply curves.

FOUR GENERAL LESSONS ABOUT RESOURCE ALLOCATION

In this chapter, we have examined several examples of government intervention in markets that might have been left unregulated. In all cases that we have examined, the government interventions generated some problems (though they may also have helped achieve certain goals). Our discussion suggests four general lessons about resource allocation.

COSTS CAN BE SHIFTED, BUT NOT AVOIDED

Production, whether in response to free-market signals or to government controls, uses resources; thus it involves costs to members of society. If it takes 5 percent of the nation's resources to provide housing at some stated average standard, those resources will not be available to produce other products. If resources are used to produce unwanted wheat, those resources will not be available to produce other products. For society as a whole, there is no such thing as free housing or free wheat.

The average standard of living depends on the amount of resources available to the economy and the efficiency with which these resources are used. It follows that *costs are real* and are incurred no matter who provides the goods. Rent controls or subsidies to agriculture can change the share of the costs paid by particular individuals or groups, lowering the share for some and raising the share for others, but they cannot make the costs go away.

Different ways of allocating the costs may also affect the total amount of resources used and thus the amount of costs incurred. For example, controls that keep prices and profits of some product below free-market levels will lead to increased quantities demanded and decreased quantities supplied. Unless government steps in to provide additional supplies, fewer resources will be allocated to producing the product. If government chooses to supply all the demand at the controlled prices, more resources will be allocated to it, which means that fewer resources will be devoted to other kinds of goods and services.

MARKET PRICES ENCOURAGE ECONOMICAL USE OF RESOURCES

Prices and profits in a market economy provide signals to both demanders and suppliers. Prices that are high (relative to other prices) provide an incentive to purchasers to economize on the product. They may choose to satisfy the want in question with substitutes whose prices have not risen so much (because they are less costly to provide) or to satisfy less of that want by shifting expenditure to the satisfaction of other wants.

On the supply side, rising prices tend to produce rising profits. High profits attract further resources into production. Short-term profits that bear no relation to current costs repeatedly occur in market economies. They cause resources to move into industries with profits until profits fall to levels that can be earned elsewhere in the economy.

Falling prices and falling profits provide the opposite motivations. Purchasers are inclined to buy more; sellers are inclined to produce less and to move resources out of the industry and into more profitable undertakings.

The price system responds to the need for a change in the allocation of resources—say, in response to an external event such as the loss of a source of a raw material or the outbreak of a war. Changing relative prices and profits signal the need for change to which consumers and producers respond.

GOVERNMENT INTERVENTION AFFECTS RESOURCE ALLOCATION

Governments intervene in the price system sometimes to satisfy generally agreed social goals and sometimes to help politically influential interest groups. Government intervention changes the allocation of resources that the price system would achieve.

Interventions have allocative consequences because they inhibit the free-market allocative mechanism. Some controls, such as rent controls, prevent prices from rising (in response, say, to an increase in demand with no change in supply). If the price is held down, the signal is not given to consumers to economize on a product that is in short supply. On the supply side, when prices and profits are prevented from rising, the profit signals that would attract new resources into the industry are never given. The shortage continues, and the movements of demand and supply that would resolve it are not set in motion.

Other controls, such as agricultural price supports, prevent prices from falling (in response, say, to an increase in supply with no increase in demand). This leads to excess supply, and the signal is not given to producers to produce less or to buyers to increase their purchases. Surpluses continue, and the movements of demand and supply that would eliminate them are not set in motion.

INTERVENTION REQUIRES ALTERNATIVE MECHANISMS

During times of shortages, allocation will be by sellers' preferences, on a first-come, first-served basis, or by some system of government rationing. During periods of surplus, there will be unsold supplies unless the government buys and stores the surpluses. Because long-run changes in demand and costs do not induce resource reallocations through private decisions, the government will have to step in. It will have to force resources out of industries in which prices are held too high, as it has tried to do in agriculture, and into industries in which prices are held too low, as it can do, for example, by providing public housing.

Intervention almost always has both benefits and costs. Economics cannot answer the question of whether a particular intervention with free markets is desirable, but it can clarify the issues by identifying benefits and costs and who will enjoy or bear them. In doing so, it can identify the competing values involved. This matter will be discussed in detail in Part 6 of this book.

SUMMARY

A. GOVERNMENT-CONTROLLED PRICES

- Government price controls are policies that attempt to hold the price of some good or service at some disequilibrium value—a value that could not be maintained in the absence of the government's intervention. A binding price floor is set above the equilibrium price; a binding price ceiling is set below the equilibrium price.
- Effective price floors lead to excess supply. Either the potential seller is left with quantities that cannot be sold, or the government must step in and buy the surplus. Effective price ceilings lead to excess demand and provide a strong incentive for black marketeers to buy at the controlled price and sell at the higher free-market price.

B. RENT CONTROLS: A CASE STUDY OF PRICE CEILINGS

- Rent controls are a persistent and widespread form of price ceiling. The major consequence of effective rent controls is a shortage of rental accommodations that gets worse because of a decline in the quantity of rental housing.
- Rent controls can be an effective response to temporary situations in which there is a ban on building or a tran-

sitory increase in demand. They usually fail when they are introduced as a response to a long-run increase in demand.

C. AGRICULTURE AND THE FARM PROBLEM

- Agricultural products are subject to wide fluctuations in market prices, which cause fluctuations in farmers' incomes. This is because of year-to-year unplanned fluctuations in supplies combined with inelastic demands, and because of cyclical fluctuations in demands combined with inelastic supplies. Where demand is inelastic, large crops tend to be associated with low total receipts for farmers, and small crops tend to be associated with high total receipts.
- To stabilize farm incomes, the government should not stabilize prices. Instead, it should buy and sell just enough to allow prices to vary in proportion to changes in quantity, thus causing the elasticity of demand for the product to be unity.
- Agricultural prices and incomes are depressed by chronic surpluses in agricultural markets. Government policies to protect farm incomes have included buying farmers' output at above free-market prices, limiting production and acreage through quotas, and paying farmers to leave crops unproduced. Such policies tend to inhibit the reallocation mechanism and thus to increase farm surpluses above what they would otherwise be and to lead to accumulating stocks.
- Canadian farm policy illustrates that government intervention to prevent the working of the market mechanisms affects resource allocation and requires alternative allocative mechanisms. While farm policy has protected farmers from certain hardships, it has slowed

the required outflow of resources that alone would solve the problem of chronic excess supply.

D. THE DETERMINATION OF IMPORTS AND EXPORTS

- For goods that are internationally traded, the equilibrium price of the good is determined by supply and demand *for the world as a whole* rather than for each country individually. This means that the world price of the good may be above or below the domestic equilibrium price *that would exist if there were no international trade.*
- A country will export goods when the domestic-market price is below the world price; a country will import goods for which the domestic-market price is above the world price.
- A tariff on some product causes conflict between domestic producers of that product, who are benefited by it, and domestic consumers, who are made worse off due to the higher prices they are forced to pay.

E. FOUR GENERAL LESSONS ABOUT RESOURCE ALLOCATION

- The examples of rent controls, farm policy, and tariffs seen in this chapter illustrate four important lessons about resource allocation.
  1. Costs can be shifted, but they cannot be avoided.
  2. Market-determined prices encourage the economical use of resources.
  3. Government intervention affects the allocation of resources.
  4. Intervention with the price mechanism means that other allocative mechanisms (often arbitrary) must be used.

KEY CONCEPTS

Price controls: floors and ceilings
Allocation by sellers' preferences and by black markets
Rent controls
Short-run and long-run supply curves of rental accommodations

The farm problem: short-run fluctuations and long-run trends
Price stabilization versus income stabilization
Quotas and supply management
Law of one price

Supply and demand curves at the world price
Imported and exported products
The effects of tariffs

DISCUSSION QUESTIONS

1. Discuss the following statements about the housing problem in Vancouver.
   a. "Zoning laws requiring that most of Vancouver be single-family dwellings reflect the exploitation of the poor by the middle class."

   b. "The world is awash with agricultural surpluses while land-starved Vancouver is prevented from spreading into much of the adjacent Fraser Valley by government 'land banks' designed to preserve agricultural land from urbanization."

c. "More than 40 percent of all rented apartments in Vancouver are illegal and would not be permitted if their owners applied for permission to rent their space legally."

2. "When an item is vital to everyone, it is easier to start controlling the price than to stop controlling it. Such controls are popular with consumers, regardless of their harmful consequences." Explain why it may be inefficient to have such controls, why they may be popular, and why, if they are popular, the government might nevertheless choose to decontrol these prices.

3. Commenting on a shortage of natural gas in the United States, the columnist William Safire called it "the unnatural shortage of natural gas." He wrote: "Be angry at the real villains: the Washington-knows-best Congressmen, the self-anointed consumer 'protectors' and the regulatory bureaucracy. They thought they could protect the consumer by breaking the laws of supply and demand, and as a result have made a classic case against government intervention." From these remarks, what do you judge the policy to have been? How would you define a "shortage?" Is there a useful distinction between a "natural shortage" and an "unnatural shortage?"

4. A top-ranked Canadian law school has 1,000 qualified applicants for 200 places in the first-year class. It is debating whether or not to institute a number of alternative admission criteria: (a) a lottery, (b) LSAT score, (c) recommendations from alumnae and alumni, (d) place of residence of applicant. An economist on the faculty determined that if the tuition level is doubled, the excess demand will disappear. Argue for (or against) using tuition fees to replace each of the other suggested criteria.

5. It is sometimes asserted that the rising costs of construction are putting housing out of the reach of ordinary citizens. Who bears the heaviest cost when rentals are kept down by (a) rent controls, (b) a subsidy to tenants equal to some fraction of their rent payments, and (c) low-cost public housing?

6. "This year the weather smiled on us, and we made a crop," says a wheat farmer near Minedosa in Manitoba. "But just as we made a crop, the economic situation changed." This quotation brings to mind the old saying, "If you are a farmer, the weather is always bad." Discuss the sense in which this saying might be true.

7. The Kenya Meat Commission (KMC) decided that it was undemocratic to allow meat prices to be out of reach of the ordinary citizen. It decided to freeze meat prices. Six months later, in a press interview, the managing commissioner of the KMC made the following statements.

a. "Cattle are scarce in the country, but I do not know why."
b. "People are eating too much beef, and unless they diversify their eating habits and eat other foodstuffs, the shortage of beef will continue."

Can you explain to the commissioner why these things have happened?

8. Consider a proposal to change trucking regulations such that trucks pulling smaller rigs (and so fewer tons) are permitted to use radar detectors while trucks pulling larger rigs (and more cargo) are prohibited from doing so. How can you interpret this as an income-support policy for the small-rig segment of the trucking industry? What are the income redistribution effects of this policy change? What is likely to be the effect on the supply curves of industries that rely on trucking to deliver raw materials or finished products?

9. During the summer of 1993, severe floods swept through the American Midwest. Although many homes that flooded that year do not typically flood, for many people this was only one in a long string of floods. However, after the waters receded, most people rebuilt their homes, despite the long history of destruction, generally with low-interest loans and disaster relief grants from the federal government. Discuss how the policy of subsidizing the reconstruction of property following floods affects the market for real estate in flood-prone areas. Is the outcome more or less efficient in the long run with such government intervention?

10. Gary Storey, a professor of agricultural economics at the University of Saskatchewan, made the following statement: "One of the sad truths of the agricultural policies in Europe and the United States is that they do very little for the future generations of farmers. Most of the subsidies get capitalized into higher land prices, creating windfall gains for current landowners (i.e., gains that they did not expect). It creates a situation where the next generation of farmers require, and ask for, increased government support."

a. Explain why subsidies to farmers would increase land values and generate windfall gains to current landowners.
b. As we have seen in this chapter, many Canadian agricultural policies are based on supply management, which involves the use of production quotas. Does such a system avoid the problem described by Professor Storey?

PART THREE

CONSUMPTION, PRODUCTION, AND COST

Why does water, which is essential to life and which we all value dearly, have such a low price? Why do diamonds, a more-or-less unnecessary part of life, have such a high price? Does this mean that the demand-and-supply apparatus that you just learned is all wrong? How many times have you heard the suggestion that a product, such as a new line of cosmetics, will sell more easily at a higher price than at a lower one? Does this mean that demand curves can have a positive slope? What determines the cost of specific products, and why does the cost sometimes depend on how many units are produced? For example, why is the production cost of a widely-used textbook significantly less than a similar textbook used only by a few universities? Why has the declining cost of computer-related equipment led some firms to reduce their number of employees? These are the sort of questions you will be able to answer after reading the next three chapters.

In Part 2, we saw that demand and supply are important for determining market prices and quantities. You also saw that the *shapes* of demand and supply curves influence the way prices and quantities respond to changes in income, technology, or commodity taxes. In the next three chapters, we go "behind the scenes" of demand and supply to examine in more detail the behaviour of consumers and the behaviour of firms. This will give you a deeper understanding of what demand and supply are all about.

In Chapter 7, you will explore the *theory of consumer behaviour*. There you will see how economists think about the way consumers make decisions. You will be introduced to the important concept of *utility*, and to the distinction between *marginal* and *total* utility. It is this distinction that explains why water has a low price and diamonds have a high price. You will also see how demand curves are derived from the underlying consumer behaviour, and you will see that (except in some very unusual cases) demand curves are indeed negatively sloped.

Chapters 8 and 9 explore the *theory of the firm*. You will learn about *profits* and *costs*, and how these terms are used differently in economics than in everyday life. The important concepts of *average cost* and *marginal cost* will be developed, at which point you will know why 50,000 textbooks can be produced at a lower cost per book than can 10,000 textbooks. You will be introduced to the *principle of substitution*, which explains why the falling cost of computers has led some firms to reduce their workforces (and increase their use of computers). Finally, you will see how changes in technology lead to changes in firms' behaviour.

CHAPTER 7

THE THEORY OF CONSUMER BEHAVIOUR

Imagine that you are walking down the aisle of a supermarket looking for something for your late-night snack (to have while you are studying!). With only a $5 bill in your pocket, you must choose how to divide this $5 between frozen burritos and cans of coke. How do you make this decision? In this chapter, we introduce you to the way economists think about such problems—the theory of consumer behaviour. Not surprisingly, economists (being consumers themselves) think about consumers as caring both about the prices of the goods and the amount of satisfaction that they get from the goods.

MARGINAL UTILITY AND CONSUMER CHOICE

Consumer *choice* is fundamental to market economies, and consumers make all kinds of decisions—they choose to drink coffee or tea (or neither), to go to the movies, to dine out, to buy excellent (or not so good) stereo equipment. As we discussed in Chapter 1, economists assume that in making their choices, consumers are motivated to maximize their **utility,** the total satisfaction that they derive from the goods and services that they consume.[1]

Neither economists nor psychologists can measure utility directly. However, it turns out that we can construct a useful theory of consumer behaviour based on utility maximization without directly measuring utility. In Chapter 1, we defined the *opportunity cost* of a given action as the benefit given up by choosing that action rather than the next best alternative. This chapter's theory of consumer behaviour is based on the idea that we can use the opportunity cost of making choices to measure the utility that consumers derive from the products they consume.

In developing our theory of consumer behaviour in general, we begin by considering the consumption of a single product. It will be useful to distinguish between the consumer's **total utility,** which is the full satisfaction resulting from the consumption of that product by a consumer, and the consumer's **marginal utility,** which is the *change* in satisfaction resulting from consuming a little more of that product. For example, the total utility of consuming seven eggs per week is the total satisfaction that those seven eggs provide. The marginal utility of the seventh egg consumed is the additional satisfaction provided by the consumption of that egg. Hence marginal utility is the difference in total utility gained by consuming six eggs per week and by consuming seven eggs per week.[2]

DIMINISHING MARGINAL UTILITY

The basic hypothesis of utility theory, often called the *law of diminishing marginal utility,* is as follows:

The utility that any consumer derives from *successive* units of a particular product diminishes as total consumption of the product increases, holding the consumption of all other products constant.

---

[1]We discuss two theories of consumer choice. In the chapter, we present the marginal utility theory of demand. In the appendix to this chapter, we present a more formal version of essentially the same theory using indifference curves.

[2]Technically, *incremental* utility is measured over a discrete interval, such as from 6 to 7, whereas *marginal* utility is a rate of change measured over an infinitesimal interval. However, common usage applies the word marginal when the last unit is involved, even if a one-unit change is not infinitesimal. [10]

Consider water. Some minimum quantity is essential to sustain life, and a person would, if necessary, give up his or her entire income to obtain that quantity of water. Thus the marginal utility of that basic quantity of water is extremely high. More than this bare minimum will be consumed, but the marginal utility of successive glasses of water drunk over a period of time will decline steadily.

Evidence for this hypothesis will be considered later, but you can convince yourself that it is at least reasonable by asking a few questions. How much money would induce you to reduce your consumption of water by one glass per week? The answer is very little. How much would induce you to reduce it by a second glass? By a third glass? To only one glass consumed per week? The answer to the last question is quite a bit. The fewer glasses you are consuming already, the higher the marginal utility of one more glass of water.

Water has many uses other than for drinking. A fairly high marginal utility will be attached to some minimum quantity for bathing, but much more than this minimum will be used for more frequent baths or longer showers than are absolutely necessary. The last weekly litre used for bathing is likely to have a low marginal utility. Again, some small quantity of water is necessary for brushing teeth, but many people leave the water running while they brush. The water going down the drain between wetting and rinsing the brush surely has a low utility. When all the extravagant uses of water by the modern consumer are considered, the marginal utility of the last, say, 30 percent of all units consumed is probably very low, even though the total utility of all the units consumed is extremely high.

UTILITY SCHEDULES AND GRAPHS

The hypothetical schedule in Table 7-1 is constructed to illustrate the assumptions that have been made about utility, using movie attendance as an example. The table shows that total utility rises as the number of movies attended (per month) rises. Everything else being equal, the more movies the consumer attends each month, the more satisfaction is obtained—at least over the range shown in the table. However, the marginal utility of each additional movie per month is less than that of the previous one, even though each movie adds something to the consumer's satisfaction. The schedule in Table 7-1 shows that mar-

TABLE 7-1
Total and Marginal Utility Schedules

Number of Movies Attended Per Month	Total Utility	Marginal Utility
0	0	
		30
1	30	
		20
2	50	
		15
3	65	
		10
4	75	
		8
5	83	
		6
6	89	
		4
7	93	
		3
8	96	
		2
9	98	
		1
10	99	

Total utility rises, but marginal utility declines as consumption increases. The marginal utility of 20, shown as the second entry in the third column, arises because total utility increases from 30 to 50—a difference of 20—with attendance at the second movie. To indicate that the marginal utility is associated with the change from one rate of movie attendance to another, the figures in the third column are recorded between the rows of the figures in the second column. When plotting marginal utility on a graph, it is plotted at the midpoint of the interval over which it is computed.

ginal utility declines as quantity consumed rises. [11] The data are graphed in the two parts of Figure 7-1.

MAXIMIZING UTILITY

A basic assumption of the theory of consumer behaviour is that consumers try to make themselves as well off as they possibly can in the circumstances in which they find themselves. In other words, the members of a household seek to maximize their total utility.

The Consumer's Decision

How can a consumer adjust expenditure so as to maximize total utility? A simple answer would be that the consumer should consume such that the marginal utility of each product is the same—that is, such that the last unit of each product consumed is valued equally. But this would make sense only if each product had the same price per unit. Consider a consumer buying two goods who must spend $3 to obtain an additional unit of one product and only $1 to obtain one unit of another. The first product would repre-

sent a poor use of money if the marginal utility of each were equal. The consumer would be spending $3 to get satisfaction equal to what could have been acquired for only $1 by buying the other good.

A consumer who is maximizing utility will allocate expenditures so that the utility obtained from the last dollar spent on each product is equal.

Imagine that the consumer is in a position in which the utility of the last dollar spent on cashews yields three times the utility of the last dollar spent on toffee. In this case, total utility can be increased by switching a dollar of expenditure from toffee to cashews and by gaining the difference between the utilities of a dollar spent on each.

The utility-maximizing consumer will continue to switch expenditure from toffee to cashews as long as a dollar spent on cashews yields more utility than a dollar spent on toffee. This switching, however, reduces the quantity of toffee consumed and, given the law of diminishing marginal utility, raises the marginal utility of toffee. At the same time, switching increases the quantity of cashews consumed and thereby lowers the marginal utility of cashews.

Eventually, the marginal utilities will have changed enough so that the utility of a dollar spent on cashews is just equal to the utility of a dollar spent on toffee. At this point, there is nothing to be gained by a further switch of expenditure from toffee to cashews. If the consumer persists in reallocating expenditure, she will further reduce the marginal utility of cashews (by consuming more of them) and raise the marginal utility of toffee (by consuming less of them). Total utility will no longer be at its maximum because the utility of a dollar spent on toffee will now exceed the utility of a dollar spent on cashews.

So much for the simple example. Now, what can we say more generally about utility maximization? Suppose we denote the marginal utility of the last unit of product X by MU_X and its price by p_X. Let MU_Y and p_Y refer, respectively, to the marginal utility of a second product Y and its price. The marginal utility per dollar of X will be MU_X/p_X. For example, if the last unit adds 30 units to utility and costs $2, its marginal utility per dollar is $30/2 = 15$.

The condition required for a consumer to be maximizing utility, for any pair of products (X and Y), is

$$\frac{MU_X}{p_X} = \frac{MU_Y}{p_Y} \qquad [1]$$

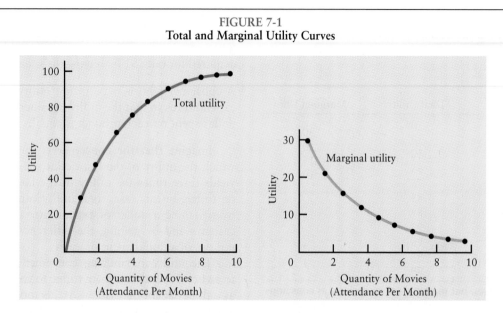

FIGURE 7-1
Total and Marginal Utility Curves

The total utility curve rises, but the marginal utility curve falls as the quantity consumed rises. The dots correspond to the values listed in Table 7-1; smooth curves have been drawn through them.

This says that the consumer will allocate expenditure so that the utility gained from the last dollar spent on each product is equal.

This is the fundamental equation of marginal utility theory. A consumer demands each good up to the point at which the marginal utility per dollar spent on it is the same as the marginal utility of a dollar spent on every other good. When this condition is met for all goods, the consumer cannot increase utility by shifting a dollar of expenditure from one product to another.

Utility and Opportunity Cost Revisited

When a consumer is deciding how much of a given product to purchase, the consumer compares the utility from that product to the utility that could be derived from spending the same money on other things. Thus for some good X, the consumer consumes to the point where the marginal utility obtained per dollar's worth of X is just equal to the marginal utility obtained per dollar of money.

The value to the consumer of consuming the last unit of some good (the marginal unit) is just equal to the opportunity cost—the value to the consumer of the money used to make the purchase.

This conclusion depends only on the assumption that the consumer maximizes utility and has preferences that exhibit diminishing marginal utility.

An Alternative Interpretation

If we rearrange the terms in Equation 1, we can gain additional insight into consumer behaviour.

$$\frac{MU_X}{MU_Y} = \frac{p_X}{p_Y} \qquad [2]$$

The right side of this equation states the *relative* price of the two goods. It is determined by the market and is outside the control of the individual consumer; the consumer reacts to these market prices but is powerless to change them. The left side states the relative ability of an additional unit of each good to add to the consumer's satisfaction. This is within the control of the consumer because in determining the quantities of different goods to buy, the consumer also determines their marginal utilities. (If you have difficulty seeing why, look again at the right side of Figure 7-1.)

If the two sides of Equation 2 are not equal, the consumer can increase total utility by rearranging purchases. To see this, suppose that the price of a unit of X is twice the price of a unit of Y ($p_X/p_Y = 2$) and that the marginal utility of a unit of X is three times that of a unit of Y ($MU_X/MU_Y = 3$). Under these conditions, it is worthwhile for the consumer to buy more of X and less of Y. For example, if the consumer reduces purchases of Y by two units, enough purchasing power is freed to buy a unit of X. Because one extra unit of X bought yields 1½ times the satisfaction of two units of Y forgone, the switch is worth making. What about a further switch of X for Y? As the consumer buys more of X and less of Y, the marginal utility of X falls and the marginal utility of Y rises. The consumer will go on rearranging purchases, reducing Y consumption and increasing X consumption, until, in this example, the marginal utility of X is only twice that of Y. At this point, total satisfaction cannot be increased further by rearranging purchases between the two products.

The example in the previous paragraph illustrates a simple general point: Consumers face a set of prices that they cannot change and maximize their utility by adjusting the things that they can change—the quantities of the various goods they purchase—until Equation 2 is satisfied for all pairs of products.

This sort of equation—one side representing the choices made available to the individual by the outside world and the other side representing the effect of those choices on the individual's welfare—recurs often in economics. It reflects the position reached when decision makers have made the best adjustment possible to the external forces that limit their choices.

All consumers face the same set of market prices when they enter the market. When all consumers are fully adjusted to these prices, each will have identical ratios of marginal utilities for each pair of goods. Of course, a rich consumer may consume more of each product than a poor consumer. However, the rich and the poor consumers (and every other consumer) will adjust their *relative* purchases of each product so that the *relative* marginal utilities are the same for all. Thus if the price of X is twice the price of Y, each consumer will purchase X and Y to the point at which, for that consumer, the marginal utility of X is twice the marginal utility of Y. Consumers with different tastes will have different marginal utility schedules and so may consume differing relative quantities of products, even though the ratios of these marginal utilities are the same for all consumers.

DERIVATION OF THE CONSUMER'S DEMAND CURVE

To derive the consumer's demand curve for a product, it is only necessary to ask what happens when there is a change in the price of that product. As an example, let us do this for cashews. Consider Equation 2 and let X represent cashews and Y represent *all other products taken together*. In this case, the price of Y is interpreted as the average price of all other products. What will happen if, with all other prices remaining constant, there is an increase in the price of cashews? When the price of cashews rises, the right side of Equation 2 increases but until the consumer adjusts consumption, the left side is unchanged. Thus, after the price changes but before the consumer reacts, the consumer will be in a position in which the following circumstance prevails:

$$\frac{MU \text{ of cashews}}{MU \text{ of } Y} < \frac{\text{price of cashews}}{\text{price of } Y} \quad [3]$$

What does the consumer do to restore the equality? The hypothesis of diminishing marginal utility tells us that as the consumer buys fewer cashews, the *marginal* utility of cashews will rise, thereby increasing the ratio on the left side. Thus in response to an increase in the price of cashews, with all other prices constant, the consumer will reduce his consumption of cashews (and increase his consumption of other goods) until the marginal utility of cashews rises sufficiently that Equation 2 is restored.[3]

The consumer began with the utility of the last dollar spent on cashews equal to the utility of the last dollar spent on all other goods, but the rise in cashew prices changes this. The consumer buys fewer cashews (and more of other goods) until the marginal utility of cashews rises enough to make the utility of the last dollar spent on cashews the same as

---

[3]For most consumers, cashews absorb only a small proportion of their total expenditures. If, in response to a change in its price, expenditure on cashews changes by $5 per month, this represents a large change in cashew consumption but only a negligible change in the consumption of other products. Hence in the text we proceed by assuming that the marginal utilities of other products do not change when the price and the consumption of cashews change.

MARKET AND INDIVIDUAL DEMAND CURVES

Market demand curves show how much is demanded by all purchasers. For example, in Figure 4-1, the market demand for carrots is 90,000 tons when the price is $40 per ton. This 90,000 tons is the sum of the quantities demanded by millions of different consumers. The demand curve in Figure 4-1 also tells us that when the price rises to $60, the total quantity demanded falls to 77,500 tons per month. This quantity, too, can be traced back to individual consumers. Notice that we have now described two points not only on the market demand curve but also on the demand curves of each of the millions of individual consumers.

The market demand curve is the horizontal sum of the demand curves of individual consumers. It is the horizontal sum because we wish to add quantities demanded at a given price, and quantities are measured in the horizontal direction on a conventional demand curve.

The figure illustrates aggregation over two consumers. At a price of $3, Consumer A purchases 2 units and Consumer B purchases 4 units; thus together they purchase 6 units, yielding one point on the market demand curve. No matter how many consumers are involved, the process is the same: Add the quantities demanded by all consumers at each price, and the result is the market demand curve.

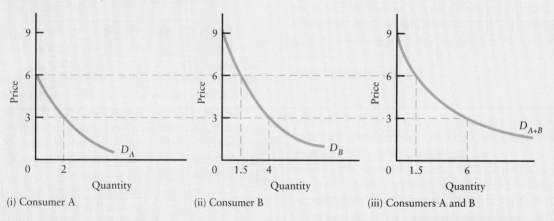

(i) Consumer A   (ii) Consumer B   (iii) Consumers A and B

it was originally. This analysis leads to the basic prediction of demand theory:

A rise in the price of a product (holding all other things constant) will lead to a decrease in the quantity of the product demanded by each consumer.

If this is what each household does, it is also what all households taken together do. Thus the theory of consumer behaviour that we have presented here predicts a negatively sloped market demand curve in addition to a negatively sloped demand curve for each individual consumer. Extension 7-1 shows how a market demand curve can be obtained by adding up the demand curves of individual consumers.

THE DISTINCTION BETWEEN TOTAL AND MARGINAL UTILITY

An instinctive appreciation for the difference between *total* utility and *marginal* utility is important for understanding demand theory. Here are three important applications which will help to illustrate this difference.

CONSUMER SURPLUS

Imagine yourself facing an either-or choice concerning some particular product, say, ice cream: You can have the amount you are now consuming, or you can have none of it. Suppose that you would be willing to pay as much as $100 per month for the 8 litres of gourmet ice cream that you now consume, rather than do without it. Further suppose that you actually buy those 8 litres for only $50 instead of $100. What a bargain! You have paid $50 less than the most you were willing to pay. Strikingly, this sort of bargain occurs every day in any economy in which prices do the rationing. Indeed, it is so common that the $50 "saved" in this example has been given a name: *consumer surplus*. In general, **consumer surplus** is the difference between the total value that consumers place on all the units consumed of some product and the payment they must make to purchase that amount of the product.

Consumer surplus is a direct consequence of negatively sloped demand curves. To illustrate this connection, suppose that we have collected the information in Table 7-2 on the basis of an interview with Mr. Wally Ranney. Our first question to Mr. Ranney is, "If you were getting no milk at all, how much would you be willing to pay for one glass per week?" With no hesitation he replies $3.00. We then ask, "If you had already consumed that one glass, how much would you pay for a second glass per week?" After a bit of thought, he answers $1.50. Adding one glass per week with each question, we discover that he would be willing to pay $1.00 to get a third glass per week and 80, 60, 50, 40, 30, 25, and 20 cents for successive glasses from the fourth to the tenth glass per week.

The sum of the values that he places on each glass of milk gives us the *total value* that he places on all 10 glasses. In this case, Mr. Ranney values 10 glasses of milk per week at $8.55. This is the amount he would be willing to pay if he faced the either-or choice of 10 glasses or none. This is also the amount he would be willing to pay if he were offered the milk one glass at a time and charged the maximum he was willing to pay for each.

However, Mr. Ranney does not have to pay a different price for each glass of milk he consumes

TABLE 7-2
Consumer Surplus on Milk Consumption by One Consumer

(1) Glasses of Milk Consumed Per Week	(2) Amount the Consumer Would Pay to Obtain This Glass	(3) Consumer Surplus on Each Glass if Milk Costs 30 Cents Per Glass
First	$3.00	$2.70
Second	1.50	1.20
Third	1.00	0.70
Fourth	0.80	0.50
Fifth	0.60	0.30
Sixth	0.50	0.20
Seventh	0.40	0.10
Eighth	0.30	0.00
Ninth	0.25	—
Tenth	0.20	—

Consumer surplus on each unit consumed is the difference between the market price and the maximum price that the consumer is willing to pay to obtain that unit. The table shows the value that one consumer puts on successive glasses of milk consumed each week. His negatively sloped demand curve shows that he would be willing to pay progressively smaller amounts for each additional unit consumed. As long as he would be willing to pay more than the market price for any unit, he obtains consumer surplus on it when he buys it. The marginal unit is the one valued just at the market price and on which no consumer surplus is earned.

each week; he can buy all he wants at the prevailing market price. Suppose that the price is 30 cents per glass. He will buy eight glasses per week because he values the eighth glass just at the market price but all earlier glasses at higher amounts. He does not buy a ninth glass because he values it at less than the market price.

Because he values the first glass at $3.00 but gets it for 30 cents, he makes a "profit" of $2.70 on that glass. Between his $1.50 valuation of the second glass and what he has to pay for it, he clears a "profit" of $1.20. He clears a "profit" of 70 cents on the third glass, and so on. This "profit", which is shown in column 3 of Table 7-2, is his consumer surplus on each glass.

His total consumer surplus of $5.70 per week can be calculated by summing his surplus on each glass; the same total can be calculated by first summing what he would pay for all eight glasses, which is $8.10, and then subtracting the $2.40 that he does pay.

The value placed by each consumer on the total consumption of some product can be estimated in at least two ways: The valuation that the consumer places on each successive unit may be summed, or the consumer may be asked how much he or she would be willing to pay to consume the amount in question if the alternative were to have none of that product.[4]

Although other consumers would put different numerical values into Table 7-2, the negative slope of the demand curve implies that the values in column 2 would be declining for each consumer. Because a consumer will go on buying additional units until the value placed on the last unit equals the market price, it follows that there will be consumer surplus on every unit consumed except the last one.

The data in columns 1 and 2 of Table 7-2 give Mr. Ranney's demand curve for milk. It is his demand curve because he will go on buying glasses of milk as long as he values each glass at least as much as the market price he must pay for it. When the market price is $3.00 per glass, he will buy only one glass; when it is $1.50, he will buy two glasses; and so on. The total valuation is the area below his demand curve, and consumer surplus is the part of the area that lies above the price line. This is shown in Figure 7-2.

Figure 7-3 shows that the same relationship holds for the smooth market demand curve that indicates the total amount that all consumers would buy at each price.[5]

Consumer surplus is an important and useful concept. Understanding it is the key to understanding the theory of demand. In other parts of this chap-

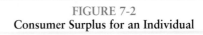

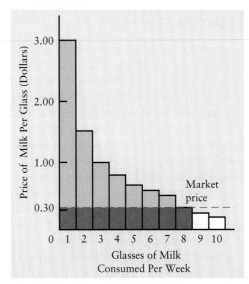

FIGURE 7-2
Consumer Surplus for an Individual

Consumer surplus is the sum of the extra valuations placed on each unit above the market price paid for each. This figure is based on the data in Table 7-2. The consumer pays the amounts shown in the dark shaded area for the eight glasses of milk he will consume per week when the market price is 30 cents per glass. The total value he places on these eight glasses is the entire shaded area. Hence his consumer surplus is the light shaded area.

ter, we will see how it helps us to explain some real-world events that on the surface seem paradoxical. Consumer surplus will also prove useful in later chapters when we evaluate aspects of the performance of the market system.

THE PARADOX OF VALUE

Early economists, struggling with the problem of what determines the relative prices of products, encountered what they called the *paradox of value*: Many necessary products, such as water, have prices that are low compared to the prices of luxury products, such as diamonds. Water is necessary to our existence, whereas diamonds are used mostly for frivolous purposes and could disappear from the face of the earth tomorrow without causing any real hardship. Does it not seem odd, then, these economists

[4]This is only an approximation, but it is good enough for our purposes. Although more advanced analysis indicates that it is sometimes necessary to account for the income effect discussed later in this chapter, no amount of refinement upsets the general result that we establish here: When consumers can buy all the units they require at a single market price, they pay less than they would be willing to pay if facing a choice between having the quantity they consume and having none.

[5]Figure 7-2 is a bar chart because we only allowed the consumer to vary his consumption in discrete units of one glass at a time. Had we allowed him to vary his consumption of milk one drop at a time, we could have traced out a continuous curve similar to the one shown in Figure 7-3.

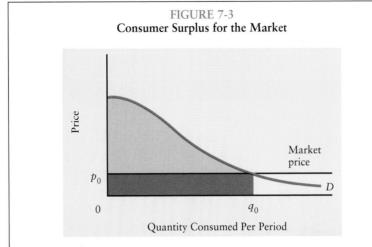

FIGURE 7-3
Consumer Surplus for the Market

Total consumer surplus is the area under the demand curve and above the price line. The demand curve shows the amount consumers would pay for each unit of the product if they had to buy their units one at a time. The area under the demand curve shows the total valuation that consumers place on all units consumed. For example, the total value that consumers place on q_0 units is the entire shaded area under the demand curve up to q_0. At a market price of p_0, the amount paid for q_0 units is the dark shaded area. Hence consumer surplus is the light shaded area.

asked, that water is so cheap and diamonds are so expensive? It took a long time to resolve this apparent paradox, so it is not surprising that even today, analogous confusions cloud many policy discussions.

The key to resolving this apparent paradox lies in the important distinction between what one would pay to avoid having one's consumption of a product *reduced to zero* and what one would pay to avoid losing the consumption of the product by *one unit*. This point involves a distinction between total and marginal values that is frequently encountered in many branches of economics.

We have seen already that the area under the demand curve shows what a consumer would pay for the product if required to purchase it unit by unit. It is thus a measure of the total value placed on all of the units that the consumer consumes. For all consumers together, the total value of q_0 units is the entire shaded area (light and dark) under the demand curve in Figure 7-3.

What about the *marginal value* that each consumer places on one more unit than is currently being consumed? This is given by the product's market

price, which is p_0 in this case. Facing a market price of p_0, each consumer buys all the units that he or she values at p_0 or greater but does not purchase any units valued at less than p_0. It follows that each consumer places on the last unit consumed of any product a value that is measured by the product's price. (Look back at Figure 7-2.)

Now look at the total *market* value of the product. This is the amount that everyone spends to purchase it. It is price multiplied by quantity. In Figure 7-3, this is the dark shaded rectangle defined by the vertical distance to p_0 and the horizontal distance to q_0.

We have seen that the total value that consumers place on a given amount of a product, as measured by the relevant area under the demand curve, is different from the total market value of a product, as given by the product's price multiplied by the quantity consumed. Not only are the two values different, but they are generally unrelated, except that the total area under the demand curve is always greater than the total market value. Figure 7-4 illustrates a case in which a good with a high total value has a low market value and vice versa.

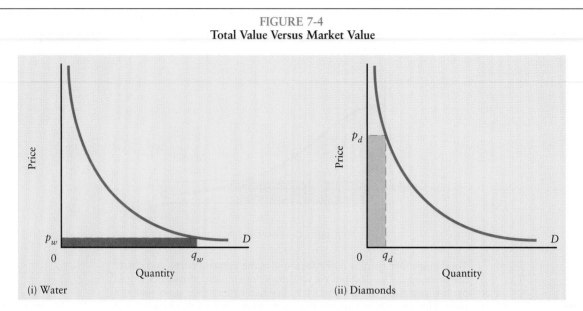

FIGURE 7-4
Total Value Versus Market Value

The market value of the amount of some product bears no necessary relationship to the total value that consumers place on that amount. The graph presents hypothetical demand curves for water and diamonds that are meant to be stylized versions of the real curves. The total value that consumers place on water, as shown by the area under the demand curve, is great—indeed, we do not even show the curve for very small quantities because people would pay all they had rather than be completely deprived of water. The total valuation that consumers place on diamonds is shown by the area under the demand curve for diamonds. This is clearly less than the total value placed on water.

The large supply of water makes water plentiful and makes water low in price, as shown by p_w in part (i) of the figure. Thus the total *market* value of water consumed, indicated by the dark shaded area, is low. The low supply of diamonds makes diamonds scarce and keeps diamonds high in price, as shown by p_d in part (ii) of the figure. Thus the total *market* value of diamonds sold, indicated by the light shaded area, is high.

The resolution of the paradox of value is that a good that is very plentiful, such as water, will have a low price and will thus be consumed to the point where all consumers place a low value on the last unit consumed, whether or not they place a high value on their total consumption of the product. By contrast, a product that is relatively scarce will have a high market price, and consumption will therefore stop at a point where consumers place a high value on the last unit consumed, regardless of the value that they place on their total consumption of the good.

We have now reached an important conclusion:

Because the market price of a product depends not only on demand but also on supply, there is nothing paradoxical in there being a product on which con-

sumers place a high total value (such as water) selling for a low price and hence having only a small amount spent on it.

FREE AND SCARCE GOODS

Consider a product for which the quantity supplied exceeds the quantity demanded at a price of zero. Such goods will not command positive prices in a market economy and hence are called **free goods.** A consumer can become better off by increasing consumption of free goods as long as the extra units consumed have positive value. It follows that free goods will be consumed up to the point at which the value that consumers place on another unit consumed is zero. At some times in some places, air, water, salt, sand, and wild fruit have been free goods.

Note that a good may be free at one time or place but not at another.

A **scarce good** is one for which the quantity demanded exceeds the quantity supplied at a price of zero. If all such goods had zero prices, the total amount that people would want to consume would greatly exceed the amount that could be produced. Such goods will therefore command positive prices in a market economy. Most goods are scarce goods.

Many people have strong views about the prices that are charged for certain products. These views are often an emotional reaction to the total values of the goods rather than to their marginal values. Here is an example: "Because water is such a complete necessity of life, both to the rich and the poor, it is wrong to make people pay for water. Instead, the government should provide free water for everyone."

When deciding between a zero price and a modest price for water, the relevant question for the consumer is not "Is water so necessary that we want everyone to be provided with some of it?" but rather "Are the marginal uses of water so important that we are willing to use scarce resources to provide the necessary quantities?" The distinction is important because the two questions have different answers.

The evidence that we have about the consumption of water at various prices suggests that the demand curve for water has a shape similar to the curve shown in part (i) of Figure 7-4. If so, the difference in consumption that results from providing water free or charging a modest price for it will be large. The additional water consumed, however, is costly to provide, and its provision requires scarce resources that could have been used to produce other goods. If the value that consumers place on the products forgone is higher than the value that they place on the extra water consumed, consumers are worse off as a result of receiving water for free. A charge for water would release resources from water production to produce goods that consumers value more highly at the margin. Of course, some minimum quantity of water could be provided free to every consumer, but the effects of this would be quite different from the effects of making *all* water free.

It follows that if we want to know the gain to consumers from consuming a little more of some product (or the loss from consuming a little less), then we need to know the *marginal value* to them of consuming the product. It is not enough simply to

know the *total value* they place on consuming all units of the product.

Similar considerations apply to food, medical services, and a host of other products that are necessities of life but that also have numerous low-value uses that will be encouraged if a scarce product is provided at a zero price.

INCOME AND SUBSTITUTION EFFECTS OF PRICE CHANGES

In the first section of this chapter, we examined the relationship between the *law of diminishing marginal utility* and the slope of the consumer's demand curve for some product. In this section, we introduce an alternative method for thinking about the slope of an individual's demand curve. From the discussion in Extension 7-1, this alternative method can also be used to think about the slope of a market demand curve.

A fall in the price of one good (let's go back to our example of ice cream) affects the consumer in two ways. First, as we have emphasized throughout this chapter, relative prices change, providing an incentive to buy *more* ice cream because it is cheaper. Second, because the price of ice cream has fallen, the consumer has more *purchasing power* available to spend on all products. Suppose that the price of premium ice cream fell from $5.00 to $4.00 per litre and your friend Emil was in the habit of eating half a litre of ice cream a day. In the course of a 30-day month, Emil could keep his ice cream habit unchanged but save $15.00, money that would be available for any purpose—more ice cream, a trip to the movies, or photocopies of your economics notes.

The price fall induces an increase in Emil's **real income,** which we define as the quantity of goods and services that can be purchased with a given amount of money income. This rise in real income in turn provides an incentive to buy more of all normal goods. (Recall from Chapter 5 that when real income rises, the consumer buys more of all normal goods and less of all inferior goods.)

In general, the *extent* of the rise in real income depends on the share of total expenditures that the

---

EXTENSION 7-2

Can demand curves have a positive slope?

What the great English economist Alfred Marshall (1842–1924) called the law of demand asserts that, other things being constant, the market price of a product and the quantity demanded in the market are negatively associated; that is, demand curves have a negative slope. Challenges to the law have taken various forms, focusing on Giffen goods, "conspicuous consumption" goods, and goods whose demands are perfectly inelastic. Let us consider each of these in turn.

GIFFEN GOODS

Great interest was attached to the apparent refutation of the law of demand by the English economist Sir Robert Giffen (1837–1910). He is alleged to have observed that when a rise in the price of imported wheat led to an increase in the price of bread, members of the British working class *increased* their consumption of bread. This meant that their demand curve for bread was positively sloped.

Two things must be true in order for a good to be a so-called **Giffen good**: The good must be an inferior good, and the good must take a large proportion of total household expenditure; that is, its in-

come effect must be both negative and large. Bread was indeed a dietary staple of the British working classes during the nineteenth century. A rise in the price of bread would cause a large reduction in their real income. This could lead to increased consumption of bread as households cut out their few luxuries in order to be able to consume enough bread to keep alive. Though possible, such cases are all but unknown in the modern world. The reason is that in all but the poorest societies, typical households do not spend large proportions of their incomes on a single inferior good.

CONSPICUOUS CONSUMPTION GOODS

Thorstein Veblen (1857–1929), in *The Theory of the Leisure Class*, noted that some products were consumed not for their intrinsic qualities but because they had "snob appeal." He suggested that the more expensive such a commodity became, the greater might be its ability to confer status on its purchaser.

Consumers might value diamonds, for example, precisely because diamonds are expensive. Thus a fall in price might lead them to stop buying dia-

---

consumer spends on each good. For example, consider the extreme case of a consumer who spends all of her income on ice cream. If the price of ice cream falls by half, she will find that her real income has doubled because she can buy twice as much as before. At the other extreme, a consumer who spends none of his income on ice cream and all of it on other things finds that his consumption opportunities are unchanged—he can still buy exactly what he bought before the price of ice cream fell. For intermediate cases where both ice cream and other goods are purchased, there will be some positive effect on real income when the price of ice cream

falls, the strength of which depends on the share of food expenditures in the consumer's budget.

THE SUBSTITUTION EFFECT

To isolate the effect of the change in relative price when the price of food falls, we can consider what would happen if we also reduce the consumer's money income to restore the original purchasing power. Suppose, in our example, that Emil's uncle sends him a monthly allowance for ice cream, and that when the price of ice cream falls, the allowance is reduced so that Emil can buy just as much ice monds and to switch to a more satisfactory object of conspicuous consumption. They may behave in the same way with respect to luxury cars, buying them *because* they are expensive.

Consumers that behave in this way will have positively-sloped *individual* demand curves for diamonds and cars. However, no one has ever observed a positively-sloped *market* demand curve for such commodities. The reason is easy to discover. The fact that countless lower-income consumers would be glad to buy diamonds or Cadillacs only if these commodities were sufficiently inexpensive suggests that positively-sloped demand curves for a few individual wealthy households are much more likely than a positively-sloped *market* demand curve for the same commodity.*

PERFECTLY INELASTIC DEMAND CURVES

Quite often, people implicitly assume that demand curves are vertical. It was once widely argued that the market demand for gasoline was almost perfectly inelastic on the grounds that people who had paid thousands of dollars for cars would not balk at pay-

ing a few cents extra for gasoline. Events have proved how wrong this argument is: Higher gasoline prices in the early 1980s led to production of smaller cars, to more car pools, to more economical driving speeds and habits, and to less pleasure driving. Falling gasoline prices in the mid-1980s led to a reversal of these trends.

MARKET DEMAND CURVES

Even if some individual consumers exhibited one or more of the "exceptions" to the law of demand discussed here, in most cases their actions would be swamped by those of consumers whose behaviour conformed to the law of demand. Thus the *market* demand curve would still be negatively sloped.

All in all, the mass of accumulated evidence confirms that demand curves generally have a negative slope. Exceptions are extremely rare.

---

*Of course, even with conspicuous consumption goods, the quantity demanded may rise when the price of the good goes down as long as its *perceived* price remains high. As one advertising slogan for a discount department store puts it: "Only you know how little you paid."

cream—and everything else—as he could before. Emil's purchasing power will be unchanged. If his behaviour remains unchanged, however, he will not be maximizing his utility. Recall that utility maximization requires that the ratio of marginal utility to price be the same for all goods. In our hypothetical example, with no change in behaviour, the quantities (and hence marginal utilities) and the prices of all goods other than ice cream are unchanged. The quantity of ice cream is also unchanged, but the price has fallen. To maximize his utility, Emil must therefore increase his consumption (reduce his marginal utility) of ice cream and reduce his consumption of all other goods.

In general, *holding purchasing power constant*, the change in the quantity demanded of a good whose relative price has changed is called the **substitution effect** of the price change.[6] With real income unchanged, consumers will always substitute toward goods whose relative prices have fallen and away from goods whose relative prices have increased.

---

[6]This measure, which isolates the substitution effect by holding the consumer's *purchasing power* constant, is known as the *Slutsky Effect*. A related but slightly different measure that holds the consumer's level of utility constant is discussed in the appendix to this chapter.

The substitution effect always increases the quantity demanded of a good whose price has fallen and always reduces the quantity demanded of a good whose price has risen.

THE INCOME EFFECT

To examine the substitution effect, we reduced Emil's *money* income following the price reduction so we could see the effect of the relative price change, holding purchasing power constant. Now we want to see the effect of the change in purchasing power, *holding relative prices constant at their new value*. To do this, suppose that after Emil has adjusted his purchases to the new price and his reduced income, he then calls his uncle and pleads to have his allowance restored to its original (higher) amount. Emil's uncle agrees, and so Emil's money income is returned to its original level. Assuming that we are dealing with normal goods, Emil will increase consumption of both ice cream and other goods. The change in the quantity of ice cream demanded as a result of the consumer's reaction to increased real income is called the **income effect.** Of course, if ice cream were an inferior good, the income effect of a price fall would lead Emil and other consumers to purchase less ice cream. This raises the possibility that demand curves could have positive slopes, which we considered in Extension 7-2.

The income effect leads consumers to buy more of a product whose price has fallen, provided that the product is a normal good.

We have now broken down the reaction to a change in the price of a product into a substitution effect and an income effect. Of course, when the price of a good falls, the consumer moves directly from the initial consumption pattern to the final one; we do not observe any "halfway" consumption pattern. By breaking this movement into two parts for analytical purposes, however, we are able to study the consumer's total change in quantity demanded as a response to a change in relative prices and a response to a change in real income.

Notice that the size of the income effect depends on the amount of income spent on the good whose price changes and on the amount by which the price changes. In our example, if Emil were initially spending one-half of his income on ice cream, a $1 fall in the price of ice cream would be equivalent to a 10 percent increase in income (20 percent of 50 percent). Now consider a different case: The price of petroleum falls by 20 percent. For a consumer who was spending only 5 percent of income on gas and oil, this is equivalent to only a 1 percent increase in purchasing power (20 percent of 5 percent).

THE SLOPE OF THE DEMAND CURVE

We have seen that the substitution effect always leads consumers to increase their demand for goods whose prices fall and to reduce their demand for goods whose prices rise. The income effect leads consumers to buy more of all normal goods whose prices fall.

Putting the income and substitution effects together gives the following support for the law of demand:

Because of the combined operation of the income and substitution effects, the demand curve for any normal commodity will be negatively sloped, indicating that a fall in price will increase the quantity demanded.

For most inferior goods, the demand curve also has a negative slope. The theoretical possibility that demand curves might not have a negative slope is considered in Extension 7-2.

SUMMARY

A. MARGINAL UTILITY AND CONSUMER CHOICE

- Marginal utility theory distinguishes between the total utility from the consumption of *all units* of some product and the incremental (or marginal) utility derived from consuming *one more unit* of the product.
- The basic assumption in marginal utility theory is that the utility that consumers derive from the consumption

of successive units of a product diminishes as the number of units consumed increases.
- Consumers are assumed to make their decisions in a way which maximizes their utility. They thus make their choices such that the utility derived from the last dollar spent on each product is equal. Another way of putting this is that the marginal utilities derived from the last unit of each product consumed will be proportional to their prices.

- Demand curves have negative slopes because when the price of one product, *X*, falls, each consumer responds by increasing purchases of *X* sufficiently to restore the ratio of that product's marginal utility to its now lower price (MU_X/p_X) to the same level achieved for all other products.

B. THE DISTINCTION BETWEEN TOTAL AND MARGINAL UTILITY

- The total value that consumers place on some quantity of a product consumed is given by the area under the demand curve up to that quantity. The market value is given by an area below the market price up to that quantity. Consumer surplus is the difference between the two. In other words, consumer surplus is the difference between what the consumers would be *prepared to pay* for some quantity of the good and what the consumers *actually pay* for that quantity of the good.
- Consumer surplus arises because a consumer can purchase every unit of a product at a price equal to the value placed on the last unit purchased. The negative slope of demand curves implies that the value that consumers place on all other units purchased exceeds the value of the last unit purchased and hence that all but the last unit purchased yields consumer surplus.
- It is important to distinguish between total and marginal values because choices concerning a bit more and a bit less cannot be predicted from a knowledge of total values. The paradox of value involves a confusion between total value and marginal value.
- Price is related to the *marginal* value that consumers place on having a bit more or a bit less of some product; it bears no necessary relationship to the *total* value that consumers place on all of the units consumed of that product.
- Consumers will consume any good that has a zero price up to the point where the marginal value that they place on further consumption is zero.

C. INCOME AND SUBSTITUTION EFFECTS OF PRICE CHANGES

- A change in the price of a product generates both an income effect and a substitution effect. The substitution effect is the reaction of the consumer to the change in relative prices, with purchasing power held constant. The substitution effect leads the consumer to increase purchases of the product whose relative price has fallen.
- The income effect is the reaction of the consumer to the change in purchasing power that is caused by the price change, holding relative prices constant. A fall in one price will lead to an increase in the consumer's purchasing power and thus to an increase in purchases of all normal goods.
- The combined income and substitution effects ensure that the quantity demanded of any normal good will increase when its money price falls, other things being equal. This means that normal goods have negatively sloped demand curves.

KEY CONCEPTS

Total utility and marginal utility
Utility maximization
Equality of *MU/p* across different
   goods

Slope of the demand curve
Consumer surplus
The paradox of value
Free goods and scarce goods

Income effect and substitution effect
The law of demand and its possible
   exceptions

DISCUSSION QUESTIONS

1. In an effort to promote responsible drinking and to encourage the use of designated drivers, many campus bars in the country have started offering soft drinks at very low prices, sometimes even free. Describe the results you would expect in terms of the income and substitution effects.

2. Describe the difference in behaviour at a campus party at which drinks are free between someone who imbibes up to the point where the *marginal* value of more alcohol consumed is zero and someone who imbibes up to the point where the *average* value of alcohol consumed is zero.

3. Between 1980 and 1994, the cost of purchasing a representative bundle of consumer goods rose by almost 100 percent, as measured by the Consumer Price Index. What else would you need to know to

find out what had happened to the average Canadian's real income?

4. Compare and contrast the consequences of the income effect of a drastic fall in food prices with the consequences of a rise in incomes when prices are constant.

5. Mary is willing to pay $10 for the first widget that she purchases each year, $9 for the second, $8 for the third, and so on down to $1 for the tenth and nothing for the eleventh. How many widgets will she buy, and what will be her consumer surplus, if widgets cost $3 each? What will happen if the price of widgets rises to $5? Can you state a generalization about the relationship between consumer surplus obtained and the price of a product?

6. Two economics professors in the United States recently estimated that a 25 percent increase in wages will cause the average individual to reduce the time that he or she spends sleeping by about 1 percent. Interpret this in terms of the substitution effect. Would you expect to find an income effect on the amount of time that a person spends sleeping?

7. Consider the following common scenario. An economist is attending a conference in an unfamiliar city. She is in the mood for a high-quality dinner and wanders through the centre of the city looking for a restaurant. After narrowing her search to two establishments, she ultimately selects the restaurant with the higher prices. Because she is an economist, we know that she is rational. What might account for this behaviour?

8. Predict the relative magnitudes of changes in consumption due to a 10 percent rise in the prices of the following commodities. Pay particular attention to the expected size of the income effects.

   a. Salt
   b. Blue jeans
   c. Gasoline
   d. Automobiles
   e. Aspirin

9. One often-touted characteristic of the "information superhighway" is the ability of consumers to have access to 500-channel cable systems. However, recent experiments by selected telecommunication companies with such super cable systems met with only lukewarm consumer response. Why might consumers not respond positively to a 200 to 500 percent increase in viewing options?

10. Medical and hospital services in Canada are provided at zero cost to all Canadians and are paid for out of general government revenues. What will be the *marginal value* of such services consumed by each Canadian if the government provides funds to meet all demand? What will differ when the government reduces the supply of these services (in order to save money to reduce their budget deficits)?

APPENDIX TO CHAPTER 7

Indifference Curve Analysis

In Chapter 7, we covered some basic material concerning the theory of demand; here we extend the treatment of demand theory by considering in more detail the assumptions about consumer behaviour that underlie the theory of demand.

The history of demand theory has seen two major breakthroughs. The first was *marginal utility theory*, which we used in Chapter 7. By distinguishing total and marginal values, this theory helped to explain the so-called paradox of value. The second breakthrough came with *indifference theory*, which showed that all that is required to develop demand theory is to assume that consumers can always say which of two consumption bundles they prefer without having to say *by how much* they prefer it.

Indifference theory, which is sometimes called the modern theory of demand, is based on *indifference curves*.

INDIFFERENCE CURVES

Start with an imaginary consumer who currently has available some specific bundle of goods, say, 18 units of clothing and 10 units of food. Now offer the consumer an alternative bundle of, say, 13 units of clothing and 15 units of food. This alternative combination of goods has 5 fewer units of clothing and 5 more units of food than the first one. Whether the consumer prefers this new bundle depends on the relative valuation that he places on 5 more units of food and 5 fewer units of clothing. If he values the extra food more than the forgone clothing, he will prefer the new bundle to the original one. If he values the extra food less than the foregone clothing, he will prefer the original bundle. If the consumer values the extra food the same as the forgone clothing, he is said to be *indifferent* between the two bundles.

Suppose that after much trial and error, we have identified several bundles between which the consumer is indifferent. In other words, each bundle gives the consumer equal satisfaction or utility. They are shown in Table 7A-1.

There will, of course, be combinations of the two products other than those enumerated in Table 7A-1 that will give the same level of satisfaction to the consumer. All of these combinations are shown in Figure 7A-1 by the smooth curve that passes through the points plotted from the table. This curve, called an **indifference curve,** shows all combinations of products that yield the same satisfaction to the consumer; the consumer is indifferent between the combinations indicated by any two points on one indifference curve.

Any points above the curve show combinations of food and clothing that the consumer would prefer to points on the curve. Consider, for example, the combination of 20 units of food and

TABLE 7A-1
Alternative Bundles Giving a Consumer Equal Utility

Bundle	Clothing	Food
a	30	5
b	18	10
c	13	15
d	10	20
e	8	25
f	7	30

These bundles all lie on a single indifference curve. Because all of these bundles of food and clothing give the consumer equal utility, the consumer is indifferent between them.

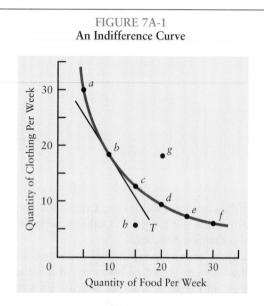

FIGURE 7A-1
An Indifference Curve

This indifference curve shows combinations of food and clothing that yield equal utility and between which the consumer is indifferent. Points *a* through *f* are plotted from Table 7A-1. The smooth curve through them is an indifference curve; each combination on it gives equal satisfaction to the consumer. Point *g* above the line is a preferred combination to any point on the line; point h below the line is an inferior combination to any point on the line. The slope of the line *T* gives the marginal rate of substitution at point *b*. Moving down the curve from *b* to *f*, the slope flattens, showing that the more food and the less clothing the consumer has, the less willing the consumer will be to sacrifice further clothing to get more food.

and to the left of the curve represent bundles that are inferior to bundles represented by points on the curve.

DIMINISHING MARGINAL RATE OF SUBSTITUTION

How much clothing would the consumer be prepared to give up to get one more unit of food? The answer to this question measures what is called the marginal rate of substitution of clothing for food. The **marginal rate of substitution (MRS)** is the amount of one product that a consumer is prepared to give up to get one more unit of another product.

The first basic assumption of indifference theory is that the algebraic value of the *MRS* is always negative.

A negative *MRS* means that to increase consumption of one product, the consumer is prepared to decrease consumption of a second product. The negative value of the marginal rate of substitution is indicated graphically by the negative slope of all indifference curves. (See, for example, the curve in Figure 7A-1.)

The second basic assumption of indifference theory is that the marginal rate of substitution between any two products depends on the amounts of the products currently being consumed.

Consider a case in which the consumer has a lot of clothing and only a little food. Common sense suggests that the consumer might be willing to give up quite a bit of plentiful clothing to get one unit more of scarce food. It suggests as well that a consumer with a little clothing and a lot of food would be willing to give up only a little scarce clothing to get one more unit of already plentiful food.

This example illustrates the hypothesis of **diminishing marginal rate of substitution.** The less of one product, A, and the more of a second product, B, that the consumer has already, the smaller the amount of A that the consumer will be willing to give up to get one additional unit of B. The hypothesis says that the marginal rate of substitution changes when the amounts of two products consumed change. The graphical expression of this is that any indifference curve becomes flatter as the consumer moves downward and to the right along the curve. In Figure 7A-1, a movement downward and to the right means that less clothing and more

18 units of clothing, represented by point *g* in Figure 7A-1. Although it may not be obvious that this bundle must be preferred to bundle *a* (which has more clothing but less food), it is obvious that it will be preferred to bundle *c* because both less clothing and less food are represented at *c* than at *g*. Inspection of the graph shows that any point above the curve will be superior to some points on the curve in the sense that it will contain both more food and more clothing than those points on the curve. However, because all points on the curve are equal in the consumer's eyes, any point above the curve must be superior to all points on the curve. By a similar argument, all points below

TABLE 7A-2
The Marginal Rate of Substitution Between Clothing and Food

Movement	(1) Change in Clothing	(2) Change in Food	(3) Marginal Rate of Substitution (1) ÷ (2)
From a to b	−12	5	−2.4
From b to c	−5	5	−1.0
From c to d	−3	5	−0.6
From d to e	−2	5	−0.4
From e to f	−1	5	−0.2

The marginal rate of substitution of clothing for food declines (in absolute value) as the quantity of food increases. This table is based on Table 7A-1. When the consumer moves from a to b, he gives up 12 units of clothing and gains 5 units of food; he remains at the same level of overall satisfaction. The consumer at point a is prepared to sacrifice 12 units of clothing for 5 units of food (i.e., 12/5 = 2.4 units of clothing per unit of food obtained). When the consumer moves from b to c, he sacrifices 5 units of clothing for 5 units of food (a rate of substitution of 1 unit of clothing for each unit of food).

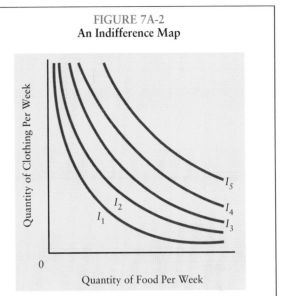

FIGURE 7A-2
An Indifference Map

Quantity of Clothing Per Week (vertical axis)

I_1, I_2, I_3, I_4, I_5

Quantity of Food Per Week (horizontal axis)

An indifference map consists of a set of indifference curves. All points on a particular curve indicate alternative combinations of food and clothing that give the consumer equal satisfaction. The farther the curve is from the orgin, the higher is the level of satisfaction it represents. For example, I_5 is a higher indifference curve than I_4, which means that all the points on I_5 yield a higher level of satisfaction than do the points on I_4.

food is being consumed. The decreasing steepness of the curve means that the consumer is willing to sacrifice less and less clothing to get each additional unit of food. [12]

The hypothesis is illustrated in Table 7A-2, which is based on the example of food and clothing in Table 7A-1. The last column of the table shows the rate at which the consumer is prepared to sacrifice units of clothing per unit of food obtained. At first, the consumer will sacrifice 2.4 units of clothing to get 1 unit more of food, but as his consumption of clothing diminishes and his consumption of food increases, the consumer becomes less and less willing to sacrifice further clothing for more food.

THE INDIFFERENCE MAP

So far, we have constructed only a single indifference curve. However, starting at any other point of Figure 7A-1, such as g, there will be other combinations that will yield equal satisfaction to the consumer. If the points indicating all of these combina-

tions are connected, they will form another indifference curve. This exercise can be repeated as many times as we wish, and we can generate as many indifference curves as we wish. The farther any indifference curve is from the origin, the higher will be the level of satisfaction given by any of the points on the curve.

A set of indifference curves is called an **indifference map**, an example of which is shown in Figure 7A-2. It specifies the consumer's tastes by showing his rate of substitution between the two products for every possible level of current consumption of these products.

When economists say that a consumer's tastes are *given*, they do not mean that the consumer's current consumption pattern is given; rather, they mean that the consumer's entire indifference map is given.

FIGURE 7A-3
A Budget Line

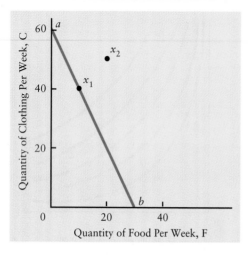

The budget line shows the quantities of goods available to a consumer given money income and the prices of goods. Any point in this diagram indicates a combination (or bundle) of so much food and so much clothing. Point x_1, for example, indicates 40 units of clothing and 10 units of food per week.

With an income of $720 a week and prices of $24 per unit for food and $12 per unit for clothing, the consumer's budget line is *ab*. This line shows all the combinations of F and C available to a consumer spending this income at these prices. The consumer could spend all of this money income on clothing and obtain 60 units of clothing and zero food each week. The consumer could likewise go to the other extreme and purchase only food, buying 30 units of F and zero units of C. The consumer could also choose an intermediate position and consume some of both goods—for example, spending $240 to buy 10 units of F and $480 to buy 40 units of C (point x_1). Points above the budget line, such as x_2, are not attainable.

THE BUDGET LINE

Indifference curves illustrate consumers' tastes. To develop a complete theory of their choices, we must also illustrate the alternatives available to them. These we show as the solid line *ab* in Figure 7A-3. That line, called a **budget line,** shows all the combinations of food and clothing that the consumer can buy if he spends a fixed amount of money, in this case his entire money income of $720 per week, at

fixed prices of the products. (It is also sometimes called an *isocost line* because all points on it represent bundles of goods with the same total cost.)

PROPERTIES OF THE BUDGET LINE

The budget line has several important properties:

1. Points on the budget line indicate bundles of products that use up the consumer's entire income. (Try, for example, the point 20C, 20F.)

2. Points between the budget line and the origin indicate bundles of products that cost less than the consumer's income. (Try, for example, the point 20C, 10F.)

3. Points above the budget line indicate combinations of products that cost more than the consumer's income. (Try, for example, the point 30C, 40F.)

The budget line shows all combinations of products that are available to the consumer given his money income and the prices of the goods that he purchases.

We can also show the consumer's alternatives with an equation that uses symbols to express the information contained in the budget line. Let E stand for the consumer's money income, which must be equal to the consumer's total expenditure on food and clothing. If P_F and P_C represent the money prices of food and clothing, respectively, and F and C represent the quantities of food and clothing chosen, then spending on clothing is equal to P_F times F, and spending on clothing is P_C times C. Thus the equation for the budget line is

$$E = P_F \times F + P_C \times C$$

THE SLOPE OF THE BUDGET LINE

Look again at the budget line shown in Figure 7A-3. The vertical intercept is 60 units of clothing, and the horizontal intercept is 30 units of food. Thus the slope is equal to −2. The minus sign means that increases in purchases of one of the goods must be accompanied by decreases in purchases of the other. The numerical value of the slope indicates how much of one good must be given up to obtain an additional unit of the other; in our example, the slope of −2 means that it is necessary to forgo the purchase of 2 units of clothing to acquire 1 extra unit of food.

Recall that in Chapter 4, we contrasted the *absolute,* or *money,* price of a product with its *relative* price, which is the ratio of its absolute price to that of some other product or group of products. One important point is that the relative price determines the slope of the budget line. In terms of our example of food and clothing, the slope of the budget line is determined by the relative price of food in terms of clothing, P_F/P_C; with the price of food (P_F) at $12 per unit and the price of clothing (P_C) at $6 per unit, the slope of the budget line (in absolute value) is −2. [13]

The significance of the slope of the budget line for food and clothing is that it reflects the *opportunity cost* of food in terms of clothing. To increase food consumption while maintaining expenditure constant, one must move along the budget line and therefore consume less clothing; the slope of the budget line determines how much clothing must be given up to obtain an additional unit of food.

The opportunity cost of food in terms of clothing is measured by the slope of the budget line, which is equal to the relative price ratio, P_F/P_C.

In the example, with fixed income and with the relative price of food in terms of clothing (P_F/P_C) equal to 2, it is necessary to forgo the purchase of 2 units of clothing to acquire 1 extra unit of food. The opportunity cost of a unit of food is thus 2 units of clothing. Notice that the relative price (in our example, $P_F/P_C = 2$) is consistent with an infinite number of absolute prices. If $P_F = \$40$ and $P_C = \$20$, it is still necessary to sacrifice 2 units of clothing to acquire 1 unit of food.[1] This shows that relative, not absolute, prices determine opportunity cost.

THE CONSUMER'S UTILITY-MAXIMIZING CHOICE

An indifference map describes the preferences of a consumer, and a budget line describes the possibili-

ties available to a consumer. To predict what a consumer will actually do, both sets of information must be combined. This is done in Figure 7A-4. The consumer's budget line is shown by the straight line, and the curves from the indifference map are also shown. Any point on the budget line is attainable, but which point will actually be chosen by the consumer?

Because the consumer wishes to maximize utility, he wishes to reach the highest attainable indifference curve. Inspection of Figure 7A-4 shows that if the consumer purchases any bundle on the budget line at a point cut by an indifference curve, a higher indifference curve can be reached. Only when the bundle purchased is such that the indifference curve is tangent to the budget line is it impossible for the consumer to reach a higher curve by altering his purchases.

The consumer's utility is maximized at the point where an indifference curve is tangent to the budget line. At that point, the consumer's marginal rate of substitution for the two goods is equal to the relative prices of the two goods.

The intuitive explanation for this result is that if the consumer values goods differently than the market does, there is room for profitable exchange. The consumer can give up some of the good that he values relatively less than the market does and take in return some of the good that he values relatively more than the market does. When the consumer is prepared to exchange goods at the same rate as they can be traded on the market, there is no further opportunity for the consumer to raise utility by substituting one product for the other.

The theory thus proceeds by supposing that the consumer is presented with market prices that he cannot change and then analyzing how the consumer adjusts to these prices by choosing a bundle of goods such that, at the margin, his own subjective evaluation of the goods coincides with the valuations given by market prices.

We now use this theory to predict the typical consumer's response to a change in income and in prices.

THE CONSUMER'S REACTION TO A CHANGE IN INCOME

A change in the consumer's money income will, *ceteris paribus,* shift the budget line. For example, if the

---

[1]Of course, with a given income, the consumer can afford much less of each at these higher money prices, but the opportunity cost of food in terms of clothing remains unchanged.

FIGURE 7A-4
The Consumer's Choice

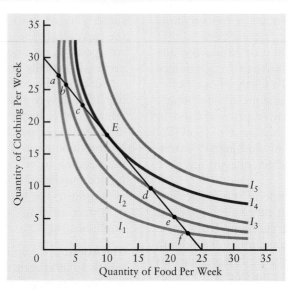

The consumer's utility is maximized at *E*, where an indifference curve is tangent to the budget line. The consumer has a money income of $750 per week and faces money prices of $25 per unit for clothing and $30 per unit for food. A combination of units of clothing and food indicated by point *a* on I_1 is attainable, but by moving along the budget line, higher indifference curves can be reached. The same is true at *b* on I_2 and at *c* on I_3. At *E*, however, where an indifference curve (I_4) is tangent to the budget line, it is impossible to reach a higher curve by moving along the budget line. A consumer who altered the consumption bundle by moving from *E* to *d*, for example, would move to the lower indifference curve I_3 and hence to a lower level of utility.

consumer's income doubles, he will be able to buy twice as much of both goods compared with any combination on his previous budget line. The budget line will therefore shift out parallel to itself to indicate this expansion in the consumer's consumption possibilities. (The fact that it will be a parallel shift is established by our previous demonstration that the slope of the budget line depends only on the relative price of the two products.)

For each level of income, there will be a utility-maximizing point at which an indifference curve is tangent to the relevant budget line. Each such utility-maximizing position means that the consumer is doing as well as possible at that level of income. If we move the budget line through all possible levels of income and if we join up all the utility-maximizing points, we will trace out what is called an **income-consumption line,** an example of which is shown in Figure 7A-5. This line shows how the consumption bundle changes as income changes, with relative prices being held constant.

THE CONSUMER'S REACTION TO A CHANGE IN PRICE

We already know that a change in the relative price of the two goods changes the slope of the budget line. Given the price of clothing, for each possible price of food there is a utility-maximizing consumption bundle for the consumer. If we connect these bundles, at a given money income, we will trace out a **price-consumption line,** as shown in Figure 7A-6. Notice that in this example, as the relative prices of food and clothing change, the relative quantities of

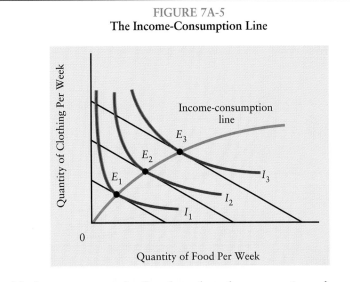

FIGURE 7A-5
The Income-Consumption Line

The income-consumption line shows how the consumer's purchases react to a change in money income with relative prices being held constant. Increases in money income cause a parallel outward shift of the budget line, moving the utility-maximizing point from E_1 to E_2 to E_3. By joining all the utility-maximizing points, an income-consumption line is traced out.

food and clothing purchased also change. In particular, as the price of food falls, the consumer buys more food and less clothing.

DERIVATION OF THE DEMAND CURVE

What happens to the consumer's demand for some product, say, gasoline, as the price of that product changes, *holding constant the prices of all other goods?*

If there were only two products purchased by consumers, we could derive a demand curve for one of the products from the price-consumption line like the one shown in Figure 7A-6. When there are many products, however, a change in the price of one product generally causes substitution toward (or away from) *all other goods.* Thus we would like to have a simple way of representing the individual's tastes in a world of many products.

In part (i) of Figure 7A-7, a new type of indifference map is plotted in which litres of gasoline per

month are measured on the horizontal axis and the *value* of all other goods consumed per month is plotted on the vertical axis. We have in effect used "everything but gasoline" as the second product. The indifference curves in this figure then show the rate at which the consumer is prepared to substitute gasoline for money (which allows him to buy all other goods) at each level of consumption of gasoline and of all other goods.

To illustrate the derivation of demand curves, we use the numerical example shown in Figure 7A-7. The consumer is assumed to have an after-tax money income of $4,000 per month. This level of money income is plotted on the vertical axis, showing that if the consumer consumes no gasoline, he can consume $4,000 worth of other goods each month. When gasoline costs $1.50 per litre, the consumer could buy a maximum of 2,667 litres per month. This gives rise to the innermost budget line. Given the consumer's tastes, utility is maximized at point E_0, consuming 600 litres of gasoline and $3,100 worth of other products.

Next let the price of gasoline fall to $1.00 per litre. Now the maximum possible consumption of

FIGURE 7A-6
The Price-Consumption Line

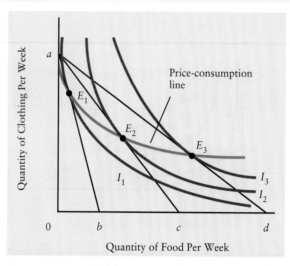

The price-consumption line shows how the consumer's purchases react to a change in one price with money income and other prices being held constant. Decreases in the price of food (with money income and the price of clothing being held constant) pivot the budget line from ab to ac to ad. The utility-maximizing bundle moves from E_1 to E_2 to E_3. By joining all the utility-maximizing points, a price-consumption line is traced out, showing more food and less clothing bought as the price of food falls.

gasoline is 4,000 litres per month, giving rise to the middle budget line in the figure. The consumer's utility is maximized, as always, at the point where the new budget line is tangent to an indifference curve. At this point, E_1, the consumer is consuming 1,200 litres of gasoline per month and spending $2,800 on all other goods. Finally, let the price fall to 50 cents per litre. The consumer can now buy a maximum of 8,000 litres per month, giving rise to the outermost of the three budget lines. The consumer maximizes utility by consuming 2,200 litres of gasoline per month and spending $2,900 on other products.

If we let the price vary over all possible amounts, we will trace out a complete price-consumption line, as shown in the figure. The points derived in the preceding paragraph are merely three points on this line.

We have now derived all that we need to plot the consumer's demand curve for gasoline, now that we know how much the consumer will purchase at each price. To draw the curve, we merely replot the data from part (i) of Figure 7A-7 onto a demand graph, as shown in part (ii) of Figure 7A-7.

Like part (i), part (ii) has quantity of gasoline on the horizontal axis. By placing one graph under the other, we can directly transcribe the quantity determined on the upper graph to the lower one. We first do this for the 600 litres consumed on the innermost budget line. We now note that the price of gasoline that gives rise to that budget line is $1.50 per litre. Plotting 600 litres against $1.50 in part (ii) produces the point x, derived from point E_0 in part (i). This is one point on the consumer's demand curve. Next we consider the middle budget line, which occurs when the price of gasoline is $1.00 per litre. We take the figure of 1,200 litres from point E_1 in part (i) and transfer it to part (ii). We then plot this quantity against the price of $1.00 to get the point y on the demand curve. Doing the same thing for point E_2

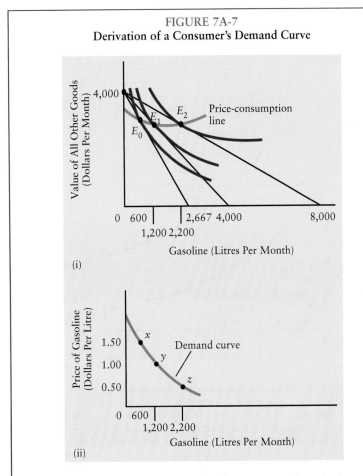

FIGURE 7A-7
Derivation of a Consumer's Demand Curve

Every point on the price-consumption line corresponds to both a price of the product and a quantity demanded; this is the information required for a demand curve. In part (i), the consumer has a money income of \$4,000 and alternatively faces prices of \$1.50, \$1.00, and \$0.50 per litre of gasoline, choosing positions E_0, E_1, and E_2 at each price. The information for litres demanded at each price is then plotted in part (ii) to yield the consumer's demand curve. The three points x, y, and z in part (ii) correspond to the points E_0, E_1, and E_2 in part (i).

yields the point z in part (ii): price 50 cents, quantity 2,200 litres.

Repeating the operation for all prices yields the demand curve in part (ii). Note that the two parts of Figure 7A-7 describe the same behaviour. Both parts measure the quantity of gasoline on the horizontal axes; the only difference is that in part (i) the price of gasoline determines the slope of the budget line, whereas in part (ii) the price of gasoline is plotted explicitly on the vertical axis.

THE SLOPE OF THE DEMAND CURVE

The price-consumption line in part (i) of Figure 7A-7 indicates that as price decreases, the quantity of gasoline demanded increases, thus giving rise to the negatively sloped demand curve in part (ii). As we saw in Chapter 7, the key to understanding the negative slope of the demand curve is to distinguish between the income effect and the substitution effect of a change in

FIGURE 7A-8
The Income Effect and the Substitution Effect of a Price Change

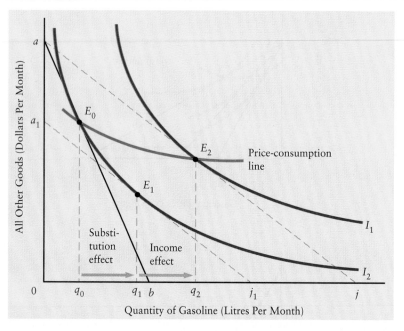

The substitution effect is defined by sliding the budget line around a fixed indifference curve; the income effect is defined by a parallel shift of the budget line. The original budget line is at ab, and a fall in the price of gasoline takes it to aj. The original utility-maximizing point is at E_0 with q_0 of gasoline being consumed, and the new utility-maximizing point is at E_2 with q_2 of gasoline being consumed. To remove the income effect, imagine reducing the consumer's money income until the original indifference curve is just attainable. We do this by shifting the line aj to a parallel line nearer the origin a_1j_1 that just touches the indifference curve that passes through E_0. The intermediate point E_1 divides the quantity change into a substitution effect q_0q_1 and an income effect q_1q_2.

price. This distinction can be made more precisely, and somewhat differently, using indifference curves.

Income and Substitution Effects

In Chapter 7, we examined the substitution effect of a reduction in price by eliminating the income effect. We did this by reducing money income until the consumer could just purchase the original bundle of goods. We then examined how the change in relative prices affected the consumer's choices. In indifference theory, however, the income effect is removed by changing money income until the *original level of utility*—the original indifference curve—can just be achieved. This results in a slightly different measure of the income effect, but the principle involved in separating the total change into an income effect and a substitution effect is exactly the same as in Chapter 7.[2]

The separation of the two effects according to indifference theory is shown in Figure 7A-8. The figure shows in greater detail part of the price-consumption line first drawn in Figure 7A-7. Points E_0 and E_2 are on the price-consumption line for gasoline. We can think of the separation occurring in the following way. After the price of the good has fallen, we reduce money income *until the original indifference curve can just be obtained*. This leads the consumer to move from point E_0 to an intermediate point E_1, and this response is defined as the substitution effect. Then, to measure the income effect, we restore money income. The consumer moves from the point E_1 to the final point E_2, and this response is defined as the income effect.

---

[2]The approach used in Chapter 7 defines constant real income as constant purchasing power. The introduction of indifference curves allows a slightly more sophisticated concept of constant real income: constant utility as captured by the original indifference curve. However, the two are very similar in practice, and indeed, in most empirical applications, the approach taken in Chapter 7 is used.

SUMMARY

A. INDIFFERENCE CURVES

- Indifference curves describe consumers' tastes or preferences. A single indifference curve joins combinations of products that give consumers equal satisfaction and among which they are therefore indifferent. An indifference map is a set of indifference curves.
- The basic hypothesis about tastes is that of *diminishing marginal rate of substitution*. This hypothesis states that the less of one good and the more of another the consumer has, the less willing she will be to give up some of the first good to get an additional unit of the second. This means that indifference curves are downward sloping and convex to the origin.

B. BUDGET LINES

- The budget line shows all combinations of products that are available to a consumer with a given amount of money income who faces given prices of the products. The slope of the budget line is determined by the relative prices of the products; the position of the budget line is determined by both prices and income.

C. UTILITY MAXIMIZATION

- Given the constraint of the budget line, the consumer's utility is maximized by consuming a bundle of goods such that the indifference curve through that bundle is tangent to the budget line.
- The income-consumption line shows how quantity consumed changes as income changes with relative prices being held constant.
- The price-consumption line shows how quantity consumed changes when the price of one product changes. When prices change, the consumer will consume more of the product whose relative price falls.
- The price-consumption line relating the purchases of one particular product to all other products contains the same information as a conventional demand curve. The horizontal axis measures quantity, and the slope of the budget line measures price. Transferring this price-quantity information to a diagram whose axes represent price and quantity yields a demand curve.
- The effect of a change in price of one product, all other prices and money income being held constant, changes not only relative prices but also real incomes. A change in price affects consumption through both the substitution effect and the income effect.

DISCUSSION QUESTIONS

1. We have all seen people who consume too much alcohol at parties. Often, even though these individuals are quite sick, they continue to drink. Draw an indifference curve for alcohol for a person who has begun to get ill but still continues to drink. Explain your representation.

2. Figure 7A-5 shows the behaviour of a hypothetical consumer as income increases. Do you think that such responses would hold globally? How might the response differ if the individual has $10,000 in income versus $1 million in income? Would there ever be a time when a person might exhibit no response to an increase in income? If so, what would the indifference map look like in that case?

CHAPTER **8**

PRODUCTION AND COST IN THE SHORT RUN

To find out how market prices and quantities are determined, we know that we must consider the interaction of demand *and* supply. In Chapter 7, we examined the theory of demand. In this chapter and the next, we build a theory of how firms behave. To understand supply, we must find out, among other things, what determines the cost of various goods and services. It turns out that for most products, cost and output are closely related. This implies that a convincing theory of cost is inextricably intertwined with a theory of the level of production. Chapters 8 and 9 develop just such a theory. Extension 8-1 considers the question of why firms even exist in the first place.

EXTENSION 8-1

WHY ARE THERE FIRMS?

Throughout this book, we study the role of markets in allocating resources. Markets work through the forces of supply and demand: People with a particular good or service to sell and people who wish to purchase that good or service satisfy their mutual desires by exchanging with each other.

However, not all mutually advantageous trade occurs through markets; often it occurs within institutions and, in particular, within firms. Most economists, like most other people, are inclined simply to take the existence of firms for granted. But in a famous article published in 1937, Professor Ronald Coase of the University of Chicago, the recipient of the 1991 Nobel Prize in economics, took up the question posed in the title of this box.*

The key to understanding Coase's argument is to recognize that there are costs associated with transactions, known, appropriately enough, as **transactions costs.** When a firm purchases something, it must identify the market and then find what different quantities and qualities are available at what prices. This takes time and money; it usually involves some uncertainty. When the firm decides instead to produce the thing itself, it uses the command principle and orders the commmodity to be made to its desired specifications. The transactions costs may be lower, but the advantages of buying in a competitive market are lost. Furthermore, as the firm gets larger, the inefficiencies of the command system tend to become large compared with the efficiencies involved in decentralizing through the market system.

The firm must choose when to transact internally and when to transact through the market. For example, a car manufacturer must decide whether to purchase a certain component by contracting with a parts manufacturer to supply it or to "supply the component to itself" by producing it. Coase viewed the firm as an institution that economizes on transactions costs, and thus he argued that the market works best when transactions costs are low, but when transactions costs are high, the firm has an incentive to use internal mechanisms in place of market transactions.

Coase's insights have stimulated a great deal of further research by economists such as Professor Oliver Williamson of the University of California at Berkeley. This research has contributed to the understanding of the interaction of institutions and markets. Organization theorists have stressed that firms sometimes require less information than do markets for certain types of transactions; for example, transactions within firms do not require that the decision makers know market prices. Some research even shows that transactions within firms sometimes generate information that is useful to the firm; for example, a close relationship between the producer of a particular component and the user might lead to improvements in its design. Another aspect is that when firms internalize a production process, they use one type of contract (say, with employees) to replace a set of often more complicated contracts with external suppliers.

Coase's analysis has proved remarkably robust over the years, and its influence has spread throughout economics. As economic historian and 1993 Nobel laureate Douglass North recently put it, "Whenever transactions costs are high, institutions become important."

---

* "The Nature of the Firm," *Economica* (1937).

PROFITS AND COSTS

The theory of the firm is based on the assumption that firms maximize profits, an assumption that we will examine and criticize in Chapter 14. An immediate corollary of the assumption that firms maximize profits is that, given any particular level of output, they minimize costs.[1]

Before we begin our analysis of how profit-maximizing (and cost-minimizing) firms behave, it is worth taking a little time to be precise about exactly what economists mean when they use the words *profit* and *cost* and to examine some general consequences of profit maximization and cost minimization.

MOTIVATION: PROFIT MAXIMIZATION

Economists predict the behaviour of firms by studying the effect that making each choice available to the firm would have on profits. They then predict that firms will select the alternative that yields the largest profits. This theory does not say that profit is the *only* factor that influences the firm's behaviour; rather, it says that profits are important enough that assuming profits to be the firm's sole objective will produce predictions that are substantially correct.

FACTORS OF PRODUCTION

Firms seek profits by producing and selling products. In order to make their products, firms purchase materials such as metal, wood, electricity, and paint. They also purchase the services of factors of production—they hire workers, purchase or rent land, and purchase or rent machines. Economists use the word **inputs** to refer to all such purchases. They refer to the goods and services that result from the production process as **outputs**. One way of looking at the production process is to regard the inputs as being combined to produce the outputs. Another equally useful way is to regard the inputs as being used up, or sacrificed, to gain the outputs.

It is important to make the distinction among the different types of inputs. For example, among the inputs used to produce automobiles are steel, rubber, spark plugs, electricity, land, machinists, cost accountants, forklift operators, managers, designers, robots, drill presses, and painters. These inputs can be grouped into four broad classes: (1) those that are inputs for the automobile manufacturer but outputs for some other manufacturer, such as spark plugs, electricity, and steel; (2) those that are provided directly by nature, such as the land used by the automobile plant; (3) those that are provided directly by households, such as the services of workers; and (4) those that are provided by machines, such as drill presses and robots.

Inputs in the first group just mentioned are called **intermediate products**. They are goods that are produced by other firms, and they appear as inputs only because the stages of production are divided among different firms so that at any one stage, some firms are using as inputs goods produced by other firms. If these products are traced back to their sources, all production can be accounted for by the services of only three kinds of inputs, which we call **factors of production**. The three fundamental factors of production are:

- **Land.** Includes all gifts of nature, such as land and raw materials.[2]

- **Labour.** All physical and mental contributions that are provided by people are called labour.

- **Capital.** All manufactured aids to further production, such as machines, are referred to as capital.

Extensive use of capital is one distinguishing feature of modern production. Instead of making consumer goods with only the aid of simple natural tools, productive effort goes into the manufacture of tools, machines, and other goods that are desired not in themselves but as aids to making other goods.

---

[1]A firm's plant and equipment can be useful in its strategic behaviour against other firms. For example, a firm may sensibly invest in *unused* capacity as a means of detering entry into the industry by other firms. In this case, the firm would not be minimizing its costs for a given level of output, though such a strategy may be a profit-maximizing one. In our basic theory we ignore such strategic behaviour by firms and assume that the only purpose of plant and equipment is to produce current output. In this case, the assumption of profit maximization implies cost minimization. We examine strategic behaviour by firms in Chapter 12.

[2]Economists have begun to distinguish between land and the natural resources found on or below the land, such as oil, natural gas, or minerals. In Chapter 17, we discuss the pricing and use of non-renewable natural resources.

THE MEANING OF COST

Profits are the difference between the value of the goods that a firm sells and the cost of producing those goods. In later chapters, we will look at the firm's sales revenues. Here we are concerned with cost. **Cost,** to the producing firm, is the *value* of inputs used to produce its output.

Notice the emphasis on the word *value* in the definition. A given output produced by a given technique, say, 6,000 cars produced each week by General Motors with its present production methods, has a given set of inputs associated with it—so many working hours of various types of labourers, supervisors, managers, and technicians; so many tons of steel, glass, and aluminum; so many kilowatt-hours of electricity; and so many hours of the time of various machines. The cost of each can be calculated, and the sum of these separate costs is the total cost to General Motors of producing 6,000 cars per week.

Although the details of economic costing vary, they are governed by the principle of *opportunity cost,* a concept introduced in Chapter 1. Recall that the opportunity cost of using something in a particular venture is the benefit forgone by not using it in its best alternative use.

THE MEASUREMENT OF OPPORTUNITY COST

To measure opportunity cost, the firm must assign to each of its inputs a monetary value equal to what it has sacrificed to use the input. Applying this principle to specific cases is not quite as easy as it may seem at first.

Purchased and Hired Factors

Assigning costs is a straightforward process when inputs purchased in one period are used up in the same period and when the price that the firm pays is determined by forces beyond its control. Inputs of intermediate products purchased from other firms fall into this category. If a firm pays $150 per ton for steel, it has sacrificed its claims to something else the $150 can buy, and thus the purchase price is a good measure of the firm's opportunity cost of using 1 ton of steel.

Inputs of hired factors of production are also in this category. Firms hire labour, and the opportunity cost is the price that must be paid for these labour services. This includes the wage rate and all related expenses, such as contributions to pension funds, unemployment and disability insurance, and other fringe benefits. Firms also use borrowed money. Interest payments measure the opportunity cost of borrowed funds because the money paid out as interest could have been used to buy something else of equivalent monetary value.

Imputed Costs

Some of the inputs that the firm uses are neither purchased nor hired for current use. Their use requires no payment to anyone outside the firm, so the costs of using them are not obvious. The opportunity cost of these inputs is the amount that the firm would earn if it were to shift the inputs to their next best use. When these costs are calculated, they are called **imputed costs,** costs that must be inferred because they are not made as money payments. The following examples all involve imputed costs.

Using the Firm's Own Money.   Consider a firm that uses $100,000 of its own money to finance production, which instead it could have loaned out for one year at 7 percent interest, yielding $7,000 in interest income. This amount should be deducted from the firm's revenue as the cost of funds used in production. If the firm earns only $6,000 over all other costs, one would not say that the firm made a profit of $6,000 but rather that it lost $1,000. If it had closed down completely and merely loaned out its money to someone else, it could have earned $7,000.

Costs of Durable Assets.   The costs of using assets owned by the firm, such as buildings, equipment, and machinery, include a charge, called **depreciation,** for the loss in value of an asset over a period of time because of its use in production, due to physical wear and tear, and to obsolescence. The economic cost of owning an asset for a year is the loss in value of the asset during the year. Accountants use several conventional methods to show depreciation based on the price originally paid for the asset, which is called its *historical cost.* One of the most common is *straight-line depreciation,* in which the same amount of historical cost is deducted in every year of useful life of the asset. Although historical cost is often a useful approximation, in some cases it may differ substantially from the depreciation required by the opportunity cost principle. Consider two examples.

1. *Assets that may be resold.* A woman buys a new automobile for $15,000. She intends to use it

for six years and then sell it for $6,000. She may think that, using straight-line depreciation, this will cost her $1,500 per year. If after one year, however, the value of her car on the used-car market is $12,000, it has cost her $3,000 to use the car during the first year. Why should she charge herself $3,000 depreciation during the first year? After all, she does not intend to sell the car for six years. The answer is that one of the purchaser's alternatives is to buy a one-year-old car and operate it for five years. Indeed, that is the position she is in after the first year. Whether she likes it or not, she has paid $3,000 for the use of the car during the first year of its life. If the market had valued her car at $14,000 after one year (instead of $12,000), the correct depreciation would have been only $1,000.

2. *Assets that cannot be resold.* In the first example, an active used-asset market was available. At the other extreme, consider an asset that has no alternative use. This is sometimes called a *sunk cost.* Suppose that a firm has a set of machines that it purchased a few years ago for $100,000. These machines were expected to last 10 years, and the firm's accountant calculates the depreciation costs of these machines by the straight-line method at $10,000 per year. Assume also that the machines can be used to make one product and nothing else. Suppose, too, that they are installed in the firm's plant, they cannot be leased to any other firm, and their scrap value is negligible. In other words, the machines have no value except to this firm in its current operation. Suppose that the machines are used to produce the product, the cost of all other factors used will amount to $25,000, and the goods produced can be sold for $29,000.

Now, if the accountant's depreciation costs of running the machines are added in, the total cost of operation comes to $35,000; with revenues at $29,000, this yields an annual loss of $6,000 per year. It appears that the goods should not be made!

The fallacy in this argument lies in adding a charge based on the sunk cost of the machines as one of the costs of current operations. The machines have no alternative uses whatsoever. This means that their *opportunity cost is zero.* The total cost of producing this line of goods is thus only $25,000 per year (assuming that all other costs have been correctly assessed), and the line of production shows an annual return over all relevant costs (that is, a profit) of $4,000, not a loss of $6,000.

To see why the second calculation leads to the correct decision, we notice that if the firm abandons this line of production as unprofitable, it will have no money to pay out and no revenue received on this account. If the firm takes the economist's advice and pursues the line of production, it will pay out $25,000 and receive $29,000, thus making it $4,000 per year better off than if it had not done so. Clearly, the production is worth undertaking. The amount that the firm happens to have paid out for the machines in the past has no bearing whatever on deciding on the correct use of the machines once they are installed on the premises.

Because they involve neither current nor future costs, sunk costs should have no influence on deciding what is currently the most profitable thing to do.

This important principle of "let bygones be bygones" extends well beyond economics and is often ignored in poker, in war, and in love. Because you have invested heavily in a poker hand, a war, or a courtship does not mean that you should stick with it if the prospects of winning become very small. At every moment of decision making, maximizing behaviour is based on how *benefits from this time forward compare with current and future costs.*

Risk Taking.   One difficulty in imputing costs has to do with risk taking. Business enterprise is often a risky affair. Uninsured risks are borne by the owners of the firm, who, if the enterprise fails, may lose the money that they have invested in the firm.

Risk must be borne by someone. When the firm bears the risk, it will not carry on production unless it is compensated for the risk. If a firm does not yield a return that is sufficient to compensate for the risks involved, it will not be able to persuade people to invest in it. Those who buy the firm's shares expect a return that exceeds what they could have obtained if they had invested their money in a virtually riskless manner, say, by buying a government bond.

Suppose that a businesswoman invests $100,000 in a class of risky ventures and expects that most of the ventures will be successful but that some will fail. In fact, she expects that about $10,000 will be a total loss. (She does not know which specific ventures will be the losers; if she did, she would not invest in them.) Suppose further that she could earn a 10 percent return on an otherwise equivalent but riskless use of her funds (such as buying a government bond). To earn a $10,000 overall profit and recover the $10,000 expected loss, she needs to earn a $20,000 profit on the $90,000 of successful investment. This is a rate of return of 22.2 percent. She charges 10 percent for the use of her funds and 12.2 percent for bearing the risk of the venture.

Patents, Trademarks, and Other Special Advantages. Suppose that a firm owns a valuable patent or a highly desirable location or produces a popular brand-name product such as Coca-Cola or Molson Canadian. Each of these involves an opportunity cost to the firm in production (even if it was acquired free) because if the firm does not choose to use the special advantage itself, it could sell or lease it to others.

THE MEANING OF ECONOMIC PROFITS

Economic profits, sometimes also called *pure profits,* are the difference between the revenues received by the firm from the sale of output and the opportunity cost of all the inputs used to make the output. If costs are greater than revenues, such "negative profits" are called **losses.**

This definition *includes* in costs the imputed returns to capital and to risk taking. By doing so, it gives a special meaning to the words *profits* and *losses* that differs considerably from everyday usage. Table 8-1 illustrates by means of an example how economists use the terms cost and profit.

Other Definitions of Profits

Firms define profits as the excess of revenues over costs as measured by the conventions of accounting. Economists' definition of profits differs from one based on pure accounting conventions in a number of ways. Some of these differences affect the meaning of profits. Accountants do not charge for risk taking and use of the owner's own capital as costs, and thus these items are recorded by the firm as part of its profits. When a firm says it needs a certain amount of profit to stay in business, it is making sense within its definition, for its profits must be large enough to pay the costs of inputs that accounting conventions do not include as costs.

Economists would express the same notion by saying that the firm needs to cover *all* of its costs, including those that are not used in accounting. If the firm is covering all of its opportunity costs, it could not do better by using its resources in any other line of activity than the one currently being followed.

TABLE 8-1
The Calculation of Economic Profits: An Example

Gross revenue from sales	$1,000
Less: direct cost of production (materials, labour, electricity, etc.)	−650
"Gross profits" (or "contributions to overhead")	350
Less: other costs (depreciation, overhead, management salaries, interest on debt, etc.)	−140
"Net profits"	210
Less: Income taxes payable	−74
After-tax "net profits"	136
Less: normal profits (imputed charges for own capital used and for risk taking)	−130
Economic profits	$6

Economic profits are less than profits as defined by accountants. The main difference between economic profits and what a firm calls its net profits is in the subtraction of the imputed charges for use of capital owned by the firm and for risk taking. Income tax is levied on whatever definition of profits the taxing authorities choose, usually closely related to net profits. Although economic profits are necessarily less than net profits, they can be greater or less than normal profits, which include only the imputed charges for capital and risk. (In this example, they are much less.)

A situation in which revenues equal costs, including opportunity costs, is one in which economic profits are zero; such a situation is consistent with the firm remaining in business because all factors, hidden as well as visible, are being rewarded at least as well as they would be in their best alternative uses.

The term profit is sometimes used in a different way. Economists often use the term **normal profits** to refer to the opportunity costs of capital and risk taking. When this definition is used, we would say that the firm must earn normal profits if it is to be willing to stay in the industry.

The income-tax authorities have yet another definition of profits, which is implicit in the thousands of rules as to what may and may not be included as a deduction from revenue in arriving at taxable income. In some cases, the taxing authorities allow more for costs than accountants recommend; in other cases, they allow less than accountants recommend.

It is important to be clear about the various meanings of the term profit, not only to avoid fruitless semantic arguments but also because a theory that predicts certain behaviour when profit is defined in one way will not necessarily predict behaviour accurately if profit is defined in another way. For example, the prediction that new firms will seek to enter an industry whenever profits are earned will not stand up if it is tested against the accountants' definition of profits. Firms may be recording accounting profits but economic losses because they are not covering the full opportunity costs of their capital. In this case, the tendency will be for firms to leave rather than enter the industry.

The definition of *economic profits* as an excess over all opportunity costs is for many purposes the most useful, but to apply it to business behaviour or to tax policy, appropriate adjustments must be made. Conversely, to apply accounting or tax data to particular economic theories requires the reverse set of adjustments.

Henceforth, when we use the word profits, unless otherwise noted, we mean economic profits.

Profits and Resource Allocation

When resources are valued by the opportunity cost principle, their costs show how much these resources would earn if they were used in their best alternative uses. If there is an industry in which revenues exceed opportunity costs, the firms in that industry will be earning profits. The owners of factors of production will want to move resources into that industry because they can earn more there than in their present uses. Conversely, if in some other industry firms are incurring losses, resources in that industry could earn more revenues in other uses, and their owners will want to move them to those other uses. Only when economic profits are zero is there no incentive for resources to move into or out of an industry.

Profits and losses play a crucial signaling role in the workings of a free-market system.

Choices open
to the firm

Every firm knows that its total costs of production are positively related to its output. If it produces more, it must pay more to hire additional workers and to buy more of other inputs. Perhaps, more interestingly, many firms also find that their costs *per unit of output* are systematically related to their outputs. Both very low and very high levels of output are usually associated with high unit costs, whereas intermediate levels that are near the plant's normal output capacity are typically associated with lower unit costs of production. In the remainder of this chapter, we will see how and why costs vary with the level of production and with changes in factor prices.

Consider a firm that is producing a single product in a number of plants. Its sales have increased, and it decides that production should be increased correspondingly. Should a single plant be operated for longer hours, using overtime shifts, or should several plants each be operated for a slightly longer period of time? Such decisions concern how best to use *existing* plants and equipment. They involve time periods that are too short in which to build new plants or to install more equipment.

Rather different decisions must be made when managers make long-range plans. Should the firm adopt a highly automated process that will greatly reduce its wage bill? Or should it continue to build new plants that use current techniques? These matters concern what a firm should do when it is changing or replacing its plant and equipment. Such decisions may take a long time to put into effect.

In the examples just given, managers make decisions from known possibilities. Many firms also have research and development (R&D) staffs whose job it is to come up with new products and new methods of production. Such firms must decide how much money to devote to R&D and in what areas the payoff for new development will be largest. For example, if a shortage of a particular labour skill or raw material is anticipated, the research staff can be told to try to find ways to economize on that input or even to eliminate it from the production process.

TIME HORIZONS
FOR DECISION MAKING

Economists organize the decisions that firms make into three classes: (1) how best to employ existing plant and equipment—the *short run;* (2) what new plant and equipment and production processes to select, given known technical possibilities—the *long run;* and (3) how to encourage, or adapt to, the development of new techniques—the *very-long run.*

The Short Run

The **short run** is a time period in which the quantity of some inputs, called **fixed factors,** cannot be increased.[3] A fixed factor is usually an element of capital (such as plant and equipment), but it might be land, the services of management, or even the supply of skilled labour. Inputs that can be varied in the short run are called **variable factors.**

The short run does not correspond to a specific number of months or years. In some industries, it may extend over many years; in others, it may be a matter of months or even weeks. In the electric power industry, for example, it takes three or more years to acquire and install a steam turbine generator. An unforeseen increase in demand will involve a long period during which the extra demand must be met with the existing capital equipment. In contrast, a machine shop can acquire new equipment or sell existing equipment in a few weeks. An increase in demand will have to be met with the existing stock of capital for only a brief time, after which it can be adjusted to the level made desirable by the higher demand.

The Long Run

The **long run** is a time period in which all inputs may be varied but in which the basic technology of production cannot be changed. Like the short run, the long run does not correspond to a specific length of time.

The long run corresponds to the situation the firm faces when it is planning to go into business, to expand the scale of its operations, to branch out into new products or new areas, or to change its method of production. The firm's *planning decisions* are long-run decisions because they are made from given technological possibilities but with freedom to choose from a variety of production processes that will use factor inputs in different proportions.

The Very-Long Run

Unlike the short run and the long run, the **very-long run** is a period of time in which the technological possibilities available to a firm will change. Modern industrial societies are characterized by continuously changing technologies that lead to new and improved products and production methods.

Some of these technological advances are made by the firm's own research and development efforts. For example, much of the innovation in computer hardware and software has been made by IBM, Apple, and Microsoft. Some firms adopt technological changes developed by others. For example, liquid crystal displays and microprocessor chips have revolutionized dozens of industries that had nothing to do with developing them. Firms must regularly decide how much to spend in efforts to change technology either by developing new techniques or by adapting techniques that have been developed by others.

CONNECTING THE RUNS: THE PRODUCTION FUNCTION

The **production function** describes the precise physical relationship between factor inputs and output.

The various runs are simply different aspects of the same basic problem: getting output from inputs efficiently. They differ in terms of what the firm is able to change.

A simplified production function in which there are only two factors of production, labour and capital, will be considered here, but the conclusions apply equally when there are many factors. In the short run, which is the focus of the remainder of this chapter, capital is taken to be the fixed factor and labour the variable one. This chapter deals with the short-run situations in which output and cost change as different amounts of the variable input, labour, are used. Long-run situations in which both factors can be varied and very-long-run situations in which the production function changes are both covered in Chapter 9.

---

[3]Sometimes it is physically impossible to increase the quantity of a fixed factor in a short time. For instance, there is no way to build a hydroelectric dam or a power plant in a few months. In other cases, it might be physically possible but prohibitively expensive to increase the quantity of a fixed factor in a short time. For example, a suit-manufacturing firm could conceivably rent a building, buy and install new sewing machines, and hire a trained labour force in a few days if money were no consideration. Prohibitive costs and physical impossibility are both determinants of fixed factors.

SHORT-RUN CHOICES FOR THE FIRM

Suppose that a firm starts with a fixed amount of capital (say, 4 units) and contemplates applying various amounts of labour to it. Table 8-2 shows three different ways of looking at how output varies with the quantity of the variable factor.

TOTAL, AVERAGE, AND MARGINAL PRODUCTS

Total product *(TP)* is the total amount that is produced during a given period of time. If the inputs of all but one factor are held constant, total product will change as more or less of the variable factor is used. This variation is shown in columns 1 and 2 of Table 8-2, which gives a total product schedule. Part (i) of Figure 8-1 shows such a schedule graphically. (The shape of the curve will be discussed shortly.)

Average product *(AP)* is the total product divided by the number of units of the variable factor used to

TABLE 8-2
Variation of Output with Fixed Capital and Variable Labour

(1) Quantity of Labour *(L)*	(2) Total Product *(TP)*	(3) Average Product *(AP)*	(4) Marginal Product *(MP)*
0	0	–	
			15
1	15	15.0	
			19
2	34	17.0	
			14
3	48	16.0	
			12
4	60	15.0	
			2
5	62	12.4	

The relationship between changes in output and changes in the quantity of labour can be looked at in three ways. Capital is assumed to be fixed at 4 units. As the quantity of labour increases, the level of output (the total product) increases. Average product increases at first and then declines. The same is true of marginal product. Marginal product is shown between the lines because it refers to the *change* in output from one level of labour input to another. When the schedule is graphed, marginal products are plotted at the midpoint of the interval. For example, the marginal product of 12 would be plotted to correspond to a quantity of labour of 3.5.

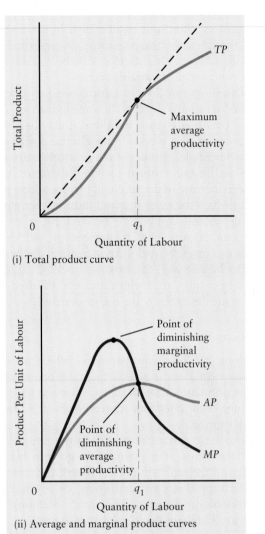

FIGURE 8-1
Total Product, Average Product, and Marginal Product Curves

(i) Total product curve

(ii) Average and marginal product curves

Total product *(TP)*, **average product** *(AP)*, and **marginal product** *(MP)* curves often have the shapes shown here. The total product curve in part (i) shows the total product steadily rising, first at an increasing rate and then at a decreasing rate. This causes both the average and the marginal product curves in part (ii) to rise at first and then to decline. The point of diminishing average productivity is q_1. At this point, $MP = AP$.

produce it. If we let the number of units of labour be denoted by L, the average product is given by

$$AP = \frac{TP}{L}$$

Notice in column 3 of Table 8-2 that as more of the variable factor is used, average product first rises and then falls. The level of output at which average product reaches a maximum (34 units of output in the example) is called the **point of diminishing average productivity.** Up to that point, average productivity is increasing; beyond that point, average productivity is decreasing.

Marginal product *(MP)*, sometimes called *incremental product* or **marginal physical product *(MPP)*,** is the change in total product resulting from the use of *one additional unit* of the variable factor:[4] **[14]**

$$MP = \frac{\Delta TP}{\Delta L}$$

Computed values of marginal product are shown in column 4 of Table 8-2. The figures in this column are placed between the other lines of the table to stress that the concept refers to the *change* in output caused by the *change* in quantity of the variable factor. For example, the increase in labour from 3 to 4 units ($\Delta L = 1$) raises output by 12 from 48 to 60 ($\Delta TP = 12$). Thus the *MP* equals 12, and it is recorded between 3 and 4 units of labour. Note that the *MP* in the example first rises and then falls as output increases. The level of output at which marginal product reaches a maximum is called the **point of diminishing marginal productivity.**

Part (ii) of Figure 8-1 plots average product and marginal product curves. Although three different schedules are shown in Table 8-2 and three different curves are shown in Figure 8-1, they are all aspects of the same single relationship described by the production function. As we vary the quantity of labour, with capital being fixed, output changes. Sometimes it is interesting to look at total product, sometimes at average product, and sometimes at the marginal product.

Finally, bear in mind that the schedules in Table 8-2 and the curves in Figure 8-1 all assume a specified quantity of the fixed factor. If the quantity of capital were, say, 10 units instead of the 4 that we assumed, there would be a different set of total product, average product, and marginal product curves. The reason is that if for any specified amount of labour there is more capital to work with, labour can then produce more output; that is, the total product will be greater.

AVERAGE AND MARGINAL PRODUCT CURVES

A great deal of important economic information is given by the shapes of the average and marginal product curves.

The Law of Diminishing Returns

The variations in output that result from applying more or less of a variable factor to a given quantity of a fixed factor are the subject of a famous economic hypothesis, referred to as the **law of diminishing returns.**

The law of diminishing returns states that if increasing amounts of a variable factor are applied to a given quantity of a fixed factor, eventually a situation will be reached in which each additional unit of the variable factor adds less to total product than the previous unit did; that is, the marginal product of the variable factor will decline.

The commonsense explanation of the law of diminishing returns is that as output is increased in the short run, more and more of the variable factor is combined with a given amount of the fixed factor. As a result, each unit of the variable factor has less and less of the fixed factor to work with. When the fixed factor is capital and the variable factor is labour, each unit of labour gets a declining amount of capital to assist it as the total output grows. It is not surprising, therefore, that sooner or later, equal increases in labour eventually begin to add less and less to total output.

It is possible that marginal product might diminish from the outset, so that the first unit of labour contributes most to total production and each successive unit contributes less than the previous unit. It is also possible for the marginal product to rise at first and to decline only at some higher level of output. In this case, the law might more accurately be described as the law of *eventually diminishing marginal returns.*

To illustrate this second case, let us consider the use of workers in a manufacturing operation. If there is only one worker, that worker must do all the tasks, shifting from one to another and becoming competent at each. As a second, third, and subsequent workers are added, each can specialize in one task, becoming expert at it. This process, as we noted in Chapter 3, is called the *division of labour.* If additional workers allow more efficient divisions of

---

[4] Δ is read "the change in." For example, ΔL is read "the change in quantity of labour."

labour, marginal product will rise: Each newly hired worker will add more to total output than each previous worker did. However, according to the law of diminishing returns, the scope for such increases must eventually disappear, and sooner or later, the marginal products of additional workers must decline. When this happens, each additional worker that is hired will increase total output by less than the previous worker did. This case, in which marginal product rises at first and then declines, is illustrated in part (ii) of Figure 8-1.

Eventually, as more and more of the variable factor is employed, marginal product may reach zero and even become negative. It is not hard to see why if you consider the extreme case, in which there would be so many workers in a limited space that additional workers would simply get in the way, thus reducing the total output.

We have so far examined the concept of diminishing *marginal* returns; but *average* returns are also expected to diminish. The *law of diminishing average returns* states that if increasing quantities of a variable factor are applied to a given quantity of fixed factors, the average product of the variable factor will eventually decrease. Diminishing marginal and average products are both illustrated in Table 8-2 and Figure 8-1. [15]

The Significance of Diminishing Returns

Empirical confirmation of both diminishing marginal and diminishing average returns occurs frequently. Some examples are illustrated in Application 8-1. But one might wish that it were not so. There would then be no reason to fear a food crisis caused by the population explosion in less-developed countries. If the marginal product of additional workers applied to a fixed quantity of land were constant, food production could be expanded in proportion to population growth merely by keeping a constant fraction of the population on farms. With fixed techniques, however, diminishing returns dictate an inexorable decline in the marginal product of each additional labourer because an expanding population must work with a fixed supply of agricultural land.

Thus, were it not for the steady improvement in the techniques of production, continuous population growth would bring with it, according to the law of diminishing returns, declining average living standards and eventually widespread famine. This gloomy prediction of the English economist Thomas Malthus (1766–1834) is discussed further in Application 9-2 in Chapter 9.

THE AVERAGE-MARGINAL RELATIONSHIP

Notice that in part (ii) of Figure 8-1, the *MP* curve cuts the *AP* curve at the *AP*'s maximum point. This is not a matter of luck or the way the artist just happened to draw the figure. Rather, it illustrates a fundamental property of the relationship between average and marginal product curves, one that is very important to understand. [16]

The average product curve slopes upward as long as the marginal product curve is *above* it; whether the marginal product curve is itself sloping upward or downward is irrelevant. If an additional worker is to raise the average product of all workers, that additional worker's output must be greater than the average output of the other workers. It is immaterial whether the new worker's contribution to output is greater or less than the contribution of the worker hired immediately before; all that matters is that the new worker's contribution to output exceeds the *average* output of all workers hired previously.

The relationship between marginal and average measures is very general. If the marginal is greater than the average, the average must be rising; if the marginal is less than the average, the average must be falling. For example, if you have a 3.6 cumulative grade point average (GPA) through last semester and in this (marginal) semester you have a 3.4, your cumulative GPA will fall. To increase your cumulative GPA, you must score better in this (marginal) semester than you have on average in the past—that is, to increase the average, the marginal must be greater than the average.

SHORT-RUN VARIATIONS IN COST

We now shift our attention from the firm's production function to its costs. The majority of firms cannot influence the prices of the inputs that they employ; instead they must pay the going market price for their inputs. For example, a shoe factory in

DIMINISHING RETURNS

The law of diminishing returns operates in a wide range of circumstances. Here are four examples.

British Columbia's Campbell River, a noted sport-fishing area, has long been the centre of a thriving, well-promoted tourist trade. As sport-fishing has increased over the years, the total number of fish caught has steadily increased, but the number of fish *per person fishing* has decreased and the average hours fished for each fish caught has increased.*

When Southern California Edison was required to modify its Mojave power plant to reduce the amount of pollutants emitted into the atmosphere, it discovered that a series of filters applied to the smokestacks could do the job. A single filter eliminated one-half of the discharge. Five filters in series reduced the discharge to the 3 percent allowed by law. When a state senator proposed a new standard that would permit no more than 1 percent of the pollutant to be emitted, the company brought in experts who testified that this would require at least 15 filters per stack and would triple the cost.

Public opinion pollsters, as well as all students of statistics, know that you can use a sample to estimate characteristics of a large population. Even a relatively small sample can provide a useful estimate—at a tiny fraction of the cost of a complete enumeration of the population. However, sample estimates are subject to sampling error. If, for example, 38 percent of a sample approves of a certain policy, the percentage of the population that approves of it is likely to be close to 38 percent, but it might well be anywhere from 36 to 40 percent. The theory of statistics shows that the size of the expected sampling error can be reduced by increasing the sample size. However, the theory also shows that successive reductions in the sampling error require larger and larger increases in the sample size. Suppose that the original sample was 400; if quadrupling the sample to 1,600 would halve the chance of an error of any given size from occurring, then to halve it again, the new sample would have to be quadrupled again—to 6,400. In other words, increasing the sample size leads to diminishing marginal returns in terms of accuracy.

During the early days of World War II, so few naval ships were available that each North Atlantic convoy had only a few escort vessels to protect it from German submarines. The escorts dashed about from one side of the convoy to the other and ended up sinking very few submarines. As the construction program made more ships available, the escorts could stay in one position in the convoy: Some could close in on the various flanks; others could hunt farther afield. Not only did the total number of submarines sunk per convoy crossing rise, but also the number of submarines sunk per escort vessel rose. Still later in the war, as each successive convoy was provided with more and more escort vessels, the number of submarines sunk per convoy crossing continued to rise, but the number of submarines sunk per escort vessel began to fall sharply.

---

*For a *given stock of fish* and increasing numbers of boats, this example is a good illustration of the law of diminishing returns. But in recent years the story has become more complicated as overfishing has depleted the stock of fish. We examine the reasons for overfishing in Chapter 18.

Montreal, a metals manufacturer in Sarnia, a rancher in Red Deer, and a boat builder in Prince Rupert are each too small a part of the total demand for the factors that they use to be able to influence their prices significantly. The firms must pay the going rent for the land that they need, the going wage rate for the labour that they employ, and the going interest rate that banks charge for loans; so it is with

EXTENSION 8-2

A SUMMARY OF SHORT-RUN COST CONCEPTS

TOTAL COSTS:

Total Cost *(TC)* = Total Fixed Cost *(TFC)* + Total Variable Cost *(TVC)*

Total Cost is the total cost to the firm of producing a given level of output.

Total Fixed Cost is the sum of all costs of production that do not vary with the level of output. Also called overhead costs.

Total Variable Cost varies directly with the level of output; it rises as more ouptut is produced and falls as less output is produced.

AVERAGE COSTS:

Average Total Cost *(ATC)* = Average Fixed Cost *(AFC)* + Average Variable Cost *(AVC)*

Average Total Cost is the total cost *per unit* of output: $ATC = \dfrac{TC}{\text{Units of Output}}$.

Average Fixed Cost is the fixed cost *per unit* of output: $AFC = \dfrac{TFC}{\text{Units of Output}}$.

Average Variable Cost is the variable cost *per unit* of output: $AVC = \dfrac{TVC}{\text{Units of Output}}$.

MARGINAL COSTS:

Marginal Cost is the increase in total cost resulting from increasing the level of output by one unit. Also called incremental cost.

$$MC = \frac{\text{Change in Total Cost}}{\text{Change in Output}} = \frac{\Delta TC}{\Delta Q}$$

Note: Since some of total costs are fixed costs, which do not change as the level of output changes, marginal cost is also equal to the increase in variable cost that results when output is increased by one unit.

most other firms.[5] Given these prices and the physical returns summarized by the product curves, the costs of different levels of output can be calculated.

COST CONCEPTS DEFINED

The following definitions of several cost concepts are closely related to the product concepts just introduced.

Total cost *(TC)* is the full cost of producing any given level of output. Total cost is divided into two parts, *total fixed cost* and *total variable cost*. **Total fixed cost** *(TFC)* does not vary with the level of output; it is the same whether output is 1 unit or 1 million units. Such a cost is also referred to as an *over-*

head cost. A cost that varies directly with output, rising as more output is produced and falling as less output is produced, is called a **total variable cost** *(TVC).* In the example in Table 8-2, labour is the variable factor of production, and wages are therefore a variable cost.

Average total cost *(ATC)*, also called **average cost** *(AC)*, is the total cost of producing any given number of units of output divided by that number. Average total cost is therefore the (average) cost *per unit of output.* ATC can be separated into **average fixed costs** *(AFC)*, fixed cost divided by quantity of output, and **average variable costs** *(AVC)*, variable cost divided by quantity of output.

Although average *variable* costs may rise or fall as production is increased, it is clear that average *fixed* costs decline continuously as output increases. A doubling of output always leads to a halving of fixed costs per unit of output. This is a process popularly known as *spreading one's overhead.*

Marginal cost *(MC)*, sometimes called *incremental cost*, is the increase in total cost resulting

---

[5]The firm that is a large enough employer of labour or user of land or capital to affect the prices of its factor services is the exception rather than the rule. The exceptions are very large firms who employ much of the world's total of a given factor and firms in isolated towns that have only one large employer. Even in these cases, the firm does not have complete control over the wages it pays, as we shall see in Chapters 15 and 16.

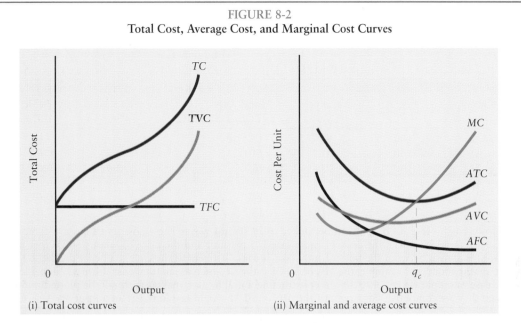

FIGURE 8-2
Total Cost, Average Cost, and Marginal Cost Curves

Total cost *(TC)*, average cost *(AC)*, and marginal cost *(MC)* curves often have the shapes shown here. Total fixed cost does not vary with output. Total variable cost and the total of all costs ($TC = TVC + TFC$) rise with output, first at a decreasing rate and then at an increasing rate. The total cost curves in part (i) give rise to the average and marginal cost curves in part (ii). Average fixed cost *(AFC)* declines as output increases. Average variable cost *(AVC)* and average total cost *(ATC)* fall and then rise as output increases. Marginal cost *(MC)* does the same, intersecting *ATC* and *AVC* at their minimum points. Capacity output is q_c, the minimum point on the *ATC* curve.

from raising the rate of production by one unit. Because fixed costs do not vary with output, marginal fixed costs are always zero. Therefore, marginal costs are necessarily marginal variable costs, and a change in fixed costs will leave marginal costs unaffected. For example, the marginal cost of producing a few more potatoes by farming a given amount of land more intensively is not affected by the rent paid for the land. [17]

See Extension 8-2 for a summary of the firm's short-run cost concepts.

SHORT-RUN COST CURVES

Using the production relationships found in Table 8-2, suppose that the price of labour is $10 per unit and that the price of capital is $25 per unit. The cost schedules that result from these values are shown in Table 8-3.

Figure 8-2 shows some hypothetical cost curves. The shape of these curves are similar to the ones that would result from plotting the data in Table 8-3. Notice that the marginal cost curve cuts the average total cost curve and the average variable cost curve at their lowest points. This is another example of the relationship between a marginal and an average curve. The *ATC* curve, for example, slopes downward as long as the *MC* curve is below it; it makes no difference whether the *MC* curve is itself sloping upward or downward.

To see this, consider an example in which 10 units are produced each week at an average cost of $5 per unit (total cost equals $50). The average cost of producing 11 units will exceed $5 if the eleventh unit adds more than $5 to total cost (*MC* exceeds *AC*) and will be less than $5 if the eleventh unit adds less than $5 to total cost (*MC* is less than *AC*). (The marginal cost of the tenth unit does not matter for this calculation. It could be above, below, or equal to the eleventh unit's marginal cost.)

Short-Run Average Variable Cost

In Figure 8-2, the average variable cost curve reaches a minimum and then rises. For given factor prices, when average product per worker is at a

TABLE 8-3
Variation of Costs with Capital Fixed and Labour Variable

(1) Labour (L)	(2) Output (q)	(3) Fixed (TFC)	(4) Variable (TVC)	(5) Total (TC)	(6) (MC)	(7) Fixed (AFC)	(8) Variable (AVC)	(9) Total (ATC)
		Total Cost ($)			Marginal Cost ($ per unit)	Average Costs ($ per unit)		
0	0	100	0	100		—	—	—
					0.67			
1	15	100	10	110		6.67	0.67	7.33
					0.53			
2	34	100	20	120		2.94	0.59	3.53
					0.71			
3	48	100	30	130		2.08	0.62	2.71
					0.83			
4	60	100	40	140		1.67	0.67	2.33
					5.00			
5	62	100	50	150		1.61	0.81	2.42

The relationship of cost to level of output can be looked at in several ways. These cost schedules are computed from the product schedule of Table 8-2, given the price of capital of $25 per unit and the price of labour of $10 per unit. Marginal cost (in column 6) is shown between the lines of total cost because it refers to the change in cost divided by the change in output that brought it about. For example, the MC of $0.71 is the $10 increase in total cost (from $120 to $130) divided by the 14-unit increase in output (from 34 to 48). In constructing a graph, marginal costs should be plotted midway in the interval over which they are computed. For example, the MC of $0.71 would be plotted at an output of 41.

maximum, average variable cost is at a minimum. **[18]** Common sense tells us that each additional worker adds the same amount to cost but a different amount to output, so when output per worker rises, the cost per unit of output must fall, and vice versa.

Eventually diminishing average productivity implies eventually increasing average variable costs.

Short-Run Average Total Cost

Short-run *ATC* curves are often U-shaped. This reflects the assumption that average productivity increases when output is low but that at some level of output, average productivity begins to fall fast enough so that average variable costs increase faster than average fixed costs are falling. When this happens, *ATC* increases.

Marginal Cost

In part (ii) of Figure 8-2, the marginal cost curve is shown as a declining curve that reaches a minimum and then rises. This is the reverse of the shape of the marginal product curve in part (ii) of Figure 8-1. The reason for the reversal is as follows: If extra units of a variable factor that is bought at a fixed price per unit result in increasing quantities of out-

put (marginal *product rising*), the cost per unit of extra output must be falling (marginal *cost falling*). However, if marginal product is falling, marginal cost will be rising.

The law of eventually diminishing marginal product implies eventually increasing marginal cost. **[19]**

Total Variable Cost

In part (i) of Figure 8-2, total variable cost is shown as an upward-sloping curve, indicating that total variable cost rises with the level of output. This is true as long as marginal cost is positive because the total variable cost of producing any given level of output is just the sum of the marginal costs of producing each unit of output up to the given level of output. **[20]**

CAPACITY

The level of output that corresponds to the minimum short-run average total cost is often called the *capacity* of the firm. In this sense, capacity is the largest output that can be produced without encountering rising average costs per unit. In part (ii) of Figure 8-2, capacity output is q_c units, but higher outputs can be achieved, provided that the firm is willing to accept the higher per-unit costs that accompany any level of output that is "above capacity." A firm that is producing at an output less than the point of minimum average total cost is said to have **excess capacity.**

The technical definition gives the word *capacity* a meaning that is different from the one used in everyday speech, in which it often means an upper limit that cannot be exceeded. The technical definition is, however, a useful concept in economic and business discussions.

SHIFTS IN SHORT-RUN COST CURVES

So far, we have seen how costs vary as output varies, with input prices being held constant. Figure 8-3 shows the effect on a firm's cost curves of a change in the price of any variable input. A rise in the price of any input used by the firm must raise the price of producing any given quantity of output. A fall in the price of any input has the opposite effect. This is a very simple relationship, but it is important nonetheless.

A change in the price of any variable input used by the firm will shift its marginal and average cost curves—upward for a price increase and downward for a price decrease.

There is thus a set of average and marginal cost curves that correspond to each price of the variable factor.

A FAMILY OF SHORT-RUN COST CURVES

A short-run cost curve shows how costs vary with output for a given quantity of the fixed factor, say, a given size of plant.

There is a different short-run cost curve for each given quantity of the fixed factor.

A small plant that manufactures nuts and bolts will have its own short-run cost curve. A medium-size plant and a large plant will each have its own short-run cost curve. If a firm expands and replaces its small plant with a medium-size plant, it will move from one short-run cost curve to another. This change from one plant size to another is a long-run change, which brings us to the next chapter, in which we discuss how short-run cost curves for plants of different sizes are related to each other.

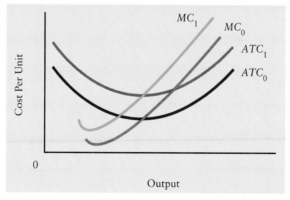

FIGURE 8-3
The Effect of a Change in Input Prices

A change in any input price shifts the average total cost curve and the marginal cost curve. The original average total cost and marginal cost curves are shown by ATC_0 and MC_0. A rise in the price of a variable input—for example, the wage rate—raises the cost of producing each level of output. As a result, the average total cost curve and the marginal cost curve shift upward to ATC_1 and MC_1.

SUMMARY

A. PROFITS AND COSTS

- The key behavioural assumption in the theory of the firm is that the firm seeks to maximize its profit.
- Production consists of transforming inputs into outputs. It is often convenient to divide factors of production into categories. One common classification is land, labour, and capital. Land includes land and natural resources, labour refers to all human services, and capital denotes all manufactured aids to further production. An outstanding feature of modern production is the use of capital goods.
- The opportunity cost of using a resource is the value of that resource in its best alternative use. Measuring opportunity cost to the firm requires *imputing* the cost of resources not purchased or hired for current use. Among these imputed costs are those for the use of the owners' money, depreciation, risk taking, and any special advantages, such as trademarks, that the firm possesses.
- A firm that is maximizing profits (the difference between revenue and the opportunity cost of all the resources that it uses) is making the best allocation of the resources under its control, according to the firm's evaluation of its alternatives. When a firm is earning zero *economic profits,* its revenue is covering all of its opportunity costs. This means that it could do just as well (but not better) by using its resources in other ways.
- Economic profits and losses provide important signals concerning the allocation of resources. Profits earned in an industry provide a signal that more resources can profitably move into the industry. Losses show that resources have more profitable uses elsewhere and serve as a signal that some of these resources should be transferred out of that industry.

B. CHOICES OPEN TO THE FIRM

- A firm's production decisions can be classified into three groups:
  - The Short Run: How best to employ existing plant and equipment
  - The Long Run: What new plant and equipment and production processes to select, given known technical possibilities
  - The Very-Long Run: How to encourage or to adapt to technological changes
- The short run involves decisions in which one or more factors of production are fixed. The long run involves decisions in which all factors are variable but technology is given. The very long run involves decisions in which technology can change.
- The production function shows the output that results from each possible combination of inputs. Short-run and long-run situations can be interpreted as implying different kinds of constraints on the production function. In the short run, the firm is constrained to use no more than a given quantity of some fixed factor; in the long run, it is constrained only by the available techniques of production.

C. SHORT-RUN CHOICES FOR THE FIRM

- The theory of short-run costs is concerned with how output varies as different amounts of the variable factors are combined with given amounts of the fixed factors. The concepts of total, average, and marginal product represent alternative relationships between output and the quantity of the variable factors of production.
- The law of diminishing returns asserts that if increasing quantities of a variable factor are combined with given quantities of fixed factors, the marginal and the average products of the variable factor will eventually decrease. For given factor prices, this hypothesis implies that marginal and average costs will eventually rise.

D. SHORT-RUN VARIATIONS IN COST

- Given physical productivity schedules and the prices of inputs, it is a matter of simple arithmetic to develop the whole family of short-run cost curves, one for each quantity of the fixed factor.
- Short-run average total cost curves are often U-shaped. Average productivity increases at low levels of outputs but eventually declines sufficiently and rapidly to offset advantages of spreading overheads. The output corresponding to the minimum point of a short-run average total cost curve is called the plant's capacity.
- Changes in factor prices shift the short-run cost curves—upward when prices rise and downward when prices fall. Thus there is a whole family of short-run cost curves, one for each set of factor prices.

KEY CONCEPTS

The role of profit maximization
Inputs and factors of production
Opportunity costs
Imputed costs
The economics of durable capital: depreciation and sunk costs
Alternative definitions of profits

Profits and resource allocation
Short run, long run, and very-long run
Total product, average product, and marginal product
The law of diminishing returns
Marginal product curves and average product curves

The relationship between productivity and cost
Total cost, marginal cost, and average cost
Short-run cost curves
Capacity and excess capacity

DISCUSSION QUESTIONS

1. Can the economic theory of the firm be of any help in analyzing the decisions of such nonprofit organizations as governments, churches, and universities? What role, if any, does the notion of opportunity cost play for them?

2. "There is no such thing as a free lunch." Can anything be free? In earlier decades, gasoline stations routinely provided many free services, including windshield cleaning, tire inflation, and road maps. Now many sell road maps and have discontinued free services. Indeed, self-service stations have become increasingly popular with motorists, who like the lower gasoline prices at these stations. Under what conditions will profit-maximizing behaviour lead to the coexistence of full-service and self-service gasoline stations? What would determine the proportions in which each occurs?

3. Having bought a used car from Smiling Sam for $2,000, you drive it for two days, and it breaks down. You now find that it requires an extra $1,500 before it will run. Assuming that the car is worth less than $3,500 repaired, should you make the repairs? How does the concept of sunk cost enter your analysis?

4. Which concept of profits is implied in the following quotations?

   a. "Profits are necessary if firms are to stay in business."
   b. "Profits are signals for firms to expand production and investment."
   c. "Accelerated depreciation allowances lower profits and thus benefit the company's owners."

5. Does the short run consist of the same number of months for increasing output as for decreasing it? Must the short run in an industry be the same length for all firms in the industry? Under what circumstances

might the short run actually involve a longer time span than the very-long run for one particular firm?

6. In 1921, a classic set of experiments with chemical fertilizers was performed at the Rothampsted Experimental Station, an agricultural research institute in Hertfordshire, England. Researchers applied different amounts of a particular fertilizer to 10 apparently identical quarter-acre plots of land. The results for one test, using identical seed grain, are listed in the following table. Compute the average and marginal product of fertilizer, and identify the (approximate) points of diminishing average and marginal productivity.

Plot	Fertilizer Dose	Yield Index*
1	15	104.2
2	30	110.4
3	45	118.0
4	60	125.3
5	75	130.2
6	90	131.4
7	105	131.9
8	120	132.3
9	135	132.5
10	150	132.8

* Yield without fertilizer = 100.

7. Indicate whether each of the following conforms to the hypothesis of diminishing returns and, if so, whether it refers to marginal returns, average returns, or both.

   a. "The bigger they are, the harder they fall."
   b. "As more and more of the population receives chicken pox vaccinations, the reduction in the

chicken pox disease rate for each additional 100,000 vaccinations becomes smaller."

c. "Five workers produce twice as much today as 10 workers did 40 years ago."

d. "Diminishing returns set in last year when the rising rural population actually caused agricultural output to fall."

8. Consider the education of a person as a process of production. Regard years of schooling as one variable factor of production. What are the other factors? What factors are fixed? At what point would you expect diminishing returns to set in? For an Einstein, would diminishing returns set in during his lifetime?

9. Suppose that you are hungry and between classes. You go to a vending machine for a candy bar, deposit the required money, and press the button for your selection. Unfortunately, you do not pay enough attention and inadvertently press a button for an empty bay. Based on the discussion in the chapter, and assuming that you have more money, what should you do next? Why?

10. A carpenter quits his job at a furniture factory to open his own cabinetmaking business. In his first two years of operation, his sales average $100,000 and his operating costs for wood, workshop and tool rental, utilities, and miscellaneous expenses average $70,000. Now his old job at the furniture factory is again available. Should he take it or remain in business for himself? How would you make this decision?

11. Suppose that a large telecommunications firm launches a set of new communications satellites that carry twice the traffic of their previous satellites. Further assume that the only costs of this decision are the initial satellite construction and launch. Discuss how the cost curves for this firm may be affected.

12. The point of minimum average cost is referred to as the capacity of the firm. Yet we draw the average cost curve extending both to the left and to the right of this point. Obviously, a firm can operate below capacity, but how can a firm operate above capacity? Are there any types of firms for which it may be desirable to have a capacity below the level at which the firm may have to produce occasionally or even relatively frequently? Explain.

PRODUCTION AND COST IN THE LONG RUN AND THE VERY-LONG RUN

In the first part of this chapter, we look at the *long run*, in which firms are free to vary all factors of production. Picking up from the end of Chapter 8, the choice that a firm faces in the long run is *which* of the family of short-run cost curves it should be on. Some firms use a great deal of capital and only a small amount of labour. Others use less capital and more labour. Here we examine the effects that these choices have on firms' costs, and we look at the conditions that determine these choices.

In the second part of the chapter, we examine the *very-long run*, in which the technology itself (the whole family of short-run cost curves) changes. The discussion concerns the improvements in technology and productivity that have dramatically increased output and incomes in all industrial countries over centuries. Firms are among the most important economic actors that cause technological advances to take place. Evidence shows that the hypotheses of profit maximization and cost minimization can help us to understand technological changes. Here, as in the short and long run, firms respond to such signals as changes in factor prices.

Throughout this chapter, we should remember that the lengths of the various runs under consideration are defined by the kinds of changes that can take place, not by calendar time. Thus we would expect actual firms in any given time period to minimize costs in the short run, as described in Chapter 8; to choose among short-run cost curves in the long run, as described in the first part of this chapter; and to change technologies as described in the latter part of this chapter.

THE LONG RUN: NO FIXED FACTORS

In the short run, in which only one factor can be varied, the only way to produce a given output is to adjust the input of the variable factor. Thus once the firm has decided on a rate of output, there is only one possible way of achieving it. In the long run, all factors can be varied, so there are numerous technically possible ways to produce any given output. The firm must decide on both a level of output *and* how to produce that output. Specifically, this means that firms in the long run must choose the type and amount of plant and equipment and the size of their labour force.

In making these choices, the firm will wish to be *technically efficient* by using no more of all inputs than necessary—that is, the firm does not want to waste any of its valuable inputs. Technical efficiency is not enough, however. To be *economically efficient,* the firm must choose from among the many technically efficient options the one that produces a given level of output at the lowest possible cost. (The distinction between various types of efficiency sometimes causes confusion, particularly when engineers and economists are involved in the same decision-making process. Extension 9-1 elaborates on this important distinction.)

Long-run planning decisions are important. A firm that decides to build a new steel mill and invest in the required machinery will choose among many alternatives. Once installed, that equipment is fixed for a long time. If the firm makes a wrong choice, its survival may be threatened; if it estimates correctly, it may be rewarded with large profits.

Long-run decisions are risky because the firm must anticipate what methods of production will be efficient not only today but also for many years in the future, when the costs of labour and raw materials will no doubt have changed. The decisions are also risky because the firm must estimate how much output it will want to produce. Is the industry to which it belongs growing or declining? Will new products emerge to render its existing products less useful than an extrapolation of past sales suggests?

PROFIT MAXIMIZATION AND COST MINIMIZATION

Any firm that is trying to maximize its profits in the long run should select the economically efficient method, which is the method that produces its output at the lowest possible cost. As we noted in the previous chapter, this implication of the hypothesis of profit maximization is called **cost minimization:** From the alternatives open to it, the profit-maximizing firm will choose the least costly way of producing whatever specific output it chooses.

Choice of Factor Mix

If it is possible to substitute one factor for another to keep output constant while reducing total cost, the firm is not using the least costly combination of factors. In such a situation, the firm should substitute one factor for another factor as long as the marginal product of the one factor *per dollar spent on it* is greater than the marginal product of the other factor *per dollar spent on it.* The firm is not minimizing its costs whenever these two magnitudes are unequal. For example, if an extra dollar spent on labour produces more output than an extra dollar spent on capital, the firm can reduce costs by spending less on capital and more on labour.

If we use K to represent capital, L to represent labour, and P_L and P_K to represent the prices per unit of the two factors, the necessary condition for cost minimization is as follows:

$$\frac{MP_K}{P_K} = \frac{MP_L}{P_L} \qquad [1]$$

Whenever the ratio of the marginal product of some factor to its price is not equal for all factors, there are possibilities for factor substitutions that will reduce costs.

EXTENSION 9-1

CONCEPTS OF EFFICIENCY

In popular discussion, business decision making, and government policies, three different types of efficiency concepts are encountered. These are engineering, technical, and economic efficiency. Each is a valid concept, and each conveys useful information. However, the use of one concept in a situation in which another is appropriate is a frequent source of error and confusion.

Engineering efficiency refers to the physical amount of some *single key input* that is used in production. It is measured by the ratio of that input to output. For example, the engineering efficiency of an engine refers to the ratio of the amount of energy in the fuel burned by the engine to the amount of usable energy produced by the engine. The difference goes in friction, heat loss, and other unavoidable sources of waste. Saying that a steam engine is 40 percent efficient means that 40 percent of the energy in the fuel that is burned in the boiler is converted into work that is done by the engine, while the other 60 percent is lost.

Technical efficiency is related to the physical amount of *all factors* used in the process of producing some product. A particular method of producing a given output is technically *inefficient* if there are other ways of producing the output that will use less of at least one input while not using more of any others.

Economic efficiency is related to the *value* (rather than the physical amounts) of all inputs used in producing a given output. The production of a given output is economically efficient if there is no other way of producing the output that will use a smaller total value of inputs.

What is the relationship between economic efficiency and these other two concepts? We have seen that engineering efficiency measures the efficiency with which a single input is used. Although knowing the efficiency of any given gasoline, electric, or diesel engine is interesting, increasing this efficiency is not necessarily economically efficient because doing so usually requires the use of other valuable resources. For example, the engineering efficiency of a gas turbine engine can be increased by using more and stronger steel in its construction. Raising the engineering efficiency of an engine saves on fuel, but at the cost of using more of other inputs. To know whether this is worth doing, the firm must compare the value of the fuel saved with the value of the other inputs used.

Technical efficiency is desirable as long as inputs are costly to the firm in any way. If a technically inefficient process is replaced by a technically efficient process, there is a saving. We do not need to put a precise value on the cost of inputs to make this judgment. All we need to know is that inputs have a positive cost to the firm, so that saving on these costs is desirable.

Usually, however, any given output may be produced in any one of many alternative technically efficient ways. Achieving technical efficiency is clearly a *necessary* condition for producing any output at the least cost. The existence of technical inefficiency means that costs can be reduced by reducing some inputs and not increasing any others. Achieving technical efficiency, however, is not a *sufficient* condition for producing at the lowest possible cost. The firm must still ask which of the many technically efficient methods it should use. This is where the concept of economic efficiency comes in. The appropriate method is the one that uses the smallest *value* of inputs. This ensures that the firm spends as little as possible producing its given output; in terms of opportunity cost, the firm sacrifices the least possible value with respect to other things that it might do with those inputs.

To see why Equation 1 must be satisfied when costs are being minimized, consider an example where the equation is *not* satisfied. Suppose that the marginal product of capital is 40 and the price of a unit of capital is $10, making the left side of Equation 1 equal to 4. Suppose also that the marginal product of labour is 20 and the price of a unit of labour is $2, making the right side equal to 10.

Thus the last dollar spent on capital adds only 4 units to output, whereas the last dollar spent on labour adds 10 units to output. In this case, it is possible for the firm to keep its output constant but reduce its costs by using more labour and less capital. Specifically, if the firm spent an additional $4 on labour, output would rise by 40 units; but then it could spend exactly $10 less on capital and output would fall back by 40 units. Making such a substitution of labour for capital would leave output unchanged but it would reduce costs by $6. Thus the original combination of factors was not a cost-minimizing one.[1]

By rearranging the terms in Equation 1, we can look at the cost-minimizing condition a bit differently.[2]

$$\frac{MP_K}{MP_L} = \frac{P_K}{P_L} \qquad [2]$$

The ratio of the marginal products on the left side compares the contribution to output of the last unit of capital and the last unit of labour. The right side shows how the cost of an additional unit of capital compares to the cost of an additional unit of labour. If the two sides of Equation 2 are the same, then the firm cannot make any substitutions between labour and capital to reduce costs (holding output constant). However, with the marginal products and factor prices used in the example above, the left side of the equation equals 2 but the right side equals 5; the last unit of capital is twice as productive as the last unit of labour but it is five times as expensive. It will thus pay the firm to switch to a method of production that uses less capital and more labour. If, however, the ratio on the right side were less than the ratio on the left, then it would pay the firm to switch to a method of production that used less labour and more capital.

We have seen that when the ratio MP_K/MP_L is greater than the ratio P_K/P_L, the firm will substitute capital for labour. This substitution is measured by changes in the **capital-labour ratio**—the amount of capital per worker used by the firm.

How far does the firm go in making this substitution? There is a limit because as the firm uses more capital, the marginal product of capital falls, and as it uses less labour, the marginal product of labour rises. Thus the ratio MP_K/MP_L falls. When the ratio of marginal products reaches the ratio of factor prices, the firm need substitute no further.

Firms adjust the elements over which they have control (the quantities of factors used and thus the marginal products of the factors) to the prices of the factors given by the market.

Long-Run Cost Minimization

The firm will have achieved its cost-minimizing capital-labour ratio when there is no opportunity for cost-reducing substitutions. This occurs when the marginal product per dollar spent on each factor is the same (Equation 1) or, equivalently, when the ratio of the marginal products of factors is equal to the ratio of their prices (Equation 2). The preceding discussion suggests that cost-minimizing firms will react to changes in factor prices by changing their methods of production. We refer to this as the **principle of substitution**.

THE PRINCIPLE OF SUBSTITUTION

Suppose that a firm is currently meeting the cost-minimizing conditions and that the cost of labour increases while the cost of capital remains unchanged. The least-cost method of producing any output will now use less labour and more capital than was required to produce the same output before the factor prices changed.

Methods of production will change if the relative prices of factors change. Relatively more of the cheaper factor and relatively less of the more expensive factor will be used.

This is called the principle of substitution, and it follows from the assumption that firms minimize their costs.

The principle of substitution plays a central role in resource allocation because it relates to the way in which individual firms respond to changes in relative factor prices that are caused by the changing relative scarcities of factors in the economy as a whole. Individual firms are motivated to use less of factors that become scarcer to the economy and more of factors that become more plentiful. Here are two examples of the principle of substitution in action.

In recent decades, the price of "smart" word processors has fallen sharply relative to the wages of clerical workers. One result of this change has

---

[1] The argument in this paragraph assumes that the marginal products do not change when expenditure changes by a small amount.
[2] The appendix to this chapter provides a graphical analysis of this condition, which is similar to the analysis of consumer behaviour in the appendix to Chapter 7.

been the near demise of the form letter, beginning "Dear Sir or Madam." Nowadays, even total strangers send you letters that are customized by name and sometimes more. Twenty years ago, such customized attention would have required that a secretary look up the information in a file and type it into a letter. Now a well-designed mail-merge program can do the job at much lower cost, and we see the result every day. Here we see the substitution toward capital and away from labour as their relative prices change.

Some countries have plentiful land and relatively small populations. Their land prices are low, and because their labour is in short supply, their wage rates are high. In response, their farmers make lavish use of the cheap land while economizing on expensive labour; thus their production processes use low ratios of labour to land. Other countries are small in area but have large populations. The demand for land is high relative to its supply, and land is relatively expensive whereas labour is relatively cheap. In response, farmers economize on land by using much labour per unit of land; thus their production processes use high ratios of labour to land.

Once again, we see the price system functioning as an automatic control system. No single firm needs to be aware of national factor surpluses and scarcities. These are reflected by market prices, so individual firms that never look beyond their own profits are led to economize on factors that are scarce to the nation as a whole and to use factors that are abundant.

This discussion suggests why methods of producing the same product differ across countries. In Canada, where labour is generally highly skilled and expensive, a farmer with a large farm may use elaborate machinery to economize on labour. In China, where labour is abundant and capital is scarce, a much less mechanized method of production is appropriate. The Western engineer who believes that the Chinese are inefficient because they are using methods long ago discarded in the West is missing the truth about efficiency in the use of resources: Where factor scarcities differ across nations, so will the most efficient methods of production.

COST CURVES IN THE LONG RUN

When all factors can be varied, there exists a least-cost method of producing each possible level of output. Thus with given factor prices, there is a minimum achievable cost for each level of output; if this cost is expressed in terms of dollars per unit of output, we obtain the long-run average cost of producing each level of output. When this cost of producing each level of output is plotted on a graph, the result is called a **long-run average cost (*LRAC*) curve**. Figure 9-1 shows one such curve.

This cost curve is determined by the technology of the industry (which is assumed to be fixed in the long run) and by the prices of the factors of production. It is a "boundary" in the sense that points below it are unattainable; points on the curve, however, are attainable if sufficient time elapses for all inputs to be adjusted. To move from one point on the *LRAC* curve to another requires an adjustment in *all* factor inputs, which may, for example, require building a larger, more elaborate factory.

The *LRAC* curve is the boundary between cost levels that are attainable, with known technology and given factor prices, and those that are unattainable.

Just as the short-run cost curves discussed in Chapter 8 relate to the *production function* describing the physical relationship between factor inputs and output, so does the *LRAC* curve. The difference is that in deriving the *LRAC* curve, there are no fixed factors of production. Thus, since all costs are variable in the long run, we do not need to distinguish between *AVC*, *AFC*, and *ATC*, as we did in the short run; in the long run, there is only one *LRAC* for any given set of input prices.

The Shape of the Long-Run Average Cost Curve

The *LRAC* curve shown in Figure 9-1 first falls and then rises. This curve is often described as U-shaped, although "saucer-shaped" might be a more accurate description of the evidence from many empirical studies. Consider the three portions of any such saucer-shaped *LRAC* curve.

Decreasing Costs. Over the range of output from zero to q_m, the firm has falling long-run average costs: An expansion of output permits a reduction of costs per unit of output. Technologies with this property are referred to as exhibiting **economies of scale**. Because the *LRAC* curve is drawn under the assumption of constant factor prices, the decline in long-run average cost occurs because output is increasing *more than* in proportion to inputs as the scale of the firm's production expands. Over this

FIGURE 9-1
A Long-Run Average Cost Curve

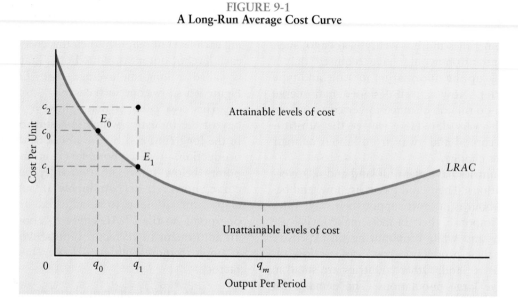

The long-run average cost *(LRAC)* curve provides a boundary between attainable and unattainable levels of costs. If the firm wishes to produce output q_0, the lowest attainable cost level is c_0 per unit. Thus point E_0 is on the *LRAC* curve. E_1 represents the lowest possible average cost of producing q_1. Suppose that a firm is producing at q_0 and desires to increase output to q_1. In the long run, a plant optimal for output q_1 can be built, and the cost of c_1 per unit can be attained. However, in the short run, it will not be able to vary all factors, and thus costs per unit will be above c_1, say, c_2. At output q_m, the firm attains its lowest possible per unit cost of production for the given technology and factor prices.

range of output, the decreasing-cost firm is often said to enjoy long-run **increasing returns.**[3]

Increasing returns may occur as a result of increased opportunities for specialization of tasks made possible by the division of labour. Adam Smith's classic discussion of this important point is given in Extension 3-2 in Chapter 3. Even the most casual observation of the differences in production techniques used in large and small plants will show that larger plants use greater specialization.

These differences arise because large, specialized equipment is useful only when the volume of output that the firm can sell justifies employment of that equipment. For example, assembly-line techniques and body-stamping machinery in automobile production are economically efficient only when individual operations are repeated thousands of times. Use of elaborate harvesting equipment (which combines many individual tasks that would otherwise be done by hand and by tractor) provides the least-cost method of production on a big farm but not on a few acres.

Typically, as the level of planned output increases, capital is substituted for labour and complex machines are substituted for simpler machines. Robotics is a contemporary example. Electronic devices can handle huge numbers of operations quickly, but unless the level of production requires such a large volume of operations, robotics or other forms of automation will not provide the least-cost method of production.

The foregoing discussion refers to the technology of production, which is one major source of increasing returns to scale. A second source lies in the geometry that is intrinsic to the three-dimensional world in which we live. To illustrate how geometry matters, consider a firm that wishes to store a gas or a liquid. The firm is interested in the *volume* of storage space. However, the materials cost of a storage container is related to the *area* of its surface. When the size of a container is increased, the storage capacity (volume) increases faster than its surface area. This is a genuine case of increasing returns—the output, in terms

---

[3]Economists shift back and forth between speaking in physical terms ("increasing returns") and cost terms ("decreasing costs"). As the text explains, the same relationship can be expressed in either terms.

of storage capacity, increases more proportionately than the increase in the costs of the required construction materials.

A third source of increasing returns consists of inputs that do not have to be increased as the output of a product is increased, even in the long run. For example, there are often large fixed costs in developing new products, such as a new generation of airplanes or a more powerful computer. These R&D costs have to be incurred only once for each product and hence are independent of the scale at which the product is subsequently produced. Even if the product's *production costs* increase in proportion to output in the long run, average total costs, including *product development costs,* will fall as the scale of output rises. The influence of such once-and-for-all costs is that, other things being equal, they cause average total costs to be falling over the entire range of output. (The significance of such once-and-for-all costs is discussed further in Chapter 12.)

Constant Costs. In Figure 9-1, the firm's long-run average costs fall until output reaches q_m and rise thereafter. Another possibility should be noted. The firm's *LRAC* curve might have a flat portion over a range of output around q_m. With such a flat portion, the firm would be encountering constant costs over the relevant range of output. This means that the firm's long-run average costs per unit of output do not change as its output changes. Because factor prices are assumed to be fixed, the firm's output must be increasing *exactly in proportion to* the increase in inputs. When this happens, the constant-cost firm is said to be exhibiting **constant returns.**

Increasing Costs. Over the range of outputs greater than q_m, the firm encounters rising long-run average costs. An expansion in production, even after sufficient time has elapsed for all adjustments to be made, is accompanied by a rise in average costs per unit of output. If factor prices are constant, the firm's output must be increasing *less than* in proportion to the increase in inputs. When this happens, the increasing-cost firm is said to encounter long-run **decreasing returns.**[4] Decreasing returns imply that the

firm suffers some *diseconomy of scale.* As its scale of operations increases, diseconomies are encountered that increase its per-unit cost of production.

Such diseconomies may be associated with the difficulties of managing and controlling an enterprise as its size increases. For example, planning problems do not necessarily vary in direct proportion to size. At first there may be scale economies as the firm grows, but sooner or later, planning and coordination problems may multiply more than in proportion to the growth in size. If so, management costs per unit of output will rise. Other sources of scale diseconomies are the possible alienation of the labour force as size increases; it becomes more difficult to provide appropriate supervision as more and more tiers of supervisors and middle managers come between the person at the top and the workers on the shop floor. Control of middle-range managers may also become more difficult. As the firm becomes larger, managers may begin to pursue their own goals rather than devote all of their efforts to making profits for the firm. Much of the "reengineering" of large firms in the 1990s has been aimed at reducing the extent to which management difficulties increase with firm size, but the problem has not been, and probably cannot be, eliminated entirely.

The Relationship Between Long-Run and Short-Run Costs

The short-run cost curves mentioned at the conclusion of Chapter 8 and the long-run curve studied in this chapter are all derived from the same production function. Each curve assumes given prices for all factor inputs. In the long run, all factors can be varied; in the short run, some must remain fixed. The long-run average cost *(LRAC)* curve shows the lowest cost of producing any output when all factors are variable. Each short-run average total cost *(SRATC)* curve shows the lowest cost of producing any output when one or more factors are held constant at some specific level.

No short-run cost curve can fall below the long-run curve because the *LRAC* curve represents the lowest attainable cost for each possible output. As the level of output is changed, a different-size plant is normally required to achieve the lowest attainable cost. This is shown in Figure 9-2, where the *SRATC* curve lies above the *LRAC* curve *at all levels of output except q_0.*

---

[4]Long-run decreasing returns differ from short-run diminishing returns. In the short run, at least one factor is fixed, and the law of diminishing returns ensures that returns to the variable factor will eventually diminish. In the long run, all factors are variable, and it is possible that physically diminishing returns would never be encountered—at least as long as it was genuinely possible to increase inputs of all factors.

FIGURE 9-2
Long-Run Average Cost and Short-Run Average Cost Curves

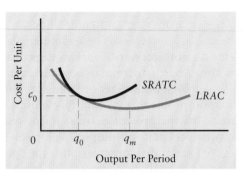

The short-run average total cost *(SRATC)* curve is tangent to the long-run average cost *(LRAC)* curve at the output for which the quantity of the fixed factors is optimal. For all other levels of output, there is either too little or too much of the fixed factors, and *SRATC* lies above *LRAC*. If output exceeds q_0, there is too little of the fixed factors; if output is less than q_0, there is too much of the fixed factor. If some level of output other than q_0 is to be sustained, costs can be reduced to the level of the long-run average cost curve when sufficient time has elapsed to adjust the plant and equipment.

As we observed at the end of Chapter 8, an *SRATC* curve is one of many such curves. The *SRATC* curve in Figure 9-2 shows how costs vary as output is varied from a base output, holding the fixed factor at the quantity most appropriate to that output. Figure 9-3 shows a family of short-run average total cost curves, along with a single long-run average cost curve. The long-run average cost curve is sometimes called an **envelope** because it encloses a series of short-run average total cost curves by being tangent to them. Each *SRATC* curve is tangent to the long-run average cost curve at the level of output for which the quantity of the fixed factor is optimal and lies above it for all other levels of output.

The relationship between the *LRAC* curve and the many different *SRATC* curves has a famous history in economics. The economist who is credited with first working out this relationship, Jacob Viner, initially made a serious mistake which ended up being published; Extension 9-2 explains his mistake and shows how it illustrates an important difference between short-run and long-run costs.

SHIFTS IN COST CURVES

The cost curves derived so far show how cost varies with output, given constant factor prices and fixed

FIGURE 9-3
The Envelope Relationship Between the Long-Run Average Cost Curve and All of the Short-Run Average Total Cost Curves

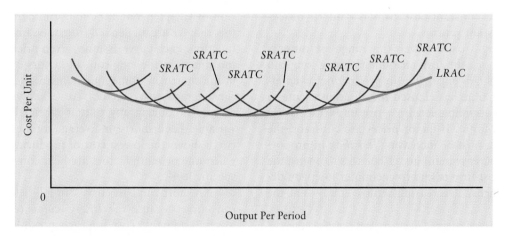

To every point on the long-run average cost *(LRAC)* curve, there is an associated short-run average total cost *(SRATC)* curve tangent at that point. Each short-run curve shows how costs vary if output varies, with the fixed factor being held constant at the level that is optimal for the output at the point of tangency.

JACOB VINER AND THE CLEVER DRAFTSMAN

Jacob Viner (1892–1970) was born in Montreal and studied economics at McGill University under Stephen Leacock (1869–1944). Viner was clearly an outstanding student and, according to some of his McGill classmates, knew much more about economics than did Leacock, who was actually better known as a humourist than an economist. Viner was such a good economist that he was the first person to work out the relationship between a firm's long-run average costs and its short-run average costs. He went on to teach economics at the University of Chicago and at Princeton University and became one of the world's leading economic theorists.

The student who finds the relationship between *SRATC* and *LRAC* hard to understand may take some comfort from the fact that when Jacob Viner first worked out this relationship, and published it in 1931, he made a crucial mistake. In preparing a diagram like Figure 9-3, he instructed his draftsman to draw the *LRAC* curve through the *minimum points* of all the *SRATC* curves, "but so as to never lie above" the *SRATC* curves. Viner later said of the draftsman: "He is a mathematician, however, not an economist, and he saw some mathematical objection to this procedure which I could not succeed in understanding. I could not persuade him to disregard his scruples as a craftsman and to follow my instructions, absurd though they might be."

Viner's mistake was to require that the draftsman connect all of the *minimum* points of the

SRATC curves rather than to construct the curve which would be the *lower envelope* of all the *SRATC* curves. The former curve can of course be drawn, but it *is not* the *LRAC* curve. The latter curve *is* the *LRAC* curve, and is tangent to each *SRATC* curve.

Since Viner's article was published in 1931, generations of economics students have experienced great satisfaction when they finally figured out his crucial mistake. Viner's famous article was often reprinted, for its fame was justly deserved, despite the importance of the mistake. But Viner always rejected suggestions that he correct the error because he did not wish to deprive other students of the pleasure of feeling one up on him.

The economic sense of the fact that tangency is *not* at the minimum points of *SRATC* rests on the subtle distinction between the *most efficient way to utilize a given plant* and the *most efficient way to produce a given level of output*. The first concept defines the minimum of any given *SRATC* curve, while the second defines a point on the *LRAC* curve for any given level of output. It is the second concept that interests us in the long run. If bigger plants can achieve lower costs per unit, there will be a gain in building a bigger plant *and underutilizing it* whenever the gains from using the bigger plant are enough to offset the costs of being inefficient in the use of the plant. If there are gains from building bigger plants (i.e., if *LRAC* is declining), there is always some underutilization that is justified.

---

technology. Changes in either technological knowledge or factor prices will cause the entire family of short-run and long-run average cost curves to shift. Loss of existing technological knowledge is rare, so technological change normally causes change in only one direction, shifting cost curves downward. Improved ways of producing existing products make lower-cost methods of production available.

Changes in factor prices can exert an influence in either direction. If a firm has to pay more for any factor that it uses, the cost of producing each level of

output will rise; if the firm has to pay less for any factor that it uses, the cost of producing each level of output will fall.

A rise in factor prices shifts the family of short-run and long-run average cost curves upward. A fall in factor prices or a technological advance shifts the entire family of average cost curves downward.

Although factor prices usually change gradually, sometimes they change suddenly and drastically. For example, in the mid 1980s, oil prices fell dramatically; the effect was to shift downward the cost curves of all users of oil and oil-related products.

Technological change is constantly occurring and is typically more gradual. To this issue we now turn.

THE VERY-LONG RUN: CHANGES IN TECHNOLOGY

In the long run, profit-maximizing firms do the best they can to produce known products with the techniques and the resources currently available. This means being *on*, rather than above, their long-run cost curves. In the very-long run, the techniques and resources that are available change. Such changes cause *shifts* in long-run cost curves.

The decrease in costs that can be achieved by choosing from among available factors of production, known techniques, and alternative levels of output is necessarily limited. Improvements by invention and innovation are potentially limitless, however, and hence sustained growth in living standards is critically linked to technological change.

Technological change refers to all changes in the available techniques of production. To measure its extent, economists use the notion of **productivity**, defined as a measure of output produced per unit of resource input. The rate of increase in productivity provides a measure of the progress caused by technological change. The significance of such growth is explored further in Application 9-1.[5]

INNOVATION, INVENTION, AND TECHNOLOGICAL CHANGE

Technological change was once thought to be mainly a random process, brought about by inventions made by crackpots and eccentric scientists working in garages and scientific laboratories. As a result of recent research by economists, we now know better.

Changes in technology are often *endogenous responses* to changing economic signals; that is, they result from responses by firms to the same things that induce the substitution of one factor for another within the confines of a given technology.

---

[5]One widely used measure of productivity is output per hour of labour. Other possible measures include output per worker, output per person, and output per unit of inputs, measured by an index number.

In our discussion of long-run demand curves in Chapter 5, we looked at just such technological changes in response to rising relative prices when we spoke of the development, in the 1970s, of smaller, more fuel-efficient cars in the wake of rising gasoline prices. Similarly, much of the move to substitute capital for labour in manufacturing, transportation, communications, mining, and agriculture in response to rising wage rates has taken the form of inventing new labour-saving methods of production.

Invention and Innovation

Invention is the creation of something new, such as a production technique or a product. **Innovation** is the introduction of an invention into methods of production. Invention is thus a precondition to innovation.

Innovation is a costly and very risky activity engaged in by firms in the hope of gaining profits; it results from responses to signals of current and expected prices and costs—that is, responses to profit incentives. Profit incentives are in turn affected by many aspects of the economic climate, among them the rate of growth of the economy, the cost and availability of money for investment, and all sorts of government policies, from taxes to regulations.

Invention is cumulative in effect. A useful invention is adopted; a useless one is discarded. The cumulative impact of many small, useful devices and techniques may be as great as the impact of one occasional dramatic mechanism such as the steam engine, the sewing machine, or the computer chip. Indeed, few famous inventions have sprung from a single act of creative genius; usually, each builds on the contributions of prior inventors. The backlog of past inventions constitutes society's technical knowledge, and that backlog in turn feeds innovation.

Kinds of Technological Change

Consider three kinds of change that influence production and cost in the very-long run.

New Techniques. Throughout the nineteenth and twentieth centuries, changes in the techniques available for producing existing products have been dramatic; this is called *process innovation*. About the same amount of coal is produced in North America today as was produced 50 years ago, but the number of coal miners is less than one-tenth what it was then. Eighty years ago, roads and railways were built by gangs of workers who used buckets, spades, and draft horses. Today, bulldozers, giant trucks, and other spe-

APPLICATION 9-1

THE SIGNIFICANCE OF PRODUCTIVITY GROWTH

Economics used to be known as the "dismal science" because some of its predictions were grim. Thomas Malthus (1766–1834) and other Classical economists predicted that the pressure of more and more people on the world's limited resources would cause a decline in output per person due to the law of diminishing returns. Human history would see more and more people living less and less well and the surplus population, which could not be supported, dying off from hunger and disease.

This prediction has proved wrong for the developed countries, for two main reasons. First, their populations have not expanded as rapidly as predicted by early economists, who were writing before birth-control techniques were widely used. Second, pure knowledge and its applied techniques have expanded so rapidly during the past 150 years that the ability to squeeze more out of limited resources has expanded faster than the population. We have experienced sustained growth in productivity that has permitted increases in output per person.

Growth in productivity permits increases in output per person and thus contributes to rising living standards.

Productivity increases are a powerful force for increasing living standards. Our great-grandparents would have regarded today's standard of living in most industrialized countries as unattainable. An apparently modest rate of increase in productivity of 2 percent per year leads to a doubling of output per hour of labour every 35 years. Productivity in Canada has increased at a rate somewhat greater than this throughout most of the twentieth century.

The growth rates of other countries have been even higher. Between 1945 and 1980, German productivity increased at 5 percent per year, doubling its output every 14 years. In Japan, it increased at more than 9 percent per year, a rate that doubles output per hour of labour approximately every 8 years! In many countries, a stable rate of productivity growth came to be taken for granted as an automatic source of ever-increasing living standards.

During the 1970s, the rate of productivity growth in most industrialized countries dropped sharply below its historical trend, and the slowdown was particularly acute in Canada and the United States. Although productivity growth has increased somewhat in the first part of the 1990s, almost no one expects the doubling of productivity in every generation to return anytime soon.

A permanent slowdown in productivity growth means that living standards rise more slowly than before.

---

cialized equipment have banished the workhorse completely from construction sites and to a great extent have displaced the pick-and-shovel worker.

An important new production technique called *lean production* (also often called *flexible manufacturing*) is rapidly replacing long-established *mass production, assembly line* techniques in many industries. Lean production, which was pioneered by the Japanese automobile industry and is spreading throughout the Western industrialized countries, is a more flexible, lower-cost method of production that produces higher-quality products and

reduces the cost of developing new products. Lean production typically has a lower long-run cost curve than conventional mass production and a more rapidly downward-shifting cost curve in the very-long run. Lean production is discussed further in Application 9-2.

New Products. New goods and services are constantly being invented and marketed; this is called *product innovation*. Videocassette players, personal computers, compact discs, and many other current consumer products did not exist a mere generation ago. Other products have changed so dra-

---

APPLICATION 9-2

THE LEAN PRODUCTION REVOLUTION*

In many industries and in many countries, production techniques are currently being revolutionized by the introduction of so-called *lean production techniques* or *flexible manufacturing*. This is the most fundamental change to occur since the introduction of mass production—a technique brought to full development by Henry Ford early in the twentieth century. To understand the lean production revolution, pioneered by the Japanese, we must distinguish the three types of production methods used today.

Craft methods employ highly-skilled workers to make nonstandardized products that are often tailor-made for individual purchasers. The result is usually an expensive product of high quality, made by artisans who get considerable job satisfaction.

Mass-production methods are based on specialization and division of labour (see Extension 3-2 in Chapter 3). They use skilled personnel to design products and production methods. They then employ relatively unskilled labour to produce standardized parts and to assemble them using highly specialized, single-purpose machines. The parts are usually manufactured in separate locations, often by distinct companies, and then assembled at a central production facility, often called an *assembly line*. The design of the product is centralized, and manufacturers bid competitively to produce parts to the stated specifications. The cost of changing the specialized equipment from the production of one product variant to another is high, and hence specific product types are

produced for as long as possible. The result is a standardized product, made in a fairly small number of variants and produced at low cost with moderate quality. The work is repetitive, and workers are regarded as variable costs to be laid off or taken on as the desired rate of production varies.

Lean production methods combine the flexibility and high-quality standards of craft production with the low cost of mass production techniques. They are lean because they use less of all inputs, including time, labour, capital, and inventories, compared with either of the other techniques. They are flexible because the costs of switching from one product line to another are minimized.

In lean production, workers are organized as teams; each worker is encouraged to do all of the tasks assigned to the team, using equipment that is less highly specialized than is used in mass production techniques. This emphasizes individuality and initiative rather than a mind-numbing repetition of one unskilled operation. It also helps workers to identify places where improvements can be made and encourages them to follow up on these.

In mass-production plants, stopping an assembly line to correct a problem at one point stops work at all points. Stopping the line is therefore regarded as a serious matter, and keeping the assembly line running is the sole responsibility of a senior line manager. To reduce stoppages, large stocks of each part are held, and defective parts are discarded. Faults in assembly, which are treated as random events, are left to be corrected after the product has been assembled—often an expensive procedure. In lean production, by contrast, every worker has the ability to stop production whenever

---

*This material is adapted from J. P. Womack, D. T. Jones, and D. Ross, *The Machine That Changed the World* (New York: Macmillan, 1990).

---

matically that the only connection they have with the "same" product that was produced in the past is the name. A 1997 Ford is very different from a 1920 Ford, and it is even different from a 1970 Ford in size, safety, and gasoline consumption. Modern jets are revolutionary compared with the first jet aircraft, which were in turn many times larger and faster than

the DC–3, the workhorse of the airlines during the 1930s and 1940s. Beyond having wings and engines, the DC–3 itself bore little resemblance to the Wright brothers' original flying machine.

Improved Inputs. Improvements in such intangibles as health and education raise the quality of labour services. Today's workers and managers are a fault is discovered. Parts are delivered by the suppliers to the work stations "just in time." Defective parts are put aside for their source to be identified, and any defects are treated as events with patterns of causes that need to be understood. When lean methods are first introduced, stoppages are frequent as problems are identified and investigated. As the sources are found and removed, work stoppages diminish, and the typical mature lean production line, in which any worker can stop the line, stops much less frequently than the typical mass production assembly line, where only the line foreman can press the stop button.

The result for labour is much more worker identification with the job and much more worker satisfaction than under mass production techniques. Employers find that their labour force develops substantial skills, and they try to hold on to workers rather than treating them as strictly variable factors. (This can often result in some transitional difficulties as both unions and management adjust to new ways of dealing with each other.)

Product design is expensive. Mass-production firms try to reduce costs by using specialist designers. For example, one person may spend a lifetime trying to improve window-opening mechanisms. Specialization creates problems both in coordinating the work of various designers and in getting good feedback from parts producers and assembly line workers to designers. Lean producers use design teams that are nonspecialized and work closely with production engineers and parts producers. This creates more flexibility and better feedback, from the practical problems that arise in production to the basic design of products.

Although lean production methods generally still have scale economies—unit costs fall as the volume of output increases—their main effect is to shift the whole long-run cost curve downward. Lean methods are also effective in the very-long run, especially in developing successful new products that can be produced efficiently and cheaply.

Japanese automobile firms using these methods have been able to achieve unit costs of production below those of mass-production-based North American car factories that have twice their volume of output. They have also been able to lead in international competition to design new products efficiently and rapidly. Lean production methods are a major source of the Japanese competitive advantage, in automobiles and in a range of other manufactured goods. The ability of firms in other countries to compete successfully with these Japanese firms may depend on the speed with which they can institute lean methods in their own production processes.

Many Canadian and U.S. firms have redesigned their systems of operation to implement lean production methods in a process referred to as "reengineering." This has often involved a reduction in middle management, whose output is of little value in a lean system, with reduced heirarchy and more participation on the part of workers. In some cases, however, reengineering has become a euphemism for widespread layoffs. "Downsizing" of a firm may or may not be associated with moving toward lean production, and it is important to look at each case to see if the changes being made are simply efforts to cut costs by increasing the load on remaining employees or if they truly change the way that the firm is organized to produce its output.

healthier and better educated than their grandparents. Many of today's unskilled workers are literate and competent in arithmetic, and their managers are apt to be trained in methods of business management and computer science.

Similarly, improvements in material inputs occur. For example, the type and quality of metals have changed. Steel has replaced iron, and aluminum substitutes for steel in a process of change that makes a statistical category such as "primary metals" seem unsatisfactory. Even for a given category, say, steel, today's product is lighter, stronger, and more flexible than the "same" product manufactured only 20 years ago.

THE CHOICES THAT FIRMS FACE IN THE VERY-LONG RUN

When firms receive signals that the economic environment they currently face and can expect to face in the future is changing, they can respond in a number of ways.

Suppose that the price of an important input rises and that this increase is expected to persist into the future. One option for the firm is to make what we have called a long-run response by substituting away from the use of the input by changing its production techniques within the confines of existing technology. Another option is to invest in research in order to develop new production techniques that innovate away from the input. Often, both responses are adopted, but because both involve the use of costly resources, the responses are often substitutes in the sense that a particular firm may have to choose one or the other.

It is important to recognize that the two options can involve quite different actions and can ultimately have quite different implications for productivity. For example, consider three possible responses to an apparently permanent increase in labour costs.

One firm might reallocate its production activities to Mexico or Southeast Asia, where labour costs are relatively low and hence labour-intensive production techniques remain quite profitable. A second firm might elect to replace existing equipment with alternative machines that are more expensive but use less labour and hence become more attractive in the face of increased labour costs. A third firm might elect to devote resources to developing new production techniques—perhaps using robotics or other new equipment—that innovate the increased labour costs away.

All three are possible reactions to the changed circumstances. The first two are largely well understood in advance and will lead to improved efficiency relative to continued reliance on the original production methods. The third response, depending on the often unpredictable results of the innovation, may reduce costs sufficiently to warrant the investment in research and development and may even lead to substantially more effective production techniques that allow the firm to maintain an advantage over its competitors for a number of years.

In trying to understand any industry's response to changes in its operating environment, it is important to consider the effects of endogenous innovations in technology as well as substitution based on changes in the use of existing technologies.

SUMMARY

A. THE LONG RUN: NO FIXED FACTORS

- There are no fixed factors in the long run. Profit-maximizing firms choose from the alternatives open to them the least-cost method of achieving any specific output. A long-run cost curve represents the boundary between attainable and unattainable levels of cost for the given technology.
- The principle of substitution says that efficient production will use cheaper factors lavishly and more expensive ones more prudently. If the relative prices of factors change, relatively more of cheaper factors and relatively less of more expensive ones will be used.
- The shape of the long-run cost curve depends on the relationship of inputs to outputs as the whole scale of a firm's operations changes. Increasing, constant, and decreasing returns lead, respectively, to decreasing, constant, and increasing long-run average costs.

- The long-run and short-run cost curves are related. Every long-run cost corresponds to some quantity of each factor and is thus on some short-run cost curve. The short-run cost curve shows how costs vary when that particular quantity of a fixed factor is used to produce outputs greater than or less than the output for which it is optimal.
- Cost curves shift upward or downward in response to changes in the prices of factors or changes in technology. Increases in factor prices shift cost curves upward. Decreases in factor prices and technological advances shift cost curves downward.

B. THE VERY-LONG RUN: CHANGES IN TECHNOLOGY

- Over the very-long run, the most important influence on costs of production and on standards of living has been increases in output made possible by technological change—all the various changes in available techniques of production that lead to an increase in measured productivity.

- Changes in technology are often *endogenous responses* to changing economic signals; that is, they result from responses by firms to the same things that induce the substitution of one factor for another in a given technology.
- Innovation is the key to productivity growth. It requires invention but also profitable opportunities for the introduction of available knowledge. The state

of the economy, the institutional climate, and differences in technological possibilities in sectors where demand is growing and declining all affect the opportunities for innovation. Innovation can lead to technological change due to the introduction of new techniques, new products, and improved inputs.

- In trying to understand any industry's response to changes in its operating environment, it is important to consider the effects of endogenous innovations in technology as well as substitution based on changes in the use of existing technologies.

KEY CONCEPTS

The implication of cost minimization

The interpretation of $MP_K/MP_L = P_K/P_L$

The principle of substitution

Increasing, decreasing, and constant returns

Economies of scale

Envelope

Technological change and productivity growth

Changes in technology as endogenous responses

Determinants of innovation

Invention and innovation

DISCUSSION QUESTIONS

1. In *The Competitive Advantage of Nations,* Professor Michael Porter of Harvard University claimed: "Faced with high relative labor cost, . . . American consumer electronics firms moved to locate labor-intensive activities in . . . Asian countries, leaving the product and production process essentially the same. . . . Japanese rivals . . . set out instead to eliminate labor through automation. Doing so involved reducing the number of components which further lowered cost and improved quality. Japanese firms were soon building assembly plants in the United States, the place American firms had sought to avoid." Discuss these reactions in terms of changes over the long run and the very-long run.

2. Why does the profit-maximizing firm choose the least-cost method of producing any given output? Might a non-profit-maximizing organization such as a university, church, or government intentionally choose a method of production other than the least-cost one?

3. The chairman of a multinational oil company recently said, "Our government has adopted a gratuitously hostile attitude. Industry has been compelled to spend more and more of its research dollars to comply with

environmental, health, and safety regulations—and to move away from longer-term efforts aimed at major scientific advance." If this is true, is it necessarily a sign that government policies are misguided?

4. Use the principle of substitution to predict the effect of each of the following.

   a. During the 1960s, salaries of professors rose much more rapidly than those of teaching assistants. During the 1970s, salaries of teaching assistants rose more than those of professors. During the 1980s, the relative salaries of these two groups did not change greatly.

   b. The ratio of land costs to building costs is much higher in big cities than in smaller cities.

   c. Gold leaf is produced by pounding gold with a hammer. The thinner it is, the more valuable it is. The price of gold is set on the world market, but the price of labour varies among countries.

   d. Wages of textile workers and shoe machinery operators are higher in Canada than in the southern United States.

5. The long-run average cost curve can be thought of as consisting of a series of points, one taken from each

of a number of short-run average total cost curves. Explain in what sense any point on the long-run average cost curve is also on some short-run average total cost curve. What is the interpretation of a move from one point on a long-run average cost curve to another point on the same curve? Contrast this with a movement along a short-run average total cost curve.

6. Israel, a very small country, imports the "insides" of its automobiles, but it manufactures the bodies. If this makes economic sense, what does it tell us about cost conditions of automobile manufacturers?

7. Name five important modern products that were not available at the time you were born. Consider to what extent the items on your list may reflect product or process innovation.

8. Each of the following is a means of increasing productivity. Discuss which groups in a society might oppose each one.

   a. A labour-saving invention that permits all goods to be manufactured with less labour than before

   b. Rapidly increasing population growth in the economy

   c. The removal of all government production safety rules

   d. A reduction in corporate income taxes

   e. A reduction in production of services and an increase in agricultural production

9. Think of an industry with which you are familiar. Discuss the characteristics that may lead to economies of scale. Discuss the characteristics that would cause diseconomies of scale as production is continually increased.

10. Many people have called the transistor and the integrated circuit, which are the heart of the modern computer, the most important inventions of this century. Discuss the process of innovation with respect to computers. How many applications has this device found? Has the application of computers to a device or a task always resulted in a downward shift in the average cost curve?

APPENDIX TO CHAPTER 9

Isoquant Analysis

The production function gives the relationship between the factor inputs that the firm uses and the output that it obtains. In the long run, the firm can choose among many different combinations of inputs that yield the same output. The production function and the long-run choices open to the firm can be represented graphically using *isoquants*.

ISOQUANTS

Table 9A-1 illustrates a hypothetical example in which several combinations of two inputs, labour and capital, can produce a given quantity of output. The data from Table 9A-1 are plotted graphically in Figure 9A-1. A smooth curve is drawn through the points to indicate that there are additional ways, which are not listed in the table, of producing the same output.

This curve is called an **isoquant**. It shows the whole set of technologically efficient factor combinations for producing a given level of output—6 units, in this case. This is an example of graphing a relationship between three variables in two dimensions. It is analogous to the contour line on a map, which shows all points of equal altitude, and to an indifference curve (discussed in the Appendix to Chapter 7), which shows all combinations of products that yield the consumer equal utility.

As we move from one point on an isoquant to another, we are *substituting one factor for another* while holding output constant. If we move from point *b* to point *c*, we are substituting 1 unit of labour for 3 units of capital. *The marginal rate of substitution measures the rate at which one factor is substituted for another with output being held con-*

TABLE 9A-1
Alternative Methods of Producing 6 Units of Output: Points on an Isoquant

Method	K	L	ΔK	ΔL	Rate of Substitution $\Delta K / \Delta L$
a	18	2			
			−6	1	−6.00
b	12	3			
			−3	1	−3.00
c	9	4			
			−3	2	−1.50
d	6	6			
			−2	3	−0.67
e	4	9			
			−1	3	−0.33
f	3	12			
			−1	6	−0.17
g	2	18			

An isoquant describes the firm's alternative methods for producing a given output. The table lists some of the methods available to produce 6 units of output. The first combination uses a great deal of capital *(K)* and very little labour *(L)*. As we move down the table, labour is substituted for capital in such a way as to keep output constant. Finally, at the bottom, most of the capital has been replaced by labour. The rate of substitution between the two factors is calculated in the last three columns of the table. Note that as we move down the table, the absolute value of the rate of substitution declines.

stant. Graphically, the marginal rate of substitution is measured by the slope of the isoquant at a particular point.[1] Table 9A-1 shows the calculation of some rates of substitution between various points on the isoquant. [21]

---

[1]Sometimes the term *marginal rate of technical substitution* is used to distinguish this concept from the analogous one for consumer theory (marginal rate of substitution) that we examined in Chapter 7. From here on, we adopt the standard convention of defining the marginal rate of substitution as the negative of the slope of the isoquant so that it is a positive number.

FIGURE 9A-1
An Isoquant for Output Equal to 6 Units

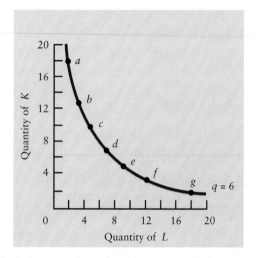

Isoquants are downward sloping and convex. The downward slope reflects the requirement of technical efficiency: Keeping the level of output constant, a reduction in the use of one factor requires an increase in the use of the other factor. The convex shape of the isoquant reflects a diminishing marginal rate of (technical) substitution. The lettered points on the graph are plotted from the data in Table 9A-1. Starting from point *a*, which uses relatively little labour and much capital, and moving to point *b*, 1 additional unit of labour can substitute for 6 units of capital (while holding production constant). However, from *b* to *c*, 1 unit of labour substitutes for only 3 units of capital. This diminishing rate is expressed geometrically by the flattening of the slope of the isoquant.

The marginal rate of substitution is related to the marginal products of the factors of production. To see how, consider an example. Suppose that at the present level of inputs of labour and capital, the marginal product of labour is 2 units of output and the marginal product of capital is 1 unit of output. If the firm reduces its use of capital and increases its use of labour to keep output constant, it needs to add only one-half unit of labour for 1 unit of capital given up. If, at another point on the isoquant with more labour and less capital, the marginal products are 2 for capital and 1 for labour, the firm will have to add 2 units of labour for every

unit of capital it gives up. The general proposition is this:

The marginal rate of (technical) substitution between two factors of production is equal to the ratio of their marginal products.

Isoquants satisfy two important conditions: They are downward sloping, and they are convex when viewed from the origin. What is the economic meaning of these conditions?

The downward slope indicates that each factor input has a positive marginal product. If the input of one factor is reduced and that of the other is held constant, output will be reduced. Thus if one input is decreased, production can be held constant only if the other factor input is increased. The marginal rate of substitution has a negative value. Decreases in one factor must be balanced by increases in the other factor if output is to be held constant.

To understand the convexity of the isoquant, consider what happens as the firm moves along the isoquant of Figure 9A-1 downward and to the right. Labour is being added and capital reduced to keep output constant. If labour is added in increments of exactly 1 unit, how much capital may be dispensed with each time? The key to the answer is that both factors are assumed to be subject to the law of diminishing returns. Thus the gain in output associated with each additional unit of labour added is *diminishing*, whereas the loss of output associated with each additional unit of capital forgone is *increasing*. It therefore takes ever-smaller reductions in capital to compensate for equal increases in labour. This implies that the isoquant is convex viewed from the origin.

AN ISOQUANT MAP

The isoquant of Figure 9A-1 is for 6 units of output. There is another isoquant for 7 units, another for 7,000 units, and a different one for every other rate of output. Each isoquant refers to a specific level of output and connects combinations of factors that are technologically efficient methods of achieving that output. If we plot a representative set of these isoquants from the same production function on a single graph, we get an *isoquant map* like that in

FIGURE 9A-2
An Isoquant Map

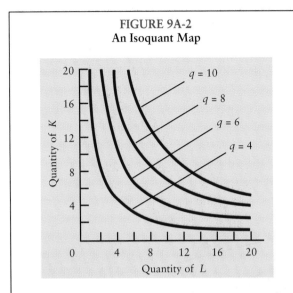

An isoquant map shows a set of isoquants, one for each level of output. Each isoquant corresponds to a specific level of output and shows factor combinations that are technologically efficient methods of producing that output.

Figure 9A-2. The higher the level of output along a particular isoquant, the farther the isoquant is from the origin.

CONDITIONS FOR COST MINIMIZATION

Finding the *economically efficient* way of producing any output requires finding the least-cost factor combination. To do this requires that when both factors are variable, factor prices be known. Suppose, to continue the example, that capital is priced at $4 per unit and labour at $1 per unit. In the Appendix to Chapter 7, a budget line was used to show the alternative combinations of goods that a household could buy; here an *isocost line* is used to show alternative combinations of factors that a firm could buy for a given total cost. Four different isocost lines appear in Figure 9A-3. The slope of each reflects *relative* factor prices, just as the slope of the budget line in Chapter 7 represented relative product prices. For

given factor prices, a series of parallel isocost lines will reflect the alternative levels of expenditure on factor purchases that are open to the firm. The higher the level of expenditure, the farther the isocost line is from the origin.

In Figure 9A-4, the isoquant and isocost maps are brought together. Recall that economic efficiency requires any given level of output to be produced at minimum possible cost. Thus, the economically efficient method of production must be a point on an isoquant that just touches (is tangent to) an isocost line. If the isoquant cuts the isocost line, it is possible to move along the isoquant and reach a lower level of cost. Only at a point of tangency is a movement in either direction along the isoquant a movement to a higher cost level. The lowest attainable cost of producing 6 units is $24. This cost level can be achieved only by operating at A, the point where the $24 isocost line is tangent to the 6-unit isoquant. The lowest average cost of producing 6 units is thus $24/6 = $4 per unit of output.

The least-cost position is given graphically by the tangency point between the isoquant and the isocost lines.

FIGURE 9A-3
Isocost Lines

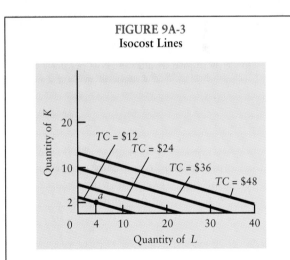

Each isocost line shows alternative factor combinations that can be purchased for a given outlay. The graph shows the four isocost lines that result when labour costs $1 per unit and capital $4 per unit and when expenditure is held constant at $12, $24, $36, and $48, respectively. The line labeled $TC = 12 represents all combinations of the two factors that the firm could buy for $12. Point a represents 2 units of K and 4 units of L.

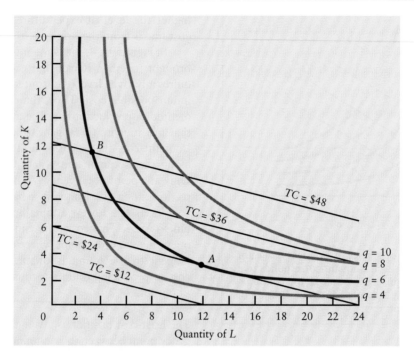

FIGURE 9A-4
The Determination of the Least-Cost Method of Production

Least-cost methods of production are represented by points of tangency between isoquant and isocost lines. The isoquant map of Figure 9A-2 and the isocost lines of Figure 9A-3 are brought together. Consider point A. It is on the 6-unit isoquant and the $24 isocost line. Thus it is possible to achieve the output $q = 6$ for a total cost of $24. There are other ways to achieve this output, for example, at point B, where $TC = \$48$. Moving along the isoquant from point A in either direction increases cost. Similarly, moving along the isocost line from point A in either direction lowers output. Thus either move would raise cost per unit.

Notice that point A in Figure 9A-4 indicates not only the lowest level of cost for 6 units of output but also the highest level of output for $24 of cost. Thus we find the same solution if we set out *either* to minimize the cost of producing 6 units of output *or* to maximize the output that can be produced for $24. One problem is said to be the *dual* of the other.

The slope of the isocost line is given by the ratio of the prices of the two factors of production. The slope of the isoquant is given by the ratio of their marginal products. When the firm reaches its least-cost position, it has equated the price ratio (which is given to it by the market) with the ratio of the marginal products (which it can adjust by varying the proportions in which it hires the factors). In symbols,

$$\frac{MP_K}{MP_L} = \frac{P_K}{P_L}$$

We have now derived this result by use of the isoquant analysis of the firm's decisions. [22] Note the similarity of this condition for a cost-minimizing firm to Equation 2 in Chapter 7 where we showed how utility maximization for a consumer requires that the ratio of marginal utilities of consuming two products must equal the ratio of the two product prices.

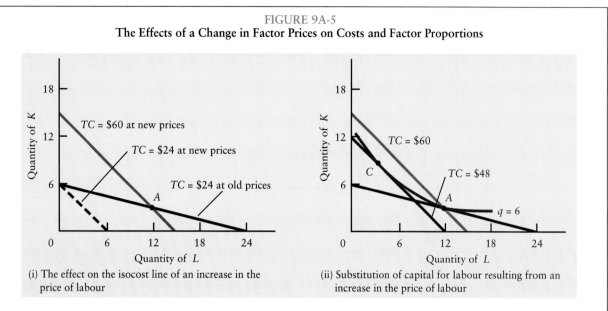

FIGURE 9A-5
The Effects of a Change in Factor Prices on Costs and Factor Proportions

(i) The effect on the isocost line of an increase in the price of labour

(ii) Substitution of capital for labour resulting from an increase in the price of labour

An increase in the price of labour pivots the isocost line inward, increasing its slope. This changes the least-cost method of producing any output. In part (i), the rise in the price of L from \$1 to \$4 per unit (with the price of K being held constant at \$4) pivots the \$24 isocost line inward to the dashed line. Any output previously produced for \$24 will cost more at the new prices if it uses any labour. The new cost of using the factor combination at A rises from \$24 to \$60. In part (ii), the steeper isocost line is tangent to the isoquant at C, not A, so that more capital and less labour is used. Costs at C are \$48, higher than they were before the price increase but not as high as they would be if the factor substitution had not occurred.

THE PRINCIPLE OF SUBSTITUTION

Suppose that with technology unchanged (that is, for a given isoquant map), the price of one factor changes. Let us say that with the price of capital unchanged at \$4 per unit, the price of labour rises from \$1 to \$4 per unit. Originally, the efficient factor combination for producing 6 units of output was 12 units of labour and 3 units of capital. Total cost was \$24. To produce that same output in the same way would now cost \$60 at the new factor prices. Figure 9A-5 shows why this is not efficient. The slope of the isocost line has changed, which makes it efficient to substitute the now relatively cheaper capital for the relatively more expensive labour. This illustrates the principle of substitution.

Changes in relative factor prices will cause a partial replacement of factors that have become relatively

more expensive by factors that have become relatively cheaper.

Of course, substitution of capital for labour cannot fully offset the effects of a rise in cost of labour, as Figure 9A-5(i) shows. Consider the output attainable for \$24. In the figure, there are two isocost lines representing \$24 of outlay—at the old and new prices of labour. The new isocost line for \$24 lies inside the old one (except where no labour is used). The \$24 isocost line must therefore be tangent to a lower isoquant. This means that if production is to be held constant, higher costs must be accepted. However, because of substitution, it is not necessary to accept costs as high as those that would accompany an unchanged factor proportion. In the example, 6 units can be produced for \$48 rather than the \$60 that would be required if no change in factor proportions were made.

This leads to the following predictions:

A rise in the price of one factor with all other factor prices being held constant will (1) shift the cost curves of products that use that factor upward and (2) lead to a substitution of factors that are now relatively cheaper for the factor whose price has risen.

Both of these predictions were stated in Chapter 9; now they have been derived formally using isoquants.

PART FOUR

PRICING AND MARKET STRUCTURE

Do wheat farmers in Saskatchewan and Manitoba compete with each other in the same way that Nike competes with Reebok? How would the Saskatchewan farmer respond to an improvement in techniques used by the Manitoba farmer? How would Nike respond to a price reduction by Reebok? Are markets with many firms different in important ways from markets with only a few firms? Why does the government sometimes worry about (and prevent) two firms from merging to form one larger firm? Are there special considerations when one of the merging firms is a foreign firm? These are the types of questions you will be able to answer after reading the next five chapters.

Chapter 10 discusses the *theory of perfect competition*. This is the theory that describes markets in which there are a very large number of firms producing very similar products, like the wheat farmers in Saskatchewan and Manitoba. You will be introduced to the important concept of *price taking*. You will see how the existence of profits in such an industry leads to the *entry* of new firms, and why such entry leads to the dissipation of those profits. Similarly, you will see why losses lead existing firms to *exit*, and why this increases the profits of the remaining firms.

Chapter 11 introduces you to *monopoly*—a situation in which there is only a single seller of a product. You will see that monopolies typically produce less ouptut and have higher prices than do firms under perfect competition. You will understand why several firms often try to join together to form a *cartel*—like the OPEC oil cartel—in which case they act as if they were a monopoly seller. You will also see why such cartels often break down.

Chapter 12 discusses the idea of *imperfect competition*, which describes markets that are in between the polar cases of perfect competition and monopoly. You will learn about industries with many firms but *differentiated products*, and you will also learn about industries with very few firms, in which *strategic behaviour* between the firms is important. It is here that you will see how economists—using simple *game theory*—think about Nike's likely response to Reebok's price reduction.

The concept of *economic efficiency* is examined in Chapter 13. You will see why perfectly competitive markets are more efficient than monopolized markets, and you will then understand why Canadian *competition policy* is designed to prevent the occurrence of some monopolies. In Chapter 14, we examine several issues related to what goes on inside firms. You will see why the *owners* of firms sometimes have different interests than the *managers* of firms, and how the *market for corporate control* enters the picture. We explore the hypothesis of *profit maximization* and examine what might happen if firms did not act to maximize profits. Finally, we look at some issues concerning the costs and benefits of *foreign investment*.

CHAPTER 10

COMPETITIVE MARKETS

Does PetroCanada compete with Esso in the sale of gasoline? Does American Express compete with Visa? Does a wheat farmer from Biggar, Saskatchewan compete with a wheat farmer from Brandon, Manitoba? If we use the ordinary meaning of the word *compete*, the answer to the first two questions is plainly yes, and the answer to the third is no.

PetroCanada and Esso both advertise extensively to persuade car drivers to buy their products. All sorts of things, from free dishes to performance-enhancing gasoline additives, are used to tempt drivers to buy one brand of gasoline rather than another. A host of world travelers in various tight spots attest on television or in magazines to the virtues of American Express, while other happy faces advise us that only with a Visa card can their pleasures be ours.

When we shift our attention to wheat farmers, however, we see that there is nothing that the Saskatchewan farmer can do to affect either the sales or the profits of the Manitoba farmer. There would be no point in doing so even if they could, since the sales and profits of the Manitoba farm have no effect on those of the Saskatchewan farm.

To sort out the questions of who is competing with whom and in what sense, it is useful to distinguish between the behaviour of individual firms and the type of market in which they operate. In everyday use, the word *competition* usually refers to competitive behaviour. Economists, however, are interested both in the competitive behaviour of individual firms and in a quite distinct concept—competitive market structure.

MARKET STRUCTURE AND FIRM BEHAVIOUR

The term **market structure** refers to all the features that may affect the behaviour and performance of the firms in a market (for example, the number of firms in the market or the type of product that they sell).

COMPETITIVE MARKET STRUCTURE

The competitiveness of the market is the extent to which individual firms have power to influence market prices or the terms on which their product is sold. *The less power an individual firm has to influence the market in which it sells its product, the more competitive that market is.*

The extreme form of competitiveness occurs when each firm has zero market power. In such a case, there are so many firms in the market that each must accept the price set by the forces of market demand and market supply. The firms perceive themselves as being able to sell as much as they choose at the prevailing market price and as having no power to influence that price. If the firm charged a higher price, it would make no sales; so many other firms would be selling at the market price that buyers would take their business elsewhere.

This extreme is called a *perfectly competitive market structure* or, more simply, a *perfectly competitive market*. In such a market there is no need for individual firms to compete actively with one another because none has any power over the market. One firm's ability to sell its product does not depend on the behaviour of any other firm. For example, the Saskatchewan and Manitoba wheat farms operate in a perfectly competitive market over which they have no power. Neither can change the market price for its wheat by altering its own behaviour.

COMPETITIVE BEHAVIOUR

In everyday language, the term *competitive behaviour* refers to the degree to which individual firms actively vie with one another for business. For example, PetroCanada and Esso clearly engage in competitive behaviour. It is also true, however, that both companies have some real power over their market. Each has the power to decide the price that people will pay for their gasoline and oil, within limits set by buyers' tastes and the prices of competing products. Either firm could raise its prices and still continue to attract some customers. So even though they actively compete with each other, they do so in a market that does not have a perfectly competitive structure.

In contrast, the Saskatchewan and Manitoba wheat farmers do not engage in competitive behaviour because the only way they can affect their profits is by changing their own outputs of wheat or their own production costs.

The distinction that we have just made between behaviour and structure explains why firms in perfectly competitive markets (e.g., the Saskatchewan and Manitoba wheat producers) do not compete actively with each other, whereas firms that do compete actively with each other (e.g., PetroCanada and Esso) do not operate in perfectly competitive markets.

THE SIGNIFICANCE OF MARKET STRUCTURE

PetroCanada and Esso are two of several large firms in the oil *industry*. They produce petroleum products and sell them in various *markets*. The terms *industry* and *market* are familiar from everyday use.

However, economists give them precise definitions that we need to understand.

We noted in Chapter 3 that a market consists of an area over which buyers and sellers can negotiate the exchange of some product. The firms that produce a well-defined product or a closely related set of products constitute an **industry**. In earlier chapters, we developed and used market demand curves; here we note that the market demand curve for any particular product is the demand curve facing the industry that produces the product.

When the managers of a firm make their production and sales decisions, they need to know what quantity of a product their firm can sell at various prices. Their concern is therefore not with the *market* demand curve for their industry's product but rather with the demand curve for their own firm's output of that product. If they know the demand curve that their own firm faces, they know the sales that their firm can make at each price it might charge, and thus they know its potential revenues. If they also know their firm's costs for producing the product, they can calculate the profits that would be associated with each rate of output. With this information, they can choose the output that maximizes profits.

Recall that economists define market structure as the characteristics that affect the behaviour and performance of firms that sell in that market. These characteristics determine, among other things, the relationship between the market demand curve for the industry's product and the demand curve that each firm in that industry faces.

To reduce the analysis of market structure to manageable proportions, economists focus on four theoretical market structures that cover most actual cases: *perfect competition, monopoly, monopolistic competition,* and *oligopoly.* Perfect competition will be dealt with in the rest of this chapter, the others in the chapters that follow.

THE THEORY OF PERFECT COMPETITION

The perfectly competitive market structure—usually referred to simply as **perfect competition**—applies directly to a number of markets. It also provides an important benchmark for comparison with other market structures.

THE ASSUMPTIONS OF PERFECT COMPETITION

The theory of perfect competition is built on a number of key assumptions relating to each firm and to the industry as a whole.

1. All the firms in the industry sell an identical product. Economists say that the firms sell a **homogeneous product.**

2. Customers know the nature of the product being sold and the prices charged by each firm.

3. The level of a firm's output at which its long-run average cost reaches a minimum is small relative to the *industry's* total output. (This is the precise way of saying that the firm is small relative to the size of the industry.)

4. Each firm in the industry is a **price taker.** This means that the firm can alter its rate of production and sales without affecting the market price of its product. This is why a firm operating in a perfectly competitive market has no power to influence that market through its own individual actions. It must passively accept whatever happens to be the ruling price, but it can sell as much as it wants at that price.[1]

5. The industry is assumed to be characterized by *freedom of entry and exit;* that is, any new firm is free to enter the industry and start producing if it so wishes, and any existing firm is free to cease production and leave the industry. Existing firms cannot bar the entry of new firms, and there are no legal prohibitions or other artificial barriers to entering or exiting the industry.

The Saskatchewan and Manitoba wheat farmers we considered earlier provide us with good illustrations of firms that are operating in a perfectly competitive market. Because each individual wheat farmer is just one of a very large number of producers who are all growing the same product, one firm's contribution to the industry's total production is a tiny drop in an extremely large bucket. Each firm will correctly assume that variations in its output

---

[1]To emphasize its importance, we identify price taking as a separate assumption, although, strictly speaking, it is implied by the first three assumptions.

have no significant effect on the world price of wheat. Thus each firm, knowing that it can sell as much or as little as it chooses at that price, adapts its behaviour to a given market price of wheat. Furthermore, there is nothing that existing farmers can do to stop another farmer from growing wheat, and there are no legal deterrents to becoming a wheat farmer. Anyone who has enough money to buy or rent the necessary land, labour, and equipment can become a wheat farmer.

The difference between the wheat farmers and PetroCanada is in the *degree of market power.* Each firm that is producing wheat is an insignificant part of the whole market and thus has no power to influence the price of wheat. The oil company does have power to influence the price of gasoline because its own sales represent a significant part of the total sales of gasoline.

THE DEMAND CURVE FOR A PERFECTLY COMPETITIVE FIRM

A major distinction between firms operating in perfectly competitive markets and firms operating in any other type of market is in the shape of the firm's own demand curve.

The demand curve that each firm in perfect competition faces is horizontal because variations in the firm's output have no noticeable effect on price.

The horizontal (perfectly elastic) demand curve does not mean that the firm could actually sell an infinite amount at the going price. It means, rather, that the variations in production *that it will normally be possible for the firm to make* will leave price unchanged because their effect on total industry output will be negligible.

Figure 10-1 contrasts the market demand curve for the product of a competitive industry with the demand curve that a single firm in that industry faces. Application 10-1 provides an example of the important difference between the firm's demand curve and the market demand curve. It shows a detailed calculation of why the demand curve facing any individual wheat farmer is very nearly perfectly elastic, even though the *market* demand for wheat is quite inelastic.

FIGURE 10-1

The Demand Curve for a Competitive Industry and for One Firm in the Industry

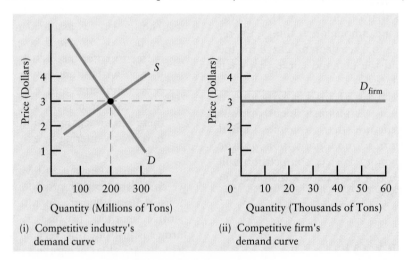

(i) Competitive industry's demand curve

(ii) Competitive firm's demand curve

The industry's demand curve is negatively sloped; the firm's demand curve is virtually horizontal. Notice the difference in the quantities shown on the horizontal scale in each part of the figure. The competitive industry has an output of 200 million tons when the price is $3. The individual firm takes that market price as given and considers producing up to, say, 60,000 tons. The firm's demand curve in part (ii) appears horizontal because the quantity scale represents a very small part of the industry's demand curve in part (i). The firm's output variation has only a tiny percentage effect on industry output. If we plotted the industry demand curve from 199,970,000 tons to 200,030,000 tons on the scale used in part (ii), the *D* curve would also appear virtually horizontal.

APPLICATION 10-1

DEMAND UNDER PERFECT COMPETITION: FIRM AND INDUSTRY

Consider an individual wheat farmer and the market for wheat. Since products have negatively sloped market demand curves, *any* increase in the industry's output (caused by a shift in supply) will cause *some* fall in the market price. However, as the calculations made below show, any conceivable increase that one wheat farm could make in its output has such a negligible effect on the industry's price that the farmer correctly ignores it—the individual wheat farmer is thus a price taker. Although the arithmetic used in reaching this conclusion is unimportant, it is crucial to understand why an individual wheat farmer is a price taker.

Here is the argument that the calculations summarize. The *market* elasticity of demand for wheat is approximately 0.25. Thus, if the quantity of wheat supplied in the world increased by 1 percent, the price of wheat would have to fall by roughly 4 percent to induce the world's wheat buyers to purchase the extra wheat.

Even huge farms produce a very small fraction of the total world crop. In a recent year, one large farm produced 1,750 metric tons of wheat. This was only 0.0035 percent of that year's world production of 500 million metric tons. Suppose that the farmer decided in one year to produce nothing and in another year managed to produce twice the normal output of 1,750 metric tons. This is an extremely large variation in one farm's output.

The increase in output from zero to 3,500 metric tons represents a 200 percent variation measured around the farm's average output of 1,750 metric tons. Yet the percentage increase in world output is only (3,500 / 500 million) × 100 = 0.0007 percent. This increase would lead to a decrease in the world price of 0.0028 percent. This price change, together with the 200 percent change in the farm's *own* output, implies that the farm's own demand curve has

an elasticity of over 71,000! This is an enormous elasticity of demand. The farm would have to increase its output by over 71,000 percent to bring about a 1 percent decrease in the price of wheat! Because the farm's output cannot be varied this much, it is not surprising that the farmer regards the price of wheat as unaffected by any change in output that he could conceivably make. For all intents and purposes, the individual farmer faces a perfectly elastic demand curve for its product and is thus a *price taker*.

CALCULATION OF THE FIRM'S DEMAND ELASTICITY FROM THE MARKET'S DEMAND ELASTICITY

We begin by taking as given the world elasticity of demand ($\eta = 0.25$) and world output (500 million metric tons). A large farm with an average output of 1,750 metric tons varies its output between 0 and 3,500 tons. The variation of 3,500 tons represents 200 percent of the farm's average output of 1,750 metric tons. This causes world output to vary by only 0.0007 percent.

Step 1: Find the percentage change in world price. We know that the market elasticity is 0.25. This means that the percentage change in price must be *four* times as big as the percentage change in *quantity*. Since world quantity changes by 0.0007 percent, world price must change by 0.0028 percent.

Step 2: Find the firm's elasticity of demand. This is the percentage change in its *own output* divided by the resulting percentage change in the world price: 200 percent divided by 0.0028 percent. Clearly, the percentage change in quantity vastly exceeds the percentage change in price, making elasticity very high. Its precise value is 200 / 0.0028 = 71,429.

TOTAL, AVERAGE, AND MARGINAL REVENUE

To study the revenues that firms receive from the sales of their products, economists define three concepts called *total, average,* and *marginal revenue.* These are the revenue counterparts of the concepts of total, average, and marginal cost that we considered in Chapter 8.

Total revenue (TR) is the total amount received by the seller from the sale of a product. If q units are sold at p dollars each, $TR = p \times q$.

Average revenue (AR) is the amount of revenue per unit sold. It is equal to total revenue divided by the number of units sold, and is thus equal to the price at which the product is sold: $AR = (p \times q)/q = p$.

Marginal revenue (MR), sometimes called *incremental revenue,* is the change in a firm's total revenue resulting from a change in its sales by 1 unit. Whenever output changes by more than 1 unit, the change in revenue must be divided by the change in output to calculate marginal revenue. For example, if an increase in output of 3 units per month is accompanied by an increase in revenue of $1,500, the marginal revenue resulting from the sale of 1 extra unit per month is $1,500/3, or $500. At any existing level of sales, marginal revenue shows what revenue the firm would gain by selling 1 unit more (or what revenue it would lose by selling 1 unit less). [23]

To illustrate each of these revenue concepts, consider a firm that is selling an agricultural product in a perfectly competitive market at a price of $3 per bushel. Total revenue rises by $3 for every bushel sold. Because every bushel brings in $3, the average revenue per bushel sold is clearly $3. Furthermore, because each *additional* bushel sold brings in $3, the marginal revenue of an extra bushel sold is also $3. Table 10-1 shows calculations of these revenue concepts for a range of outputs between 10 and 13 bushels.

The important point illustrated in Table 10-1 is that as long as the firm's own level of output cannot affect the price of the product it sells, then the firm's marginal revenue is equal to its average revenue (which is *always* equal to price). Thus, for a price-taking firm, $AR = MR = $ price. Graphically, as shown in part (i) of Figure 10-2, average revenue and marginal revenue are the same horizontal line drawn at the level of market price. Because the firm can sell any quantity it chooses at this price, the horizontal line is also the *firm's demand curve;* it shows that

TABLE 10-1
Revenue Concepts for a Price-Taking Firm

Price p	Quantity q	$TR = p \times q$	$AR = TR/q$	$MR = \Delta TR/\Delta q$
$3	10	$30	$3	
3	11	33	3	$3
3	12	36	3	3
3	13	39	3	3

When the firm is a price taker, $AR = MR = p$. Marginal revenue is shown between the lines because it represents the change in total revenue (e.g., from $33 to $36) in response to a change in quantity (from 11 to 12 units): $MR = (36 - 33)/(12 - 11) = $3 per unit.

any quantity the firm chooses to sell will be associated with this same market price.

If the market price is unaffected by variations in the firm's output, then the firm's demand curve, its average revenue curve, and its marginal revenue curve all coincide in the same horizontal line.

This result can be stated in a slightly different way that turns out to be important for our later study:

For a firm in perfect competition, price equals marginal revenue.

This means, of course, that total revenue rises in direct proportion to output, as shown in part (ii) of Figure 10-2.

SHORT-RUN DECISIONS

We learned in Chapters 8 and 9 how each firm's costs vary with its output. In the short run, the firm has one or more fixed factors, and the only way in which it can change its output is by using more or less of its variable factor inputs. Thus the firm's short-run cost curves are relevant to its decision regarding output.

RULES FOR ALL PROFIT-MAXIMIZING FIRMS

We have just learned how the revenues of each price-taking firm vary with its output. The next step is to combine information about the firm's costs and revenues to determine the level of output that will

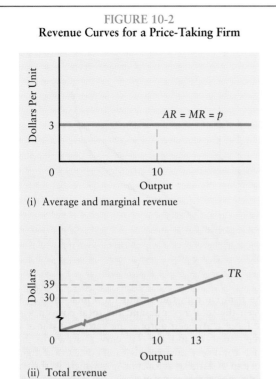

FIGURE 10-2
Revenue Curves for a Price-Taking Firm

(i) Average and marginal revenue

(ii) Total revenue

This is a graphical representation of the revenue concepts in Table 10-1. Because price does not change as a result of the *firm* changing its output, neither marginal revenue nor average revenue varies with output. When price is constant, total revenue (which is price times quantity) is an upward-sloping straight line starting from the origin.

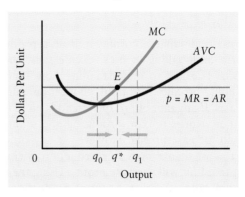

FIGURE 10-3
The Short-Run Profit-Maximizing Output Choice of a Competitive Firm

The firm chooses the output for which $p = MC$ above the level of AVC. When $p = MC$, as at q^*, the firm would decrease its profits if it changed its output. At any point to the left of q^*, say, q_0, price is greater than the marginal cost, and it is worthwhile for the firm to increase output (as indicated by the arrow on the left). At any point to the right of q^*, say, q_1, price is less than the marginal cost, and it is worthwhile for the firm to reduce output (as indicated by the arrow on the right).

maximize its profits. We start by stating two rules that apply to *all* profit-maximizing firms, whether or not they operate in perfectly competitive markets. The first determines whether the firm should produce at all, and the second determines how much it should produce.

Should the Firm Produce at All?

The firm always has the option of producing nothing. If it exercises this option, it will have an operating loss that is equal to its fixed costs. If it decides to produce, it will add the variable cost of production to its costs and the receipts from the sale of its product to its revenue. Therefore, since it must pay its fixed costs in any event, it will be worthwhile for the firm to produce as long as it can find some level of

output for which revenue exceeds *variable* cost. However, if its revenue is less than its variable cost at every level of output, the firm will actually lose more by producing any level of output than by not producing at all.

Rule 1: A firm should not produce at all if for *all* levels of output, the total variable cost of producing that output exceeds the total revenue derived from selling it or, equivalently, if the average variable cost of producing the output exceeds the price at which it can be sold. [24]

The price at which the firm can just cover its average variable cost, and so is indifferent between producing and not producing, is often called the **shut-down price.** At any price below this price, the firm will shut down. Such a price is shown in part (i) of Figure 10-5. (We will return in a moment to Figures 10-3 and 10-4.) At the price of $2, the firm can just cover its average variable cost by producing q_0 units. At this price, any other output would not produce enough revenue to cover variable costs. For any price below $2, there is no output at which variable costs can be covered. The price of $2 in part (i) is therefore the shut-down price.

How Much Should the Firm Produce?

If a firm decides that, according to Rule 1, production is worth undertaking, it must decide *how much* to produce. The key to understanding how much the firm should produce is to think about it on a unit-by-unit basis. If any unit of production adds more to revenue than it does to cost, producing and selling that unit will increase profits. However, if any unit adds more to cost than it does to revenue, producing and selling that unit will decrease profits. Using the terminology introduced earlier, a unit of production raises profits if the *marginal* revenue obtained from selling it exceeds the *marginal* cost of producing it; it lowers profits if the marginal revenue obtained from selling it is less than the marginal cost of producing it.

Now let a firm with some existing rate of output consider increasing or decreasing that output. If a further unit of production will increase the firm's profits, the firm should expand its output. However, if the last unit produced reduced profits, the firm should contract its output. From this it follows that the only time the firm should leave its output unaltered is when the last unit produced adds the same amount to revenues as it does to costs (i.e., $MR = MC$).

The results in these two paragraphs can be combined in the following rule:

Rule 2: Assuming that it is worthwhile for the firm to produce at all, the firm should produce the output at which marginal revenue equals marginal cost. [25]

The two rules that we have stated refer to each firm's own costs and revenues, and they apply to all profit-maximizing firms, whatever the market structure in which they operate.[2]

Rule 2 Applied to Price-Taking Firms

Rule 2 tells us that any profit-maximizing firm that produces at all will produce at the point where marginal cost equals marginal revenue. However, we

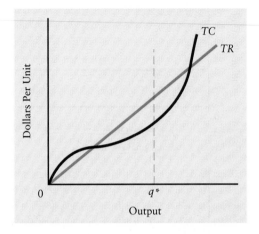

FIGURE 10-4
The Short-Run Profit-Maximizing Output Choice of a Firm Using Total Cost and Revenue Curves

The firm chooses the output for which the gap between the total revenue and the total cost curves is the largest. At each output, the vertical distance between the *TR* and the *TC* curves shows by how much total revenue exceeds total cost. In the figure, the gap is largest at output q^*, which is thus the profit-maximizing output.

have already seen that for price-taking firms, marginal revenue is the market price. Combining these two results gives us an important conclusion:

A firm that is operating in a perfectly competitive market will produce the output that equates its marginal cost of production with the market price of its product (as long as price exceeds average variable cost).

In a perfectly competitive industry, the market determines the price at which the firm sells its product. The firm then picks the quantity of output that maximizes its profits. We have seen that this is the output for which price equals marginal cost. When the firm has reached a position where its profits are maximized, it has no incentive to change its output. Therefore, unless prices or costs change, the firm will continue to produce this output because it is doing as well as it can do, given the market situation. This is illustrated in Figures 10-3 and 10-4.

The perfectly competitive firm is a quantity-adjuster, adjusting its level of output in response to changes in the price which are determined in the market.

Figure 10-3 shows the profit-maximizing choice of the firm using average cost and revenue curves. We

---

[2]A third rule is needed to distinguish between profit-maximizing and profit-*minimizing* positions: The marginal cost curve must cut the marginal revenue curve from below. This rule is not, however, needed for the discussion that follows, so we say nothing further about it. We consider only situations in which it is met.

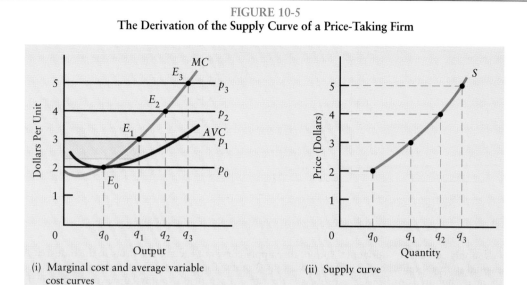

FIGURE 10-5
The Derivation of the Supply Curve of a Price-Taking Firm

(i) Marginal cost and average variable cost curves

(ii) Supply curve

The supply curve of the price-taking firm, shown in part (ii), is the same as its MC curve, shown in part (i). For prices below $2, output is zero because there is no output at which AVC can be covered. Thus the point E_0, where the price of $2 is just equal to AVC, is the point at which the firm will shut down. As price rises to $3, $4, and $5, the profit-maximizing point changes to E_1, E_2, and E_3, taking output to q_1, q_2, and q_3. At any of these prices, the firm's revenue exceeds its variable costs of production. An example of the excess is shown in part (i) of the figure by the shaded area associated with price p_1 and output q_1. This amount is available to help cover fixed costs and, once these are covered, to provide a profit.

can, if we wish, show the same result using total cost and revenue curves as done in Figure 10-4. Figure 10-4 combines the total cost curve first drawn in Figure 8-2 with the total revenue curve first shown in Figure 10-2. It shows the profit-maximizing output as the output with the largest positive difference between total revenue and total cost. This must of course be the same output as we located in Figure 10-3 by equating marginal cost and marginal revenue.

SHORT-RUN SUPPLY CURVES

We have seen that in a perfectly competitive market, the firm responds to a price that is set by the forces of demand and supply. By adjusting the quantity it produces in response to the current market price, the firm helps to determine the market supply. The link between the behaviour of the firm and the behaviour of the competitive market is provided by the *market supply curve*.

The Supply Curve for One Firm

The firm's supply curve is derived in part (i) of Figure 10-5, which shows a firm's marginal cost curve and

four alternative prices. The horizontal line at each price is the firm's demand curve when the market price is at that level. The firm's marginal cost curve gives the marginal cost corresponding to each level of output. We require a supply curve that shows the quantity that the firm will supply at each price. For prices below average variable cost, the firm will supply zero units (Rule 1). For prices above average variable cost, the firm will equate price and marginal cost (Rule 2, modified by the proposition that $MR = p$ in perfect competition). This leads to the following conclusion:

In perfect competition, the firm's supply curve is given by its marginal cost curve for those levels of output for which marginal cost exceeds average variable cost.

The Supply Curve for an Industry

To illustrate what is involved, Figure 10-6 shows the derivation of an industry supply curve for an industry containing only two firms. The general result is as follows:

In perfect competition, the industry supply curve is the horizontal sum of the marginal cost curves

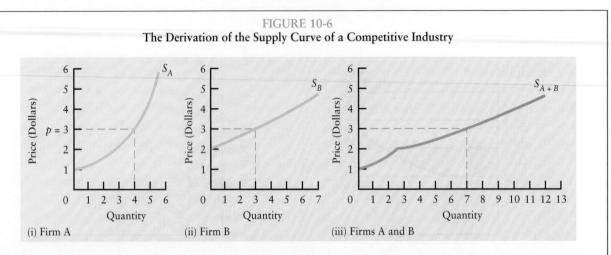

FIGURE 10-6
The Derivation of the Supply Curve of a Competitive Industry

(i) Firm A   (ii) Firm B   (iii) Firms A and B

The industry's supply curve is the horizontal sum of the supply curves of each of the firms in the industry. At a price of $3, Firm A would supply 4 units and Firm B would supply 3 units. Together, as shown in part (iii), they would supply 7 units. If there are hundreds of firms, the process is the same. Each firm's supply curve (derived as in Figure 10-5) shows what the firm will produce at any given price p. The industry supply curve relates the price to the sum of the quantities produced by each firm. In this example, because Firm B does not enter the market at prices below $2, the supply curve S_{A+B} is identical to S_A up to price $2 and is the sum of S_A and S_B above $2.

(above the level of average variable cost) of all firms in the industry.

The reason for this is that each firm's marginal cost curve shows how much that firm will supply at each given market price, and the industry supply curve is the sum of what each firm will supply.

This supply curve, based on the short-run marginal cost curves of all the firms in the industry, is the industry's supply curve that was first encountered in Chapter 4. We have now established the profit-maximizing behaviour of individual firms that lies behind that curve. It is sometimes called a **short-run supply curve** because it is based on the short-run, profit-maximizing behaviour of all the firms in the industry. It should not be confused with the long-run industry supply curve, which relates quantity supplied to the price that exists *when the industry is in long-run equilibrium* (which we will study later in this chapter).

SHORT-RUN EQUILIBRIUM IN A COMPETITIVE MARKET

The price of a product sold in a perfectly competitive market is determined by the interaction of the industry's short-run supply curve and the market demand curve. Although no single firm can influence the market price significantly, the collective actions of all

firms in the industry (as shown by the industry supply curve) and the collective actions of households (as shown by the market demand curve) together determine the equilibrium price. This occurs at the point where the market demand curve and the industry supply curve intersect.

When a perfectly competitive industry is in **short-run equilibrium,** each firm is producing and selling a quantity for which its marginal cost equals price. No firm is motivated to change its output in the short run. Because total quantity demanded equals total quantity supplied, there is no reason for market price to change in the short run.

Short-Run Profitability of the Firm

We know that when an industry is in short-run equilibrium, each firm is maximizing its profits. However, we do not know *how large* these profits are. It is one thing to know that a firm is doing as well as it can, given its particular circumstances; it is another thing to know how well it is doing.

Figure 10-7 shows three possible positions for a firm when the industry is in short-run equilibrium. In all cases, the firm is maximizing its profits by producing where price equals marginal cost, but in part (i) the firm is suffering losses, in part (ii) it is just

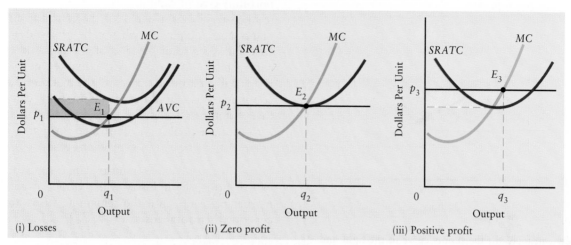

FIGURE 10-7
Alternative Short-Run Profits of a Competitive Firm

(i) Losses   (ii) Zero profit   (iii) Positive profit

When the industry is in short-run equilibrium, a competitive firm may be suffering losses, breaking even, or making profits. The diagrams show a firm with given costs that faces three alternative prices p_1, p_2, and p_3. In each part of the figure, $MC = MR$ = price. Because in all three cases price exceeds AVC, the firm produces positive output in each case.

In part (i), price is p_1 and the firm is suffering losses, shown by the shaded area, because price is below average total cost. Because price exceeds average variable cost, it is worthwhile for the firm to keep producing, but it is not worthwhile for it to replace its capital equipment as it wears out.

In part (ii), price is p_2 and the firm is just covering its total costs. It is worthwhile for the firm to replace its capital as it wears out, since it is covering the full opportunity cost of its capital.

In part (iii), price is p_3 and the firm is earning profits, shown by the shaded area.

covering all of its costs (breaking even), and in part (iii) it is making profits because average revenue exceeds average total cost. In part (i), we could say that the firm is minimizing its losses rather than maximizing its profits, but both statements mean the same thing. In all three cases, the firm is doing as well as it can, given its costs and the market price.

LONG-RUN DECISIONS

Although Figure 10-7 shows three possible positions for a typical firm when the industry is in short-run equilibrium, not all of them are possible outcomes in the long run.

THE EFFECT OF ENTRY AND EXIT

The key difference between a perfectly competitive industry in the short run and in the long run is the entry or exit of firms. We have seen that firms may be making profits, suffering losses, or just breaking even when the industry is in short-run equilibrium. Because costs include the opportunity cost of capital, firms that are just breaking even are doing as well as they could do by investing their capital elsewhere. Hence there will be no incentive for such firms to leave the industry. Similarly, if new entrants expect just to break even, there will be no incentive for firms to enter the industry, because capital can earn the same return elsewhere in the economy. If, however, existing firms are earning revenues in excess of all costs, including the opportunity cost of capital, new capital will enter the industry to share in these profits. Conversely, if existing firms are suffering losses, capital will leave the industry because a better return can be obtained elsewhere in the economy. Let us now consider this process in a little more detail.

An Entry-Attracting Price

First, suppose that there are 100 firms in a competitive industry, all in the position of the firm shown in part (iii) of Figure 10-7. New firms, attracted by the profitability of existing firms, will enter the industry.

FIGURE 10-8
The Effect of New Entrants

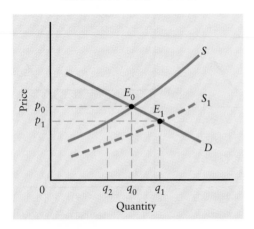

New entrants shift the supply curve to the right and lower the equilibrium price. Initial equilibrium is at E_0. The entry of new firms shifts the supply curve to S_1. Equilibrium price falls to p_1, while output rises to q_1. Before the entry of new firms, only q_2 would have been produced had the price been p_1. The extra output is supplied by the new productive capacity.

Suppose that in response to the high profits that the 100 existing firms are making, 20 new firms enter. The market supply curve that formerly added up the outputs of 100 firms must now add up the outputs of 120 firms. At any price, more will be supplied because there are more producers. This is a rightward shift in the industry supply curve.

With an unchanged market demand curve, this shift in the short-run industry supply curve means that the previous equilibrium price will no longer prevail. The shift in supply will lower the equilibrium price, and both new and old firms will have to adjust their output to this new price. This is illustrated in Figure 10-8. New firms will continue to enter, and the equilibrium price will continue to fall, until all firms in the industry are just covering their total costs. All firms will then be in the position of the firm shown in part (ii) of Figure 10-7, which is called a *zero-profit equilibrium*.

Profits in a competitive industry are a signal for the entry of new firms; the industry will expand, pushing price down until profits fall to zero.

An Exit-Inducing Price

Now suppose that all of the firms in the industry are in the position of the firm shown in part (i) of Figure 10-7. Although the firms are covering their variable costs, the return on their capital is less than the opportunity cost of capital. They are not covering their total costs. This is a signal for the exit of firms. Old plants and equipment will not be replaced as they wear out. As a result, the industry's short-run supply curve shifts leftward, and the market price rises. Firms will continue to exit, and the market price will continue to rise, until the remaining firms can cover their total costs—that is, until they are all in the zero-profit equilibrium illustrated in part (ii) of Figure 10-7. The exit of firms then ceases.

Losses in a competitive industry are a signal for the exit of firms; the industry will contract, driving the market price up until the remaining firms are just covering their total costs.

LONG-RUN EQUILIBRIUM IN A COMPETITIVE MARKET

Because firms exit when they are motivated by their losses and enter in pursuit of profits, we get the following conclusion:

The long-run equilibrium of a competitive industry occurs when firms are earning zero profits.

When a perfectly competitive industry is in long-run equilibrium, each firm will be like the firm in part (ii) of Figure 10-7. For such firms, the price P_z is sometimes called the **break-even price**. It is the price at which all costs, including the opportunity cost of capital, are being covered. The firm is just willing to stay in the industry. It has no incentive to leave, nor do other firms have an incentive to enter.

In the preceding analysis, we see profits serving the function of providing signals that guide the allocation of scarce resources among the economy's industries. It is also worth noting that freedom of entry will tend to push profits toward zero in any industry, whether it is perfectly competitive or not.

Conditions for Long-Run Equilibrium

The previous discussion suggests four conditions for a competitive industry to be in long-run equilibrium.

1. Existing firms must be maximizing their profits, given their existing capital. This means that short-run marginal costs of production must be equal to market price.

2. Existing firms must not be suffering losses. If they are suffering losses, they will not replace their capital and the size of the industry will decline over time.

3. Existing firms must not be earning profits. If they are earning profits, then new firms will enter the industry and the size of the industry will increase over time.

4. Existing firms must not be able to increase their profits by changing the size of their production facilities. This implies that each existing firm must be at the minimum point of its long-run average cost curve.

This last condition is new to our discussion. Figure 10-9 shows that if the condition does not hold, a firm can increase its profits. Although the firm is maximizing its profits with its existing production facilities, there are unexploited economies of scale. By building a new plant with a larger capacity than its existing plant, the firm can reduce its average cost. Because in its present position, average cost is just equal to price, any reduction in average cost must yield profits.

For a price-taking firm to be maximizing its long-run profits, it must be producing at the minimum point on its *LRAC* curve.

The level of output at which *LRAC* reaches a minimum is known as the firm's **minimum efficient scale (MES)**.[3]

When each firm in the industry is producing at the minimum point of its long-run average cost curve and just covering its costs (i.e., each is in the position shown in Figure 10-10), the industry is in long-run equilibrium. Because marginal cost equals price, no firm can improve its profits by varying its output in the short run. Because *LRAC* is above price at all possible outputs except the current one, where it is equal to the price, there is no incentive for any existing firm to move along its long-run cost curve by al-

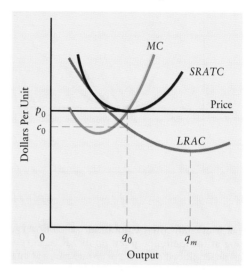

FIGURE 10-9
Short-Run Versus Long-Run Profit Maximization for a Competitive Firm

A competitive firm that is not at the minimum point on its *LRAC* curve is not maximizing its long-run profits. A competitive firm with short-run cost curves *SRATC* and *MC* faces a market price of p_0. The firm produces q_0, where *MC* equals price and total costs are just being covered. However, the firm's long-run average cost curve lies below its short-run curve at output q_0. The firm could produce output q_0 at cost c_0 by building a larger plant so as to take advantage of economies of scale. Profits would rise, because average total costs of c_0 would then be less than price p_0. The firm cannot be maximizing its long-run profits at any output below q_m because with any such output, average total costs can be reduced by building a larger plant. The output q_m is the *minimum efficient scale* of the firm.

tering the scale of its operations. Because there are neither profits nor losses, there is no incentive for entry into or exit from the industry.

In long-run competitive equilibrium, each firm's average cost of production is the lowest attainable, given the limits of known technology and factor prices.

To summarize, the conditions for long-run equilibrium for a competitive industry are as follows: (1) Existing firms produce at the point where marginal cost equals price, (2) existing firms are not making losses and thus have no incentive to exit, (3) existing firms are not making positive profits, and thus potential new firms have no incentive to enter, and (4)

---

[3]With a U-shaped cost curve, as in Figure 10-10, there is only one point of efficient scale, so the qualification "minimum" is redundant. In Chapter 12, however, we will encounter cost curves that are flat over a range of minimum average cost. The qualification "minimum" is then needed to indicate the *smallest* output at which average costs are minimized.

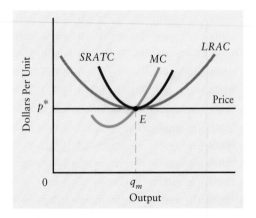

FIGURE 10-10
A Typical Firm When the Industry is in Long-Run Equilibrium

In long-run competitive equilibrium, each firm is operating at the minimum point on its *LRAC* curve. In long-run equilibrium, each firm must be (1) maximizing short-run profits, $MC = p$; (2) earning profits of zero on its existing plant, $SRATC = p$; and (3) unable to increase its profits by altering the scale of its operations. These three conditions can be met only when the firm is at E, the minimum point on its *LRAC* curve, with price p^* and output q_m.

existing firms produce at the minimum point on their long-run average cost curve. This is the position shown in Figure 10-10.

THE LONG-RUN INDUSTRY SUPPLY CURVE

Consider a competitive industry that is in long-run equilibrium. Suppose now that the market demand for the industry's product increases. The reactions to this demand shift should by now be a familiar story. First, price will rise, and in response, existing firms will increase their outputs and earn profits. New firms then enter the industry, attracted by the profits. As the industry's output expands, price will fall, and this process continues until profits have been eliminated. At that time, existing firms will once again be just covering their full costs. Note that in *both* of the long-run equilibrium positions just discussed—the one before and the one after the change in demand—all firms in the industry are producing at the lowest point on their *LRAC* curves.

This is now familiar ground, but there is one further question that we could ask. When all the dust has settled, will the new long-run equilibrium price be higher than, lower than, or the same as the price at the initial long-run equilibrium? A similar analysis could be made for a fall in demand, and the same question could be asked.

The adjustment of a competitive industry to the types of changes that we have just discussed is shown by what is sometimes called the **long-run industry supply *(LRS)* curve**. This curve shows the relationship between the market price and the quantity produced in a competitive industry *when it is in long-run equilibrium*. Note, however, that the curve does not take *very* long-run reactions into account and so is drawn on the assumption that technological knowledge is constant. (Changes in technology will *shift* the *LRS* curve.) Figure 10-11 shows the derivation of this curve and its various possible shapes.

Horizontal Long-Run Supply Curve. In part (i) of the figure, the *LRS* curve is horizontal. This indicates that the industry will adjust its size to provide whatever quantity is demanded at a constant price. An industry with a horizontal *LRS* curve is said to be a **constant-cost industry.** This situation occurs when the long-run expansion of the industry, due to the entry of new firms, leaves the long-run cost curves of existing firms unchanged. Because new firms have access to the same technology and face the same factor prices as existing firms, their cost curves will be the same as those of existing firms. It follows that the cost curves of all firms, new or old, will be unaffected by expansion or contraction of the industry. Thus long-run equilibrium can be reestablished only when price returns to its original level. In other words, because cost curves are unaffected by the expansion or contraction of the industry, each firm must start from, and return to, the long-run equilibrium position shown in Figure 10-10—*which means that market price must also do the same.*

Upward-Sloping Long-Run Supply Curve. When an increase in demand for an industry's product leads that industry to expand, more of its inputs will be needed. The increase in demand for these inputs tends to bid up their prices.

If costs rise with increasing levels of industry output, so too must the price at which the producers are able to cover their costs. As the industry ex-

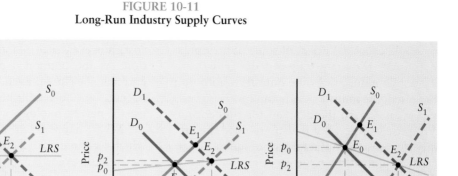

FIGURE 10-11
Long-Run Industry Supply Curves

(i) Constant cost (ii) Increasing cost (iii) Falling cost

The long-run industry supply curve may be horizontal, positively sloped, or negatively sloped. In all three parts, the initial curves are at D_0 and S_0, yielding equilibrium at E_0, with price p_0 and output q_0. A rise in demand shifts the demand curve to D_1, taking the short-run equilibrium to E_1. New firms now enter the industry, shifting the supply curve outward, pushing down price until pure profits are no longer being earned. At this point, the supply curve is S_1 and the new equilibrium is E_2, with price at p_2 and output q_2.

In part (i), price returns to its original level, making the long-run industry supply curve horizontal. In part (ii), profits are eliminated, and a new long-run equilibrium acheived, at a price higher than p_0. This gives the *LRS* curve a positive slope. In part (iii), the price falls below its original level before profits are eliminated, giving the *LRS* curve a negative slope.

pands, the short-run supply curve shifts outward, but the firms' *SRATC* curves shift upward because of rising factor prices. The expansion of the industry comes to a halt when price is equal to minimum *LRAC* for existing firms. Because costs have risen, this must occur at a higher price than prevailed before the expansion began, as illustrated in part (ii) of Figure 10-11. A competitive industry with rising long-run supply prices is often called an **increasing-cost industry.**

Downward-Sloping Long-Run Supply Curve. So far we have suggested that the long-run supply curve may be flat or upward sloping. Could it ever be downward sloping, thereby indicating that higher outputs were associated with lower prices in long-run equilibrium?[4]

It is tempting to answer yes because of the opportunities of more efficient scales of operation using greater mechanization and more effective specilization of labour. However, this answer would not be correct for perfectly competitive industries because in long-run equilibrium each firm must already be at the lowest point on its *LRAC* curve. If a firm could lower its costs by building a larger, more mechanized plant, it would be profitable to do so without waiting for an increase in demand. Because any single firm perceives that it can sell all it wishes at the going market price, it will be profitable for the firm to expand the scale of its operations as long as it is on the downward-sloping portion of its *LRAC*.

The scale economies that we have just considered are within the control of the firm; they are said to be **internal economies of scale.** A perfectly competitive industry might, however, have falling long-run costs if industries that supply its inputs have increasing returns to scale. Such effects are outside the control of the perfectly competitive firm and are called **external economies of scale.** Whenever expansion of an industry leads to a fall in the prices of some of its

---

[4]The discussion of economies of scale in Chapter 9 is relevant here.

inputs, the firms will find their cost curves shifting downward as they expand their outputs.

As an illustration of how the expansion of one industry could cause the prices of some of its inputs to fall, consider the early stages of the growth of the automobile industry. As the output of automobiles increased, the industry's demand for tires grew greatly. This increased the demand for rubber and tended to raise its price, but it also provided the opportunity for tire manufacturers to build larger plants that exploited the scale economies available in tire production. These economies were large enough to offset any factor price increases, and tire prices charged to automobile manufacturers fell. Thus automobile costs fell because of lower prices of an important input. This case is illustrated in part (iii) of Figure 10-11. An industry that has a declining long-run supply curve is often called a **declining-cost industry.**

Notice in this example that although the economies of scale were *external* to the automobile industry, they were *internal* to the tire industry. This in turn requires that the tire industry *not* be perfectly competitive; if it were, all of its scale economies would already have been exploited as firms locate at the minimum of their *LRAC* curves in the long run. So this case refers to a perfectly competitive industry that uses an input produced by a non-perfectly-competitive industry whose own scale economies have not yet been fully exploited because demand is insufficient.

We can now use our long-run theory to understand the behaviour of firms in two commonly encountered but often misunderstood situations—changes in technology and declining industries.

CHANGES IN TECHNOLOGY

Consider a competitive industry in long-run equilibrium. Because the industry is in long-run equilibrium, each firm must be earning zero profits. Now suppose that some technological development lowers the cost curves of newly built plants. Because price is just equal to the average total cost *for the existing plants,* new plants will be able to earn profits, and some of them will now be built. The resulting expansion in capacity shifts the short-run supply curve to the right and drives price down.

The expansion in industry output and the fall in price will continue until price is equal to the short-

run average total cost of the *new* plants. At this price, old plants will not be covering their long-run costs. As long as price exceeds their average variable cost, however, such plants will continue in production. As the outmoded plants wear out, they will gradually be closed. Eventually, a new long-run equilibrium will be established in which all plants will use the new technology.

What happens in a competitive industry in which technological change does not occur as a single isolated event but instead happens more or less continuously? Plants built in any one year will tend to have lower costs than plants built in any previous year. This common occurrence is illustrated in Figure 10-12.

Industries that are subject to continuous technological change have three common characteristics. The first is that plants of different ages and at different levels of efficiency exist side by side. This characteristic is dramatically illustrated by the many different vintages of farm equipment found in the agricultural sector; some farms have much newer and better equipment than others. Indeed, even any individual farm that has been established for a long time will have various vintages of equipment, all of which are in use. In this case, and in many others that you can think of, different vintages of plant and equipment, each with different efficiencies, exist side by side; older models are not discarded as soon as a better model comes on the market.

Critics who observe the continued use of older, less efficient plants and equipment often urge that something be done to "eliminate these wasteful practices." These critics miss the point of economic efficiency. If the plant or piece of equipment is already there, it can be profitably operated as long as its revenues more than cover its *variable* costs. As long as a plant or equipment can produce goods that are valued by consumers at an amount above the value of the resources currently used up for their production (variable costs), the value of society's total output is increased by using it.

A second characteristic of a competitive industry that is subject to continuous technological change is that price is governed by the minimum *ATC* of the *most efficient* plants. Firms will enter the industry until plants of the latest vintage are just expected to earn normal profits over their lifetimes. The benefits of the new technology are passed on to consumers because all of the units of the product, whether pro-

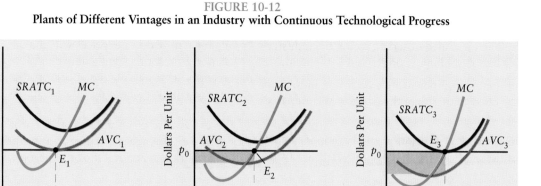

FIGURE 10-12
Plants of Different Vintages in an Industry with Continuous Technological Progress

Entry of progressively lower-cost firms forces price down, but older plants with higher costs remain in the industry as long as price covers average variable cost. Plant 3 is the newest plant with the lowest costs. Long-run equilibrium price will be determined by the average total costs of plants of this type because entry will continue as long as the owners of the newest plants expect to earn profits from them. Plant 1 is the oldest plant in operation. It is just covering its AVC, and if the price falls any further, it will be closed down. Plant 2 is a plant of intermediate age. It is covering its variable costs and earning some contribution toward its fixed costs. In parts (ii) and (iii), the excess of revenues over variable costs is indicated by the shaded area.

duced by new or old plants, are sold at a price that is related solely to the $ATCs$ of the new plants. Owners of older plants find that their returns over variable costs fall steadily as more and more efficient plants drive the price of the product down.

A third characteristic is that old plants are discarded (or "mothballed") when the price falls below their $AVCs$. This may occur well before the plants are physically worn out. In industries with continuous technological progress, capital is usually discarded because it is *economically obsolete,* not because it is physically worn out. Old capital is obsolete when the market price of output does not even cover its average variable cost of production. Thus a steel mill that is still fully capable of producing top-quality steel may be shut down for perfectly sensible reasons; if the price of steel cannot cover the average variable cost of the steel produced, then profit-maximizing firms will shut down the plant.

DECLINING INDUSTRIES

What happens when a competitive industry in long-run equilibrium begins to suffer losses due to a con-

tinual decrease in the demand for its products? One example of this might be a long-term change in tastes that leads households to substitute away from red meat and toward fish and poultry. As market demand for red meat declines, market price falls, and firms that were previously covering average total costs are no longer able to do so. They find themselves in the position shown in part (i) of Figure 10-7. Firms suffer losses instead of breaking even; the signal for the exit of capital is given, but exit takes time.

The Response of Firms

The economically efficient response to a steadily declining demand is to continue to operate with existing equipment as long as its variable costs of production can be covered. As equipment becomes obsolete because it cannot cover even its variable cost, it will not be replaced unless the new equipment can cover its total cost. As a result, the capacity of the industry will shrink. If demand keeps declining, capacity must keep shrinking.

Declining industries typically present a sorry sight to the observer. Revenues are below long-run total costs, and as a result, new equipment is not brought in to replace old equipment as it wears out. The average age of equipment in use thus rises steadily. The untrained observer, seeing the industry's plight, is likely to blame it on the old equipment.

The antiquated equipment in a declining industry is often the effect rather than the cause of the industry's decline.

An interesting illustration of the importance of the distinction between fixed and variable costs—one that is familiar to many hotel users—is given in Application 10-2.

The Response of Governments

Governments are often tempted to support declining industries because they are worried about the resulting job losses. Experience suggests, however, that propping up genuinely declining industries only delays their demise—at significant national cost. When the government finally withdraws its support, the decline is usually more abrupt and hence more difficult to adjust to than it would have been had the industry been allowed to decline gradually under the market force of steadily declining demand.

Once governments recognize the decay of certain industries and the collapse of certain firms as an inevitable aspect of economic growth, a more effective response is to provide retraining and income-support schemes that cushion the impacts of change. These can moderate the effects on the incomes of workers who lose their jobs and make it easier for them to transfer to expanding industries. Intervention that is intended to increase mobility while reducing the social and personal costs of mobility is a viable long-run policy; trying to freeze the existing industrial structure by shoring up an inevitably declining industry is not.

THE APPEAL OF PERFECT COMPETITION

Consider an economy in which all markets are perfectly competitive. In this economy, there are many firms and many households. Each is a price taker, responding as it sees fit to signals that are sent to it by the market. No single firm or consumer has any power over the market; instead, each is a passive quantity adjuster that merely responds to market signals. Yet the impersonal force of the market produces an appropriate response to all changes. If tastes change, for example, prices will change, and the allocation of resources will change in the appropriate direction. Throughout the entire process, no one firm has any power over any other firm. Dozens of firms react to the same price changes, and if one firm refuses to react, countless other profit-maximizing firms will be eager to make the appropriate changes.

Market reactions, not public policies, eliminate shortages or surpluses. There is need neither for regulatory agencies nor for bureaucrats to make arbitrary decisions about who may produce what, how to produce it, or how much it is permissible to charge for the product. If there are no government officials to make such decisions, no bribes will be necessary to influence their decisions.

In the impersonal decision-making world of perfect competition, neither private firms nor public officials wield economic power. The market mechanism, like an invisible hand, determines the allocation of resources among competing uses.

The theory of perfect competition is an intellectual triumph in showing how a price system can work to coordinate the decisions of millions of decentralized households and firms. The price system allows all necessary adjustments to occur, despite the fact that no single individual foresees them or provides any overall plan for them. Moreover, as we shall see in Chapter 13, a perfectly competitive economy will generally be economically efficient.

The British historian Lord Acton once observed, "Power tends to corrupt; absolute power corrupts absolutely." To someone who fears power, either in the hands of the state or in such private organizations as large firms, the perfectly competitive model has a strong appeal. It describes an economy that functions effectively without any private or public group exercising any significant market power.

Economic and social policy would be much simpler if the entire economy were perfectly competitive. Although the price system often allocates resources in ways that are quite similar to the perfectly competitive economy, and although some markets are indeed perfectly competitive, in our world many groups have power over many markets. Large firms often set

APPLICATION 10-2

THE PARABLE OF THE SEASIDE INN

Why do some resort hotels stay open during the off-season, even though to do so they must offer bargain rates that do not even cover their "full costs?" Why do the managers of other hotels allow them to fall into disrepair even though they are able to attract enough customers to stay in business? Are the former being overly generous, and are the latter being irrational penny-pinchers?

To illustrate what is involved, consider an imaginary resort hotel called the Seaside Inn. Its revenues and costs of operating during the four months of the high-season and during the eight months of the off-season are shown in the accompanying table. When the profit-maximizing price for its rooms is charged in the high-season, the hotel earns revenues of $58,000 and incurs variable costs equal to $36,000. Thus there is an "operating profit" of $22,000 during the high-season. This surplus goes toward meeting the hotel's fixed costs of $24,000. There is then $2,000 of the fixed costs which need yet to be paid.

If the Seaside Inn were to charge the same rates during the off-season, it could not attract enough customers even to cover its costs of maids, bell-hops, and managers. However, the hotel discovers that by charging lower rates during the off-season, it can rent some of its rooms and earn revenues of $20,000. Its costs of operating (variable costs) during the off-season are $18,000. So, by operating at reduced rates in the off-season, the hotel is able to contribute another $2,000 toward its annual fixed costs, thereby eliminating the shortfall. Therefore, the hotel stays open during the whole year by offering off-season bargain rates to grateful guests.

(Indeed, if it were to close during the off-season, it would not be able to cover its total fixed and variable costs solely through its high-season operations.)

Now assume that the off-season revenues fall to $19,000 (everything else remaining the same). The short-run condition for staying open, that total revenue *(TR)* must exceed total variable cost *(TVC)*, is met both for the high-season and for the off-season. However, the long-run condition is not met, since the *TR* over the whole year of $77,000 is less than the total costs of $78,000, all of which are variable in the long run. The hotel will remain open as long as it can do so with its present capital—it will produce in the short run. However, it will not be worthwhile for the owners to replace the capital as it wears out.

It will become one of those run-down hotels about which guests ask, "Why don't they do something about this place?"—but the owners are behaving quite sensibly. They are operating the hotel as long as it covers its variable costs, but they are not putting any more investment into it because it cannot cover its fixed costs. Sooner or later, the fixed capital will become too old to be run, or at least to attract customers, and the hotel will be closed.

The Seaside Inn: Total Costs and Revenues ($)

Season	Total Revenue *(TR)*	Total Variable Cost *(TVC)*	Contribution to Fixed Costs *(TR-TVC)*	Total Fixed Costs
High-Season	58,000	36,000	22,000	
Off-Season	20,000	18,000	2,000	
Total	78,000	54,000	24,000	24,000

prices, determine what will be produced, and decide what research will take place. Labour unions often influence wages by offering or withdrawing their labour services. Governments influence many markets by being the dominant purchaser, as well as by regulating

many others. As it is, observers who fear the concentration of market power can only regret that the perfectly competitive model does not describe the world in which we live; so many problems would disappear if only it did.

SUMMARY

A. MARKET STRUCTURE AND FIRM BEHAVIOUR

- Market behaviour is concerned with the degree to which individual firms compete against one another; market structure is concerned with the type of market in which firms operate. Market structure affects the degree of power that individual firms have to influence the price of the product.

B. THE THEORY OF PERFECT COMPETITION

- Five key assumptions of the theory of perfect competition are as follows:

  1. All firms produce a homogeneous product.
  2. Purchasers know the nature of the product and the price charged for it.
  3. Each firm's minimum efficient scale occurs at a level of output that is small relative to the industry's total output.
  4. Firms are price takers.
  5. The industry displays freedom of entry and exit.

- Any profit-maximizing firm will produce at a level of output at which (a) price is at least as great as average variable cost and (b) marginal cost equals marginal revenue. In perfect competition, firms are price takers, so marginal revenue is equal to price. Thus a profit-maximizing firm operating in a perfectly competitive market equates marginal cost to price.

C. SHORT-RUN DECISIONS

- If a profit-maximizing firm is to produce at all, it must be able to cover its variable costs. However, such a firm may be suffering losses (price is less than average total cost), making profits (price is greater than average total cost), or just breaking even (price is equal to average total cost).
- Under perfect competition, each firm's short-run supply curve is identical to its marginal cost curve above average variable cost. The perfectly competitive industry's short-run supply curve is the horizontal sum of the supply curves of the individual firms (the horizontal sum of the firms' marginal cost curves).

D. LONG-RUN DECISIONS

- In the long run, profits or losses will lead to the entry or the exit of capital into or out of the industry. This pushes any competitive industry to a long-run, zero-profit equilibrium and moves production to the level that minimizes average cost.
- The long-run response of an industry to steadily changing technology is the gradual replacement of less efficient plants by more efficient ones. Older plants will be discarded and replaced by more modern ones only when price falls below average variable cost.
- The long-run response of a declining industry will be to continue to satisfy demand by employing its existing plants as long as price exceeds short-run average variable cost. Despite the antiquated appearance that results, this response is the correct one.

E. THE APPEAL OF PERFECT COMPETITION

- The great appeal of perfect competition as a means of organizing production lies in the decentralized decision making of myriad firms and households. No individual firm or household exercises power over the market. At the same time, it is not necessary for the government to intervene to determine resource allocation and prices.

KEY CONCEPTS

Competitive behaviour and competitive market structure
Rules for maximizing profits
Perfect competition
Price taking and a horizontal demand curve

Average revenue, marginal revenue, and price under perfect competition
The relationship of supply curves to marginal cost curves
Short-run and long-run equilibrium of competitive industries

Entry and exit in achieving long-run equilibrium
Long-run industry supply curves
Constant, increasing, and decreasing cost industries

DISCUSSION QUESTIONS

1. A number of agricultural products, such as milk, eggs, and chickens, are produced under conditions that come close to perfect competition whenever governments do not regulate these markets. What are the main features of these industries that make them perfectly competitive? Use the theory you have learned in this chapter to predict the consequences of the introduction of government supply-management schemes that attempt to raise farmers' incomes by restricting total output through a system of quotas.

2. Discuss the common allegation that when all firms in an industry are charging the same price, this indicates the absence of competition and the presence of some form of price-setting agreement.

3. Which of the five assumptions of the theory of perfect competition does the following newspaper story relate to?

   Recently, Ken Chapman booked a $932 round-trip ticket at noon. While he slept that night, a new computer program searched for a better deal. Sixteen hours later, a new fare became available, and Chapman is now ticketed to travel for $578.

   Will this new procedure make the airline industry more or less competitive? Will it make it perfectly competitive? Why or why not?

4. Which of the following observed facts about an industry are inconsistent with its being a perfectly competitive industry?

   a. Different firms use different methods of production.
   b. The industry's product is extensively advertised by a trade association.
   c. Individual firms devote a large fraction of their sales receipts to advertising their own product brands.
   d. There are 24 firms in the industry.
   e. The largest firm in the industry makes 40 percent of the sales, and the next largest firm makes 20 percent of the sales, but the products are identical, and there are 61 other firms.
   f. All firms made large profits in 1995.

5. In which of the following sectors of the Canadian economy might you expect to find competitive behaviour? In which might you expect to find industries that are classified as operating under perfectly competitive market structures?

   a. Manufacturing
   b. Agriculture
   c. Transportation and public utilities
   d. Wholesale and retail trade
   e. Illegal drugs

6. The typical office in 1997 contains personal computers of various vintages, with the newest machines having the largest output per unit of cost. There are also old machines that, though still able to function, are not in use at all. What determines the secondhand price of the older machines? What is the economic value of the machines that are no longer used?

7. Suppose that entry into an industry is not artificially restricted but takes time because of the need to build plants, acquire technical know-how, and establish a marketing organization. Can such an industry be characterized as perfectly competitive? Does ease of entry imply ease of exit, and vice versa?

8. What, if anything, does each one of the following tell you about ease of entry into or exit from an industry?

   a. Profits have been very high for two decades.
   b. No new firms have entered the industry for 20 years.
   c. The average age of the firms in the 40-year-old industry is less than 7 years.
   d. Most existing firms are using obsolete equipment alongside newer, more modern equipment.
   e. Profits are low or negative; many firms are still producing, but from steadily aging equipment.

9. Suppose all of the potentially arable land in Canada was currently being used for growing either wheat or barley. Both crop markets are in equilibrium. Discuss exactly how decentralized competitive markets would respond to shift resources from wheat to barley production following a report that barley helps to reduce cancer risk.

10. Discuss the entry and exit histories of the following industries. What are the implications of this with respect to these markets' competitive behaviour?

    a. Canadian automobile manufacturing
    b. Canadian passenger air travel
    c. Mail and small package delivery
    d. Breakfast cereal
    e. Local telephone service

11. Explain why perfectly competitive agricultural industries may have external economies of scale—and thus may be declining-cost industries—arising from the behaviour of the farm machinery industry. Is it relevant that the farm machinery industry is dominated by a small number of very large firms?

MONOPOLY

Perfect competition is at one end of the spectrum of market structures. At the other end is monopoly. The word **monopoly** comes from the Greek words *monos polein*, which mean "alone to sell". Economists say that a monopoly occurs when the output of an entire industry is produced and sold by a single firm, called a **monopolist** or a *monopoly firm*. Examples of monopoly are rare at the national level but are much more common for smaller geographical areas. The company that supplies electric power to your home is almost certainly a monopoly, as is the firm that provides local (but not long-distance) telephone service. Because monopoly is the market structure that allows for the maximum possible exercise of market power on the part of the firm, monopoly markets and perfectly competitive markets provide two extremes of behaviour that are useful to economists as they study market structure.

A SINGLE-PRICE MONOPOLIST

The first part of this chapter deals with a monopoly firm that charges a single price for its product. The firm's profits, like those of all firms, will depend on the relationship between its production costs and its sales revenues.

COST AND REVENUE IN THE SHORT RUN

We saw in Chapter 8 that U-shaped short-run cost curves are a consequence of the law of diminishing returns. Because this law applies to the conditions under which goods are produced rather than to the market structure in which they are sold, monopolists have U-shaped short-run cost curves for the same reasons as do perfectly competitive firms.

Because a monopolist is the sole producer of the product that it sells, its demand curve is simply the market demand curve for that product. The market demand curve, which shows the total quantity that buyers will purchase at each price, also shows the quantity that the monopolist will be able to sell at each price. Thus the monopolist, unlike the perfectly competitive firm, faces a negatively sloped demand curve. This means that it faces a trade off between the price it charges and the quantity it sells. Sales can be increased only if price is reduced, and price can be increased only if sales are reduced.

Average Revenue and Marginal Revenue

Starting with the market demand curve, the monopolist's average and marginal revenue curves can be readily derived. When the monopolist charges the same price for all units sold, average revenue per unit is equal to price. Thus the market demand curve is also the firm's *average revenue* curve.

Now consider the monopolist's *marginal revenue*—the revenue resulting from the sale of an additional (or marginal) unit of production. Because its demand curve is negatively sloped, the monopolist

TABLE 11-1
A Numerical Example of a Monopolist's Average, Marginal, and Total Revenues

(1) Price (Average Revenue)	(2) Quantity Sold	(3) Total Revenue ($p \times q$)	(4) Change in Total Revenue ΔTR	(5) Marginal Revenue $\Delta TR/\Delta q$
10	0	0		
9	10	90	90	9
8	20	160	70	7
7	30	210	50	5
6	40	240	30	3
5	50	250	10	1
4	60	240	−10	−1
3	70	210	−30	−3
2	80	160	−50	−5
1	90	90	−70	−7
0	100	0	−90	−9

Marginal revenue is less than price because price must be lowered to sell an extra unit. Columns 1 and 2 of the table give specific points on the demand curve shown in Figure 11-1. The data show that every time the firm lowers its price by $1, its sales increase by 10 units. Column 3 gives the total revenue associated with each price, which is that price multiplied by the quantity sold. Column 4 gives the change in total revenue as the price is altered by $1. To calculate the change in revenue associated with a unit change in quantity, the change in column 4 must be divided by 10 to get the change in revenue *per unit change in quantity*. The result is recorded in column 5, which is the marginal revenue.

must lower the price that it charges on *all* units in order to sell an extra unit.

It follows that the addition to its revenue resulting from the sale of an extra unit is less than the price that it receives for that unit (less by the amount that it loses as a result of cutting the price on all the units that it was selling already).

The monopolist's marginal revenue is less than the price at which it sells its output. [26]

The relationship between marginal revenue and price is shown in detail in Table 11-1 and Figure 11-1. Consider Table 11-1 first. Notice that the numbers in columns (4) and (5) are both plotted between the rows that refer to specific prices. This is done because the figures refer to what happens when the price is changed between the amounts shown in two adjacent rows.

Notice also that when price is reduced starting from $10, total revenue rises at first and then falls. The maximum total revenue is reached in this exam-

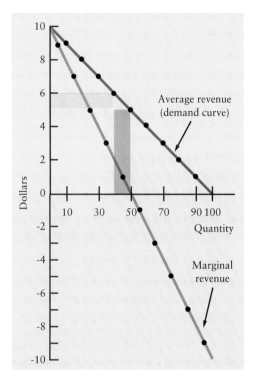

FIGURE 11-1
**A Monopolist's Average
and Marginal Revenue Curves**

**Marginal revenue is less than price because the price
at which existing units are sold must be reduced in
order to sell more units.** The figure shows an example of a demand curve that a monopolist faces and
the associated marginal revenue curve. The specific
points shown by the black dots on the *AR* curve and
the *MR* curve are recorded in Table 11-1.

the specific points on it that were calculated in the
table. For purposes of illustration, a straight-line demand curve has been chosen.[1]

Notice that marginal revenue is positive up to 50
units of sales, indicating that reductions in price between $10 and $5 increase total revenue. Notice also
that marginal revenue is negative for sales greater
than 50 units, indicating that reductions in price below $5 cause total revenue to fall.

The figure also illustrates the two opposing
forces that are present whenever the price is changed.
As an example, consider the reduction in price from
$6 to $5. First, the units already sold bring in less
money at the new lower price than at the original
higher price. This loss in revenue is the amount of
the price reduction multiplied by the number of units
already being sold (40 units × $1 per unit = $40).
This is shown in the blue shaded area in the figure.
The second force, operating in the opposite direction, is that new units are sold, which brings in more
revenue. This gain in revenue is given by the number
of new units sold multiplied by the price at which
they are sold (10 units × $5 = $50). This is shown in
the purple shaded area. The *net change* in total revenue is the *difference* between these two amounts
($10). In the example shown in the figure, the increase resulting from the sale of new units exceeds
the decrease resulting from existing sales now being
made at a lower price. Marginal revenue is thus positive. Furthermore, the change in total revenue is $10
whereas the change in the number of units sold is 10
units. Thus marginal revenue, given by $\Delta TR/\Delta q$, is
equal to $10/10 = $1.

The proposition that marginal revenue is always
less than average revenue, which has been illustrated
numerically in Table 11-1 and graphically in Figure
11-1, provides an important contrast with perfect
competition. Recall that in perfect competition, the
firm's marginal revenue from selling an extra unit of
output is *equal to* the price at which that unit is sold.
The reason for the difference is not difficult to understand. The perfectly competitive firm is a price taker;
it can sell all it wants at the given market price. In
contrast, the monopolist faces a negatively sloped

ple at a price of $5. Because marginal revenue gives
the change in total revenue resulting from the sale of
one more unit of output, marginal revenue is positive
whenever total revenue is increased by selling more,
but it is negative when total revenue is reduced by
selling more.

The method of calculating marginal revenue
shown in the table involves subtracting the total revenue associated with one price from the total revenue
associated with another price and then dividing this
change by the change in the number of units sold.

Now look at Figure 11-1. It plots the entire demand curve that gave rise to the individual figures
for price and quantity shown in Table 11-1. It also
plots the entire marginal revenue curve and locates

[1]When drawing these curves, note that if the demand curve is a
negatively sloped straight line, the *MR* curve also has a negative
slope but is twice as steep. Its price intercept (where $q = 0$) is the
same as that of the demand curve, and its quantity intercept
(where $p = 0$) is one-half that of the demand curve. [27]

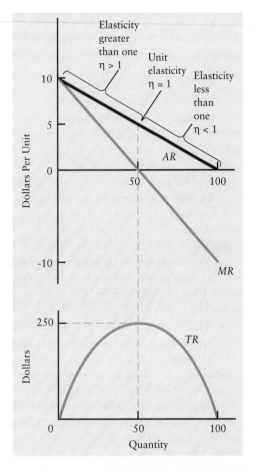

FIGURE 11-2
The Relationship Between Total, Average, and Marginal Revenue and Elasticity of Demand

For a monopolist, *MR* is always less than price. When *TR* is rising, *MR* is greater than zero and elasticity is greater than one. When *TR* is falling, *MR* is less than zero and elasticity is less than one. The monopolist's demand curve is its *AR* curve; the *MR* curve is below the *AR* curve because the demand curve has a negative slope.

11-1.[2] In Chapter 5, we discussed the relationship between the elasticity of the market demand curve and the total revenue derived from selling the product. Figure 11-2 summarizes this earlier discussion and extends it to cover marginal revenue.

Over the range in which the demand curve is elastic, total revenue rises as more units are sold; marginal revenue must therefore be positive. Over the range in which the demand curve is inelastic, total revenue falls as more units are sold; marginal revenue must therefore be negative.

SHORT-RUN PROFIT MAXIMIZATION FOR A MONOPOLIST

To show the profit-maximizing position of a monopolist, we bring together information about its revenues and its costs and then apply the two rules developed in Chapter 10: (1) The firm should not produce at all unless there is some level of output for which price is at least equal to total variable cost, and (2) if the firm does produce, its output should be set at the point where marginal cost equals marginal revenue.

When the monopolist equates marginal cost with marginal revenue, its situation is as shown in Figure 11-3. The output is found as the quantity for which marginal cost equals marginal revenue. The price is read off the demand curve, which shows the price corresponding to that output.

Notice that because marginal revenue is always less than price for the monopolist, when marginal revenue is equated with marginal cost, both are less than price.

When a monopolist is maximizing its profit, its marginal cost is always less than the price it charges for its output.

Monopoly Profits

The fact that a monopolist produces the output that *maximizes* its profits tells us nothing about *how*

demand curve; it must reduce the market price to increase its sales.

Marginal Revenue and Elasticity

Now look at Figure 11-2. This duplicates the demand and marginal revenue curves shown in Figure

---

[2]To fit the figure onto the page, the scale on the vertical price axis has been shrunk somewhat. This makes the curve look flatter than the curve in Figure 11-1, even though they each show *exactly* the same data. This illustrates the point made in Chapter 5 that the apparent steepness of one curve is not a good guide to its elasticity because that steepness can be altered merely by changing the scale on the axes.

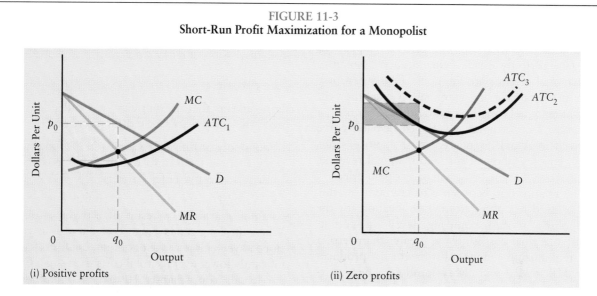

FIGURE 11-3
Short-Run Profit Maximization for a Monopolist

The profit-maximizing output is q_0, where $MR = MC$; price is p_0, which is above MC at that output. The rules for profit maximization require $MR = MC$ and $p > AVC$. (AVC is not shown in the graph, but it must be below ATC.) Whether profits at q_0 are positive or negative (or zero) depends on the position of the ATC curve. In part (i), where average total cost is ATC_1, there are positive profits, as shown by the shaded area. In part (ii), where average total cost is ATC_2, profits are zero. If average total costs were ATC_3, the monopolist would suffer the losses shown by the purple shaded area.

large these profits will be or even whether there will be any profits at all. Profits may be positive, as shown in part (i) of Figure 11-3. As part (ii) of Figure 11-3 shows, however, the profit-maximizing monopolist may break even or suffer losses. Nothing guarantees that a monopolist will make profits in the short run, but if it suffers persistent losses, it will eventually go out of business.

No Supply Curve for a Monopolist

In describing the monopolist's profit-maximizing behaviour, we did not introduce the concept of a supply curve, as we did in the discussion of perfect competition. In perfect competition, the industry short-run supply curve depends only on the marginal cost curves of the individual firms. This is true because under perfect competition, profit-maximizing firms equate marginal cost with price. Given marginal costs, it is possible to know how much will be produced at each price. This is not the case, however, with a monopoly firm.

For a monopolist, there is no unique relationship between market price and quantity supplied.[3]

Firm and Industry

Because the monopolist is the only producer in an industry, there is no need for separate theories about the firm and the industry, as is necessary with perfect competition. The monopolist *is* the industry. Thus the short-run, profit-maximizing position of the firm, as shown in Figure 11-3, is also the short-run equilibrium of the industry.

---

[3]This can be proved by drawing a monopolist's marginal cost curve and any marginal revenue curve to intersect the MC curve at some output that we call q^*. Now draw as many other different MR curves as you like, all of which intersect MC at q^*. All of these curves give rise to profit-maximizing output of q^*, but because each MR curve is different, each must be associated with a different demand curve and hence a different price at which q^* is sold. This shows that a given quantity may be associated with many different prices, depending on the slope of the demand curve that the monopolist faces.

Competition and Monopoly Compared

The comparison of a monopoly firm with firms in perfect competition is important. In perfect competition, firms face perfectly elastic demand curves, so price and marginal revenue are the same. Thus when they equate marginal cost and marginal revenue, they ensure that marginal cost also equals price. In contrast, a monopolist faces a negatively sloped demand curve for which marginal revenue is less than price. Thus when it equates marginal cost and marginal revenue, it ensures that marginal cost will be less than price.

The relationship between elasticity and revenue just discussed has an interesting implication for the monopolist's profit-maximizing level of output. Because marginal cost is always greater than zero, a profit-maximizing monopolist (which produces where $MR = MC$) will always produce where marginal revenue is also greater than zero—that is, where demand is elastic. If the firm were producing where demand was inelastic, it could reduce its output, thereby increasing its total revenue and reducing its total costs.

A profit-maximizing monopolist will never produce a level of output where the demand curve is inelastic.

Note that no such restriction applies to firms in perfect competition. Each adjusts to its own perfectly elastic demand curve, not to the market demand curve. Thus equilibrium in a perfectly competitive industry can occur where the market demand curve is either elastic or inelastic.

LONG-RUN EQUILIBRIUM IN A MONOPOLIZED INDUSTRY

In a monopolized industry, as in a perfectly competitive one, losses and profits provide incentives for exit and entry.

If the monopoly is suffering losses in the short run, it will continue to operate as long as it can cover its variable costs. In the long run, however, it will leave the industry unless it can find a scale of operations at which its full opportunity costs can be covered.

If the monopoly is making profits, other firms will wish to enter the industry in order to earn more than the opportunity cost of their capital. If such entry occurs, the monopoly's position shown in part (i) of Figure 11-3 will change, and the firm will cease to be a monopoly.

In order for positive monopoly profits to lead to the entry of new firms into the industry, these new firms must *be able* to enter the industry. This leads us to a discussion of *entry barriers*.

Entry Barriers

Impediments that prevent entry are called **entry barriers;** they may be either natural or created.

If monopoly profits are to persist in the long run, the entry of new firms into the industry must be prevented by effective entry barriers.

Natural Entry Barriers. Natural barriers most commonly arise as a result of economies of scale. When the long-run average cost curve is negatively sloped over a large range of output, big firms have significantly lower average total costs than small firms.

Recall from Chapter 10 that the *minimum efficient scale (MES)* is the smallest-size firm that can reap all of the economies of large-scale production. It occurs at the level of output where the firm's long-run average total cost curve reaches a minimum.

Now suppose that the technology of an industry is such that one firm's *MES* would be 10,000 units per week at an average total cost of $10 per unit. Further assume that at a price of $10, the quantity demanded in the entire market is 11,000 units per week. Under these circumstances, only one firm can operate at or near its *MES*.

A **natural monopoly** occurs when the industry's demand conditions allow only one firm, at most, to cover its costs while producing at its *MES*. In a natural monopoly, there is no price at which two firms can both sell enough to cover their total costs at *MES*. Electrical power transmission is a natural monopoly—it will always be cheaper to have only one set of power lines (rather than two or more) serving a given region.

Another type of natural barrier is *setup cost*. If a firm could be catapulted fully grown into the market, it might be able to compete effectively with the existing monopolist. However, the cost to the new firm of entering the market, developing its products, and establishing such things as its brand image and its dealer network may be so large that entry would be unprofitable.

Created Entry Barriers. Many entry barriers are created by conscious government action and are therefore condoned by it. Patent laws, for instance, may prevent entry by conferring on the patent holder the sole legal right to produce a particular product for a specific period of time.

Patent protection has led to a major and prolonged battle among nations fought out in international organizations that seek to enforce conditions for fair trade and investment. The major developed countries, where much of the research and development is done, have sought to extend patent rights to other countries. They argue that without the temporary monopoly profits that a patent creates, the incentive to develop new products will be weakened. The less-developed countries have sought to maintain weak or nonexistent patent laws. This allows them to produce new products under more competitive conditions and so avoid paying monopoly profits to the original patent holders in developed countries.

A firm may also be granted a charter or a franchise that prohibits competition by law. Canada Post, for example, has a government-sanctioned monopoly on the delivery of mail. In other cases the regulation and/or licensing of firms severely restricts entry. Professional organizations for dentists or engineers, for example, might restrict the number of places in acredited dental or engineering schools, and thus restrict entry into those industries.

Other barriers can be created by the firm or firms already in the market. In extreme cases, the threat of force or sabotage can deter entry. The most obvious entry barriers of this type are encountered in organized crime, where operation outside of the law makes available an array of illegal but potent barriers to new entrants. Law-abiding firms must use legal tactics in an attempt to increase a new entrant's setup costs. Such tactics range from the threat of price cutting—designed to impose unsustainable losses on a new entrant—to heavy brand-name advertising. (These and other created entry barriers will be discussed in more detail in Chapter 12.)

The Significance of Entry Barriers

Because there are no entry barriers in perfect competition, profits cannot persist in the long run. In monopolized industries, however, profits can persist in the long run whenever there are effective barriers to entry.

In competitive industries, profits attract entry, and entry erodes profits. In monopolized industries, entry barriers frustrate the adjustment mechanism that would otherwise push profits to zero in the long run.

THE VERY-LONG RUN AND CREATIVE DESTRUCTION

In the very-long run, technology changes. New ways of producing old products are invented, and new products are created to satisfy both familiar and new wants. This is related to the concept of entry barriers; a monopoly that succeeds in preventing the entry of new firms capable of producing its product will sooner or later find its barriers circumvented by innovations. One firm may be able to use new processes that avoid some patent or other barrier that the monopolist relies on to bar entry of competing firms. Another firm may compete by producing a somewhat different product that satisfies the same need as the monopolist's product. Yet another firm might get around a natural monopoly by inventing a technology that produces at a low *MES* and ultimately allows several firms to enter the market and still cover costs.

One distinguished economist, Joseph Schumpeter (1883–1950), took the view that entry barriers were not a serious problem in the very-long run. He argued that monopoly profits provide one of the major incentives for people who risk their money by financing inventions and innovations. In his view, the large short-run profits of a monopoly provide a strong incentive for others to try to usurp some of these profits for themselves. If a frontal attack on the monopolist's entry barriers is not possible, the barriers will be circumvented by such means as the development of similar products against which the monopolist will not have entry protection.

Schumpeter called the replacement of one monopolist by another through the invention of new products or new production techniques the *process of creative destruction*. "Creative" referred to the rise of new products; "destruction" referred to the demise of the existing monopoly. Schumpeter argued that this process prevents the very-long run persistence of barriers to entry into industries that earn large profits.

He pushed this argument further and argued that because creative destruction thrives on innovation, the existence of monopoly profits is a major incentive to economic growth. A key part of his argument can be found in the following words:

> What we have got to accept is that it [monopoly] has come to be the most powerful engine of progress and in particular of the long-run expansion of total output not only in spite of, but to a

considerable extent through, this strategy [of creating monopolies], which looks so restrictive when viewed in the individual case and from the individual point of time.

In this respect, perfect competition is not only impossible but inferior, and has no title to being set up as a model. It is hence a mistake to base the theory of government regulation of industry on the principle that big business should be made to work as the respective industry would work in perfect competition.[4]

Schumpeter was writing at a time when the two dominant market structures studied by economists were perfect competition and monopoly. His argument easily extends, however, to any market structure that allows profits to exist in the long run. Today, pure monopolies are few, but there are many industries in which profits can be earned for long periods of time. Such industries, which are called *oligopolies,* are candidates for the operation of the process of creative destruction. We study these industries in detail in Chapter 12. In the mean time, see Application 11-1 for some everyday examples of the process of creative destruction.

CARTELS AS MONOPOLIES

So far in our discussion, a monopoly has meant that there is only one firm in an industry. A second way a monopoly can arise is for many firms in an industry to agree to cooperate with one another, to behave as if they were a single seller, in order to maximize joint profits, eliminating competition among themselves. Such a group of firms is called a **cartel.** A cartel that includes *all* the firms in the industry can behave in the same way as a single-firm monopoly. The firms can agree among themselves to restrict their total output to the level that maximizes their joint profits.[5]

---

[4]Joseph Schumpeter, *Capitalism, Socialism, and Democracy,* 3rd ed. (New York: Harper & Row, 1950), p. 106.
[5]In this chapter, we deal with the simple case in which *all* of the firms in a perfectly competitive industry form a cartel in order to act as if they were a monopoly. Cartels are sometimes formed by a group of firms that account for a significant part, but not all, of the total supply of some product. The effect is to create what is called an *oligopoly.* The most famous example of this type is the Organization of Petroleum Exporting Countries (OPEC). We examine this type of cartel in Chapter 12.

THE EFFECTS OF CARTELIZATION

Because perfectly competitive firms are price takers, they accept the market price as given and increase their output until their marginal cost equals price. In contrast, a monopolist knows that increasing its output will depress the market price. Taking account of this, the monopolist increases its output only until marginal revenue is equal to marginal cost. If all the firms in a perfectly competitive industry form a cartel, they too will be able to take account of the effect of their *joint output* on price. They can agree to restrict industry output to the level that maximizes their joint profits (where the industry's marginal cost is equal to the industry's marginal revenue). The incentive for firms to form a cartel lies in the cartel's ability to restrict output, thereby raising price and increasing profits.

When a perfectly competitive industry is cartelized, the firms can agree to restrict their joint output to the profit-maximizing level. One way to do this is to establish a quota for each firm's output. Say that the joint-profit-maximizing output is two-thirds of the perfectly competitive output. When the cartel is formed, each firm could be given a quota equal to two-thirds of its competitive output.

The effect of cartelizing a perfectly competitive industry and of reducing its output through production quotas is shown in more detail in Figure 11-4.

PROBLEMS THAT CARTELS FACE

Cartels encounter two characteristic problems. The first is ensuring that members follow the behaviour that will maximize the industry's *joint* profits. The second is preventing these profits from being eroded by the entry of new firms.

Enforcement of Output Restrictions

The managers of any cartel want the industry to produce its profit-maximizing output. Their job is made more difficult if individual firms either stay out of the cartel or enter and then cheat on their output quotas. Any one firm, however, has an incentive to do just this—to be either the one that stays out of the organization or the one that enters and then cheats on its output quota. For the sake of simplicity, assume that all firms enter the cartel, so enforcement problems are concerned strictly with cheating by its members.

If Firm X is the only firm to cheat, it is in the best of all possible situations. All other firms restrict

---

APPLICATION 11-1

SOME EVERYDAY EXAMPLES OF THE PROCESS OF CREATIVE DESTRUCTION

Creative destruction, the elimination of one product by a superior product and one production process by a superior process, is a major characteristic of all advanced countries. It eliminates the strong market position of the firms and workers who make the threatened product or operate the threatened process.

The steel-nibbed pen eliminated the quill pen with its sharpened bird's feather nib. The fountain pen eliminated the steel pen and its accompanying ink well. The ball-point pen virtually eliminated the fountain pen. Who knows what will come next in writing implements?

The silent films eliminated vaudeville. The talkies eliminated the silent film and colour films have all but eliminated black and white. The TV seriously reduced the demand for films (and radio) while not eliminating either of them. Cable greatly reduced the demand for direct TV reception by offering better pictures and a more varied selection. The satellite is threatening to eliminate cable by offering much more selection. Predictably, the cable operators appealed to the Canadian regulators to protect their market by disallowing satellite TV.

For long-distance passenger travel by sea, the steamship eliminated the sailing vessel around the turn of the twentieth century. The airplane eliminated the ocean liner in the 1950s and 1960s. For passenger travel on land, the train eliminated the stage coach while the bus competed with the train without eliminating it. The airplane wiped out the passenger train in most of North America while leaving the bus still in a low-cost niche used mainly for short and medium distances.

The above are all product innovation. Production process also undergoes the same type of creative destruction. The laborious hand-setting of metal type for printing was replaced by the linotype that allowed the type to be set by a keyboard operator but which still involved a costly procedure for making corrections. The linotype was swept away by computer typesetting and much of the established printing shop operations have recently been replaced by desktop publishing.

Masses of assembly-line workers, operating highly specialized and inflexible machines replaced the craftsman when Henry Ford perfected the techniques of mass production. A smaller number of less specialized flexible manufacturing workers, operating sophisticated and less specialized machinery, have replaced the assembly line workers who operated the traditional factory.

The cases can be extended almost indefinitely and they all illustrate the same general message. Technological change transforms the products we consume, how we make those products, and how we work. It continually sweeps away positions of high income and economic power established by firms that were in the previous wave of technological change and by those who work for them. It is an agent of dynamism in our economy, an agent of change and economic growth, but it is not without its dark side in terms of the periodic loss of privileged positions on the part of the replaced firms and their workers.

---

output and hold the industry price up near its monopoly level. They earn profits but only by restricting output. Firm X can then reap the full benefit of the other firms' output restraint and sell some additional output at the high price that has been set by the cartel's actions. However, if all of the firms cheat, the price will be pushed back to the competitive level, and all of the firms will return to their competitive position.

This conflict between the interests of the group and the interests of the individual firm is the cartel's main dilemma. Provided that enough firms cooperate in restricting output, all firms are better off than they would be if the industry remained perfectly

FIGURE 11-4
The Effect of Cartelizing a Perfectly Competitive Industry

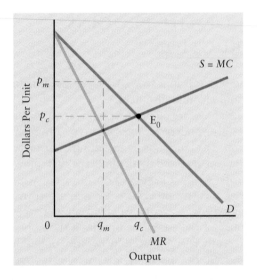

Cartelization of a perfectly competitive industry can always increase that industry's profits. Equilibrium for a perfectly competitive industry occurs at E_0, where the supply and the demand curves intersect. Equilibrium price and output are p_c and q_c. Because the industry demand curve is negatively sloped, marginal revenue is less than price.

If the industry is cartelized, profits can be increased by reducing output. All units between q_m and q_c add less to revenue than to cost—the marginal revenue curve lies below the marginal cost curve. (Recall from Figure 10-6 that the industry's supply curve is the sum of the supply curves, and hence of the marginal cost curves, of each of the firms in the industry.) If the units between q_m and q_c are not produced, output is reduced to q_m and price rises to p_m. This price-output combination maximizes the industry's profits because it is where industry marginal revenue equals industry marginal cost.

competitive. Any one firm, however, is even better off if it remains outside or if it enters and cheats. However, if all firms act on this incentive, all will be worse off than if they had joined the cartel and restricted output.

Cartels tend to be unstable because of the incentives for individual firms to violate the output quotas needed to enforce the monopoly price.

The conflict between the motives for cooperation and for independent action is analyzed in more detail in Figure 11-5. In Chapter 12, we present an

explicit theory, called *game theory*, that economists use to analyze conflicts of this kind.

Cartels and similar output-restricting arrangements have a long history. For example, schemes to raise farm incomes by limiting crops bear ample testimony to the accuracy of the predicted instability of cartels. Industry agreements concerning crop restriction often break down, and prices fall as individual farmers exceed their quotas. This is why most crop restriction plans are now operated by governments rather than by private cartels. Government marketing boards of the type discussed in Chapter 6, backed by the full coercive power of the state, can force monopoly behaviour on existing producers and can effectively bar the entry of new ones.

Restricting Entry

A cartel must not only police the behaviour of its members but must also be able to prevent the entry of new producers. An industry that can support a number of individual firms must have no overriding natural entry barriers. Thus if it is to maintain its profits in the long run, a cartel of many separate firms must create barriers that prevent the entry of new firms that are attracted by the cartel's profits. Successful cartels are often able to license the firms in the industry and to control entry by restricting the number of licenses. This practice is often used by professionals, from physicians to beauticians. At other times, the government has operated a quota system and has given it the force of law. If no one can produce without a quota and the quotas are allocated among existing producers, entry is successfully prevented.

Application 11-2 discusses how technical change has severely lowered the entry barriers into the high-fashion industry. Though the industry was never fully monopolized, the lowering of entry barriers has naturally led to the quick erosion of profits as new firms enter the industry.

A MULTIPRICE MONOPOLIST: PRICE DISCRIMINATION

So far in this chapter, we have assumed that the monopolist charges the same price for every unit of its product, no matter where or to whom it sells that

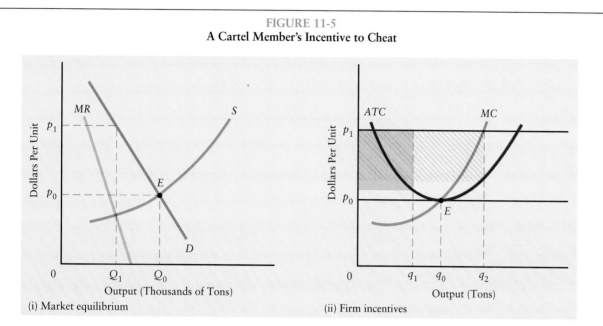

FIGURE 11-5
A Cartel Member's Incentive to Cheat

Cooperation leads to the monopoly price, but individual self-interest leads to production in excess of the monopoly output. Market conditions are shown in part (i), and the situation of a typical firm is shown in part (ii). (Note the change of scale between the two graphs.) Initially, the market is in competitive equilibrium with price p_0 and quantity Q_0. The individual firm is producing output q_0 and is just covering its total costs.

The cartel is formed and then enforces quotas on individual firms that are sufficient to reduce the industry's output to Q_1, the output where the supply curve cuts the marginal revenue curve. Q_1 is thus the output that maximizes the joint profits of the cartel members. Price rises to p_1 as a result. The typical firm's quota is q_1. The firm's profits rise from zero to the amount shown by the gray shaded area in part (ii). Once price is raised to p_1, however, the individual firm would like to increase output to q_2, where marginal cost is equal to the price set by the cartel. This would allow the firm to earn profits, shown by the diagonally striped area. However, if all firms increase their outputs above their quotas, industry output will increase beyond Q_1, and the profits earned by all firms will fall.

product. But as we shall soon see, a monopolist will find it profitable to sell different units of the same product at different prices whenever it gets the opportunity. This practice is prevalent in oligopolistic markets as well as monopoly, and so the range of examples we will discuss cover both types of market structure.

Airlines often charge less to people who stay over a Saturday night than to those who come and go within the week. Raw milk is often sold at one price when it is to be used as fluid milk but at a lower price when it is to be used to make ice cream or cheese. In countries where medical services are provided by the market, physicians in private practice often charge for their services according to the incomes of their patients. Movie theaters often have lower admission prices for children than for adults, and typically also have lower prices for seniors.

Railroads charge different rates for different products. Electric companies sell electricity at one rate to homes and at a different rate to firms.

Price discrimination occurs when a producer charges different prices for different units of the same product for reasons not associated with differences in cost. Not all price differences represent price discrimination. Quantity discounts, differences between wholesale and retail prices, and prices that vary with the time of day or the season of the year may not represent price discrimination because the same product sold at a different time, in a different place, or in different quantities may have different costs. If an electric power company has unused capacity at certain times of the day, it may be cheaper for the company to provide service at those hours than at peak demand hours. If price differences reflect cost differences, they are not discriminatory.

EASE OF ENTRY AND TECHNICAL CHANGE: THE CASE OF FASHION KNOCKOFFS

Once upon a time, the *haute couture* (high fashion) industry maintained a franchise of exclusivity and profits by its lead in the introduction of new fashions. For women who wanted to be in step with the trends set on the fashion runways of Paris and Milan, it was necessary to pay the high prices of designer originals, often in excess of $10,000 for a dress. A substantial time lag separated the introduction of the "designer original" and the arrival of the *knockoff*—a more affordable copy of the designer original—at local department stores.

The entry of high technology and global communications into the fashion industry has eroded the ability of designers to extract these high prices for their new collections. As the *Wall Street Journal* noted, "A photograph snapped at a fashion show in Milan can be faxed overnight to a Hong Kong factory, which can turn out a sample in a matter of hours. That sample can be FedExed back to a New York showroom the next day, ready for retail buyers to preview." In economic terms, the increased ease of replicating haute couture designs has meant that the costs of entry have been dramatically reduced.

Designers such as Donna Karan and Yves Saint-Laurent worry that the disappearance of the lag between the presentation of the designer originals and the arrival of the knockoffs will make it more difficult to recoup the cost of investment and development of the new designs.

Forgery of designer products (claiming that a knockoff is in fact the real thing), such as the imitation Gucci scarves and handbags that are often sold on the streets in major metropolitan areas, is illegal under Canadian and U.S. trademark law. However, substantiating in court that a dress or suit has been plagiarized is very difficult because fashion is a derivative art that often revives motifs from earlier periods. Moreover, knockoffs may duplicate a general style, such as bell bottoms or a latex miniskirt, without copying a designer's work exactly—for example, by adding or subtracting a button or by slightly altering the color scheme.

While some sceptics in the fashion industry fear that the current increase in knockoffs may lead to the demise of the long tradition of haute couture, others believe that the industry will adapt. For example, the designer Bill Blass has addressed the challenge by issuing ready-to-wear knockoffs of his own couture stock. Realizing that a pearl-strapped black cocktail dress priced at nearly $2,000 could be easily replicated, he countered by releasing a $150 copy of this dress in his lower-priced collection. For designers, such two-tier pricing may constitute a viable response to the growth of knockoffs so long as designers are able to maintain some differentiation between the copy and the original.

The phenomenon of knockoffs is by no means unique to women's fashion, though the very short time lag between the arrival of the original and the entry of the copy is somewhat anomalous. Product imitation occurs in all sorts of industries. In the computer industry, a wave of "clones" followed IBM's introduction of the PC in 1984. Similarly, generic drugs are knockoffs in the pharmaceutical industry, though the mechanisms of patent protection and regulation explicitly define the time lag between the launch of the original and the entry of the copy.

When a price difference is based on different buyers' valuations of the same product, it is discriminatory. It does not cost a movie theater operator less to fill seats with children than with adults, but it may be worthwhile for the movie theater to let the children in at a discriminatory low price if few of them would attend at the full adult fare and if they take up seats that would otherwise be empty.

DIFFERENT FORMS OF PRICE DISCRIMINATION

Why should a firm want to sell some units of its output at a price that is well below the price that it receives for other units of its output? The simple answer is because it is profitable to do so. Why should it be profitable?

Persistent price discrimination is profitable either because different buyers are willing to pay different amounts for the same product or because one buyer is willing to pay different amounts for different units of the same product. The basic point about price discrimination is that in either of these circumstances, sellers may be able to capture some of the consumer surplus that would otherwise go to buyers. (Review the discussion of consumer surplus in Chapter 7.) We first discuss the ideas behind each type of price discrimination; we then examine its implications.

Discrimination Among Units of Output

Look back to Table 7-2 in Chapter 7, which shows the consumer surplus received by one consumer when buying eight glasses of milk at a single price. If the firm could sell the consumer each glass separately, it could capture this consumer surplus. It would sell the first unit for $3.00, the second unit for $1.50, the third unit for $1.00, and so on until the eighth unit was sold for 30 cents. The firm would get total revenues of $8.10 rather than the $2.40 obtained from selling eight units at the single price of 30 cents each. In this example, the firm is able to discriminate perfectly and to extract all of the consumer surplus.

Perfect price discrimination occurs when the entire consumer surplus is obtained by the firm. This usually requires that each unit be sold at a separate price. In practice, perfect discrimination is seldom possible. Suppose, however, that the firm could charge two different prices, one for the first 4 units sold and one for the next 4 units sold. If it sold the first 4 units for 80 cents and the next 4 units for 30 cents, it would receive $4.40—less than it would receive if it could discriminate perfectly but more than it would receive if it sold all units at 30 cents.

Discrimination Among Buyers

Think of the demand curve in a market that is made up of individual buyers, each of whom has indicated the maximum price that he or she is prepared to pay for a single unit. Suppose, for the sake of simplicity, that there are only four buyers for the product; the first is prepared to pay any price up to $4 for one unit of the good, the second is prepared to pay up to $3, the third up to $2, and the fourth up to $1. Suppose that the product has a marginal cost of production of $1 per unit for all units. If the selling firm is limited to a single price, we know it will maximize its profits by setting marginal revenue equal to marginal cost. It will thus charge $3, sell 2 units, and earn profits of $4. (You can compute for yourself the firm's marginal revenue schedule.)

However, if the seller is able to discriminate among the buyers, it could charge the first buyer $4 and the second $3, thus increasing its profits from the first 2 units to $5. Moreover, it could also sell the third unit for $2, thus increasing its profits to $6. It would be indifferent about selling a fourth unit because the price would just cover marginal cost.

Discrimination Among Markets

Suppose now that the monopolist sells its product in two different markets. For example, it might be the only seller in a tariff-protected home market while in foreign markets it sells in competition with so many other firms that it is a price taker. In this case, the firm would equate its marginal cost to the price in the foreign market but to marginal revenue in the domestic market. As a result, it would charge a higher price on sales in the home market than on sales abroad.

Price Discrimination More Generally

Demand curves have a negative slope because different units are valued differently, either by one individual or by different individuals. This fact, combined with a single price for a product, gives rise to consumer surplus.

The ability to charge multiple prices gives a seller the opportunity to capture some (or, in the extreme case, all) of the consumer surplus.

In general, the larger the number of different prices that can be charged, the greater the firm's ability to increase its revenue at the expense of consumers. This is illustrated in Figure 11-6.

It follows that if a selling firm is able to discriminate through price, it can increase revenues received (and thus also profits) from the sale of any

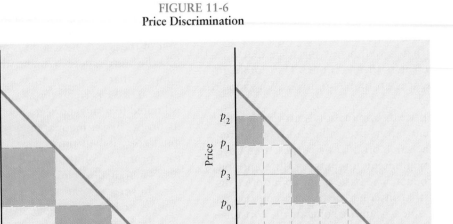

FIGURE 11-6
Price Discrimination

(i) Two prices charged

(ii) Four prices charged

Multiple prices permit a seller to capture consumer surplus. Suppose in either graph that if a single price were charged, it would be the price p_0. Quantity q_0 would be sold, and consumer surplus would be the entire area above p_0 and below the demand curve.

Part (i) assumes that the market can be segregated in such a way that two prices are charged: p_1 for the first q_1 units and p_0 for the remaining q_1q_0 units. Consumer surplus is reduced to the two light blue triangles, and the seller's revenue is increased by the dark blue square.

Part (ii) assumes that the market can be segregated in such a way that four prices are charged: p_2 for the first q_2 units, p_1 for the units between q_2 and q_1, and so on. Consumer surplus is reduced to the light blue triangles, and the seller's revenue is further increased by the two dark blue squares. At the extreme, if a different price could be charged for each unit, producers could extract every bit of the consumer surplus, and the price discrimination would be perfect.

given quantity. [28] However, price discrimination is not always possible, even if there are no legal barriers to its use.

WHEN IS PRICE DISCRIMINATION POSSIBLE?

Discrimination *among units of output* sold to the same buyer requires that the seller be able to keep track of the units that a buyer consumes in each period. Thus the tenth unit purchased by a given buyer in a given month can be sold at a price that is different from the fifth unit *only* if the seller can keep track of who buys what. This can be done by an electric company through its meter readings or by a magazine publisher by distinguishing between renewals and new subscriptions. It can also be done by distributing certificates or coupons that allow, for example, a car wash at a reduced price on a return visit.

Discrimination *among buyers* is possible only if the buyers who face the low price cannot resell the goods to the buyers who face the high price. However, even though the local butcher might like to charge the banker twice as much for steak as he charges the taxi driver, he cannot succeed in doing so. The banker can always shop for meat in the supermarket, where her occupation is not known. Even if the butcher and the supermarket agreed to charge her twice as much, she could hire the taxi driver to shop for her. The surgeon, however, may succeed in discriminating (especially if other reputable surgeons do the same) because it will not do the banker much good to hire the taxi driver to have her operation for her.

Price discrimination is possible if the seller can either distinguish individual units bought by a single buyer or separate buyers into groups such that resale between groups is impossible.

The ability to prevent resale tends to be associated with the nature of the product or the ability to classify buyers into readily identifiable groups. Services are less easily resold than goods; goods that require installation by the firm (e.g., heavy equipment or cable TV service) are less easily resold than movable goods such as household appliances. One simple example of nonresalability occurs in the case of plate glass. Small pieces of plate glass are much cheaper to buy per square metre than bigger pieces, but the person who needs glass for a picture window that is 2 metres by 4 metres obviously cannot use four pieces of glass that are each 1 by 2 metres. Thus the seller can succesfully price discriminate by charging more *per square metre* for large plate glass than for small plate glass.

In general, transportation costs, tariff barriers, and import quotas are among the factors that separate groups of buyers geographically and may make discrimination possible.

Of course, it is not enough to be able to separate different buyers or different units into separate groups. The seller must also be able to control the supply going to each group. For example, there is no point in asking more than the competitive price from some buyers if they can simply go to other firms who sell the good at the competitive price.

THE CONSEQUENCES OF PRICE DISCRIMINATION

The consequences of price discrimination are summarized in the following two propositions.

For any given level of output, the most profitable system of discriminatory prices will provide higher total revenue (and higher profits) to the firm than the profit-maximizing single price.

This first proposition, which was illustrated in Figure 11-6, requires only that the demand curve have a negative slope. To see that the proposition is correct, remember that a monopolist with the power to discriminate could produce exactly the same

quantity as a single-price monopolist and charge everyone the same price. Therefore, it need never receive less revenue, and it can do better if it can raise the price on even one unit sold, as long as the price need not be lowered on any other.

Output under price discrimination will be larger than under a single-price monopolist.

To understand this second proposition, remember that a monopolist that must charge a single price for a product will produce less than would all the firms in a perfectly competitive industry. It does this because it knows that selling more depresses the price. Price discrimination allows it to avoid this disincentive. To the extent that the firm can sell its output in separate blocks, it can sell another block without spoiling the market for blocks that are already sold. In the case of perfect price discrimination, in which every unit of output is sold at a different price, the profit-maximizing monopolist will produce every unit for which the price charged is greater than or equal to its marginal cost. *A perfect-price-discriminating monopolist will therefore produce the same quantity of output as would all firms combined in a perfectly competitive industry.*

NORMATIVE ASPECTS OF PRICE DISCRIMINATION

The predicted combination of higher average revenue and higher output does not in itself have any *normative* significance. It will typically lead to a different distribution of income and a different level of output than when the seller is limited to a single price. The ability of the discriminating monopolist to capture some of the consumer surplus will seem undesirable to consumers but obviously not to the monopolist. How outsiders view the transfer may depend on who gains and who loses.

For instance, when railroads discriminate against small farmers, the results arouse public anger. It seems acceptable to many people, however, that doctors practice price discrimination in countries where medical services are provided by the market, charging lower prices to poor patients than to wealthy ones. Not everyone disapproves when airlines discriminate by giving senior citizens and vacationers lower fares than business travelers.

An interesting further example comes from abroad. For many years, government policy prevented British railways from discriminating among passengers in different regions. To prevent discrimination, a fixed fare per passenger-kilometre was specified and charged on all lines, regardless of passenger traffic or elasticity of demand for the services of the particular line. In the interests of economy, branch lines that could not cover costs were closed. Some lines stopped operating, even though their users preferred rail transport to any alternatives and the strength of their preference was such that they would have willingly paid a price that would have allowed the line to operate profitably. However, the lines were closed because it was thought to be inequitable to "discriminate against" the passengers on these lines.

Two quite separate issues are involved in evaluating any particular example of price discrimination. One is the effect of discrimination on the level of output, and the other is the effect of discrimination on the distribution of income. Price discrimination results in a higher output than would occur if a single price were charged. Often, however, it is the effect of discrimination on income distribution that accounts for people's strong emotional reactions to it. By increasing the seller's profits, price discrimination transfers income from buyers to sellers. When buyers are poor and sellers are rich, this may seem undesirable. However, as we saw in the case of doctors' fees and senior citizens' discounts, discrimination sometimes allows lower-income people to buy a product that they would be unable to afford if it were sold at the single price that maximized the producers' profits.

SUMMARY

A. A SINGLE-PRICE MONOPOLIST

- Monopoly is a market structure in which an entire industry is supplied by a single firm. The monopolist's own demand curve is identical to the market demand curve for the product. The market demand curve is the monopolist's average revenue curve, and its marginal revenue curve always lies below its demand curve.
- A single-price monopolist is maximizing its profits when its marginal revenue is equal to marginal costs. Since marginal costs are positive, profit maximization means that marginal revenue is positive. This in turn means that elasticity of demand is greater than unity at the monopolist's profit-maximizing level of output.
- The amount of profits that a monopoly earns may be large, small, zero, or negative in the short run, depending on the relationship between demand and cost.
- For monopoly profits to persist in the long run, there must be effective barriers to the entry of other firms. Entry barriers can be natural or created.
- Monopoly power is limited by the presence of substitute products, the development of new products, and the entry of new firms. In the very-long run, it is difficult to maintain entry barriers in the face of the process

of creative destruction—the invention of new processes and new products to attack the entrenched position of existing monopolies.

B. CARTELS AS MONOPOLIES

- A group of firms may form a cartel by agreeing to restrict their joint output to the monopoly level. Cartels tend to be unstable because of the strong incentives for each individual firm to cheat by producing more than its quota allows.

C. A MULTIPRICE MONOPOLIST: PRICE DISCRIMINATION

- A price-discriminating monopolist can capture some of the consumer surplus that exists when all of the units of a product are sold at a single price. Successful price discrimination requires that the firm be able to control the supply of the product offered to particular buyers and to prevent the resale of the product.
- A profit-maximizing monopolist that can enforce discriminatory prices will produce higher output and earn larger profits than will a single-price monopolist.

KEY CONCEPTS

The relationship between price and marginal revenue for a monopolist

The relationships among marginal revenue, total revenue, and elasticity for a monopolist

Short-run monopoly profits
Natural and created entry barriers
Cartels as monopolies
The instability of cartels

The causes and consequences of price discrimination
Perfect price discrimination

DISCUSSION QUESTIONS

1. Suppose that only one professor teaches economics at your university. Would you say that this professor is a monopolist who can exact any "price" from students in the form of readings assigned, tests given, and material covered? Suppose now that two additional professors have been hired. Has the original professor's monopoly power been decreased? What if the three professors form a cartel agreeing on common reading lists, workloads, and the like?

2. Three of the four companies that manufacture matzos—the unleavened bread eaten during the Jewish Passover celebration—recently combined to control 90 percent of the total market. When the owner of the new firm was approached by a marketing specialist about doing special promotions, he replied, "Why? We already own the market." What does this tell you about the new firm's attitude with respect to competitive behaviour? In analyzing the firm's price and output decisions, would it be reasonable to use monopoly theory? What does the quotation tell you about the firm's belief about the sensitivity of market demand to promotion schemes?

3. Imagine a monopolist that has fixed costs but no variable or marginal costs. For example, consider a firm that owns a spring of water that can produce indefinitely once certain pipes are installed in an area where no other source of water is available. What would be the firm's profit-maximizing price? What elasticity of demand would you expect at that price? Would this seem to be an appropriate pricing policy if the water monopoly were instead owned by the municipal government, and operated in the interests of the residents of the municipality?

4. Which of these industries—licorice candy, copper wire, outboard motors, coal, or the local newspaper—would it be most profitable to monopolize? Why? Does your answer depend on several factors or

on just one or two? Which would you as a consumer least like to have monopolized by someone else? If your answers to the two questions are different, explain why.

5. Aristotle Murphy owns movie theatres in two towns of roughly the same size, 100 kilometres apart. In Monopolia, he owns the only chain of theatres; in Competitia, there is no theatre chain, and he is only one of a number of independent theatre operators. Would you expect movie prices to be higher in Monopolia or in Competitia in the short run? In the long run? If differences occur in his prices, would Murphy be discriminating in price?

6. Liquor retailing is a competitive industry in most U.S. states but a government-owned monopoly in most Canadian provinces. In what ways would you expect the industry in the two countries to be different? In Alberta, the previously government-owned retail liquor stores were privatized. What would you expect to happen to the price and quantity of retail liquor in Alberta after the privatization?

7. Airline fares to Europe are higher in summer than in winter. Some railroads charge lower fares during the week than on weekends. Electric companies charge consumers lower rates the more electricity they use. Are these all examples of price discrimination? What additional information would you like to have before answering this question?

8. Discuss whether each of the following represents price discrimination. In your view, which are the most socially harmful?

   a. Weekend airline fares that are less than full fare
   b. First-class fares that are 50 percent higher than tourist fares, recognizing that two first-class seats use the space of three tourist seats

c. Discounts negotiated from list price, for which sales personnel are authorized to bargain and to get as much in each transaction as the traffic will bear

d. Higher tuition for out-of-state students at state-supported colleges and universities in the United States.

e. Higher tuition for law students than for graduate students in economics.

9. Acme Department Store has a sale on luggage. It is offering $30 off any new set of luggage to customers who trade in an old suitcase. Acme has no use for the old luggage and throws it away at the end of each day. Is this price discrimination? Why or why not? Which of the conditions necessary for price discrimination are or are not met?

10. The world price of coffee has declined in real terms over the past 40 years. In 1950, coffee was priced at just under $3 per pound (in 1994 U.S. dollars), whereas by 1995 the world price had fallen to just over $1 per pound. On July 29, 1995, *The Economist* magazine reported that,

> On July 26 the Association of Coffee Producing Countries agreed in New York to limit exports to 60m bags for 12 months. The current level is 70m bags. . . . Coffee prices rallied a bit on the news, but few expect the pact to last: some big coffee producers such as Mexico have not signed up, and even those who have will probably cheat.

Explain why "few expect the pact to last", keeping in mind the two characteristic problems for cartels that were discussed in this chapter.

CHAPTER 12

IMPERFECT COMPETITION AND STRATEGIC BEHAVIOUR

The two market structures that we have studied so far—perfect competition and monopoly—are polar cases; they define the two extremes of a firm's market power over an industry. Under perfect competition, firms are price takers, price is driven to the level of marginal cost, and economic profits in the long run are zero, which means that firms are just covering the opportunity cost of their capital. Under monopoly, the firm is a price setter, it sets price above marginal cost, and it may earn more than the opportunity cost of its capital.

Although they provide important insights, these two polar cases are insufficient for understanding the behaviour of all firms. Indeed, most of the products that we easily recognize—computers, breakfast cereals, automobiles, photographic equipment, and fast food, to name a few—are produced by firms that have *some* market power but are neither perfect competitors or monopolists.

This chapter is devoted to the discussion of the theory of industries that are neither perfectly competitive nor monopolistic. Before discussing the theory, however, we turn to a brief discussion of some characteristics of the Canadian economy.

THE STRUCTURE OF THE CANADIAN ECONOMY

Most industries in the Canadian economy lie between the two extremes of monopoly and perfect competition. Within this spectrum of market structure we can divide Canadian industries into two broad groups—those with a large number of relatively small firms and those with a small number of relatively large firms.

INDUSTRIES WITH MANY SMALL FIRMS

About two-thirds of Canada's gross domestic product is produced by industries made up of firms that are either small in absolute size, as most independent retailers are, or small relative to the size of the market in which they sell, like even the largest of Canadian farms.

The perfectly competitive model, extended to allow for the impact of government intervention where necessary, does quite well in explaining the behaviour of some of these industries. These are the ones in which individual firms produce more-or-less identical products and so are price takers. Forest and fish products provide many examples. Agriculture also fits fairly well in most ways since individual farmers are clearly price takers. Entry into farming is easy, and exit does occur, often making news when it happens on a large scale. Many basic raw materials, such as iron ore, tin, and copper, are sold on world markets where most individual firms lack significant market power and prices fluctuate continually in response to changing market conditions.

Other industries, however, do not exhibit the behaviour that is predicted by the perfectly competitive model, even though they contain many firms. In retail trade and in services, for example, most firms have some influence over prices. The local grocery, supermarket, discount house, and department store not only consider weekend specials and periodic sales to be important to their success, but also spend a good deal of money advertising—something that they would not have to do if they faced perfectly-elastic demand curves. Moreover, each store in these industries has a unique location that may give it some local monopoly power over nearby customers. In wholesaling, the sales representative is regarded as a key figure who must compete with other representatives to sell to reluctant purchasers.

As a result, industries with many relatively small firms can be divided into two categories. In one category, the firms' behaviour can be explained by the perfectly competitive model; in the other category, the perfectly competitive model does not apply because the firms, though small, are not price takers. It is this second group of industries that we examine in this chapter.

INDUSTRIES WITH A FEW LARGE FIRMS

About one third of Canada's gross domestic product is produced by industries that are dominated by either a single firm or a few large ones.

The most striking cases of single-firm monopolies in today's economy are the electric utilities and the firms which provide local telephone service. In the first case they are typcially owned by provincial governments; in the second they are subject to government regulation (which we examine in Chapter 13). Other than these and similar cases in which government ownership or regulation plays an important role, cases of single-firm monopoly are very rare in Canada today. However, there are some notable examples of monopoly (or near monopoly) from many years ago. For example, the Eddy Match Company was virtually the sole producer of wooden matches in Canada between 1927 and 1940, and Canada Cement Limited produced nearly all of the output of cement until the 1950s.

This type of market dominance by a single large firm is now largely a thing of the past. Most modern industries which are dominated by large firms contain several. Their names are part of the average Canadian's vocabulary: Canadian National and Canadian Pacific; Canadian Airlines and Air Canada; Banque National, Toronto Dominion, and Scotia Bank; Imperial Oil, Petro Canada, and Irving; Stelco, Dofasco, and Alcan; Falconbridge and INCO; Abitibi Price and MacMillan Bloedel; and Ford, Chrysler, and GM. Many service industries that used to be dominated by small independent producers have in recent decades seen the development of large firms operating on a world-wide basis. In accounting, firms such as Price-Waterhouse and Deloitte-Touche are enormous and clearly have some market power. SNC-Lavalin and Acres are two examples of very large engineering firms that have business contracts all over the world.

INDUSTRIAL CONCENTRATION

An industry that is highly concentrated contains few firms, whereas an industry that has a low degree of concentration contains many firms. Recall that monopoly and perfect competition lie at the two extremes of concentration; a monopoly is an industry with only one firm, and perfect competition is an industry with so many firms that no one of them has any influence on market price. As we have just seen, most industries lie between these two extremes of concentration.

Concentration Ratios

When measuring whether an industry has power concentrated in the hands of only a few firms or dispersed over many, it is not sufficient to count the number of firms. For example, an industry with one enormous firm and 29 small ones is more concentrated in any meaningful sense than an industry with only five equally-sized firms. One approach to this problem is to calculate what is called a **concentration ratio,** which shows the fraction of total market sales controlled by the largest sellers. Common types of concentration ratios cite the share of total market sales made by the largest four or eight firms.

One important problem associated with using concentration ratios is to *define the market* with reasonable accuracy. On the one hand, the market may be much smaller than the whole country. For example, concentration ratios in national cement sales are low, but they understate the market power of cement companies because high transportation costs divide the cement *industry* into a series of regional *markets,* with each having relatively few firms. On the other hand, the market may be larger than one country. This is a particularly important consideration in a small trading country such as Canada.

Indeed, the globalization of competition brought about by the falling costs of transportation and communication has been one of the most significant developments in the world economy in recent decades. As the world has "become smaller" through the advances in communication technologies, the nature of domestic markets has changed dramatically. The presence of only a single firm in one industry in Canada in no way implies monopoly power when it is in competition with five foreign firms that can easily sell in the Canadian market. Application 12-1 discusses how the communication revolution which has taken place in the past two decades has altered the nature of production and competition in Canada and around the world.

However, the use of concentration ratios, adjusted appropriately to correctly define the relevant

GLOBALIZATION AND THE COMMUNICATION REVOLUTION

A mere 150 years ago, people and news traveled by sailing ship, and it took months to communicate across various parts of the world. Advances in the first 60 years of the twentieth century sped up both communications and travel. In the past three decades, the pace of change in communication technology has accelerated. The world has witnessed a communication revolution that has dramatically changed the way business decisions are made and implemented.

Four decades ago, telephone links were labouriously and unreliably connected by operators, satellites were newfangled and not especially useful toys for rocket scientists, photocopying and telecopying were completely unknown, mail was the only way to send hard copy and getting it to overseas destinations often took weeks, computers were in their infancy, and jets were just beginning to replace the much slower and less reliable propeller aircraft. Today, direct dialing is available to most parts of the world, at a fraction of what long-distance calls cost 40 years ago, and faxes, satellite links, jet travel, computer networks, cheap courier services, and a host of other developments have made communication that is reliable and often instantaneous available throughout the world.

The communication revolution has been a major contributor to the development of what has become known as the "global village," a term first used by Canadian author Marshall McLuhan in his writing about the social implications of changes in communication technology. Three important characteristics of the global village are a *globalization* of production, an increase in competition, and a decline in the power of the nation-state.

PRODUCTION

The communication revolution has allowed many large international companies, known as *transnational corporations (TNCs),* to decentralize their production process. They are now able to locate their research and development (R&D) where the best scientists are available. They can produce various components in dozens of places, locating each activity in a country where costs are cheapest for that type of production. They can then ship all the parts, as they are needed, to an assembly factory where the product is "made."

The globalization of production has brought employment, and rising real wages, to people in many less-developed countries. At the same time, it has put

market, can give us useful information about the degree to which production in a given market is concentrated in the hands of a few firms.

Industrial Concentration in Canada

The concentration ratios that are typical of various sectors of the Canadian economy differ greatly from one sector to another. In agriculture, concentration ratios are very low. The market structure is close to perfectly competitive, except where government supply-management schemes have created cartels. In forestry, four firms account for approximately 20 percent of the total sales, but the remainder is ac-

counted for by numerous small firms. Most of these firms, large and small, sell in highly competitive international markets. In transportation, communication, and energy utilities, the degree of concentration is higher. There are two firms in rail transportation and two main firms (with some fringe competitors) in air transport and in television networks. There is either monopoly or publicly owned firms in telecommunication, electric energy, and water and natural gas pipelines. Various parts of the wholesale trade have relatively low degrees of concentration, while in the retail trades, the ratios range from low to high. In community, business, and personal services, concentration tends to be quite low (except perhaps in small less-skilled labour in the developed countries under strong competitive pressures.

COMPETITION

The communication revolution has also caused a globalization of competition in almost all industries. National markets are no longer protected for local producers by high costs of transportation and communication or by the ignorance of foreign firms. Walk into a local supermarket or department store today, and you will have no trouble finding products representing most nations of the world.

Consumers gain by being able to choose from an enormous range of well-made, low-priced goods and services. Firms that are successful gain worldwide sales. Firms that fall behind even momentarily may, however, be wiped out by competition coming from many quarters. Global competition is fierce, and firms need to be fast on the uptake—of other people's new ideas or their own—if they are to survive.

ECONOMIC POLICY

The international character of TNCs means that national economic policies have been seriously constrained. Much international trade takes place between segments of single TNCs. This gives them the opportunity, through their accounting practices, to localize their profits in countries where corporate taxes are lowest and to localize their costs in countries where cost write-offs are highest.

The globalization of production also allows TNCs to shift production around the world. Tough national policies that reduce profitability in one country may be self-defeating as firms move production elsewhere. Generous policies that seek to attract production may succeed in attracting only small and specialized parts of it. For example, Sweden has given generous tax treatment to R&D expenditures, seeking to attract firms to do their high-tech, high-wage production in that country. Instead, however, many firms have come to Sweden to do their R&D and then have transferred the knowledge to countries where production costs are lower. The net result is that Swedish taxpayers are subsidizing world consumers by paying for R&D that is generating production in other countries.

The examples given here illustrate an important development: Globalization of production, and consequently of competition, means a great reduction in the scope for individual countries, especially small countries like Canada, to implement distinctive economic policies.

---

towns). In insurance and real estate, concentration is quite low, while in the financial industries concentration is typically quite high.

This is quite a varied story, and we can gain further insight into this experience of concentration by examining the Canadian manufacturing sector in detail.

Even in the Canadian manufacturing sector, the degree of concentration ranges from very high to very low. Table 12-1 shows the four-firm concentration ratios in selected Canadian manufacturing industries. Few, if any, of the industries shown in the table come close to monopoly. None of the industries in the table have a concentration ratio of 100 percent for four firms, let alone for one firm.

At the other extreme, there are many industries with low concentration ratios. The perfectly competitive model could conceivably fit these industries. But even here there are doubts. Manufacturers of clothing, for example, have some control over price because of style and fashion. This is also true for furniture manufacturers. Yet in both cases the four-firm concentration ratios are less than 10 percent.

Although similarities in standards of living, consumption patterns, and education in Canada and the United States have led to many similarities in industrial structure, the Canadian manufacturing sector is substantially *more concentrated* than the American.

TABLE 12-1
Four-Firm Concentration Ratios for Selected Canadian Manufacturing Industries, 1988

Industry	Percent of Revenue Controlled by Leading Four Firms
Tobacco Products	98.9
Petroleum and Coal Products	74.5
Transportation Equipment	68.4
Primary Metals	63.3
Beverages	59.2
Metal Mining	58.9
Paper and Allied Industries	38.9
Textile Mills	32.5
Electrical Products	32.1
Chemical Products	25.5
Food	19.6
Wood Industries	17.8
Knitting Mills	11.4
Machinery	11.3
Furniture Industries	7.6
Clothing Industries	6.6

Source: Douglas West, *Modern Canadian Industrial Organization* (HarperCollins, 1994), p. 37.

TABLE 12-2
Distribution of Concentration Ratios for 140 Canadian Manufacturing Industries

Concentration ratio categories (%)	Number of Industries in Each Group	
	Official data	Adjusted data
0–24.9	17	41
25–49.9	50	58
50–74.9	45	34
75–100	28	7
All industries	140	140

The standard concentration ratios overstate the degree of concentration in Canadian industries due to the openness of the Canadian economy. The first column shows the range for the four-firm concentration ratio. For example, the first row indicates a low degree of concentration, since the four largest firms account for less than 25 percent of the sales, whereas the last row indicates a high level of concentration, with the four largest firms accounting for more than 75 percent of all sales. The second column gives the number of industries in each concentration ratio class according to the official figures. The last column gives the distribution of the same industries when corrections are made for plants with multi-industry outputs and for the importance of imports in the Canadian market. When the corrected figures are substituted for the official ones, the fall in measured concentration of the typical Canadian industry is striking.

(Source: John Baldwin, Paul Gorecki, and John McVey, *Economic Council of Canada, Discussion Paper #263, 1984.)*

This is partly because the small size of the Canadian economy leaves room for fewer firms operating at minimum efficient scale than does the larger American economy. (Recall from Chapter 10 that minimum efficient scale is the level of output where *LRAC* is minimized.) Working in the other direction, however, is the fact that the Canadian economy is a very *open economy,* and for many industries the relevant market includes foreign countries, especially the United States.

Some economists have corrected the "official" concentration ratios (i.e., those published by Statistics Canada) to allow for foreign as well as domestic competition. They estimate market size on the basis of what is sold, whether or not it is produced in Canada. The importance of one firm in that market is estimated on the basis of what it sells in that market no matter where these goods were produced.

Table 12-2 gives the results based on the official four-firm concentration ratios for Canada as well as the corrected figures. It shows that when the corrections are made, there is significantly *less concentration* in Canadian manufacturing than one would infer by inspecting the published data alone. In particular, they find that correcting for the openness of the Canadian economy results in more industries having low concentration ratios and fewer industries having high concentration ratios.

The data used in Table 12-2 is from 1979, and thus the study is considerably dated. Unfortunately, the data required to carry out such a correction are not easily available, and are not available on an ongoing basis. But the changes in the structure of the Canadian economy over the past twenty years actually serve to reinforce the central point. The trend toward more international trade, partially driven by the FTA and NAFTA, have made Canada a more open economy today than it was in 1979. Thus a similar study today would likely find that there is *even less* industrial concentration than suggested in Table 12-2.

The table shows that even with the corrected data, in about 70 percent of Canadian manufacturing industries, the four largest firms control over 25 percent of the value of sales. Such industries are not monopolies, because there are several firms in the industry, and these firms engage in rivalrous behaviour. But neither do these firms operate in perfectly competitive markets. Often there are only a few major rival firms in an industry, but even when there are many, they are not price takers. Virtually all consumer goods are differentiated products, and any one firm will typically have several lines of a product that differ more or less from one another and from competing lines produced by other firms. To explain and predict behaviour in these markets, we must go beyond simple concentration ratios; we need to develop theories of the behaviour of firms in market structures other than monopoly and perfect competition.

IMPERFECTLY COMPETITIVE MARKET STRUCTURES

The market structures that we are now going to study are called *imperfectly competitive*. The word *competitive* emphasizes that we are not dealing with monopoly, and the word *imperfect* emphasizes that we are not dealing with perfect competition (in which firms are price takers). What is referred to, then, is rivalrous competitive behaviour among firms that have some amount of market power.

We begin by noting a number of important characteristics of behaviour that are typical of imperfectly competitive firms. To help organize our thoughts, we classify these under two main headings. First, firms choose the *variety* of the product that they produce and sell. Second, firms choose the *price* at which they will sell that product.

FIRMS SELECT THEIR PRODUCTS

If a new farmer enters the wheat industry, the full range of products that can be produced is already in existence. In contrast, if a new firm enters the snack food industry, that firm must decide on the characteristics of the new snacks that it is to produce. It will not produce snacks that are identical to those already in production. Rather, it will develop variations on existing snack foods or even a totally new food. Each of these will have its own distinctive characteristics. As a result, firms in the snack food industry sell an array of differentiated products, no two of which are identical.

The term **differentiated product** refers to a group of commodities that are similar enough to be

called the same product but dissimilar enough that they can be sold at different prices. For example, although one brand of face soap is similar to most others, soaps differ from each other in chemical composition, colour, smell, softness, brand name, packaging, reputation, and a host of other characteristics that matter to customers. So all face soaps taken together can be regarded as one differentiated product.

Most (but not all) firms in imperfectly competitive markets sell differentiated products. In such industries, the firm itself must decide on what characteristics to give the products that it will sell.

FIRMS CHOOSE THEIR PRICES

Because firms in perfect competition sell a homogeneous product, they face a market price that they are unable to influence. In all other market structures, firms have negatively sloped demand curves and thus face a trade off between the price that they charge and the quantity that they sell.

Whenever different firms' products are not perfect substitutes, each firm must decide on a price to quote. For example, no market sets a single price for razor blades or television sets by equating overall demand with overall supply. What is true for razor blades and for television sets is true for virtually all consumer goods and many capital goods. Any one manufacturer will typically have several product lines that differ from each other and from the competing product lines of other firms. Each product has a price that must be set by its producer. Of course, a certain amount of haggling is possible, particularly at the retail level, but this is usually within well-defined limits set by the price charged by the manufacturer.

In such circumstances, economists say that firms *administer* their price. An **administered price** is a price set by the conscious decision of an individual firm rather than by impersonal market forces. Firms that administer their prices are said to be **price makers.**

Each firm has expectations about the quantity it can sell at each price that it might set. *Unexpected* market fluctuations then cause unexpected variations in the quantities that are sold at the administered prices.

In market structures other than perfect competition, firms set their prices and then let demand determine sales. Changes in market conditions are signaled to

the firm by changes in the quantity that the firm sells at its current administered price.

The changed conditions may or may not then lead firms to change their prices.

One striking contrast between perfectly competitive markets, on the one hand, and markets for differentiated products, on the other, concerns the behaviour of prices. In perfect competition, prices change continually in response to changes in demand and supply. In markets where differentiated products are sold, prices often change less frequently. Manufacturers' prices for automobiles, radios, television sets, and men's suits do not change with anything like the frequency that prices change in markets for basic materials or stocks and bonds.

Modern firms that sell differentiated products typically have hundreds, and sometimes even thousands, of distinct products on their price lists. Changing such a long list of administered prices at the same frequency that competitive market prices change would be extremely costly if not impossible. Even changing them only occassionally involves costs. These include the costs of printing new list prices and notifying all customers, the difficulty of keeping track of frequently changing prices for purposes of accounting and billing, and the loss of customer and retailer goodwill due to the uncertainty caused by frequent changes in prices. These costs are often a significant consideration to multiproduct manufacturing firms.

Because producers of differentiated products must administer their own prices, firms must decide on the *frequency* with which they change these prices. In making this decision, the firm will balance the cost of making price changes against the revenue lost by not making price changes. Clearly, the likelihood that the firm will make costly price changes rises with the size of the disturbance to which it is adjusting and the probability that the disturbance will not be reversed.

Thus transitory fluctuations in demand may be met by changing output with prices constant, while changes in costs that accompany inflation are typically passed on through price increases. Because few firms expect inflationary price increases to be reversed, they know that they must raise their prices to cover them. Even in these cases, however, they do so periodically, rather than continuously, because of the costs incurred in making such changes.

OTHER ASPECTS OF FIRM BEHAVIOUR

Several other important aspects of the observed behaviour of firms in imperfect competition could not occur under either perfect competition or monopoly.

Nonprice Competition

Many firms spend large sums of money on advertising. They do so in an attempt both to shift the demand curves for the industry's products and to attract customers from competing firms. Many firms engage in a variety of other forms of non-price competition, such as offering competing standards of quality and product guarantees. Any kind of sales-promotion activity undertaken by a single firm would not happen under perfect competition; any such scheme directed at competing firms in the same industry is, by definition, inconsistent with monopoly.

Unexploited Scale Economies

Many firms in industries that contain more than one firm appear to be operating on the downward-sloping portions of the long-run average cost curves for many of the individual product lines that they produce. Although this is possible under monopoly, firms in perfect competition must, in the long run, be at the minimum point of their long-run average cost curves. (See Figure 10-10 in Chapter 10.)

One set of reasons is found in high development costs and short product lives. Many modern products involve large development costs and are sold for only a few years before they are replaced by new, superior products. For example, for Ford, Toyota or any of the other car manufacturers it takes many millions of dollars (and several years) to develop each new model-year, and many of the changes that are introduced into a new model-year are eliminated the very next year. In such cases, firms face steeply falling long-run average cost curves. The more units that are sold, the less the fixed development costs per unit. Given perfect competition, these firms would go on increasing outputs and sales until rising marginal costs of production balanced the falling fixed unit costs. As it is, they often face falling average cost curves all through the product's life cycle.

Entry Prevention

Firms in many industries engage in activities that appear to be designed to hinder the entry of new firms, thereby preventing existing pure profits from being eroded by entry. We will consider these activities in much more detail later in the chapter.

MONOPOLISTIC COMPETITION

The theory of **monopolistic competition** was originally developed to deal with the phenomenon of product differentiation.[1] This market structure is similar to perfect competition in that the industry contains many firms and exhibits freedom of entry and exit. It differs, however, in one important respect: Whereas firms in perfect competition sell a *homogeneous product* and are price takers, firms in monopolistic competition sell a *differentiated product* and have some power over setting price.

Product differentiation leads to, and is enhanced by, the establishment of brand names and advertising, and it gives each firm a degree of monopoly power over its own product. Each firm can raise its price, even if its competitors do not, without losing all its sales. This is the *monopolistic* part of the theory. However, each firm's monopoly power is severely restricted in both the short run and the long run. The short-run restriction comes from the presence of similar products sold by many competing firms; this causes each firm's demand curve to be very elastic. The long-run restriction comes from free entry into the industry. These restrictions comprise the *competition* part of the theory.

THE ASSUMPTIONS OF MONOPOLISTIC COMPETITION

The theory of monopolistic competition is based on three key assumptions.

1. *Each firm produces one specific variety, or brand, of the industry's differentiated product.*

Each firm thus faces a demand curve that, although it is negatively sloped, is highly elastic because competing firms produce many close substitutes.

2. *The industry contains so many firms that each one ignores the possible reactions of its many competitors when it makes its own price and output decisions.* There are so many firms in the industry that each is negligibly affected by the actions of any other one firm, and thus each firm ignores the actions of the others. In this way, firms in monopolistic competition are similar to firms in perfect competition. They make decisions based on their own demand and cost conditions and do not consider interdependence between their own decisions and those of the other firms in the industry. This is the key aspect that distinguishes the market structure of monopolistic competition from the market structure of oligopoly, which we discuss later in the chapter.

3. *There is freedom of entry and exit in the industry.* If profits are being earned by existing firms, new firms have an incentive to enter. When they do, the demand for the industry's product must be shared among more brands, and this is assumed to take demand equally from all existing firms.

PREDICTIONS OF THE THEORY

Product differentiation, which is the *only* thing that makes monopolistic competition different from perfect competition, has important consequences for behaviour in both the short and the long run.

The Short-Run Decision of the Firm

In the short run, a firm that is operating in a monopolistically competitive market structure is similar to a monopoly. It faces a negatively sloped demand curve and maximizes its profits by equating marginal cost with marginal revenue. If the demand curve cuts the average total cost curve, as is shown in part (i) of Figure 12-1, the firm can make pure profits over and above the opportunity cost of its capital.

The Long-Run Equilibrium of the Industry

Profits, as shown in part (i) of Figure 12-1, provide an incentive for new firms to enter the industry. As

---

[1]This theory was first developed by the U.S. economist Edward Chamberlin in his pioneering book, *The Theory of Monopolistic Competition* (Cambridge, Mass.: Harvard University Press, 1933).

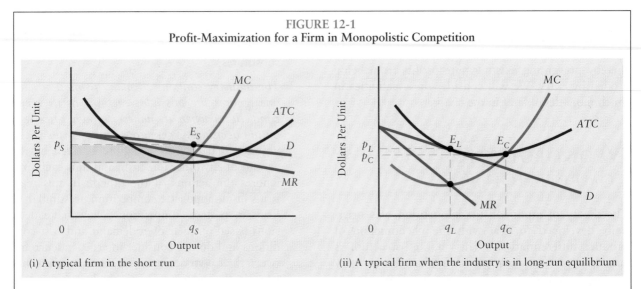

FIGURE 12-1
Profit-Maximization for a Firm in Monopolistic Competition

(i) A typical firm in the short run

(ii) A typical firm when the industry is in long-run equilibrium

The short-run position for a monopolistically competitive firm is similar to that of a monopolist. In the long run, firms in a monopolistically competitive industry have zero profits and excess capacity. Short-run profit-maximization occurs in part (i) at E_S, the output for which $MR = MC$. Price is p_S and quantity is q_S. Profits may exist; in this example they are shown by the shaded area. Starting from the short-run position shown in part (i), entry of new firms shifts the firm's demand curve to the left and eliminates profits. In part (ii), point E_L, where demand is tangent to ATC, is the position of each firm when the industry is in long-run equilibrium. Price is p_L and quantity is q_L. Price is greater and quantity is less than the perfectly competitive equilibrium price and quantity (p_C and q_C). When the industry is in long-run equilibrium, each monopolistically competitive firm has excess capacity of q_Lq_C.

they do so, the total demand for the industry's product must be shared among this larger number of firms, so each gets a smaller share of the total market. This shifts the demand curve for each existing firm's product to the left. Entry, and the consequent leftward shifting of the existing firms' demand curves, continues until profits are eliminated. When this has occurred, each firm is in the position shown in part (ii) of Figure 12-1. Its demand curve has shifted to the left until the curve is *tangent* to the average total cost curve. At this output, the firm is just covering all of its costs. At any other output, it would be suffering losses because average total costs would exceed average revenue.

To see why this "tangency solution" provides the only possible equilibrium for the industry, consider the two possible alternatives. First, suppose that the firm's demand curve *nowhere touched* the average total cost curve. There would then be no output at which costs could be covered, and exit would occur. The exit of firms from the industry would then lead each *remaining* firm's demand curve to shift to the right, until it eventually touched the average total cost curve. Second, suppose that the demand curve

cut the average total cost curve. There would then be a range of output over which profits could be earned. These profits would lead firms to enter the industry, and this would shift each *remaining* firm's demand curve to the left until it was just tangent to the average total cost curve.

The Excess-Capacity Theorem

Part (ii) of Figure 12-1 makes it clear that monopolistic competition results in a long-run equilibrium of zero profits, even though each individual firm faces a negatively sloped demand curve. It does this by forcing each firm into a position in which it has *excess capacity;* that is, each firm is producing an output less than that corresponding to the lowest point on its long-run average cost ($LRAC$) curve. If the firm were to increase its output, it would reduce its cost per unit, but it does not do so because selling more would reduce revenue by more than it would reduce cost. This result is often called the **excess-capacity theorem.**

In monopolistic competition, commodities are produced at a point where average total costs are falling, in contrast to perfect competition, where they are produced at their lowest possible cost.

EVALUATION OF THE THEORY

Alleged Inefficiency

The excess-capacity theorem once aroused passionate debate among economists because it seemed to show that all industries that sell differentiated products would produce them at a higher cost than was necessary. Because product differentiation is a characteristic of virtually all modern consumer goods industries, this suggested that modern market economies were systematically inefficient. A few decades ago, many critics of market economies called for government intervention to eliminate unnecessary product differentiation, thereby ensuring cost-minimizing levels of production in consumer goods industries.

Subsequent analysis by economists has shown that the charge of inefficiency has not been proved. The excess capacity of monopolistic competition does not necessarily indicate a waste of resources because when firms can choose the characteristics of their own products, minimizing the costs of producing a *given set of products* is not necessarily the best thing to do. Differentiated products provide consumers with a choice among a variety of products, and it is clear that consumers have different tastes and needs with respect to differentiated products.[2]

From society's point of view, there is a trade off between producing more brands to satisfy diverse tastes and producing fewer brands at a lower cost per unit.

Monopolistic competition produces a wider range of products but at a somewhat higher cost per unit than perfect competition. Consumers clearly value variety, so the benefits of variety must be

matched against the extra cost that variety imposes in order to find the *socially optimal* amount of product differentiation. Product differentiation is wasteful only if the costs of providing variety exceed the benefits conferred by providing that variety.

The socially optimal number of varieties of a differentiated product is attained when the gain to consumers from adding one more variety equals the loss from having to produce each existing variety at a higher cost because less of each is produced.

Depending on consumers' tastes and firms' costs, monopolistic competition may result in too much, too little, or the optimal amount of product variety.

Empirical Relevance

A long controversy raged over several decades as to the empirical relevance of monopolistic competition. Of course, product differentiation is an almost universal phenomenon in industries producing consumer goods and capital goods. Nonetheless, many economists maintained that the monopolistically competitive market structure was almost never found in practice.

To see why, we need to distinguish between products and firms. Single-product firms are extremely rare in manufacturing industries. Typically, a vast array of differentiated products is produced by each of the few firms in the industry. Most of the vast variety of breakfast cereals, for example, is produced by only three firms (Kellogg's, Nabisco, and General Foods). Similar circumstances exist in soap, chemicals, cigarettes, and numerous other industries where many competing products are produced by a few very large firms. These industries are clearly not perfectly competitive and neither are they monopolies. Are they monopolistically competitive? The answer is no because they contain few enough firms for each to take account of the others' reactions when determining its own behaviour. Furthermore, these firms often earn large profits without attracting new entry (thereby violating the third assumption of monopolistic competition). In fact, they operate under the market structure called *oligopoly,* which we consider in the next section.

Although monopolostic competition is not applicable to differentiated products produced in industries with high concentration, the theory remains useful for analyzing industries where concentration

---

[2]By saying that consumers clearly value variety we are not saying that *each* consumer necessarily values variety. You might like only one of the many brands of dish soap, for example, and thus you might be better off if only that one brand were produced and the price were lower. But other consumers would prefer one of the other brands. Thus it is the differences in tastes *across many consumers* that gives rise to the social value of variety, and the price of that greater variety is the higher price per unit.

ratios are low and products are differentiated, as in the cases of restaurants and gas stations.

The 1980s witnessed a great outburst of theorizing concerning all aspects of product differentiation. The newer theories are consistent with Edward Chamberlin's (1899–1967) famous propositions that it pays firms to differentiate their products, to advertise heavily, and to engage in many other forms of competitive behaviour. These are characteristics to be found in the world, but not in perfect competition. Most modern industries that sell differentiated products, however, contain only a few firms. This is the market structure of oligopoly, to which we turn now.

OLIGOPOLY

Table 12-2 indicates that 41 Canadian manufacturing industries have four-firm concentration ratios that exceed 50 percent—that is, in these industries the largest four firms account for over 50 percent of the industry's total output.

The market structure that embraces such industries is called *oligopoly,* from the Greek words *oligos polein,* meaning "few to sell." An **oligopoly** is an industry that contains two or more firms, at least one of which produces a significant portion of the industry's total output. Whenever there is a high concentration ratio for the firms that are serving one particular market, that market is oligopolistic.

CHARACTERISTICS OF OLIGOPOLY

The market structures of oligopoly, monopoly, and monopolistic competition are similar in that firms in all of these markets face negatively sloped demand curves.

In contrast to a monopoly (which has no competitors) and to a monopolistically competitive firm (which has many competitors), an oligopolistic firm faces only a few competitors. The number of competitors is small enough for each firm to realize that its competitors may respond to anything that it does and that it should take such possible responses into account. In other words, *oligopolists are aware of the interdependence among the decisions made by the various firms in the industry.*

This is the key difference between oligopolists on the one hand and perfect or monopolistic competitors and monopolies, on the other. Oligopolists are

aware of their impact on competing firms, and they may take their competitors' expected reactions into account when deciding on any course of action. We say that they exhibit **strategic behaviour,** which means that they take explicit account of the impact of their decisions on competing firms and of the reactions they expect competing firms to make. In contrast, firms in perfect competition or monopolistic competition engage in **nonstrategic behaviour,** which means they make decisions based on their own costs and their own demand curves without considering any possible reactions from their large number of competitors. Monopolists also do not engage in strategic behaviour—simply because they have no competitors to worry about.

Oligopolistic industries are of many types. In some industries, there are only a few firms. In others, there are many firms, but only a few dominate the market. For example, there are 38 manufacturers of mixed fertilizers, of which the largest 4 account for 70 percent of total sales. Oligopoly is consistent with a large number of small sellers, called a "competitive fringe," as long as a "big few" dominate the industry's production.

In oligopolistic industries, prices are typically administered. Products are usually differentiated. The intensity and the nature of rivalrous behaviour vary greatly from industry to industry and from one period of time to another. This variety has invited extensive theorizing and empirical study.

WHY BIGNESS?

Several factors contribute to explaining why so many industries are dominated by a few large firms. Some are "natural," and some are created by the firms themselves.

Natural Causes of Bigness

Economies of Scale. Much factory production uses the principle of the division of labour that we first studied in Chapter 3. The production of a commodity is broken up into hundreds of simple, repetitive tasks. This type of division of labour is the basis of the assembly line, which revolutionized the production of many goods in the early twentieth century, and it still underlies economies of large-scale production in many industries. Such division of labour is, as Adam Smith observed long ago, dependent on the size of the market (see Extension 3-2 in

Chapter 3). If only a few units of a product can be sold each day, there is no point in dividing its production into a number of tasks, each of which can be done in a few minutes. So big firms with large sales have an advantage over small firms with small sales whenever there are opportunities for economies based on an extensive division of labour.

Economies of Scope. Modern industries produce many differentiated products that give rise to a different type of large-scale advantage. It is costly to develop a new product, and it may be only a matter of a few years before it is replaced by some superior version of the same basic product. These *fixed costs* of product development must be recovered in the revenues from sales of the product. The larger the firm's sales, the less the fixed cost that has to be recovered from each unit sold. Consider a product that costs $1 million to develop and to market. If 1 million units are to be sold, $1 of the selling price of each unit must go toward recovering the development costs. If, however, the firm expects to sell 10 million units, each unit need contribute only 10 cents to these costs, and the market price can be lowered accordingly. With the enormous development costs of some of today's high-tech products, firms that can sell a large volume have a distinct pricing advantage over firms that sell a smaller volume.

Other economies of scope are related to financing and to marketing. It is costly to enter a market, to establish a sales force, and to make consumers aware of a product. These costs are often nearly as high when a small volume is being marketed as when a large volume is being marketed. Thus the smaller the volume of the firm's sales, the higher the price must be if the firm is to cover all of these costs. Notice that these economies, which are related to the size of the firm, are related neither to the amount the firm produces of any one of its differentiated products nor to the size of any one of its plants. Economies that depend on the overall size of the *firm* rather than on the size of its *plants* or the volume of production of any one commodity are called **economies of scope.**

Where size confers a cost advantage through economies of either scale or scope, there may be room for only a few firms, even when the total market is quite large. This cost advantage of size will dictate that the industry be an oligopoly unless government regulation prevents the firms from growing to their efficient size.

Firm-Created Causes of Bigness

The number of firms in an industry may be decreased while the average size of the survivors rises due to strategic behaviour of the firms themselves. Firms may grow by buying out rivals (acquisitions) or merging with them (mergers) or by driving rivals into bankruptcy through predatory practices. This process increases the size and market shares of the survivors and may, by reducing competitive behaviour, allow them to achieve larger profit margins.

The surviving firms must then be able to create and sustain barriers to entry where natural ones do not exist. The industry will then be dominated by a few large firms only because they are successful in preventing the entry of new firms that would lower the industry's concentration ratio.

Is Bigness Natural or Firm-Created?

Most observers would agree that bigness results from a mix of both natural and firm-created causes. Some industries have high concentration ratios because the efficient size of the firm is large relative to the overall size of the industry's market. Other industries may have higher concentration ratios than efficiency considerations would dictate because the firms are seeking enhanced market power through entry restriction. The issue that is debated is the relative importance of these two forces, the one coming from efficiencies of scale and scope and the other coming from the desire of firms to create market power by growing large.

Harvard economist Alfred D. Chandler Jr. is a champion of the view that the major reason for the persistence of oligopolies in the manufacturing sector is the efficiency of large-scale production. His monumental work, *Scale and Scope: The Dynamics of Industrial Capitalism,* argues this case in great detail for the United States, the United Kingdom, and Germany.[3]

The set of laws in the United States designed to promote competition among firms—known as antitrust laws—is based on the presumption that large firms are undesirable and are not justified by the benefits of scale and scope economies. If Chandler is right, however, size efficiency is the most important reason for high concentration ratios, and although strategic reasons are probably important in some cases, they are of secondary importance as an overall explanation. Canadian competition policy is more in

---

[3]A. D. Chandler Jr., *Scale and Scope: The Dynamics of Industrial Capitalism* (Cambridge, Mass.: Harvard University Press, 1990).

line with Chandler's views, since the policy condemns neither size nor high market shares per se. We examine Canadian competition policy in the next chapter.

STRATEGIC BEHAVIOUR AND THE BASIC DILEMMA OF OLIGOPOLY

Oligopoly behaviour is necessarily strategic behaviour. Oligopolists must take into account the ways in which their rivals will react to what they do. In deciding on strategies, oligopolists face a basic dilemma between *competing* and *cooperating*.

The firms in an oligopolistic industry will make more profits as a group if they cooperate; any one firm, however, may make more profits for itself if it defects while the others cooperate.

This result is similar to the one established in Chapter 11 for the cartelization of a perfectly competitive industry.[4] In a perfectly competitive industry, however, there are so many firms that they cannot reach a cooperative outcome unless some central governing body is formed, by either themselves or the government, to force the necessary behaviour on all firms. In contrast, the few firms in an oligopolistic industry will themselves recognize the possibility of cooperating to avoid the loss of profits that will result from competitive behaviour.

Cooperative and Noncooperative Outcomes

If the firms in an oligopolistic industry cooperate, either overtly or tacitly, to produce among themselves the monopoly output, they can maximize their joint profits. If they do this, they will reach what is called a **cooperative outcome,** which is the position that a single monopoly firm would reach if it owned all the firms in the industry.

We have seen that if all the firms in an oligopolistic industry are at the cooperative outcome, it will usually be worthwhile for any one of them to cut its price or to raise its output, as long as the others do not do so. However, if everyone does the same thing, they will be worse off as a group and may all be worse off individually. An industry outcome that is reached when firms proceed by calculating only their

own gains, without considering the reactions of others, is called a **noncooperative outcome.**

An Example from Game Theory

Game theory is used to study decision making in situations in which a number of players compete, each knowing that others will react to their moves and each taking account of others' expected reactions when making moves. For example, suppose that a firm is deciding whether to raise, lower, or maintain its price. Before arriving at an answer, it asks: "What will the other firms do in each of these cases, and how will their actions affect the profitability of whatever decision I make?" Game theory has become increasingly important in economics and is a very active area of economic research. The 1994 Nobel Prize in Economics went to three important contributors to game theory: John Harsanyi, John Nash, and Reinhard Selten.

When game theory is applied to oligopoly, the players are firms, their game is played in the market, their strategies are their price or output decisions, and the payoffs are their profits.

An illustration of the basic dilemma of oligopolists, to cooperate or to compete, is shown in Figure 12-2 for the case of a two-firm oligopoly, called a **duopoly.** In this simplified game there are only two strategies for each firm: to produce an output equal to either one-half of the monopoly output or two-thirds of the monopoly output. Even this simple game, however, is sufficient to illustrate several key ideas in the modern theory of oligopoly.

Figure 12-2 presents what is called a *payoff matrix*. The data in the matrix show that if both firms cooperate, *each* producing one-half of the monopoly output, they achieve the cooperative outcome and jointly earn the monopoly profits by *jointly* producing the output that a monopolist would produce. As a group, they can do no better.

Once the cooperative outcome is attained, the data in the figure show that if A cheats and produces more, its profits will increase. However, B's profits will be reduced: A's behaviour drives the industry's price down, so B earns less from its unchanged output. Because A's cheating takes the firms away from the joint-profit-maximizing monopoly output, their joint profits must fall. This means that B's profits fall by more than A's rise.

Figure 12-2 shows that similar considerations also apply to B. It is worthwhile for B to depart from the joint-profit-maximizing output, as long as A does

---

[4]The basic reason is that when only one firm increases its output by 1 percent, the price falls by less than when all firms do the same. Thus when the point is reached at which profits will be reduced if all firms expand output together, it will still pay one firm to expand output if the others do not do the same.

FIGURE 12-2
The Oligopolist's Dilemma: To Cooperate or to Compete?

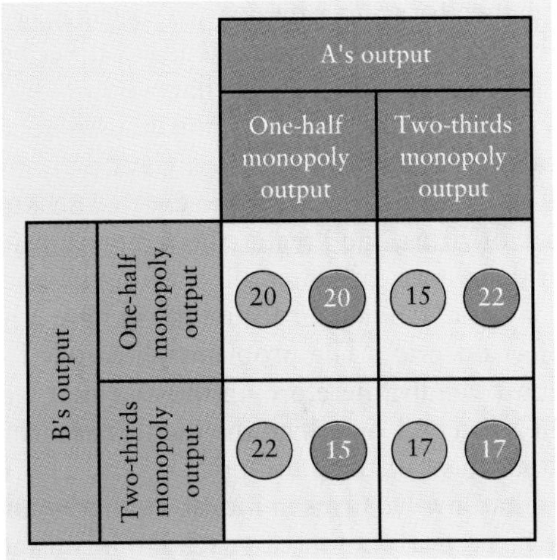

		A's output	
		One-half monopoly output	Two-thirds monopoly output
B's output	One-half monopoly output	20 20	15 22
	Two-thirds monopoly output	22 15	17 17

Cooperation to determine the overall level of output can maximize joint profits, but it leaves each firm with an incentive to alter its production. The figure gives what is called a payoff matrix for a two-firm duopoly game. Only two levels of production are considered in order to illustrate the basic problem. A's production is indicated across the top, and its payoffs (profits in millions of dollars) are shown in the blue circles within each square. B's production is indicated down the left side, and its payoffs are shown in the red circles within each square. For example, the top right square tells us that if B produces one-half while A produces two-thirds of the output that a monopolist would produce, A's profits will be 22, while B's will be 15.

If A and B cooperate, each produces one-half the monopoly output and receives a payoff of 20, as shown in the upper left box. However, at that position, known as the cooperative outcome, each firm can raise its profits by producing two-thirds of the monopoly output, provided that the other firm does not do the same.

Now assume that A and B make their decisions noncooperatively. A reasons that whether B produces either one-half or two-thirds of the monopoly output, A's best output is two-thirds. B reasons similarly. In this case, they reach the noncooperative outcome, where each produces two-thirds of the monopoly output, and each makes less than it would if the two firms cooperated. In this example, the noncooperative outcome is a Nash equilibrium.

has an incentive to do so as well. When each follows this "selfish" strategy, both reach the noncooperative outcome at which they jointly produce $1\frac{1}{3}$ times as much as the monopolist would. Each then has profits that are lower than at the cooperative outcome.

Nash Equilibrium. The noncooperative outcome shown in Figure 12-2 is called a **Nash equilibrium**, after the U.S. mathematician John Nash, who developed the concept in the 1950s and received the Nobel Prize in Economics in 1994 for this work. In a Nash equilibrium, each firm's best strategy is to maintain its present behaviour *given the present behaviour of the other firms.*

It is easy to see that there is only one Nash equilibrium in Figure 12-2. In the bottom-right cell, the best decision for each firm, given that the other firm is producing two-thirds of the monopoly output, is to produce two-thirds of the monopoly output itself. Between them, they produce a joint output of $1\frac{1}{3}$ times the monopoly output. Neither firm has an incentive to depart from this position except through cooperation with the other. In any other cell, each firm has an incentive to alter its output *given the output of the other firm.*

The basis of a Nash equilibrium is rational decision-making in the absence of cooperation. Its particular importance in oligopoly theory is that it is the only type of self-policing equilibrium. It is self-policing in the sense that there is no need for group behaviour to enforce it. Each firm has a self-interest to maintain it because no move will improve its profits, given what other firms are currently doing.

If a Nash equilibrium is established by any means whatsoever, no firm has an incentive to depart from it by altering its own behaviour.

Strategic Behaviour. We have seen how the Nash equilibrium in Figure 12-2 can be arrived at when both firms cheat on an agreement to reach the cooperative outcome. The same equilibrium will be attained if each firm behaves strategically by choosing its optimal strategy taking into account what the other firm may do. Let us see how this works.

Suppose that Firm A reasons as follows: "B can do one of two things; what is the best thing for me to do in each case? First, what if B produces one-half of the monopoly output? If I do the same, I receive a profit of 20, but if I produce two-thirds of the monopoly output, I receive 22. Second, what if B produces two-thirds of the monopoly output? If I produce one-half of the monopoly output, I receive a

not do so. So both A and B have an incentive to depart from the joint-profit-maximizing level of output.

Finally, Figure 12-2 shows that when either firm does depart from the cooperative outcome, the other profit of 15, whereas if I produce two-thirds, I receive 17. Clearly, my best strategy is to produce two-thirds of the monopoly output in either case."

B will reason in the same way. As a result, they end up producing 1 ⅓ times the monopoly output between themselves, and each earns a profit of 17. This type of game, in which the noncooperative equilibrium makes *both players worse off* than if they were able to cooperate, is called a *prisoner's dilemma*. The reason for this curious name, and some further applications, are discussed in Extension 12-1.

COOPERATION OR COMPETITION?

We have seen that although oligopolists have an incentive to cooperate, they may be driven, through their own individual decisions, to produce more and earn less than they would if they cooperated. Our next step is to look in more detail at the types of cooperative and competitive behaviour that oligopolists may adopt. We can then go on to study the forces that influence the balance between cooperation and competition in actual situations.

Types of Cooperative Behaviour

When firms agree to cooperate in order to restrict output and raise prices, their behaviour is called **collusion.** Collusive behaviour may occur with or without an explicit agreement to collude. Where explicit agreement occurs, economists speak of *overt or covert collusion,* depending on whether the agreement is open or secret. Where no explicit agreement actually occurs, economists speak of *tacit collusion.* In this case, all firms behave cooperatively without an explicit agreement to do so. They merely understand that it is in their mutual interest to restrict output and to raise prices.

In terms of Figure 12-2, Firm A decides to produce one-half of the monopoly output, hoping that Firm B will do the same. Firm B does what A expects, and they achieve the cooperative outcome without ever explicitly cooperating.

Explicit Collusion.   The easiest way for firms to ensure that they will all maintain their joint-profit-maximizing output is to make an explicit agreement to do so. Such collusive agreements have occurred in the past, although they have been illegal among privately owned firms in Canada for a long time. When they are discovered today, they are rigorously prose-

cuted. We shall see, however, that such agreements are not illegal everywhere in the world, particularly when they are supported by national governments.

We saw in Chapter 11 that when a group of firms get together to act in this way, it is called a *cartel.* Cartels show in stark form the basic conflict between cooperation and competition that we just discussed. Full cooperation always allows the industry to achieve the result of monopoly. It also always presents individual firms with the incentive to cheat. The larger the number of firms, the greater the temptation for any one of them to cheat. After all, cheating by one small firm may not be noticed because it will have a negligible effect on price. The problems all cartels face are seen most vividly, therefore, in the case that we studied in Chapter 11, in which the number of firms is so large that most of them are price takers. This is why cartels that involve firms in industries that would otherwise be perfectly competitive tend to be unstable.

Cartels may also be formed by a group of firms that would otherwise be in an oligopolistic market. The smaller the group of firms that forms a cartel, the more likely that the firms will let their joint interest in cooperating guide their behaviour. Although cheating may still occur, the few firms in the industry can easily foresee the outcome of an outbreak of rivalrous behaviour among themselves.

The most famous modern example of a cartel that encourages explicit cooperative behaviour among oligopolists is the Organization of Petroleum Exporting Countries (OPEC). This cartel is discussed in more detail in Application 12-2.

Tacit Collusion.   Although collusive behaviour that affects prices is illegal, a small group of firms that recognize the influence that each has on the others may act without any explicit agreement to achieve the cooperative outcome. In such tacit agreements, the two forces that push toward cooperation and competition are still evident.

First, firms have a common interest in cooperating to maximize their joint profits at the cooperative solution. Second, each firm is interested in its own profits, and any one of them can usually increase its profits by behaving competitively.

Types of Competitive Behaviour

Although the most obvious way for a firm to violate the cooperative solution is to produce more than its share of the joint-profit-maximizing output, there are other ways in which rivalrous behaviour can occur.

EXTENSION 12-1

THE PRISONER'S DILEMMA

The game shown in Figure 12-2 is often known as a prisoner's dilemma game. This is the story that lies behind the name:

> Two men, John and William, are arrested for jointly committing a crime and are interrogated separately. They know that if they both plead innocence, they will get only a light sentence, and if they both admit guilt they will both receive a medium sentence. Each is told, however, that if *either* protests innocence while the *other* admits guilt, the one who claims innocence will get a severe sentence while the other will be released with no sentence at all.

Here is the payoff matrix for that game:

		John's Plea	
		Innocent	Guilty
William's Plea	**Innocent**	J light sentence / W light sentence	J no sentence / W severe sentence
	Guilty	J severe sentence / W no sentence	J medium sentence / W medium sentence

John reasons as follows: William will plead either guilty or innocent. First assume that he pleads innocent. I get a light sentence if I also plead innocent but no sentence at all if I plead guilty, so guilty is my better plea. Now assume that he pleads guilty. I get a severe sentence if I plead innocent and a medium sentence if I plead guilty. So once again guilty is my preferred plea. William reasons in the same way and, as a result, they both plead guilty and

get a medium sentence, whereas if they had been able to communicate and coordinate their pleas, they could both have agreed to plead innocent and get off with a light sentence.

Another example of a prisoner's dilemma can arise when two firms are making sealed bids on a contract. For simplicity, suppose that only two bids are permitted, either a high or a low price. The high price yields a profit of $10 million, whereas the low price yields a profit of $7 million. If they put in the same price, they share the job, and each earns half the profits. If they give different bids, the firm submitting the lower bid gets the job and all the profits. You should have no trouble in drawing up the payoff matrix and determining the outcomes under noncooperative and cooperative behaviour.

The prisoner's dilemma has been used to consider aspects of social behaviour that seem far removed from economics. For example, Professor Robert Axelrod of the University of Michigan has used the model to study the *evolution of cooperation*. In particular, he showed that in a *repeated* prisoner's dilemma, where the same players played the game many times, the best strategy was one that would support both players' cooperating rather than defecting. It turns out that the very simple rule of "tit for tat" works well: Cooperate if the other player cooperated on the most recent move, and defect (don't cooperate) if the player defected on the most recent move. In an environment with many players, those who use the tit-for-tat strategy will generally reap benefits of cooperation, while still effectively preventing themselves from being exploited by players who routinely do not. Thus players of the tit-for-tat strategy can come to dominate a population. This idea has been extended to a wide variety of human behaviours and of the behaviour of other organisms.*

---

*See Robert Axelrod, *The Evolution of Cooperation* (New York: Basic Books, 1984), and Robert Axelrod and Douglas Dion, "The Further Evolution of Cooperation", *Science* 242 (1988): p.1385–1389.

APPLICATION 12-2

EXPLICIT COOPERATION IN OPEC

The experience of the Organization of Petroleum Exporting Countries (OPEC) in the 1970s and 1980s illustrates the power of cooperative behaviour to create short-run profits, as well as the problems of trying to exercise long-run market power in an industry without substantial entry barriers.

OPEC did not attract worldwide attention until 1973, when its members voluntarily restricted their output by negotiating quotas among themselves. In that year, OPEC countries accounted for about 70 percent of the world's supply of crude oil and 87 percent of the world's oil exports. So although it was not a complete monopoly, the cartel came close to being one. By reducing output, the OPEC countries were able to drive up the world price of oil and to earn massive profits both for themselves and for non-OPEC producers, who obtained the high prices without having to limit their output. After several years of success, however, OPEC began to experience the typical problems of cartels.

ENTRY

Entry became a problem for the OPEC countries. The high price of oil encouraged the development of new supplies, and within a few years, new productive capacity was coming into use at a rapid rate in non-OPEC countries.

LONG-RUN ADJUSTMENT OF DEMAND

The short-run demand for oil proved to be highly inelastic. Over time, however, adaptations to reduce the demand for oil were made within the confines of existing technology. Homes and offices were insulated more efficiently, and smaller, more fuel-efficient cars became popular. This is an example of the distinction between the short-run and long-run demand for a commodity first introduced in Chapter 5.

INNOVATION IN THE VERY-LONG RUN

Innovation further reduced the demand for oil in the very-long run. Over time, technologies that were more efficient in their use of oil, as well as alternative energy sources, were developed. Had the oil prices stayed up longer than they did, major breakthroughs in solar and geothermal energy would surely have occurred.

This experience in both the long run and the very-long run shows the price system at work, signal-

---

Competition for Market Shares.   Even if *joint* profits are maximized, there is the problem of market shares. How is the profit-maximizing level of sales to be divided among the colluding firms? Competition for market shares may upset the tacit agreement to hold to joint-profit-maximizing behaviour. Firms often compete for market shares through various forms of non-price competition, such as advertising and variations in the quality of their product. Such costly competition may reduce industry profits.

Covert Cheating.   In an industry that has many differentiated products and in which sales are often by contract between buyers and sellers, covert rather than overt cheating may seem attractive. Secret discounts and rebates can allow a firm to increase its

sales at the expense of its competitors while appearing to hold to the tacitly agreed monopoly price.

Very-Long-Run Competition.   As we first discussed in Chapter 11, very-long-run considerations may also be important. When technology and product characteristics change constantly, there may be advantages to behaving competitively. A firm that behaves competitively may be able to maintain a larger market share and earn larger profits than it would if it cooperated with the other firms in the industry, even though all the firms' joint profits are lower. In our world of constant change, a firm that thinks it can *keep* ahead of its rivals through innovation has an incentive to compete even if that competition lowers the joint profing the need for adaptation and providing the incentives for that adaptation. It also provides an illustration of Schumpeter's concept of creative destruction, which we first discussed in Chapter 11. To share in the profits generated by high energy prices, new technologies and new substitute products were developed, and these destroyed much of the market power of the original cartel.

CHEATING

At first, there was little incentive for OPEC countries to violate quotas. Members found themselves with such undreamed-of increases in their incomes that they found it difficult to use all of their money productively. As the output of non-OPEC oil grew, however, OPEC's output had to be reduced to hold prices high. Incomes in OPEC countries declined sharply as a result.

Many OPEC countries had become used to their enormous incomes, and their attempts to maintain them in the face of falling output quotas brought to the surface the instabilities inherent in all cartels. In 1981, the cartel price reached its peak of U.S. $35 per barrel. In real terms, this was about five times as high as the 1972 price, but production quotas were

less than one-half of OPEC's capacity. Eager to increase their oil revenues, many individual OPEC members gave in to the pressure to cheat and produced in excess of their production quotas. In 1984, Saudi Arabia indicated that it would not tolerate further cheating by its partners and demanded that others share equally in reducing their quotas yet further. However, agreement proved impossible. In December 1985, OPEC decided to eliminate production quotas and let each member make its own decisions about output.

AFTER THE COLLAPSE

OPEC's collapse as an output-restricting cartel led to a major reduction in world oil prices. Early in 1986, the downward slide took the price to $20 per barrel, and it fell to $11 per barrel later in the year. Allowing for inflation, this was around the price that had prevailed just before OPEC introduced its output restrictions in 1973. Prices have been volatile since then, oscillating between about $12 per barrel, which is close to the perfectly competitive price, and $20 per barrel, which seems to be all that can be sustained under the modest output restrictions that can currently be obtained.

its of the whole industry. Such competitive behaviour contributes to the long-run growth of living standards and may provide social benefits over time that outweigh any losses due to the restriction of output at any point in time.

For these and other reasons, there are often strong incentives for oligopolistic firms to compete rather than to maintain the cooperative outcome, even when they understand the inherent risks to their joint profits.

Cooperative or Noncooperative Outcomes?

Empirical research by economists suggests that the relative strengths of the incentives to cooperate and

to compete vary from industry to industry in a systematic way, depending on observable characteristics of firms, markets, and products. What are some of the characteristics that will affect the strength of the two incentives?

The tendency toward joint maximization of profits is greater for smaller numbers of sellers than for larger numbers of sellers. This involves both motivation and ability. When there are few firms, they will know that one of them cannot gain sales without inducing retaliation by its rivals. Also, a few firms can tacitly coordinate their policies with less difficulty than a large number of firms.

The tendency toward joint maximization of profits is greater for producers of similar products than for producers of sharply differentiated products. The more nearly identical the products of sellers, the closer the direct rivalry for customers and the less able one firm is to gain a lasting advantage over its rivals. Such sellers will tend to prefer joint efforts to achieve a larger pie over individual attempts to increase their own shares.

The tendency toward joint maximization of profits is greater in a growing market than in a contracting market. When demand is growing, firms can produce at full capacity without any need to "steal" customers from their rivals. When firms have excess capacity, they are tempted to give price concessions to attract customers. When their rivals retaliate, price cuts become general.

The tendency toward joint maximization of profits is greater when the industry contains a dominant firm rather than a group of more-or-less equal competitors. A dominant firm may become a **price leader,** setting the industry's price while all other firms fall into line. Even if a dominant firm is not automatically a price leader, other firms may look to it for judgment about market conditions, and its decisions may become a tentative focus for tacit agreement.

The tendency toward joint maximization of profits is greater when non-price rivalry is absent or limited. When firms are not competing with each other through price, rivalry will tend to break out in other forms. Firms may seek to increase their market shares through extra advertising, changes in the quality of the product, the establishment of new products, giveaways, and a host of similar schemes that leave their prices unchanged but increase their costs and so reduce their joint profits.

The tendency toward joint maximization of profits is greater when the barriers to entry of new firms are greater. The high profits of existing firms attract new entrants, who will drive down price and reduce profits. The greater the barriers to entry, the less this will occur. Thus the greater the entry barriers, the closer the profits of existing firms can be to their joint maximizing level without being reduced by new entrants.

THE IMPORTANCE OF ENTRY BARRIERS

Suppose that firms in an oligopolistic industry succeed in raising prices above long-run average costs and earn substantial profits that are not completely eliminated by nonprice competition. In the absence of significant entry barriers, new firms will enter the industry and erode the profits of existing firms, as they do in monopolistic competition. Natural barriers to entry were discussed in Chapter 11. They are an important part of the explanation of the persistence of profits in many oligopolistic industries.

Where such natural entry barriers do not exist, however, oligopolistic firms can earn profits in the long run only if they can *create* entry barriers. To the extent this is done, existing firms can move toward joint profit maximization without fear that new firms, attracted by the high profits, will enter the industry. We discuss next some types of created entry barriers.

Brand Proliferation

By altering the characteristics of a differentiated product, it is possible to produce a vast array of variations on the general theme of that product. Think, for example, of automobiles with a little more or a little less acceleration, braking power, top speed, cornering ability, fuel efficiency, and so on, compared with existing models.

Although the multiplicity of existing brands is no doubt partly a response to consumers' tastes, it can have the effect of discouraging the entry of new firms. To see why, suppose that the product is the type for which there is a substantial amount of brand switching by consumers. In this case, the larger the number of brands sold by existing firms, the smaller the expected sales of a new entrant.

Suppose, for example, that an industry contains three large firms, each selling one brand of cigarettes, and say that 30 percent of all smokers change brands in a random fashion each year. If a new firm enters the industry, it can expect to pick up one-third of the smokers who change brands (a smoker who switches brands now has three *other* brands to choose between). This would give the new firm 10 percent (one-third of 30 percent) of the total market the first year merely as a result of picking up its share of the random switchers, and it would keep increasing its share for some time thereafter. If, however, the existing three firms have five brands each, there would be 15 brands already available, and a new firm selling one new brand could expect to pick up only one-fifteenth of the brand switchers, giving it only 2 percent of the total market the first year, with smaller gains also in subsequent years. This is an extreme case, but it illustrates a general result.

The larger the number of differentiated products that are sold by existing oligopolists, the smaller the market share available to a new firm that is entering with a single new product. Brand proliferation can therefore be an effective entry barrier.

Setup Costs

Existing firms can create entry barriers by imposing significant fixed costs on new firms that enter their market. This is particularly important if the industry has only weak natural barriers to entry because the minimum efficient scale occurs at an output that is low relative to the total output of the industry.

Advertising is one means by which existing firms can impose heavy setup costs on new entrants. Advertising, of course, serves purposes other than that of creating barriers to entry. Among them, it performs the useful function of informing buyers about their alternatives, thereby making markets work more smoothly. Indeed, a new firm may find that advertising is essential, even when existing firms do not advertise at all, simply to call attention to its entry into an industry in which it is currently unknown.

Nonetheless, advertising can also operate as a potent entry barrier by increasing the setup costs of new entrants. Where heavy advertising has established strong brand images for existing products, a new firm may have to spend heavily on advertising to create its own brand images in consumers' minds. If the firm's sales are small, advertising costs *per unit sold* will be large, and price will have to be correspondingly high to cover those costs. Consider Nike, Reebok, and their competitors. They advertise not so much the quality of their athletic shoes as images that they wish consumers to associate with the shoes. The ads are lavishly produced and photographed. They constitute a formidable entry barrier for a new producer.

Figure 12-3 illustrates how heavy advertising can shift the cost curves of a firm with a low minimum efficient scale *(MES)* to make it one with a high *MES*. In essence, what happens is that a high *MES* of advertising is added to a low *MES* of production, with the result that the overall *MES* is raised.

A new entrant with small sales but large setup costs finds itself at a substantial cost disadvantage relative to its established rivals.

Any one-time cost of entering a market has the same effect as a large initial advertising expenditure.

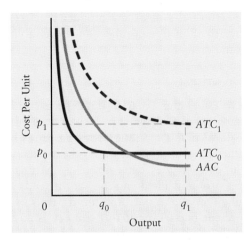

FIGURE 12-3
Advertising Cost as a Barrier to Entry

Large advertising costs can increase the minimum efficient scale *(MES)* of production and thereby increase entry barriers. The ATC_0 curve shows that the *MES* without advertising is at q_0. The curve *AAC* (for average advertising cost) shows that advertising cost per unit falls as output rises. Advertising increases average total cost to ATC_1, which is downward sloping over its entire range. The new *MES* is given by q_1. Advertising has given a scale advantage to large sellers and has thus created a barrier to entry.

For example, with many consumer goods, the cost of developing a new product that is similar but not identical to existing products may be quite substantial. Even if there are few economies of scale in the production of the product, its large fixed *development* cost can lead to a falling long-run average cost curve over a wide range of output.

An Example

The combined use of brand proliferation and advertising as an entry barrier helps to explain one apparent paradox of everyday life—that one firm often sells multiple brands of the same product, which compete actively against one another as well as against the products of other firms.

The soap and beer industries provide classic examples of this behaviour. Because all available scale economies can be realized by quite small plants, both industries have few natural barriers to entry. Both contain a few large firms, each of which produces an array of heavily advertised products. The numerous existing products make it harder for a new entrant to obtain a large market niche with a single new product. The heavy advertising, although directed against existing products, creates an entry barrier by increasing the setup costs of a new product that seeks to gain the attention of consumers and to establish its own brand image.

Predatory Pricing

A firm will not enter a market if it expects continued losses after entry. One way in which an existing firm can create such an expectation is to cut prices below costs whenever entry occurs and to keep them there until the entrant goes bankrupt. The existing firm sacrifices profits while doing this, but it sends a discouraging message to potential future rivals, as well as to present ones. Even if this strategy is costly in terms of lost profits in the short run, it may pay for itself in the long run by creating *reputation effects* that deter the entry of new firms at other times or in other markets that the firm controls.

Predatory pricing is controversial. Some economists argue that pricing policies that appear to be predatory can be explained by other motives and that existing firms only hurt themselves when they engage in such practices instead of accommodating new entrants. Others argue that predatory pricing has been observed and that it is in the long-run interests of existing firms to punish the occasional new entrant even when it is costly to do so in the short run.

The courts have taken the position that predatory pricing does indeed occur and a number of firms have been convicted of using it as a method of restricting entry. Canadian competition policy is discussed in Chapter 13.

CONTESTABLE MARKETS

We have been discussing the role played by entry barriers in determining the long-run characteristics of an oligopolistic industry. In general, we expect profits made by existing firms to lead new firms to enter the industry. Such entry will, in turn, reduce profits toward their competitive level. We now turn to a theory which emphasizes not the role of *actual entry*, but rather the role of *potential entry* in keeping industry profits near their competitive level.

The theory of *contestable markets* holds that markets do not have to contain many firms or expe-

rience *actual* entry for profits to be held near the competitive level. *Potential* entry can do the job just as well as actual entry, as long as (1) entry can be easily accomplished and (2) existing firms take potential entry into account when making price and output decisions.

The Theory of Contestable Markets

Entry is usually costly to the entering firm. It may have to build a plant, develop new versions of the industry's differentiated product, or advertise heavily to call attention to its product. These and many other initial expenses are often called *sunk costs of entry*. A sunk cost of entry is a cost that a firm must incur to enter the market and that *cannot be recovered if the firm subsequently exits*. For example, if an entering firm builds a product-specific factory that has no resale value, this is a sunk cost of entry. However, the cost of a factory that is not product-specific and can be resold for an amount that is close to its original cost is not a sunk cost of entry.

A market in which new firms can enter and leave without incurring any sunk costs of entry is called a perfectly **contestable market.** A market can be perfectly contestable even if the firm must pay some costs of entry, as long as these can be recovered when the firm exits. Because all markets require at least some sunk costs of entry, contestability must be viewed as a variable. The lower the sunk costs of entry, the more contestable the market.

In a contestable market, the existence of profits, even if they are due to transitory causes, will attract entry. Firms will enter to gain a share of these profits and will exit when the transitory situation has changed.

As an example, consider the market for air travel in the lucrative Toronto-Ottawa-Montreal triangle. This market would be quite contestable *if* counter and loading space were available to new entrants at the three cities' airline terminals. An airline that was not currently serving the cities in question could shift some of its existing planes to the market with small sunk costs of entry. Some training of personnel would be needed for them to become familiar with the route and the airport. This is a sunk cost of entry that could not be recovered if the cities in question were no longer to be served. However, most of the airline's costs are not sunk costs of entry. If it were to subsequently decide to leave a city, the rental of terminal space would stop and the airplanes and the ground equipment could be shifted to another location.

Sunk costs of entry constitute a barrier to entry, and the larger these are, the larger the profits of existing firms can be without attracting new entrants. The flip side of this coin is that firms operating in markets without large sunk costs of entry will not earn large profits. Strategic considerations will lead them to keep prices near the level that would just cover their total costs. They know that if they charge higher prices, firms will enter to capture the profits while they last and then exit.

Contestability, where it is possible, is a force that can limit the profits of existing oligopolists. Even if entry does not occur, the ease with which it can be accomplished may keep existing oligopolists from charging prices that would maximize their joint profits.

Contestability is just another example, in somewhat more refined form, of the key point that the possibility of entry is the major force preventing the exploitation of market power to restrict output and to raise prices.

Empirical Relevance

Most economists take the view that although the theory of contestable markets is an elegant extension of the theory of competitive markets, there are at least *some* barriers to entry in almost all real markets and very large barriers in many markets. Setting up an effective organization to produce or sell almost anything incurs sunk costs. In the case of airlines, for instance, the new company at a given airport must hire and train staff, advertise extensively to let customers know that it is in the market, set up baggage-handling facilities, and overcome whatever loyalties customers have to the preexisting firms. New firms in almost all industries face entry costs that are analogous to these. Entering a manufacturing industry usually requires a large investment in industry-specific (and sometimes product-specific) plants and equipment, in addition to considerable expenditures in product-development and marketing.

These considerations suggest that contestability, in practice, is something to be measured rather than simply asserted. The higher the sunk costs of entry, the less contestable the market, and the higher the profits that existing firms can earn without inducing entry. Current evidence suggests that a high degree of contestability is in practice quite rare.

OLIGOPOLY: AN OVERVIEW

Oligopoly is found in many industries and in all advanced economies. It typically occurs in industries where both perfect and monopolistic competition are made impossible by the existence of major economies of scale or scope (or both). In such industries, there is simply not enough room for a large number of firms all operating at or near their minimum efficient scales.

Three questions are important for the evaluation of the performance of the oligopolistic market structure. First, do oligopolistic markets allocate resources very differently than perfectly competitive markets? Second, in their short-run and long-run price-output behaviour, where do oligopolistic firms typically settle between the extreme outcomes of earning zero profits and earning the profits that would be available to a monopolist? Third, how much do oligopolists contribute to economic growth by encouraging innovative activity in the very-long run? We consider each of these questions in turn.

The Market Mechanism Under Oligopoly

We have seen that under perfect competition, prices are set by the impersonal forces of demand and supply, whereas firms in oligopolistic markets administer their prices. The market signaling system works slightly differently when prices are administered rather than being determined by the market. Changes in the market conditions for both inputs and outputs are signaled to the perfectly competitive firm by changes in the prices of its inputs and its outputs. Changes in the market conditions for inputs are signaled to oligopolistic firms by changes in the prices of their inputs. Changes in the market conditions for the oligopolist's output, however, are typically signaled by changes in the volume of sales at administered prices.

Increases in costs of inputs will shift cost curves upward, and oligopolistic firms will be led to raise prices and lower outputs. Increases in demand will cause the sales of oligopolistic firms to rise. Firms will then respond by increasing output, thereby increasing the quantities of society's resources that are allocated to producing that output. They will then decide whether or not to alter their administered prices.

The market system reallocates resources in response to changes in demands and costs in roughly the same way under oligopoly as it does under perfect competition.

Profits Under Oligopoly

Some firms in some oligopolistic industries succeed in coming close to joint profit maximization in the short run. In other oligopolistic industries, firms compete so intensely among themselves that they come close to achieving competitive prices and outputs.

In the long run, those profits that do survive competitive behaviour among existing firms will tend to attract entry. These profits will persist only insofar as entry is restricted either by natural barriers, such as large minimum efficient scales for potential entrants, or by barriers created, and successfully defended, by the existing firms.

Very-Long-Run Competition

Once we allow for the effects of technological change, we need to ask which market structure is most conducive to the sorts of very-long-run changes that we discussed in Chapter 9. These are the driving force of the economic growth that has so greatly raised living standards over the past two centuries. They are intimately related to Schumpeter's concept of creative destruction, which we first encountered in our discussion of entry barriers in Chapter 11.

As we saw in Application 11-1, examples of creative destruction abound. In the nineteenth century, railways began to compete with wagons and barges for the carriage of freight. In the twentieth century, trucks operating on newly-constructed highways began competing with trains. During the 1950s and 1960s, airplanes began to compete seriously with trucks and trains.

The slide rule is an example of a product that had its market destroyed by a new one, which resulted in the elimination of a firm's monopoly power. Keuffel & Esser had achieved a dominant position in the manufacture and sale of slide rules, which were essential tools for engineers and applied scientists. Its dominant position and highly-profitable operations were wiped out, not by a better slide rule, but by the pocket calculator. When they were first introduced in the early 1970s, pocket calculators were relatively expensive, often costing over $100. They were also relatively crude in their capabilities. Nonetheless, they proved to be popular; sales and profits rose, and firms rushed to enter the lucrative new field. Competition led simultaneously to product improvements and price reductions. Today, calculators that perform basic calculations can be bought for a few dollars, and sophisticated scientific and programmable pocket calculators can be bought for under $20. Few of today's university students have heard of Keuffel & Esser, but most of them know about Texas Instruments and Hewlett-Packard.

In recent years, the development of facsimile transmission and electronic mail eliminated the monopoly of the postal service in delivering hard-copy (printed) communications. In their myriad uses, microcomputers for the home and the office swept away the markets of many once-thriving products and services. For instance, in-store computers answer customer questions, decreasing the need for salespeople. Aided by computers, "just in time" inventory systems greatly reduce the investment in inventories required of existing firms and new entrants alike. Computer-based flexible manufacturing systems allow firms to switch production easily and inexpensively from one product line to another, thereby reducing the minimum scale at which each can be produced profitably. One day soon, your textbooks may be replaced by computers.

An important defense of oligopoly relates to this process of creative destruction. Some economists have adopted Joseph Schumpeter's concept of creative destruction to develop theories that intermediate market structures, such as oligopoly, lead to more innovation than would occur in either perfect competition or monopoly. They argue that the oligopolist faces strong competition from existing rivals and cannot afford the more relaxed life of the monopolist. At the same time, however, oligopolistic firms expect to keep a good share of the profits that they earn from their innovative activity.

The empirical evidence is broadly consistent with this view. Professor Jesse Markham of Harvard University concluded a survey of empirical findings with the following:

> If technological change and innovational activity are, as we generally assume, in some important way a product of organized R&D activities financed and executed by business companies, it is

clear that the . . . payoffs that flow from them can to some measurable extent be traced to the doorsteps of large firms operating in oligopolistic markets.

Everyday observation provides some confirmation of this finding. Leading North American firms that operate in highly concentrated industries, such as Alcan, Bombardier, Du Pont, Kodak, General Electric, Northern Telecom, and Xerox, have been highly innovative over many years.

This is not meant to suggest that *only* oligopolistic industries are innovative. Much innovation is also done by very small new firms; and if today's new firms are successful in their innovation, they may become tomorrow's corporate giants. For example,

Hewlett-Packard, Microsoft, and Apple, which are enormous firms today, barely existed two decades ago; their rise from new start-up firms to corporate giants reflects their powers of innovation.

A Final Word

Oligopoly is an important market structure in modern economies because there are many industries in which the minimum efficient scale is simply too large to support many competing firms. The challenge to public policy is to keep oligopolists competing, rather than colluding, and using their competitive energies to improve products and to lower costs, rather than merely to erect entry barriers.

SUMMARY

A. THE STRUCTURE OF THE CANADIAN ECONOMY

- Most industries in the Canadian economy lie between the two extremes of monopoly and perfect competition. Within this spectrum of market structure we can divide Canadian industries into two broad groups—those with a large number of relatively small firms and those with a small number of relatively large firms. Such intermediate market structures are called imperfectly competitive.
- When measuring whether an industry has power concentrated in the hands of only a few firms or dispersed over many, it is not sufficient to count the number of firms. Instead, economists consider the concentration ratio, which shows the fraction of total market sales controlled by the largest group of sellers.
- One important problem associated with using concentration ratios is to define the market with reasonable accuracy. Since many goods produced in Canada compete with foreign-produced goods, the concentration ratios of Canadian industries should be adjusted to include foreign production. Such an adjustment significantly reduces the estimated concentration ratios in many Canadian industries.

B. IMPERFECTLY COMPETITIVE MARKET STRUCTURES

- Most firms operating in imperfectly competitive market structures sell differentiated products whose characteristics they choose themselves. They also administer their

prices, do not change their prices as often as prices change in perfectly competitive markets, engage in non-price competition, sometimes have unexploited economies of scale, and sometimes take actions designed to prevent the entry of new firms.

C. MONOPOLISTIC COMPETITION

- Monopolistic competition is a market structure that has the same characteristics as perfect competition except that the many firms each sell one variety of a differentiated product rather than all selling a single homogeneous product. Firms face negatively sloped demand curves and may earn monopoly profits in the short run.
- As in a perfectly competitive industry, the long run in monopolistic competition sees new firms enter the industry whenever profits can be made. Long-run equilibrium in the industry requires that each firm earns zero profits. But unlike perfect competition, the long-run equilibrium in monopolistic competition has each firm producing less than its minimum-cost level of output. This is because firms with differentiated products face downward-sloping demand curves. Zero profits then requires that the demand curve is tangent to the average total cost curve, which in turn means that the firm will be on the downward-sloping part of its average total cost curve. This is the excess-capacity theorem associated with monopolistic competition.
- Such excess capacity in the long-run equilibrium of monopolistic competition does not necessarily result in inefficiency. Even though each firm produces at a cost

that is higher than the minimum attainable cost, the resulting product choice is valued by consumers and so may be worth the extra cost.

D. OLIGOPOLY

- Oligopolies are dominated by a few large firms that usually sell differentiated products and have significant market power. They can maximize their joint profits if they cooperate to produce the monopoly output. By acting individually, each firm has an incentive to depart from this cooperative outcome, but rivalrous behaviour reduces profits and may lead to a noncooperative Nash equilibrium from which no one firm has an incentive to depart.
- Strategic behaviour, in which each firm chooses its best strategy in light of other firms' possible decisions, may also lead to a Nash equilibrium. Economists use game theory to study strategic behaviour.
- Tacit cooperation is possible but often breaks down as firms struggle for market share, indulge in non-price competition, and seek advantages through the introduction of new technology. Oligopolistic industries are likely to come closer to the joint-profit-maximizing cooperative outcome (a) the smaller the number of firms in the industry, (b) the less differentiated their products, (c) when the industry's demand is growing rather than shrinking, (d) when the industry contains a dominant firm, (e) the less the opportunity for non-price competition, and (f) the smaller the barriers to entry.
- Oligopolistic industries will exhibit profits in the long run only if there are significant barriers to entry. Natural barriers relate to the economies of scale and scope in production, finance and marketing, and also to large entry costs. Firm-created barriers can be created by proliferation of competing brands, heavy brand-image advertising, and the threat of predatory pricing when new entry occurs.
- The theory of contestable markets holds that *potential* entry may be sufficient to hold profits down and emphasizes the importance of sunk costs as an entry barrier.
- In the presence of major scale economies, oligopoly may be the best of the feasible alternative market structures. Evaluation of oligopoly depends on how much interfirm competition (a) drives the firms away from the cooperative, profit-maximizing solution and (b) leads to innovations in the very-long run.

KEY CONCEPTS

Concentration ratios
Reasons for the persistence of large firms
Administered prices
Product differentiation
Monopolistic competition
The excess-capacity theorem

The alleged inefficiency of monopolistic competition
Strategic behaviour
Cooperative and noncooperative outcomes
Game theory
Nash equilibrium

Explicit and tacit collusion
OPEC as a cartel
Natural and firm-created entry barriers
Contestable markets
The social benefits of oligopoly in the very-long run.

DISCUSSION QUESTIONS

1. It is sometimes said that there are more drugstores and gasoline stations than are needed. In what sense might this be correct? Does the consumer gain anything from this plethora of retail outlets?

2. Do you think any of the following industries might be monopolistically competitive? Why or why not?

   a. Textbook publishing (more than 50 elementary economics textbooks are in use on campuses in North America this year)
   b. Postsecondary education
   c. Cigarette manufacturing
   d. Restaurant operation
   e. Automobile retailing

3. What bearing did each of the following have on the eventual inability of OPEC to maintain a monopoly price for oil?

   a. Between 1979 and 1985, OPEC's share of the world oil supply decreased by half.

   b. "Saudi Arabia's interest lies in extending the life span of oil to the longest possible period," said Sheik Yamani.

   c. During the 1970s, government policies in many oil-importing countries protected consumers from oil price shocks by holding domestic prices well below OPEC levels.

   d. To earn Western currency to pay for grain, the Soviet Union increased its oil exports to the West during the 1980s, becoming the world's second largest oil exporter.

   e. In the late 1980s, Iran became increasingly concerned with maximizing its oil revenues in order to pay for its war with Iraq.

   f. Iraq in 1990 occupied Kuwait, and many wells there were set on fire before Iraq was driven out in 1991 by Operation Desert Storm.

   g. Other OPEC countries are able to make up for the lost Kuwait production by raising their outputs at a marginal cost far below the current world price.

4. "The periods following each of the major OPEC price shocks proved to the world that there were many available substitutes for gasoline, among them bicycles, car pools, moving closer to work, cable TV, and Japanese cars." Discuss how each of these may be a substitute for gasoline.

5. Can you think of other examples of competition among a few firms that might be of the prisoner's dilemma type?

6. The Canadian airline industry is essentially a duopoly (an oligopoly with two firms). Do the firms price-discriminate? Why or why not? Which features of the market facilitate price discrimination, and which make it difficult or impossible? Does the behaviour of the firms seem likely to get them close to or far away from the cooperative outcome? Until recently, European airlines operated under a price-setting arrangement. How would you expect prices to differ between Canada and Europe?

7. Compare the effects on the automobile and the wheat industries of each of the following. In light of your answers, discuss general ways in which oligopolistic industries fulfill the same general functions as perfectly competitive industries.

   a. A large rise in demand

   b. A large rise in the costs of production

   c. A temporary cut in supplies coming to market due to a three-month rail strike

   d. A rush of cheap foreign imports

8. Evidence suggests that the profits earned by all the firms in many oligopolistic industries are less than the profits that would be earned if the industry were monopolized. What are some reasons why this might be so?

9. Assume that you operate one of two self-service photocopying firms in your market. Due to space constraints, the businesses must be set up right next to each other, and each has room for only five identical machines. The only dimension on which you can compete is price. In fact, your services are so similar that if your competitor charges 1 cent less than you per copy, all customers will go to your competition. If the marginal cost per copy is 5 cents for each of you, what price do you think will dominate in the market?

10. What is the key difference between monopolistic competition and oligopoly? Assume that you are in an industry that is monopolistically competitive. What actual steps might you take to transform your industry into a more oligopolistic form?

CHAPTER 13

ECONOMIC EFFICIENCY AND PUBLIC POLICY

Monopoly has long been regarded with suspicion. In *The Wealth of Nations*, Adam Smith (1723–1790) developed a stinging attack on monopolists. Since then, most economists have criticized monopoly and advocated competition.

In this chapter, we first consider what economic theory has to say about the relevant advantages of the two polar market structures of monopoly and perfect competition. Next we examine intermediate market forms and then go on to study public policies that are directed at encouraging competition and discouraging monopoly.

Part of the appeal of competition and the distrust of monopoly is noneconomic, being based on a fear of concentration of power. This was discussed in Chapter 11. Much of the attraction of competition and the dislike of monopoly, however, has to do with the understanding that competition is efficient in ways that monopoly is not. To understand the issue, we must first define *efficiency*.

Economic efficiency

Economic *efficiency* requires that resources not be wasted. In this context, when economists speak of avoiding the waste of resources, they are *not* referring to those situations where labour is unemployed or factories are idle (as occurs in recessions). Though situations of such idleness might be viewed as wasteful in the sense that valuable resources are not being used, when defining economic efficiency economists usually consider situations where factors are *fully employed*. However, full employment of resources by itself is not enough to prevent the waste of resources. Even when resources are fully employed, they may be used inefficiently. Let us look at three examples of inefficiency in the use of fully employed resources.

1. If firms do not use the least-cost method of producing their chosen outputs, they waste resources. For example, a firm that produces 30,000 pairs of shoes at a resource cost of $400,000 when it could have been done at a cost of only $350,000 is using resources inefficiently. The lower-cost method would allow $50,000 worth of resources to be transferred to other productive uses.

2. If within an industry, the cost of producing its last unit of output is higher for some firms than for others, the industry's overall cost of producing its output is higher than necessary.

3. If too much of one product and too little of another product are produced, resources are being used inefficiently. To take an extreme example, suppose that so many shoes are produced that every consumer has all the shoes he or she could possibly want and so places a zero value on obtaining an additional pair of shoes. Further sup-

pose that fewer coats are produced relative to demand, so that each consumer places a positive value on obtaining an additional coat. In these circumstances, each consumer can be made better off if resources are reallocated from shoe production, where the last shoe produced has a low value in the eyes of each consumer, to coat production, where one more coat produced would have a higher value to each consumer.

PRODUCTIVE AND ALLOCATIVE EFFICIENCY

These examples suggest that we must refine our ideas of the waste of resources beyond the simple notion of ensuring that all resources are employed. The sources of inefficiency just outlined suggest important conditions that must be fulfilled if economic efficiency is to be attained. These conditions are conveniently collected into two categories, called *productive efficiency* and *allocative efficiency*, which were studied in the nineteenth century by the Italian economist Vilfredo Pareto (1848–1923). Indeed, efficiency in the use of resources is often called Pareto-optimality or Pareto-efficiency in his honour.

Productive Efficiency

Productive efficiency has two aspects, one concerning production within each firm and one concerning the allocation of production among the firms in an industry.

The first condition for productive efficiency is that each firm should produce *any given level of output* at the lowest possible cost. In the short run, with only one variable factor, the choice of technique is not a problem for the firm. It merely uses enough of the variable factor to produce the desired level of output. In the long run, however, more than one method of production is available. Productive efficiency requires that the firm use the least costly of the available methods of producing any given output. This means that firms will be located on, rather than above, their long-run average cost curves.

In Chapter 9, we studied the condition for productive efficiency within the firm:

Productive efficiency requires that each firm produce its given output by combining factors of production so that the ratios of the marginal products of each pair of factors equals the ratio of their prices.

This is the same thing as saying that $1 spent on every factor should yield the same output. If this were not so, the firm could reduce the resource costs of producing its given output by altering the inputs it uses. It could substitute the input for which $1 of expenditure yields the higher output for the input for which $1 of expenditure yields the lower output.[1]

Any firm that is not being productively efficient is producing at a higher cost than is necessary. This must reduce its profits. It follows that any profit-maximizing firm will seek to be productively efficient no matter which market structure it operates within—perfect competition, monopoly, oligopoly, or monopolistic competition.

There is a second condition for productive efficiency. It ensures that the total output of each industry is allocated among its individual firms in such a way that the total cost of producing the industry's output is minimized.

Productive efficiency at the level of the industry requires that the marginal cost of production must be the same for each firm.

If an industry is productively *inefficient*, it is possible to reduce the industry's total cost of producing any given output by reallocating production among the industry's firms. To illustrate, suppose that the Jones Brothers shoe manufacturing firm has a marginal cost of $70 for the last shoe of some standard type that it produces, while Gonzales, Inc., has a marginal cost of only $65 for the same type of shoe. If the Jones plant were to produce one less pair of shoes and the Gonzales plant were to produce one more, total shoe output is unchanged, but total industry costs are reduced by $5. Thus $5 worth of resources would be released to increase the production of other goods.

Clearly, this cost saving can go on as long as the two firms have different marginal costs. However, as the Gonzales firm produces more shoes, its marginal cost rises, and as the Jones firm produces fewer shoes, its marginal cost falls. (By producing more,

the Gonzales firm is moving upward along its given *MC* curve, whereas by producing less, the Jones firm is moving downward along its given *MC* curve.) Say, for example, that after the Gonzales firm increases its production by 1,000 shoes per month, its marginal cost rises to $67, whereas when Jones Brothers reduces its output by the same amount, its marginal cost falls to $67. Now there are no further cost savings to be obtained by reallocating production between the two firms.

Figure 13-1 shows a production possibility curve of the sort that was first introduced in Chapter 1. Productive *inefficiency* implies that the economy is at some point *inside* the production possibility curve. In such a situation, it is possible to produce more of some goods without producing less of others. *Thus productive efficiency implies being on, rather than inside, the economy's production possibility curve.*

Allocative Efficiency

Allocative efficiency concerns the relative quantities of the products to be produced. It concerns the choice between alternative points on the curve such as points *b*, *c*, and *d* in Figure 13-1.

Allocative efficiency is defined as a situation in which it is impossible to change the allocation of resources in such a way as to make someone better off without making someone else worse off. Changing the allocation of resources implies producing more of some goods and less of others, which in turn means moving from one point on the production possibility curve to another. This is called changing the *mix* of production.

From an allocative point of view, resources are said to be used *inefficiently* when using them to produce a different bundle of goods makes it *possible* for at least one person to be better off while making no other person worse off. Conversely, resources are said to be used *efficiently* when it is *impossible*, by using them to produce a different bundle of goods, to make any one person better off without making at least one other person worse off.

This tells us what is meant by allocative efficiency, but how do we find the efficient point on the production possibility curve? For example, how many shoes, dresses, and hats should be produced to achieve allocative efficiency? The answer is as follows:

The economy is allocatively efficient when, for each good produced, its marginal cost of production is equal to its price.

---

[1]As we saw in Extension 9-1, producing at least cost within the firm also involves a more obvious type of efficiency, called *technical efficiency*. Technical efficiency requires that the firm not adopt a method of production if there exists another method that uses *less of all inputs*. Productive efficiency then ensures that the firm chooses the method that uses the lowest *value* of resources from among the technically efficient methods.

FIGURE 13-1
Productive and Allocative Efficiency

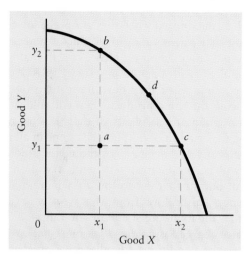

Any point on the production possibility curve is productively efficient; not all points on this curve are allocatively efficient. The curve shows all combinations of two goods X and Y that can be produced when the economy's resources are fully employed and being used with productive efficiency.

Any point inside the curve, such as a, is productively inefficient. If the inefficiency exists in industry X, production could be reallocated among firms in that industry in such a way as to raise production of X from x_1 to x_2. This would take the economy from point a to point c, raising production of X without any reduction in production of Y. Similarly, if the inefficiency exists in industry Y, production of Y could be increased from y_1 to y_2, which would take the economy from point a to point b. If both industries are productively inefficient, production can be increased to take the economy to some point on the curve between b and c, thereby increasing the production of both products.

Allocative efficiency concerns being at the most efficient point on the production possibility curve. Assessing allocative efficiency requires comparing various points on the curve, such as b, c, and d. Usually only one such point will be allocatively efficient (though all of them are productively efficient).

To understand the reasoning behind this answer, we need to recall a point that was established in our discussion of consumer surplus in Chapter 7. The price of any product indicates the value that each consumer places on the last unit consumed of that product. Faced with the market price of some product, the consumer goes on buying units until the last one is

valued exactly at its price. Consumer surplus arises because the consumer would be willing to pay more than the market price for all but the last unit that is bought. On the last unit bought (the marginal unit), however, the consumer only "breaks even" because the valuation placed on it is just equal to its price.

Now let us return to our shoe example. Suppose that shoes sell for $60 per pair but the marginal cost is $70. If one less pair of shoes were produced, the value that all households would place on the pair of shoes not produced would be $60. Using the concept of opportunity cost, however, we see that the resources that would have been used to produce that last pair of shoes could instead produce another good (say, a coat) valued at $70. If society can give up something that its members value at $60 and get in return something that its members value at $70, the original allocation of resources is inefficient. Someone can be made better off, and no one need be worse off.

This is easy to see when the same consumer gives up the shoes and gets the coat, but it follows even when different consumers are involved. In this case, the market value of the gains to the household that gets the coat exceeds the market value of the loss to the household that gives up the shoes. The gaining household *could afford* to compensate the losing household and still come out ahead.

Suppose next that shoe production is cut back until the price of a pair of shoes rises from $60 to $65, while its marginal cost falls from $70 to $65. Efficiency is achieved in shoe production because $p = MC = \$65$. Now if one less pair of shoes were produced, $65 worth of shoes would be sacrificed, while at most, $65 worth of other products could be produced with the freed resources.

In this situation, it is not possible to change the allocation of resources to shoe production to make someone better off without making someone else worse off. If one household were to sacrifice one pair of shoes, it would give up goods worth $65 and would then have to obtain for itself all of the new production of the alternative commodity produced just to break even. It cannot gain without making another household worse off. The same argument can be repeated for every product, and it leads to the conclusion that we have stated already: The allocation of resources is efficient when each product's price equals its marginal cost of production.

One final comment about allocative efficiency. Whereas an individual firm or an individual industry may be *productively efficient*, it does not make sense to say that a given firm or industry is *allocatively efficient*. Allocative efficiency is a property of the overall economy, concerning the relative outputs of its various industries, and it is achieved when price equals marginal cost in *all* industries. Thus if we were to observe price greater than marginal cost in some individual industry, we would know that the economy is not allocatively efficient. But if we were to see price equal to marginal cost in that one industry, we must still check *all* other industries before we know whether the economy is allocatively efficient.

EFFICIENCY IN PERFECT COMPETITION AND MONOPOLY

We now know that for productive efficiency, marginal cost should be the same for all firms in any one industry and that for allocative efficiency, marginal cost should be equal to price in each industry. Do the market structures of perfect competition and monopoly lead to productive and allocative efficiency?

Perfect Competition

Productive Efficiency. We saw in Figure 10-9 that in the long run under perfect competition, each firm produces at the lowest point on its long-run average cost curve. Therefore, no one firm could lower its costs by altering its own production.

We also know that in perfect competition, all firms in an industry face the same price of their product and that they equate marginal cost to that price. It follows immediately that marginal cost will be the same for all firms. Because all firms in the industry have the same cost of producing their last unit of production, no reallocation of production among the firms could reduce the total industry cost of producing a given output. Thus productive efficiency is achieved under perfect competition because all firms in an industry have identical marginal costs and identical minimum costs in long-run equilibrium.

Allocative Efficiency. We have already seen that perfectly competitive firms maximize their profits by equating marginal cost to price. Thus when perfect competition is the market structure for the whole economy, price is equal to marginal cost in each line of production, resulting in allocative efficiency.

Monopoly

Productive Efficiency. Monopolists have an incentive to be productively efficient because their profits will be maximized when they adopt the lowest-cost method that can be used to produce whatever level of output they choose. Hence profit-maximizing monopolists will operate on their *LRAC* curves. Furthermore, when they have more than one plant producing the same product, they will allocate production among those plants so that the cost of producing the last unit of output is the same in all plants.

Allocative Efficiency. Although a monopoly firm will be productively efficient, it will choose a level of output that is too low to achieve allocative efficiency. This follows from what we saw in Chapter 11—that the monopolist chooses an output at which the price charged is *greater than* marginal cost. This violates the conditions for allocative efficiency because the amount that consumers pay for the last unit of output exceeds the opportunity cost of producing it.

Consumers would be prepared to buy additional units for an amount that is greater than the cost of producing these units. Some consumers could be made better off, and none need be made worse off, by shifting extra resources into production of the monopolized product, thus increasing the output of the product. From this follows the classic efficiency-based preference for competition over monopoly:

Monopoly creates allocative inefficiency because the monopolist's price always exceeds its marginal cost.

This result has important policy implications for economists and for policymakers, as we shall see later in this chapter.

Efficiency in Other Market Structures

Note that the result just stated extends beyond the case of a simple monopoly. Whenever a firm has any power over the market, in the sense that it faces a negatively sloped demand curve rather than one that is horizontal, its marginal revenue will be less than its price. Thus when it equates marginal cost to marginal revenue, as all profit-maximizing firms do, marginal cost will also be less than price. This implies allocative inefficiency. Thus oligopoly and monopolistic competition are also allocatively inefficient.

Oligopoly is an important market structure in today's economy because in many industries the minimum efficient scale is simply too high to support a large number of competing firms. Although oligopoly does not achieve the conditions for allocative efficiency, it may nevertheless produce more satisfactory results than monopoly. We observed one reason why this might be so in Chapter 12: Competition among oligopolists may encourage very-long-run adaptations that result in both new products and cost-reducing methods of producing old ones.

An important defense of oligopoly as an acceptable market structure is that it may be the best of the available alternatives when minimum efficient scale is large. As we observed at the end of Chapter 12, the challenge to public policy is to keep oligopolists competing and using their competitive energies to improve products and to lower costs rather than to restrict interfirm competition and to erect entry barriers. As we shall see later in this chapter, much public policy has just this purpose. What economic policymakers call *monopolistic practices* include not only output restrictions operated by firms with complete monopoly power but also anticompetitive behaviour among firms that are operating in oligopolistic industries.

ALLOCATIVE EFFICIENCY AND TOTAL SURPLUS

By using the concepts of price and marginal cost, we have established the basic points of productive and allocative efficiency. A different way of thinking about allocative efficiency—though completely consistent with the first approach—is to use the concepts of consumer and producer surplus.

Consumer and Producer Surplus

Recall from Chapter 7 that consumer surplus is the difference between the total value that consumers place on all the units consumed of some product and the payment that they actually make for the purchase of that product. Consumer surplus is shown once again in Figure 13-2.

Producer surplus is analogous to consumer surplus. It occurs because all units of each firm's output are sold at the same market price, while, given an upward-sloping supply curve, each unit except the last is produced at a marginal cost that is less than the market price.

Producer surplus is defined as the amount that producers are paid for a product minus the total

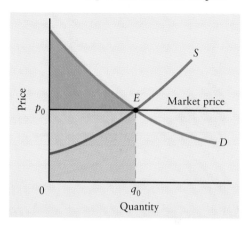

FIGURE 13-2
Consumer Surplus and Producer Surplus

Consumer surplus is the area under the demand curve and above the market price line. Producer surplus is the area above the supply curve and below the market price line. The total value that consumers place on q_0 of the commodity is given by the sum of the three shaded areas. The amount they pay is the rectangle p_0q_0. The difference, shown as the dark blue shaded area, is consumer surplus.

The receipts to producers from the sale of q_0 units are also p_0q_0. The area under the supply curve, the red shaded area, is the minimum amount producers require to supply the output. The difference, shown as the light blue shaded area, is producer surplus.

variable cost of producing the product. The total variable cost of producing any output is shown by the area under the supply curve up to that output.[2] Thus producer surplus is the area above the supply curve and below the market price line. Producer surplus is also shown in Figure 13-2.

The Allocative Efficiency of Perfect Competition Revisited

If the total of consumer and producer surplus is not maximized, the industry's output could be altered to

---

[2]Marginal cost is the change in total cost caused by producing one more unit of output. Summing these additions over each unit of output, starting with the first, yields the total variable cost of output. Graphically, this process of summation is shown by the whole area under the marginal cost curve. Because, as we have already seen, the industry supply curve under perfect competition is merely the sum of the marginal cost curves of all the firms in the industry, the area under that supply curve up to some given output is the total of all the firms' variable costs of producing that output.

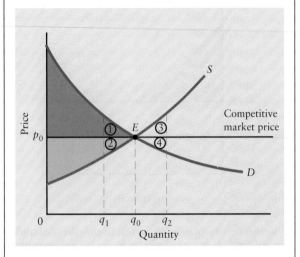

FIGURE 13-3
The Allocative Efficiency of Perfect Competition

Competitive equilibrium is allocatively efficient because it maximizes the sum of consumer and producer surplus. The competitive equilibrium occurs at the price-output combination $p_0 q_0$. At this equilibrium, consumer surplus is the dark shaded area above the price line, while producer surplus is the light shaded area below the price line.

For any output that is less than q_0, the sum of the two surpluses is less than at q_0. For example, reducing the output to q_1 but keeping price at p_0 lowers consumer surplus by area 1 and lowers producer surplus by area 2.

For any output that is greater than q_0, the sum of the surpluses is also less than at q_0. For example, if producers are forced to produce output q_2 and to sell it to consumers, who are in turn forced to buy it at price p_0, producer surplus is reduced by area 3 (the amount by which variable costs exceed revenue on those units), while the amount of consumer surplus is reduced by area 4 (the amount by which expenditure exceeds consumers' satisfactions on those units).

Only at competitive output q_0 is the sum of the two surpluses maximized.

increase that total. The additional surplus could then be used to make some consumers better off without making any others worse off.

Allocative efficiency occurs where the sum of consumer and producer surplus is maximized.

The allocatively efficient output occurs under perfect competition where the demand curve intersects the supply curve—that is, the point of equilibrium in a competitive market. This is shown in Figure 13-3. For any output that is less than the com-

petitive output, the demand curve lies above the supply curve, which means that the value that consumers put on the last unit of production exceeds its marginal cost of production. Suppose that the current output of shoes is such that consumers value at $70 an additional pair of shoes that adds $60 to costs. If it is sold at any price between $60 and $70, both producers and consumers gain; there is $10 of potential surplus to be divided between the two groups. In contrast, the last unit produced and sold in a competitive equilibrium adds nothing to either consumer or producer surplus because consumers value it at exactly its market price, and it adds the full amount of the market price to producers' costs.

If production were pushed beyond the competitive equilibrium, the sum of the two surpluses would fall. Suppose, for example, that firms were forced to produce and sell further units of output at the competitive market price and that consumers were forced to buy these extra units at that price. (Note that neither group would do so voluntarily.) Firms would lose producer surplus on those extra units because their marginal costs of producing the extra output would be above the price that they received for it. Purchasers would lose consumer surplus because the valuation that they placed on these extra units, as shown by the height of the demand curve, would be less than the price that they would have to pay.

The sum of producer and consumer surplus is maximized only at the perfectly competitive level of output. This is the only level of output that is allocatively efficient.

The Allocative Inefficiency of Monopoly Revisited

We have just seen in Figure 13-3 that the output in perfectly competitive equilibrium maximizes the sum of consumer and producer surplus. It follows that the lower monopoly output must result in a smaller total of consumer and producer surplus.

The monopoly equilibrium is not the outcome of a voluntary agreement between the one producer and the many consumers. Instead, it is imposed by the monopolist by virtue of the power it has over the market. When the monopolist chooses an output below the competitive level, market price is higher than it would be under perfect competition. As a result, consumer surplus is diminished, and producer surplus is increased. In this way, the monopolist gains at the expense of consumers. This is not the whole story, however.

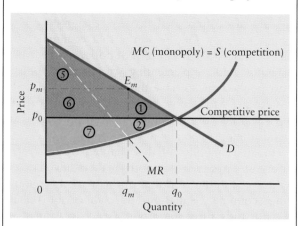

FIGURE 13-4
The Allocative Inefficiency of Monopoly

Monopoly is allocatively inefficient because it produces less than the competitive output and thus does not maximize the sum of consumer and producer surplus. If this market were perfectly competitive, price would be p_0, output would be q_0, and consumer surplus would be the sum of areas 1, 5, and 6 (the blue shaded areas). When the industry is monopolized, price rises to p_m and consumer surplus falls to area 5. Consumers lose area 1 because that output is not produced; they lose area 6 because the price rise has transferred it to the monopolist.

Producer surplus in a competitive equilibrium would be the sum of areas 7 and 2 (the gray shaded areas). When the market is monopolized and price rises to q_m, the surplus area 2 is lost because the output is not produced. However, the monopolist gains area 6 from consumers (6 is known to be greater than 2 because p_m maximizes profits).

Whereas area 6 is surplus that is transferred from consumers to producers by the price rise, areas 1 and 2 are lost altogether. They represent the deadweight loss resulting from monopoly and account for its allocative inefficiency.

When output is below the competitive level, there is always a *net loss* of surplus: More surplus is lost by consumers than is gained by the monopolist. Some surplus is lost because output between the monopolistic and the competitive levels is not produced. This loss of surplus is called the *deadweight loss of monopoly*. It is illustrated in Figure 13-4.

It follows that there is a conflict between the private interest of the monopoly producer and the public interest of all the nation's consumers. This creates grounds for government intervention to prevent the formation of monopolies or at least to control their behaviour.

ALLOCATIVE EFFICIENCY AND MARKET FAILURE

We have seen that perfect competition is allocatively efficient and that monopoly, in general, is not. Most of the remainder of the chapter discusses ways in which public policy has attempted to deal with problems raised by monopoly. Before we go on, however, it is important to reemphasize that perfect competition is a theoretical ideal that is at best only approximated in actual market economies and that the markets for many products do not even closely resemble this ideal. Hence to say that perfect competition is allocatively efficient is not to say that real-world market economies are ever allocatively efficient.

In Chapter 18, we provide a detailed analysis of the most important ways (other than monopoly) that market economies may fail to produce efficient outcomes. In Chapters 19 and 20, we discuss and evaluate the most important public policies that have been used to try to correct for these *market failures*. The most important problems arise when market transactions—production and consumption—impose costs or confer benefits on economic agents who are not parties to the transaction. Cases like these, which are called *externalities* because they involve economic effects that are external to the transaction, generally raise the possibility that market outcomes will be allocatively inefficient.

A simple example can illustrate the problem. We have argued that markets for agricultural commodities are highly competitive, with many relatively small producers who are unable to affect the price of the goods that they are producing. At the same time, it turns out that the technology of agricultural production involves the extensive use of fertilizers that pollute nearby streams and rivers. This pollution in turn imposes costs on downstream fisheries and on households downstream who use the water for drinking and cleaning. Because these costs are not taken into account in the market for the agricultural products, they will be external to transactions in those markets. Generally, when production of a good or service causes pollution, the quantity produced in a perfectly competitive industry will exceed the efficient amount.

One of the most important issues in public policy is whether, and under what circumstances, government action can increase the allocative efficiency of market outcomes.

As we will see later in this book, there are many circumstances in which there is room to increase the efficiency of market outcomes, but there are also many cases in which the cure is worse than the disease. In the remainder of this chapter, we consider an important set of examples of both of these phenomena—those arising from public policy toward monopoly and competition.

ECONOMIC REGULATION TO PROMOTE EFFICIENCY

Monopolies, cartels, and price-fixing agreements among oligopolists, whether explicit or tacit, have met with public suspicion and official hostility for over a century. These and other noncompetitive practices are collectively referred to as *monopoly practices*. Such practices go far beyond what actual monopolists do and include noncompetitive behaviour of firms that are operating in other market structures. The laws and other instruments that are used to encourage competition and discourage monopoly practices make up **competition policy** and are used to influence both the market structure and the behaviour of individual firms. By and large, Canadian competition policy has sought to create more competitive market structures where possible, to discourage monopolistic practices, and to encourage competitive behaviour where competitive market structures cannot be established. In addition, federal, provincial, and local governments all employ *economic regulations*, which prescribe the rules under which firms can do business and in some cases determine the prices that businesses can charge for their output. Railway freight rates, passenger airline fares, cable television, and local telephone service are examples of services that are subject to this kind of regulation.

The quest for allocative efficiency provides rationales both for competition policy and for economic regulation. Competition policy is used to promote allocative efficiency by increasing competition in the marketplace. Where effective competition is not possible (as in the case of a natural monopoly, such as an electric power company), economic regulation of privately owned firms or public ownership can be used as a substitute for competition. Consumers can then be protected from the high prices and reduced output that result from the use of monopoly power.[3]

Public policies are indeed used in these ways, but they are also often used in ways that reduce economic efficiency. One reason is that economic efficiency is not the only concern of policymakers when designing and implementing competition policy. Most public policies have the potential to redistribute income, and people often use them for private gain, regardless of their original public purpose. This is studied more generally in Chapter 18.

In the remainder of this chapter, we look at a variety of ways in which policymakers have chosen to intervene in the workings of the market economy using economic regulation and competition policy. We will study three important aspects of Canadian policy: the control of natural monopolies, the control of oligopolies, and the creation of competitive conditions.

DIRECT CONTROL OF NATURAL MONOPOLIES

The clearest case for public intervention arises with what is called a **natural monopoly**—an industry in which scale effects are so dominant that there is room for *at most* one firm to operate at the minimum efficient scale. (Indeed, scale effects could be so important that even a single firm could satisfy the entire market demand before reaching its minimum efficient scale.) In the past, there have been many natural monopolies. Today, they are found mainly in public utilities, such as electricity generation and cable television.

One response to natural monopoly is for government to assume *ownership* of the single firm. In Canada, such government-owned firms are called **crown corporations**. In these cases, the government appoints managers and directors who are supposed to set prices guided by their understanding of the national interest. Another response to the problem of natural monopoly is to allow private ownership but to regulate the monopolist's behaviour. In Canada, both government ownership (e.g., Canada Post and the provincial hydro authorities) and regulation (e.g.,

---

[3] A second kind of regulation, *social regulation*, involves the legislated rules that require firms to consider the health, safety, environmental, and other social consequences of their behaviour. Social regulation is discussed in Chapter 19.

cable television and local telephone) are used actively. In the United States, with a few notable exceptions, regulation has been the preferred alternative.

Whether the government owns or merely regulates natural monopolies, the industry's pricing policy is determined by the government. The industry is typically asked to follow some pricing policy that conflicts with the goal of profit maximization. We will see that such government intervention must deal with problems that arise in the short run, the long run, and the very-long run.

Short-Run Price and Output

In the short run, there are three general types of pricing policies that the natural monopoly—either state owned or privately owned but regulated—might be required to follow. These are *marginal-cost pricing, two-part tariffs,* and *average-cost pricing.* We discuss them in turn.

Marginal-Cost Pricing. Sometimes the government dictates that the natural monopoly should try to set price equal to short-run marginal cost in an effort to maximize the sum of consumer and producer surplus in that industry. In principle, this policy, called **marginal-cost pricing,** induces the allocatively efficient level of output (i.e., where price equals marginal cost). This is not, however, the profit-maximizing output (which is where marginal cost equals marginal revenue). Thus marginal-cost pricing sets up a tension between the regulators' desire to achieve the allocatively efficient level of output and the monopolist's desire to maximize profits.

Marginal-cost pricing creates different problems in each of two important cases. In the first case, the natural monopoly has unexploited economies of scale when producing the allocatively efficient output because it is still operating on the downward-sloping portion of its average total cost curve. In this case, marginal cost will be less than average total cost. It follows that when price is set equal to marginal cost, price will therefore be less than average cost, and so marginal-cost pricing will lead to losses. This is shown in part (i) of Figure 13-5.

In the second case, demand is sufficient to allow the firm to produce a level of output beyond its minimum efficient scale and thus on the upward-sloping portion of its average total cost curve. At any such level of output, marginal cost exceeds average total cost. Thus if the firm is directed to equate price with

marginal cost, it is clear that price will be above average total cost. Marginal-cost pricing will therefore lead the firm to earn positive profits. This is shown in part (ii) of the figure.[4]

When a natural monopoly with falling average costs sets price equal to marginal cost, it will suffer losses. When a natural monopoly with rising average costs sets price equal to marginal cost, it will earn positive profits.

Two-Part Tariff. Though marginal-cost pricing achieves allocative efficiency, a natural monopoly with declining average costs cannot be expected to incur losses indefinitely. One way of trying to cover total costs in this case is to allow the firm to charge a **two-part tariff** in which customers pay one price to gain access to the product and a second price for each unit consumed. Consider the case of a regulated electric utility. In principle, the "hookup fee" covers fixed costs, and then each unit of output can be priced at marginal cost. In practice, some electric utilities use a modified form of the two-part tariff. Each customer pays a high price for the first block of kilowatts of electricity consumed each month and then pays a price that is closer to marginal cost for the remaining consumption. This is referred to as *block pricing.*

Average-Cost Pricing. Another method of regulating a natural monopoly is to set prices just high enough to cover total costs, thus earning neither profits nor losses. This means that the firm produces to the point where average revenue equals average total cost, which is where the demand curve cuts the average total cost curve. Part (i) of Figure 13-5 shows that for a firm with declining costs, this pricing policy requires producing at less than the optimal output. The firm's financial losses that would occur under marginal-cost pricing are avoided by producing less than

---

[4]Sometimes a natural monopoly is defined as one where long-run costs are falling when price equals marginal cost. This, however, is only *sufficient* for a natural monopoly; it is not *necessary.* Demand may be such that one firm is producing, when price equals marginal cost, on the rising portion of its long-run cost curve, while there is no price at which two firms could both cover their total costs. For example, if a firm's minimum efficient scale is 1 million units of output and demand is sufficient to allow the firm to cover costs at 1.2 million units, there may be no price at which two firms, with their combined *MES* of 2 million units, can cover their full costs.

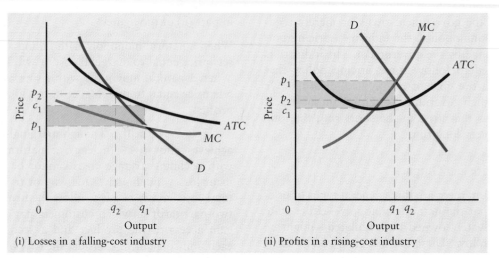

FIGURE 13-5
Pricing Policies for Natural Monopolies

(i) Losses in a falling-cost industry

(ii) Profits in a rising-cost industry

Marginal-cost pricing leads to profit or losses, whereas average-cost pricing violates the efficiency condition. In each part, the output at which marginal cost equals price is q_1 and price is p_1.

In part (i), average costs are falling at output q_1, so marginal costs are less than the average cost c_1. There is an average loss of $c_1 - p_1$ on each unit, making a total loss equal to the shaded area.

In part (ii), average cost c_1 is less than price at output q_1. There is an average profit of $p_1 - c_1$ on each unit sold, making a total profit equal to the shaded area.

In each part of the diagram, the output at which average cost equals price is q_2 and the associated price is p_2. In part (i), marginal cost is less than price at q_2, so output is below its optimal level. In part (ii), marginal cost exceeds price at q_2, so output is greater than its optimal level.

the efficient output.[5] Part (ii) shows that for a firm with rising costs, the policy requires producing at more than the optimal output. The profits that would occur under marginal-cost pricing are dissipated by producing more than the efficient output.

Generally, average-cost pricing will not result in allocative efficiency because price will not equal marginal cost.

On what basis do we choose between marginal-cost pricing and average-cost pricing? One the one hand, marginal-cost pricing generates allocative efficiency, but the firm may incur losses. In this case, the firm will eventually go out of business unless someone is prepared to cover the firm's costs. If the government is unwilling to do so, seeing no reason why

taxpayers should subsidize the users of the product in question, then average-cost pricing is preferable to monopoly pricing. It provides the lowest price that can be charged and the largest output that can be produced, given the requirement that sales revenue must cover the total cost of producing the product.

Long-Run Investment

So far, we have examined the implications for different pricing policies in the short run. Recall that in the short run the level of the firm's capital is fixed. The allocatively efficient pricing policy sets price equal to short-run marginal cost. The position of the short-run marginal cost curve depends, however, on the amount of fixed capital that is currently available to be combined with the variable factors. What should determine the long-run investment decision to accumulate capital?

The efficient answer follows from comparing the current market price with the *long-run* marginal cost of producing the product. The current market price

---

[5]Note that the losses are financial losses, not social welfare losses. Every unit produced between the points where AC equals price and MC equals price brings private financial losses to the producer even though total (consumer plus producer) surplus increases.

reflects the value consumers place on one additional unit of output. The long-run marginal cost reflects the full resource cost (including capital costs) of providing an extra unit of output. Thus if the current price exceeds long-run marginal cost, then the natural monopoly should increase its capacity; if current price is less than long-run marginal cost, the natural monopoly should allow its capacity to decline as its capital wears out.

For given capacity in the short run, the allocatively efficient pricing system determines output by setting price equal to the short-run marginal cost of production. It also adjusts capacity in the long run until the long-run marginal cost of production is equal to the price.

Application 13-1 discusses the example of provincial hydro authorities and the long-run investment problems associated with average-cost pricing.

Very-Long-Run Innovation

Natural monopoly is a long-run concept, meaning that given *existing technology,* there is room for only one firm to operate profitably. In the very-long run, however, technology changes. Not only does today's competitive industry sometimes become tomorrow's natural monopoly, but today's natural monopoly often becomes tomorrow's competitive industry.

A striking example is found in the telecommunications industry. Thirty years ago, hard-copy message transmission was close to a natural monopoly belonging to the post office. Today, technological developments such as satellite transmission, electronic mail, and fax machines have made this activity highly competitive. In many countries, an odd circumstance has now arisen: Publicly owned, or privately owned but regulated, post offices seek to maintain their profitability by prohibiting entry into what would otherwise become a highly competitive industry. Because it has the full force of the legal system behind it, the government-sanctioned monopolist may be more successful than the unregulated privately owned firm would have been in preserving its monopoly long after technological changes have destroyed its "naturalness." What started out as policies to facilitate efficiency of a natural monopoly ends up being a protection of an artificial monopoly against would-be competitors.

Not only is this true of many publicly owned or regulated post offices around the world, but it is also true of a number of other industries that once were natural monopolies but that could now be highly competitive. For example, many countries continue to operate such artificial monopolies in railways, airlines, telephones, and the generation of electricity (the *distribution* of electricity continues to be a natural monopoly). The basic lesson is this: Market economies change continually under the impacts of innovation and growth; to be successful, government policy must also adapt continually to keep it relevant to the ever-changing environment.

DIRECT CONTROL OF OLIGOPOLIES

Governments have from time to time intervened in industries that were oligopolies (rather than natural monopolies), seeking to enforce the type of price and entry behaviour that was thought to be in the public interest. Such intervention has typically taken two distinct forms. In the United Kingdom, it was primarily nationalization of whole oligopolistic industries such as railways, steel, and coal mining, which were then to be run by government-appointed boards. In the United States, firms such as airlines, railways, and electric power companies were left in private hands, but their decisions were regulated by government-appointed bodies that set prices and regulated entry. As so often happens, Canada followed a mixture of British and American practices. Many Canadian crown corporations were set up, and many firms that remained in private hands were regulated. For example, in the regulated railway industry, Canadian Pacific was privately owned while Canadian National, until very recently, was a crown corporation.

Scepticism About Direct Control

Policymakers have become increasingly sceptical of their ability to improve the behaviour of oligopolistic industries by having governments control the details of their behaviour either through ownership or regulation. Three main experiences have been important in developing this scepticism.

Oligopolies and Economic Growth. First, oligopolistic market structures have provided much of the economic growth in the twentieth century. New products and new ways of producing old products have followed each other in rapid succession, all lead-

| APPLICATION   13-1 |

PRICING IN THE PROVINCIAL POWER AUTHORITIES

The use of average-cost pricing in natural monopolies tends to distort investment decisions. One example which illustrates this idea is the case of the provincially-owned power authorities, such as Manitoba Hydro, Ontario Hydro, or New Brunswick Power. There are essentially three different methods of generating electricity used by the power authorities: hydroelectric, fuel burning (coal, oil, and other fuels), and nuclear power. Across the various provincial hydro authorities, there is considerable variation in the methods used. For example, in British Columbia and Manitoba almost all power is hydroelectric; Ontario makes considerable use of nuclear power; and almost all electricity in Alberta is generated in fuel-burning plants. New Brunswick is the most diversified of the power authorities, having large amounts of its electricity being produced by each of the three methods.

COSTS OF PRODUCTION

The three methods of generating electricity differ markedly in their costs. Producing hydroelectricity involves high fixed costs but extremely low marginal costs—this reflects the high cost of building a dam but the very low costs of having an extra unit of water flow through a turbine. Fuel-burning plants have smaller fixed costs, but higher marginal costs—a fuel-burning plant can be easily built, but expensive fuel must be used for every unit of power produced. Nuclear plants have extremely high fixed costs, but do not have the advantage of the very low marginal costs typical of hydro plants—uranium and heavy water are important and expensive *variable* factors of production.

The combination of these very different cost structures is that hydro plants tend to produce electricity at the lowest average total cost, with power from fuel-burning plants being slightly more expensive. The extreme fixed costs of building nuclear plants (and storage facilities for the spent fuel bundles) tend to give nuclear power the highest average total costs.

AVERAGE-COST PRICING

Now consider a typical problem faced by the hydro authorities—especially Ontario Hydro—until the early 1990s. Suppose that there are no sites in Ontario where new hydroelectric plants can be built, and that new fuel-burning plants are considered undesirable on environmental grounds. This means that any new capacity which is to be built must come from new high-cost nuclear plants.

If Ontario Hydro uses a policy of average-cost pricing, then the price of each unit of electricity sold (a kilowatt hour) is set equal to the average total cost of *all* units produced. With all three methods of electricity generation being used, the policy of average-cost pricing implies that the price of electricity is greater than the average cost from the hydro and fuel-burning plants but less than the average cost from the nuclear plants.

Now suppose that when Ontario Hydro follows this policy of average-cost pricing, it finds that there is excess demand for electricity. That is, when price is set equal to overall average cost, the quantity of electricity demanded exceeds what Ontario Hydro can currently provide. In this situation, should Ontario Hydro build new capacity?

ing to higher living standards and higher productivity. Many of these innovations have been provided by firms in oligopolistic industries such as automobiles, agricultural implements, steel, petroleum refining, chemicals, and telecommunications. As long as oli-

gopolists continue to compete with each other, rather than cooperating to produce monopoly profits, most economists see no need to regulate such things as the prices at which oligopolists sell their products and the conditions of entry into oligopolistic industries.

The relevant test is not the existence of excess demand at the current price (which equals average cost), because the long-run cost of providing more electricity exceeds the current price. The relevant cost is the long-run *marginal* cost of providing electricity *from nuclear plants* (which includes the high fixed costs of nuclear plants). On efficiency grounds, another plant should be built only if there is excess demand at a price that equals that long-run marginal cost.

This case illustrates the inefficient policies often adopted by nationalized and regulated industries that face rising long-run costs. If they priced at marginal cost, they would make profits on all units of output except the marginal one. Instead, they price at average cost. As a result, market price does not then provide the correct signal about the social value of further investment. If a regulated or nationalized firm installs capacity to satisfy all of the demand when price is set equal to average cost, then there will be more capacity than what is socially optimal. Such socially wasteful policies were adopted by several of the provincial power authorities, including Ontario Hydro.

NEW PROBLEMS

Technological improvements and deregulation have introduced new problems for the provincial power authorities in the past few years. First, technological improvements in the generation of electricity have removed many of the economies of scale that for many years were typical of this industry. In particular, the development of small-scale gas-combustion turbines has permitted the inexpensive construction of small generating stations that can produce electricity at a lower average cost than the much larger existing stations owned by the power authorities. This improvement in technology has led regulators to the view that the provincial power authorities should be deregulated and forced to face competition from private power generators.

Such competition introduces serious problems for the power authorities. Faced with low-price competition from the private power producers, the provincial power authorities have been forced to reduce their prices. But such price reductions imply that price is no longer high enough to cover their high fixed costs, especially those associated with nuclear plants. The result is that competition has driven prices down—which is clearly good for consumers—but has left the provincial power authorities unable to cover their average costs.

This situation is now occurring in some of the provincial power authorities in Canada, especially those like Ontario Hydro that use so much nuclear power. How the provincial authorities will respond is not yet known, but there are two broad possibilities, neither of which are promising. The first is that the power authorities will continue to produce power with their large facilities and sell it at a price below their average cost. The losses incurred will be absorbed by the shareholders of the companies—which in these cases are the provincial taxpayers. The second possibility is that the power authorities will moth-ball their high-fixed-cost production facilities. This is the so-called *stranded investment* problem—the ownership of capacity that is unable to compete with the new small-scale private power generators and is therefore economically obsolete.

Over the next few years we will see how the provincial power authorities deal with this difficult situation.

Cross Subsidization. Second, many regulatory bodies have imposed policies that were not related to the cost of each of the services being priced. These prices involved what is called *cross subsidization,* whereby profits that are earned in the provision of one service are used to subsidize the provision of another at a price below cost. When they were in control, regulators typically required that long-distance telephone calls subsidize local calls, first-class mail subsidize third-class mail, and long-haul airline rates subsidize short-haul rates. These pricing policies forced users of the profitable service to subsidize users of the unprofitable service. When these users are firms that compete with firms in other countries where regulators do not require cross subsidization, international competitiveness can be reduced. Furthermore, cross subsidizing is never welfare maximizing. Instead, it reduces the sum of producer and consumer surplus because price exceeds marginal cost in some lines of output but is less than marginal cost in others.

Protection from Competition. Third, the record of postwar government intervention into regulated industries seemed poorer in practice than its supporters had predicted. Research by the University of Chicago Nobel Laureate George Stigler (1911–1991) and others established that in many industries, regulatory bodies were "captured" by the very firms that they were supposed to be regulating. As a result, the regulatory bodies that were meant to ensure competition often acted to enforce monopoly practices that would have been illegal if instituted by the firms themselves.

For example, Canadian and U.S. railroad rates were originally regulated in order to keep profits down by establishing schedules of *maximum* rates. By the 1930s, however, concern had grown over the depressed economic condition of the railroads and the emerging vigorous competition from trucks and barges. The regulators then became the protectors of the railroads, permitting them to establish *minimum* rates for freight of different classes, allowing price discrimination, and encouraging other restrictive practices.

The regulators also advocated including trucking under the regulatory umbrella. Restricting entry into trucking and setting minimum rates for trucks was unmistakably designed to protect the producers, not the consumers. The only reason for regulating the large carriers was to control their competition with the railroads. Regulation limited the big road carriers' routes and set *floors* to the prices they could charge. As a result, they became targets for small, unregulated truckers, who could cut rates and thus draw away customers without fear of retaliation. To eliminate the rate competition, regulation was extended to small truckers.

Airline regulation in Canada and the United States provides another example. When airline routes and fares were first regulated, it was possible to argue that demand was too low to permit effective competition among many firms. Whatever the validity of that argument in earlier times, by the mid 1960s the regulation was plainly protecting the industry, allowing it to charge higher fares, earn higher profits, and pay higher wages than it would under more competitive conditions. For decades, Canadian and U.S. regulation of airline prices consistently prevented price competition. For example, until recently airlines other than Air Canada and Canadian Airlines were prevented from introducing cheap fares between Canada and Europe. This regulation could not be explained as protecting the interests of passengers against the predatory behaviour of the carriers.

Why did regulatory bodies shift from protecting consumers to protecting firms? One reason is that the regulatory commissions were gradually captured by the firms they were supposed to regulate. In part, this capture was natural enough. When regulatory bodies were hiring staff, they needed people who were knowledgeable in the industries they were regulating. Where better to go than to people who had worked in these industries? Naturally, these people tended to be sympathetic to firms in their own industries. Also, because many of them aspired to go back to those industries once they had gained experience within the regulatory bodies, they were not inclined to arouse the wrath of industry officials by imposing policies that were against the firms' interests.

Deregulation and Privatization

The 1980s witnessed a movement in many advanced industrial nations to reduce the level of government control over industry. Various experiences in these countries have been pushing in this direction:

- The realization that regulatory bodies often sought to reduce, rather than increase, competition

- The dashing of the hopes that publicly owned industries would work better than privately owned firms in the areas of efficiency, productivity growth, and industrial relations

- The realization that replacing a private monopoly with a publicly owned one would not greatly change the industry's performance and that replacing privately owned oligopolists by a publicly owned monopoly might actually worsen the industry's performance

- The awareness that falling transportation costs and revolutions in data processing and communications exposed local industries to much more widespread international competition than they had previously experienced domestically

The natural outcomes of these revised views were deregulation, intended, among other things, to leave prices and entry free to be determined by private decisions, and the privatization of publicly operated activities such as municipal garbage collection and the operation of local transit services.

Privatization went a long way in the United Kingdom. In the United States, where regulation rather than government ownership had been the adopted policy, many industries were deregulated. In Canada, hundreds of crown corporations that the government had acquired for a variety of reasons, but were neither natural monopolies nor operating in highly concentrated industries, were sold off. Also, many large crown corporations operating in oligopolistic industries, such as Air Canada, Petro Canada, and Canadian National, were privatized. (In 1995, the federal government began exploring the privatization of the air traffic control network and the various ports.) Also, many industries, such as airlines and gas and oil, were deregulated. Prices were freed, to be set by the firms in the industries, and entry was no longer restricted by government policy.

The effects (and thus the wisdom) of these changes are the subject of both economic analysis and political debate. A considerable lapse of time is needed, however, before any industry settles into a stable post-regulation pattern, at which point a more informed debate about the effects of deregulation can take place.

INTERVENTION TO KEEP FIRMS COMPETING

The least stringent form of government intervention is designed neither to force firms to sell at particular prices nor to regulate the conditions of entry and exit; it is designed, instead, to create conditions of competition by preventing firms from merging unnecessarily or from engaging in anticompetitive practices such as colluding to set monopoly prices. This is referred to as **competition policy**. Here the policy seeks both to create the most competitive market structure possible and to prevent firms from reducing competition by engaging in certain forms of cooperative behaviour. We discuss the details of Canadian competition policy in the next section.

CANADIAN COMPETITION POLICY

Laws designed for the purposes of preventing anticompetitive behaviour are called **combine laws** in Canada. They have provided the main thrust of Canadian competition policy since its inception in the nineteenth century. They prohibit monopolies, attempts to monopolize, and conspiracies in restraint of trade. Throughout the history of Canadian competition policy, legislation has been directed chiefly at the misuse of market power by single firms or groups of firms and only rarely at mergers per se.

This acceptance of the need for relatively large firms in the business sector was partly a function of the small size of the Canadian economy in the days when most production was solely for the domestic market. Firms that were large enough to exploit the available economies of scale were likely to be large in relation to the total market. This meant that there would be fewer firms in Canadian industries dominated by scale effects than would be found in similar industries in such relatively large economies as the United States.

THE EVOLUTION OF CANADIAN POLICY

The first Canadian combine laws were adopted in 1889 and 1890, when legislation made it an offense to combine, to agree to lessen competition unduly, or to restrain trade. Because the proscribed behaviour was illegal, an offense was a criminal act to be handled by the criminal justice system. The laws have been changed frequently since that time, but their basic procompetition stance still prevails in current legislation.

By the 1950s, Canadian anticombine laws had evolved to make illegal three broad classes of activity:

- combinations, such as price-fixing agreements that unduly lessen competition

- mergers or monopolies that may operate to the detriment of the public interest

- unfair trade practices

Many cases of unfair trade practices were successfully pursued under these laws, but compared to the United States, few cases were brought against mergers, and none of those that were brought were successful. The reason most often cited for this lack of success was the inability of criminal legislation to cope with complex economic issues. Under criminal law, the government must prove *beyond a reasonable doubt* that the accused party has committed the offense. As an added complication, Canadian courts have been much less willing than American courts to assess economic evidence.

A major review of Canadian legislation was undertaken in the late 1960s by the now-disbanded Economic Council of Canada. Its recommendations, published in a report in 1969, together with those of a committee of experts appointed by the then-named Department of Consumer and Corporate Affairs, formed the basis of the amendments to the Combines Investigation Act that are still in force. Of the recommendations that were accepted, some were put into effect in 1976 and the remainder in 1986.

The 1976 amendments included several provisions:

- extending the Combines Investigation Act to service industries

- allowing *civil* (rather than criminal) actions to be brought for damages resulting from contravention of the act

- strengthening legislation against misleading advertising

Claims about product quality must now be based on adequate tests. Advertising a product at a bargain price when the supplier does not supply the product in reasonable quantities is prohibited. Also prohibited is the supplying of a product at a price higher than the advertised price. In 1992, the court levied a record fine against one individual of $500,000 for seriously misleading advertising. Also, the Restrictive Trade Practices Commission was given the power to protect customers by prohibiting suppliers from (1) refusing to supply without good

reason, (2) requiring exclusive dealerships, (3) restricting the way a good is sold, or (4) requiring tied sales. As a result, retailing practices for many goods have changed considerably.

In 1986, after four previous attempts had failed, the final set of amendments to the Combines Investigation Act were passed. The resulting Act—now called the Competition Act—has three central themes: economic efficiency, adaptability, and international trade. The new Act creates a specialized Competition Tribunal to deal with civil matters now that competition policy has been taken out of the sphere of the criminal law. This tribunal is empowered to hear applications and issue orders in respect of reviewable practices contained in the Act.

The Competition Tribunal can also accept consent orders from the director of investigations on terms agreed on by the parties involved without hearing further evidence. When this happens, Canadian procedures, which used to be very public ones (what economists call *transparent*), now go on very much behind closed doors in private negotiations between the firms involved and the Director of Investigations. Furthermore, in the important case of the takeover of Texaco Oil Company by Imperial Oil, a carefully worked out agreement among the parties and the director of investigations was seriously amended by the tribunal. This showed that the tribunal was unwilling merely to rubber-stamp agreements worked out behind the scenes under the auspices of the director.

Perhaps the most important of the 1986 amendments was the one which placed mergers under civil (rather than criminal) law—the statutory test being whether or not the merger "substantially lessens competition." For the first time in Canada, economic considerations are stated to be directly relevant in judging the acceptability of a merger. When reviewing a merger, the Director of Investigations is obliged to consider such things as effective competition after the merger, the degree of foreign competition, barriers to entry, the availability of substitutes, and the financial state of the merging firms. Furthermore, an allowable defense of a merger is that the gains in efficiency more than offset any reductions in competition.

This new merger legislation has had some substantial effects on business mergers for the first time in the history of Canadian competition policy. Many firms have consulted with the Director of

Investigations before concluding a merger. As a result, some proposed mergers have been amended, and a few have been abandoned. Many mergers that have gone forward have been investigated, and the terms of some have been substantially modified.

Several provisions of the Act have been challenged in the courts, and many times these cases reached the Supreme Court of Canada. In summarizing the effects of the Supreme Court's rulings, the Director of Investigation and Research of the Bureau of Competition Policy had this to say:[6]

> The recent case law, together with the release of enforcement guidelines concerning mergers (April 1991), price discrimination (September 1992), predatory pricing (May 1992) and misleading advertising (September 1991), have considerably advanced the important objectives of providing guidance to the business and legal communities with respect to the enforcement of Canada's competition law. Enforcement guidelines, in particular, have become an important

tool in the Bureau of Competition Policy's efforts towards articulating and clarifying enforcement policies and practices.

Looking Forward

The 1986 Competition Act will not be the end of the evolution of Canadian competition policy, but it appears to have marked the end of a major chapter. Canadian legislation has for a long time provided substantial protection to consumers against the misuse of market power by large firms. For the first time, it now also seems to provide some substantial protection against the creation, through mergers, of market power that is not justified by gains to efficiency or international competitiveness. Many observers are optimistic that these laws, no doubt to be further refined in the future, will provide more protection to consumers than direct government intervention did—either through government ownership of particular firms or through government control of prices and conditions of entry.

SUMMARY

A. ECONOMIC EFFICIENCY

- Economists distinguish two main kinds of efficiency: productive and allocative.
- Productive efficiency exists for given technology when whatever output is being produced is being produced at the lowest attainable cost. This requires, first, that firms be on, rather than above, their relevant cost curves and, second, that all firms in an industry have the same marginal cost.
- Allocative efficiency is achieved when it is impossible to change the mix of production in such a way as to make someone better off without making someone else worse off. The allocation of resources will be efficient when each product's price equals its marginal cost.
- Perfect competition achieves both productive and allocative efficiency. Productive efficiency is achieved because the same forces that lead to long-run equilibrium lead to production at the lowest attainable cost. Allocative efficiency is achieved because in competitive equilibrium, price equals marginal cost for every product.
- The economic case against monopoly rests on its allocative inefficiency, which arises because profit maximization for a monopolist implies that price exceeds marginal cost. Some economists (notably Joseph Schumpeter) have argued that the incentive to innovate is so much greater under monopoly that monopoly is to be preferred to perfect competition, despite its allocative inefficiency. Though few modern economists go that far, the empirical evidence suggests that technological change and innovation can to a measurable extent be traced to the efforts of large firms operating in oligopolistic industries.

B. ECONOMIC REGULATION TO PROMOTE EFFICIENCY

- There are two broad types of policies designed to promote allocative efficiency in imperfectly competitive markets. These can be divided into *economic regulations* and *competition policy*. Economic regulation is used both in the case of a natural monopoly and in the case of an oligopolistic industry. Competition policy applies more to the latter.

---

[6]Public Lecture, Fordham Corporate Law Institute, New York, October 22, 1992.

- Efficient operation of natural monopolies requires that price be set equal to short-run marginal cost (marginal-cost pricing) and that investment be undertaken whenever that price exceeds the full long-run marginal cost of production. Average-cost pricing results in too little output in the short run and too little investment in the long run in falling-cost industries and too much output and too much investment in rising-cost industries.
- Direct control of pricing and entry conditions of some key oligopolistic industries has been common in the past, but deregulation is reducing such control. The move to deregulation is largely the result of the experiences that oligopolistic industries are a major engine of growth, as long as their firms are kept competing; that direct control of such industries has produced disap-

pointing results in the past; and that forced cross subsidization can have serious consequences for some users.

C. CANADIAN COMPETITION POLICY

- Canadian combine laws have always recognized the need for firms that are large in relation to the domestic market if economies of scale and scope are to be exploited. Such laws seek to restrict growth in size through mergers where the size is not justified by efficiencies and seek to prevent the unwarranted exploitation of market power.
- In 1976, such laws were removed from the criminal code, where enforcement proved difficult, and placed in the civil code, where enforcement appears to be easier.

KEY CONCEPTS

Productive and allocative efficiency	The inefficiency of monopoly	Regulation and effects on innovation
Consumer and producer surplus	Regulation of natural monopolies	Deregulation
The efficiency of competition	Marginal- and average-cost pricing	Canadian competition policy

---

DISCUSSION QUESTIONS

1. Suppose that allocative inefficiency of some economy amounts to 5 percent of the value of production. What does this statement mean? If it is true, would consumers *as a whole* be better off if policy measures were successful in moving the economy to an allocatively efficient outcome? Would *every* consumer be better off if the economy moved to an allocatively efficient outcome?

2. If the many plants producing a product were built at different times, with different levels of capacity and different cost curves, is it possible that the industry can ever be productively efficient? Use a diagram of the various firms' marginal cost curves to show why or why not.

3. When theme parks charge a price of admission and then a price for each ride, what type of pricing policy are they following? What alternative pricing policies

might be available? What are the advantages or disadvantages of each policy to the operators?

4. Would combine laws be necessary in an economy of perfect competition? Would they be beneficial in an economy of natural monopoly?

5. Evaluate the wisdom of having the Bureau of Competition Policy use profits as a measure of monopoly power in deciding whether to prosecute a case. Would such a rule be expected to affect the behaviour of firms with high profits? In what ways might any changes induced by such a rule be socially beneficial, and in what ways might they be socially harmful?

6. It is often asserted that whenever a regulatory agency is established, ultimately it will become controlled by the people whom it was intended to regu-

late. (This argument raises the question of who regulates the regulators.) Can you identify why this might happen? How might the integrity of regulatory boards be protected?

7. The chapter identifies several strategies for dealing with natural monopolies and their associated inefficiencies. Alternatively, assume that you are a regulator and that the monopoly you face is able to price discriminate—perhaps perfectly. Does this change the options you have for encouraging the efficient level of production? Would you choose to use this additional option? Why or why not?

8. Until 1983, AT&T was the sole provider of long-distance telephone service in the United States—a position enforced by U.S. federal law. What are some arguments that might have been in favour of supporting such a monopoly with government action early in this century? Which of these arguments do you think are

no longer valid? What has been the consequence of such structural changes?

9. "Canadian air travellers opting for U.S. carriers were [partly] responsible for Canadian airlines deregulation."—C. D. Howe Institute.

   "Canadian consumers crossing the border to buy cheap U.S. agricultural products may be responsible for the end of supply management in Canada."—Canadian economist

   What market forces lie behind each of these quotations? What difficulties do they reveal for the regulation of particular industries?

10. "Allocative efficiency is really about whether the economy 'has the quantities right'—it is not really about prices at all. Prices are only important in a discussion about allocative efficiency because *in a free market* changes in prices bring about the efficient allocation of resources." Comment.

CHAPTER 14

INSIDE THE FIRM

Up to now, we have abstracted from much of the rich detail that distinguishes one firm from another, treating all firms merely as entities that assemble resources to produce goods and services with the ultimate objective of maximizing profits. But other than profit maximization, we have said nothing about what goes on inside firms, about how firms raise the necessary financial capital to conduct their business, or about the potentially different roles of managers versus owners.

In this chapter, we look at some of the details that are important in specific situations. We look in particular at how firms are organized and financed. We also see how the markets of many firms have expanded from just the country in which they are located to include international sales which, in many cases, now cover the entire world. We also consider why the management of firms may not succeed in maximizing profits and what may happen if they do not.

THE ORGANIZATION OF FIRMS

FORMS OF BUSINESS ORGANIZATION

There are three major forms of business organization in the private sector: the single proprietorship, the partnership, and the corporation. In the **single proprietorship,** one owner makes all the decisions and is personally responsible for all of the firm's actions and debts. In the **partnership,** there are two or more joint owners, each of whom may make binding decisions and may be personally responsible for all of the firm's actions and debts. In the **corporation,** the firm has a legal existence separate from that of the owners. The owners are the firm's shareholders, and they risk only the amount of money that they put up to purchase their shares. The owners elect a board of directors, which hires managers to run the firm under the board's supervision.

In manufacturing, transportation, public utilities, and finance, corporations do almost all of the nation's business. In trade and construction, they do about one-half of the total business. Only in agriculture and in services is the corporation relatively unimportant, and its importance has been increasing in these sectors as well.

The Single Proprietorship and the Partnership

The major advantage of the single proprietorship is that the owner is the boss who maintains full control over the firm. The disadvantages are, first, that the size of the firm is limited by the amount of capital that the owner can personally raise and, second, that the owner is personally responsible by law for all debts of the firm; this is called *unlimited liability.*

The partnership overcomes to some extent the first disadvantage of the single proprietorship but not the second. Ten partners may be able to finance a much bigger enterprise than one owner could, but

they are still subject to unlimited liability. Each partner is fully liable for all of the debts of the firm. Partnerships are traditional in many professions, including law, dentistry, engineering, and (until recently) brokerage. Partnerships survive in these professions partly because they depend heavily on a relationship of trust between owners and clients, and the partners' unlimited liability for one another's actions is thought to enhance public confidence in the firm.

The **limited partnership,** which has two classes of partners, general and limited, provides protection against some of the risks of the general partnership. The firm's *general partners,* who are responsible for the operation of the firm, have unlimited liability; the firm's *limited partners* are liable only for the amount that they have invested; this is called **limited liability.** Limited partners can neither participate in the running of the firm nor make agreements on its behalf.

The Corporation

The corporation is regarded by law as an entity separate from the individuals who own it. It can enter into contracts, sue and be sued, own property, contract debts, and generally incur obligations that are the legal obligations of the corporation but *not* of its owners. The corporation's right to be sued may not seem to be an advantage; but it is, because it allows others to enter into enforceable contracts with the corporation that otherwise would not take place.

Although some corporations are owned by just a few persons, who also manage the business, the most important type of corporation is one that sells shares to the general public. The people who invest their money by buying its stock, called its **stockholders** or **shareholders,** are the corporation's owners. All profits belong to the stockholders. Profits that are paid out to them are called **dividends;** profits that are retained to be reinvested in the firm's operations are called **undistributed profits** or **retained earnings.**

Stockholders, who are entitled to one vote for each share that they own, elect a board of directors. This board of directors defines general policy and hires senior managers whose job it is to translate this general policy into detailed decisions. This chain of command, from owner to director to manager, gives rise to what is called a *principal-agent problem—* wherein managers do not always have the incentive to act in the best interests of the shareholders. The principal-agent problem is discussed later in this chapter.

Should the corporation go bankrupt, the personal liability of any one stockholder is limited to whatever money that stockholder has actually invested in the firm. Thus from a stockholder's viewpoint, one of the most important aspects of the corporation is its limited liability.

The limited liability corporation was one of the great institutional inventions of early capitalism. Its advantage over the proprietorship or partnership is that it can raise capital from a large number of individuals. Each of the individuals who invest money in the firm shares in the firm's profits but has no personal liability beyond risking the loss of the amount invested. Thus investors know how much they have at risk. Because shares are easily transferred from one person to another, a corporation has a continuity of life that is unaffected by changes in investors. Without limited liability, the large amounts of capital needed for many trading and manufacturing enterprises would have been difficult if not impossible to amass.

Fifty years ago, most corporations had a physical presence in only one country. Of course, many corporations exported some or even all of their production, and some corporations imported some of their inputs, but they did not produce outside of the country in which they were incorporated. Today, a great deal of production takes place in **transnational corporations (TNCs)**, which have a physical presence in more than one country. This development has many important implications for the functioning of the economy. TNCs are discussed later in this chapter.

THE RISE OF THE MODERN CORPORATION

The direct predecessors of the modern corporation were the English chartered companies of the sixteenth century. The Muscovy Company, chartered in 1555; the East India Company, chartered in 1600; and the Hudson's Bay Company, chartered in 1609 and still operating in Canada nearly 400 years later, are famous examples of early joint-stock ventures with limited liability. Their need for many investors to finance a ship that would not return with its cargo for years—if it returned at all—made this form of organization desirable.

In the next three centuries, the need to commit large amounts of capital for long periods of time and to diversify risks was felt in other fields, and charters were granted for insurance, turnpikes and canals, and banks, as well as for foreign trade. Exploiting the new techniques of the Industrial Revolution required the growth of large firms in many branches of manufacturing. The increasing need for large firms led to the passage of laws permitting incorporation with limited liability *as a matter of right rather than as a special grant of privilege*. Such laws became common in England and in North America during the late nineteenth century.

In their widely-read book, *How the West Grew Rich*, economic historians Nathan Rosenberg and L. E. Birdzell argue the importance of these institutional innovations in response to changing circumstances. Countries that develop new institutions that are better suited to the circumstances of the changing world environment, and in particular to the rapid developments in information and communication technology, may gain a large competitive advantage; some commentators argue that new management techniques and industrial structure explain much of Japan's rapid growth in the past quarter century.

THE FINANCING OF FIRMS

The money that a firm raises for carrying on its business is sometimes called its **financial capital** (or *money capital*). This is distinct from its **real capital** (or *physical capital*), the physical assets of the firm that constitute plant, equipment, and inventories. Financial capital may be broken down into **equity capital,** which refers to funds provided by the owners of the firm, and **debt,** which refers to the funds that have been borrowed from persons or institutions who are not owners of the firm.

Use of the term *capital* is sometimes confusing—economists use *capital* to refer to an amount of money, but they also use it to refer to a physical input to the production process (like plant and equipment). Fortunately, it is usually clear from the context which concept is being referred to. Notice also that the two uses are not entirely independent, for much of the financial capital raised by a firm will be used to purchase the physical capital that the firm requires for production.

Equity Financing

The firm can raise equity capital in two ways. One is to sell newly issued shares. The other is to reinvest, or plow back, some of its own profits. Although shareholders do not receive reinvested profits directly as their dividend income, they benefit from the rise in value of their shares (called *capital gains*) that occurs if the funds are reinvested profitably. Reinvestment has become an important source of funds in modern times.

Debt Financing

Firms can also raise money by issuing debt, either by selling bonds or by borrowing from financial institutions. A **bond** is a promise to pay interest each year and to repay the principal at a stated time in the future (say, 20 years hence). Bank loans are often short-term; sometimes the firm even commits to repaying the principal on demand. Debtholders are *creditors*, not owners, of the firm: They have loaned money to the firm in return for the firm's promise to pay interest on the loan and, of course, to repay the principal. The commitment to make interest payments is a legal obligation that must be met independently of whether profits are made. Many firms that would have survived a temporary crisis had all their capital been equity-financed have been forced into bankruptcy because they could not meet their contractual obligations to pay interest to their creditors. Creditors have the first claim on the firm's funds. Only when they have been repaid in full can the stockholders attempt to recover anything for themselves.

THE GOALS OF MODERN FIRMS

One hundred years ago, the single-proprietor firm, whose manager was its owner, was common in many branches of industry. In such firms, the single-minded pursuit of profits would be expected. Today, however, ownership is commonly diversified among thousands of stockholders, and the firm's managers are rarely its owners. Arranging matters so that managers always act in the best interests of stockholders is, as we shall see, anything but straightforward.

Thus there is potential for managers to maximize something other than profits.

THE SEPARATION OF OWNERSHIP FROM CONTROL

In corporations, the stockholders elect directors, and those directors then appoint managers. Directors are supposed to represent stockholders' interests and to determine broad policies that the managers will carry out. To conduct the complicated business of running a large firm, a full-time professional management group must be given broad powers of decision making. Although managerial decisions can be reviewed from time to time, they cannot be closely monitored on a day-to-day basis. The links between the directors and the managers are typically weak enough so that top management often truly controls the corporation over long periods of time.

As long as directors have confidence in the managerial group, they accept and ratify their proposals. Stockholders in turn elect and reelect directors who are proposed to them. If the managerial group does not satisfy the directors' expectations, it may be replaced. Until recently, boards of directors replaced managers only very rarely. In the past few years, boards have become somewhat more active, and in a number of cases, the top management of major firms has been removed by directors. Examples of leadership changes initiated by board action include the replacement of CEOs at GM, Eastman Kodak, IBM, and American Express. Still, such action remains unusual.

Within fairly broad limits, then, effective control of the corporation's activities generally resides with the managers. Although the managers are legally employed by the stockholders, they remain largely independent of them. Indeed, the management group typically asks for, and gets, the *proxies* of enough stockholders to elect directors who will reappoint it, and thus it perpetuates itself in office. (A proxy authorizes a person who is attending a stockholders' meeting to cast a stockholder's vote.) In the vast majority of cases, nearly all votes cast are in the form of proxies.

None of this matters unless the managers pursue different interests from those of the stockholders. Do the interests of the two groups diverge? To study this question, we need to look at what is called principal-agent theory.

PRINCIPAL-AGENT THEORY

If you (the *principal*) hire a girl down the block (your *agent*) to mow your lawn while you are away, all you can observe is how the lawn looks when you come back. She could have mowed it every 10 days, as you agreed, or she could have waited until two days before you were due home and mowed it only once. By prevailing on a friend or a neighbor to *monitor* your agent's behaviour, you could find out what she actually did, but only at some cost.

When you visit a doctor for a diagnosis and for treatment of your lower back pain, it is almost impossible for you to monitor the physician's effort and diligence on your behalf. You have not been to medical school, and much of what the physician does will be a mystery to you.

This latter situation is close to the relationship that exists between stockholders and managers. The managers have information and expertise that the stockholders do not have—indeed, that is why they are the managers. The stockholders can observe profits, but they cannot directly observe the managers' efforts. To complicate matters further, even when the managers' behaviour can be observed, the stockholders do not generally have the expertise to evaluate whether that behaviour was the best available. Everyone can see how well the firm performs, but it takes very detailed knowledge of the firm and the industry to know how well it *could have performed*. Boards of directors, who represent the firm's stockholders, can acquire some of the relevant expertise and monitor managerial behaviour, but, again, this is costly.

These examples illustrate the **principal-agent problem**—the problem of designing mechanisms that will induce agents to act in their principals' interests. In general, unless there is close monitoring of the agent's behaviour, the problem cannot be completely solved. Hired managers (like hired gardeners) will generally wish to pursue their own goals. They cannot ignore profits because if they perform badly enough, they will lose their jobs. Just how much latitude they have to pursue their own goals at the expense of profits will depend on many things, including the degree of competition in the industry and the possibility of takeover by more profit-oriented management.

Principal-agent analysis shows that when a firm's ownership and control are separated, the self-interest of agents will tend to make profits lower than in a "perfect" world in which principals act as their own agents.

We know that in the case of firms, the principals (the stockholders) are interested in maximizing profits. What different motives might their agents (the managers) have, and what market forces might limit their ability to act on these motives?

Sales Maximization

If agents do not maximize profits on behalf of the principals, what do they do? One alternative is that they seek to maximize *sales*. Suppose that the managers need to make some minimum level of profits to keep the stockholders satisfied. Beyond this, they are free to maximize their firm's sales revenue. This might be a sensible policy on the part of management because salary, power, and prestige all rise with the size of a firm as well as with its profits. Generally, the manager of a large, normally profitable corporation will earn a salary that is considerably higher than the salary earned by the manager of a small but highly profitable corporation.

The sales-maximization hypothesis says that managers of firms seek to maximize their sales revenue, subject to a profit constraint.

Sales maximization subject to a profit constraint leads to the prediction that a firm's managers will sacrifice some profits by setting price below and output above their profit-maximizing levels. See Figure 14-1 for a demonstration of this point.

Failure to Minimize Costs

The sales-maximization hypothesis implies that the firm's managers will choose to produce more than the profit-maximizing level of output. It is also possible that firms will produce their chosen output at greater than minimum cost. Why would a firm's managers fail to minimize costs?

There are many possible answers, but the most straightforward one is that minimizing costs can demand a great deal of detailed managerial attention, and if management can avoid doing so, it would prefer not to make the necessary effort. Moreover, it is usually costly for a firm to change its routine behaviour. If this is so, one firm may operate at a higher cost than another, but it will still not be worthwhile for the first firm to copy the behaviour of the second firm. The *transactions costs* of making the change

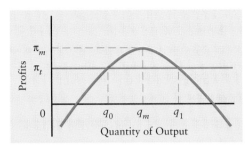

FIGURE 14-1

Output of the Firm Under Profit Maximizing, Sales Maximizing, and Satisficing Behaviour

The "best" level of output depends on the motivation of the firm. The curve shows the level of profits associated with each level of output. A profit-maximizing firm produces output q_m and earns profit π_m. A sales-maximizing firm, with a minimum profit constraint of π_t, produces the output q_1.

A satisficing firm with a target level of profits of π_t is willing to produce any output between q_0 and q_1. Thus satisficing allows a range of outputs on either side of the profit-maximizing level, whereas sales maximization results in a higher output than profit maximization.

could outweigh the benefits. As with sales maximization, pressure from stockholders, competition from other firms, and threat of takeover will limit the extent to which economic or technological inefficiency can survive, but they may not eliminate inefficiency.

THE MARKET FOR CORPORATE CONTROL

Managers who stray too far from profit maximization face the risk that their firms will be taken over by more profit-oriented ownership. **Mergers** and **takeovers** can be interpreted as transactions in a **market for corporate control.** This market, like any other, has both buyers (people who would acquire the rights to control a firm) and sellers (the current stockholders of the firm). As in other markets, the expected outcome is that the assets being bought and sold will wind up in the hands of the parties who value them most. These will tend to be those who can come closest to maximizing the firm's profits.

A takeover begins when the management of the acquiring firm makes a **tender offer** to the stockholders of the target firm. Tender offers are promises to purchase stock at a specified price for a limited period of time, during which the acquiring firm hopes to gain control of the target company. Typically, the prices offered are considerably higher than the prevailing stock market price. This action is called a *hostile takeover* when the current management of the target firm opposes it.

Do takeovers improve economic efficiency? The main argument in their favour is that after a takeover, the new management can make more efficient use of the target firm's assets. The acquiring firm should be able to exploit profit opportunities that the target management is not exploiting. This can be done by such means as operating the target firm more efficiently, providing funds that the target firm could not obtain, or providing access to markets that would be too expensive for the target firm to open up on its own. If this is true, the value of the target firm will rise in response to a takeover, reflecting the expectation of increased future profits.[1] Further, if the *acquiring* firm's managers are acting in the best interest of *their* stockholders, the value of the acquiring firm should also rise when it is successful in a takeover bid.

Although stock values of acquiring and acquired firms show considerable variability following takeovers, most economists believe that takeovers provide a useful discipline that helps to restrain managers from acting in non-profit-maximizing ways. Such discipline helps to improve the allocation of resources as managers are under pressure to use the assets under their management in the most efficient way. In the absence of evidence to show that takeovers reduce economic efficiency (either productive or allocative), most economists would probably favour leaving the market for corporate control free from major government intervention.

NONMAXIMIZING THEORIES

Many students of corporate behaviour, particularly economists based in business schools, criticize the profit-maximization assumption from a perspective different from that given by principal-agent theory. They argue that there are other reasons for doubting that modern corporations are "simple profit-maximizing computers." They believe that corporations

---

[1] Any takeover bid is likely to raise the value of a firm on the stock market. A profitable takeover raises these values permanently; a misjudged takeover does so only temporarily.

are *profit-oriented* in the sense that, other things being equal, more profits are preferred to less profits. They do not believe, however, that corporations are profit *maximizers.*

A major group of critics of profit maximization develop their argument as follows: Firms operate in highly uncertain environments. Their long-term success or failure is determined largely by their ability to administer innovation and change. But the risks of innovation are large, and the outcomes are highly uncertain. Rational firms therefore tend to be quite risk-averse. They develop routines of behaviour that they follow as long as they are successful. Only when profits fall low enough to threaten their survival do they significantly change their course of action.

Supporters of this view argue on the basis of considerable evidence that firms react to the "stick" of threatened losses of existing profit more than to the "carrot" of possible increases in profit. Others argue that firms simply cannot handle the task of scrutinizing all possibilities, calculating the probable outcomes, and then choosing among these so as to maximize their expected profits. Instead, in their view, firms carry on with existing routines as long as these produce satisfactory profits, and only when profits fall to unacceptably low levels do the firms search for new ways of doing old things or new lines of activity.

One way of formalizing these views is the *theory of satisficing.* It was first put forward by Professor Herbert Simon of Carnegie-Mellon University, who in 1978 was awarded the Nobel Prize in Economics for his work on the behaviour of firms. He wrote, "We must expect the firm's goals to be not maximizing profits but attaining a certain level or rate of profit, holding a certain share of the market or a certain level of sales." In general, a firm is said to be **satisficing** if it does not change its behaviour, provided that a *satisfactory* (rather than optimal) level of performance is achieved.

According to the satisficing hypothesis, firms could produce any one of a range of outputs that produce profits at least equal to the target level. This contrasts with the unique output that is predicted by profit-maximizing theory. Figure 14-1 compares satisficing behaviour with sales- and profit-maximizing behaviour.

The theory of satisficing predicts not a unique level of output but a range of possible outputs that includes the profit-maximizing output.

THE IMPORTANCE OF NONMAXIMIZING BEHAVIOUR

An impressive array of empirical and theoretical evidence can be gathered in support of nonmaximizing theories. What would be the implications if they were accepted as being better theories of the behaviour of the economy than the "standard model," which is based on the assumption of profit maximization?

The Implications of Nonmaximizing Behaviour

To the extent that existing non-profit-maximizing theories are accurate, the economic system does not perform with the delicate precision that follows from profit maximization. Firms will not always respond quickly and precisely to small changes in market signals from either the private sector or government policy. Nor are they certain to make radical changes in their behaviour even when the profit incentives to do so are large.

The nonmaximizing theories imply that in many cases, firms' responses to small changes in market signals will be of uncertain speed and direction.

According to all existing theories, maximizing and nonmaximizing, firms will tend to sell more when demand increases and less when it decreases. They will also tend to alter their prices and their input mixes when they face sufficiently large changes in input prices. Moreover, there are limits to the extent to which the nonmaximizing behaviour can survive in the marketplace. Failure to respond to profit opportunities can lead to takeover by a more profit-oriented management. Although this does not mean that profits are being precisely maximized at all times, it does put real limits on the extent to which firms can ignore profits.

Profits are a potent force in the life and death of firms. The resilience of profit-maximizing theory and its ability to predict the economy's reactions to many major changes (such as the dramatic variations in energy prices that have occurred over the past two decades) suggest that firms are at least strongly motivated by the pursuit of profits.

Three key points are at issue here.

1. The extent to which firms respond predictably to changes in such economic signals as output and input prices, taxes, and subsidies

2. The extent to which nonmaximizing behaviour provides the opportunity for profit-oriented takeovers, mergers, and buyouts

3. The way in which firms manage very-long-run change

Regarding the third point, one of the most important lessons learned by economists in the past decade is that much oligopolistic competition takes place over the very-long run. How the firm performs relative to its domestic or foreign competitors with respect to product and process innovation will be the major determinant of its competitive performance over a decade or so. These matters require making decisions on highly uncertain issues. Many investigators believe that the performance of firms in these matters is best understood by theories that take account of the firm's organizational structure and the routines that it uses to guide its decision making.

Over the past decade or so, the question of how firms behave in detail has received renewed attention from both economists and organization theorists. Almost everyone in the field agrees that firms do not *exactly* maximize profits at all times and in all places. At the same time, almost everyone agrees that firms cannot stray too far from the goal of profit maximization. Just how far is too far depends on the circumstances in which firms operate and the mechanisms that firms' owners can use to influence managers. Just how much firms' nonmaximizing behaviour influences how they manage change is another important unsettled issue. These areas are at the frontier of current economic research.

Profit Maximization as an Evolutionary Equilibrium

U.S. economist Armen Alchian has suggested that in long-run equilibrium, firms will evolve to become profit maximizers. The basic argument is based on the principle of *survival of the fittest*. In a competitive environment, firms that pursue goals or adopt rules that are inconsistent with profit maximization will be unable to stay in business; firms that either choose or happen upon rules that are closer to profit maximization will displace those that do not. Eventually, only the profit-maximizing firms will survive in the marketplace.

A similar kind of argument can be applied to firms that operate in oligopolistic or monopolistic markets. Here it is not competition that forces the firm toward profit maximization in the long run but the possibility of a takeover. A firm that does not maximize profits will be less valuable than one that does maximize profits. Thus the non-profit-maximizing firm can be bought by profit-maximizing managers, who will increase its value as they increase its profits, as described earlier in this chapter.

Alchian's argument suggests the following conclusion:

Even if no firm starts out with the intention of maximizing profits, in the long run the firms that survive in the marketplace will tend to be the profit maximizers.

This view provides an apparent synthesis of maximizing and evolutionary theories of the firm. The distinction between the theories is not so stark as it might seem.

In contrast, many organization theorists point out that evolutionary equilibrium is unlikely ever to be achieved. As technology and tastes change over time, so does the behaviour that will maximize profits. Without a fixed target, a firm's behaviour will continually evolve (generally toward profit maximization) but will never reach an equilibrium. The target refuses to stay put.

Foreign investment

When takeovers involve a domestic firm being taken over by a foreign firm, a further consideration is added: How much should we worry about the nationality of the owners of firms that operate in our country? This question arises not only when foreign takeovers occur, but also when a domestic firm *merges* with a foreign firm. It pertains more generally to all **foreign direct investment (FDI)**—that is, investment which gives foreign owners control over the behaviour of firms in which the investment is made. In Canada's case, FDI gives foreign owners control over the decisions of producers located in Canada (just as Canadian FDI made abroad gives Canadian owners control over the decisions of producers located in foreign countries). In contrast, the other major category of foreign investment, called **portfolio investment**, involves no control. Major components of portfolio investment are foreign holdings of government and private-sector bonds. Portfolio investment does not usually arouse the popular concerns that are associated with FDI. The latter often causes great concern, whether it is the formation of a new foreign-owned firm in Canada, new investment by an existing foreign-owned firm (*greenfield* investment), or a takeover of a Canadian-owned firm by a foreign-owned firm (*brownfield* investment).

In the past, the major form of foreign investment was greenfield investment, and it is still important, for instance, in the establishment of Japanese transplant automobile factories in North America. In the last decade or so, more and more FDI has taken the form of mergers or acquisitions of domestically-owned firms by foreign-owned firms. Large companies have deemed it necessary to have a physical presence in each of what are called the triad set of countries: Canada and the United States; Japan and Southeast Asia; and the countries of Western Europe. Developing that presence is usually done through takeovers and mergers rather than by greenfield investment. More and more stand-alone companies found it hard to compete in the globalizing marketplace, so they welcomed mergers with firms operating throughout the triad.

For example, in 1991, 22 percent of the mergers in the United States involved at least one foreign-owned company, while the comparable figure in Canada was 73 percent. There are two interesting things about these figures. First, these figures are historically high for both countries—the participation of foreign-owned firms in mergers was significantly less 20 years earlier; this reflects the trend toward increasing globalization. Second, the much smaller size of the Canadian economy explains why, in a globalizing world, a higher proportion of Canadian than American mergers will involve foreign firms. Both figures illustrate the key development of the past two decades that much FDI took the form of international mergers as transnational corporations sought to position themselves in the markets of the world's major economies.

ATTITUDES TOWARD FOREIGN INVESTMENT

Foreign investment has long been a major factor in world development. The residents of newly settled areas, such as North and South America in the seventeenth, eighteenth, and nineteenth centuries, could not hope to generate enough savings to finance the rapid development of their vast potential. Investment funds were required in large amounts to build *infrastructure* (such as roads, dams, city halls, post offices, and bridges), *private productive facilities* (such as factories, machines, and offices), and *housing* both for rental and for ownership. In the first instance, the economic growth of all such countries was financed largely by foreign investment.

As these economies grew, they produced larger and larger flows of their own domestic saving. This saving financed an increasing proportion of domestic investment, helped to buy back much of the foreign-owned assets in their country, and provided a flow of foreign investment going to other, newer countries. This was the pattern in the United States, which was a net importer of capital from abroad until the early part of the twentieth century but became, as the century advanced, a net exporter of capital.[2]

The same pattern has been observed in Canada, but it has not yet gone as far as in the United States. This is due mainly to Canada's smaller size in relation to the investment needed to exploit its huge resources. Canada has always been a recipient of a great deal of foreign investment. As the Canadian economy grew, however, the flow of domestic saving increased. This increase in domestic saving led to an increasing proportion of new investment in Canada being financed by domestic rather than by imported capital. It also led to an increasing Canadian investment abroad as successful Canadian firms expanded into foreign markets and private Canadian investors added foreign investments to their asset portfolios.

Table 14-1 shows the stock of foreign direct investment in Canada (and the stock of Canada's direct investment abroad) as a share of the flow of Canadian GDP since 1960. As the table shows, the importance of foreign ownership in Canada has declined significantly since 1960. In 1960, the value of foreign-owned assets was about 35 percent of GDP, whereas by 1994 foreigners owned assets in Canada worth only 20 percent of Canadian GDP. Thus over the past 35 years, the Canadian economy has grown more quickly than has foreign ownership of domestic assets. Note also the increasing importance of Canada's ownership of assets located in foreign countries. In 1960, the value of foreign-located assets owned by Canadians amounted to only 5 per-

---

[2]In the 1980s the pattern was reversed, with the United States once again becoming a net importer of capital. By 1990, it was home to more foreign capital than any other country in the world.

TABLE 14-1
Foreign Direct Investment in Canada and Canadian
Direct Investment Abroad, 1960–1994

Year	Foreign Direct Investment as a percentage of Canadian GDP	Canadian Direct Investment Abroad as a percentage of Canadian GDP
1960	34.5	6.3
1970	30.8	7.0
1980	20.9	8.7
1990	19.6	13.7
1994	19.7	16.7

Expressed in terms of the size of the Canadian economy, foreign direct investment in Canada has been declining and Canadian direct investment abroad has been increasing. The numbers shown are the value of the *stocks* of foreign-owned assets in Canada (or Canadian-owned assets abroad) divided by the *flow* of Canadian GDP.

(*Source:* Statistics Canada, 67–202)

cent of GDP, but by 1994 the value of Canadian direct investment abroad was almost 17 percent of GDP. Thus over the past 35 years, Canadian direct investment abroad has grown much more quickly than the Canadian economy.

World Attitudes to Foreign Investment

World attitudes toward foreign investment have been fairly tolerant throughout most of the period since the Industrial Revolution. Most people saw such investment as a benign force leading to more rapid growth, both in total output and in output per person, than could be financed through domestic savings alone.

In the late 1950s and the 1960s, many countries became more hostile to foreign investment. The change in attitude was partly the result of the growth of what was then called the *multinational enterprise,* now called the *transnational corporation (TNC).* These are firms that have locations in more than one (and often many) countries. A domestic firm may engage in international trade by selling in many countries; a transnational corporation has production facilities in many countries. In the 1960s, the vast majority of the world's TNCs were U.S.-owned.

In the 1950s and 1960s, the rise of TNCs was seen in many parts of the world as an ominous development. People correctly perceived that TNCs would make it more difficult for individual countries to

maintain economic policies that differed from those of their trading partners. For example, TNCs have some ability, through internal accounting, to shift costs to areas where local tax laws permit the greatest cost write-offs and to shift profits to areas where profit taxes are lowest. They can also often shift research and development (R&D) to where tax advantages or subsidies are largest and then make the results of this R&D available throughout their entire organization—which often means throughout the entire world.

These powers imply an inevitable weakening of the power of the individual state. It also provides a pressing reason for the creation of larger political units such as the European Union (EU) to provide the political scope necessary to exercise some control over TNCs.

In the 1960s, the rise of TNCs also aroused worldwide concern over what was perceived as U.S. economic imperialism. Because many of the most successful early TNCs were U.S.-owned, many observers in other countries feared the spread of U.S. economic dominance and cultural influence. Influential books in Europe decried the growth of U.S. economic and cultural imperialism and urged that TNCs be kept out as a defense. Today, with North American firms often on the defensive against Japanese and European TNCs, the fear of U.S. dominance seems but a quaint reminder of the human tendency to think that whatever is happening now will persist forever.

TNCs have become increasingly important over the years and now account for the majority of international trade and foreign investment. Indeed, much international trade is between different units of the same TNC (intra-TNC trade). Also, the typical organization of a TNC has undergone changes. The typical form in earlier times was a highly centralized firm. Today, with the demands for specialized products carefully tailored to the specific needs of each country and with the ability to produce small runs of each product variation efficiently thanks to computer-assisted production, internationally decentralized organizations are becoming increasingly prevalent.

By the 1980s, world attitudes toward TNCs had become tolerant again. Several developments were responsible for this softening of attitudes. First, it was clear to industrial nations that TNCs were here to stay. As world trade became more and more globalized under the impact of the communication and computer revolutions, TNCs became increasingly important until it became apparent that no advanced country could do without them. Second, less-developed countries came to the same realization and put out a welcome mat. As the executive director of the United Nations centre on TNCs said:[3]

> The 1980s have witnessed major changes in the world production system, with TNCs being the principal forces shaping the future of technological innovation. At the same time, a more pragmatic and businesslike relationship between host governments and TNCs has emerged within the past decade. Many developing countries, burdened by debt and economic stagnation, have liberalized their policies towards TNCs while these corporations have displayed greater sensitivity to the development and economic goals of host countries. The era of confrontation has receded and been replaced by a practical search for a meaningful and mutually beneficial accommodation of interests.

Canadian Attitudes to Foreign Investment

Official Canadian views have matched these swings in world views. Until the 1960s, Canada welcomed foreign investment as a means to achieving economic growth that would have been impossible had it been required to rely on domestic saving alone. Then, in the 1960s, suspicion of foreign (particularly American) investment grew. This resulted in the formation of the Foreign Investment Review Agency (FIRA) in the 1970s. This agency had the right to screen all new foreign direct investment coming into Canada. It turned down about 5 percent of the applications that it reviewed—quite a high rejection rate by international standards. It imposed requirements with respect to domestic production and exports on many of the investments that it did accept. Its presence also discouraged some unknown number of other firms from applying in the first place, making its overall effect in limiting foreign investment in the country hard to discern.

In line with the change in world opinion toward TNCs in the 1980s, the Canadian government replaced FIRA with an organization called Investment Canada (which has since been replaced by the Investment Review Division within Industry Canada). With the demise of FIRA, Canadian officials announced that Canada once again welcomed foreign investment. Although the Canadian government still has the power to review foreign takeovers of Canadian firms, it has turned down no applications in the past dozen years. It has, however, insisted on some conditions before approving some deals. For example, when the Canadian laser company Lumonics was taken over by the Japanese conglomerate Sumatoma (because Lumonics could not raise sufficient capital in Canada), Investment Canada insisted on a number of assurances designed to keep the creative activities of Lumonics located in Canada.

In the Canada-U.S. Free Trade Agreement (FTA) which began in 1989, Canada agreed to raise the threshold of review of U.S. takeovers of Canadian firms from a firm size of $5 million to $150 million. Critics decried this reduction in ability to screen foreign takeovers of Canadian firms. Supporters pointed out, first, that fully 80 percent of nonfinancial capital in Canada was located in firms larger than $150 million and so was still subject to review and, second, that in return for this Canadian concession, the United States had in effect exempted Canadian firms wishing to operate in that country from any review that the United States might subsequently initiate.

FDI IN CANADA: FACTS AND DEBATES

Canada is still heavily reliant on foreign direct investment. During 1994, Canada received an inflow of foreign direct investment equal to $8 billion; by the end of that year, foreigners owned a total of $148 billion worth of plant, buildings, and equipment physically located in Canada. To put this number in perspective, (see Table 14-1) this value represented just under 20 percent of the *flow* of Canadian GDP in 1994.

Canada is not just a recipient of foreign direct investment; Canadian firms are also very active investors in foreign countries. During 1994, Canada made $9.1 billion worth of new foreign direct investment; by the end of that year, Canadians owned a total of $125.2 billion worth of physical capital lo-

---

[3]United Nations Centre on Transnational Corporations, *Transnational Corporations in World Development: Trends and Prospects* (New York: United Nations, 1988).

cated abroad (a value equal to almost 17 percent of Canadian GDP in 1994).

Not surprisingly—given Canada's proximity to the United States—there is a great deal of foreign investment which crosses the 49th parallel. Canada is the largest single host country for U.S. foreign investment. By the end of 1993, the accumulated stock of U.S. investment in Canada was $95 billion—about 68 percent of total FDI in Canada. The United States once accounted for over 75 percent of the stock of all foreign direct investment in Canada, but this share has been gradually declining for many years.

Many people are surprised to learn of the amount of Canadian direct investment made in the United States. Canadian foreign direct investment in the United States totaled $65 billion by the end of 1993 (about 52 percent of Canada's total direct investment abroad). The gap between the two countries' holdings in each other's investment has been steadily narrowing since 1975. In recent years, Canadian TNCs have been far more aggressive investors in the United States than vice versa. As a result, Canadian direct investment in the United States grew by over 800 percent in the period 1977–1993, while U.S. direct investment in Canada grew by only about 250 percent over the same period. If present trends continue, Canadian investors will own as much of the U.S. capital stock as U.S. investors own of the Canadian capital stock shortly after the start of the twenty-first century.

Potential Benefits of Foreign Investment

By and large, but with some notable exceptions, economists have been skeptical of the view that Canada loses by foreign investment. Among the benefits attributed to foreign investment are these:

- More total investment than could be possible if all investment had to be financed by domestic saving, hence more domestic production than could otherwise be achieved

- A higher rate of growth due to a more rapid rise in the capital available for each worker

- Participation in the world's division of labour as brought about by TNCs

- Transfer of superior technology and superior management and labour practices

- Higher wages through use of best-practice technology

The first two listed advantages are important in countries, such as Canada, where domestic saving is insufficient to finance the domestic investment needed to produce a high rate of economic growth.

The third point is key in today's globalized world. The growth of global production and globalized competition, with its attendant growth of the TNCs, means that many individual firms are developing a presence over the entire trading world. If ownership of TNCs is spread evenly over several major trading countries, no single country can expect to own all of the capital in the TNCs that are operating within its borders. So if Canada is to own substantial investment in other countries, it must expect the TNCs of other countries to own substantial investments within Canada.

The fourth point concerns the transfer of new technology related to new products and new production processes. These are developed at home by Canadian firms and are then used at home as well as being taken to foreign countries. They are also developed in foreign countries and then used there as well as being brought to Canada. Just as most economists see foreign trade as mutually beneficial, most see foreign direct investment (FDI) as mutually beneficial to the countries owning and receiving the investment. Where Canadian firms have superior technology, they can gain by using it to produce *wherever* it can be profitably employed. If foreign countries have superior technology, Canada gains when this technology is brought to Canada to provide income, employment, and new knowledge. For example, the Japanese technology of lean production, which proved superior to the older assembly-line techniques, was to a significant extent transferred to Canada through the operation of the so-called Japanese transplant automobile factories. As these techniques became more widely appreciated within Canada, their use spread more rapidly to Canadian-owned firms.

The more that best-practice technology is diffused throughout the world, the higher world production is and the larger are the benefits to trading among nations. As technological know-how has spread, world income and the volume of trade have risen greatly. Countries that take part in this trade have seen both their exports and their imports rising.

Today, trade and investment tend to go together, so that a rising volume of foreign trade brings with it a rising volume of FDI. Generally, both inward- and outward-bound FDI are part of the globalizing of competition, technology diffusion, and trade from which all trading nations tend to gain.

The fifth point concerns the high wages that are generally paid by firms using the best-practice technology. Normally, labour that is employed in firms that use less up-to-date technological processes earn lower wages than labour that is employed in firms using the most productive techniques. Generally, when TNCs come to a less-developed country bringing advanced technology, wages rise (though they do not always achieve the levels of advanced countries because the productivity of labour is held down by other characteristics of the country, such as poor infrastructure). This is clear when one looks at less-developed countries whose technology is well below the state of the art, but it is also true in advanced countries. This is the point that Harvard's Robert Reich makes when he argues that the location of TNCs is more important than their ownership. According to Reich, having TNCs located in one's country using the most productive techniques that produce the highest-valued products and pay the highest wages is more important than who owns these firms.

Alleged Costs of Foreign Investment

Among the alleged costs of foreign direct investment are:

- Profits earned by foreigners rather than domestic owners
- Loss of control over resource development
- Loss of control over one's own economy
- Loss of good managerial and research jobs to foreign locations favoured by TNCs.

We consider each of these in turn.

Loss of Profits to Foreigners.   Insofar as the industries are competitive, profits are merely normal returns on capital. If foreigners provide capital that domestic sources cannot or will not provide, they get only the normal return. Employment, wages, and many other benefits stay in Canada.

More recently, however, economists have been interested in the pure profits that accompany innovations in oligopolistic industries. If innovating firms can earn large profits, these profits accrue to the firms' owners. In this case, ownership matters. This is not, however, an argument for locating Canadian-owned enterprises in Canada and keeping foreign enterprises out. What matters is the *share* of those innovating enterprises that is owned domestically. Where they operate does not matter. Indeed, to maximize the profits that the Canadian owners earn from their firms' innovations, the firms should use their new technology everywhere in the world where it is profitable to do so. If Canadian firms lose out to foreign TNCs and own a shrinking share of these innovating enterprises, Canadian income will fall relative to foreign income. But it does not matter *where* that competition occurs. The result is the same whether these Canadian firms lose market share in foreign markets or in the Canadian market.

Loss of Control over Domestic Resources.   All industries in Canada are subject to Canadian law. For example, Canada can regulate the rate of resource extraction in oil and gas and impose that regulation equally on Canadian- and foreign-owned firms operating within Canada. It can also have tough environmental laws and others that impose requirements on all firms operating within Canada.

However, TNCs do pose a serious problem called *extraterritoriality*. This occurs when the laws of a TNC's home country are extended to cover the activities of the TNC in other countries. The United States, however, has championed the principle of extraterritoriality by sometimes trying to make U.S. multinationals that operate in other countries follow U.S. laws rather than host-country laws. Thus, for example, if the United States has prohibitions against trading with Cuba (or, as it did not so long ago, with China), it tries to apply these laws not only to foreign TNCs operating within the United States but also to U.S. TNCs operating in such foreign countries as Canada and Britain. Host countries have resisted these attempts by the United States to extend its legal jurisdiction beyond its own borders, and the issue remains unresolved.

Many people worried that the Canada-U.S. Free Trade Agreement (FTA) which began in 1989, and the NAFTA which followed it, would erode Canadian sovereignty with respect to control over TNCs. Defenders of the FTA argued that such concerns were based on a misunderstanding of the principle of "national treatment," which allows Canada and the United States each to impose its own requirements on firms operating within its borders. These requirements may differ between the two countries; all that is required by national treatment is that foreign and domestic firms be treated equally *within any one country*. The only thing neither country can do is use its laws to discriminate by applying tougher laws to foreign-owned than to domestically-owned firms. So the FTA and NAFTA would appear to have introduced no new reason why foreign investment should limit Canada's ability to control its economy and its environment as it wishes.

Loss of Key Activities.   Some industries are located in a country by virtue of natural advantages. For example, Canadian natural gas must be extracted in Canada, and Canadian lumber must be cut in Canada. Thus the gas and lumber industries are firmly rooted in Canada as long as supplies of these important natural resources exist. Other industries—high-tech ones are important examples—are much more flexible. They can be moved among countries to wherever the economic climate and economic policies are most favourable to them. The key characteristic of these industries is that they are knowledge-intensive. When head offices determine the location of R&D and other knowledge-intensive activities, they make decisions that influence the course of a country's economic development. They could conceivably direct the types of production with the highest values to their home countries and keep lower-value production, which produces lower wages, in host countries. But insofar as they are profit maximizers, they will choose the most profitable location, whether it be domestic or foreign.

A similar issue relates to what are called *key industries*. Some observers believe that certain industries have important *spillovers* to the rest of the economy. Keeping these key industries at home will favourably affect the value of economic activity elsewhere in the economy. If a foreign TNC takes over one of these key industries, it may relocate the industry to its own country, thereby harming the economy of the original country. Shipbuilding and steel production were thought to be key industries in the 1960s, and many people believe that automobiles and such high-tech industries as high-definition television and computers are key industries today.

These are important and unresolved issues. No one is sure how important these possibilities are.

Furthermore, it is not easy to see what practical policy measures should be recommended if these possibilities were shown to be significant.

What Could Be Done?

Suppose we conclude—when all aspects of the issue are considered—that foreign investment is harmful for Canada. What could be done?

It would be impractical to prohibit all, or even most, foreign investment. First, this would greatly reduce the amount of capital available in Canada, with adverse effects on Canadian economic growth. Second, this would deny Canada's participation in the large segment of international trade that is dominated by TNCs, most of which cannot be owned by Canadians. For a small trading nation such as Canada, with over 35 percent of its GDP generated by exports, that would be a serious matter.

Given the volume of Canadian savings, the most that could be done would be to redirect foreign investment from some industries into others. This would be done by discouraging foreign investment in some key industries, hoping both that Canadian investment would flow into these industries and that foreign investment would fill in the gaps where the Canadian investment would otherwise have gone. For such a policy to be successful, bureaucrats must be able to discern the areas where it is advantageous to prevent foreign investment, Canadian capital must flow into these areas, and foreign capital must fill the gaps created by the reallocation of Canadian investment. Such a policy is full of risks, of which the following are merely illustrative.

First, because Canadian investment did not flow into the designated activities in the first place, there is a risk that it may not do so after the restrictions are imposed. Second, there is a risk that the activities will be transferred abroad if foreign TNCs are prevented from engaging in them in Canada. This is particularly likely where a foreign takeover of a Canadian firm is designed to make it a part of a large international organization with the linkages necessary for the firm's success. In this case, the substitution is not of Canadian-owned for foreign-owned activity in Canada but rather of foreign-located for Canadian-located activity. Third, politicians and administrators must be able to identify and promote those activities that are best held in Canadian ownership. Large firms, such as Canadian Pacific, Air

Canada, and Noranda, are the ones that would cause the most political problems if they were taken over by foreigners. Unfortunately, these most visible and best-known companies are not necessarily the ones with the greatest potential payoff from restricting foreign ownership, since they are likely to be only normally profitable. If there is a case to hold ownership at home, it is likely to be stronger for small and midsize industries that are not yet household names but are at the forefront of industrial development. Yet it is not clear that these are the industries that the political process would hold at home if foreign investment were once again to be seriously controlled.

Conclusion

Throughout most of the world, the debate about the value of foreign investment is not as heated as it was a decade or two ago. Most countries have come to accept that foreign investment contributes to their economic growth. There is an awareness of how easy it is to kill the goose that lays the golden eggs by adopting attitudes and passing laws that drive TNCs to relocate elsewhere. It is also accepted that TNCs play a key part in today's globalized economy. Because most TNCs can no longer be owned by any one single country, all countries that play a major part in the globalized economy must have substantial presences of foreign-owned TNCs within their boundaries.

There is debate about the need to encourage domestic ownership of certain key industries and about the need to control the activities of TNCs within one country by such means as requiring local R&D expenditure.

The prevailing view among economists during the 1980s and early 1990s has been that foreign investment is generally beneficial and that it should be subject to only a minimum of constraints. According to this view, TNCs are profit maximizers who will locate activities where it is most profitable to do so rather than hold them in their home country as a matter of course. In that case, the market activities of TNCs will produce the most efficient international allocation of resources and the highest possible living standards, both at home and in host countries. Furthermore, according to this view, the international economy with globalized competition is so complex and sophisticated that intervention to regulate investment is all too likely to do more harm than good.

Critics are not so sure. They advocate controls to hold certain key industries under domestic ownership and certain key activities, such as R&D, in home locations.

SUMMARY

A. THE ORGANIZATION OF FIRMS

- The firm is the economic unit that produces and sells commodities. The definition of the firm used in economics abstracts from real-life differences in the size and form of the organization of firms.
- The single proprietorship, the partnership, and the corporation are the major forms of business organization in Canada today. The corporation is by far the most common wherever large-scale production is required. The corporation is recognized as a legal entity; the liability of its owners (shareholders) is limited to the amount of money that they have invested in the organization. Corporate ownership is readily transferred by the sale of shares of the company's stock in securities markets.
- Firms can raise money through equity financing or debt financing. A firm's owners provide equity capital both when they purchase newly-issued shares and when the firm reinvests its profits. The firm obtains debt financing from creditors either by borrowing from financial institutions or by selling bonds to the public.

B. THE GOALS OF MODERN FIRMS

- Principal-agent theory gives support to the idea that corporate managers do not always operate in the best interests of the stockholders; that is, the managers may pursue their own interests rather than simply maximizing profits. Sales maximization is an example of such a pursuit.
- In the market for corporate control, would-be buyers of firms deal with would-be sellers (in friendly takeovers and mergers) as well as with reluctant sellers (in hostile takeovers). Buyers who believe that they can

operate a firm more profitably than can its present management can afford to pay more than the present market value of the firm's equities to acquire it. The possibility of such purchases provides an incentive for current managers to come close to maximizing the firm's profits and encourages their replacement by new buyers when they do not.

- Even if individual firms do not always maximize profits, it is possible that the industry will be characterized by behaviour that is approximately profit maximizing. The reason is that the firms that come closest to maximizing profits will prosper and grow while those further away from profit maximization will shrink or fail altogether.

C. FOREIGN INVESTMENT

- Foreign investment has played a large part in helping less-developed countries to develop over the past few centuries. In their time, Canada and the United States were less developed than the United Kingdom and some other European countries and were the recipients of large amounts of foreign investment that flowed from Europe to the New World.

- As the countries of the New World grew, they were able to generate an increasing flow of domestic saving, which reduced their need for foreign investment, repatriated some old foreign investment, and provided a flow of investment to newer, less-developed countries.

- The growth of transnational corporations means that no country can hope to own all of the capital that is devoted to the production of internationally traded commodities within its borders. TNCs are a major means by which technologies that are developed in one country are transferred to other countries. TNCs also have the power to avoid many national policies by shifting profits, costs, R&D, production, and investment around the world in response to relative incentives in different countries. This reduces the effectiveness of many national policies designed to give advantages to the initiating country.

- Although there is debate in Canada about the benefits and costs of foreign investment, such investment could not be dispensed with in today's world of globalized production and competition.

KEY CONCEPTS

Single proprietorship, partnership, and corporation
Advantages of the corporation
Debt and equity financing

Principal-agent theory
Sales maximization
Satisficing behaviour
Mergers, takeovers, and buyouts

Transnational corporations
Foreign direct investment

DISCUSSION QUESTIONS

1. In light of principal-agent theory, why might dentists and attorneys be required to subscribe to professional codes of ethics that prevent (or at least limit) their ability to sell unneeded services to their clients? Why do we not see similar codes of ethics for automobile mechanics?

2. Comment on these lead lines of recent newspaper stories.

   a. "Critic calls takeovers and mergers fiscal roulette that does nothing to contribute to Canadian national income."

   b. "The candidate called on Canadians to take back their country by ending all foreign ownership."

   c. "Union leaders worry that concern over Quebec separation may cause exodus of foreign investment from Canada."

3. Assume that each of the following assertions is factually correct. Taken together, what would they tell you about the prediction that big business is increasing its control of the North American economy?

   a. The share of total manufacturing assets owned by the 100 largest corporations has been rising over the past 25 years.

   b. The number of new firms begun each year has increased over the past 25 years.

   c. The share of manufacturing in total production has been decreasing for 40 years.

   d. Profits as a percentage of national income are no higher now than half a century ago.

4. In his now-famous article "Who Is Us?" Robert Reich criticizes U.S. policy for giving assistance to domestically-owned rather than domestically-located TNCs.

Why, he asks, should a domestically-owned firm get R&D assistance for research done in Taiwan to produce goods in Singapore that is denied to a Japanese-owned firm doing research on the West Coast to develop new products to be produced in the Midwest? Who gains the benefits from subsidies provided by governments (and paid for by taxpayers) to each of these types of firms?

5. "Our list prices are really set by our accounting department: They add a fixed markup to their best estimates of fully accounted cost and send these to the operating divisions. Managers of these divisions may not change those prices without permission of the board of directors, which is seldom given. Operating divisions may, however, provide special discounts if necessary to stay competitive." Does this testimony by the president of a leading manufacturing company suggest that his firm is a profit maximizer?

6. The leading automobile tire manufacturers sell original-equipment tires to automobile manufacturers at a price below the average total cost of all the tires they make and sell. This happens year after year. Is this consistent with profit-maximizing behaviour in the short run? In the long run? If it is not consistent, what does it show? Do original-equipment tires compete with replacement tires?

PART FIVE

THE MARKETS
FOR FACTORS
OF PRODUCTION

Why do university professors typically get paid more than elementary-school teachers? Why does an acre of land outside Kamloops rent for less than an acre of land in downtown Vancouver? Are governments successful in their attempts to equalize income across the various Canadian regions or in their attempts to equalize the earnings of people in different occupations? What are the effects of legislating a minimum wage? What do unions do? Is there discrimination in the labour market and, if so, what can be done about it? Should we be alarmed at the overall trend in Canada (and other countries) toward fewer manufacturing jobs but more service jobs? What is the connection between the interest rate and firms' investment in physical capital? What determines the interest rate? These are the sort of questions you will be able to answer after reading the next three chapters.

In Chapter 15, you are introduced to the way economists think about markets for *factors of production*. Not surprisingly, demand and supply play a key role. You will see several reasons for *factor-price differentials*. It is here that you will learn why the acre of land in Kamloops rents for less than the one in Vancouver. You will also see the importance of *factor mobility*, and why this mobility can thwart government efforts to reduce income inequality across regions.

Chapter 16 examines labour markets in detail. You will see how *working conditions* and *human capital* can combine to explain why some workers get paid more than others. You will learn about the effects of *legislated minimum wages*, and about the objectives of *labour unions*. You will also examine the important issue of *discrimination* in labour markets, and you will learn about government policies to redress it. Finally, you will see whether the decline of the manufacturing sector (and the rise of the service sector) is necessarily a bad thing.

Chapter 17 begins by discussing the market for *physical capital*. You will see why firms choose to buy less capital when the *interest rate* rises (and more when the interest rate falls). You will learn how the *equilibrium* interest rate is determined, and how it is affected by changes in technology. The chapter then goes on to discuss the pricing of *nonrenewable resources*, such as oil, natural gas, or minerals. You will learn how the market system works as a *conservation mechanism*—the idea that rising prices of nonrenewable resources encourage the conservation of these scarce resources.

CHAPTER 15

FACTOR PRICING AND FACTOR MOBILITY

Most people spend a considerable amount of their time working. Some of those people are fortunate enough to earn good wages, and thus have good incomes which enable them to afford some of the "good things in life." Others are not so fortunate, and earn only low wages (or are unable to find jobs at all). What determines the wages that individuals earn? What explains why professors usually get paid more than high-school teachers, or why doctors get paid more than nurses? Labour is not the only factor of production, of course. Physical capital is also important, as are land and natural resources. What determines the payments that these factors earn? Why does an acre of farm land in Northern Saskatchewan rent for far less than an acre of land in downtown Toronto? Not surprisingly, understanding why different factors of production earn different payments requires us to understand both demand-side and supply-side aspects of the relevant factor markets.

In this chapter we examine the issue of factor pricing and the closely related issue of factor mobility. Understanding what determines the payments to different factors of production will help us to understand the overall distribution of income in the economy, which is our first topic.

INCOME DISTRIBUTION AND FACTOR PRICING

The founders of Classical economics, Adam Smith (1723–1790) and David Ricardo (1772–1823), were concerned with the distribution of income among what were then the three great social classes: workers, capitalists, and landowners. They defined three factors of production as labour, capital, and land. The return to each factor was treated as the income of the respective social class.

Smith and Ricardo were interested in what determined the income of each class relative to the total national income. Their theories predicted that as society progressed, landlords would become relatively better off and capitalists would become relatively worse off. Karl Marx (1818–1883) had a different theory which predicted that as growth occurred, capitalists would become relatively better off and workers would become relatively worse off (until the whole capitalist system collapsed).

TABLE 15-1
Functional Distribution of National Income in Canada, 1994

Type of Income	Billions of Dollars	Percentage of Total
Employee Compensation	410.3	72.4
Corporate Profits	57.4	10.1
Proprietor's Income (including rent)	43.0	7.6
Interest	56.4	9.9
Total	567.1	100.0

Total income is classified here according to the nature of the factor service that earned the income. Although these data show that employee compensation accounts for over 72 percent of national income, this does not mean that workers and their families receive only that proportion of national income. Many households will have income in more than one category listed in the table.
(*Source:* Statistics Canada, 13-001.)

These nineteenth-century debates focused on what is now called the **functional distribution of income,** defined as the distribution of total income among the major factors of production. Table 15-1 presents data for the functional distribution of income in Canada in 1994.

Although functional distribution categories (wages, rent, profits) pervade current statistics, modern economists have shifted their emphasis to another way of looking at differences in incomes, called the **size distribution of income.** This refers to the distribution of income among different households without reference to the source of the income or the "social" class of the household. Tables 15-2 and 15-3 show that there is substantial inequality in the distribution of income across families, but that the system of government taxes and transfers are effective in reducing the extent of this inequality.

Inequality in the distribution of income is shown graphically in Figure 15-1, which displays the information contained in the second column of Table 15-3. This curve of income distribution, called a **Lorenz curve,** shows how much of total income is accounted for by given proportions of the nation's households. If every household had the same income, then the Lorenz curve would lie exactly along the diagonal. The farther the curve bends away from the diagonal, the less equal the distribution of income. The curve shows, for example, that in 1993 the bottom 20 percent of all Canadian households received 7.7 percent of all after-tax income.

TABLE 15-2
After-Tax Incomes of Canadian Families, 1993

Income Category	Percentage of families
Less than $9,999	2.1
$10,000–$19,999	11.8
$20,000–$29,999	18.5
$30,000–$39,999	19.2
$40,000–$49,999	16.7
$50,000–$59,999	12.0
$60,000 and over	19.7

Although average family after-tax income in 1993 was just under $40,000, many families received much less than this, and some received a great deal more. While almost 20 percent of Canadian families had very comfortable incomes of more than $60,000, 14 percent had to subsist on incomes below $20,000.

(*Source:* Statistics Canada, 13-210.)

Today, most economists devote more attention to the size distribution of income than to the functional distribution. After all, some capitalists (such as the owners of small retail stores) are in the lower part of the income scale, and some wage earners (such as professional athletes) are at the upper end of the income scale. Moreover, if someone is poor, it matters little whether that person is a landowner or a worker.

TABLE 15-3
Inequality in Family Income Distribution, 1993

Family Income Rank	Percentage of Aggregate Income	
	Before taxes and transfers	After taxes and transfers
Lowest fifth	6.4	7.7
Second fifth	12.0	13.2
Middle fifth	17.6	18.1
Fourth fifth	24.1	23.8
Highest fifth	39.9	37.2

The distribution of income is unequal before and after taxes. The first column shows the inequality of income produced by market forces. The second column shows that the Canadian system of taxes and transfers reduced income inequalities to some extent. The distribution of income is more equal in the second column because the share of total income going to the lowest three income groups increased, while the share going to the highest two groups decreased.

(*Source:* Statistics Canada, 13-207 and 13-210.)

To understand the size distribution of income, we must first study how individual incomes are determined. Superficial explanations of differences in income, such as "People earn according to their ability," are clearly inadequate. Incomes are distributed much more unequally than any *measured* index of ability, be it IQ, physical strength, or typing skill. The best professional sports players may only score twice as many points as the average players, but their salary is many times more than the average salary. Something other than simple ability is at work here. However, if answers that are couched in terms of ability are easily refuted, so are answers such as "It's all a matter of luck" or "It's just the system." In this chapter, we look beyond such superficial explanations.

FACTOR PRICING

In this chapter, we confine ourselves to goods and factor markets that are perfectly competitive. This means that individual firms are price takers in both markets. They face a given price for the product they produce, and that price is both their average revenue and their marginal revenue. Similarly, they face a given price of each factor that they buy, and that price is both the average cost and the marginal cost of the factor.

Dealing first with firms that are price takers in product and factor markets allows us to study the principles of factor-price determination in the simplest context. Once these are understood, it is relatively easy to allow for monopolistic elements in either or both types of markets. This is done in Chapter 16.

The income that a factor earns depends on the price charged for its services and on the quantity that is employed. To determine factor incomes, therefore, we need to ask how markets determine these prices and quantities. To anticipate, the answer is that factor prices and quantities are determined in just the same way as the prices and quantities of goods—by the interaction of demand and supply. What is new about factor pricing arises from the *determinants* of factor demands and factor supplies.

THE LINK BETWEEN OUTPUT AND INPUT DECISIONS

In Chapters 8 and 9, we saw how firms' costs varied with their outputs and how they could achieve cost

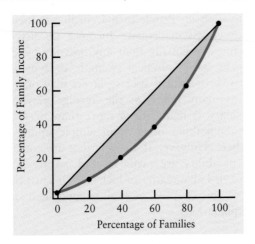

FIGURE 15-1
A Lorenz Curve of Family Income in Canada, 1993

The size of the shaded area between the Lorenz curve and the diagonal is a measure of the inequality of income distribution. If there were complete income equality, the bottom 20 percent of income receivers would receive 20 percent of the income, and so forth, and the Lorenz curve would coincide with the diagonal line. Because the lowest 20 percent receive less than 8 percent of the income, the Lorenz curve lies below the diagonal line. The extent to which it bends away from the straight line indicates the amount of inequality in the distribution of income. This Lorenz curve graphs the data from the second column in Table 15-3.

minimization by finding the least-cost combination of factors to produce any given output. In Chapter 10, we saw that firms in perfect competition decided how much to produce by equating their marginal costs to given market prices. We also saw how the market supply curve interacted in each product's market with the market demand curve of consumers. This interaction determines the market price as well as the quantity that is produced and consumed.

These events in goods markets have implications for factor markets. The decisions of firms on how much to produce and how to produce it imply specific demands for various quantities of the factors of production. These demands, together with the supplies of the factors of production (which are determined by the owners of the factors), come together in factor markets. Together they determine the quantities of the various factors of production that are employed, their prices, and the incomes earned by their owners.

The foregoing discussion shows that there is a close relationship between the production and pricing of the goods and services produced by firms on the one hand and the pricing, employment, and incomes earned by the factors of production they hire on the other hand. They are two aspects of a single set of economic activities relating to the production of goods and services and the allocation of the nation's resources among their various possible uses. This discussion provides a brief introduction to one of the great insights of economics:

When demand and supply interact to determine the allocation of resources among various lines of production, they also determine the incomes of the factors that are used in producing the goods.

The rest of this chapter is an elaboration of this important theme. We first study the demand for factors, then their supply, and finally how demand and supply come together to determine factor prices and quantities.

THE DEMAND FOR FACTORS

Firms require the services of land, labour, capital, and natural resources to be used as inputs. Firms also use as inputs the products of other firms, such as steel, legal services, and electricity.

If we investigate the production of these produced inputs, we will find that they, too, are made by using land, labour, capital, natural resources, and other produced inputs. If we continue following through the chain of products used as inputs, we can account for all of the economy's output in terms of inputs of the basic factors of production—land, labour, capital, and natural resources. The theory of factor pricing applies to *all* inputs used by a firm. The theory of distribution explains the division of total national income among the owners of the basic factors: land, labour, capital, and natural resources. It also explains the division of income between the *different types* of labour (such as highly skilled or less-skilled workers) and the different types of other factors (such as arable land and poor land, or new capital equipment and obsolete capital equipment).

Firms require inputs not for their own sake but as a means to produce goods and services. For example, the demand for computer programmers and technicians is growing as more and more computers are used. The demand for carpenters and building materials rises and falls as the amount of housing construction rises and falls. The demand for any input is therefore *derived from the demand* for the goods and services that it helps to produce; for this reason, the demand for a factor of production is said to be a **derived demand.**

Derived demand provides a link between the markets for output and the markets for inputs.

THE FIRM'S MARGINAL DECISION ON FACTOR USE

What determines whether an individual firm will choose to hire one extra worker, or whether the same firm will decide to use one extra machine, or an extra kilowatt-hour of electricity? Since we are considering whether the firm will use one *extra unit* of some factor, we refer to this as the firm's *marginal decision* on factor use.

We start by deriving a famous relation that holds for every factor employed by profit-maximizing firms. In Chapter 10, we established the rules for the maximization of a firm's profits in the short run. When one factor is fixed and another is variable, the profit-maximizing firm increases its output until the last unit produced adds just as much to cost as to revenue, that is, until marginal cost equals marginal revenue. Another way of stating that the firm maximizes profits is to say that the firm will increase production up to the point at which the last unit of the variable factor employed adds just as much to revenue as it does to cost.

The addition to total cost resulting from employing one more unit of a factor is that factor's price. (Recall that the firm is assumed to buy its factors in competitive markets.) So if one more worker is hired at a wage of $15 per hour, the addition to the firm's costs is $15. The amount that a unit of a variable factor adds to revenue is the amount that the unit adds to total output multiplied by the change in revenue caused by selling an extra unit of output.

In Chapter 8, we introduced the concept of *marginal product*—the amount by which output increased when the variable factor was increased by one unit. When dealing with factor markets, economists use the term **marginal physical product (MPP)** to avoid confusion with the revenue concepts that they also need to use. The change in revenue caused

by selling one extra unit of output is just the price of the output, *P* (because the firm is a price taker in the market for its output). The resulting amount, which is $MPP \times P$, is called the factor's **marginal revenue product (MRP).**[29] For example, if the variable factor's marginal physical product is 2 units per hour and the price of a unit of output is $7.50, the factor's marginal revenue product is $15 ($7.50 × 2).

We can now restate the condition for a firm to be maximizing its profits in two ways. First:

$$\begin{array}{ccc} \text{Marginal} & & \text{Marginal} \\ \text{Cost of the} & = & \text{Revenue Product} \\ \text{Factor} & & \text{of the Factor} \end{array} \quad [1]$$

Because the firm is a price taker in both its input and output markets, we can restate Equation 1 by noting that the left-hand side is just the price of a unit of the variable factor, which we call *w*, and the right-hand side is the factor's marginal physical product, multiplied by the price at which the output is sold. In words, this gives us

$$\begin{array}{ccc} \text{Price of} & & \text{Factor's Marginal} \\ \text{a Unit of} & = & \text{Physical Product} \\ \text{the Factor} & & \text{times its Price} \end{array} \quad [2a]$$

Expressed in symbols, this is

$$w = MPP \times P \quad [2b]$$

To check your understanding of Equation 2, consider an example. Suppose that the factor is available to the firm at a cost of $10 a unit (*w* = $10). Suppose also that employing another unit of the factor adds 3 units to output (*MPP* = 3). Suppose further that output is sold for $5 a unit (*P* = $5). Thus the additional unit of the factor adds $15 to the firm's revenue and $10 to its costs. Hiring one more unit of the factor brings in $5 more than it costs. *The firm will take on more of the factor whenever its marginal revenue product exceeds its price.*

Now assume, however, that the last unit of the factor taken on by the firm has a marginal physical product of 1 unit of output—it adds only one extra unit to output—and so adds only $5 to revenue. Clearly, the firm can increase profits by cutting back on its use of the factor because laying off 1 unit reduces revenues by $5 while reducing costs by $10. *The firm will lay off units of the factor whenever its marginal revenue product is less than its price.*

Finally, assume that another unit of the factor taken on or laid off changes revenue by $10. Now the firm cannot increase its profits by altering its employment of the variable factor in either direction.

The firm cannot increase its profits by altering employment of the factor whenever the factor's marginal revenue product equals its price.

This example illustrates what was said earlier, and we are doing nothing that is essentially new—instead, we are merely looking at the firm's profit-maximizing behaviour from the point of view of its inputs rather than its output. In Chapters 10 and 11, we saw the firm varying its output until the marginal cost of producing another unit was equal to the marginal revenue derived from selling that unit. Now we see the same profit-maximizing behaviour in terms of the firm's varying its inputs until the marginal cost of another unit of input is just equal to the revenue derived from selling that unit's marginal product.

THE FIRM'S DEMAND CURVE FOR A FACTOR

We now know what determines the quantity of a variable factor a firm will buy when facing some specific price of the factor and some specific price of its output. Next we wish to derive the firm's *entire* demand curve for a factor, which tells us how much of the factor the firm will buy at *each* price.

To derive a firm's demand curve for a factor, we start by considering the right-hand side of Equation 2b, which tells us that the factor's marginal revenue product is composed of a physical component and a value component. We examine these two separate components in turn.

The Physical Component of *MRP*: *MPP*

As the quantity of the variable factor changes, output will change. The hypothesis of diminishing returns, first discussed in Chapter 8, predicts what will happen: As the firm adds further units of the variable factor to a given quantity of the fixed factor, the additions to output will eventually get smaller and smaller. In other words, the factor's marginal physical product declines. This is illustrated in part (i) of Figure 15-2. The negative slope of the *MPP* curve reflects the operation of the law of diminishing returns: Each unit of labour adds less to total output than the previous unit.

The Value Component of *MRP*: *MR*

To convert the marginal physical product curve of Figure 15-2(i) into a curve showing the marginal rev-

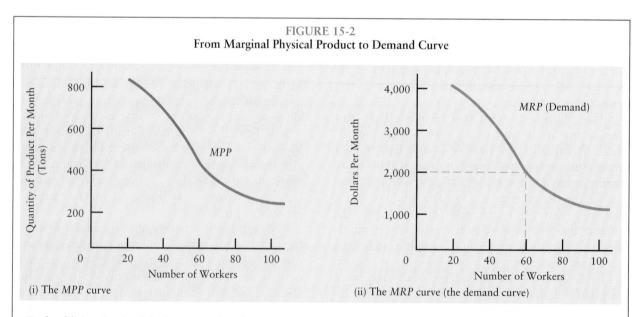

FIGURE 15-2
From Marginal Physical Product to Demand Curve

(i) The *MPP* curve

(ii) The *MRP* curve (the demand curve)

Each additional unit of the factor employed adds a certain amount to total product, as shown in part (i), and hence a certain amount to total revenue, as shown in part (ii). This determines the amount of the factor that firms will demand at each price.

enue product of the variable factor, we need to know the dollar value of the extra physical product. As long as the firm sells its output in a competitive market, the dollar value of *one extra* unit of output (marginal revenue) is simply the market price of the product. In this case, the marginal revenue product of the factor is simply the marginal physical product multiplied by the market price of output.

Part (ii) of Figure 15-2 shows a marginal revenue product curve for labour on the assumption that the firm sells its product in a competitive market at a price of $5 per unit. This curve shows—for each level of total employment of the factor—how much would be added to revenue by employing one more unit of the factor. Thus, the *MRP* curve represents *MPP* × *MR* for each additional unit of the factor. Since the *MR* for a firm in perfect competition is simply equal to price, the *MRP* curve has the same shape as the *MPP* curve.

Note, however, that if the firm were not perfectly competitive, then *MR* would not be equal to price. If *MR* declines as output increases (as it does whenever the firm is not a price taker), then the *MRP* curve will be steeper than the *MPP* curve; this is because the increase in output produced by the extra unit of the factor leads to a fall in the price of the product.

From *MRP* to the Demand Curve

Equation 2a states that the profit-maximizing firm will employ additional units of the factor up to the point at which the *MRP* equals the price of the factor. For example, in Figure 15-2, if the price of the variable factor were $2,000 per month, the profit-maximizing firm would employ 60 workers. (There is no point in employing a sixty-first because that would add less than $2,000 to revenue but a full $2,000 to costs.) So the profit-maximizing firm hires the quantity of the variable factor that equates the marginal revenue product with the price of the variable factor. Thus the curve that relates the quantity of the variable factor employed to its *MRP* is also the curve that relates the quantity of the variable factor the firm wishes to employ to its price.

The *MRP* curve of the variable factor is the firm's (derived) demand curve for that variable factor.

ELASTICITY OF FACTOR DEMAND

The elasticity of demand for a factor measures the *degree* of the response of the quantity demanded to a change in its price. The preceding sections have explained the *direction* of the response; that is, that quantity demanded is negatively related to price. But you should not be surprised to hear that the magnitude of the response depends on the strength of various effects. For example, the extent of diminishing returns to labour, and the ability of the firm to substitute between labour and other factors of production, will both affect the firm's elasticity of demand for labour. This section presents the four principles of derived demand that come from the work of the English economist Alfred Marshall (1842–1924).

Diminishing Returns

The first influence on the slope of the demand curve for a factor is the diminishing marginal productivity of that factor. If marginal productivity declines rapidly as more of a variable factor is employed, a fall in the factor's price will not induce many more units to be employed. Conversely, if marginal productivity falls only slowly as more of a variable factor is employed, there will be a large increase in quantity demanded as price falls.

For example, both labour and fertilizers are used by farmers who produce vegetables for sale in nearby cities. For many crops, additional doses of fertilizers add significant amounts to yields over quite a wide range of fertilizer use. Although the marginal product of fertilizer does decline, it does so rather slowly as more and more fertilizer is used. In contrast, although certain amounts of labour are needed for planting, weeding, and harvesting, there is only a small range over which additional labour can be used productively. The marginal product of labour, although high for the first units, declines rapidly as more and more labour is used. Under these circumstances, such farmers will have a more elastic demand for fertilizer than for labour.

Substitution Between Factors

In the long run, all factors are variable. If one factor's price rises, firms will try to substitute relatively cheaper factors for it. For this reason, the slope of the demand curve for a factor is influenced by the ease with which other factors can be substituted for the factor whose price has changed.

The ease of substitution depends on the substitutes that are available and on the technical conditions of production. It is often possible to vary factor proportions in surprising ways. For example, in automobile manufacturing and in building construction, glass and steel can be substituted for each other simply by varying the dimensions of the windows. Another example is that construction materials can be substituted for maintenance labour in the case of most durable consumer goods. This is done by making the product more or less durable and more or less subject to breakdowns by using more or less expensive materials in its construction.

Such substitutions are not the end of the story. Plant and equipment are being replaced continually, which allows more or less capital-intensive methods to be built into new plants in response to changes in factor prices. Similarly, engines that use less gasoline per kilometre tend to be developed when the price of gasoline rises severely.

Importance of the Factor

Other things being equal, the larger the fraction of the total costs of producing some commodity that are made up of payments to a particular factor, the greater the elasticity of demand for that factor.

To see this, suppose that wages account for 50 percent of the costs of producing a good and raw materials account for 15 percent. A 10 percent rise in the price of labour raises the cost of producing the commodity by 5 percent (10 percent of 50 percent), but a 10 percent rise in the price of raw materials raises the cost of the commodity by only 1.5 percent (10 percent of 15 percent). The larger the increase in the cost of production, the larger the shift in the commodity's supply curve and hence the larger the decreases in quantities demanded of both the commodity and the factors used to produce it.

Elasticity of Demand for the Output

Other things being equal, the more elastic is the demand for the commodity that the factor is used to produce, the more elastic is the demand for the factor.

If an increase in the price of the commodity causes a large decrease in the quantity demanded—that is, if the demand for the commodity is highly elastic—there will be a large decrease in the quantity of a factor needed to produce it in response to a rise in the factor's price. However, if an increase in the price of a commodity causes only a small decrease in the quantity demanded—that is, if the demand for the commodity is inelastic—there will be only a

small decrease in the quantity of the factor required in response to a rise in its price.

In Extension 15-1, the forces affecting the elasticity of the derived demand curves that have just been discussed are related more specifically to the market for the industry's output.

THE SUPPLY OF FACTORS

When we consider the supply of any factor of production, we can consider supply at three different levels of aggregation:

- the amount supplied to the economy as a whole

- the amount supplied to a particular use (such as a particular industry or occupation)

- the amount supplied to a particular user (such as a particular firm)

The elasticity of supply of a factor will normally be different at each of these levels of aggregation. This is because the amount of factor mobility is very different at these different levels of aggregation; a given factor of production is often very mobile between firms within a given industry, less mobile between different industries, and almost completely immobile from the perspective of the entire economy. As an example, an electrician may be very mobile between industries within a given city, reasonably mobile between provinces, but it may be very difficult for that electrician to move to another country to find a job. In this section, we examine the relationship between factor mobility and the supply of factors of production. We start with the highest level of aggregation, the supply of each factor to the economy as a whole.

THE TOTAL SUPPLY OF FACTORS

At any one time, the total supply of each factor of production is given. For example, in each country, the labour force is of a certain size, so much arable land is available, and there is a given supply of discovered petroleum. However, these supplies can and do change in response to both economic and noneconomic forces. Sometimes the change is very gradual, as when a climatic change slowly turns arable land into desert or when medical advances re-

EXTENSION 15-1

MARSHALL'S PRINCIPLES OF DERIVED DEMAND

The great English economist Alfred Marshall (1842–1924) referred to the two propositions derived here as the principles of **derived demand**.

1. The larger the proportion of total costs accounted for by a factor, the more elastic the demand for it.

Consider the figure on the left. The demand curve for the industry's product is D and, *given the factor's original price,* the industry supply curve is S_0. Equilibrium is at E_0 with output at q_0.

Suppose that the factor's price then falls. If the factor accounts for a small part of the industry's total costs, each firm's marginal cost curve shifts downward by only a small amount. So also does the industry supply curve, as illustrated by the supply curve S_1. Output expands only a small amount to q_1, which implies only a small increase in the quantity of the factor demanded.

If the factor accounts for a large part of the industry's total costs, each firm's marginal cost curve shifts downward a great deal. So also does the indus-

try supply curve, as illustrated by the curve S_2. Output expands to q_2, which implies a large increase in the quantity of the factor demanded.

2. The more elastic the demand curve for the product made by a factor, the more elastic the demand for the factor.

Now consider the figure on the right. The original demand and supply curves for the industry's product intersect at E_0 to produce an industry output of q_0. A fall in the price of a factor causes the industry supply curve to shift downward to S_1.

When the demand curve is relatively inelastic, as shown by the curve D_i, industry output increases by only a small amount, to q_1. The quantity of the factor demanded only increases by a correspondingly small amount.

When the demand curve is relatively elastic, as shown by the curve D_e, industry output increases by a large amount to q_2. The quantity of the factor demanded then increases by a correspondingly large amount.

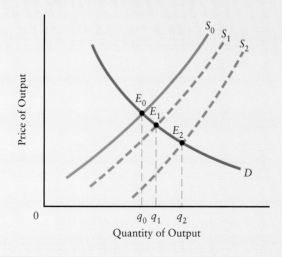

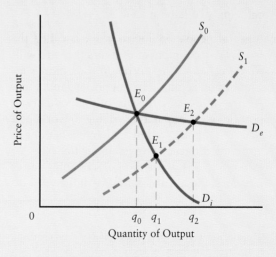

duce the rate of infant mortality and hence increase the rate of population growth, thereby eventually increasing the supply of adult labour. Sometimes the changes can be quite rapid, as when a boom in busi-

ness activity brings retired persons back into the labour force or a rise in the price of agricultural produce encourages the draining of marshes to add to the supply of farmland.

The Total Supply of Capital

The supply of capital in a country consists of the stock of existing machines, plants, and equipment.[1] Capital is a manufactured factor of production, and its total supply is in no sense fixed, although it changes only slowly. Each year, the stock of capital goods is diminished by the amount that becomes physically or economically obsolete and is increased by the amount that is newly produced. The difference between these is the net addition to (or net subtraction from) the capital stock. On balance, the trend has been for the capital stock to grow from decade to decade over the past few centuries. We will consider the determinants of investment in capital in Chapter 17.

The Total Supply of Land

The total area of dry land in a country is almost completely fixed, but the supply of *fertile* land is not fixed.[2] Considerable care and effort are required to sustain the productive power of land. If farmers earn low incomes, they may not provide the necessary care, and the land's fertility may be destroyed within a short time. In contrast, high earnings from farming may provide the incentive to increase the supply of arable land by irrigation and other forms of reclamation.

The Total Supply of Labour

The number of people willing to work is called the labour force; the total number of hours they are willing to work is called the *supply of effort* or, more simply, the **supply of labour**. The supply of labour depends on three influences: the size of the population, the proportion of the population willing to work, and the number of hours worked by each individual. Each of these is partly influenced by economic forces.

Population.   The population of a country varies over time, and these variations are influenced to some extent by economic forces. There is some evidence, for example, that the birthrate and the net immigration rate (immigration minus emigration) are higher in good times than in bad.

Labour-Force Participation.   The proportion of the total population that is willing to work is called the *labour-force participation rate*. We can also define participation rates for subgroups, such as women or youths. Participation rates vary in response to many influences, including changes in attitudes and tastes. The enormous rise in female participation rates in the past four decades is one example. Another is a lowering of the retirement age, which has the effect of reducing the overall labour-force participation rate.

Forces other than tastes also play a role in determining the labour-force participation rate. For example, a rise in the demand for labour, and an accompanying rise in the wage, will lead to an increase in the proportion of the population willing to work. More married women and elderly people enter the labour force when the demand for labour is high. For the same reasons, the labour force tends to decline when earnings and employment opportunities decline.[3]

Hours Worked.   The wage rate not only influences the number of *people* in the labour force, but it is also a major determinant of the number of *hours* worked for each person. When workers sell their leisure services to employers, they are trading leisure for income. By giving up leisure in order to work, they obtain income with which to buy goods. They can therefore be thought of as trading leisure for goods.

A rise in the wage implies a change in the relative price of goods and leisure. Goods become cheaper relative to leisure because each hour worked buys more goods than before. Or, looked at the other way around, an increase in the wage means that leisure becomes more expensive relative to goods, because each hour of leisure consumed is at the cost of more goods forgone.

---

[1]Recall the distinction between *financial capital* (the money that a firm raises to carry on its business) and *physical capital* (the assets of the firm like buildings and equipment). In this chapter, whenever we use the term "capital" we are referring to physical capital.
[2]Although natural resources are often included with land as a single factor of production, they have so many important special characteristics that it is sometimes worthwhile treating them as a separate factor. Some of the issues involved with pricing natural resources are discussed in Chapter 17.

[3]Economists sometimes refer to the decline in labour-force participation in bad economic times when there are few job opportunities as the *discouraged-worker effect*. When there is a temporary decline in family income, perhaps because one member of the family loses a job in a recession, the number of family members seeking market work may increase; this is known as the *added-worker effect*. Generally, the discouraged-worker effect is larger than the added-worker effect during recessions; the labour-force participation rate declines during recessions and increases during periods of economic recovery.

It is not necessarily the case, however, that an increase in the wage increases the amount of hours worked. This is because an increase in the wage generates both income and substitution effects (see Chapter 7), and these effects typically work in opposite directions. As the wage rises, the substitution effect leads the individual to consume more goods and less leisure because leisure is now relatively more expensive (in terms of foregone goods). The income effect of a higher wage, however, leads the individual to consume more goods *and* more leisure. Since the income and substitution effects work in the same direction for the consumption of goods, we can be sure that a rise in the wage rate will lead to a rise in goods consumed. However, because the two effects work in the opposite direction for leisure, the following is true:

A rise in the wage rate leads to less leisure being consumed (more hours worked) when the substitution effect is the dominant force and to more leisure consumed (fewer hours worked) when the income effect is the dominant force.

Much of the long-run evidence suggests that as real hourly wage rates rise for the economy as a whole, people wish to *reduce* the number of hours they work, indicating that the income effects of wage increases dominate the substitution effects. Extension 15-2 provides a more detailed treatment of these two effects using indifference curves. (Recall the Appendix to Chapter 7.)

THE SUPPLY OF FACTORS TO A PARTICULAR USE

Most factors have many uses. A given piece of land can be used to grow any one of several crops, or it can be subdivided for a housing development. A computer programmer living in the Ottawa valley can work for one of several firms, for the government, or for Carleton University. A lathe can be used to make many different products, and it requires no adaptation when it is turned for one use or another.

One industry or occupation can attract a factor away from another industry or occupation, even though the total supply of that factor may be fixed. Thus a factor's elasticity of supply to a particular use is larger than its elasticity of supply to the entire economy.

Factor Mobility

When considering the supply of a factor for a particular use, the most important concept is **factor mobility**. A factor that shifts easily between uses in response to small changes in incentives is said to be *mobile*. Its supply to any one of its uses will be elastic because a small increase in the price offered will attract many units of the factor from other uses. A factor that does not shift easily from one use to another, even in response to large changes in remuneration, is said to be *immobile*. It will be in inelastic supply in any one of its uses because even a large increase in the price offered will attract only a small inflow from other uses. Often a factor may be immobile in the short run but mobile in the long run.

An important key to factor mobility is time: The longer the time interval, the easier it is for a factor to convert from one use to another.

Consider the factor mobility among particular uses of each of the three key factors of production.

Capital.   Some kinds of capital equipment—lathes, trucks, and computers, for example—can be shifted readily among uses; many others are comparatively unshiftable. A great deal of machinery is quite specific: Once built, it must be used for the purpose for which it was designed, or it cannot be used at all. Indeed, it is the immobility of much fixed capital equipment that makes the exit of firms from declining industries the slow and difficult process described in Chapter 10.

In the long run, however, capital is highly mobile. When capital goods wear out, a firm may simply replace them with identical goods, or it may exercise other options. It may buy a newly designed machine to produce the same goods, or it may buy machines to produce totally different goods. Such decisions lead to changes in the long-run allocation of a country's stock of capital among various uses.

Land.   Land, which is physically the least mobile of factors, is one of the *most mobile* in an economic sense. Consider agricultural land. In a given year, one crop can be harvested and a totally different crop can be planted. A farm on the outskirts of a growing city can be sold for subdivision and development on short notice. Once land is built on, its mobility is much reduced. A site on which a hotel has been built can be converted into a warehouse site, but it takes a large differential in the value of land use to make that transfer worthwhile because the hotel must be torn down.

EXTENSION 15-2

THE SUPPLY OF LABOUR

The discussion in the text can be formalized for readers who have studied indifference curves in the appendix to Chapter 7. The key proposition is this:

Because a change in the wage rate has an income effect and a substitution effect that work in opposite directions, the supply curve of labour may have a positive or a negative slope.

Part (i) of the figure plots leisure on the horizontal axis and the consumption of goods (measured in dollars) on the vertical axis. The budget line always starts at 24, indicating that all individuals are endowed with 24 hours a day that they may either consume as leisure or trade for goods by working.

At the original wage rate, the individual could obtain q_a of goods by working 24 hours (i.e., the hourly wage rate is $q_a/24$). The outcome is at point E_0, where the individual consumes l_0 of leisure and works $24 - l_0$ hours in return for q_0 of goods.

The wage rate now rises so that q_b becomes available if 24 hours are worked (i.e., the hourly wage rate rises to $q_b/24$). The individual now chooses point E_1, where the consumption of leisure

falls to l_1 and the individual works $24 - l_1$ hours in return for a consumption of q_1 of goods. The rise in wages increases hours worked.

The hourly wage rate now rises further to $q_c/24$, and the individual chooses point E_2. Consumption of leisure rises to l_2, and $24 - l_2$ hours are worked in return for an increased consumption of q_2 of goods. This time, therefore, the rise in the wage rate lowers hours worked.

Part (ii) of the figure shows the same behaviour as in part (i), using a supply curve. It plots the number of hours worked against the wage rate. At wage rates of up to $\underline{w}$, the individual is not in the labour force, for no work is offered. As the wage rate rises from $\underline{w}$ to w^*, more and more hours are worked, so the supply curve of effort has the normal positive slope. The wage rates that result in E_0 and E_1 in part (i) of the figure lie in this range. Above w^*, the quantity of effort falls as wages rise so that the supply curve has a negative slope. This latter case is often referred to as a *backward-bending supply curve of labour*. The wage that gives rise to point E_2 in part (i) lies in this range.

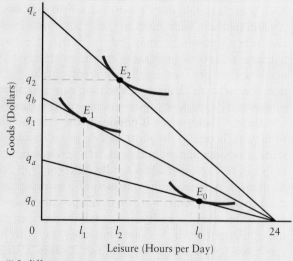

(i) Indifference curves

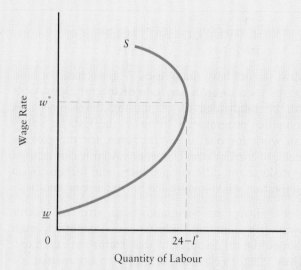

(ii) A supply curve of effort

Although land is highly mobile among alternative uses, it is completely immobile as far as location is concerned. There is only so much land within a given distance of the center of any city, and no increase in the price paid can induce further land to be located within that distance. This locational immobility has important consequences, including high prices for desirable locations and the tendency to build tall buildings to economize on the use of scarce land, as in the centre of large cities.

Labour.   Labour is unique as a factor of production in that the supply of the service often requires the physical presence of the person who supplies it.[4]

Absentee landlords, while continuing to live in the place of their choice, can obtain income from land that is located in remote parts of the world. Investment can be shifted from iron mines in South Africa to mines in Labrador while the owners commute between Calgary and Hawaii. However, when a worker who is employed by a firm producing men's ties in Montreal decides instead to supply his or her labour services to a firm producing women's shoes in Winnipeg, the worker must physically travel to Winnipeg. This has an important consequence.

Because of the need for labour's physical presence when its services are provided for the production of many commodities, nonmonetary considerations are much more important for the supply of labour than for other factors of production.

People may be satisfied with or frustrated by the kind of work that they do, where they do it, the people with whom they do it, and the social status of their occupations. Because these considerations influence their decisions about what they will do with their labour services, they will not always move just because they could earn a higher wage.

Nevertheless, labour does move among industries, occupations, and areas in response to changes in the signals provided by wages and opportunities for employment. The ease with which movement occurs depends on many forces. For example, it is not difficult for a secretary to shift from one company to another in order to take a job in Red Deer, Alberta, instead of Regina, Saskatchewan, but it can be difficult for a secretary to become an editor, a model, a machinist, or a doctor within a short period of time. Workers who lack ability, training, or inclination find certain kinds of mobility difficult or impossible.

Some barriers to movement may be virtually insurmountable once a person's training has been completed. It may be impossible for a farmer to become a surgeon or for a truck driver to become a professional athlete, even if the relative wage rates change greatly. However, the children of farmers, doctors, truck drivers, and athletes, when they are deciding how much education or training to obtain, are not nearly as limited in their choices as their parents, who have already completed their education and are settled in their occupations.

In any given year, some people enter the labour force directly from school, and others leave it through retirement or death. The turnover in the labour force owing to these causes is 3 or 4 percent per year. Over a period of 10 years, the allocation of labour can change dramatically merely by directing new entrants to jobs other than the ones that were left vacant by workers who left the labour force.

The role of education in helping new entrants to adapt to available jobs is important. In a society in which education is provided to all, it is possible to achieve large increases in the supply of any needed labour skill within a decade or so. These issues are discussed at greater length in the first part of Chapter 16.

The labour force as a whole is mobile, even though many individual members in it are not.

THE SUPPLY OF FACTORS TO A PARTICULAR FIRM

Most firms usually employ a small proportion of the total supply of each factor that they use. As a result, they can usually obtain their factors at the going market price. This is true both in the case of less-skilled workers and in the case of highly skilled workers. For example, a firm of management consultants can usually augment its clerical staff by placing an ad in the local newspaper and paying the going rate for clerks. A university which is hoping to expand its economics department can similarly place

---

[4]Labour must be physically present if it is helping in the direct production of most goods, such as automobiles, and of some services, such as haircuts. In other cases, however, labour services, such as consulting, design of a product, or writing advertising copy, can be supplied at a distance and its product communicated to the purchaser by such means as phone, fax, or mail.

an ad in *The Economist* or in a professional journal; it would also find itself paying the going rate for economics professors. In neither case will the employer's hiring actions affect the rate of pay earned by clerks (or professors) in its area.

Most firms are price takers in factor markets.

THE OPERATION OF FACTOR MARKETS

Once you have mastered the basic analysis of demand and supply in Chapters 4 through 6, the determination of the price, quantity, and income of a factor in a single market poses no new problems. Figure 15-3 shows a competitive market for a factor where the intersection of the demand and the supply curve determine the factor's price and the quantity of it that is employed. The price times quantity is the factor's total income, and that amount, divided by the

total income earned by all factors in the economy, represents that factor's share of the nation's total income.

In this section, we explore three issues relating to factor pricing. First, what explains the differences in payments received by different units of the same factor? For example, why do some workers get paid more than others? Second, what is the effectiveness of policies designed to reduce these differences? For example, can policies that promote "pay equity" eliminate these differences? Finally, we explore the important concept of *economic rent*.

DIFFERENTIALS IN FACTOR PRICES

Why is it that airline pilots typically get paid more than auto mechanics? Why does an acre of land in downtown Calgary rent for much more than an acre of land 150 kilometres away in the Crowsnest Pass? Do such differences in factor payments reflect some aspect of the factor markets that is not functioning properly, or are such *factor-price differentials* to be expected in well-functioning markets?

If every labourer were the same, if all benefits were monetary, and if workers moved freely among markets, the price of labour would tend to be the same in all uses. Workers would move from low-priced jobs to high-priced ones. The quantity of labour supplied would diminish in occupations in which wages were low, and the resulting labour shortage would tend to force those wages up; the quantity of labour supplied would increase in occupations in which wages were high, and the resulting surplus would force wages down. The movement would continue until there were no further incentives to change occupations—that is, until wages were equalized in all uses.

In fact, however, wage differentials commonly occur. These differentials may be divided into two distinct types: those that exist only temporarily and those that persist in long-term equilibrium.

As it is with labour, so it is with other factors of production. If all units of any factor of production were identical and moved freely among markets, all units would receive the same remuneration in equilibrium. In fact, however, different units of any one factor receive different payments.

Temporary Differentials

Some factor-price differentials reflect temporary disturbances. They are brought about by circumstances

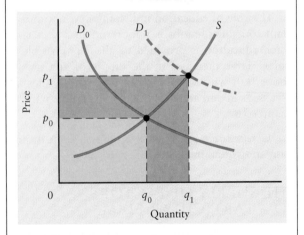

FIGURE 15-3
The Determination of Factor Price and Income in a Competitive Factor Market

In competitive factor markets, demand and supply determine factor prices, quantities of factors used, and factor incomes. With demand and supply curves D_0 and S, the price of the factor will be p_0 and the quantity employed will be q_0. The total income earned by the factor is the light gray shaded area. A shift in demand from D_0 to D_1 raises equilibrium price and quantity to p_1 and q_1, respectively. The income earned by the factor rises by an amount equal to the dark gray shaded area.

such as the growth of one industry and the decline of another. The differentials themselves lead to reallocation of factors, and such reallocations in turn act to eliminate the differentials.

Consider the effect on factor prices of a rise in the demand for air transport and a decline in the demand for rail transport. The airline industry's demand for factors increases while the railroad industry's demand for factors decreases. Relative factor prices will go up in airlines and down in railroads. The differential in factor prices causes a net movement of factors away from the railroad industry and toward the airline industry, and this movement causes the differentials to lessen and eventually to disappear. How long this process takes will depend on how easily factors can be reallocated from one industry to the other—that is, on the degree of factor mobility.

Equilibrium Differentials

Some factor-price differentials persist without generating any forces that eliminate them. These *equilibrium differentials* can be explained by intrinsic differences in the factors themselves and, for labour, by differences in the cost of acquiring skills and by different nonmonetary advantages of different occupations.

Intrinsic Differences.   If various units of a factor have different characteristics, the price that is paid may differ among these units. If dexterity is required to accomplish a task, manually dexterous workers will earn more than less dexterous workers. If land is to be used for agricultural purposes, highly fertile land will earn more than poor land. These differences will persist even in long-run equilibrium.

Acquired Differences.   If the fertility of land can be increased by costly methods, then more fertile land must command a higher price than less fertile land. If it did not, landowners would not incur the costs of improving fertility. The same holds true for labour since it is costly to acquire most skills. For example, a mechanic must train for some time, and unless the earnings of mechanics remain sufficiently above what can be earned in less skilled occupations, people will not incur the cost of training.

Nonmonetary Advantages.   Whenever working conditions differ among various uses for a single factor, that factor will earn different equilibrium amounts in its various uses. The difference between a test pilot's wage and a chauffeur's wage is only partly a matter of skill; the rest is compensation to the

worker for facing the higher risk of testing new planes as compared to driving a car. If both were paid the same, there would be an excess supply of chauffeurs and a shortage of test pilots.

Academic researchers commonly earn less than they could earn in the world of commerce and industry because of the substantial nonmonetary advantages of academic employment. If chemists were paid the same in both sectors, many chemists would prefer academic to industrial jobs. Excess demand for industrial chemists and excess supply of academic chemists would then force chemists' wages up in industry and down in academia until the two types of jobs seemed equally attractive on balance.

The same forces account for equilibrium differences in regional earnings of otherwise identical factors. People who work in remote logging or mining areas are paid more than people who do jobs requiring similar skills in large cities. Without higher pay, not enough people would be willing to work at sometimes dangerous jobs in unattractive or remote locations. Similarly, because many people prefer living in the Maritimes to living in the Yukon, equilibrium wages in comparable occupations are lower in the Maritimes than in the Yukon.

Differentials and Factor Mobility: Equalizing Net Advantage

The distinction between temporary and equilibrium differentials is closely linked to factor mobility.

Temporary differentials lead to, and are eroded by, factor movements; equilibrium differentials are not eliminated by factor mobility.

The behaviour that causes the erosion of disequilibrium differentials is summarized in the hypothesis of the *maximization of net advantage:* The owners of factors of production will allocate those factors to uses that maximize the net advantages to themselves, taking both monetary and nonmonetary rewards into consideration. If net advantages were higher in occupation A than in occupation B, factors would move from B to A. The increased supply in A and the lower supply in B would drive factor earnings down in A and up in B until net advantages would be equalized, after which no further movement would occur. This analysis gives rise to the prediction of *equal net advantage:* In equilibrium, units of each kind of factor of production will be allocated among alternative possible uses in such a way that the net advantages in all uses are equalized.

Although nonmonetary advantages are important in explaining differences in levels of pay for labour in different occupations, they tend to be quite stable over time. As a result, monetary advantages, which vary with market conditions, lead to *changes* in net advantage.

A change in the relative price of a factor between two uses will change the net advantages of the uses. It will lead to a shift of some units of that factor to the use for which relative price has increased.

This implies an upward-sloping supply curve for a factor in any particular use. When the price of a factor rises in that use, more will be supplied to that use. This factor supply curve (like all supply curves) can also *shift* in response to changes in other variables. For example, an improvement in the safety record in a particular occupation improves the attractiveness of that occupation and thus shifts to the right the labour-supply curve to that occupation. We examine some of the consequences of this in Chapter 19.

POLICY ISSUES

The distinction between temporary and equilibrium factor-price differentials raises an important consideration for policy. Trade unions, governments, and other bodies often have explicit policies about earnings differentials, sometimes seeking to eliminate them in the name of equity. The success of such policies depends to a great extent on the kind of differential that is being attacked. One general lesson here is the following: Policies that attempt to eliminate *equilibrium* differentials will encounter severe difficulties. Here are two examples.

Pay Equity

Recent government legislation has sought to require *equal pay for work of equal value,* or **pay equity.** Such policy is designed to eliminate the wage differentials that exist between workers *in different jobs* but who are deemed to have approximately the same skills and responsibilities. For example, a policy of pay equity might require that a nurse with 10 years of experience receive the same salary as a teacher with 10 years of experience. Whatever the social value of such laws, they run into trouble whenever

they require equal pay for jobs that have different nonmonetary advantages.

To illustrate the nature of the problem encountered by such legislation, consider the following example. Suppose that two jobs demand equal skills, training, and everything else that is taken into account when deciding what constitutes work of equal value but that, in a city with an extreme climate, one is an outside job and the other is an inside job. If legislation requires equal pay for both jobs, there will be a shortage of people who are willing to work outside and an excess of people who want to work inside. Employers will seek ways to attract outside workers. Higher pensions, shorter hours, longer holidays, overtime paid for but not worked, and better working conditions may be offered. If these are allowed, they will achieve the desired result but will defeat the original purpose of equalizing the monetary benefits of the inside and outside jobs; they will also cut down on the number of outside workers that employers will hire because the total cost of an outside worker to an employer will have risen. If the jobs are unionized or if the government prevents such "cheating," the shortage of workers for outside jobs will remain.

In Chapter 16, we discuss the effects of race and sex discrimination on wage differentials. Although these effects can be important, it remains true that many factor-price differentials are a natural market consequence of supply and demand conditions that have nothing to do with inequitable treatment of different groups in the society. Generally, mobility of factors tends to establish factor prices at which temporary differentials are eliminated but equilibrium differentials are stabilized.

Policies that seek to eliminate factor-price differentials without consideration of what causes them or how they affect the supply of the factor often have perverse results.

Regional Income Equalization

Canada's various regions differ markedly in their wealth. For example, the oil resources in Alberta have contributed considerably to that province's wealth over the past several decades; in contrast, the dramatic decline of the Atlantic fishery over the past decade has been one contributing factor to falling real incomes in the Atlantic provinces, especially

Newfoundland. Over the years, the federal government has developed several policies designed to reduce regional differences in per capita incomes. (In Chapter 20 we will see that such regional disparities are part of the motivation behind Canada's program of *equalization payments*.) The problems that these policies encounter are most easily seen by asking if it would be possible to equalize per capita incomes and unemployment rates across the provinces. The answer to this question is almost certainly no—at least when we consider the kinds of policy tools likely to be available to any foreseeable Canadian government. The reason is because as long as provinces differ in their nonmonetary attractiveness, there will be equilibrium differences in their per capita incomes and/or unemployment rates. And, as we saw above, trying to eliminate *equilibrium* factor-price differentials is problematic.

To illustrate the problem in this context, consider the following example. Suppose that Province A—despite strong physical, climatic, and social attractions—has a set of natural endowments that will not produce as high an income per person employed as Province B.[5] Suppose also that because of migration costs, cultural and language differences, climatic advantages, or other local amenities, many people choose to live in Province A even though they earn lower incomes there. In short, living in Province A has nonmonetary advantages over living in Province B. Markets can adjust to such regional differences in two basic ways; one way when wages are flexible, and another when wages are inflexible.

Flexible Wages. If wages and prices are flexible, real wages and incomes will fall in Province A for the kinds of workers who are in excess supply. The falling real wages will give the province an advantage in new lines of production. Real wages will continue to fall until everyone who is willing to stay in Province A at the lower wage has a job and those who are not have migrated. In long-run equilibrium, Province A is a low-wage, low-income province, but it has no special unemployment problem. Those who do not value Province A's amenities as much as

they value the higher incomes to be earned in Province B, or who are subject to lower migration costs, will have left. What the price system does is equalize total advantages. It does not equalize factor payments, because the nonmonetary advantages of living in Province A exceed those of living in Province B.

Inflexible Wages. The second possibility arises when wages are *not* totally flexible. Minimum-wage laws, national unions, and nationwide pay scales for the federal civil service put substantial restraints on possible interprovincial wage differentials. People who prefer Province A remain there, yet wages do not fall to create a wage incentive to employ more people in A or for those people to move to B. Instead, unemployment rates in A rise until (1) the extra uncertainty of finding a job and (2) the lower lifetime income expectations because of bouts of unemployment just balance both the nonmonetary advantages that Province A enjoys over Province B and the costs of moving from A to B. In long-run equilibrium, those who are willing to stay in spite of the higher unemployment remain, and the others leave.

Suppose now that the government of Province A attempts to battle against the high unemployment in its region by introducing some labour-market policies. Could policies close the unemployment gap between the two provinces? In these circumstances, market restrictions (such as laws that require the employment of local labour only) and labour-market policies (such as employment subsidies) will not reduce the unemployment *rate* in Province A, although they will increase the *level* of employment. As new jobs are created in Province A, the rate of emigration slows so that the rate of unemployment is unchanged. The local supply rises as fast as the local demand for labour, and the unemployment rate is left unchanged. This is because in the long run, A's unemployment rate must remain sufficiently above B's to balance the nonmonetary advantages that A enjoys over B.

The foregoing argument does not imply that we should ignore regions that have lower incomes or higher unemployment rates. However, it is important to realize that if the differential is an *equilibrium* phenomenon, no amount of policy intervention will remove it. If the policies continue to be strengthened as long as these differentials in unemployment persist, expenditures will continue to rise, but the ultimate goal of equalization will continue to prove elusive.

---

[5]Deficiencies in economic opportunities in a particular province might arise for many reasons: an inadequate resource base; technological backwardness; slow growth in demand for one region's products; or rapid natural growth of the labour force.

Some Evidence of Labour Mobility in Canada

This chapter has emphasized the importance of factor mobility. In particular, in the previous examples policy interventions to eliminate equilibrium differentials were thwarted *because of the mobility of labour.* In the first case, the requirement that outside jobs earned the same wage as inside jobs induced workers to reduce their supply of labour to the outside job and to increase their supply of labour to the inside job. This is labour mobility across jobs. In the second example, the policy designed to reduce the unemployment gap between two regions induced workers to move into the high-unemployment region, thereby leaving the unemployment rate in that region unchanged. This is labour mobilty across regions.

But does this kind of labour mobility really take place? The answer is yes. Table 15-4 shows some data on the amount of net migration between Canadian provinces and territories from 1970 to 1992. The first column shows the net migration between provinces for the year 1992 in particular. The second column shows the cumulative net flow from 1970 to 1992.

Over the 22-year period, there was a net migration of over 800,000 individuals between the provinces. But even this large number understates the actual amount of interregional labour mobility, for three reasons. First, these data do not include individuals who emigrated from Canada or who arrived to Canada from foreign countries. Second, the data do not include individuals who moved from one location in a region to another location within the same region. For example, an individual who moves from Lethbridge in Southern Alberta to Grand Prairie in Northern Alberta does not show up in this table. These two problems suggest that both the data from 1992 and the cumulative data for 1970–1992 understate the true amount of labour mobility. The third reason applies to the cumulative data, but less so to the annual data. The cumulative data does not show the migration that "reverses itself" during the period. For example, the many individuals who moved from Ontario to Alberta in the mid 1970s, and then returned to Ontario in the mid 1980s, do not show up in the cumulative data, but would show up in the annual data. Partly for this reason, the migration numbers for 1992 are much more than one-twenty-second of the migration numbers for the entire 1970–1992 period.

TABLE 15-4
Net Canadian Interregional Migration

Region	Net Change	Cumulative Net Change
	(number of individuals)	
	1992	1970–1992
Newfoundland	− 3,626	− 63,265
P.E.I.	504	1,711
Nova Scotia	− 2,132	3,444
New Brunswick	− 1,890	− 3,526
Quebec	− 15,497	− 429,820
Ontario	− 2,956	156,059
Manitoba	− 6,513	− 129,821
Saskatchewan	− 8,472	− 168,679
Alberta	− 1,278	185,342
British Columbia	41,240	454,140
Yukon/N.W.T.	620	− 5,585
Net Total Movers	42,364	800,696

The past few decades have seen significant migration of individuals between Canadian regions. In the 1970–1992 period, a cumulative net flow of 429,820 people left Quebec and settled in some other Canadian province or territory; in contrast, a cumulative net flow of 454,140 people arrived in B.C. from other Canadian regions. The numbers in the table sum to zero because each person who emigrates from one province also immigrates to another. The total number of movers is the total amount of emigration (or immigration). For the three reasons given in the text, these numbers understate the actual amount of interregional labour mobility in Canada.

(*Source:* Richard Chaykowski, *Modern Labour Economics,* HarperCollins 1994.)

For these three reasons, even the relatively large amount of labour mobility suggested by Table 15-4 understates the actual amount of interregional labour mobility in Canada.

ECONOMIC RENT

One of the most important concepts in economics is that of *economic rent.*

A factor must earn a certain amount in its present use to prevent it from moving to another use—Alfred Marshall called this amount the factor's *transfer earnings.* If there were no nonmonetary advantages in alternative uses, the factor would have to earn its opportunity cost (what it could earn elsewhere) to prevent it from moving elsewhere. This is usually true for capital and land. Labour, however, gains important nonmonetary advantages in various jobs, and it must earn in one use enough to equate the two jobs' total advantages, both monetary and nonmonetary.

Any excess that a factor earns over the minimum amount needed to keep it at its present use is called its **economic rent.** Economic rent is analogous to economic profit as a surplus over the opportunity cost of capital. The concept of economic rent is crucial in predicting the effects that changes in earnings have on the movement of factors among alternative uses. However, the terminology is confusing because economic rent is often called simply *rent,* which can

of course also mean the price paid to hire something, such as a machine, a piece of land, or an apartment. How the same term came to be used for these two very different concepts is explained in Extension 15-3.

How Much of Factor Earnings is Rent?

In most cases, economic rent makes up part of the actual earnings of a factor of production. The distinction is most easily seen, however, by examining

---

EXTENSION 15-3

ORIGIN OF THE TERM "ECONOMIC RENT"

In the early nineteenth century, there was a public debate about the high price of wheat in England. The price was causing great hardship because bread was a primary source of food for the working class. Some people argued that wheat had a high price because landlords were charging high rents to tenant farmers. In short, it was argued that the price of wheat was high because the rents of agricultural land were high. Some of those who held this view advocated restricting the rents that landlords could charge.

David Ricardo (1772–1823), a great British economist who was one of the originators of Classical economics, argued that the situation was exactly the reverse. The price of wheat was high, he said, because there was a shortage, caused by the Napoleonic Wars. Because wheat was profitable to produce, there was keen competition among farmers to obtain land on which to grow wheat. This competition in turn forced up the rental price of wheat land. Ricardo advocated removing the existing tariff on wheat so that imported wheat could come into the country, thereby increasing its supply in England and lowering both the price of wheat and the rent that could be charged for the land on which it was grown.

The essentials of Ricardo's argument were these: The supply of land was fixed. Land was regarded as having only one use, the growing of wheat. Nothing had to be paid to prevent land from transferring to a use other than growing wheat because it had no other

use. No landowner would leave land idle as long as some return could be obtained by renting it out. Therefore, all the payment to land, that is, rent in the ordinary sense of the word, was a surplus over and above what was necessary to keep it in its present use.

Given a fixed supply of land, the price of land depended on the demand for land, which depended in turn on the demand for wheat (i.e., the demand for land was *derived from* the demand for wheat). *Rent,* the term for the payment for the use of land, thus became the term for a surplus payment to a factor over and above what was necessary to keep it in its present use.

Later, two facts were realized. First, land often had alternative uses, and, from the point of view of any one use, part of the payment made to land would necessarily have to be paid to keep it in that use. Second, factors of production other than land also often earned a surplus over and above what was necessary to keep them in their present use. Television stars and great athletes, for example, are in short and fairly fixed supply, and their potential earnings in other occupations often are quite moderate. However, because there is a huge demand for their services as television stars or athletes, they may receive payments greatly in excess of what is needed to keep them from transferring to other occupations. This surplus is now called *economic rent,* whether the factor is land, labour, or a piece of capital equipment.

FIGURE 15-4
The Determination of Rent in Factor Payments

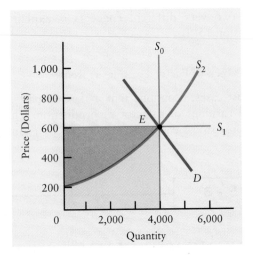

The amount of rent in factor payments depends on the shape of the supply curve. A single demand curve is shown with three different supply curves. In each case, the competitive equilibrium price is $600, and 4,000 units of the factor are hired. The total payment ($2.4 million) is represented by the entire shaded area.

When the supply curve is vertical (S_0), the whole payment is economic rent because a decrease in price would not lead any units of the factor to move elsewhere.

When the supply curve is horizontal (S_1), none of the payment is rent because even a small decrease in price offered would lead all units of the factor to move elsewhere.

When the supply curve is positively sloped (S_2), part of the payment is rent. As shown by the height of the supply curve, at a price of $600, the 4,000th unit of the factor is receiving just enough to persuade it to offer its services in this market, but the 2,000th unit, for example, is earning well above what it requires to stay in this market. The aggregate of economic rents is shown by the red shaded area, whereas the aggregate of what must be paid to keep all 4,000 units in this market is shown by the entire shaded area.

crease, no matter how low the price goes. This indicates that the factor has no alternative use, and thus requires no minimum payment to keep it in its present use. In this case, the whole of the payment is economic rent. The price actually paid allocates the fixed supply to whoever is most willing to pay for it.

When the supply curve is perfectly elastic (horizontal), none of the price paid is economic rent. If any lower price is offered, nothing whatsoever will be supplied since all units of the factor will transfer to some other use.

The more usual situation is that of an upward-sloping supply curve. A rise in the factor's price serves the allocative function of attracting more units of the factor into the market in question, but the same rise provides additional economic rent to all units of the factor that are *already employed*. We know that the extra pay that is going to the units already employed is economic rent because the owners of these units were willing to supply them at the lower price. The general result for a positively sloped supply curve is stated as follows.

If the demand for a factor in any of its uses rises relative to the supply available to that use, its price will rise in that use. This will serve the allocative function of attracting additional units into that use. It will also increase the economic rent to all units of the factor already in that use.

Various Perspectives on Economic Rent

The proportion of a given factor payment that is economic rent varies from situation to situation. We cannot point to a factor of production and assert that some fixed fraction of its income is always its economic rent. The proportion of its earnings that is rent depends on the alternatives that are open to it.

Focus first on a narrowly defined use of a given factor, say, its use by a particular firm. From that firm's point of view, the factor will be highly mobile, as it could readily move to another firm in the same industry. The firm must pay the going wage or risk losing that factor. Thus from the perspective of the single firm, a large proportion of the payment made to a factor is needed to prevent it from transferring to another use.

two extreme cases. In one, everything a factor earns is rent; in the other, none is rent.

The possibilities are illustrated in Figure 15-4. When the supply curve is perfectly inelastic (vertical), the same quantity is supplied, whatever the price. Evidently, the quantity supplied does not de-

Focus now on a more broadly defined use, for example, the factor's use in an entire industry. From the industry's point of view, the factor is less mobile because it would be more difficult for it to gain employment quickly outside the industry. From the perspective of the particular *industry* (rather than the specific *firm* within the industry), a larger proportion of the payment to a factor is economic rent.

From the even more general perspective of a particular *occupation*, mobility is likely to be even less, and the proportion of the factor payment that is economic rent is likely to be more. It may be easier, for example, for a carpenter to move from the construction industry to the furniture industry than to retrain to be a computer operator.

As the perspective moves from a narrowly defined use of a factor to a broadly defined use of a factor, the mobility of the factor decreases; as mobility decreases, the share of the factor payment that is economic rent increases.

Consider how this applies to the often controversial large salaries that are received by some highly specialized types of labourers, such as recording stars and professional athletes. These performers have a style and a talent that cannot be duplicated, whatever the training. The earnings that they receive are mostly economic rent from the viewpoint of the occupation: These performers generally enjoy their occupations and would pursue them for much less than the high remuneration that they actually receive. For example, Shaquille O'Neal would probably choose basketball over other alternatives even at a much lower salary. However, because of O'Neal's amazing skills as a basketball player, most NBA teams would pay handsomely to have him on their rosters, and he is able to command a high salary from the team he does play for. From the perspective of the individual firm, the Orlando Magic, most of O'Neal's salary is required to keep him from switching to another team and hence is not economic rent. From the point of view of the basketball "industry," however, much of his salary is economic rent.

Notice also that O'Neal's salary is largely determined by the demand for his services. The supply is perfectly inelastic—no one else possesses his particular combination of skills. So the market-clearing price is determined by the position of the demand curve. This is generally the case with economic rent—supply is fixed, so price is determined by demand.

A FINAL WORD

This chapter has examined the operation of factor markets. You should now be able to answer the questions that we posed in the opening paragraph. Here are some of the key points for two of those questions.

What explains why professors usually get paid more than high-school teachers? Part of the answer surely lies in the fact that to be a university professor typically requires nine years of university education (four for the bachelor's degree plus five for the completion of the doctorate) whereas to be a teacher usually requires only four or five years. Since that extra education is costly and time-consuming, it is not surprising that fewer people are willing to become university professors than teachers. This lower supply for professors, other things equal, leads to a higher wage.

Why does an acre of farm land in Northern Saskatchewan rent for far less than an acre of land in downtown Toronto? To answer this, just think about the alternative uses for the farm land, and compare them to the alternative uses for the acre in downtown Toronto. The acre of farm land has very few alternative uses. Or, more correctly, it has many alternative uses, but there is little demand to use that particular piece of land to build a skyscraper, shopping mall, or baseball stadium. But one acre of land in downtown Toronto has many alternative uses—there always seems to be demand for additional space for parking garages, office buildings, shopping malls, and many other things. Since the piece of farm land in Saskatchewan must stay where it is, its rental price is determined by demand. Since there is little demand for the land, its rental price is low. Similarly, the land in downtown Toronto cannot move anywhere, and so its rental price is determined by demand. And since there is lots of demand for an acre in downtown Toronto, its rental price is high.

Having learned about factor markets in general, we are now ready to examine some specific factor markets. In Chapter 16, we examine some details about labour markets, such as minimum wages, discrimination, and labour unions. In Chapter 17, we examine the pricing of physical capital and of nonrenewable resources.

SUMMARY

A. INCOME DISTRIBUTION AND FACTOR PRICING

- The functional distribution of income refers to the shares of total national income going to each of the major factors of production; it focuses on sources of income. The size distribution of income refers to the shares of total national income going to various groups of households; it focuses only on the amount of income, not its source.
- The income of a factor of production is composed of two elements: the price paid per unit of the factor and the quantity of the factor used. The determination of factor prices and quantities is an application of the same price theory that is used to determine product prices and quantities.

B. THE DEMAND FOR FACTORS

- The firm's decisions on how much to produce and how to produce it imply demands for factors of production, which are said to be derived from the demand for goods that they are used to produce.
- A profit-maximizing firm will hire units of a factor until the last unit adds as much to cost as it does to revenue. This means that the marginal cost of the factor would be equated with that factor's marginal revenue product. Marginal revenue product is equal to the marginal physical product multiplied by the revenue associated with the sale of another unit of output (i.e., marginal revenue).
- When the firm is a price taker in input markets, the marginal cost of the factor is its price per unit. When the firm sells its output in a competitive market, the marginal revenue product is the factor's marginal physical product multiplied by the market price of the output.
- A price-taking firm's demand for a factor is negatively sloped because the law of diminishing returns implies that the marginal physical product of a factor declines as more of that factor is employed (with other inputs held constant).
- The industry's demand for a factor will be more elastic (a) the faster the marginal physical product of the factor declines as more of the factor is used, (b) the easier it is to substitute one factor for another, (c) the larger the proportion of total variable costs accounted for by the cost of the factor in question, and (d) the more elastic the demand for the good that the factor helps to produce.

C. THE SUPPLY OF FACTORS

- The total supply of each factor is fixed at any moment but varies over time. The supply of labour depends on the size of the population, the participation rate, and hours worked.
- A rise in the wage rate has a substitution effect, which tends to induce more work, and an income effect, which tends to induce less work (more leisure consumed).
- The supply of a factor to a particular industry or occupation is more elastic than its supply to the whole economy because one industry can bid units away from other industries. The elasticity of supply to a particular use depends on factor mobility, which tends to be greater the longer the time allowed for a reaction to take place.

D. THE OPERATION OF FACTOR MARKETS

- Factor-price differentials often occur in competitive markets. Temporary differentials in the earnings of different units of factors of production induce factor movements that eventually remove the differentials. Equilibrium differentials reflect differences among units of factors as well as nonmonetary benefits of different jobs; they can persist indefinitely.
- Equal net advantage is a theory of the allocation of the total supply of factors to particular uses. Owners of factors will choose the use that produces the greatest net advantage, allowing for monetary and nonmonetary advantages of a particular employment. In so doing, they will cause temporary factor price differentials to be eliminated.
- Some amount must be paid to a factor to prevent it from transferring to another use. This amount is the factor's transfer earnings. Economic rent is the difference between that amount and a factor's actual earnings. Whenever the supply curve is positively sloped, part of the total pay going to a factor is needed to prevent it from transferring to another use, and part of it is rent. The proportion of each depends on the mobility of the factor. The more narrowly defined the use, the larger the fraction that is transfer earnings and the smaller the fraction that is economic rent.

KEY CONCEPTS

Functional distribution and size distribution of income

Derived demand for a factor

Marginal physical product

Marginal revenue product

The determinants of elasticity of factor demand

Factor mobility

Temporary versus equilibrium factor-price differentials

Equal net advantage

Transfer earnings

Economic rent

DISCUSSION QUESTIONS

1. Other things being equal, how would you expect each of the following events to affect the size distribution of after-tax income? Do any lead to clear predictions about the functional distribution of income?

   a. An increase in unemployment
   b. Rapid population growth in an already crowded city
   c. An increase in food prices relative to other prices
   d. An increase in social insurance benefits and taxes
   e. Elimination of the personal income-tax exemption for interest earned within an RRSP.

2. Consider the effects on the overall level of income inequality of each of the following situations.

   a. Increasing participation of women in the labour force as many women shift from work in the home to full-time jobs in the workplace
   b. Increasing use by fruit growers of migrant workers who are in the country on temporary visas
   c. Increasing numbers of minority group members studying law and medicine
   d. Cuts in the rates of income tax, together with the elimination of some personal income tax deductions

3. How much of the following payments for factor services is likely to be economic rent?

   a. The $750 per month that a landlord receives for an apartment leased to students
   b. The salary of the Canadian Prime Minister
   c. The large annual income of recording stars such as Rod Stewart, Céline Dion, and Bryan Adams
   d. The salary of a window cleaner who says, "It's dangerous and dirty work, but it beats driving a truck."

4. Which of the following are temporary differentials and which are equilibrium differentials in factor prices?

   a. Differences in earnings of football coaches and wrestling coaches

   b. A "bonus for signing on" offered by a construction company seeking carpenters in a tight labour market
   c. Differences in monthly rent charged for three-bedroom houses in different parts of the same metropolitan area
   d. Higher prices per square foot of condominium space in Vancouver compared with Halifax

5. A labour dispute has broken out at a university between the faculty and the university's board of governors. One of the issues is the faculty's complaint that summer school teaching salaries are below the regional average and hence too low. The trustees argue that considering that they have more professors asking to teach summer school at the current pay than they have courses for these faculty to teach, the pay is adequate. Comment.

6. Jim Kelly, quarterback for the Buffalo Bills, is paid many millions of dollars a year to play football. However, Kent Hull, the starting center, is paid only a few hundred thousand dollars per year, even though without Hull's efforts, Kelly would not be able to pass the ball. What can explain these differences in pay, despite the fact that in a team sport such as football, both players' efforts are arguably of "equal value"?

7. The demands listed here have been increasing rapidly in recent years. What derived demands would you predict have also risen sharply? Where will the extra factors of production that are demanded be drawn from?

   a. Demand for natural gas
   b. Demand for medical services
   c. Demand for international and interregional travel

8. Consider the large-scale substitution of jumbo jets, each of which has a seating capacity of about 350, for jets with a seating capacity of about 125. What kinds of labour service would you predict will experience an increase in demand, and what kinds will experience a decrease? Under what conditions would airplane pi-

lots (as a group) be made better off economically by virtue of this substitution?

9. A recent *Wall Street Journal* article asks, "Why do baseball players earn millions of dollars a year for their negligible contribution to society while major contributors—such as schoolteachers, policemen, firemen, and ambulance drivers—earn barely enough to survive?" Can you offer an answer based on what was discussed in this Chapter?

10. For most of the years in the past two decades, the unemployment rate in the province of Quebec has been higher than the Canadian average. It has also been higher than the unemployment rate in next-door Ontario. Given that there are almost no legal restrictions on the flow of labour across Canadian provincial boundaries, provide an explanation for how such a gap in unemployment rates can persist for so long.

LABOUR MARKETS

The competitive theory of factor-price determination, presented in Chapter 15, tells us a great deal about factor prices, factor movements, and the distribution of income. In this chapter, we apply this theory to the most important of factor markets, the labour market. In the process, we extend the theory to cover situations in which suppliers and demanders of labour have some market power in the labour market, and are thus not price takers. We also examine the effects of legislated minimum wages, the role of labour unions, and the effects of employers' discrimination between different types of workers. The chapter closes with a discussion of the often-heard claim that Canada and other developed countries have been gaining "bad jobs" at the expense of "good jobs."

LABOUR MARKETS AND WAGE DIFFERENTIALS

We observed in Chapter 15 that the need for most workers to be physically present when their labour services are used differentiates labour from other factors of production. As a result, nonmonetary considerations, such as location of employment and other working conditions, are more important in the labour market than in markets for other factors of production.

Considerations other than material advantage also enter the relationship between employer and employee, for it is a relationship that involves loyalty, fairness, appreciation, and justice along with paycheques and productivity. It is also a relationship that may involve both actual and perceived discrimination on the basis of such things as gender, race, and age. The performance of labour markets will be affected by all of these noneconomic considerations and more.

Labour unions, employers' associations, collective bargaining, and government intervention in wage determination are important features of labour markets. They influence wages and working conditions and affect the levels of employment and unemployment in many industries. This means that the basic theory of factor-price determination from Chapter 15 must be augmented before it can be applied to the full range of problems concerning the determination of wages.

CONDITIONS FOR A SINGLE WAGE

All workers would receive the same wage if the following conditions held.

- All jobs had the same working conditions
- All workers were identical
- Labour markets were perfectly competitive

If these three conditions were satisfied, then everyone would earn the same wage in equilibrium and that wage would be equal to the marginal revenue prod-

uct of labour. In reality, however, wages vary enormously. Some people work full time and are in poverty; others are able to live very well on what they earn from working. Generally, the more education and experience a worker has, the higher are his or her wages. Given equal education and experience, women on average earn less than men. In the United States, blacks on average earn less than similarly-educated whites. Workers in highly unionized industries tend to get paid more than workers with similar skills and experience in nonunionized industries. Such differentials arise because workers are not all identical, jobs are not all identical, and because many important noncompetitive forces operate in labour markets. We now look more systematically at the reasons why different types of labour earn different wages.

WAGE DIFFERENTIALS IN COMPETITIVE MARKETS

Where there are many employers (buyers) and many workers (sellers), there is a competitive labour market of the kind discussed in Chapter 15. Under competitive conditions, the wage rate and level of employment are set by supply and demand. No worker or group of workers, and no firm or group of firms, is able to affect the market wage. In practice, there are many kinds of workers and many kinds of jobs, even within individual industries or occupations. When considering these, we can think of a series of related labour markets rather than a single national market. In competitive equilibrium, we can distinguish several major sources of wage differentials.

Working Conditions

Given identical skills, those working under relatively onerous or risky conditions earn more than those working in pleasant or safe conditions. For example, construction workers who work the "high iron," assembling the frames for skyscrapers, are paid more than workers who do similar work at ground level. The reason is simple: Risk and unpleasantness reduce the supply of labour, thus raising the wage above what it would otherwise be. Another example is that a university professor who teaches at a "big-name" university might earn less than he would earn doing exactly the same job at a less well-known university. Again, the reason is simple: The nonmonetary advantages of being on staff at a famous university increase the supply of labour and reduce the wages relative to those at the less famous universities. Different working conditions in different jobs thus lead to wage differentials—these are *equilibrium* differentials as discussed in Chapter 15.

In competitive labour markets, supply and demand set the equilibrium wage, but the wage will differ according to the nonmonetary aspects of the job.

Luck

Large incomes will be earned by people who have scarce skills that cannot be taught and that are highly valued—for example, the physical ability to be an NBA basketball player. In this case, the combination of a small and inelastic supply and a large enough demand of the relevant kind of labour cause the market-clearing wage to be high. There are also less extreme cases. Some people are endowed with the ability to make others feel good—they make superior salespersons and therapists. Some people enjoy working hard more than others; they are thus more valuable on the job and often get paid more. All of these are also equilibrium differentials in the sense discussed in Chapter 15.

Inherited skills, which are mostly beyond the individual's control, can have important effects on the ability to earn income.

Human Capital

A machine is physical capital. It requires an investment of time and money to create it, and once created, it yields valuable services over a long time. In the same way, labour skills require an investment of time and money to acquire, and once acquired, they yield an increased income to their owner over a long time. Since investment in labour skills is similar to investment in physical capital, acquired skills are called **human capital**. The supply of some particular skill increases when more people find it worthwhile to acquire the necessary human capital; the supply decreases when fewer do so. The more costly it is to acquire the skill required for a particular job, the higher its pay must be to attract people to train for it.

The stock of skills acquired by individual workers is called human capital; investment in human capital is usually costly, and the return is usually in terms of higher labour productivity and hence higher earning power.

The two main ways in which human capital is acquired are through formal education and through on-the-job training.

Formal Education. Compulsory education is an attempt to provide some minimum human capital for all citizens. Some people, either through luck in the school they attend or through their own efforts, profit more from their early education than others. They acquire more human capital than their less fortunate contemporaries. Subsequent income differentials reflect these differences in human capital acquired in the early stages of education.

Those who decide to stay in school beyond the years of compulsory education are deciding to invest voluntarily in acquiring further human capital. The (opportunity) cost is measured by the income that could have been earned if the person had entered the labour force immediately, plus any out-of-pocket costs for such items as tuition fees and equipment. The return is measured by the higher income earned when a better job is obtained. (Recall Application 1-1 in Chapter 1.)

If the demand for labour with more human capital rises, the earnings of such labour will rise. This will raise the expected return to those currently deciding whether to make the investment themselves. If the demand for labour with low amounts of human capital falls, the earnings of such persons will fall. This lowers the opportunity costs of staying on in school and acquiring more capital because the earnings forgone by not going to work are reduced. A rise in unemployment will also lower the costs because the probability of earning a steady income will be reduced, and this will reduce the expected loss from not entering the labour force early.

Market forces adjust the overall costs and benefits of acquiring human capital, and individuals respond according to their varying personal assessments of costs and benefits.

The evidence suggests that in most advanced industrialized countries the demand for people with a college or university education has been rising relative to the demand for those without post-secondary education. Thus the wages for highly educated people have been rising relative to the wages of less-educated people. For example, Table 16-1 shows how the real returns to higher education changed for Canadian men and women from 1984 to 1992. For every year shown in the table, the real earnings for college graduates are significantly higher than for those with only

TABLE 16-1
Real Returns to Education for Full-Year, Full-Time Workers, 1984–1992

| Year | Real Mean Earnings, Men Aged 35–44 Years | | Real Mean Earnings, Women Aged 35–44 Years | |
	High School	College	High School	College
1984	$29,858	$45,396	$18,656	$32,455
1986	28,902	46,296	18,455	34,174
1988	30,780	45,642	17,818	32,988
1990	29,140	46,221	20,589	33,469
1992	30,307	46,884	20,582	35,140

Real earnings for college graduates have been rising relative to real earnings for those with only high-school diplomas. The data show for various years the real earnings (in 1986 dollars) for men and women with different levels of education. Real earnings for high-school graduates were roughly constant from 1984 to 1992, whereas real earnings for college graduates have increased by between 3 percent (for men) and 8 percent (for women). Note also that there is a considerable difference in any given year between the real earnings for men and women.
(*Source:* Statistics Canada, *Earnings of Men and Women,* 13-217.)

a high-school diploma. Furthermore, the earnings for college graduates increased by between 3 and 8 percent over that period (for men and women, respectively), but remained roughly constant for those with only a high-school education. Thus the *relative earnings* of more highly educated workers increased over this period.

The evidence also suggests that more people stay on to complete more education when times are bad than when times are good. The reason is that the opportunity cost of education, measured in terms of expected earnings forgone, is lower when unemployment rates are high and earnings are depressed than when unemployment rates are low and earnings are buoyant.

In the long run, decisions to acquire human capital help to erode differentials in income. Market signals change the costs and benefits of acquiring human capital in such specific forms as skill in electronics, accountancy, law, or medicine. By reacting to these signals, young people help to increase the supplies of high-income workers and reduce the supplies of low-income workers, thereby eroding the differentials that exist at a given time.

Of course, people's ability to acquire human capital is limited by their innate abilities and their past experiences. Those with below-average cognitive abilities are unlikely to become computer programmers. Those handicapped by inadequate elementary and high school education will find it difficult to become highly skilled technicians. (A few dedicated and highly intelligent people may manage to do so later in life, but for most, the handicaps of bad early training are too great to overcome.)

On-the-Job Education.   Differentials according to age are readily observable in most firms and occupations. To a significant extent, these differentials are a response to human capital acquired on the job.

Acquiring this type of human capital is important in creating rising wages for employees and for making firms competitive. Evidence suggests that people who miss on-the-job training early in life are handicapped relative to others throughout much of their later working careers. This makes prolonged unemployment early in one's potential working career more serious than just the wages lost at the time. It also appears that different countries' firms have different practices with respect to investing in their employees' human capital. For example, Japanese auto companies operating in North America spend substantially more on employee training than do the North American auto companies. To some extent, this is because the Japanese methods of flexible manufacturing (discussed in Application 9-2 in Chapter 9) require more worker flexibility and training than do the North American mass-production methods.

Gender and Race

Crude statistics show that incomes vary by race and gender. (Indeed, referring again to Table 16-1, it is clear that for every year in the table, and for either of the two education levels shown, the average real earnings for men exceeds that for women.) More detailed studies suggest that a significant part of these differences can be explained by such considerations as the amount of human capital acquired through both formal education and on-the-job experience. When all such explanations are taken into account, however, differentials that are consistent with discrimination based on race and sex seem to remain. We discuss discrimination in some detail later in this chapter.

WAGE DIFFERENTIALS IN NONCOMPETITIVE MARKETS

So far we have examined four broad explanations for why wage differentials exist in competitive labour markets. Another explanation for wage differentials is that the labour market may *not* be competitive. In Chapters 10 through 12, we distinguished different *structures* for the markets in which firms sell their outputs. The inputs that firms use are also bought in markets that can have different structures. Although some markets are perfectly competitive, many show elements of market power on either the demand or the supply side.

To study the influence of different labour market structures on wages, we consider the case of an industry that employs identical workers for only one kind of job. In this way, we eliminate the possibility that any wage differentials are caused by differences between workers or differences between jobs—we thus highlight the role of market structure.

We examine two general cases. The first is when workers get together in a group and exercise some market power over setting the wage. The second is when the firm does not have to compete with other firms to hire workers. We examine these cases in turn.

Monopoly: A Union in a Competitive Market

For the purposes of our discussion of labour markets, a **union** (or *trade union* or *labour union*) is an association that is authorized to represent workers in negotiations with their employers. We examine unions in greater detail later in this chapter. For now we take the simple view that when workers are represented by a labour union, there is essentially only a single supplier of labour.

Suppose that a union enters a competitive labour market to represent all of the workers. As the single seller of labour for many buyers, the union is a monopolist, and it can establish a wage below which no one will work, thus changing the supply curve of labour. The industry can hire as many units of labour as are prepared to work at the

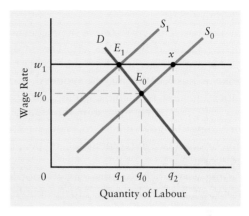

FIGURE 16-1
Effect on Wages of Union Entry in a Competitive Labour Market

A union can raise the wages of people who continue to be employed but only by reducing the number of people employed. The competitive equilibrium is at E_0, the wage is w_0, and employment is q_0. If a union enters this market and sets a wage of w_1, a new equilibrium will be established at E_1. The supply curve has become $w_1 x S_0$. At the new wage w_1, employment will be q_1, and there will be $q_1 q_2$ workers who would like to work but whom the industry will not hire. The decrease in employment due to the wage increase is $q_1 q_0$.

The wage w_1 can be achieved without generating a pool of persons who are seeking but unable to find work. To do so, the union must restrict entry into the occupation and thus shift the supply curve to the left to S_1. Employment will again be q_1.

This figure can also be used to illustrate the effect of the government imposing a minimum wage of w_1 on the market where the competitive equilibrium is at E_0. The q_1 workers who remain employed benefit by the wage increase. The $q_1 q_0$ workers who lose their jobs in this industry suffer to the extent that they fail to find new jobs at a wage of w_0 or more.

union wage but no one at a lower wage. Thus the industry (and each firm) faces a supply curve that is horizontal at the level of the union wage up to the maximum quantity of labour that is willing to work at that wage.

If the union uses its monopoly power, it will negotiate a wage above the competitive level. This situation is shown in Figure 16-1, in which the intersection of this horizontal supply curve and the demand curve establishes a higher wage rate and a lower level of employment than the competitive equilibrium.

There will be some workers who would like to obtain work in the industry or occupation but cannot. A conflict of interest has been created between serving the interests of the union's employed and unemployed members.

An alternative way to achieve the higher wage is to shift the supply curve to the left. The union may do this by restricting entry into the occupation by methods such as lengthening the required period of apprenticeship and reducing openings for trainees. Alternatively, the union may shift the supply curve by persuading the government to impose restrictive licensing or certification requirements on people who wish to work.

Raising wages by restricting entry is not limited to unions, of course. It occurs, for example, with many professional groups, including doctors. Because professional standards have long been regarded as necessary to protect the public from incompetent practitioners, doctors have found it publicly acceptable to control supply by limiting entry into their profession. Physicians' incomes are among the highest of any profession partly because of barriers to entry, including the difficulties of getting into an approved medical school, the high costs of setting up new medical schools, and various certification requirements applying to students, schools, and practitioners.

Monopsony: A Single Buyer in the Market

A **monopsony** is a market in which there is only one buyer; monopsony is to the buying side of the market what monopoly is to the selling side. Although cases of monopsony are not very common, it does sometimes arise. Monopsony sometimes occurs in small towns which contain only one industry and often only one large plant or mine. For example, the towns of Iroquois Falls in Ontario and Pine Falls in Manitoba are small towns where the principal employer is a single firm (Abitibi Price) which operates a newsprint plant. Although both towns provide alternative sources of employment in retailing and service establishments, the large industrial employer has some monopsony power over the local labour market. In other cases, local labour markets may contain only a few large industrial employers. Individually, each has substantial market power, and if they all act together, either explicitly or tacitly, they can behave as if they were a single monopsonist. Our analysis applies whenever employers have substantial monopsony power, but for concreteness, we consider a case in which the few firms operating in one labour market form an employers' hiring association in order to act as a single buying unit. We therefore refer to a single monopsonist.

Monopsonistic Labour Markets in the Absence of Unions. Suppose that there are many potential workers and that they are not members of a union. The monopsonist can offer any wage rate that it chooses, and the workers must either accept employment at that rate or find a different job.

Suppose that the monopsonist decides to hire some specific quantity of labour. The labour supply curve shows the wage that it must offer. To the monopsonist, this wage is the *average cost curve* of labour. In deciding how much labour to hire, however, the monopsonist is interested in the *marginal cost* of hiring additional workers. The monopsonist wants to know how much its total costs will increase as it takes on additional units of labour.

Whenever the supply curve of labour slopes upward, the marginal cost of employing extra units will exceed the average cost. It exceeds the wage paid (the average cost) because the increased wage rate necessary to attract an extra worker must also be paid to *everyone already employed*. [30]

For example, assume that 100 workers are employed at $8.00 per hour and that to attract an extra worker, the wage must be raised to $8.01 per hour. The marginal cost of the 101st worker is not the $8.01 per hour paid to the worker but $9.01 per hour—made up of the extra 1 cent per hour paid to the 100 existing workers and $8.01 paid to the new worker. Thus the marginal cost is $9.01 whereas the average cost is $8.01.[1]

The profit-maximizing monopsonist will hire labour up to the point at which the marginal cost just equals the amount that the firm is willing to pay for an additional unit of labour. That amount is determined by labour's marginal revenue product and is shown by the demand curve illustrated in Figure 16-2.

Monopsonistic conditions in a labour market will result in a lower level of employment and a lower wage

---

[1]This marginal cost of hiring an extra worker must not be confused with the marginal cost of *producing an extra unit of output*. Suppose that the extra worker in the example increased total output by 3 units. Because the worker adds $9.01 to cost and 3 units to output, the marginal cost of producing 1 extra unit of output is 9.01/3, which is approximately $3.00.

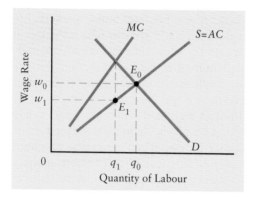

FIGURE 16-2
Monopsony in a Labour Market

A monopsonist lowers both the wage rate and employment below their competitive levels. D and S are the competitive demand and supply curves, respectively. In competition, equilibrium is at E_0, the wage rate is w_0, and the quantity of labour hired is q_0. The marginal cost of labour (MC) to the monopsonist is above the average cost. The monopsonistic firm will maximize profits at E_1. It will hire only q_1 units of labour. At q_1, the marginal cost of the last worker is just equal to the amount that the worker adds to the firm's revenue, as shown by the demand curve. The wage that must be paid to get q_1 workers is only w_1

rate than would exist when labour is purchased under competitive conditions.

The intuitive explanation is that the monopsonistic employer is aware that by trying to purchase more, it is responsible for driving up the wage. It will therefore stop short of the point that is reached when the wages are negotiated by many separate firms, no one of which can exert a significant influence on the wage rate.

Bilateral Monopoly: A Union in a Monopsonistic Market. Suppose that the workers in this industry organize themselves under a single union so that the monopsonistic employer's organization now faces a monopoly union. This situation is often referred to as one of *bilateral monopoly* since both sides of the market have considerable market power. In this case, the two sides will settle the wage through a process known as *collective bargaining*. The outcome of this bargaining process will depend on each side's objective and on the skill that each has in bargaining for its objective. We have seen that left to itself, the employer's organization will set the monopsonistic wage shown in Figure 16-2. To un-

derstand the possible outcomes for the wage after the monopoly union enters the market, let us ask what the union would do if it had the power to set the wage unilaterally. The result will give us insight into the union's objectives in the actual collective bargaining that does occur.

Suppose then that the union can set a wage below which its members will not work. Here, just as in the case of a wage-setting union in a competitive market, the union presents the employer with a horizontal supply curve (up to the maximum number of workers who will accept work at the union wage). As demonstrated in Figure 16-3, if the union sets the wage above the monopsony wage but below the competitive wage, the union can raise wages *and employment* above the monopsonistic level.

However, the union may not be content merely to neutralize the monopsonist's power. It may choose to raise wages further above the competitive level. If it does, the outcome will be similar to that shown in Figure 16-1. If the wage is raised above the competitive level, the employer will no longer wish to hire all the labour that is offered at that wage. The amount of employment will fall, and unemployment will develop. This is also shown in Figure 16-3. Notice, however, that the union can raise wages substantially above the competitive level before employment falls to a level as low as it was in the preunion monopsonistic situation.

We now know that the employers would like to set the monopsonistic wage (w_1) while the union would like a wage *no less than* the competitive wage (w_0). The union may target for a still higher wage, depending on how it trades off employment losses against wage gains. If the union is happy with an amount of employment as low as would occur at the monopsonistic wage, it could target for a wage substantially higher than the competitive wage.

Simple demand and supply analysis can take us no further. The actual outcome will, as we have already observed, depend on such other things as what target wage the two sides actually set for themselves, their relative bargaining skills, how each side assesses the costs of concessions, and how serious a strike would be for each. We discuss unions in more detail in the next section of this chapter.

LEGISLATED MINIMUM WAGES

We have examined wage differentials arising in competitive and noncompetitive labour markets.

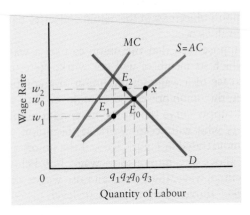

FIGURE 16-3
Effects of Union Entry
in a Monopsonistic Labour Market

By presenting a monopsonistic employer with a fixed wage, the union can raise both wages and employment over the monopsonistic level. The monopsony position before the union enters is at E_1 (from Figure 16-2), with a wage rate of w_1 and q_1 workers hired. A union now enters and sets the wage at w_0. The supply curve of labour becomes w_0E_0S, and wages and employment rise to their competitive levels of w_0 and q_0 without creating a pool of unemployed workers. If the wage is raised further, say, to w_2, the supply curve will become w_2xS, the quantity of employment will fall below the competitive level to q_2, and a pool of unsuccessful job applicants of q_2q_3 will develop.

This figure can also be used to illustrate the effect of the government imposing a minimum wage of w_0 or w_2 on a monopsonistic labour market where the equilibrium wage was initially w_1.

Government policy can also affect observed wage differentials by legislating minimum wages. We explore this possibility now.

Governments in Canada and many other countries legislate specific **minimum wages**, which define the lowest wage rates that may legally be paid. In Canada, industries under federal jurisdiction—such as airlines, trucking, and railways—are subject to the Canadian Labour Code, which in 1995 had a minimum wage of $4.00 per hour. Most Canadian workers, however, are employed in industries covered by provincial legislation. In 1995, the provincial minimum wages ranged from $4.75 per hour in Newfoundland and Prince Edward Island to $7.00 per hour in British Columbia and parts of the Northwest Territories.

For a large proportion of all employment covered by the law, the minimum wage is below the actual market wage, and thus in such cases the minimum wage is *not binding*. Some workers, however, are employed in industries in which the free-market wage would be below the legal minimum, and so the legislated minimum wage is *binding*. It is in these cases only where the effects of minimum wages are of interest.

Although legislated minimum wages are now an accepted part of the labour scene in Canada and many other industrialized countries, economists are often sceptical about the benefits from such a policy. To the extent that the minimum wages are binding, they clearly raise the wages of employed workers. However, as our analysis in Chapter 6 indicated, a binding price floor in a competitive market leads to a market surplus of the product—in this case, an excess supply of labour, or unemployment. Thus a policy which legislates minimum wages is likely to benefit some workers only by hurting others.

The problem is more complicated than the analysis of Chapter 6 would suggest, however, both because not all labour markets are competitive and because minimum-wage laws do not cover all employment. Moreover, those groups in the labour force that tend to have the lowest wages, such as youth and minorities, are affected more than the average worker.

Employment Effects of a Minimum Wage

Suppose that minimum-wage laws apply uniformly to all occupations. The occupations and the industries in which minimum wages are binding will be the lowest paying in the country; they usually involve unskilled or semiskilled labour. In most of them, the workers are not members of unions. Thus the situations in which minimum wages are likely to be binding include competitive labour markets and those in which employers exercise monopsony power. The effects on employment are different in the two cases.

Competitive Labour Markets. The consequences for employment of a binding minimum wage are unambiguous when the labour market is competitive. By raising the wage that employers must pay, minimum-wage legislation leads to a reduction in the quantity of labour that is demanded and an increase in the quantity of labour that is supplied. As a result, the actual level of employment falls, and unemployment is generated. This situation is exactly analogous to the one that arises when a union succeeds in setting a wage above the competitive equilibrium wage, as illustrated in Figure 16-1. The excess supply of labour at the minimum wage also creates incentives for people to evade the law by working "under the table" below the legal minimum wage.

Monopsonistic Labour Markets. The minimum-wage law can simultaneously increase both wages and employment in monopsonistic labour markets. The circumstances in which this can occur are the same as those in which a union facing a monopsonistic employer is able to increase both the wage and the level of employment, as shown in Figure 16-3. Of course, if the minimum wage is raised above the competitive wage, employment will start to fall, as in the union case. When it is set at the competitive level, however, the minimum wage can protect workers against monopsony power *and* lead to increases in employment.

Evidence on the Effects of Minimum Wages

Empirical research on the effects of minimum-wage laws reflects these mixed theoretical predictions. There is some evidence that people who keep their jobs gain when the minimum wage is raised. There is some evidence that some groups suffer a decline in employment consistent with raising the wage in a fairly competitive market. At other times and places, there is evidence that both wages earned and employment rise when the minimum wage rises, consistent with monopsonistic labour markets.

Employment Effects. Several Canadian studies have examined the relationship between minimum wages and employment (or unemployment). Though the studies differ in their approaches and data used, there is a broad concensus that minimum wages decrease the level of employment (and raise unemployment), particularly for low-wage groups such as women and teenagers. In this sense, the Canadian results confirm the theoretical predictions of the effects of minimum wages in competitive labour markets.

Some recent research in the United States, however, has produced quite different results. David Card and Alan Krueger, both of Princeton University, traced the effects of minimum-wage increases in California during 1988 and New Jersey during 1992 and found that substantial rises in these states' minimum wages not only increased wages but were also associated with small employment gains for

teenagers. Card and Krueger argue that these findings are inconsistent with a competitive labour market and thus take the results as evidence in support of the view that firms have some monopsony power in the labour market.

The Card and Krueger results have not been widely accepted, however. One criticism relates to the quality of their data. Another relates to the short span of time covered by their study. The argument is that firms will not immediately reduce the level of employment in response to an increase in the minimum wage—they will instead choose *not to replace* workers who leave their jobs in the natural process of "turnover" that occurs in labour markets. Thus it is not surprising to see few employment losses (or slight gains) when examining the labour market immediately before and immediately after the change in legislation. Proponents of this view argue that the total employment effects of minimum wages can only be detected by examining the data over longer periods of time.[2]

Distributional Effects. The primary concern in research about minimum wages has been the effect on the total level of employment. A related issue, however, is how the effects of a legislated minimum wage are *distributed* over the labour force. Professors Charles Beach and Michael Shannon have recently examined this distributional issue by analysing the effects of a proposed change in the Ontario minimum wage, from $5.40 per hour to $6.75 per hour.[3] They showed that approximately 20 percent of all Ontario workers would be affected by the increase. Of those workers affected, 62 percent were women, 59 percent were under the age of 25, and 66 percent had no more than a high-school education. These findings confirm the idea that the effects of legislated minimum wages are more likely to fall on low-wage workers than on high-wage workers. Beach and Shannon also showed that the proposed increase in minimum wages would generate a reduction of employment of about 80,000 jobs, a reduction of approximately 1.3 percent.

---

[2]See, for example, "The Effects of Minimum Wages in the Canadian Labour Market: 1975–1993," by Michael Baker, Dwayne Benjamin and Shuchita Stanger, University of Toronto, mimeo, 1994.

[3]Michael Shannon and Charles Beach, "Distributional Employment Effects of Ontario Minimum-Wage Proposals: A Microdata Approach," *Canadian Public Policy XXI*, 284–303.

APPLICATION 16-1

THE PUZZLE OF INTERINDUSTRY WAGE DIFFERENTIALS IN CANADA

Differences in wages across industries have been observed for as long as information on wages has been collected. But only in the past decade or so have economists looked closely at the wage differentials in an attempt to understand whether they could be explained by differences in skills, differences in jobs, or differences in market structure. In Canada, a recent study published by Surendra Gera and Gilles Grenier shows the extent of these wage differentials in 1986. Their approach follows closely that of two American economists who have explored the same issue (and found broadly similar results) in the United States.*

The table shows results from their study for selected industries; for each industry, the number in the table shows the amount by which wages in that industry are above or below the average wage across all industries. These numbers are referred to as the industry's *wage premium,* and reflect the differences in wages across industries *that cannot be explained* by differences in such factors as the worker's education, years of experience, age, gender, marital status, occupation, region of country, or union status. The challenge is to explain such wage premia.

COMPETITIVE WAGE DIFFERENTIALS

Following our discussion in the text, three possible explanations of these wage differentials are consistent with the labour market being competitive.

The first possibility is that these observed wage differentials for 1986 may reflect temporary shifts in the pattern of labour demand or supply across industries. If wages are slow to adjust to such shifts, or if labour is slow to move between industries, then such

shifts could indeed lead to differentials. For example, a large increase in the demand for labour in the forestry industry that occurs together with a large decline in the demand for labour in the textiles industry, could account for some of the data in the table. To address this possible explanation, Gera and Grenier examine Canadian census data for 1970, 1980, and 1985. They find that the pattern of interindustry wage differentials is very similar across these three periods, suggesting that the observed wage differentials are not simply temporary phenomena.

The second possibility is that the wage differentials can actually be explained by differences in the quality of the workers, but many of these differences are not observable to the economist when conducting such a study. For example, we are not able to observe whether a worker is "highly motivated," "innovative," or "a good problem solver." But many of these characteristics *are* observable to potential employers, either by watching the individual work for a short period of time, or by asking previous employers who know the worker. To examine this explanation, Gera and Grenier examine the group of individuals in their sample that move from a job in one industry to a job in a different industry. For example, if high wages to a particular worker in the Tobacco industry are due to that worker's unobserved skills, then when that worker switches to the Clothing industry, the high wage should persist. But Gera and Grenier find the opposite. A worker that moves from a high-wage industry to a low-wage industry tends to suffer a fall in wage; similarly, a worker that moves from a low-wage industry to a high-wage industry tends to experience a rise in the wage. This suggests that the observed wage differentials are not due mainly to unobserved labour quality.

The final possible explanation consistent with a competitive labour market is that the observed wage differentials reflect different characteristics of the *jobs.* Thus, maybe the jobs in the high-wage industries are less pleasant jobs—longer hours, less job security, less safe—than those in the low-wage industries. Gera and Grenier offer two pieces of evidence

---

*S. Gera and G. Grenier, "Interindustry Wage Differentials and Efficiency Wages: Some Canadian Evidence," *Canadian Journal of Economics,* 1994. A. Krueger and L. Summers, "Efficiency Wages and the Interindustry Wage Structure," *Econometrica,* 1988.

against this explanation. First, they note that workers in *similar occupations* receive very different wages in different industries, and it is difficult to believe that working conditions for, say, a clerk are very different in the Tobacco industry than in the Textiles industry. Second, if the observed wage differentials just reflect different job characteristics, then in competitive equilibrium workers are indifferent between (pleasant) jobs in the low-wage industries and (unpleasant) jobs in the high-wage industries. But this is hard to reconcile with the observation that workers appear to quit jobs in the high-wage industries much less frequently than they quit jobs in the low-wage industries. In other words, workers *appear* to view the high-wage jobs as valuable relative to the low-wage jobs. This, of course, suggests that the observed wage differentials are reflecting more than just differences in working conditions.

OTHER EXPLANATIONS?

Maybe the explanation for these observed wage differentials lies in a noncompetitive market structure. Perhaps unions have a large presence in some industries and little or no presence in others. When Gera and Grenier examine this possibility, they find that the interindustry wage differentials are just as marked among unionized workers as they are among nonunionized workers.

If the observed wage differentials across Canadian industries cannot be explained by considering different characterstics of the workers, jobs, or market structures, then what is the explanation? One explanation that is starting to attract considerable attention among economists is based on the theory of *efficiency wages*. According to this theory, firms in even a competitive labour market *pay more than the competitive wage* to their workers. The reason firms do this is that they perceive that a higher wage will make their workers more productive. Since workers are receiving more than is required to attract their services, they are earning *economic rents*. The fact that workers are receiving rents, in turn, explains why they are reluctant to leave these good jobs—and thus their quit rates from such jobs are low.

Though the efficiency-wage theory offers one possible explanation for why some workers might earn rents, it does not directly offer an explanation for why these rents might be different across industries. In order for the efficiency-wage theory to explain the observed interindustry wage differentials, it must explain why firms' incentives to pay higher wages are greater in some industries than in others. So far, proponents of the theory have not come up with convincing reasons.

The efficiency-wage theory is still young and still generates considerable disagreement among economists. But there is little debate that there exist significant wage differentials across industries, even after taking account of observable characteristics of workers and jobs. As more data become available, perhaps we will find better explanations for the interindustry wage differentials that do exist.

1986 Industry Wage Premia in Canada
(percentage above average wage)

Tobacco Products	33.4
Mineral Fuels	25.5
Forestry	18.9
Electric Power, Gas, and Water Utilities	14.4
Paper and Allied Products	12.0
Communications	10.5
Rubber and Plastics	7.1
Transportation Equipment	7.0
Wholesale Trade	3.8
Electrical Products	2.6
Education and Related Services	−1.0
Health and Welfare	−3.1
Food and Beverages	−3.5
Insurance and Real Estate Agencies	−4.1
Clothing	−8.1
Fishing and Trapping	−9.5
Personal Services	−16.7
Retail Trade	−11.1
Textiles	−19.0
Accommodation and Food Services	−20.3

Economists have not reached a definitive conclusion regarding the desirabilty or the effects of legislated minimum wages. Given its mixed economic effects, support for and opposition to the minimum wage might be understood as arising largely from political and sociological motives. Organized labour has consistently pressed for a broad, relatively high minimum wage. There is some economic reason for this, in that there is evidence that the minimum wage "trickles up" to higher-wage workers, both unionized and not. Arguably, however, the support dates back to the 1930s, when organized labour was still fighting for its position in North American society. Enactment of a minimum wage was then a great political victory, and the minimum wage still has symbolic significance.

A FINAL WORD

We have examined several explanations for why some workers get paid more than others. The explanations include differences in workers' educations and skills, differences in job characteristics, and differences in the structure of the various labour markets. But this apparent abundance of explanations should not lead you to believe that economists understand *all* wage differentials that are observed in the labour market. Recent studies, both in Canada and in the United States, have revealed significant differences in wages across industries that appear to defy explanations based on the sort of arguments we have examined. Application 16-1 discusses the puzzle of interindustry wage differentials in Canada.

TABLE 16-2
Union Membership in Canada, Selected Years, 1921–1992

Year	Total (thousands)	Percent of Labour Force
1921	313	9.4
1931	311	7.5
1941	462	10.3
1951	1,029	19.7
1962	1,423	21.5
1972	2,388	27.6
1982	3,617	30.4
1992	4,089	29.7

Union membership in Canada grew steadily from the 1920s until peaking in the early 1980s; it has dropped slightly since then.

(*Source:* Richard Chaykowski, *Modern Labour Economics,* HarperCollins 1994.)

LABOUR UNIONS

Unions currently represent fewer than 30 percent of workers in Canada. Of those workers employed in the public sector, however, approximately 80 percent are unionized. Table 16-2 shows how union membership has changed in Canada over the past several decades. Table 16-3 shows unionization rates by industry in 1990. As is clear from the table, unionization is most common in the public and educational sectors, and least common in agriculture, finance, and business services.

There is considerable variation across countries in the degree of unionization. In 1988, Canada's unionization rate (expressed as a share of the non-agricultural labour force) was 36.5 percent. This was far below the unionization rates in Sweden (96 percent), Italy (62.7 percent) and Australia (53 percent), but considerably more than the United States (16 percent) and France (12 percent).

Despite the relatively low degree of unionization among Canada's private-sector workers, unions have

TABLE 16-3
Unionization Rates by Industry, 1990

Industry	Membership as Percentage of Paid Workers
Agriculture	1.8
Forestry	58.8
Fishing & Trapping	33.4
Mining	28.4
Manufacturing	36.7
Construction	59.6
Transportation, Communication and other utilities	54.8
Trade	11.6
Finance, Real Estate and Insurance	3.5
Services	
Business	3.1
Educational	77.0
Health and Social	50.8
Other	11.6
Public Administration	80.6
Total	34.7

There is considerable variation across industries of the extent of unionization. The public sector and the educational services sector are the most unionized; agriculture, finance, and business services are the least unionized.

(*Source:* Richard Chaykowski, *Modern Labour Economics,* HarperCollins 1994.)

a considerable influence in the private sector. One reason is the impact that union wage contracts have on other labour markets. When, for example, the Canadian Auto Workers negotiate a new contract with an automobile producer in Oshawa, its provisions set a pattern that directly or indirectly affects other labour markets, both in Ontario and in other provinces. A second reason is the major leadership role that unions have played in the past 50 years in the development of labour market practices and in lobbying for legislation that applies to all workers.

In this section, we discuss the process of *collective bargaining* and, in particular, examine the inherent conflict that unions face between striving for higher wages or for increased employment. Extension 16-1 examines the historical development of labour unions in Canada.

COLLECTIVE BARGAINING

The process by which unions and employers (or their representatives) arrive at and enforce their agreements is known as **collective bargaining.** This process has an important difference from the theoretical models with which we began this chapter. In those models, we assumed that the union had the power to set the wage unilaterally; the employer then decided how much labour to hire. In real-world collective bargaining, however, the firm and union typically bargain over the wage. There is usually a substantial range over which an agreement can be reached, and the actual result in particular cases will depend on the strengths of the two bargaining parties and on the skill of their negotiators.[4]

Wages Versus Employment

Unions seek many goals when they bargain with management. They may push for higher wages, higher fringe benefits, more stable employment, or less onerous working conditions. Whatever their specific goals, unless they face a monopsonist across the

bargaining table, they must deal with a fundamental dilemma.

There is an inherent conflict between the level of wages and the size of the union itself.

The more successful a union is in raising wages, the more management will attempt to reduce the size of its work force, substituting capital for labour. This will lead to lower union membership. However, if the union does not provide some wage improvement for its members, they will have little incentive to stay around.

The Union Wage Premium

Despite the costs to unions (i.e., reduced membership) of pushing for higher wages, there is clear evidence in Canada of a *union wage premium*—that is, a higher wage attributed only to the union status of the job. It is not an easy task to measure this wage premium, however, because it is not appropriate simply to compare the average wage of unionized workers with the average wage of non–unionized workers. After all, unions may occur mainly in industries where workers have higher skills or where working conditions are less pleasant. And we know from the first section of this chapter that differences in skills or working conditions can lead to wage differentials. Economists have therefore been forced to use complicated statistical techniques to identify this union wage premium. The consensus of these studies appears to be that the union wage premium in Canada is somewhere between 10 and 25 percent—that is, unionized workers with a particular set of skills in particular types of jobs get paid 10 to 25 percent more than *otherwise identical workers* that are not members of unions.

There is also evidence that the size of this union wage premium differs across industries. Given that workers in different industries and with different occupations are often represented by different unions, this cross-industry difference in the union wage premium may simply reflect the differences in unions' preferences for higher wages versus higher employment.

UNION RESPONSES TO CHANGING CONDITIONS

A union that, through the bargaining process, pushes the wage above the competitive level is making a

---

[4]In terms of Figure 16-3, it may be that the firm wants the wage to be w_1 and the union wants the wage to be w_2. Depending on each side's market power, and on their bargaining tactics, the final agreed-upon wage may be anywhere in between. Note that while real-world collective bargaining has the firm and union bargaining over the wage, it is typically the case that the firm retains the "right to manage"—meaning that the firm can decide how much labour it wants to employ at the bargained wage.

EXTENSION 16-1

THE DEVELOPMENT OF UNIONS IN CANADA

Early Canadian unionization was strongly dominated by the influence of international unions, which had their headquarters and an overwhelming proportion of their membership outside Canada. The creation of Canadian locals of American unions began in the 1860s, and by 1911, the earliest date for which figures are available, 90 percent of Canadian workers who were union members belonged to international unions.

During the first half of the twentieth century, there was strong pressure, first, toward a single national federation, and second, to achieve autonomy from American unions. The issues became intertwined when conflicts in the United States arose between craft and industrial unions. Until the 1930s, *craft unions*—which cover persons in a particular occupation—were the characteristic form of collective action in the United States. In Canada, meanwhile, trade unionists were attracted to the principle of *industrial unions* that embraced unskilled workers as well as skilled craftsmen in one industry such as steel making.

Because of the impossibility of establishing bargaining strength by controlling the supply of unskilled workers, the rise of industrial unionism in Canada was associated with political action as an alternative means of improving the lot of the membership. In general, social and political reform were given much more emphasis by Canadian unionists than by their American counterparts. Political action here extended to the support for social democratic political parties: first, the Cooperative Commonwealth Federation (CCF), established in 1932, and later its successor, the New Democratic Party (NDP), formed in 1961.

The late Senator Eugene Forsey, a former director of research for the Canadian Labour Congress, viewed the unification of the bulk of Canadian unions under the CLC in 1956 as the beginning of virtual autonomy for Canadian locals from their U.S. head offices—the CLC has guidelines for the conduct of international unions operating in Canada. Throughout the postwar period, the percentage of total Canadian union membership represented by international unions fell: In the mid 1950s, it was about 70 percent, and by the mid 1990s, it was just over 30 percent.

One factor in the increased share of national unions is the growth of membership in the two unions representing government workers, the Canadian Union of Public Employees and the Public Service Alliance. Another major component of non-international union membership has arisen out of the distinct aspirations of French-Canadian workers. More recently, the formation of the Canadian Auto Workers, independent of the American Auto Workers, represented a significant further reduction of membership in international unions.

Rapid gains in union membership in Canada occurred in the years during World War II. This led to pressure for the rights of workers to organize and to elect an exclusive bargaining agent. These rights were established by provisions of the Wartime Labour Relations Regulations Act of 1944.

Government intervention in industrial disputes in Canada has a history dating back to the early years of the twentieth century. The earliest legislation applied only to public utilities and coal mining. It provided that before a strike or a lockout could be initiated, the parties were required to submit any dispute to a conciliation board. This system of compulsory conciliation and compulsory delay in work stoppage was extended to a much larger segment of the economy under special emergency powers adopted by the government of Canada during World War II. In the postwar period, jurisdiction over labour policy reverted to the provinces, but the principles established have been carried over into provincial legislation.

choice of higher wages for some workers and unemployment for others. Should the union strive to maximize the earnings of the group that remains employed? If it does, some of its members will lose their jobs, and the union's membership will decline. Should it instead maximize the welfare of its present members? Or should it seek to expand employment opportunities (perhaps by a low-wage policy) so that the union membership grows? Different unions decide these questions differently.

Severe strains developed between Canadian and American members of international unions as a result of different views of how to respond to the difficult economic conditions of the 1980s. Two key differences typified a range of differences in attitudes.

American unions were willing to reopen contracts and accept wage cuts when the alternative seemed to be plant closures or company liquidations. They were also willing to consider schemes designed to move away from the traditional pattern where wages are relatively stable over the business cycle while employment does most of the adjusting to fluctuating demand. The alternative is to have wages vary more over the cycle in order to maintain a more stable employment pattern. One way of doing this is to move toward the Japanese arrangement whereby wages are to some extent linked to profits.

Canadian unions have been more inclined to stick with traditional approaches. First, they argue that contracts should not be reopened before they expire. Even if the agreed wages threaten to cause plant closures, the sanctity of the contract is a more important principle than the saving of specific jobs. Second, profit sharing is often viewed as selling out to the bosses. Canadian unions believe that the traditional system should be maintained, in which wages are stable over the cycle and most of the adjustment to variations in demand occurs through variations in employment.

The Canadian Automobile Workers (CAW) eventually split with the United Automobile Workers (UAW) over these and related issues. A separate Canadian union was set up, and its different approach to bargaining soon became apparent.

Since the breakaway, the CAW has been significantly more hostile to changes in work organization than the UAW has been. The CAW's National Policy Statement issued in October 1989 explicitly rejected such innovations as flexible job classifications and supervisor-worker interchanges that appear to have contributed greatly to productivity in the Japanese automobile industry. Because the North American automobile industry is under immense challenges from Japanese and other foreign producers, this statement seemed to many observers to be an open invitation to automobile firms to invest in the United States rather than Canada. However, the policy statement and the actual policies adopted by the CAW differed: Faced, for example, with the real possibility of the closure of a major GM plant in Ste. Thérèse, Québec, the union was considerably more flexible about agreeing to a number of changes in work arrangements than its policy statement would have suggested.

DISCRIMINATION IN LABOUR MARKETS

The economic effects of discrimination against minorities and women take many forms. Labour market discrimination does not wholly explain, but surely contributes to, lower wages and higher unemployment rates for those discriminated against. Both lower wages and greater unemployment lead to lower incomes for the workers involved.

Discrimination may also have powerful indirect effects on attitudes toward the workplace and toward society. It affects not only the workers discriminated against but also their children, whose ability, aspirations, and willingness to undertake the education and training required to succeed may be adversely affected. Indeed, it may change their definition of success. There are many subtle ways in which discrimination can become part of the way in which a society functions, and these can be as important in their effects as overt (and now generally illegal) direct discrimination.

The problems of race discrimination and gender discrimination differ, but there are similarities as well. It is helpful to look first at how both kinds of discrimination lead to important economic effects.

A MODEL OF LABOUR-MARKET DISCRIMINATION

To isolate the effects of discrimination, we begin by building a simplified picture of a nondiscriminating labour market and then introduce discrimination between two sets of equally qualified workers. The discussion here is phrased in terms of males and females but the analysis applies equally well to any situation in which workers are distinguished on grounds *other than* their ability, such as race or skin colour, citizenship, religion, or political beliefs.

Suppose that half of the people are male and the other half are female. Each group has the same proportion who are educated to various levels, identical distributions of talent, and so on. Suppose also that there are two occupations. Occupation E (*elite*) requires people of above-average education and skills, and occupation O (*ordinary*) can use anyone. Finally, suppose that the nonmonetary aspects of the two occupations are the same.

In the absence of discrimination, the labour markets that we are studying are competitive. The theory of competitive factor markets that we have developed suggests that the wages in E occupations will be bid up above those in O occupations in order that the E jobs attract the workers of above-average skills. Men and women of above-average skill will take the E jobs, while the others, both men and women, will have no choice but to seek O jobs. Because skills are equally distributed, each occupation will employ one-half men and one-half women.

Now suppose that discrimination enters in an extreme form. All E occupations are hereafter open only to men, but O occupations are open to either men or women. The immediate effect is to reduce by 50 percent the supply of job candidates for E oc-

cupations; candidates must now be *both* men and above average. The discrimination also increases the supply of applicants for O jobs by 50 percent; this group now includes all women and the below-average men.

Wage Level Effects

Suppose that labour is perfectly mobile among occupations, that everyone seeks the best job that he or she is eligible for, and that wage rates are free to vary so as to equate supply and demand. The analysis is shown in Figure 16-4. Wages rise in E occupations and fall in O occupations. The take-home pay of people in O occupations falls, and the O group is now approximately two-thirds women.

Discrimination, by changing supply, can decrease the wages and incomes of a group that is discriminated against.

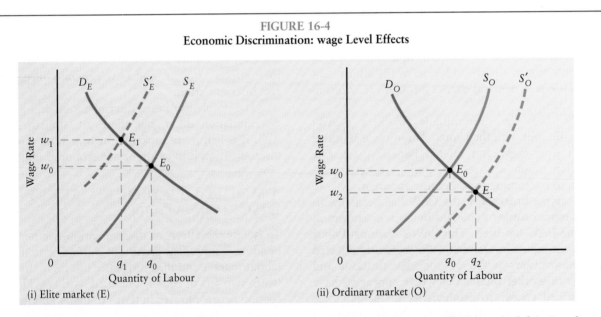

FIGURE 16-4
Economic Discrimination: wage Level Effects

(i) Elite market (E)

(ii) Ordinary market (O)

If market E discriminates against one group and market O does not, the supply curve will shift to the left in E and to the right in O. Market E requires above-average skills, while market O requires only ordinary skills. When there is no discrimination, demand and supply are D_E and S_E in market E and D_0 and S_0 in market O. Initially, the wage rate is w_0 and employment is q_0 in each market. (w_0 in market E will be higher than w_0 in market O because the workers in E have higher skills than those in O.) When all women are barred from E occupations, the supply curve shifts to S'_E, and the wage earned by the remaining workers, all of whom are men, rises to w_1. Women put out of work in the E occupations now seek work in the O occupations. The resulting shift in the supply curve to S'_0 brings down the wage to w_2 in the O occupations. Because all women are in O occupations, they have a lower wage rate than many men. The average male wage is higher than the average female wage.

Discrimination also hurts members of the favoured group who cannot obtain E jobs.

In the longer run, further changes may occur. Notice that total employment in the E jobs falls. Employers may find ways to use slightly below average labour and thus lure the next best qualified men out of O occupations. Although this will raise O wages slightly, it will also make these occupations increasingly "female occupations." If discrimination has been in effect for a sufficient length of time, women will learn that it does not pay to acquire above-average skills. Regardless of ability, women are forced by discrimination to work in unskilled jobs.

Now suppose that a long-standing discriminatory policy is reversed. Because they will have responded to discrimination by acquiring fewer skills than men, many women will be locked into the O occupations, at least for a time. Moreover, if both men and women come to expect that women will have less education than men, employers will tend to look for men to fill the E jobs. This will reinforce the belief of women that education does not pay. Such subtle discrimination can persist for a very long time, making the supply of women to O jobs higher than it would be in the absence of discrimination, thereby depressing the wages of women and below-average men.

Employment Effects

For a number of reasons, labour-market discrimination may have adverse employment effects that are even more important than the effects on wages. Labour is not perfectly mobile, wages are not perfectly flexible downward, and not everyone who is denied employment in an E occupation for which he or she is trained and qualified will be willing to take a "demeaning" O job. We continue the graphical example in Figure 16-5.

If wages do not fall to the market-clearing level, possibly because of minimum-wage laws, the increase in the supply of labour to O occupations will cause excess supply, which will result in unemployment in O occupations. Because women dominate these occupations, women will bear the brunt of the extra unemployment, as illustrated in Figure 16-5(i).

A similar result will occur if labour is not fully mobile between occupations. For example, many of the O jobs might be in places to which the women are unable or unwilling to move. (Discrimination in housing markets may be one reason for this.) See Figure 16-5(ii). Potential O workers who cannot move to places where jobs are available become unemployed or withdraw from the labour force. Quite apart from any discrimination, long-term technological changes tend to decrease the demand for less skilled labour of the kind that is required in O occupations. Occupation O then becomes increasingly oversupplied. This possibility is outlined in Figure 16-5(iii).

The kind of discrimination that we have considered in our model is extreme. It is similar to the South African apartheid system that was dismantled in the 1980s and 1990s, in which blacks were excluded by law from prestigious and high-paying occupations. In Canada and the United States, labour-market discrimination against a specific group usually occurs in somewhat less obvious ways. First, it may be difficult (but not impossible, as in our model) for members of the group to get employment in certain jobs. Second, members of groups subject to discrimination may receive lower pay for a given kind of work than members of groups not subject to discrimination.

Indeed, the first type of discrimination may encourage the second type. How might this happen? First, if discrimination makes it difficult for a qualified woman to get a good job, she may be more willing to accept such a job even if the pay and working conditions are poorer than those given to men in the same job. Even under relatively unfavourable terms, the job will still be better than the alternative (an O job). Second, employers who are seeking to fill E jobs and who have no taste for discrimination will nonetheless be able to hire qualified women at wages that, although higher than O wages, are lower than E wages for men. As long as there is some discrimination of the first type (in the extreme, apartheid), there will be pressures coming from both the supply and the demand sides of the labour market for discrimination of the second type.

Can Discrimination Exist in Equilibrium?

We have seen that in the absence of discrimination, competitive labour markets will tend to equalize the wages of the two groups, men and women in our example above. (Note in Figure 16-4 that wages in E jobs are higher than those in O jobs because workers in E jobs—both men and women—have higher skills

FIGURE 16-5
Economic Discrimination: Employment Effects

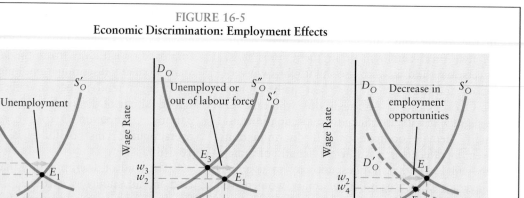

(i) Wage rigidities (or minimum wage)

(ii) Immobile labour (or withdrawal from labour force)

(iii) Declining demand

Increasing supply or decreasing demand in occupations in which the people discriminated against are the major sources of labour can increase unemployment. In each part of the diagram, the curves D_0 and S_0 are those from part (ii) of Figure 16-4; they show the market for O workers after the discriminatory policies are put into effect. Equilibrium is at E_1. In each case, the wage w_2 would clear the market and provide employment of q_2.

In part (i), if the wage rate cannot fall below w_3, perhaps because of a legislated minimum wage, employment will fall to q_3, and unemployment will occur in the amount shown by the arrows.

In part (ii), if some of the potential workers in the O occupations are unable or unwilling to take employment in O jobs, the supply curve will not be S'_0 but S''_0. Equilibrium will be at E_3. Although O wages will rise somewhat to w_3, employment will be only q_3, and a number of workers, shown by the arrows, will not be employed. Whether they are recorded as "unemployed" or as having withdrawn from the labour force will depend on the official definitions.

In part (iii), if demand is declining in O occupations over time, say, from D_0 to D'_0, either wages and employment will fall to the new equilibrium E_4 with w_4 and q_4, or wages will be maintained but employment will fall to q_3. The arrows illustrate the latter case, where the fall in employment is q_3q_2.

than workers in O jobs.) Some economists go further than this and argue that under perfect competition, discrimination *cannot be sustained in equilibrium,* and thus if it exists at all it must only be a temporary phenomenon. This theory, most forcefully propounded by Thomas Sowell of the Hoover Institution and Nobel Laureate Gary Becker of the University of Chicago, works like this: Employers of workers in E jobs who pay high wages (w_1) can increase their profits if they hire qualified women at any lower wage. If women have the same distribution of qualifications as men (as they do in our model above), under discrimination there will be plenty of workers who will be willing to work in E jobs at any wage that is greater than the low wage level in the O market (w_2)—much less than the going wage for men. If some employers take advantage of this opportunity, there will be competitive pressure that, all other things being equal, works against the

maintenance of discrimination. As firms who hire qualified women at wages below w_1 (but above w_2) earn profits, they will grow, and other firms will have to imitate them or go out of business. Eventually, the discrimination will disappear in competitive equilibrium.

This argument shows the important pressures that act against discrimination in competitive markets. However, the proposition that competitive equilibrium is completely inconsistent with the practice of discrimination fails to take into account a number of important phenomena. One of these is the indirect effect of discrimination on both the acquisition of skills and on the expectations of employers. There may also be direct market effects. For example, prejudiced workers may be less productive if women are treated as equals in the workplace. Another example—though perhaps a bit extreme in this context—is that prejudiced customers may refrain from buying the products of firms that employ women in E occupations. (A less extreme example is that some customers in southern U.S. states may boycott firms that employ blacks in service jobs.) In these cases, it is customers and workers whose prejudices matter, and employers may thus have powerful economic incentives to discriminate, even if they have no prejudice of their own.

In any event, the history of both race and sex discrimination in Canada, the United States, and elsewhere suggests that however strong are the competitive forces working against discrimination in the labour market, they are not strong enough to *eliminate* it.

MALE-FEMALE WAGE DIFFERENTIALS IN CANADA

The model of labour-market discrimination that we have discussed helps us to think about discrimination that may occur in actual labour markets. We discuss briefly the male-female wage differential in Canada, and how much of this differential can be attributed to discrimination.

There is no doubt that some discrimination does occur. For example, psychologists have conducted many studies that suggest a bias against women that could easily lead to discriminatory pay differences. In one experiment, university department heads were given identical files, one with a male name and the other with a female name. They were 10 percent more likely to select the male for a job offer than the female with the identical resume. In another experiment, *female* college students were asked to rank paintings on a scale from 1 to 10. The same picture consistently got a higher rating when it had a male name attached than when it was ascribed to a female artist.

How does this discrimination translate into different labour-market performance of men versus women? Despite obvious gains that women have made in the labour market over the past few decades, the average earned income of females in the labour force is well below that of males of similar ages. The female-to-male earnings ratio has risen slightly from approximately 0.59 in 1960 to about 0.70 in 1995. The persistence of the remaining salary gap for females is due to a combination of causes in addition to straightforward discrimination: Women are still underrepresented in high-status occupations, proportionately fewer women than men reach higher-paying jobs in the occupations in which both

work, and those who do reach higher-paying jobs do so more slowly.

Most empirical studies of male-female wage differentials show that a considerable portion of the difference between men's and women's wages is due to differences in such objective considerations as educational requirements and years of experience in the work force and on the job. When all such factors have been taken into account, however, there remains a "residual" that is consistent with some direct sex discrimination.

Discrimination Within Occupations. To what extent do differences in pay levels of men and women within an occupation reflect direct discrimination against women? To what extent do they reflect other sex-linked characteristics, the most important of which is the persistent difference in lifetime patterns of labour-force participation? The evidence shows that, on average, women have fewer years of work experience than men of the same age. The average working female is less mobile occupationally and geographically than her male counterpart. These facts reflect, at least in part, *labour-market attachment*. For example, many women withdraw from the labour force or work only part time in order to have and raise children.

The causes of gender differences in labour-market attachment have attracted attention from both social psychologists and economists. There is some evidence that *sex-role socialization* is an important factor. To the extent that women and men are socialized to accept the view that women should be the primary caretakers of young children, some social scientists argue that differences in labour-market attachment arise from a form of indirect discrimination. However important this may be, it arises from differences in the way in which boys and girls are raised, not from the direct behaviour of the labour market.

The extent of direct discrimination within an occupation may be measured by comparing the pay status of groups with similar characteristics. Studies of the sources of male-female pay differences in Canada have found that between one-third and one-half of the differences in earnings can be explained by differences in education, work experience, and labour-market attachment.[5] Analysts attribute the remaining one-half to two-thirds of the male-female pay differentials to direct sex discrimination.

---

[5]Much of this literature is summarized in University of Toronto economist Morley Gunderson's "Male-Female Wage Differentials and Policy Responses," *Journal of Economic Literature* 27, 1989.

Interoccupational Discrimination. For many years, women were refused admission to (or were discouraged from seeking entry into) certain occupations; for example, women were urged into nursing rather than medicine, social work rather than law, and secretarial schools rather than managerial training programs. The result of this is called *occupational segregation*. Similarly, girls were raised in a culture in which their education seemed less important than that of their brothers or in which they were trained to think of themselves as potential homemakers and were thus less likely to acquire the skills for many high-paying occupations that were wholly within their capabilities. This is a form of sex-role socialization.

Differences in pay among occupations reflect, as we have seen, differences in supply and demand, including nonmonetary considerations. Might they not also reflect discrimination, if one occupation is predominantly female and the other predominantly male? This is certainly possible, and a number of studies have shown that such an effect exists; that is, if one uses the characteristics of workers (education, training, experience, etc.) to explain their wages, the fraction of female workers in the occupation has a significant negative effect. Moreover, this effect exists for both men and women. Men (and women) who work in predominantly female occupations are paid less than men (and women) with the same training and experience in predominantly male occupations. For this reason, many have urged that attention be paid to interoccupational pay differences under the general term *pay equity*. Determining how much observed differences reflect discrimination is extremely difficult, because so many different considerations affect the pay levels of, say, firefighters and librarians.

GOVERNMENT POLICIES TO REDRESS DISCRIMINATION

Governments have long had policies to eliminate discrimination between men and women *doing the same job*. Such policies require that a man and a woman doing a job with the same job description must receive the same pay. These policies are relatively easy to administer, as long as it is easy to identify that two individuals are indeed doing the same job (i.e., same hours, same factory, same health risk, etc.).

A much harder case arises when an attempt is made to remove alleged discrimination *between jobs*. If one job is staffed primarily with women and another primarily with men (such as nurses and firefighters), do differences between the wages paid in the two jobs represent differences in market conditions, or are they due to discrimination?

Much of the persistence of male-female pay differentials results from wages in male-dominated occupations exceeding those in female-dominated ones. As a way of eliminating these differentials, the federal government and many of the provinces have enacted legislation that mandates wage adjustments to eliminate disparities between jobs of "comparable worth" or "equal value."

Pay-equity policy relies on a job evaluation program that measures the *intrinsic value* of different occupations. In practice, this involves assigning "worth points" to various attributes of a given job (typically effort, initiative, skill, training, responsibility, and conditions of work). These points can then be summed to obtain a "total job score"; comparing scores for different jobs allows a comparison of their intrinsic values. Pay equity then requires that two jobs judged to be of equal value receive equal pay.

Needless to say, pay-equity policies have been controversial. Supporters argue that they do not go far enough and that significant differentials will persist even after full implementation. Critics argue that the evaluation schemes are often arbitrary and always imperfect. Simple schemes are easy to administer but give poorer results; more complex schemes are, in principle, more accurate but harder to administer. Implementation problems such as definition of an establishment, determination of criteria to include in the evaluation program and the weights to assign to them, and definition of gender dominance plague most schemes currently in place.

Economists are often concerned that the policies fail to distinguish between temporary and equilibrium differentials as stressed in Chapter 15. They fear that misguided attempts to eliminate equilibrium differentials will lead to the emergence of excess demand in some occupations and excess supply in others, with associated efficiency costs for the economy.

Supporters of pay-equity policy often argue that job evaluation and comparison play an important role in any big firm's employment policy, implicitly and often explicitly. Hence, they argue, pay-equity legislation merely formalizes in law procedures that already play an important role in labour markets. Economists point out, however, that market-oriented job evaluation policies of individual firms, whether explicit or implicit, have the major advantage of reacting quickly to market forces. Such evaluations are only a guideline to determining wages. If changes occur to make previously determined evaluations no longer consistent with market balance, and surpluses or shortages arise, firms will respond quickly by altering their guidelines and changing relative wages. Legislated comparisons determining wages may cause shortages or surpluses to persist for long periods of time.

Professor Roberta Robb of Brock University identifies three potential costs of pay-equity legislation: economic efficiency losses (including allocation distortions and implementation costs), private costs of employers (including higher wages for some female employees and administration costs), and private costs of employees (including adverse employment effects for females). Potential benefits include increased productivity of females (resulting from the incentive effects of increased earnings) and a reduced male-female wage differential. The latter is viewed as a benefit in its own right, and it has been suggested that current legislation may succeed in reducing the male-female earnings differential by about 10 percentage points (out of a total differential in 1995 of about 30 percentage points).[6]

Is pay-equity policy "progressive pragmatism," as one supporter put it, or is it "a profoundly flawed concept," as a critic pronounced? The answer will depend on the magnitude of the resource misallocation caused by setting relative wages through a system that does not attempt to balance demand and supply and on one's view of whether this lost efficiency is a price worth paying in the name of equity. As Professor Robb concludes, "This kind of legislation is likely to have a very significant impact on individual perceptions of what women's jobs are worth. This result is clearly important if one believes that part of the role of this policy is to break the cycle of systematically undervaluing women's jobs."

---

[6]Roberta Robb, "The Costs and Benefits of Canadian Pay Equity Policy," in Richard Chaykowski, ed. *Pay Equity Legislation* (Kingston, Ont.: Queen's University Industrial Relations Centre, 1990).

THE "GOOD JOBS–BAD JOBS" DEBATE

We saw in Chapter 1 (see Figure 1-5) how the composition of Canadian employment has changed dramatically over the past century. Similar changes have also occurred in the United States and in many other industrialized countries. This changing composition of the labour force has led to some concerns in recent years. The specific change which has received considerable attention in Canada and elsewhere is the decline in the share of total employment in the manufacturing sector since the Second World War, and the simultaneous increase in the share of total employment in the service sector.

Some people fear that productivity is lower and the opportunities for growth are much more limited in some service industries than in goods-producing industries. They argue that the possibilities for using more capital per unit of labour employed, which raises labour productivity, are less in the service sector than in the manufacturing sector. Another concern is that many of the "good jobs" in the manufacturing sector appear to have been replaced by "bad jobs" in the service sector, where such "bad jobs" are characterized by low pay and little job security.

Should these dramatic changes in the composition of employment worry us? Is there something undesirable about the fact that fewer Canadian workers are now producing manufactured goods than forty years ago? Or that more Canadian workers are working in the service sector than forty years ago? Are the good jobs in Canada being replaced by bad jobs? This final section of the chapter addresses this issue.

FOUR OBSERVATIONS

There are four reasons why the decline in the manufacturing sector may not necessarily reflect anything "wrong" with the economy. First, we need to keep a sense of perspective about the emergence of low-paying service jobs. As is apparent in Figure 1-5, the trend toward services has been going on for over a century. Yet real income per hour worked has been rising throughout this period (recall Figure 1-4); as a nation, we are getting wealthier, not poorer. Further, the size distribution of income has not changed dramatically over this period, so the increased wealth has been experienced by individuals in *all* income classes.

Second, to a considerable extent, the decrease in the share of manufacturing in total employment is a result of that sector's dynamism. More and more manufactured goods have been produced by fewer and fewer workers, leaving more workers to produce services. This movement is analogous to the one out of agriculture earlier in the century (see Figure 1-5 again). At the turn of the century, nearly 50 percent of the Canadian labour force worked on farms. Today that number is less than 5 percent, yet they produce more total output than did the 50 percent in 1900. This movement away from agricultural employment freed workers to move into manufacturing, raising our living standards and transforming our way of life. In like manner, the movement away from manufacturing is freeing workers to move into services, and by replacing the grimy blue-collar jobs of the smokestack industries with more pleasant white-collar jobs in the service industries, it will once again transform our way of life.

Third, to a considerable extent, the decrease in the share of manufacturing in total employment also follows from consumers' tastes. Just as consumers in the first half of the century did not want to go on consuming more and more food products as their incomes rose, today's consumers do not wish to spend all of their additional income on manufactured products. Households have chosen to spend a high proportion of their increased incomes on services, thus creating employment opportunities in that sector. This simply reflects the fact that many products of the service sector—like restaurant meals, hotel stays, and airline flights—are products which have a high income elasticity of demand. Thus as the income of the average Canadian household increases, so too does that household's demand for these products of the service sector.

Finally, it is easy to underestimate the scope for quality, quantity, and productivity increases in services. As one example of productivity increases, consider your ability to make an automatic cash withdrawal from your bank account in Truro, Nova Scotia, while you are on vacation in Brazil. Now compare that to the apprehension your parents faced twenty years ago when they had to get to the bank before 3:00 pm on a Friday afternoon to make sure that they had enough cash for the weekend. As another example, note that since 1950, output per full-time worker has grown about *twice as fast* in the communication industry as it has in manufacturing.

CONTINUING CHANGE

The service sector is changing quickly. There has been some trend toward the mass-production techniques that provided much of the basis for productivity growth in the goods sector earlier in this century. This should increase productivity further. Services are also becoming globalized, so international trade will provide more opportunity for specialization and, hence, increased productivity. Also, much of the recent growth in demand for services comes as an input into goods-producing industries—either indirectly in the form of bundling sales with, say, maintenance contracts, or directly through productivity-enhancing management skills, inventory control methods, and the like. These contribute to the value added of the goods sector and hence to real national income.

It is also the case that many quality improvements in services go unrecorded. Today's hotel room is vastly more comfortable than a hotel room of 40 years ago, yet this quality improvement does not show up in our national income statistics. Measuring such technological improvements is even more difficult when they take the form of entirely new products. Airline transportation, telecommunication, fast-food chains, and financial services are prominent examples. The resulting increase in output is not always properly captured in our existing statistics.

It is easy to become concerned when looking at the official statistics, which show low wages earned in some service jobs. Indeed, the shift in employment toward services is, like most changes that hit the economy, a mixed blessing. It entails a significant increase in the number of "bad" service-sector jobs with low pay or low job security. Further, such transitions often generate temporary unemployment as workers get laid off from a contracting manufacturing sector and only slowly find jobs in the expanding service sector. Such transitions suggest a role for government policy to maintain the income of those workers temporarily unemployed (we discuss unemployment insurance and other income-support programs in Chapter 20). However, if we focus on the *overall economy*, and consider the growth in the real living standards of the *average* Canadian household, we are reminded that average real income has continued to rise, not only throughout the shift from agriculture to manufacturing, but also throughout the shift from manufacturing to services. There is little reason to think that the continued growth of the service sector will stand in the way of this slow but steady improvement in Canadians' living standards.

S U M M A R Y

A. LABOUR MARKETS AND WAGE DIFFERENTIALS

- In a competitive labour market, wages are set by the forces of supply and demand. Differences in wages will arise because some skills are more valued than others, because some jobs are more onerous than others, because of varying amounts of human capital, and because of discrimination based on such factors as gender and race.
- A union entering a competitive market acts as a monopolist and can raise wages, but only at the cost of reducing employment and creating a pool of unemployed who would like to work at the going wage rate but are unable to find employment in that market.
- A monopsonistic employer entering a competitive labour market will reduce both the wage and the level of employment.
- A union in a monopsonistic labour market—a case of bilateral monopoly—may increase both employment and wages relative to the pure monopsony outcome. If the union sets wages above the competitive level, however, it will create a pool of workers who are unable to get the jobs that they want at the going wage.
- Governments set some wages above their competitive levels by passing minimum-wage laws. In competitive labour markets, these laws raise the incomes of many employees, and cause unemployment for some of those with the lowest levels of skills. In monopsonistic labour markets, a legislated minimum wage (as long as it is not too high) can raise both wages and employment.

B. LABOUR UNIONS

- Labour unions seek many goals when they bargain with management. They may push for higher wages, higher fringe benefits, more stable employment, or less onerous working conditions. Whatever their specific goals, unless they face a monopsonist across the bargaining table, they must recognize the inherent conflict between the level of wages and the size of the union itself.
- Despite the costs to unions (i.e., reduced membership) of pushing for higher wages, there is clear evidence in Canada of a union wage premium. The union wage premium in Canada is somewhere between 10 and 25 percent—that is, unionized workers with a particular set of skills in particular types of jobs get paid 10 to 25 percent more than otherwise identical workers that are not members of unions.

C. DISCRIMINATION IN LABOUR MARKETS

- Discrimination has played an important role in labour markets, as it has in other aspects of life in Canada, the United States, and other industrialized countries. Direct discrimination affects wages and employment opportunities in part by limiting labour supply in the best-paying occupations and by increasing it in less attractive occupations.
- Some economists take the view that under perfect competition, discrimination cannot be sustained in equilibrium. This view is based on the argument that if some employers discriminate against certain types of workers, then this represents an opportunity for other employers. By taking advantage of this opportunity, those other employers create competitive pressure that works against the maintenance of discrimination.

D. THE "GOOD JOBS–BAD JOBS" DEBATE

- The past few decades have witnessed an increase in the share of total employment in the service sector and a decline in the share of employment in manufacturing. Some people are concerned that "good" manufacturing jobs are being replaced by "bad" service jobs.

- There are four reasons why the decline of the manufacturing sector is *not* necessarily a problem.

  1. Real disposable income per employed person has continued to rise throughout this period of decline in manufacturing employment.
  2. The decline in manufacturing employment is partly a result of the dynamism of that sector.

  3. Some of the decline in manufacturing reflects consumers' increased desires for services as their real income grows.
  4. It is easy to underestimate the importance of productivity improvements in the service sector. This is partly because the output of services is sometimes very hard to measure.

KEY CONCEPTS

Wage differentials in competitive labour markets
Labour unions as monopolists
Single employer as monopsonist
Effects of legislated minimum wages

Collective bargaining
Union goals: wages versus employment
Union wage premium
Effects of discrimination on wages and employment

Direct and indirect discrimination
"Comparable worth" and "pay equity"
"Good jobs" vs. "bad jobs"
Growth of the service sector

DISCUSSION QUESTIONS

1. "Because firms' demand curves for labour are downward-sloping, raising the minimum wage must reduce employment." Why is this statement wrong? When would raising the minimum wage reduce employment, and when might it increase employment?

2. Interpret the following statements or practices in terms of the subject matter of this chapter.

   a. A requirement that one must pass an English-language proficiency test to be a carpenter in Vancouver
   b. A statement by an official of a textile workers' union in New England (U.S.): "Until we have organized the southern [U.S.] textile industry, we will be unable to earn a decent wage in New England."
   c. A statement by an official of a steel-workers union in Hamilton: "Things are getting rough in our locals because the youngsters have different views about wages than the old-timers."

3. "The great increase in the number of women entering the labour force for the first time means that relatively more women than men earn beginning salaries. It is therefore not evidence of discrimination that the average wage earned by females is less than that earned by males." Discuss.

4. During the late 1980s and early 1990s, North American industry underwent an apparent restructuring that saw the elimination of many middle-management jobs. As a result, a relatively large group of workers in their forties and fifties were thrown back into the job market. Many of these people had difficulty finding new work and attributed this problem to age discrimination. What are some factors *other than prejudice* that could place such workers at a competitive disadvantage relative to their younger counterparts?

5. Physicians are among the highest-paid of workers. However, in addition to a bachelor's degree, would-be physicians must attend four years of medical school, three years of residency, and up to seven additional years of residency for some specialists. How does this change your perception with respect to how much physicians are paid? What additional information would you need to determine whether physicians' real pay is higher than that of other professionals?

6. This chapter discusses several supply-side origins of discrimination in the labour market. Recall from Chapter 15 that the demand for a factor of production is equal to that factor's marginal revenue product. In light of this, can you identify any sources of discrimination that originate on the demand side of the labour market? Discuss how these forces would lead to discrimination.

7. The United States Supreme Court recently ruled on a case in which a company had a policy of prohibiting women of childbearing age from working in jobs where they would be exposed to lead, which has been shown to be damaging to fetal development. The company argued that the policy simply protected its employees.

The plaintiffs in the case, women who had been excluded from these relatively high-paying jobs, argued that the policy was discriminatory. What do you think?

8. In considering the distributional impact of a higher minimum wage, economists have grown increasingly concerned about the composition of the population working at the minimum wage. For example, one commentator suggested, "Much of the gain from a higher minimum wage would go to surfboards and stereos—not into rent and baby formula." In what respects would we expect to see different behavioural responses to changes in the minimum wage when the affected population is largely teenagers working for discretionary income or adults who are the primary earners in their families?

9. Former U.S. President Ronald Reagan stated that the minimum wage "has caused more misery and unemployment than anything since the Great Depression." What evidence would we need to support or refute Reagan's statement?

10. "One can judge the presence or absence of discrimination by looking at the proportion of the population in different occupations." Does such information help? Does it suffice? Consider each of the following examples. Relative to their numbers in the total population, there are

a. Too many blacks and too few Jews among professional athletes
b. Too few male secretaries
c. Too few female judges
d. Too few female prison guards
e. Too few male school teachers

11. "Equal pay for work of equal value" is a commonly held goal, but "equal value" is hard to define. What would be the consequences of legislation that enforces equal pay for what turns out to be work of unequal value?

12. One critic of pay-equity legislation argues that it confuses "value determined *at the margin* by supply and demand" with a "job evaluator's concept of the *average* value of the inputs required to do the job." Reread the discussion of the paradox of value in Chapter 7, and then comment on this criticism of pay-equity legislation.

CHAPTER 17

CAPITAL AND NONRENEWABLE RESOURCES

In this chapter, we discuss capital and nonrenewable resources. These are similar factors of production in that each is a stock of valuable things that gets used up in the process of producing goods and services. They are also similar in that the optimal level of capital used by firms and the optimal level of extraction of a nonrenewable resource depend on the interest rate. They are different in that capital can be replaced, whereas nonrenewable resources cannot. A new machine can always be built to replace one that wears out, but a barrel of petroleum used represents a permanent reduction in the total stock of petroleum in the world—no more can be created to replace what has been used.

Resources that can be replaced, either through human effort, as with machines, or through natural reproduction, as with trees, humans, or fish, are called renewable resources. Resources that cannot be renewed, as with fossil fuels or minerals, are called nonrenewable resources or exhaustible resources.

CAPITAL AND THE INTEREST RATE

Capital is a produced factor of production. The nation's capital stock consists of all produced goods that are used in the production of other goods and services. Factories, machines, tools, computers, roads, bridges, and railroads are but a few of the many examples.

We begin our study of capital by exploring an important complication that arises because factors of production are durable—a machine lasts for years, a labourer for a lifetime, and land more or less forever. It is convenient to think of a factor's lifetime as being divided into the shorter periods that we refer to as *production periods* or *rental periods*. The present time is the current period. Future time is one, two, three, and so on, periods hence.

The durability of factors makes it necessary to distinguish between the factor itself and the *flow of services* that it provides in a given production period. For example, we can rent a piece of land for use over some period of time, or we can buy the land outright. This distinction is just a particular instance of the general distinction between flows and stocks that we first encountered in Chapter 4.

Although what follows applies to any durable factor, applications to capital are of most importance, so we limit the discussion to capital. Extension 17-1 discusses some of these issues as they apply to labour.

TWO PRICES OF CAPITAL

If a firm hires a piece of capital equipment for use over some period of time—for example, one truck

---

EXTENSION 17-1

THE RENTAL AND PURCHASE PRICE OF LABOUR

If you wish to farm a piece of land, you can buy it yourself, or you can rent it for a specific period of time. If you want to set up a small business, you can buy your office and equipment, or you can rent them. The same is true for all capital and all land; a firm often has the option of buying or renting.

Exactly the same would be true for labour if we lived in a slave society. You could buy a slave to be your assistant, or you could rent the services either of someone else's slave or of a free person. Fortunately, slavery is illegal throughout most of today's world. As a result, the labour markets that we know deal only in the *services* of labour; we do not go to a labour market to buy a worker, only to hire his or her services.

You can, however, hire the services of a labourer for a long period of time. In professional sports, multiyear contracts are common, and 10-year contracts

are not unknown. The late Herbert von Karajan was made conductor for life of the Berlin Philharmonic Orchestra. Publishers sometimes tie up their authors in multibook contracts, and movie and television production firms often sign up their actors on long-term contracts. In all cases of such *personal services contracts,* the person is not a slave, and his or her personal rights and liberties are protected by law. The purchaser of the long-term contract is nonetheless buying ownership of the factor's *services* for an extended period of time. The price of the contract will reflect the person's expected earnings over the contract's lifetime. If the contract is transferable, the owner can sell these services for a lump sum or rent them out for some period. As with land and capital goods, the price paid for this stock of labour services depends on the expected rental prices over the contract period.

for one month—it pays a price for the privilege of using that piece of capital equipment. If the firm buys the truck outright, it pays a different (and higher) price for the purchase. Consider each of these prices in turn.

Rental Price

The *rental price of capital* is the amount that a firm pays to obtain the services of a capital good for a given period of time. The rental price of one week's use of a piece of capital is analogous to the weekly wage rate that is the price of hiring the services of labour.

Just as a profit-maximizing firm operating in a competitive labour market continues to hire labour until its marginal revenue product (*MRP*) equals the wage, so will the firm go on hiring capital until its *MRP* equals its rental price, which we call *r*. Because in a competitive market each firm faces the same market-determined rental price, and each hires capital until *MRP* equals *r*, it follows that each profit-maximizing firm will have the same *MRP* of capital.

A capital good may also be used by the firm that owns it. In this case, the firm does not pay out any rental fee. However, the rental price is the amount that the firm could charge if it leased its capital to another firm. The rental price is thus the *opportunity cost* to the firm of using the capital good itself. This rental price is the *implicit* price that reflects the value to the firm of the services of its own capital that it uses during the current production period.

Whether the firm pays the rental price explicitly or calculates it as an implicit cost of using its own capital, the rental price of a capital good over the current production period is equal to its marginal revenue product.

Purchase Price

The price that a firm pays to buy a capital good is called the *purchase price of capital*. When a firm buys a capital good outright, it obtains the use of the good's services over the whole of that good's lifetime. What the capital good will contribute to the firm is a flow that is equal to the marginal revenue product of the capital good's services over its lifetime. The price that the firm is willing to pay for the capital good, naturally enough, is related to the total value that it places now on this stream of *expected* receipts to be received over future time periods. The term *expected* emphasizes that the firm is usually uncertain about

the prices at which it will be able to sell its outputs in the future.

In order to compute the value that the firm places on receiving a future stream of benefits (the *MRP* of the capital good), we must examine the concept of *present value*. The following discussion proceeds under the simplifying assumption that the firm knows the future *MRP*s. This allows us to develop the central insights about *present value* without dealing with the complications arising from uncertainty.

THE PRESENT VALUE OF FUTURE RETURNS

Consider the stream of future income that is provided by a capital good. How much is that stream worth *now*? How much would someone be willing to pay now to buy the right to receive that flow of future payments? The answer is called the good's *present value*. In general, present value (*PV*) refers to the value now of one or more payments to be received in the future.

The Present Value of a Single Future Payment

One Period in the Future.   To learn how to find the present value, we start with the simplest possible case. How much would a firm be prepared to pay now to purchase a capital good that will produce a marginal revenue product (*MRP*) of $100 in one year's time, after which time the capital good will be useless? One way to answer this question is to ask a somewhat *opposite* question: How much would the firm have to lend now in order to have $100 a year from now? Suppose for the moment that the interest rate is 5 percent, which means that $1.00 invested today will be worth $1.05 in one year's time.[1]

If we use *PV* to stand for this unknown amount, we can write $PV \times (1.05) = \$100$. Thus $PV = \$100/1.05 = \$95.24$. This tells us that the present value of $100, receivable in one year's time, is $95.24 when the interest rate is 5 percent. Anyone who lends out $95.24 for one year at 5 percent interest will receive $95.24 back plus $4.76 in interest, which makes $100 in total. When we calculate this present value, the interest rate is used to *discount* (reduce to its present value) the $100 to be received in one year's time. The maximum price that a firm would be willing to pay for this capital good is

---

[1]The analysis in the rest of this chapter assumes *annual* compounding of interest.

$95.24 (assuming that the interest rate relevant to the firm is 5 percent).

To see why, let us start by assuming that firms are offered the capital good at some other price. Suppose that the good is offered at $98. If, instead of paying this amount for the capital good, a firm lends its $98 out at 5 percent interest, it would have at the end of one year more than the $100 that the capital good will produce. (At 5 percent interest, $98 yields $4.90 in interest, which, together with the principal, makes $102.90.) Clearly, no profit-maximizing firm would pay $98—or, by the same reasoning, any sum in excess of $95.24—for the capital good. It could do better by using its funds in other ways.

Now suppose that the good is offered for sale at $90. A firm could borrow $90 to buy the capital good and would pay $4.50 in interest on its loan. At the end of the year, the good yields $100. When this is used to repay the $90 loan and the $4.50 in interest, $5.50 is left as profit to the firm. Clearly, it would be worthwhile for a profit-maximizing firm to buy the good at a price of $90 or, by the same argument, at any price less than $95.24.

The actual present value that we have calculated depended on our assuming that the interest rate is 5 percent. What if the interest rate is 7 percent? At that interest rate, the present value of the $100 receivable in one year's time would be $100/1.07 = $93.46.

These examples are easy to generalize. In both cases, we have found the present value by dividing the sum that is receivable in the future by 1 plus the rate of interest.[2] In general, if the interest rate is i per year, then the present value of the MRP (in dollars) received one year hence is

$$PV = MRP/(1 + i) \qquad [1]$$

Several Periods in the Future. Now we know how to calculate the present value of a single sum that is receivable one year hence. The next step is to ask what would happen if the sum were receivable at a later date. For example, what is the present value of $100 to be received *two* years hence when the interest rate is 5 percent? This is $100/[(1.05)(1.05)] = $90.70. We can check this by seeing what would happen if $90.70 were lent out for two years. In the first year, the loan would earn interest of

(0.05)($90.70) = $4.54, and hence after one year, the firm would receive $95.24. In the second year, the interest would be earned on this entire amount; interest earned in the second year would equal (0.05)($95.24) = $4.76. Hence, in two years the firm would have $100.

In general, the present value of MRP dollars received t years in the future when the interest rate is i per year is

$$PV = MRP/(1 + i)^t \qquad [2]$$

All that this formula does is discount the sum MRP by the interest rate, repeatedly, once for each of the t periods that must pass until the sum becomes available. If we look at the formula, we see that the higher is i or t, the higher is the whole term $(1 + i)^t$. This term, however, appears in the denominator, so PV is *negatively* related to both i and t.

The formula $PV = MRP/(1 + i)^t$ shows that the present value of a given sum payable in the future will be smaller the more distant the payment date and the higher the rate of interest.

The Present Value of a Stream of Payments

Now consider the present value of a stream of receipts that continues indefinitely. Indeed, this is essentially the question that we are interested in when examining the firm's decision to purchase a capital good since that capital good will typically generate a stream of benefits long into the future. At first glance, the PV in this case might seem very high because the total amount received grows without reaching any limit as time passes. The preceding section suggests, however, that people will not value the far-distant payments very highly.

To find the PV of $100 a year, payable forever, we ask: How much would you have to invest now, at an interest rate of i percent per year, to obtain $100 each year in interest earnings? This is simply $i \times PV = \$100$, where i is the interest rate and PV the sum required. Dividing through by i shows the present value of the stream of $100 a year forever:

$$PV = \$100/i \qquad [3]$$

For example, if the interest rate is 10 percent, the present value would be $1,000. This merely says that $1,000 invested at 10 percent yields $100 per year

---

[2]In this type of formula, the interest rate i is expressed as a decimal fraction where, for example, 7 percent is expressed as 0.07, so that $1 + i$ equals 1.07.

forever. Notice that, as in the preceding sections, *PV* is negatively related to the rate of interest: The higher the interest rate, the lower the present value of the stream of future payments.

Conclusions

From the foregoing discussion we can put together three important propositions about the rental and purchase prices of capital.

1. The rental price of capital paid in each period is the flow of net receipts that the capital good is expected to produce during that period—that is, the marginal revenue product of the capital good.

2. The maximum purchase price that a firm would pay for a capital good is the discounted present value of the flow of net receipts (rental values) that the good is expected to produce over its lifetime.

3. The maximum purchase price that a firm would pay for a capital good is positively associated with its rental price and negatively associated with both the interest rate and the amount of time that the owner must wait for payments to accrue.

THE FIRM'S DECISION

An individual firm faces a given interest rate and a given purchase price of capital goods. The firm can vary the quantity of capital that it employs, and as a result, the marginal revenue product of its capital varies. The law of diminishing returns tells us that the more capital the firm uses, the lower its *MRP*.

The Decision to Purchase a Unit of Capital

Consider a firm that is deciding whether or not to add to its capital stock and facing an interest rate of *i* at which it can borrow or lend money. The first thing the firm has to do is to estimate the expected marginal revenue product of the new piece of capital over its lifetime. Then it discounts this at the interest rate of *i* per year to find the present value of the stream of receipts the machine will generate. Having computed the *PV* of the stream of *MRPs*, the firm then compares this *PV* with the purchase price of the capital good. If the purchase price is less than the *PV*, then the firm buys the capital good; if *PV* is less than the purchase price, the firm will not buy the capital good.

Consider the following simple example. Suppose that a machine has an *MRP* of $1,000 each period—that is, by buying this machine the firm can produce and sell an extra $1,000 worth of output each period. Suppose further that the machine lasts for 3 periods—after that, the machine is completely worn out and worth nothing. Finally, suppose the interest rate is 10 percent per year. The *PV* of this stream of *MRPs* is then equal to

$$PV = \$1,000 + \$1,000/(1 + 0.10) \\ + \$1,000/(1 + 0.10)^2 = \$2,735.53.$$

The present value, by its construction, tells us how much any flow of future receipts is worth now. If the firm can buy the machine for less than its *PV*—that is, for any amount less than $2,735.53—then this machine is a good buy. If it must pay more, the machine is not worth its price.

It is always worthwhile for a firm to buy another unit of capital whenever the present value of the stream of future *MRPs* that the capital provides exceeds its purchase price.

The Firm's Optimal Capital Stock

Because the *MRP* declines as the firm's capital stock rises, the firm will go on adding to its stock of capital until the *present value* of the flow of *MRPs* generated by the *last unit* added is equal to the purchase price of that unit.

The profit-maximizing capital stock of the firm is such that the present value of the flow of *MRPs* that is provided by the marginal unit of capital is equal to its purchase price.

Now suppose the firm has achieved its profit-maximizing stock of capital. What would then lead the firm to wish to increase that stock? Given the price of the machines, anything that increases the present value of the flow of income that the machines produce will have that effect. Two things will do this. First, the *MRPs* of the capital may rise. That would happen if technological changes make capital more productive so that each unit produces more than before. (This possibility is dealt with later in the chapter.) Second, the interest rate may fall, causing an increase in the *present value* of any given stream of future *MRPs*. For example, suppose that next

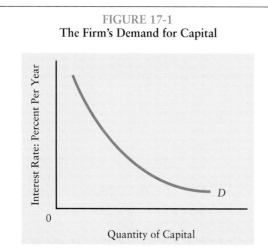

FIGURE 17-1
The Firm's Demand for Capital

Interest Rate: Percent Per Year

0

Quantity of Capital

D

The lower the rate of interest, the larger is the firm's desired capital stock. The lower the interest rate, the higher is the present value of any given stream of marginal revenue products and hence the more capital that the firm will wish to use.

year's *MRP* is $1,000. This has a *PV* of $909.09 when the interest rate is 10 percent and $952.38 when the interest rate falls to 5 percent.

So when the interest rate falls, the firm will wish to add to its capital stock. It will go on doing so until the decline in the *MRPs* of successive additions to its capital stock, according to the law of diminishing returns, reduces the present value of the *MRP* at the new lower rate of interest to the purchase price of the capital.

The size of a firm's desired capital stock increases when the rate of interest falls, and it decreases when the rate of interest rises.

This relationship is shown in Figure 17-1. It can be thought of as the firm's demand curve for capital plotted against the interest rate. It shows how the desired stock of capital varies with the interest rate. (It is sometimes called the **marginal efficiency of capital curve.**)

One final comment about the firm's decision. We have shown that changes in the interest rate lead to changes in the firm's desired capital stock. When you go on to study *macroeconomics*, however, you will learn that the presence of *inflation* forces economists to make a distinction between the *real* interest rate

and the *nominal* interest rate. All of our discussion here has been about the real interest rate. See Extension 17-2 for a more detailed discussion of inflation and interest rates.

THE EQUILIBRIUM INTEREST RATE

The analysis that we used for a single firm in the previous section also applies for the entire economy. This is because the aggregate or total demand for capital goods is simply the sum of all the individual firms' demands. Thus the higher is the market interest rate, the lower will be the total quantity of capital goods demanded. Also, changes in technology which make each unit of capital more productive lead to an increase in the total demand for capital goods.

The important difference between the analysis of a single firm and the analysis of the entire economy is that whereas any individual firm takes the market interest rate as given, the interest rate is determined *in equilibrium* for the economy as a whole. This is exactly analogous to each competitive firm taking the product price as given, whereas the product's price is determined *in equilibrium* in the market as a whole.

Short-Run Equilibrium

In the short run, the *economy's* capital stock is given. Though any given firm can change its own capital stock relatively easily—by buying or selling capital goods to or from other firms—the economy as a whole can adjust its capital stock only slowly. To reduce the aggregate capital stock, firms must allow their capital goods to wear out, or *depreciate;* to increase the aggregate capital stock, new capital goods must be built, some of which—buildings, bridges, etc.—take a considerable time to complete.

Figure 17-2 shows the economy's fixed short-run supply of capital as well as the total demand for capital goods, which is negatively related to the interest rate. Since the aggregate capital stock is fixed in the short run, equilibrium is achieved through changes in the interest rate, as opposed to changes in the level of capital.

For the economy as a whole, the condition that the present value of the MRPs should equal the price of capital goods determines the equilibrium interest rate.

EXTENSION 17-2

INFLATION AND INTEREST RATES

Inflation means the prices of all goods in the economy are rising. More correctly, it means that the prices of goods are rising on *average*—some prices may be rising and others may be falling, but if there is inflation then the price of the average good is rising. Economists refer to the average price of all goods as the *price level*. When the price level is rising, inflation is positive; if prices are rising at a rate of 5 percent per year, we say that the rate of inflation is 5 percent. When the price level is falling, inflation is negative. If prices are falling at a rate of 2 percent per year, we say that the rate of inflation is −2 percent.

REAL AND NOMINAL INTEREST RATES

In the presence of inflation, it becomes very important to distinguish between the **real interest rate** and the **nominal interest rate.** The nominal interest rate is measured simply in dollars paid. If you pay me $7 interest for a $100 loan for one year, the nominal interest rate is 7 percent.

Consider further my one-year loan to you of $100 at the nominal rate of 7 percent. The real rate that I earn depends on what happens to the price level during the course of the year. If the price level remains constant over the year, then the real rate that I earn is also 7 percent. This is because I can buy 7 percent more real goods and services with the $107 that you repay me than with the $100 that I lent you. However, if the price level were to rise by 7 percent during the

year, the real rate would be zero because the $107 you repay me will buy exactly the same quantity of real goods as did the $100 I gave up. If I were unlucky enough to have lent money at a nominal rate of 7 percent in a year in which prices rose by 10 percent, the real rate would be −3 percent. The real rate of interest concerns the ratio of the purchasing power of the money returned to the purchasing power of the money borrowed, and it will be different from the nominal rate whenever inflation is not zero.

The real interest rate is the difference between the nominal interest rate and the rate of inflation.

If lenders and borrowers are concerned with the real costs measured in terms of purchasing power, the nominal interest rate will be set at the real rate they require plus an amount to cover any expected rate of inflation. Consider a one-year loan that is meant to earn a real return to the lender of 3 percent. If the expected rate of inflation is zero, the nominal interest rate for the loan will also be 3 percent. If, however, a 10 percent inflation is expected, the nominal interest rate will have to be set at 13 percent in order that the real return be 3 percent.

To provide a given expected real rate of interest the nominal interest rate will have to be set at the desired real rate of interest plus the expected rate of inflation.

This point is often overlooked, and as a result people are surprised at the high nominal interest rates that exist during periods of high inflation. But it is the

Let us see how this comes about. If the price of capital is less than the present value of its stream of future *MRPs*, it would be worthwhile for all firms to borrow money to invest in capital. For the economy as a whole, however, the stock of capital cannot change quickly, so the effect of this demand for borrowing would be to push up the interest rate until the present value of the *MRPs* equals the price of a unit of capital goods. Conversely, if the price of capital is above its present value, no one would

wish to borrow money to invest in capital, and the rate of interest would fall. This is illustrated in Figure 17-2.[3]

---

[3]In the macroeconomics part of this textbook, we see that if prices are inflexible in the short run, then actions taken by the central bank can also affect the interest rate. For now, we continue our assumption that all prices (for goods and factors) rise or fall quickly to clear markets, so that the short-run equilibrium interest rate is determined only by the economy's marginal product of capital.

real interest rate that matters more to borrowers and lenders. Inflation is currently quite low in Canada (below 2 percent in 1997), but it has not always been that way. For example, in 1981 the rate of inflation was 12.4 percent and the nominal interest rate to prime borrowers was an unprecedented 19.3 percent! The real interest rate was then 6.9 percent. By 1993, the rate of inflation had fallen to 1.8 percent and the nominal rate to prime borrowers had fallen to 5.9 percent; the real rate was then 4.1 percent.

UNEXPECTED INFLATION

If an inflation is fully expected, the nominal interest rate can be set to give any desired real interest rate. Problems arise, however, when the inflation rate changes unexpectedly. Consider, for example, a loan contract in which the parties wish to carry a 3 percent real rate of interest. If a 7 percent inflation rate is expected, the nominal interest rate will be set at 10 percent. But what if the inflationary expectations turn out to be wrong? If the inflation rate ends up being only 4 percent, the real interest rate will be 6 percent. If, on the other hand, the inflation rate is 12 percent, the real interest rate will be −2 percent; the lender, even after paying the interest on the loan, will give back less purchasing power at the end of the period than he or she borrowed at the beginning.

Unexpected changes in the rate of inflation cause the real rate of interest on contracts already drawn up to vary in unexpected ways. An unexpected fall in the inflation rate is beneficial to lenders; an unexpected rise is beneficial to borrowers.

Such unexpected changes in inflation have happened in Canada. In the mid 1970s, for example, the massive increase in the world price of oil, driven by the actions of the OPEC oil cartel, contributed to a sudden increase in the rate of inflation. During these years, the real interest rate was actually negative—reflecting the fact that actual inflation was much greater than people had expected.

BACK TO CAPITAL

In this chapter, we have examined the firm's decision to buy capital stock, and we emphasized the importance of the interest rate to this decision. Though we did not say it explicitly in the text, all of our discussion about the interest rate was about the *real* interest rate. Thus the central conclusion about the firm's decision can be restated more accurately: *The size of the firm's desired capital stock increases when the real interest rate falls, and it decreases when the real interest rate rises.*

When you go on to study *macroeconomics*, in Chapters 21–38 of this book, you will learn more about what causes inflation, and thus what forces us to make the distinction between real and nominal interest rates. For now, however, keep in mind that in this chapter we are supposing that there is no inflation, so real and nominal interest rates are the same.

Changing Capital and Technology

In the long run, the economy's capital stock is free to change, but technology is constant. If capital is accumulated over time, then the MRP will fall, and the equilibrium interest rate will also fall. Conversely, the aggregate capital stock is allowed to wear out, then the MRP will rise and so will the equilibrium interest rate. This is shown in Figure 17-2, where the aggregate capital stock changes between K_0 and K_1, holding the demand for capital goods constant.

In the very-long run, technology changes. As a result, the capital stock becomes more productive as the old, obsolete capital is replaced by newer, more efficient capital. This shifts the MRP curve outward, which tends to increase the equilibrium interest rate associated with any particular size of the capital stock. In contrast, the accumulation of capital moves the economy downward to the right along any given MRP curve, and that tends to lower the interest rate associated with any one MRP curve. The net effect

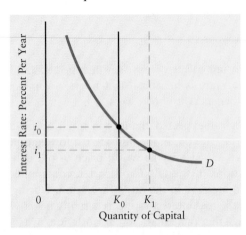

FIGURE 17-2
The Equilibrium Interest Rate

In the short run, the interest rate fluctuates to equate the demand and supply of capital; in the long run, the interest rate falls as more capital is accumulated. The economy's desired capital stock is negatively related to the interest rate, as shown by the curve D. In the short run, the aggregate capital stock is given. When the capital stock is K_0, the equilibrium interest rate is i_0. Above that rate firms will not want to hold all of the available capital; below that rate firms will want to borrow and add to their capital. In the long run, as the capital stock grows to K_1, the equilibrium interest rate falls to i_1.

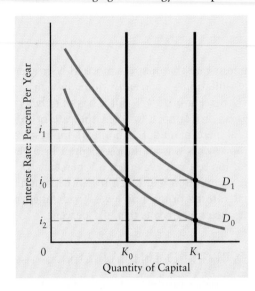

FIGURE 17-3
The Effect of Changing Technology and Capital Stock

Technological changes which increase the marginal product of capital, and changes in the capital stock itself, have opposite effects on the equilibrium interest rate. The original capital stock is K_0 and the original technology gives rise to the demand for capital given by D_0. Thus, the equilibrium interest rate is i_0. Technological changes which increase the marginal product of capital shift the demand curve to D_1 and, with a constant capital stock, would increase the interest rate to i_1. Alternatively, an increase in the capital stock to K_1, holding technology constant, lowers the interest rate to i_2. If technology improves *and* the capital stock increases, then the interest rate could rise or fall. In the figure, the two effects exactly offset each other so that the interest rate is unchanged at i_0.

on the interest rate of both of these changes may be to raise it, to lower it, or to leave it unchanged, as shown in Figure 17-3.

In almost all industrialized countries, there have been enormous increases in the aggregate capital stock over the past century. Yet, there *have not* been large decreases in the interest rate over the same period. This fact is explained easily by examining Figure 17-3. Technological change has improved the marginal productivity of capital goods and has thus led to increases in the aggregate demand for capital. This fact, taken alone, would lead to increases in the equilibrium interest rate. Working in the other direction, however, is the continual accumulation of capital, which tends to push down the equilibrium interest rate. The observation that the aggregate capital stock has increased dramatically, combined with the absence of a clear trend in the interest rate, suggests that these forces are offsetting each other more-or-less equally. The very-long-run effects of changing technology, combined with a growing capital stock, are studied further in Chapter 33.

NONRENEWABLE RESOURCES

So far, we have discussed the pricing of factors, such as labour and capital, that can be replaced as they wear out. As older people leave the labour force because of retirement or death, young persons, seeking their first jobs, enter. As an existing piece of capital equipment is retired because of depreciation or obsolescence, it is replaced by a new piece of equipment. Such resources are called **renewable resources**.

We now consider factors of production that are available in fixed amounts. For each such factor, the total stock is given, and every unit that is used today permanently reduces the stock that is available for future use. Such a factor is called a **nonrenewable resource** or an *exhaustible resource*.

In practice, few, if any, resources are completely nonrenewable. Although there is only a fixed stock of oil, coal, or iron ore that is known to exist at any given time, new discoveries add to the known stock, and extraction subtracts from it. It is, however, possible to imagine exhausting all of the world's supplies of oil, natural gas, or coal. In this sense, they are nonrenewable resources.

THE EXTRACTION RATE OF A RESOURCE

To focus on the basic issues, it is easiest to think of a resource that is completely nonrenewable. Suppose for the moment that all of the petroleum in existence has been discovered so that every unit that is used permanently diminishes the available stock by 1 unit.

Suppose that many firms own the land that contains the oil supply. They have invested money in discovering the oil, drilling wells, and laying pipelines. Their current extraction costs are virtually zero; all they have to do is turn their taps on, and the oil flows at any desired rate to the oil markets.[4]

Profit-Maximizing Firms

What should each firm do? It could extract all of its oil in a great binge of production this year, or it could save the resource for some future rainy day and produce nothing this year. In practice, it is likely to adopt some intermediate policy, producing and selling some oil this year and holding stocks of it in the ground for extraction in future years. But *how much* should it extract this year and *how much* should it carry over for future years? What will the decision imply for the price of oil over the years?

The firms that own land with petroleum underneath it are holding a valuable resource. Holding it, however, has an opportunity cost: It could have been extracted and sold this year, yielding revenue to the firms in the same year. A firm will be willing to leave the resource in the ground only if it earns a return equal to what it can earn in alternative investments. This alternative return is measured by the interest rate. To see why, consider two cases.

First, suppose that the price of oil is expected to rise by less than the interest rate. For example, suppose the interest rate is 10 percent per year but the price of oil is expected to increase by only 5 percent per year. Oil extracted and sold now will in this case have a higher value than oil left in the ground, since revenues from current sales could be earning 10 percent in a bank account. Firms will therefore extract more oil this year. Because the demand curve for oil has a negative slope, raising the extraction rate will lower this year's price. Production will rise, and the current price will fall until the expected price rise between this year and next year is equal to the interest rate.[5] The firms will then be indifferent between producing another barrel this year and holding it for production next year.

Second, suppose that the price is expected to rise by more than the interest rate. Firms will in this case prefer to leave more in the ground, where they earn a higher return than could be earned by selling the oil this year and investing the proceeds at the current interest rate. Thus firms will cut their rate of production for this year, which will raise this year's price. When the current price has risen so that the gap between the current price and next year's expected price is equal to the interest rate, firms will value equally a barrel of oil extracted and one left in the ground.

In a perfectly competitive industry for a nonrenewable resource, the equilibrium occurs when the last unit currently produced earns just as much for each firm as it would if it had been left in the ground for future sales.

To illustrate these important relations, suppose that next year's price is expected to be $1.05 and that the rate of interest is 5 percent. First, suppose that

---

[4]It is, of course, a simplification of any real case to assume that current production costs are actually zero. The assumption, however, is not too far from reality in the case of such a resource as oil, where the fixed costs of discovery, extraction, and distribution account for the bulk of total costs. When extraction costs are nonzero, all statements about prices in the text refer to the margin by which price exceeds the current cost of extraction.

[5]The discussion is simplified by assuming next year's expected price to be given. The decision to produce more this year may also affect next year's price. If the total supplies are small, next year's expected price may rise. The argument proceeds exactly as in the text, except that the equilibrium gap between two prices is achieved by the present price falling and the expected future price rising rather than by having next year's expected price remaining constant and all the adjustment coming through this year's price.

the current price is $1.04 per barrel. It clearly pays to produce more now because the $1.04 that is earned by selling a barrel now can be invested to yield approximately $1.09 ($1.04 × 1.05), which is more than the $1.05 that the oil would be worth in a year's time if it is left in the ground. Second, suppose that the current price is $.90 cents per barrel. Now it pays to reduce production because oil left in the ground will be worth 16.66 percent more next year [(1.05/0.90) × 100]. Extracting it this year and investing the money will produce a gain of only 5 percent. Finally, let the current price be $1.00. Now oil producers make the same amount of money whether they leave $1.00 worth of oil in the ground to be worth $1.05 next year or they sell the oil for $1.00 this year and invest the proceeds at 5 percent interest.

Market Pricing

What we have established so far determines the *rate of increase* of prices over time: If stocks are given and unchanging, prices should rise over time at a rate equal to the rate of interest. But what about the *level* of prices? Will they start low and rise to only moderate levels over the next few years, or will they start high and then rise to even higher levels? The answer depends on the total stock of the resource that is available (and, where some new discoveries are possible, on the expected additions to that stock in the future). The scarcer the resource relative to the demand for it, the higher its market price at the outset.

A resource's price tends to rise over time at a rate equal to the rate of interest; the current price will depend on the resource's scarcity relative to current demand.

Socially Optimal Behaviour: Hotelling's Rule

Petroleum is a scarce resource, and the value to consumers of one more barrel produced now is the price that they would be willing to pay for it, which is the current $1.00 market price of the oil. If the oil is extracted this year and the proceeds are invested at the rate of interest (5 percent), they will produce $1.05 worth of valuable goods next year. If that barrel of oil is not produced this year and is left in the ground for extraction next year, its value to consumers at that time will be next year's price of oil. It is not socially optimal, therefore, to leave the oil in the ground unless it will be worth at least $1.05 to consumers next year. More generally, society obtains in-

creases in the value of what is available for consumption by conserving units of a nonrenewable resource only if the price of the units is expected to rise at a rate that is at least as high as the interest rate.

This answer to the question "How much of a nonrenewable resource should be consumed now?" was provided many years ago by the U.S. economist Harold Hotelling. His answer—now referred to as **Hotelling's Rule**—is very simple, yet it specifically determines the optimal pattern of prices over the years. It is interesting that the answer applies to *all* nonrenewable resources. It does not matter whether there is a large or a small demand or whether that demand is elastic or inelastic. In all cases the answer is the same:

The rate of extraction of any nonrenewable resource should be such that its price increases at a rate equal to the interest rate.

For example, if the rate of interest is 4 percent, the price of the resource should be rising 4 percent per year. If it is rising by more, there is too much current extraction; if it is rising by less, there is not enough current extraction. We have already seen that this is the rate of extraction that will be produced by a competitive industry.

The Rate of Extraction

Hotelling's Rule does not tell us exactly how many barrels of oil should be extracted each year. Instead, it only tells us that the year's extraction rate *should be such that* the market price rises at a rate equal to the interest rate. What then should the actual extraction rate be if the competitive market fulfills Hotelling's Rule for optimal extraction rates? The answer to this question *does* depend on market conditions. Specifically, it depends on the position and the slope of the demand curve. If the quantity demanded at all prices is small, the rate of extraction will be small. The larger the quantity demanded at each price, the higher the rate of extraction will tend to be.

Now consider the influence of the demand elasticity. A highly inelastic demand curve suggests that there are few substitutes and that purchasers are prepared to pay large sums rather than do without the resource. This will produce a relatively even rate of extraction, with small reductions in each period being sufficient to drive up the price at the required rate. A relatively elastic demand curve suggests that people can easily find substitutes once the price rises.

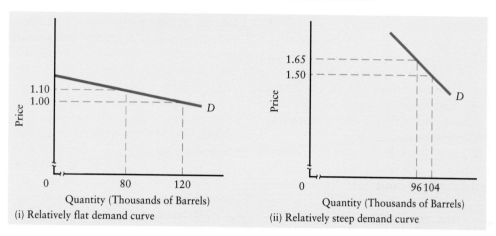

FIGURE 17-4
The Extraction Rate for a Nonrenewable Resource

(i) Relatively flat demand curve

(ii) Relatively steep demand curve

The shape of the demand curve determines the extraction pattern over time. In the example in this figure, the interest rate is assumed to be 10 percent, and there is a fixed supply of 200,000 barrels of oil that can be extracted from the ground at zero variable cost. (All costs are fixed costs.) The oil is available for extraction either in the current period or in the next period, after which it spoils.

In part (i) of the figure, the demand curve is relatively flat. The two conditions—that the whole supply be used over two periods and that the price rise by 10 percent between the two periods—dictate that the quantities be 120,000 barrels in the first period, with a price of $1.00 per barrel, and 80,000 in the second period, with a price of $1.10 per barrel.

In part (ii), the demand curve is rather steep. The same two conditions now dictate that the quantities be 104,000 barrels in the first period, with a price of $1.50 per barrel, and 96,000 barrels in the second period, with a price of $1.65 per barrel.

This will encourage a great deal of consumption now and a rapidly diminishing amount over future years because large reductions in consumption are needed to drive the price up at the required rate.

Figure 17-4 illustrates this working of the price mechanism with a simple example in which the whole stock of oil must be consumed in only two periods, this year and next year. The general point is this:

The more inelastic the demand curve, the more even the rate of extraction (and hence the rate of use) will be over the years; the more elastic the demand curve, the more uneven the rate of extraction will be over the years.

An elastic demand curve will lead to large consumption now and a rapid fall in consumption over the years. An inelastic demand curve will lead to lower consumption now and a less rapid fall in consumption over the years.

Rents to Natural Resources

The incomes earned by the owners of petroleum are rents in the sense defined in Chapter 15: The owners would be willing to produce the oil at any price that covers the direct costs of extraction, which in this example is zero.[6] Although these incomes serve no function in getting the product produced, since any nonzero price would do that, they do fulfill the important function of determining the extraction rate, and hence the use of the resource, *over time*. As we have seen, the pattern of prices determines the use of the resource and hence the amount of resources allocated to its production *over time*.

CONSERVATION THROUGH THE PRICE SYSTEM

In this discussion, we see the price system playing its now familiar role of coordinator. By following private profit incentives, firms are led to conserve the resource in a manner that is consistent with society's needs.

The Role of Rising Prices

From society's viewpoint, the optimal extraction pattern of a nonrenewable resource occurs when its

---

[6]In real cases, the direct cost of extracting the resource is positive, and the rent is the income earned above that amount.

price rises each year at a rate equal to the interest rate. If the price is prevented from rising, the resource is depleted much too fast. The rising price fulfills a number of useful functions.

First, the rising price encourages conservation. As the resource becomes scarcer and its price rises, users will be motivated to be more and more economical in its use. Uses with low yields may be abandoned altogether, and uses with high yields will be pursued only as long as their value at the margin is enough to compensate for the high price.

Second, the rising price encourages the discovery of new sources of supply—at least in cases in which the world supply is not totally fixed and already known.

Third, the rising price encourages innovation. New products that will do the same job may be developed, as well as new processes that use alternative resources.

How Might the Price System Fail?

We now examine three basic ways in which the price system might fail to produce the optimal rate of resource extraction. First, private owners may not have sufficient information to determine the optimal extraction rate. Second, deficiencies in property rights may result in firms' having incentives to extract the resource too fast. Third, markets may not correctly reflect social values. We look at examples of each of these and ask if they justify government intervention.[7]

Ignorance. Private owners might not have enough knowledge to arrive at the best estimate of the rate at which prices will rise. If they do not know the world stocks of their commodity and the current extraction rate, they may be unable to estimate the rate of the price rise and thus will not know when to raise or lower their current rates of extraction. For example, if all firms think that prices will rise only slowly in the future, but prices actually end up rising quickly, they will all produce too much now and conserve too little for future periods.

In this situation, however, there is no reason to think that the government could do any better, unless it has access to some special knowledge that private firms do not possess. If it does have such knowledge, the government can make it public; further intervention is unnecessary if a competitive industry is maximizing profits on the basis of the best information available to it. In practice, what knowledge does exist about both the proven reserves of nonrenewable resources and their current extraction rates is usually freely and openly available.

Inadequate Property Rights. Some nonrenewable resources have the characteristics of what is called *common property*. Such property cannot be exclusively owned and controlled by one person or firm. For example, one person's oil-bearing land may be adjacent to another person's, and the underground supplies may be interconnected. In such a case, if one firm holds off producing now, the oil may end up being extracted by the neighbour. In such cases, which are sometimes encountered with petroleum, there is a tendency for a firm to extract the resource too fast because a firm's oil that has been left in the ground may not be available to that firm at a future date. (Similar issues arise with any common-property resource such as fishing grounds—we examine this further in Chapter 18.)

What is being described here is a problem of *inadequate property rights*. Because the resource will be worth more in total value when it is exploited at the optimal extraction rate than when small firms exploit it too quickly, there will be an incentive for individual owners to combine until each self-contained source of supply is owned by only one firm. After that, the problem of overexploitation will no longer arise. Government ownership is not necessary to achieve this result. What is needed, at most, is intervention to ensure that markets can work to provide the optimal size of individual units so that proper extraction management can be applied by the private owners.

Political uncertainty can be another source of inadequate property rights. For example, the owners of the resource may fear that a future election or a revolution will establish a government that will confiscate their property. They will then be motivated to exploit the resource too quickly, on the grounds that certain revenue now is more valuable than uncertain revenue in the future. The current rate of extraction will tend to increase until the expected rate of price rise exceeds the interest rate by a sufficient margin to compensate for the risks of future confiscation of supplies left in the ground.

Unequal Market and Social Values. In a competitive world, the market interest rate indicates the

---

[7]This discussion partly anticipates the analysis in Part 6, which investigates market successes and market failures in more general terms.

rate at which it is optimal to discount the future. Society's investments are beneficial if they earn at least the market rate of return; they are not beneficial if they earn less (because the resources could be used in other ways to produce more value to consumers). In certain circumstances, however, the government may have reasons to adopt a different rate of discount. It is then said that the *social rate of discount*—the discount rate that is appropriate to the society as a whole—differs from the private rate, as indicated by the market rate of interest. In such circumstances, there is reason for the government to intervene to alter the rate at which the private firms would exploit the resource.

Critics are often ready to assume that profit-hungry producers will despoil most exhaustible resources by using them up too quickly. They argue for government intervention to conserve the resource by slowing its rate of extraction. Yet unless the social rate of discount is below the private rate, there is no clear social gain in investing by holding resources in the ground where they will yield only, say, a 2 percent return when perhaps 5 percent can be gained on other investments.

Because governments must worry about their short-term popularity and their chances of reelection, there is no presumption that government intervention will slow the rate of extraction even if the social discount rate exceeds the private rate. Instead, governments might extract resources faster than market forces alone would.

ACTUAL PRICE MOVEMENTS

Many nonrenewable resources do not seem to have the steadily rising prices predicted by Hotelling's Rule. The price of oil, having been raised artificially by the OPEC cartel in the 1970s, returned in the late 1980s to an inflation-adjusted level that was not far from where it was in 1970. Indeed, it has since been held somewhat above that price only insofar as the producing countries have succeeded in intermittently enforcing some output restrictions. The price of coal has not soared; nor has the price of iron ore. In many cases, the reason lies in the discovery of new supplies, which have prevented the total known stocks of many resources from being depleted. In the case of petroleum, for example, the ratio of known reserves to one year's consumption is no lower now than it was two or even four decades ago. Furthermore, most industry experts believe that

large quantities of undiscovered oil exist under both the land and the sea.

In other cases, the invention of new substitute products has reduced the demand for some of these resources and has thus prevented prices from rising as quickly as they otherwise would have. For example, plastics have replaced metals in many uses, and fiber optics have replaced copper wire in many types of message transmission.

In yet other cases, the reason is to be found in government pricing policy. An important example of this type is the use of nonrenewable water for irrigation in much of the United States. Though vast underground reserves of water lie in aquifers beneath many areas of the United States, they are being used up at a rate that will exhaust them in a matter of decades. The water is often supplied by government water authorities at a price that covers only a small part of total cost and that does not rise steadily to reflect the dwindling stocks. Current U.S. water policy will have strong effects on Canada, which controls a large *renewable* supply of fresh water from rivers and lakes.

Such a constant-price policy for *any* nonrenewable resource creates three characteristic problems. First, the resource will be exhausted much faster than if the price were to rise over time. With a given demand, a constant price will lead to a constant rate of extraction to meet the quantity demanded at that price until the resource is completely exhausted. Second, since the price is not allowed to rise, no signals go out to induce conservation, innovation, and exploration. Third, when the supply of the resource is finally exhausted, the adjustment will have to come all at once. If the price had risen steadily each year under free-market conditions, adjustment would have taken place little by little each year. The controlled price, however, gives no signal of the ever-diminishing stock of the resource until all at once the supplies run out. The required adjustment will then be much more painful than it would have been if it had been spread over time in response to steadily rising prices.

When governments intervene to keep the price of a nonrenewable resource below its free-market value, the current users of the resource are essentially obtaining a subsidy from future users, who, if the policy continues, will have to make many adjustments abruptly while paying much higher prices for the resource.

SUMMARY

A. CAPITAL AND THE INTEREST RATE

- Because capital goods are durable, it is necessary to distinguish between the stock of capital goods and the flow of services provided by them and thus between their purchase price and their rental price. The rental price is the amount that is paid to obtain the flow of services that a capital good provides for a given period. The purchase price is the amount that is paid to acquire ownership of the capital.

- The linkage between the rental price and the purchase price relies on the ability to assign a present value to future returns. The present value of a future payment will be lower when the payment is more distant and the interest rate is higher.

- An individual firm will invest in capital goods as long as the present value of the stream of future net returns that is provided by another unit of capital exceeds its purchase price. For a single firm and for the economy as a whole, the profit-maximizing size of the capital stock varies negatively with the rate of interest.

- Whereas individual firms take the market interest rate as given, the interest rate is determined in equilibrium for the economy as a whole. Long-run increases in the aggregate capital stock, holding technology constant, lead to reductions in the equilibrium interest rate. Changes in technology which increase the marginal product of capital lead to increases in the equilibrium interest rate.

B. NONRENEWABLE RESOURCES

- The socially optimal rate of extraction for a nonrenewable resource occurs when its price rises at a rate equal to the rate of interest. This is Hotelling's Rule. This rate of price increase is also the rate that will be established by profit-maximizing firms in a competitive industry.

- Resources for which the demand is highly elastic will have a high rate of extraction in the near future and a fairly rapid falloff over time. Resources for which the demand is highly inelastic will have a lower rate of extraction in the near future and a smaller falloff over time.

- Rising prices act as a conservation device by rationing consumption over time according to people's preferences. As prices rise, conservation, discovery of new sources of supply, and innovation to reduce demand are all encouraged.

- The price system can fail to produce optimal results if (a) people lack the necessary knowledge, (b) property rights are inadequate to protect supplies left for future use by their owners, or (c) the social rate of discount differs significantly from the market rate.

- Controlling the price of an exhaustible resource at a constant level speeds up the rate of extraction and removes the price incentives to react to its growing scarcity.

KEY CONCEPTS

Rental price and purchase price
of capital
Present value

Marginal efficiency of capital
The interest rate and the capital stock
The equilibrium interest rate

Hotelling's Rule
The role of rising prices of exhaustible
resources

DISCUSSION QUESTIONS

1. Suppose you are offered, free of charge, one from each of the following pairs of assets. What considerations would determine your choice?

   a. A perpetuity that pays $20,000 per year forever or an annuity that pays $100,000 per year for five years

   b. An oil-drilling company that earned $100,000 after corporate taxes last year or Canadian government bonds that paid $100,000 in interest last year

   c. A 1 percent share in a new company that has invested $10 million in a new cosmetic that is thought to appeal to middle-income women or a $100,000 bond that has been issued by the same company

2. How would you go about evaluating the present value of each of the following?

   a. The existing reserves of a relatively small oil company
   b. The total world reserves of an exhaustible natural resource with a known completely fixed supply
   c. A long-term bond, issued by a very unstable third-world government, that promises to pay the bearer $1,000 per year forever
   d. A lottery ticket that your neighbour bought for $10, which was one of 1 million tickets sold for a drawing to be held in one year's time that will pay $2 million to the single winner

3. Can you think of any resources that are renewable if they are exploited at one rate and nonrenewable if they are exploited at other, higher rates?

4. Some Canadians opposed the 1989 Free Trade Agreement (FTA) between Canada and the United States because they wished to prohibit the export of Canadian oil and natural gas to the U.S. and instead to save it for use by future generations of Canadians. What would have been the economic gains and losses resulting from following the courses of action advocated by these people?

5. Outline some of the main events that would follow if no further significant discoveries of oil were ever made after 1997.

6. Your parents argue that it makes more sense for you to take taxis and, on occasion, to rent a car while you are at school because you will be spending most of your time in the library and your need for a car should be minimal. Make an argument based on the rental price of transportation (not on the other advantages of having the car) that it may be cheaper for you to buy a car for use while you are at school.

7. It is possible to rent a movie such as *Casablanca* for 24 hours for $3. Alternatively, you can buy the tape for about $20. How many times would you need to plan on viewing the movie to justify purchasing it? How would the interest rate and interval between viewings affect your calculations? How would the transactions costs of going to the video rental store affect your calculations?

8. There are many examples of resources that are technically renewable—such as the stock of old-growth forests—but may not be replenished within your lifetime if the current stock is depleted. Explain how you would expect the market to price such resources.

9. Species that are on the verge of extinction—beluga whales, African elephants, mountain gorillas, and the California condor—might be classified as nonrenewable resources; once they disappear, there will be no regeneration. Does the market create appropriate incentives to ensure that extinction will not occur?

10. Why would Americans be interested in gaining control over Canadian water supplies in the future? Why would the Canadian government have resisted granting such control in the text of the Canada-U.S. Free Trade Agreement?

PART SIX

GOVERNMENT POLICY IN THE MARKET ECONOMY

When is there a role for government to intervene in the market economy? Is government action necessary to reduce sulphur dioxide emissions, or can the market economy handle that problem itself? Why doesn't the private sector provide things like national defense? Why do some people believe that government actions to improve equity in the economy almost surely reduce efficiency? Is government action needed to ensure that workers have safe workplaces, or will firms find it in their own interests to have safe working conditions? How does the Canadian government raise the money it needs to finance its expenditures, and on what does the Canadian government spend? What is the financial relationship between the federal government and the various provincial governments, and how has this relationship affected the design and operation of Canada's social programs? These are the sort of questions you will be able to answer after reading the next three chapters.

Chapter 18 examines the case for free markets. You will see the reasons why economists often argue in favour of free markets and against government intervention. You will then explore the case for government intervention which is based on the concept of a *market failure*—a situation in which the free market fails to produce the socially desirable outcome. It is here that you will see that the free market typically cannot be relied upon to solve the problem of pollution; you will also learn why the private sector does not provide national defense. You will then learn about the process of government intervention, and about the reasons why there are *government failures*.

In Chapter 19 you are introduced to the economics of pollution. You will learn about the *rationale for regulating pollution* and about the various methods of pollution control that have been tried. You will learn about *tradable pollution permits*—the most recent (and most controversial) method for dealing with pollution. The chapter then examines government regulation for health and safety. One of the key points made in this chapter is that firms often can be counted on to provide adequate safety for their workers; one exception, however, is when there is *imperfect information* about the dangers in the workplace.

Chapter 20 then examines the taxation and expenditure patterns of Canadian governments. You will learn about the Canadian tax system, and about how to evaluate a tax system from the standpoints of both efficiency and equity. You will learn about the concept of *fiscal federalism*, upon which many Canadian programs are based. You will then examine the programs which make up Canadian social policy, and you will learn about the continuing pressures to reform these programs.

CHAPTER 18

BENEFITS AND COSTS OF GOVERNMENT INTERVENTION

There are two extreme views of the Canadian economy. In one, Canada is a stronghold of free enterprise, with millions of people in a mad and brutal race for the almighty dollar. In the other, Canadian business people, workers, and consumers are seen as strangling slowly in a web of red tape spun by the spider of government regulation. Neither of these extreme views is accurate.

Many aspects of economic life in Canada are determined by the free-market system. Private preferences, expressed through private markets and influencing private profit-seeking enterprises, determine much of what is produced, how it is produced, and the incomes of productive factors. But even casual observation makes it clear that public policies and public decisions also play a large role in the economic life of the Canadian populace. Laws restrict what people and firms may do, and taxes and subsidies influence their choices. Much public expenditure is not market determined, and this influences the distribution of the national product. Canada's economy, like all others, is a mixed economy.

The general case for some reliance on free markets is that allowing decentralized decision making is more desirable than having all economic decisions made by a centralized planning body. Indeed, much of the political upheaval in Eastern Europe in the past decade arose from the weak performance of planned economies. (Recall Application 1-2 in Chapter 1.)

The general case for some public intervention is that almost no one wants to let markets decide everything about our economic affairs. Most people's moral and practical sense argues for some state intervention to mitigate the disastrous results that the market deals out to some. Most people believe that there are areas in which markets do not function well and in which state intervention can improve the general social good. Indeed, even when there is maximum reliance on the market economy, government is needed to enforce contracts and prevent theft. For such reasons, there is no known economy in which the people have opted for complete free-market determination of all economic matters and against any kind of government intervention.

The operative choice today is not between an unhampered free-market economy and a fully centralized command economy. It is rather the choice of *which mix* of markets and government intervention best suits people's hopes and needs. Although all economies are mixed, the mixture varies greatly among them and over time. Whether the existing mixture could be improved—and, if so, how—is debated continually and is a major political issue. But even the most passionate advocates of free markets agree that government must provide for enforcement of the rules under which private firms and persons make contracts. Without well-defined property rights, the enforcement of contracts, and a reasonable assurance that goods and services will not be stolen, market economies cannot function. In the modern mixed economy, however, government does a great deal more than act as a "traffic cop" for the private sector.

In this chapter, we discuss the role of the government in market-based economies, making the case both for and against government intervention. In the following two chapters, we look at the principal types of intervention in more detail. Before turning to the cases for and against government intervention in market economies, it is useful to briefly review the fundamental function of markets—coordinating the decisions of large numbers of decentralized private decision makers.

How markets coordinate

Any economy consists of thousands upon thousands of individual markets. There are markets for agricultural goods, for manufactured goods, and for consumers' services; there are markets for intermediate goods such as steel and lumber, which are outputs of some industries and inputs of others; there are markets for raw materials such as iron ore, trees, bauxite, and copper; there are markets for land and for thousands of different types of labour; there are markets in which money is borrowed and in which securities are sold.

COORDINATION: SIGNALS AND RESPONSES

An economy is not, however, a series of markets functioning in isolation—it is an interlocking system in which events in one market affect tens of thousands of others. Any change, such as an increase in demand for a particular product, requires many further changes and adjustments. Should the quantity produced change? If it should, by how much and by what means? Any change in the output of one product will generally require changes in other markets. Someone or something must decide what is to be produced, how, and by whom, and what is to be consumed and by whom.

The essential characteristic of the market system is that its coordination occurs in an unplanned and decentralized way. Millions of people make millions of independent decisions concerning production and consumption every day. Most of these decisions are not motivated by a desire to contribute to the social good or to make the whole economy work well; instead, these decisions are motivated by the fairly immediate considerations of self-interest. The price system coordinates these decentralized decisions, making the whole system fit together and respond to the wishes of individual consumers and producers.

The basic insight into how a market system works is that decentralized decision makers, acting in their own interests, respond to such *signals* as the prices of what they buy and sell. Economists have long emphasized the signaling feature of free-market prices. When a commodity becomes scarce, its free-market price rises. Firms and households that use the commodity are led to economize on it and to look for alternatives. Firms that produce it are led to produce more of it. How the price system informs these decisions has been examined at many places in this book.

THE ROLE OF PROFITS AND LOSSES

If prices are the signals to which firms and consumers respond, economic profits may be thought of as the engine that drives the economy. Except when there is monopoly or oligopoly (in which cases entry barriers might allow profits to exist in the long run) economic profits and losses are symptoms that a market is not in long-run equilibrium. Economic profits or losses represent the underlying motivation behind the economy's response to change.

A rise in demand for a commodity or a fall in production costs creates profits for that commodity's producers. Profits make an industry attractive to new investment. They signal that there are too few resources allocated to that industry. In search of these profits, more resources enter the industry, increasing output and driving down price until profits

are driven to zero. A fall in demand or a rise in production costs creates losses. Losses reveal that too many resources are allocated to the industry. Resources will leave the industry until those left behind are no longer suffering losses.

The importance of profits and losses is that they set in motion forces that tend to move the economy toward a new equilibrium.

Individual households and firms respond to common signals according to their own best interests. Yet these individuals and firms are decentralized—there is nothing intentionally coordinated about their actions. However, when a shortage of some product causes its price to rise, individual buyers begin to reduce the quantities that they demand and individual firms begin to increase the quantities that they supply. As a result, the shortage begins to lessen. As it does, price begins to come back down, and profits are reduced. These signals in turn are seen and responded to by firms and households. Eventually, when the shortage has been eliminated, there are no profits to attract further increases in supply. The chain of adjustments to the original shortage is completed.

Notice that in the sequence of signal-response-signal-response, no single individual has to foresee at the outset the final price and quantity, nor does any government agency have to specify who will increase production and who will decrease consumption. Some firms respond to the signals for more output by increasing production, and they keep on increasing production until it is no longer profitable to do so. Some buyers withdraw from the market when they think that prices are too high, perhaps to return when (in their view) prices become more reasonable. Households and firms, responding to market signals, not to the orders of government bureaucrats, determine who will increase production and who will limit consumption. No one is forced to do something against his or her best judgment. Voluntary responses collectively produce the end result.

Because the economy is adjusting to shocks continuously, a snapshot of the economy at any given moment reveals substantial positive profits in some industries and substantial losses in others. A snapshot at any other moment will also reveal profits and losses, but their locations will be different.

The price system, like an "invisible hand" (Adam Smith's famous phrase), coordinates the responses of

individual decision makers who seek only their own self-interests. Because they respond to signals that reflect market conditions, their responses are coordinated without any conscious planning.

Notice that the price system coordinates responses even to prices that are set by monopolistic producers or pegged by government controls. The process of signal-response-signal-response occurs in a price system even when the prices have not been determined in freely competitive markets. The details of the outcomes will be somewhat different under monopoly and oligopoly than with competition, but when market signals change, the responses will usually be in the same direction. Although monopoly and government controls usually lead to allocative inefficiency (recall our discussion in Chapter 13), they do not prevent the tendency of prices to rise when things are scarce, nor do they stop the tendency for producers to minimize costs. It is these reactions that are at the heart of a price system's ability to coordinate economic behaviour.

THE CASE FOR FREE MARKETS

In presenting the case for free-market economies, economists have used two quite different approaches. The first of these may be characterized as the "formal defense," and is based on the concept of allocative efficiency, introduced in Chapter 13. The essence of the formal defense of free-market economies is that if all markets are perfectly competitive, and if governments allow all prices to be determined by demand and supply, then resources will be allocated in the *optimal* manner. That is, prices will equal marginal cost for all products and thus the economy will be allocatively efficient—it would be impossible to make any individual better off without at the same time making somebody else worse off.

The other defense of free markets—what might be called the "informal defense"—is at least as old as Adam Smith and is meant to apply to market economies whether or not they are perfectly competitive. It is based on the theme that markets are a very effective mechanism for coordinating the decisions of decentralized decision makers. The informal defense is intuitive in that it is not laid out in equations representing a formal model of an economy, but it does

follow from some hard reasoning, and it has been subjected to much intellectual probing.

This informal defense of free markets is based on four central arguments, which we examine in turn.

1. Free markets are flexible and provide automatic coordination of the actions of decentralized decision makers.

2. The pursuit of profits which is central to free markets provides a stimulus to innovation and economic growth.

3. Free markets are self-correcting so that situations of disequilibrium are only temporary.

4. Free markets permit a decentralization of economic power.

FLEXIBLE AND AUTOMATIC COORDINATION

Defenders of the market economy argue that, compared with the alternatives, the decentralized market system is more flexible and leaves more scope for adaptation to change at any moment in time and for quicker adjustment over time.

Suppose, for example, that the price of oil rises. One household might prefer to respond by maintaining a high temperature in its house and economizing on its driving; another household might do the reverse. A third household might give up air-conditioning instead. This flexibility can be contrasted with centralized control, which would force the same pattern on everyone, say, by fixing the price, by rationing heating oil and gasoline, by regulating permitted temperatures, and by limiting air-conditioning to days when the temperature exceeded 27°C.

Furthermore, as conditions continue to change, prices in a market economy will continue to change, and decentralized decision makers can react continually. In contrast, government quotas, allocations, and rationing schemes are much more difficult to adjust. As a result, there are likely to be shortages and surpluses before adjustments are made. One great value of the market is that it provides automatic signals *as a situation develops* so that not all of the consequences of an economic change have to be anticipated and allowed for by a body of central planners. Millions of adaptations to millions of changes in tens of thousands of markets are required every year, and it would be a herculean task to anticipate and plan for them all.

A market system allows for coordination *without anyone needing to understand how the whole system works*. As Professor Thomas Schelling put it:

> The dairy farmer doesn't need to know how many people eat butter and how far away they are, how many other people raise cows, how many babies drink milk, or whether more money is spent on beer or milk. What he needs to know is the prices of different feeds, the characteristics of different cows, the different prices . . . for milk . . . , the relative cost of hired labor and electrical machinery, and what his net earnings might be if he sold his cows and raised pigs instead.[1]

It is, of course, an enormous advantage that all the producers and consumers of a country collectively can make the system operate without any one of them, much less all of them, having to understand how it works. (Such a lack of knowledge becomes a disadvantage, however, when people have to vote on schemes for interfering with market allocation.)

STIMULUS TO INNOVATION AND GROWTH

Technology, tastes, and resource availability are changing all the time, in all economies. Thirty years ago, there was no such thing as a personal computer or a digital watch. Front-wheel drive was a curiosity in North America. Students carried their books in briefcases or in canvas bags that were anything but waterproof. Manuscripts only existed as hard copy, not as electronic files in a computer. To change one word in a manuscript, one usually had to retype an entire page. Videocassettes did not exist, nor did compact discs.

Digital watches, personal computers, front-wheel drive cars and compact discs are all products that were invented or developed by individuals or firms in pursuit of profits. An entrepreneur who correctly "reads" the market and perceives that there may be a demand for some product will be inclined to develop it.

The next 20 years will also surely see changes great and small. Changes in technology may make an

idea that is not practical today practical five years from now. New products and techniques will be devised to adapt to shortages, gluts, and changes in consumer demands and to exploit new opportunities made available by new technologies. Fibre optics, for example, is likely to change radically the nature of communication, permitting widespread availability of inexpensive, two-way video transmission.

In a market economy, individuals risk their time and money in the hope of earning profits. While many fail, some succeed. New products and processes appear and disappear. Some are fads or have little impact; others become items of major significance. The market system works by trial and error to sort them out and allocates resources to what prove to be successful innovations.

In contrast, planners in more centralized systems have to guess which innovations will be productive and which goods will be strongly demanded. Centrally planned effort may achieve wonders by permitting a massive effort in a chosen direction, but central planners also may guess incorrectly about the direction and put too many eggs in the wrong basket or reject as unpromising something that will turn out to be vital. Perhaps the biggest failure of centrally planned economies was their inability to encourage the experimentation and innovation that has proved to be the driving force behind long-run growth in advanced market economies. It is striking that the last decade has seen most centrally planned economies abandon their system in favour of a price system in one fell swoop while the only remaining large planned economy, China, is increasing the role of markets in most aspects of its economy.

SELF-CORRECTION OF DISEQUILIBRIUM

Equilibrium of the economic system is continually disrupted by change. If the economy did not "pursue" equilibrium, its behaviour in equilibrium would be of little interest. An important characteristic of the price system is its ability to set in motion forces that tend to correct disequilibrium.

To review the advantages of the price system in this respect, imagine operating without a market mechanism. Suppose that planning boards make all market decisions. The Planning Board for Men's Clothing somehow learns that pleated shirts are all the rage in neighbouring countries. It orders a certain

---

[1]Schelling, T.C. *Micro Motives and Macro Behavior* (New York: Norton, 1978).

proportion of clothing factories to make pleated shirts instead of the traditional men's dress shirt. Conceivably, the quantities of pleated shirts and traditional shirts produced could be just right, given shoppers' preferences. But what if the Board guesses wrong and orders the production of too many traditional shirts and not enough pleated shirts? Long lines would appear at pleated-shirt counters, while mountains of traditional shirts would pile up. Once the Board sees the lines for pleated shirts, it could order a change in quantities produced. Meanwhile, it could store the extra traditional shirts for another season or ship them to a country with different tastes.

Such a system can correct an initial mistake, but it may prove inefficient in doing so. It may use a lot of resources in planning and administration that could instead be used to produce commodities. Further, many consumers may be greatly inconvenienced if the Board is slow to correct its error. In such a system, the members of the Board may have no incentive to admit and correct a mistake quickly. Indeed, if the authorities do not like pleated shirts, the Board may get credit for having stopped the craze before it went too far!

In contrast, suppose that in a market system, a similar misestimation of the demand for pleated shirts and traditional shirts is made by firms in the men's clothing industry. Lines develop at pleated-shirt counters, and inventories of traditional shirts accumulate. Stores raise the prices of pleated shirts and at the same time lower them for traditional shirts. Consumers could then get bargains by buying traditional shirts. Pleated-shirt manufacturers could earn profits by raising prices and running extra shifts to increase production. Some traditional-shirt producers would be motivated to shift production quickly to pleated shirts and to make traditional shirts more attractive to buyers by cutting prices. Unlike the planning board, the producers in a market system would be motivated to correct their initial mistakes as quickly as possible. Those who were slowest to adjust would lose the most money and might even be forced out of business.

DECENTRALIZATION OF POWER

Another important part of the case for a market economy is that it tends to decentralize power and thus requires less coercion of individuals than any other type of economy. Of course, even though markets tend to diffuse power, they do not do so completely; large firms and large unions clearly have and exercise substantial economic power.

Though the market power of large corporations and unions is not negligible, it tends to be constrained both by the competition of other large entities and by the emergence of new products and firms. This is the process of creative destruction that was described by Joseph Schumpeter (see Application 11-1 in Chapter 11). In any case, say defenders of the free market, even such aggregations of private power are far less substantial than government power.

Governments must coerce if markets are not allowed to allocate people to jobs and commodities to consumers. Not only will such coercion be regarded as arbitrary (especially by those who do not like the results), but the power creates major opportunities for bribery, corruption, and allocation according to the tastes of the central administrators. If, at the going prices and wages, there are not enough apartments or coveted jobs to go around, the bureaucrats can allocate some to those who pay the largest bribe, some to those with religious beliefs, hairstyles, or political views that they like, and only the rest to those whose names come up on the waiting list.

This line of reasoning has been articulated forcefully by the Nobel laureate and conservative economist Milton Friedman, who was for many years a professor of economics at the University of Chicago. Friedman argues that economic freedom—the ability to allocate resources through private markets—is essential to the maintenance of political freedom.[2] Many other economists and social theorists have challenged this proposition.

THE CASE FOR GOVERNMENT INTERVENTION

Free markets do all of the good things that we have just discussed; yet there are many circumstances in which the free market does not produce the most desirable outcomes. When this happens, economists say that markets have *failed*. The case for intervening

[2]Milton Friedman, *Capitalism and Freedom* (Chicago: The University of Chicago Press: 1982).

in free markets turns in large part on identifying the conditions that lead to **market failure.** Much of the following discussion is devoted to this task.

Care must be taken when using the expression *market failure* because the word *failure* may convey the wrong impression. Market failure does not mean that nothing good has happened—but rather that the *best attainable outcome* has not been achieved.

The concept of a market failure is used to apply to two quite different sets of circumstances. One is the failure of the market system to achieve efficiency in the allocation of society's resources. The other is the failure of the market system to serve social goals other than allocative efficiency, such as a desirable distribution of income or the preservation of value systems. We treat each in turn.

Four broad types of phenomena lead to a failure of allocative efficiency: *monopoly power, externalities, public goods,* and *information asymmetries.* Recall that allocative efficiency requires that the marginal cost for society of producing each good equals the marginal benefit to society of that good. In each of these four cases, the free market does not generate an allocatively efficient outcome because the marginal benefit to society does not equal the marginal cost to society.

MONOPOLY POWER

As we discussed in Chapter 11, firms that face downward-sloping demand curves will maximize profits at an output where price exceeds marginal cost, leading to allocative inefficiency. Although some market power is maintained through artificial barriers to entry, such power can also arise naturally because in some industries the least costly way to produce a good or a service is to have few producers relative to the size of the market. The standard government remedies are competition policy and regulation, which, as discussed in Chapter 13, present problems of their own.

EXTERNALITIES

Recall that in order for the economy to be allocatively efficient, price must equal marginal cost for all products. But whose costs are relevant here? Firms that are maximizing their *own* profits are interested only in their own costs of production—they are not interested in any costs that their actions might impose on others. An **externality** occurs whenever actions taken by firms

or consumers impose costs or confer benefits on *others that are not involved in the transaction.* When you smoke a cigarette in a restaurant, you might impose costs on others present; when you cut your lawn early on a weekend morning you might impose costs on sleeping neighbours. Externalities are also called *third-party effects* because parties other than the two primary participants in the transaction (the buyer and the seller) are affected.

Private and Social Costs

The foregoing discussion suggests the importance of the distinction between *private cost* and *social cost.* **Private cost** measures the best alternative use of the resource available to the private decision maker. **Social cost** includes the private cost (since the decision maker is a member of society) but also includes the best use of all resources available to society.

In general, discrepancies between private cost and social cost occur when there are externalities. The presence of externalities, even when all markets are perfectly competitive, leads to allocatively inefficient outcomes.

Private producers and consumers make their decisions about production and consumption based on private marginal cost and market price. When they neglect to take into account the social costs involved in the transaction, they arrive at an outcome where the market price does not reflect *social cost,* and thus allocative efficiency is not achieved. This is shown in Figure 18-1.

Externalities arise in many different ways, and they may be harmful or beneficial to the third parties. When they are harmful they are called *negative externalities;* when they are beneficial, they are called *positive externalities.* Here are two examples.

Consider the case of a firm whose production process for steel generates harmful smoke as a byproduct. Individuals who live and work near the firm bear real costs due to the firm's production. In addition to the disutility of enduring the smoke and of any adverse health effects, they may be forced to invest in air conditioners so that they can keep the noxious fumes out of their homes. When the firm makes its decision concerning how much steel to produce, it ignores these costs that it imposes on other people. This is a negative externality. In this case, because the firm ignores those parts of social cost that are not its own private cost, the firm will produce too much steel relative to what is allocatively efficient.

FIGURE 18-1
Private and Social Cost

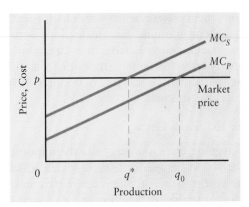

A competitive firm will produce output to the point where its private marginal cost equals the market price. In this case, every unit of output produced imposes *external costs*, equal to the distance between MC_P (private marginal cost) and MC_S (social marginal cost).

The profit-maximizing competitive firm chooses to produce q_0, the output where price equals private marginal cost. If the full social cost of production were taken into account, only q^* would be produced. Notice that for each unit of output between q^* and q_0, the cost incurred by society exceeds the value to consumers, which is given by the market price. Thus in this example, the profit-maximizing firms end up producing *too much* of the good compared to what is allocatively efficient (q^*).

Now consider what happens when an individual renovates her home and thus improves its external appearance. Such improvements enhance the neighbours' view and the value of their property. Yet the individual renovator ignores the benefits that her actions have on the neighbours. This is a positive externality. In this case, because the renovator ignores those parts of **social benefits** that are not her own private benefits, there will be too little home renovation done relative to what is allocatively efficient.

Externalities, whether adverse or beneficial to the third parties, cause market outcomes to be inefficient because they cause marginal social benefit to differ from marginal social cost.

In those cases where the production of a good generates *negative* externalities, private producers will produce too much of the good relative to what is allocatively efficient. This is because the private producer ignores the costs imposed on the rest of society. In those cases where the production of a good gener-

ates *positive* externalities, private producers will produce too little of the good relative to what is allocatively efficient. This is because the private producer ignores the benefits conferred on the rest of society.

The Importance of Property Rights

Economist and Nobel laureate Ronald Coase has argued that when property rights are well defined (e.g., the law is clear on whether a polluter has rights to determine the emissions from a smokestack), third parties will be able to negotiate with the producers of externalities in order to ensure that the producers take all relevant valuations of their behaviour into account. In such cases, externalities would not be a source of market failure because social marginal cost and social marginal benefit would be included in the supply and demand curves of the parties engaged in the externality-producing activity. Since social marginal cost and social marginal benefit would then be equalized, the free market would generate the allocatively efficient outcome.

An example will help to clarify this important idea—known as the **Coase Theorem.** Suppose there is a paper mill that dumps toxic waste in a nearby river and there is a privately owned beach resort on the shore of the river downstream from the paper mill. Suppose further that for every ton of paper produced there is an accompanying barrel of toxic waste dumped in the river, and this imposes a $100 cost on the downstream resort owner. The social marginal cost of paper production is thus $100 more than the private marginal cost of paper production.

Coase's insight is that *as long as property rights are well defined*, this situation need not result in allocative inefficiency. For example, if the owners of the paper mill also owned the river, then they would clearly have the "right" to dump their toxic waste there. However, the downstream resort owner would be prepared to pay $100 for every ton of paper that the paper mill *did not produce*. The paper mill would therefore face an incentive to reduce the output of paper. Indeed, since the paper mill would gain $100 for each ton *not produced*, the paper mill's private marginal cost of production would equal the social marginal cost of production. The market outcome would therefore be allocatively efficient.

Note, however, that the efficient result does not depend on ownership over the river being given to the paper mill. Perhaps the most striking part of the Coase Theorem is that the allocatively efficient outcome is also achieved if the resort owner were awarded ownership over the river. To see this, note that if the resort owner owned the river, then he could force the paper mill to pay for the right to dump toxic waste in the river. If the resort owner charged the paper mill $100 per barrel of waste dumped in the river, then the paper mill would be forced to recognize the costs that its activities incur on the rest of society. That is, the paper mill's private marginal cost would now equal the social marginal cost, and hence the market outcome would be allocatively efficient.

The practical application of the Coase Theorem depends in large part on the *number* of third parties affected. In cases where there is only one (or a few), as in the example above, it is quite plausible that careful definition of property rights would be sufficient to permit private markets to deal efficiently with the externality. Where there are millions of third parties affected, however, as often is the case with air pollution in urban areas, it is hard to see how the negotiations could proceed except with government acting on behalf of the third parties. Another example is where the externalities cross international boundaries. The smokestack industries of the U.S. industrial midwest are commonly thought to be responsible for the problems of acid rain in Canada and New England. It is difficult to believe that any practical definition of property rights could eliminate the effects of these externalities.

Thus since many externalities in real-world economies will have large numbers of third parties involved, it seems reasonable to conclude that many externalities will indeed lead to allocative inefficiency and thus provide a motivation for government intervention.

PUBLIC GOODS

Public goods are sometimes called *collective consumption goods* because many people can consume them simultaneously. The total cost of providing public goods therefore does not necessarily increase as the number of consumers increases. Public goods also have a property that makes it difficult to exclude somebody from using them. The classic case of a public good is national defense. Adding to the population of Canada does not diminish the extent to which each Canadian citizen is defended by a given size and quality of armed forces. Nor would it be possible to exclude any one individual from consuming the benefits of national defense.

Information is also a public good. Suppose a certain food additive causes cancer. The cost of discover-

ing this needs to be borne only once. The information is then of value to everyone who might have used the additive, and the cost of making the information available to one more consumer is essentially zero. Furthermore, once the information of the newly discovered carcinogen is available, it is impossible to prevent people from using that information. Other public goods include lighthouses, weather forecasts (a type of information), the provision of clean air, streetlighting, public parks, and outdoor band concerts.

All of these examples raise what is called the *free-rider problem*, which follows from the fact that it is difficult to prevent people from using public goods once they are produced. The private market will generally not produce efficient amounts of the public good because once the good is produced, it is impractical (or impossible) to make people pay for its use. Indeed, free markets may fail to produce public goods at all. The obvious remedy in these cases is for the government to provide the good, financed from its tax revenues.

How much of a public good should the government provide? It should provide up to the point where the *sum of everyone's individual valuations* of the good is just equal to the marginal cost of providing the good. To see why we must add up everyone's marginal valuation, consider a simple example. Suppose that Andy, Bibbi, Carol, and Dick are all thinking of renting a video. Watching the video will be a collective consumption good for the four of them because the cost will be the same no matter how many of them decide to watch. Suppose that each honestly expresses his or her value of watching the tape. Say it is worth $1.00 to Andy, $2.00 each to Bibbi and Carol, and 50 cents to Dick. If the rental charge for the tape is $5.50 or less, it is worth renting because the total value to all four consumers will be at least equal to the cost.

This example also illustrates the free-rider problem. If the cost of renting the tape is only $3.00, everyone will have an incentive to understate the value that they place on watching the tape, hoping to get the others to pay for their "free ride."

Sometimes it is possible to eliminate the free-rider problem by charging a fee for using a public good. In our example, the videotape rental would have been covered if the group decided to charge each member of the group $1.00 to watch the video. Doing this, however, would have been inefficient. Dick, who would be willing to pay 50 cents to see the video, would be excluded. The marginal benefit from letting Dick see the video is 50 cents, and the marginal cost is zero. It is plainly inefficient to exclude him because 50 cents worth of value is forgone, at no cost, when he is excluded.

Parks, roads, and bridges often are financed through fees or tolls that lead to *inefficient exclusion*. Exclusion in these cases is inefficient for exactly the same reason that it was inefficient to exclude Dick from watching the video. Efficiency requires that social marginal cost be equal to social marginal benefit. For a road with little or no traffic, the marginal cost of use is very close to zero. Charging a toll that pays for construction of a road excludes users who value its use at more than the marginal cost of their using it but less than the toll.

Even where getting around the free-rider problem is technically possible, doing so is usually inefficient. As in cases in which the private market would not produce a public good at all, the obvious remedy is government provision.

Efficient provision of public goods requires that consumers pay the marginal cost of their consumption—zero. Private markets will never provide goods at a price of zero and thus will always underprovide public goods.

An important example of a problem which is related both to public goods and to externalities—the overfishing of the world's oceans—is discussed in Application 18-1.

ASYMMETRIC INFORMATION

The role of information in the economy has received increasing attention from economists in recent years. Information is, of course, a valuable commodity, and markets for information and expertise are well developed, as every college student is aware. Markets for expertise are conceptually identical to markets for any other valuable service. They can pose special problems, however. One of these we have already discussed: Information is often a public good and thus will tend to be underproduced by a free market because once the information is known to anyone, it is extremely cheap to make it available to others.

Even where information is not a public good, markets for expertise are prone to market failure. The reason for this is that one party to a transaction can often take advantage of special knowledge in ways that change the nature of the transaction itself. The two important sources of market failure that arise when privately held information is bought and sold are *moral hazard* and *adverse selection*.

Moral Hazard

In general, **moral hazard** exists when one party to a transaction has both the *incentive* and the *ability* to shift costs onto the other party. Moral hazard problems often arise from insurance contracts. The classic example is the homeowner who does not bother to shovel snow from his walk because he knows that his insurance will cover the cost if the mail carrier should fall and break a leg. The costs of the homeowner's lax behaviour will be borne largely by others, including the mail carrier and the insurance company. Individuals and firms who are insured against loss will often take less care to prevent that loss than they would in the absence of insurance. They do so because they do not bear all of the marginal cost imposed by the risk, while they do bear all of the marginal cost of taking action to reduce the risk.

As in all of the cases of market failure that we have considered, the failure arises because the marginal private benefit of an action is not equal to the marginal social cost of that action. The existence of insurance markets, which ideally merely spread existing risk, will also increase the total amount of risk present because of moral hazard.

Insurance is not the only context in which moral hazard problems arise. Another example is professional services. Suppose that you ask a dentist whether your teeth are healthy or a lawyer whether you need legal assistance. The dentist and the lawyer both face moral hazard in that they both have a financial interest in giving you answers that will encourage you to buy their services, and it is difficult for you to find out if their advice is good advice. A similar situation occurs when you ask your mechanic what is wrong with your engine. In all of these cases, one party to the transaction has special knowledge that he or she could use to change the nature of the transaction in his or her favour. As long as the auto mechanic is merely selling her expertise in repairing cars, there is no problem, but when she uses her expertise to persuade the consumer to demand more repairs than are warranted, there is a moral hazard problem. Codes of professional ethics and licensing and certification practices, both governmental and private, are reactions to concerns about this kind of moral hazard.

Adverse Selection

Closely related to moral hazard is the problem of **adverse selection**—the tendency of people who are most at risk to buy the most insurance. A person who is

OVERFISHING AND THE TRAGEDY OF THE COMMONS

In March 1995, the Spanish fishing trawler *Estai* was fishing off the coast of Newfoundland just outside of Canada's 200-nautical-mile "economic zone" when a Canadian fisheries-protection vessel fired across its bow and then forced it into harbour in St. John's. The European Union, of which Spain is a member, accused Canada of piracy. Canada in turn accused Spain of overfishing and of depleting the value of Canada's turbot fishery.

This was an unusually dramatic event in the Canadian fishing industry, but it revealed problems and frustrations that have been present for many years. The problem of Canada's fisheries (and other countries' fisheries as well) has two sources. The first relates to the special public-good nature of the fishery; the second relates to technological advance. Each of these has given rise to overfishing by both Canadian and foreign fishing fleets off of Newfoundland (and of almost all other fisheries in the world).

COMMON-PROPERTY RESOURCE

The North Atlantic fishery represents a special kind of public good. Fish are obviously mobile and cannot be confined to international boundaries. Thus even if Canada has a well-defined 200-mile limit, there is nothing preventing the "Canadian fish" from being caught outside of the limit by fishing fleets from other countries. The same problem has also led to disputes in the Pacific salmon fishery when U.S. fishing fleets in U.S. or international waters catch the salmon that are returning to spawn in Canada's rivers. A resource which everyone has access to—like the fish in international waters—is known as a *common-property resource*.

The public-good nature of the fishery illustrates an important example of an externality. The externality is that fishermen catching fish today deplete the stock of fish available both for other fishermen and for future generations. Thus they impose costs on other potential users of the resource. Since their private marginal cost of catching fish is less than the social marginal cost of catching fish, the free market will result in overuse of the fishery—that is, too many fish being caught.

A 1994 article in *The Economist* captured the problem succinctly:

A fisherman who tries to conserve stock by leaving fish in the sea has no reason for thinking

that he will gain by his investment: the fish he has spared, or their offspring, will probably be caught by someone else. On the contrary, if he catches more fish now he will be the richer for it. Although there will be fewer fish next year, the cost will not be borne by him alone, but spread over the entire fleet. Without regulation, in other words, fisherman have an incentive to overfish.*

TECHNOLOGICAL ADVANCE

Technological advance exacerbates the fundamental problem stemming from the public-good nature of the fishery. With technological advancements and the growth of the fishing fleets, fisherman have caught more fish than are naturally replenished, leading to serious declines in the stocks of many species. Many observers argue that the only way to make commercial fishing in the North Atlantic viable in the twenty-first century is to stop fishing entirely until the fish population increases. Indeed, Canada closed the entire Newfoundland cod fishery in 1993 so that cod stocks could replenish themselves. In 1994, the multinational Northwest Atlantic Fisheries Organization set the allowable yearly catch of turbot to only 27,000 tonnes, less than half of the normal catch only a few years earlier. Not surprisingly, shutting down the fishery in this way imposes considerable hardship on those that earn their living either from fishing or processing the fish products.

GENERAL PRINCIPLE

The result of overfishing in the North Atlantic is just one example of what is known as "the tragedy of the commons," which refers to the tragic results from having unregulated access to a common-property resource. Another example is that ranchers who are given unlimited access to public grazing land will overgraze and thus deplete the value of that resource. In both cases, appropriate regulation will lead to a more efficient allocation of resources than would occur in an unregulated free market. Such regulation would require that users of the resource are forced to pay the costs that their actions impose on future users of the resource.

---

*"The Tragedy of the Oceans," *The Economist*, March 19, 1994.

suffering from a heart condition may seek to increase his life insurance coverage by purchasing as much additional coverage as is available without a medical examination. People who buy insurance almost always know more about themselves as individual insurance risks than do their insurance companies. The company can try to limit the variation in risk by requiring physical examinations (for life or health insurance) and by setting up broad categories based on variables, such as age and occupation, over which actuarial risk is known to vary. The rate charged is then different across categories and is based on the average risk in each category, but there will always be much variability of risk *within* any one category.

People who know that they are well above the average risk for their category are offered a bargain and will be led to take out more car, health, life, or fire insurance than they otherwise would. Their insurance premiums will also not cover the full expected cost of the risk that they are insuring against. Once again, their private cost is less than social cost. On the other side, someone who knows that she is at low risk and pays a higher price than the amount warranted by her risk is motivated to take out less insurance than she otherwise would. In this case, her private cost is more than the social cost.

In both cases, resources are allocated inefficiently because the marginal private benefit of the action (taking out insurance) is not equal to the social cost.

More generally, whenever either party to a transaction lacks information that the other party has or is deceived by claims made by the other party, market results will tend to be changed, and such changes may lead to inefficiency. Economically (but not legally), it is but a small step from such unequal knowledge to outright fraud. The arsonist who buys fire insurance before setting a building on fire and the business person with fire insurance who decides that a fire is preferable to bankruptcy are extreme examples of moral hazard.

Asymmetric information is involved in many other situations of market failure. The *principal-agent problem,* which we discussed in Chapter 14, is one example. In its classic form, the firm's managers act as agents for the stockholders, who are the legal principals of the firm. The managers are much better informed than the principals are about what they do and what they can do. Indeed, the managers are hired for their special expertise. Given that it is expensive for the shareholders (principals) to monitor what the managers (agents) do, the managers have latitude to pursue goals other than maximizing the

firm's profits. The private costs and benefits of their actions will thus be different from the social costs and benefits, with the usual consequences for the allocative efficiency of the market system.

A second example of market failure due to asymmetric information is the apparent overdiscounting of the prices of used cars because of the buyer's risk of acquiring a "lemon." See the discussion of this problem in Application 18-2.

FAILURE TO ACHIEVE SOCIAL GOALS

We have examined four general ways in which free markets may fail to produce allocatively efficient outcomes. But suppose that the market *did* generate the allocatively efficient outcome. That is, suppose that all markets were perfectly competitive and that there were no problems of externalities, public goods or asymmetric information. In such an extreme world, does the achievement of allocative efficiency mean that the free-market outcome is desirable? The answer, in general, is no.

It should not be surprising that even when the free-market system generates an allocatively efficient outcome, it may not always achieve broader social goals. Some of these goals (for example, the desire for an "equitable" income distribution) are basically economic. Some, especially notions that people in a given society should have shared values, such as patriotism or a belief in basic human rights, are clearly not economic. In either set of cases, however, markets are not very effective, precisely because the goods in question are not of the kind that can be exchanged in decentralized transactions. (Indeed, if we stretch the definition a bit, these are public goods, and we have seen that markets tend to underproduce such goods.)

Income Distribution

An important characteristic of a market economy is the *distribution of income* that it determines. People whose services are in heavy demand relative to supply, such as good television anchors and outstanding hockey players, earn large incomes, whereas people whose services are not in heavy demand relative to supply, such as doctorates in classics and high-school graduates without work experience, earn much less.

The distribution of income produced by the market can be looked at in the long run or in the short run. In the long run, in an efficiently operating free-market economy, similar efforts of work or invest-

---

APPLICATION 18-2

USED-CAR PRICES: THE "LEMONS" PROBLEM

It is common for people to regard the large loss of value of a new car in the first year of its life as a sign that consumers are overly style-conscious and will always pay a big premium for the latest in anything. Professor George Akerlof of the University of California at Berkeley suggests a different explanation based on the proposition that the flow of services expected from a one-year-old car that is *purchased on the used-car market* will be lower than those expected from an *average* one-year-old car on the road. Consider his theory.

Any particular model year of automobiles will include a certain proportion of "lemons"—cars that have one or more serious defects. Purchasers of new cars of a certain year and model take a chance on their car turning out to be a lemon. Those who are unlucky and get a lemon are more likely to resell their car than those who are lucky and get a quality car. Hence in the used-car market, there will be a disproportionately large number of lemons for sale. (Also, not all cars are driven in the same manner; those that are driven for long dis-

tances or under bad conditions are much more likely to be traded in or sold as used cars than those that are driven on good roads and for moderate distances.)

Thus buyers of used cars are right to be on the lookout for low-quality cars, while salespeople are quick to invent reasons for the high quality of the cars they are selling ("It was owned by a little old lady who drove it only on Sundays"). Because it is difficult to identify a lemon or a badly treated used car before buying it, the purchaser is prepared to buy a used car only at a price that is low enough to offset the increased probability that it is of poor quality.

This is a rational consumer response to uncertainty and may explain why one-year-old cars typically sell for a discount that is much larger than can be explained by the physical depreciation that occurs in one year in the *average* car of that model. The large discount reflects the lower services that the purchaser can expect from a used car because of the higher probability that it will be a lemon.

---

ment by similar people will tend to be similarly rewarded everywhere in the economy. Of course, dissimilar people, or people in dissimilar jobs, will be dissimilarly rewarded. (Recall our discussion of equilibrium factor-price differentials in Chapter 15.)

In the short run, however, similar people making similar efforts may be dissimilarly rewarded. People in declining industries, areas, and occupations suffer the "punishment" of low earnings through no fault of their own. Those in expanding sectors earn the "reward" of high earnings through no extra effort or talent of their own. But these differentials are likely to be temporary, eliminated by the mobility of workers across industries, occupations, or regions.

These rewards and punishments serve the important function in decentralized decision making of motivating people to adapt. The advantage of such a system is that individuals can make their own decisions about how to alter their behaviour when mar-

ket conditions change; the disadvantage is that temporary rewards and punishments are dealt out as a result of changes in market conditions that are beyond the control of the affected individuals.

Moreover, even equilibrium differences in income may seem unfair. A free-market system rewards certain groups and penalizes others. Because the workings of the market may be stern, even cruel, society often chooses to intervene. Should heads of households be forced to bear the full burden of their misfortune if, through no fault of their own, they lose their jobs? Even if they lose their jobs through their own fault, should they and their families have to bear the whole burden, which may include starvation? Should the ill and the aged be thrown on the mercy of their families? What if they have no families? Both private charities and a great many government policies are concerned with modifying the distribution of income that results from such things as where one starts, how able one is, how lucky one is, and how one fares in the labour market.

We might all agree that it is desirable to have a more equal distribution of income than the one generated by the free market. We would probably also agree that the pursuit of allocative efficiency is a good thing. It is important to understand, however, that the goal of a more equitable distribution of income invariably conflicts with the goal of allocative efficiency. To understand why this is so, see Extension 18-1 which discusses Arthur Okun's famous analogy of the "leaky bucket."

Preferences for Public Provision

Police protection and justice could in principle be provided by private-market mechanisms. Security guards, private detectives, and bodyguards all provide police-like protection. Privately hired arbitrators, "hired guns," and vigilantes of the Old West represent private ways of obtaining "justice." Yet the members of society may believe that a public police force is *preferable* to a private one and that public justice is preferable to justice for hire. The question of the boundary between public and private provision of any number of goods and services became an important topic of debate during the 1980s, and the debate shows no sign of waning. In Canada, the United States and Western Europe, the issue is framed as *privatization*. In the formerly Socialist countries of Eastern Europe, the disposition of much of the productive capacity of entire countries is currently under dispute. In all of these cases, part of the debate is about the magnitude of the efficiency gains that could be realized by private organization, and part is about less tangible issues, such as changes in the nature and distribution of goods and services that may take place when production is shifted from one sector to the other.

Protecting Individuals from Others

People can use and even abuse other people for economic gain in ways that the members of society find offensive. Child labour laws and minimum standards of working conditions are responses to such actions. Yet direct abuse is not the only example of this kind of market failure. In an unhindered free market, the adults in a household would usually decide how much education to buy for their children. Selfish parents might buy no education, while egalitarian parents might buy the same education for all of their children, regardless of their abilities. The rest of society may want to interfere in these choices, both to protect the child of the selfish parent and to ensure that some of the scarce educational resources are distributed according to the ability and the willingness to use them rather than according to a family's wealth. All households are forced to provide a minimum of education for their children, and a number of inducements are offered—through public universities, scholarships, and other means—for talented children to consume more education than they or their parents might choose if they had to pay the entire cost themselves.

Paternalism

Members of society, acting through government, often seek to protect adult (and presumably responsible) individuals, not from others, but from themselves. Laws prohibiting the use of addictive drugs and laws prescribing the installation and use of seat belts are intended primarily to protect individuals from their own ignorance or shortsightedness. This kind of interference in the free choices of individuals is called **paternalism.** Whether such actions reflect the wishes of the majority in the society or whether they reflect the actions of overbearing governments, there is no doubt that the market will not provide this kind of protection. Buyers do not buy what they do not want, and sellers have no motive to provide it.

Social Obligations

In a free-market system, if you can pay another person to do things for you, you may do so. If you persuade someone else to clean your house in return for $35, presumably both parties to the transaction are better off (otherwise neither of you would have voluntarily conducted the transaction). Normally, society does not interfere with people's ability to negotiate mutually advantageous contracts.

Most people do not feel this way, however, about activities that are regarded as social obligations. For example, when military service is compulsory, contracts similar to the one between you and a housekeeper could also be negotiated. Some persons faced with the obligation to do military service could no doubt pay enough to persuade others to do their military service for them.[3] By exactly the same argument as we just used, we can presume that both par-

---

[3]During the U.S. Civil War, it was common practice for a man to avoid the draft by hiring a substitute to serve in his place.

ARTHUR OKUN'S "LEAKY BUCKET"

Economists recognize that government actions can affect both the allocation of resources and the distribution of income. Resource allocation is easier to talk about simply because economists have developed precise definitions of *efficient* and *inefficient* allocations. Distribution is more difficult because we cannot talk about *better* or *worse* distributions of income without introducing normative considerations. (Recall the important distinction between *positive* and *normative* statements discussed in Chapter 2.) Partly because of this, much of economics concerns efficiency and neglects the effects on the distribution of income. Many disagreements about economic and social policy can be understood in terms of differences in emphasis on efficiency and distribution. Distribution, of course, is often more important as a political matter because distribution (especially one's own share) is what people care about most, not the overall efficiency with which the economy is operating.

Moreover, to the extent that society chooses to redistribute income, it is generally the case that allocative efficiency will be reduced. Arthur Okun (1928–1980)—a noted economist at Yale University—developed the image of a "leaky bucket" to illustrate this problem. Suppose we have a well-supplied reservoir of water and we wish to get some water to a household that is not able to come to the reservoir. The only vessel available for transporting the water is a leaky bucket; it works, in that water is deliverable to the intended location, but it works at a cost, in that some of the water is lost on the trip. Thus to get a litre of water to its destination, more than a litre of water has to be removed from the reservoir. It may be possible to design better or worse buckets, but all of them will leak somewhat (if only via evaporation of water from the surface).

The analogy to an economy is this: The act of redistribution (carrying the water) reduces the total value of goods and services available to the economy (by the amount of water that leaks on the trip). Getting a dollar to the poor reduces the resources

available to everyone else by more than a dollar. This means that pursuing social goals—like the redistribution of income—conflicts with the goal of allocative efficiency.

Why is the bucket always leaky? Because there is no way to redistribute income without changing the incentives that private households and firms face. Generally, a program that takes from the rich and gives to the poor will reduce the incentives of both the rich and the poor to produce income. A policy of subsidizing goods that are deemed to be important, such as food, shelter, or oil, will cause the market prices of those goods to be lower than marginal costs, implying that resources used to produce those goods could be used to produce goods of higher value elsewhere in the economy. (This is the basic efficiency argument that we first discussed in Chapter 13.)

Measuring the efficiency costs of redistribution is an important area of economic research. Most economists would agree that programs that directly redistribute income are more efficient (per dollar of resources made available to a given income group) than programs that subsidize the prices of specific commodities. One reason for this is that price subsidies apply even when high-income households purchase the commodities in question.

Redistribution virtually always entails some efficiency cost, and price subsidies are generally less efficient than direct income transfers. However, this does *not* imply that such programs should not be undertaken. (That buckets leak surely does not imply that they should not be used to transport water, given that we want to transport water and that the buckets we have are the best available tools.) Whatever the social policy regarding redistribution of income, economics has an important role to play in measuring the efficiency costs and distributional consequences of different programs of redistribution. Put another way, it has useful things to say about the design and deployment of buckets.

ties will be better off if they are allowed to negotiate such a trade. Yet such contracts are usually prohibited by law. They are prohibited because there are values to be considered other than those that can be expressed in a market. In times when it is necessary, military service by all healthy males is usually held to be a duty that is independent of an individual's tastes, wealth, influence, or social position. It is felt that everyone *ought* to do this service, and exchanges between willing traders are prohibited.

Military service is not the only example of a social obligation. Citizens cannot buy their way out of jury duty or legally sell their voting rights to others, even though in many cases they could find willing trading partners.

We have discussed how the free market may fail to achieve social goals that members of society deem to be desirable. This discussion suggests the following general principle:

Even if the price system generated allocatively efficient outcomes, members of a society may not wish to rely solely on the market if they have social goals that they wish to achieve. Furthermore, there is generally a trade off between allocative efficiency and the achievement of these social goals.

GOVERNMENT INTERVENTION

Private collective action can sometimes remedy the failures of private individual action. For example, private charities can help the poor, volunteer fire departments can fight fires, or insurance companies can guard against adverse selection by more careful classification of clients. However, by far the most common remedy for market failure is government intervention.

Since markets sometimes *do* fail, there is a potential scope for governments to intervene in beneficial ways. Whether government intervention is warranted in any particular case depends both on the magnitude of the market failure that the intervention is designed to correct and on the costs of the government action itself.

The benefits of some types of government intervention (e.g., the advantages of having a publicly provided justice system) are both difficult to quantify and potentially very large. Further, government intervention often imposes difficulties of its own. For many types of government activity, however, *benefit-cost analysis,* developed by economists to consider the consequences of economic projects undertaken by governments, can be helpful in considering the general question of when governments ought to intervene and to what extent.

The idea behind **benefit-cost analysis** is simple: Add up the (opportunity) costs of a given policy, then add up the benefits, and implement the policy if the benefits outweigh the costs. In practice, however, benefit-cost analysis is usually quite difficult for three reasons. First, it may be difficult to ascertain what will happen when an action is undertaken. Second, many government actions involve costs and benefits that will occur only in the distant future. The evaluation of future events raises both technical and normative problems for the analyst. Third, some benefits and costs (e.g., the benefits of prohibiting actions that would harm members of an endangered species of animal) are very difficult to quantify. Indeed, many people would argue that they cannot be and should not be quantified, as they involve values that are not commensurate with money. The practice then is to use benefit-cost analysis to measure the things that can be measured and to be sure that the things that cannot be measured are not ignored when collective decisions are made. By narrowing the range of things that must be determined by informal judgment, benefit-cost analysis can still play a useful role.

In this chapter, we have been working toward a benefit-cost analysis of government intervention. We have made a general case against it (free markets are great economizers on information and coordination costs). We have made a general case for it (free markets will fail to produce allocative efficiency when there are public goods, externalities, or information asymmetries and may also not achieve social goals). We now turn to the more specific questions of what governments do when they intervene, what the costs of government intervention are, and under which circumstances government interventions may fail to improve on even imperfect private markets.

THE TOOLS OF GOVERNMENT INTERVENTION

The legal power of governments to intervene in the workings of the economy is limited only by the Charter of Rights (as interpreted by the courts), the willingness of legislatures to pass laws, and the willingness of the government to enforce them. There are numerous ways in which one or another level of government can prevent, alter, complement, or replace the workings of the unrestricted market economy.

Public Provision. National defense, the criminal justice system, public schools, the highway system, air traffic control, and national parks are all examples of goods or services that are directly provided by governments in Canada. Public provision is the most obvious remedy for market failure to provide public goods, but it is also often used in the interest of redistribution (e.g., hospitals) and other social goals (e.g., public schools). We shall consider public spending in detail in Chapter 20.

Redistribution and Social Insurance Programs. Taxes and spending are often used to provide a distribution of income that is different from that generated by the private market. Government transfer programs affect the distribution of income in this way. We examine the distributive effects of the Canadian tax system in Chapter 20.

Regulation. Government regulations are public rules that apply to private behaviour. In Chapter 13, we saw that governments regulate private markets to limit monopoly power. In Chapter 19, we will focus on regulations designed to deal with environmental quality and with workplace safety. Among other things, government regulations prohibit minors from consuming alcohol, require that children attend school, penalize racial discrimination in housing and labour markets, and require that new automobiles have passive passenger restraints. Government regulation is used to deal with all of the sources of market failure that we have discussed in this chapter; it applies at some level to virtually all spheres of modern economic life.

Structuring Incentives. Almost all government actions, including the kinds we have discussed here, change the incentives that consumers and firms face. If the government provides a park, people will have a weakened incentive to own large plots of land of their own. Fixing minimum or maximum prices (as we saw in the discussion of rent control and agriculture in Chapter 6) affects privately chosen levels of output.

The government can adjust the tax system to provide subsidies to some kinds of behaviour and penalties to others. In the United States, for example, deductible mortgage interest makes owned housing relatively more attractive than other assets that a person might purchase. In Canada, tax exemptions for contributions to Registered Retirement Saving Plans (RRSPs) may lead individuals to increase their total

saving. Such tax treatment sends the household different signals from those sent by the free market. Scholarships to students to become nurses or teachers may offset barriers to mobility into those occupations. Fines and criminal penalties for breaking the law are another part of the incentive structure. By providing direct or indirect fines or subsidies, the government can (in principle) correct externalities, induce private production of public goods, change the income distribution, and encourage behaviour that is deemed socially desirable. However, as we shall see, interventions of this kind are not always successful, and they often do as much (or more) harm than good.

THE COSTS OF GOVERNMENT INTERVENTION

Consider the following argument: The market system is working imperfectly; government has the legal means to improve the situation; therefore, the public interest will be served by government intervention.

This appealing argument is deficient because it neglects three important considerations. First, government intervention is itself costly since it uses scarce resources; for this reason alone, not every market failure is worth correcting because the intervention itself may use up more resources than are being wasted in the (inefficient) free-market outcome. Second, government intervention may be imperfect. Just as markets sometimes succeed and sometimes fail, so government interventions sometimes succeed and sometimes fail. Third, deciding what governments are to do and how they are to do it is also costly and intrinsically imperfect. These are among the messages that can be drawn from a relatively new speciality in economics and political science, called *social choice theory*. Extension 18-2 provides an example of the problems that can arise when social choices are made on the basis of majority rule.

For the remainder of the discussion in this section, note that the *benefit* of government intervention is the value of the market failures that the intervention will correct. Imagine that such a failure has been identified and evaluated. The question at hand, then, is whether the benefits of the intervention will exceed the costs.

Large potential benefits do not necessarily justify government intervention, nor do large potential costs necessarily make it unwise. What matters is the balance between benefits and costs.

EXTENSION 18-2

ARROW'S IMPOSSIBILITY THEOREM

Nobel laureate Kenneth Arrow from Stanford University has shown that it is generally impossible to construct a set of rules for making social choices that is at once comprehensive, democratic, efficient, and consistent. Arrow's theorem has led to decades of work on the part of economists, philosophers, and political scientists, who have tried to find conditions under which democracy can be expected to yield efficient (or otherwise favoured) allocations of resources. The news is generally not good. Unless individual preferences or their distribution in the population meet fairly unlikely criteria, either democracy or efficiency must be sacrificed in the design of social choice mechanisms.

The Arrow theorem can be illustrated by a simple case, depicted in the following table.

Density of Trees	Voter		
	A	B	C
Sparse (1)	3	1	2
Medium (2)	1	2	3
Thick (3)	2	3	1

Imagine that we have a society that consists of three voters who are choosing how many trees to plant in the local park. The three possibilities are as follows: (1) Plant very few trees in one corner. This would make the park suitable for Frisbee and soccer but not for walks in the woods. (2) Plant trees in moderate density throughout the park. In this case, the park would be nice for playing tag and jogging but not usable for most sports. (3) Plant trees densely everywhere. This would make the park a pleasant place to get away from it all (for whatever reasons) but not a good place to jog. Voter A loves jogging, hates Frisbee, and likes walking in the woods. His ranking of the alternatives is 2–3–1. Voter B likes the wide open spaces. His ranking is 1–2–3. Voter C likes to play Frisbee, likes solitude even more, and has little taste for a park that provides neither. Her ranking is 3–1–2.

Suppose that the electorate gets to choose between alternatives that are presented two at a time. What does majority rule do? It depends on which two alternatives are presented. In a choice of 1 versus 2, 1 wins, getting votes from B and C. When the choice is between 2 and 3, 2 wins, getting votes from A and B. When 3 is pitted against 1, 3 wins with the support of A and C. Thus the social choice mechanism of majority rule is *inconsistent*. It tells us that 1 is preferred to 2, 2 is preferred to 3, and 3 is preferred to 1. There is no way to make a choice without arbitrarily (i.e., undemocratically) choosing which set of alternatives to offer the electorate.

There are several different costs of government intervention. We divide these costs into two categories—*direct resource costs* and *indirect costs*.

Direct Resource Costs

Government intervention uses real resources that could be used elsewhere. Civil servants must be paid. Paper, photocopying, and other trappings of bureaucracy; the steel in the navy's ships; the fuel for the army's tanks; and the pilot of the Prime Minister's jet all have valuable alternative uses. The same is true of the accountants who administer the social security system, the economists who are employed by the Bureau of Competition Policy, and of the educators who retrain displaced workers.

Similarly, when government inspectors visit plants to monitor compliance with federally imposed standards of health, industrial safety, or environmental protection, they are imposing costs on the public in the form of their salaries and expenses. When regulatory bodies develop rules, hold hearings, write opinions, or have their staff prepare research reports, they are incurring costs. The costs of the judges, clerks, and court reporters who hear, transcribe, and review the evidence are likewise costs imposed by government regulation. All these activities use valuable resources that could have provided very different goods and services.

All forms of government intervention use real resources and hence impose direct costs.

This type of cost is fairly easy to identify, as it almost always involves expenditure of public funds. Other costs of intervention are less apparent but no less real.

Indirect Costs

Most government interventions in the economy impose some costs on firms and households. The nature and the size of the extra costs borne by firms and households vary with the type of intervention. A few examples will illustrate what is involved.

Changes in Costs of Production. Government safety and emission standards for automobiles have raised the costs of both producing and operating cars. These costs are much greater than the direct budgetary costs of administering the regulations. Taxes used to finance the provision of public goods must be paid by producers and consumers and often increase the cost of producing or selling goods and services. Less direct, but also important, is the possibility that some kinds of regulation deter potential innovation because the innovation might not be approved by the regulators. This, too, could increase the costs of production in the long run.

Costs of Compliance. Government regulation and supervision generates a flood of reporting and related activities that are often referred to collectively as *red tape.* The number of hours of business time devoted to understanding, reporting, and contesting regulatory provisions is enormous. Pay Equity, occupational safety, and environmental control have all increased the size of nonproduction payrolls. The legal costs alone of a major corporation sometimes can run into tens or hundreds of millions of dollars per year. While all this provides lots of employment for lawyers and economic experts, it is costly because there are other tasks these professionals could do that would add more to the production of consumer goods and services.

Households also bear compliance costs directly. A recent study found that the time and money cost of filling out individual income-tax returns was about 8 percent of the total revenue that is collected. In addition to costs of compliance, there are costs borne as firms and households try to avoid regulation. There

will be a substantial incentive to find loopholes in regulations. Resources that could be used elsewhere will be devoted by the regulated to the search for such loopholes and then, in turn, by the regulators to counteracting such evasion.

Rent Seeking. A different kind of problem arises from the mere existence of government and its potential to use its tools in ways that affect the distribution of economic resources. This phenomenon has been dubbed **rent seeking** by economists because private firms, households, and business groups will use their political influence to seek economic rents from the government. These valuable rents can come in the form of favourable regulations, direct subsidies, and profitable contracts. Democratic governments are especially vulnerable to manipulation of this kind because they respond to well articulated interests of all sorts.

Rent seeking is endemic to mixed economies. Because of the many things that governments are called on to do, they have the power to act in ways that transfer resources among private entities. Because they are democratic, they are responsive to public pressures of various kinds. If a government's behaviour can be influenced, whether by voting, campaign contributions, lobbying, or bribes, real resources will be used in trying to influence government behaviour.

THE CAUSES OF GOVERNMENT FAILURE

Our conceptual benefit-cost analysis of government intervention is almost complete. First, we identify each market failure. Then we make our best estimate of the benefits of a government intervention designed to correct that failure—in most cases, the best that we can do is less than the maximum potential benefit. Then we calculate the costs of the government intervention, as outlined in the preceding section. If the benefits exceed the costs, the intervention is warranted. Unfortunately, things are never this simple. For one thing, as we have already noted, many of the benefits of government intervention are extremely difficult to quantify. Even in the easy cases, however, where the benefits and the direct costs of intervention can be measured and the indirect costs are unimportant, governments, like private markets, are imperfect. Often they will fail, in the same sense that markets do, to achieve their potential.

The reason for government failure is not that public-sector employees are less able, honest, or virtuous than people who work in the private sector. Rather, the causes of government failure are inherent in government institutions, just as the causes of market failure stem from the nature of markets. Importantly, some government failure is an inescapable cost of democratic decision making.

Inefficient Public Choices

At the core of most people's idea of democracy is that each citizen's vote should have the same weight. One of the insights of social choice theory is that resource allocation, based on the principle of one vote per person will generally be inefficient because it fails to take into account the *intensity of preferences*. Consider three farmers, A, B, and C, who are contemplating building access roads. Suppose that the road to A's farm is worth $7,000 to A and that the road to B's farm is worth $7,000 to B. (C's farm is on the main road, which already exists.) Suppose that under the taxing rules currently in effect, each road would cost A, B, and C $2,000 each. It is plainly efficient to build both roads because each generates net benefits of $1,000 ($7,000 gross benefits to farmers A and B less $6,000 total cost). But each road would be defeated 2-1 in a simple majority vote. (B and C would vote against A's road; A and C would vote against B's road.)

Now suppose that we allow A and B to make a deal: "I will vote for your road if you will vote for mine." Although such deals are often decried by political commentators, the deal enhances efficiency: Both roads now get 2–1 majorities, and both roads get built. However, such deals can just as easily reduce efficiency. If the gross value of each road were $5,000 instead of $7,000, and farmers A and B again make their deal, each road will still command a 2–1 majority, but building the roads will now be inefficient. (The gross value of each road is now only $5,000, but the cost is still $6,000.) A and B will be using democracy to appropriate resources from C while reducing economic efficiency.

Special Interests

The case in the preceding paragraph can be interpreted in a different way. Instead of being the third farmer, C might be all of the other voters in the country. Instead of bearing one-third of the costs, A and B each might bear only a small portion of the costs. To the extent that A and B are able to forcefully articulate the benefits that they would derive from the roads, they may be able to use democracy to appropriate resources from taxpayers in general. Much of the concern with the power of "special interests" stems from the fact that the institutions of representative democracy tend to be responsive to benefits (or costs) that focus on particular, identifiable, and articulate groups. Often costs that are borne diffusely by taxpayers or voters in general are hardly noticed.

This potential bias applies to regulations as well as to direct government provisions. Chapter 13 discussed a number of cases in which economic regulations are used to benefit the affected industry. Similarly, as we saw in Chapter 6, rent control can be interpreted, at least in part, as benefiting existing tenants at the expense of future potential tenants; the latter group tends to have no political power at all.

Governments as Monopolists

Governments face the same problems of cost minimization that private firms do but often operate in an environment where they are monopoly producers without stockholders. Large governments (provinces, big cities, the federal government) face all of the organizational problems faced by large corporations. They tend to use relatively rigid rules and hence to respond slowly to change. Building codes are an example of this type of problem. Most local governments have detailed requirements regarding the materials that must go into a new house, factory, or office. When technology changes, the codes often lag behind. For example, plastic pipe, which is cheaper and easier to use than steel pipe, was prohibited by building codes for decades after its use became efficient. Similarly, much antipollution regulation specifies the type of control equipment that must be employed. Changes in technology may make a regulation inefficient, but the regulation may stay in place for some time.

Like those of large private enterprises, a government's "organization chart" will often be out of date. For example, for most of this century the Canadian government has regulated freight rates charged by railroads. With the advent of buses and trucks, the government should have turned to developing a healthy *transportation system*. Yet for years, the imposed rate structure favoured the railroads. The same kind of problem—a misclassification of the relevant economic issue—might well have arisen when the purchasing division in a large corporation, which used typewriters exclusively, was confronted with modern word-processing technology. In the private sector, market forces often push the corporation into revising its view of the problem at hand, whereas there is ordinarily no market mechanism to force governments to use relatively efficient rules of thumb and organizational structures. Put in the language of Chapter 14, the scope for satisficing governments to depart from optimal behaviour is generally greater than that for satisficing firms. Put another way, much government failure arises precisely because governments do not have competitors and are not constrained by the "bottom line."

Principal-Agent Problems in Government

Governments face the same kinds of principal-agent problems that firms do, but the problem in the case of governments can be more serious for two reasons. First, the possibility of a hostile takeover, although quite powerful as applied to elected officials (they can be removed from office), is very weak as applied to bureaucracies. Second, the principal in the case of government is all of its citizens, and this group will generally be unable to agree on what government *should* do. Stockholders can all agree that the firm should maximize profits. Citizens who vote, by contrast, are not expected to agree on any simple mission for their elected representatives. This lack of agreement makes it that much more difficult for the agents to serve their principals and that much easier for agents who do not perform well to get away with it.

HOW MUCH SHOULD GOVERNMENT INTERVENE?

The theoretical principles for determining the optimal amount of government intervention are individually accepted by almost everyone. What they add up to, however, is more controversial. Moreover, the issue is often framed ideologically. Those on the "right wing" tend to compare heavy-handed government with a hypothetical and perfectly operating competitive market. In contrast, those on the "left wing" tend to compare hypothetical and ideal government intervention with a laissez-faire economy rife with market failures.

Evaluating the costs and the benefits of government intervention requires a comparison of the private economic system as it is working (not as it might work ideally) with the pattern of government intervention as it is likely to perform (not as it might perform ideally).

The cases that we have made for and against government intervention are both valid, depending on time, place, and the values that are brought to bear. At this point, we turn to the issue of what government actually does, something that will perhaps illuminate the question of what it ought to do. In Chapter 13, we discussed government action that is designed to affect monopoly and competition. In the next two chapters, we will discuss in some detail three other important types of intervention in the Canadian economy today: environmental and safety regulation, taxation, and public spending.

SUMMARY

A. HOW MARKETS COORDINATE

- The various markets in the economy are coordinated in an unplanned, decentralized way by the price system. Profits and losses play a key role in achieving a coordinated market response. Changes in prices and profits, resulting from emerging scarcities and surpluses, lead to responses by consumers and producers. Such responses tend to correct the shortages and surpluses as well as to change the market signals of prices and profits.

- Important features of a market economy include voluntary responses to market signals, the limited informa-

tion required by any individual, and the fact that coordination will occur under any market structure.

B. THE CASE FOR FREE MARKETS

- The case for free markets can be made in two different ways. The "formal defense" is based on the concept of allocative efficiency. This was the basis for the appeal of competitive markets as discussed in Chapter 13.

- The "informal defense" of free markets is not specifically based on the idea of allocative efficiency, and thus applies to market structures other than just perfect competition. The informal defense of free markets is based on four central arguments:

1. Free markets are flexible and provide automatic co-ordination of the actions of decentralized decision makers.
2. The pursuit of profits which is central to free markets provides a stimulus to innovation and economic growth.
3. Free markets are self-correcting so that situations of disequilibrium are only temporary.
4. Free markets permit a decentralization of economic power.

C. THE CASE FOR GOVERNMENT INTERVENTION

- Markets do not always work perfectly. Dissatisfaction with market results often leads to government intervention. Five main sources of market failure are

   1. monopoly
   2. externalities
   3. public goods
   4. information asymmetries
   5. failure to achieve social goals

- Pollution is an example of an externality. A producer who pollutes the air or water does not pay the social cost of the pollution and is therefore not motivated to avoid the costs. Private producers will therefore produce too much pollution relative to what is allocatively efficient.
- National defense is an example of a public good (or collective consumption good). Markets fail to produce public goods because the benefits of such goods are available to people whether they pay for them or not.

- Information asymmetries cause market failure when one party to a transaction is able to use personal expertise to manipulate the transaction in his or her own favour. Moral hazard, adverse selection, and principal-agent problems are all consequences of information asymmetries.
- Changing the distribution of income is one of the roles for government intervention that members of a society may desire. Others include values that are placed on public provision for its own sake, on protection of individuals from themselves or from others, and on recognition of social obligations.

D. GOVERNMENT INTERVENTION

- Microeconomic policy concerns activities of the government that alter the unrestricted workings of the free-market system in order to affect either the allocation of resources or the distribution of income. Major tools of microeconomic policy include (a) public provision, (b) redistribution, (c) regulation, and (d) structuring incentives. (The first two are the subject of Chapter 20.) Regulation can take various forms. Incentives can be structured in a number of ways, including the use of fines, subsidies, taxes, and effluent charges (which are discussed in Chapter 19).
- The costs and benefits of government intervention must be considered in deciding whether, when, and how much intervention is appropriate. Among the costs are the direct costs that are incurred by the government, the costs that are imposed on the parties who are regulated, directly and indirectly, and the costs that are imposed on third parties. These costs are seldom negligible and are often large.
- The possibility of government failure must be balanced against the potential benefits of removing market failure. It is neither possible nor efficient to correct all market failure; neither is it always efficient to do nothing.

KEY CONCEPTS

Market coordination	Coase theorem	Benefits and costs of government intervention
Differences between private and social valuations	Public goods	
Market failure	Information asymmetries	Rent seeking
Externalities	Moral hazard and adverse selection	Government failure
	Benefit-cost analysis	

DISCUSSION QUESTIONS

1. Should the free market be allowed to determine the price for the following, or should government intervene? Defend your choice for each.

   a. Transit fares
   b. Garbage collection
   c. Postal delivery of newspapers and magazines
   d. Fire protection for churches
   e. Ice cream

2. The following activities have known harmful effects. In each case, identify any divergence between social and private costs.

   a. Cigarette smoking
   b. Driving a car at the speed limit of 100 km per hour
   c. Private ownership of guns
   d. Drilling for offshore oil

3. The size of commercial fishing fleets has fallen markedly in recent years. Suppose there are many boats engaged in fishing a given area. Use the idea of externalities to show that each boat can be expected to fish more than the socially optimal amount.

4. Suppose the facts asserted here are true. Should they trigger government intervention? If so, what policy alternatives are available?

   a. The proportion of total national income taken up in medical and hospital costs in Canada has been rising more rapidly than in any other country (except the United States).
   b. The cost of an average one-family house in Vancouver is now about $300,000—an amount that is out of the reach of most people.
   c. Cigarette smoking reduces the smoker's life expectancy by eight years.
   d. Saccharin in large doses has been found to cause cancer in mice.

5. Consider the possible beneficial and adverse effects of each of the following forms of government intervention.

   a. Charging motorists a tax for driving in the downtown areas of large cities and using the revenues to provide peripheral parking and shuttle buses

   b. Prohibiting juries from awarding large malpractice judgments against doctors
   c. Mandating no-fault automobile insurance, in which the automobile owner's insurance company is responsible for damage to his or her vehicle no matter who causes the accident
   d. Requiring that automobile manufacturers rather than tire manufactures warrant the tires on cars that they sell

6. The president of Goodyear Tire and Rubber Company complained that government regulation had imposed $30 million per year in "unproductive costs" on his company, as listed here. How would one determine whether these costs were "productive" or "unproductive?"

   a. Environmental regulation, $17 million
   b. Occupational safety and health, $7 million
   c. Motor vehicle safety, $3 million
   d. Personnel and administration, $3 million

7. Your local government almost certainly provides a police department, a fire department, and a public library. What are the market imperfections, if any, that each of these seeks to correct? Which of these are closest to being public goods? Which are furthest?

8. Suppose that for $100, a laboratory can accurately assess a person's probability of developing a fairly rare disease that is costly to treat. What would be the likely effects of such a test on health insurance markets?

9. What market failures do public support of higher education seek to remedy? How would you go about evaluating whether the benefits of this support outweigh the costs?

10. What government failure might be involved when professional organizations encourage a provincial government to stiffen the requirements necessary to be licensed to practice a profession? What market failure might such requirements correct? How would you weigh arguments for and against stiffening the requirements?

CHAPTER 19

ENVIRONMENTAL AND SAFETY REGULATION

In almost everything we do, we are subject to some form of government regulation. The system of criminal law regulates our interactions with people and property. Local zoning ordinances regulate the ways in which the land that we own may be used. Insurance commissions must approve both the insurance contracts that we sign and the rates that we are charged. Regulatory commissions set rates for electricity, natural gas, local telephone service, and a host of other goods and services. Seat belts, brake lights, turn signals, air bags, internal door panels, bumpers, and catalytic converters are all subjects of regulation in just one industry. The number of electrical outlets per room, the material used for plumbing, and the spacing of the vertical supports in an interior wall are usually dictated by local building codes. The list goes on and on. A good case can be made that various governments in Canada have more effect on the economy through regulation than through taxing and spending.

In Chapter 18, we identified a number of types of market failure that might be addressed by government policy. Regulation of economic activity is used to address each of them. Market failure arising from natural monopoly has led to public regulation, as discussed in Chapter 13. *Externalities*, especially the negative externalities of industrial pollution, are the motivation for environmental regulation, a major topic of this chapter.

Regulation of advertising and much health and safety regulation are designed to deal with market failures arising from *information asymmetries*.

There is no easy way for a consumer to know whether the paint on a child's toy can cause lead poisoning, so a government body regulates the market for children's toys. Occupational licensing is defended on the same grounds; in most provinces, professionals as different as barbers and psychiatrists must undergo specified courses of training before they are allowed to ply their trades. The idea is to prevent "just anyone" from claiming and abusing alleged expertise.

Information about a professional's training is a *public good:* Once the information is available to one consumer, it can be made available to all very cheaply. Occupational licensing is a way to produce this public good—in the form of the familiar diploma that hangs on the wall of the barbershop, physician's office, or repair garage.

Regulations can also be used to change the *distribution of income.* This is the purpose of such regulations as rent controls, minimum wages, and agricultural supply-management policies. Finally, the laws and regulations that enforce private contracts are pure public goods that are essential to the operation of a market economy. Without reliably enforceable contracts, many transactions would be so risky that they would not take place.

The principal topic of this chapter is **social regulation.** Social regulation does not mean the regulation of social behaviour such as the clothes we wear or the words we use. Rather, it is the regulation of economic behaviour to advance social goals in circumstances in which neither competition nor economic regulation can be expected to do the job.

In this chapter, we consider both the market failures that social regulation addresses and the effectiveness and costs of different kinds of regulation in correcting these market failures. We start by extending the analysis of negative externalities in Chapter 18 to the problem of environmental pollution.

THE ECONOMICS OF POLLUTION CONTROL

Pollution is a negative externality. As a consequence of producing or consuming goods and services, "bads" are produced as well. Steel plants produce smoke in addition to steel. Farms produce chemical runoff as well as food. Households produce human

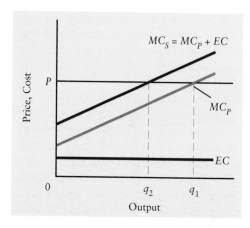

Internalizing an externality can correct market failure. The private marginal cost curve MC_P is the conventional marginal cost for a firm that is producing output in a competitive market. The external cost curve EC depicts marginal cost that the firm's production imposes on people other than its owners, employees, and customers. Because the firm is maximizing profits, it will ignore EC and produce output q_1, where the market price p equals private marginal cost. Adding EC and MC_P yields social marginal cost, MC_S. The socially optimal level of output is q_2, where price is equal to MC_S.

Suppose that the firm is required to pay a tax of $\$EC$ per unit of output. Its MC_P curve will now become the MC_S curve. The externality will be *internalized,* and the profit-maximizing firm will be motivated to reduce its output to the socially optimal level, q_2. It does this because with the tax added to its private marginal cost, q_2 is the profit-maximizing level of output.

waste and garbage as they consume goods and services. In all of these cases, the technology of production and consumption automatically generates pollution. Indeed, there are few human endeavors that do not have negative pollution externalities.

THE ECONOMIC RATIONALE FOR REGULATING POLLUTION

When firms use resources that they do not regard as scarce, they fail to consider the cost of those resources. This is a characteristic of most examples of pollution, including the case that is illustrated in Figure 19-1. When a paper mill produces pulp for the world's newspapers, more people are affected than its suppliers, employees, and customers. Its water-discharged effluent hurts the fishing boats that ply nearby waters, and its smog makes many resort areas less attractive, thereby reducing the tourist revenues that local motel operators and boat renters can expect. The profit-maximizing paper mill neglects these external effects of its actions because its profits are not affected by them.

Allocative efficiency requires that the price (the value that consumers place on the marginal unit of output) be just equal to the marginal social cost (the value of resources that society gives up to produce the marginal unit of output). When there are harmful externalities, marginal *social* cost and marginal *private* cost (the cost born by the producer) will diverge, because the firm is not charged for its contamination of the water.

By producing where price equals marginal private cost and thereby ignoring the externality, the firm is maximizing profits but producing too much output. The price that consumers pay just covers the marginal private cost but does not pay for the external damage. The *social benefit* of the last unit of output (the market price) is less than the social cost (marginal private cost plus the social cost imposed by the externality). Reducing output by 1 unit would reduce both social benefit and social cost but would reduce social cost by more because social cost is larger. Reducing output by 1 unit would save economic resources and increase allocative efficiency.

Making the firm bear the entire social cost of its production is called **internalizing** the externality. This will cause it to produce at a lower output. Indeed, at the optimal output, where the externality is completely internalized, consumer prices would just cover all of the marginal *social* cost of production—marginal private cost plus the externality. We would have the familiar condition for allocative efficiency that marginal benefits to consumers are just equal to the marginal cost of producing these benefits. The difference here is that some of the marginal social cost takes the form of an externality.

As an example, suppose that Great Cabinets Inc. produces kitchen cabinets and that residue from painting the cabinets is washed into a stream that runs beside the plant. The stream is part of the municipal water supply, which is treated at a water purification plant before it is sent into people's homes. Suppose that each cabinet produced increases the cost of running the water treatment plant by $1. In terms

of the previous analysis, the external cost is $1 per cabinet, and thus the social cost per cabinet is exactly $1 above the private cost per cabinet—that is, social marginal cost exceeds private marginal cost by $1.

In practice, the external cost is often quite difficult to measure. This is especially so in the case of air pollution, where the damage is often spread over hundreds of thousands of square kilometres and can have real but small effects on millions of people. Another difficulty arises because the cost that is imposed by pollution will generally depend on the mechanisms that are used to undo the damage that it causes. Pollution-control mechanisms are themselves costly, and their costs must also be counted as part of the social cost of pollution. Nevertheless, the basic analysis of Figure 19-1 applies to these more difficult cases.

The socially optimal level of output is at the quantity where all marginal costs, private plus external, equal the marginal benefit to society.

Notice that the optimal level of output is not the level at which there is no pollution. Rather, it is the level at which the beneficiaries of pollution (the consumers and producers of Great Cabinets' kitchen cabinets, in our example) are just willing to pay the marginal social cost that is imposed by the pollution.

Unregulated markets will generally produce excessive amounts of environmental damage. Zero environmental damage, however, is neither technologically possible nor economically efficient.

POLLUTION CONTROL IN THEORY AND PRACTICE

The economics of determining how much pollution to prohibit, and therefore how much to allow, is summarized in Figure 19-2, which depicts the benefits and costs of pollution control. The analysis might be thought of as applying, say, to water pollution in a specific watershed. It is drawn from the perspective of a public authority that has been charged with maximizing social welfare.

Note that the figure is drawn in terms of the amount of pollution that is prevented (or abated) rather than in terms of the total amount of pollution. This is because pollution *abatement* (rather than pollution) is a "good" of economic value, and we are used to applying the concepts of supply and demand for goods with positive values. If no pollution is

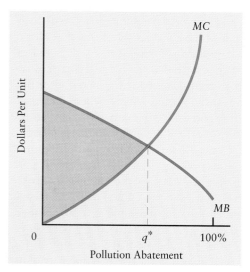

FIGURE 19-2
The Optimal Amount of Pollution Abatement

The optimal amount of pollution abatement occurs where the marginal cost of reducing pollution is just equal to the marginal benefits from doing so. *MB* represent the marginal benefit that is achieved by pollution prevention in some activity. *MC* represents the marginal cost of preventing pollution; it rises sharply as more and more pollution is eliminated. The optimal level of pollution control is q^*, where $MB = MC$. *Notice that not all pollution is eliminated.* For each unit up to q^*, the marginal benefit derived from pollution abatement exceeds the marginal cost. The total net benefit from the optimal amount of pollution abatement is given by the shaded area—the sum of the difference between marginal benefit and marginal cost at each level of abatement. Any further reductions in pollution beyond q^* would add more to costs than to benefits.

abated, the watershed will be subjected to the amount of pollution that would occur in an unregulated market. The greater the amount of pollution prevented, the smaller the amount of pollution that remains.

The marginal cost of preventing pollution is likely to be small at low levels of abatement but to rise steeply after some point. This is the upward-sloping line shown in Figure 19-2. There are two reasons for believing that this shape is generally accurate. First is the familiar logic behind increasing marginal costs. For each firm that pollutes, there will be some antipollution measures that can be taken fairly easily, so the first portion of pollution reduction will be cheap relative to later portions. In addi-

tion, it is likely that pollution reduction of any degree will be easier for some firms than for others. New facilities are likely to run cleaner than old ones, for example. Reducing pollution from a factory that was designed in the era of environmental concern may be much easier than obtaining similar reductions from an older factory. After some point, however, the easy fixes are exhausted, and the marginal cost of reducing pollution further rises steeply.

The downward-sloping curve in Figure 19-2 is the "demand" for pollution abatement, and reflects the marginal benefit of pollution reduction. The curve slopes downward for much the same reason that the typical demand curve slopes downward. Starting at any nonlethal level of pollution, people will derive some benefit from reducing the level of pollution, but the marginal benefit from a given amount of reduction will be lower, the lower the level of pollution. Put another way, in a very dirty environment, a little cleanliness will be much prized, but in a very clean environment, a little more cleanliness will be of only small additional value.

The optimal amount of pollution reduction occurs where the marginal benefit is equal to the marginal cost—where "supply" and "demand" in Figure 19-2 intersect. In trying to reach this optimum, the pollution control authority faces three serious problems.

First, although Figure 19-2 looks like a supply-demand diagram, we have already seen that the private sector will not by itself create a market in pollution control. Hence the government must intervene in private-sector markets if the optimal level of control shown in Figure 19-2 is to be attained.

The second problem is that the optimal level of pollution abatement is not easily known because the marginal benefit and the marginal cost curves shown in Figure 19-2 are not usually observable. In practice, the government can only estimate these curves, and accurate estimates are often difficult to obtain, especially when the technology of pollution control is changing rapidly and the health consequences of various pollutants (e.g., chemicals that are new to the marketplace) are not known.

The third problem is that the available techniques for regulating pollution are themselves imperfect. Even when the optimal level of pollution control is known, there are both technical and legal impediments to achieving that level through regulation.

In what follows we examine three different types of policies designed to bring about the optimal amount of pollution abatement (or the optimal amount of pollution). These are *direct controls, emissions taxes,* and *tradable emissions permits.*

Direct Controls

Direct control is the form of environmental regulation that is used most often. Automobile emissions standards are direct controls that are familiar to most of us. The standards must be met by all new cars that are sold in Canada. They require that emissions per kilometre of a number of noxious chemicals and other pollutants be less than certain specified amounts. The standards are the same no matter where the car is driven. The marginal benefit of reducing carbon monoxide emissions in rural Saskatchewan, where there is relatively little air pollution, is certainly much less than the marginal benefit in Montreal, where there is already a good deal of carbon monoxide in the air. Yet the standard is the same in both places.

Direct controls also often require that specific techniques be used to reduce pollution. For example, coal-fired electric plants were sometimes required to use devices called "scrubbers" to reduce sulfur dioxide emissions, even in cases where other techniques could have achieved the same level of pollution abatement at lower cost.

Another form of direct control is the simple prohibition of certain polluting behaviours. For example, many cities and towns prohibit the private burning of leaves and other trash because of the air pollution problem that the burning would cause. A number of communities have banned the use of wood stoves. Similarly, the government gradually reduced the amount of lead allowed in leaded gasoline and then eliminated leaded gasoline altogether.

Problems with Direct Controls.   Direct controls are likely to be economically inefficient; in most cases, more pollution could be abated at the same economic cost as that imposed by direct controls. Suppose that pollution of a given waterway is to be reduced by a certain amount. Regulators will typically apportion the required reduction among all of the polluters according to some roughly equitable criterion. The regulators might require that every polluter reduce its pollution by the same percentage. Alternatively, every polluter might be required to install a certain type of control device or to ensure that each litre of water that is dumped into the watershed

meets certain quality criteria. Although any of these rules might seem reasonable, each of them will be inefficient *except in the extreme case where all polluters face identical pollution abatement costs.*

To see this, consider two firms that face different costs of pollution abatement, as depicted in Figure 19-3. Suppose that Firm A's marginal cost of pollution abatement is everywhere below Firm B's. Such a circumstance is quite likely when one recalls that pollution comes from many different industries. It may be easy for one industry to cut back on the amount that it uses of some pollutant; in another industry, the pollutant may be an integral part of the production process. The most efficient way to reduce pollution would be to have Firm A cut back on its pollution until the marginal cost of further reductions is just equal to Firm B's marginal cost of reducing its first (and cheapest to forgo) unit of pollution. Once their marginal costs of reducing pollution are equalized, *further* reductions in pollution will be efficient only if this equality is maintained. To see this, suppose that the marginal costs of abatement are different for the two firms. By reallocating some pollution abatement from the high-marginal-cost firm to the low-cost firm, total pollution abatement could be kept constant while the real resources used to abate pollution would be reduced. Alternatively, one could hold the resource cost constant and increase the amount of abatement.

Direct pollution controls are usually inefficient in that they do not minimize the cost of a given amount of pollution abatement. This implies that they also do not abate the most pollution possible for a given cost.

When direct controls require that firms adopt specific techniques of pollution abatement, a second type of inefficiency arises. Regulations of this kind tend to change only slowly: The regulators will often mandate today's best techniques tomorrow, even if something more effective has come along.

Both of these sources of inefficiency in direct controls are examples of *government failure,* discussed in Chapter 18. In both cases, the government does not do as well as it could in pursuing its important social objectives. In terms of Figure 19-2, government failure would add to the marginal cost of pollution reduction. Thus the less efficient the method used to control pollution the lower the opti-

FIGURE 19-3
The Potential Inefficiency of Direct Pollution Controls

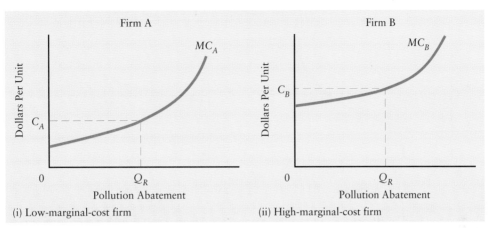

(i) Low-marginal-cost firm

(ii) High-marginal-cost firm

Requiring equal amounts of pollution abatement from different polluters is inefficient when the different polluters have different technologies of pollution abatement. Firm A is able to reduce its emissions according to the marginal cost curve MC_A. Firm B, which operates at the same scale but in a different kind of factory, has a higher marginal cost of abatement, MC_B. Suppose that a regulatory authority requires that the two firms reduce pollution by the same amount, Q_R. Firm A will have a marginal cost of pollution abatement of C_A, whereas firm B's marginal cost will be C_B, which is larger than C_A.

To see that this outcome is inefficient, consider what happens if firm A reduces its pollution (increases its pollution abatement) by 1 unit while firm B increases its pollution by 1 unit. Total pollution remains the same, but total costs fall. Firm A incurs added costs of C_A, and firm B saves a greater amount, C_B. Because the total amount of pollution is unchanged, the total social cost of pollution and pollution abatement is lower.

mal amount of pollution abatement and hence the higher the optimal level of pollution.

A final problem that arises with direct controls in practice is that they are expensive to monitor and to enforce. The regulatory agency has to check, factory by factory, farm by farm, how many pollutants of what kinds are being emitted. It then also needs a mechanism for penalizing offenders. Accurate monitoring of all potential sources of pollution requires a level of resources that is much greater than has ever been made available to the relevant regulatory agencies. Moreover, the existing system of fines and penalties, in the view of many critics, is not nearly harsh enough to have much effect. A potential polluter, required to limit emissions of a pollutant to so many kilograms or litres per day, will take into account the cost of meeting the standard, the probability of being caught, and the severity of the penalty before deciding how to behave. If the chances of being caught and the penalties for being caught are small, the direct controls may have little effect.

Monitoring and enforcement of direct pollution controls is costly, and this reduces the effectiveness of the controls.

Emissions Taxes

An alternative method of pollution control is to levy a tax on emissions at the source. The great advantage of such a procedure is that it internalizes the pollution externality so that decentralized decisions can lead to allocatively efficient outcomes. Again, suppose that Firm A can reduce emissions cheaply, while it is more expensive for Firm B to reduce emissions. If all firms are required to pay a tax of t for each unit of pollution they produce, then t is equal to the marginal benefit of pollution reduction. The goal of profit maximization will then lead firms to reduce emissions to the point where the marginal cost of further reduction is just equal to t. This means that Firm A will reduce emissions much more than Firm B and that both will then have the same

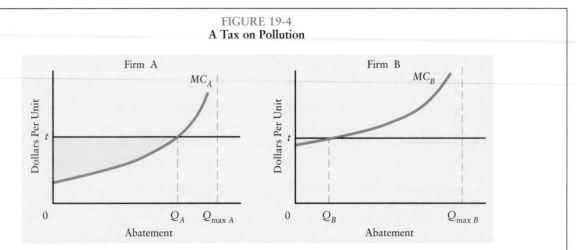

FIGURE 19-4
A Tax on Pollution

Taxes on pollution can lead to efficient pollution abatement. As in Figure 19-3, firm A faces a lower marginal cost of pollution abatement than does firm B. Suppose that the regulatory authority imposes a tax of t dollars per unit of pollution. Since each firm must then pay t dollars for each unit of pollution it produces, t can be viewed as the firm's marginal benefit of pollution abatement—for each unit of pollution it *does not produce* it avoids paying taxes equal to t.

Firm A will choose to reduce its pollution by Q_A. Up to this point, the tax saved by reducing pollution exceeds the marginal cost of reducing pollution. If firm A chooses not to reduce pollution at all, it would pay $t \times Q_{maxA}$ in pollution taxes, where Q_{maxA} is the firm's total pollution if it does nothing to prevent pollution. By abating its pollution by Q_A, firm A saves an amount that is given by the shaded area in the panel on the left.

Firm B chooses to abate only a small amount of pollution, Q_B. Any further abatement would require that the firm incur costs along MC_B, which would be greater than the benefits of taxes saved.

marginal cost of further abatement, which is required for allocative efficiency. This is illustrated in Figure 19-4.

Note that if the regulatory agency is able to obtain a good estimate of the marginal damage that is done by pollution, it could set the tax rate just equal to that amount. In such a case, polluters would be forced by the tax to internalize the full pollution externality. A second great advantage of using emissions taxes is that they do not require that regulators specify anything about *how* polluters should abate pollution. Rather, polluters themselves can be left to find the most efficient abatement techniques. The profit motive will lead them to do so because they will want to avoid paying the tax.

Emissions taxes can, in principle, perfectly internalize pollution externalities so that profit-maximizing firms will produce the allocatively efficient amount of pollution abatement. Furthermore, unlike direct controls, emissions taxes minimize the total cost of a given amount of pollution abatement.

Application 19-1 discusses a simple type of pollution tax that is becoming quite common in many U.S. cities—charging for household garbage by the bag.

Problems With Emissions Taxes. Emissions taxes can work only if it is possible to measure emissions accurately. For some kinds of pollution-creating activities, this does not pose much of a problem, but for many other types of pollution, good measuring devices that can be installed at reasonable cost do not exist. Obviously, in these cases, emissions taxes cannot work, and direct controls are the only feasible approach.

When there is good reason to prohibit a pollutant altogether, direct controls are obviously better than taxes. Municipal bans on the burning of leaves fall in this category, as do the occasional emergency bans on some kinds of pollution that are invoked during an air pollution crisis in cities such as Los Angeles and Vancouver.

Another problem with emissions taxes involves setting the tax rate. Ideally, the regulatory agency

---

CHARGING FOR GARBAGE BY THE BAG

One of the most common forms of pollution is household garbage. The economic theory of pollution externalities discussed in the text suggests that a tax on household trash should reduce the volume of pollution. In a number of communities in the United States, per-bag charges on household garbage have led to reductions in the amount of trash generated. The waste that is not going into the costly bags is going into compost heaps and into recycling. Communities vary in the way that charges are assessed and in the degree of support that they provide for alternative uses of waste. Typically, the municipal garbage trucks will only pick up trash if the trash bag (or other type of garbage) carries a special sticker. The stickers are sold by the municipal authorities; the fewer a household uses, the less money it spends on having its trash picked up. Fees of $1 to $2 per bag are not uncommon. In one U.S. community (High Bridge, New Jersey), a fee of $1.25 per bag has led to a 25 percent reduction in the volume of garbage.

The externality in this case is the use of landfills. Especially in the more populated areas of the United States, landfills for solid waste are becoming scarce and, consequently, expensive. By charging residents something for use of the landfill, alternative means of dealing with waste are encouraged, and a solid waste facility of given size can last longer.

Even in this case, the problem of finding the optimal charge per bag of garbage poses serious technical difficulties. There are also enforcement problems: Rather than pay the charge, some households will illegally dump their trash, adding to environmental damage. However, the pollution itself is very easy to measure, and it is plain that the optimum charge is greater than zero.

---

would obtain an estimate of the marginal social damage caused per unit of each pollutant and set the tax equal to this amount. This would perfectly internalize the pollution externality. However, the information that is needed to determine the marginal social damage curve shown in Figure 19-1 is often difficult to obtain. If society is currently far away from the optimum, it may be very difficult to estimate what the marginal social damage will be at the optimum. If the regulatory agency sets the tax rate too high, too many resources will be devoted to pollution control (the outcome will be beyond q^* in Figure 19-2). If the tax is set too low, there will be too much pollution. In many practical cases, regulators may have a much better idea of the acceptable level of pollution than of the tax rate that would lead to that result. Further, when the technology of pollution abatement changes, the tax rate would have to change as well, and governments are often very slow to adjust tax rates.

A potentially serious problem with emissions taxes is that information necessary to determine the optimal tax rate is often unavailable.

Tradable Emissions Permits

One great advantage of direct controls is that the regulators can set the standards to limit the total quantity of pollution in a given geographical area. This can be done without knowing the details of either the marginal benefit or the marginal cost curve in Figure 19-2. The great advantage of emissions taxes is that they allow for decentralized decision making, providing firms with an incentive to internalize the negative externality of pollution. **Tradable emissions permits** can combine both of these advantages and thus have the potential for being superior to either direct controls or emissions taxes.

In Figure 19-3, we noted that direct pollution controls would generally be inefficient because the marginal cost curves for pollution abatement would vary across firms. Tradable permits can solve this problem. To see this, we must first figure out how much pollution to allow. This involves reformulating the regulator's problem. Start with the same conditions as those in Figure 19-3, and permit each firm to pollute exactly the same amount as would be allowed by the direct controls in Figure 19-3. Now suppose that the firms are allowed to buy and to sell tradable emissions permits which are simply "rights to pollute." Trades among firms will lead to discovery of the lowest-cost means of achieving the permitted level of pollution.

To see how the outcome is changed in the presence of tradable emissions permits, note that at the initial allowed amounts of pollution (Q_R), the marginal cost of pollution for Firm A is lower than that for Firm B. Firm B would be willing to pay up to C_B for the right to pollute 1 more unit, and Firm A would be willing to sell that right for any amount that exceeded C_B. Notice that if such a trade were made, the total amount of pollution would be unchanged, the total cost of abating pollution would fall (by $C_B - C_A$), and both firms would be at least as well off as before. We would thus have a clear efficiency improvement. No one is made worse off, and at least one party is made better off.

Once the firms are allowed to exchange rights to pollute, they will do so until their marginal abatement costs are equalized. At this point, there is no further gain from trading permits. Notice that the new outcome is identical to that depicted in Figure 19-4, with the equilibrium price of an emissions permit just equal to the emissions tax shown in that figure. However, with tradable permits, regulators do not need to calculate the optimal pollution tax. Given the permitted quantity of pollution, the market in permits will calculate the equivalent to the tax through the voluntary trades of firms.

Tradable emissions permits can be used to achieve the same allocation of resources as would occur with emissions taxes, with much less information required of the regulatory authorities.

One problem with both pollution taxes and tradable permits is more political than economic, but it is certainly important in explaining why such

policies are so rare. Opponents of tradable permits often argue that by providing permits, rather than simply outlawing pollution above some amount, the government is condoning crimes against society. Direct controls, according to this argument, have much greater normative force because they say that violating the standards is simply wrong. Emissions taxes and markets for pollution make violating the standards just one more element of cost for the firm to consider as it pursues its private goals.

Most economists find arguments of this kind unpersuasive. An absolute ban on pollution is impossible, and in choosing how much pollution to allow, society must trade pollution abatement against other valuable things. Economic analysis has a good deal to say about how a society might minimize the cost of *any* degree of pollution abatement or maximize the amount of pollution abated for any given cost that the society is willing to bear.

Problems with Tradable Emissions Permits. Tradable permits pose formidable problems of implementation. Some of these involve technical difficulties in measuring pollution and in designing mechanisms to ensure that firms and households comply with regulations (some of these problems also exist for emissions permits). Furthermore, the potential efficiency gains arising from tradable permits cannot be realized if regulatory agencies are prone to change the rules under which trades may take place. This has been a problem in the past, but it is a problem that can be corrected.

Although they have been seriously discussed in Canada, most experimentation with tradable pollution permits has so far been conducted in the United States. The U.S. Environmental Protection Agency and a number of state regulatory agencies have allowed limited trading of emissions permits for the past two decades. One study that examined the most important of these programs estimated that they had saved as much as $12 billion in the cost of pollution control, with approximately the same result for environmental quality as the costlier direct controls that

---

[1]Robert W. Hahn, "Economic Prescriptions for Environmental Problems", *Journal of Economic Perspectives* 3 (Spring 1989): 95–115.

APPLICATION 19-2

A MARKET FOR SO₂ EMISSIONS IN THE UNITED STATES

In 1991, the Chicago Board of Trade, which oversees the most important commodity market in the United States, voted to create a market in rights to emit sulfur dioxide (SO_2). The Board's decision can be traced directly to the U.S. Clean Air Act of 1990, which adopted a market approach to dealing with the problem of acid rain.

Coal-burning electric power plants are the major cause of acid rain. They emit sulfur dioxide through their tall smokestacks, and the sulfur dioxide, which stays in the air for two to five days, becomes acidic when it combines with moisture. Two to five days in the atmosphere, with prevailing winds from the southwest, turns Ohio Valley and Midwest emissions into a Canadian and New England pollution problem. Acid rain (and snow) harms the ability of lakes to sustain aquatic life and damages agricultural crops, forests, and even buildings.

The U.S. Clean Air Act of 1990 sets targets for sulfur dioxide emissions and implements those targets by issuing a fixed number of "permits to pollute." The total number of permits is fixed such that by the year 2000, emissions will be less than half the 1980 level. After 2000, the allowed emissions will be sharply reduced again. Most of the permits will be allocated to plants based on the plants' fuel use between 1985 and 1987. Thus the largest plants will get the most permits, but virtually all "dirty" plants will be required to reduce their emissions substantially.

Once firms have their permits in hand, they may use them or sell them as they please. Of course, for the new system to be effective, the level of emissions must be measured. All utilities subject to the new law were required to install continuous monitoring equipment by 1992. If a firm pollutes without a permit, it is subject to a $2,000 fine for each ton of excess emissions and must make up the overpollution by underpolluting by the same amount in the future.

No one yet knows what the market price of the emissions permits will be. And there is every reason to believe that it will not be constant over time. As technology for operating power plants with reduced sulfur dioxide emissions improves, the price of both the technology and the permits will surely fall. As a result, utilities will face interesting choices. On the one hand, they may choose to buy permits early and wait for improvements in technology. On the other, if they adopt emissions-reducing technology early, they could sell their permits and pocket the proceeds.

---

they replaced.[1] Application 19-2 discusses how the U.S. Clean Air Act of 1990 has created a national market in tradable permits for sulfur dioxide, the major cause of acid rain.

Governmental creation of a market in "bads" may become one of the most promising strategies for efficiently overcoming the market failure that leads to environmental pollution.

Despite the view held by most economists that market-based schemes—such as emissions taxes or tradable emissions permits—are both efficient and practical ways of regulating pollution in a market economy, many people remain unconvinced. Extension 19-1 examines why.

REGULATION FOR HEALTH AND SAFETY

The federal government (through the Department of Consumer and Corporate Affairs) approves the marketing of both prescription and nonprescription drugs

EXTENSION 19-1

RESISTANCE TO MARKET-BASED ENVIRONMENTAL POLICIES

Despite the many advantages that can be identified for market-based approaches to environmental protection, such approaches encounter considerable resistance from firms, members of the public, and environmentalists. Why?

PRODUCERS

1. *Some firms object to the costs that they are asked to pay in terms of emissions taxes or the purchase prices of emissions permits.* However, there is no reason why payments to government under any market-based scheme need to be an unjustified "tax grab." Emissions taxes need not be in excess of the costs imposed on society by the industry's activities. If government uses the introduction of a market-based scheme to raise general revenue—and thus levies emissions taxes in excess of the costs generated by the pollution—firms can oppose the extra tax burden without opposing the market-based scheme itself.

2. *The introduction of market-based measures may signal the end of a free ride that producers have been taking at society's expense.* If the firms in an industry were bearing none of the cost of its pollution, almost any antipollution scheme will impose a burden on them—but only to the extent of forcing them to bear the costs of their own activities. The difference between using direct controls and the market-based solution, however, is that the former will cost the average firm in the industry more than the market solution. (This just reflects the fact that direct controls are generally less efficient than emissions taxes or emissions permits.)

3. *Under market-based schemes (rather than direct controls), many firms feel a sense of unfairness because their competitors continue polluting while they must clean up.* Their complaints ignore the fact that those firms that continue to pollute have paid for the right to do so, either by paying effluent taxes or by buying pollution rights, and that the complaining firm could do the same if it wished (it does not do so because cleaning up is cheaper for it than paying to pollute, as the competitors are doing).

This points to a key issue in assessing market-based solutions: Such solutions must not be judged relative to a "no action" policy. Given a government's decision to reduce pollution, the market solution must be compared with other alternatives *that lower pollution by the same amount.* When this is done, much of the opposition from producers fades away.

THE PUBLIC

1. *Some members of the public have a moral opposition to selling anyone the right to pollute.* Since it involves human survival, dealing in rights to pollute seems evil to many people. This view makes difficult

in Canada. The National Transportation Agency requires that automobiles have brake lights and seat belts. Consumer and Corporate Affairs can remove dangerous goods from the marketplace. It can also set standards for product safety, such as requiring "dead man" controls that automatically stop engines in lawn mowers when the operator lets go of the handle. It also regulates "truth in advertising." The Workers' Compensation Board is broadly responsible for health and safety in the workplace. It sets detailed standards designed to reduce workers' exposure to injury and to health risks, such as asbestos.

What all of these examples have in common is that the market failure they address is in the market for information. A consumer will generally have difficulty determining if a cold remedy has dangerous side effects, what the effect of brake lights is on the chances of having an accident, or how likely a child's pajamas are to catch fire. An individual worker may be in no position to assess the risks of working with a the rational evaluation of alternative plans for dealing with a serious social problem.

2. *Opposition to the outcome where those who have the highest costs of cleaning up continue to pollute while those with the lowest costs do the cleaning up.* Morality may dictate to many observers that the biggest polluters should do the cleaning up. Economists cannot show this reaction to be wrong; they can only point out the cost in terms of higher prices, lower employment, unnecessary resource use, and less overall pollution abatement that follow from adopting such a position.

ENVIRONMENTALISTS

1. *Many environmentalists are sceptical about the efficiency and desirability of markets.* Some do not understand economists' reasoning as to why markets can be, and often are, efficient mechanisms for allocating scarce resources. Others understand the economists' case but reject it, although few complete the argument by trying to demonstrate that direct government controls will be more effective.

2. *Many environmentalists do not like the use of self-interest incentives to solve what they would regard as "social" rather than "economic" issues.* Economists who point to the voluminous evidence of the importance of self-interest incentives are often accused of ignoring higher motives such as social duty, self-sacrifice, and compassion. Although such motives are absent from the simple theories that try to explain the everyday behaviour of buyers and sellers, economists since Adam Smith have been aware that these higher motives often do exert strong influences on human behaviour.

Such higher motives are very powerful at some times and in some situations, but they do not govern many people's behaviour in the course of day-to-day living. If we want to understand how people behave in the aftermath of a flood, or an earthquake, or a war, we need motives in addition to self-interest; if we want to understand how people behave day after day in their buying and selling, we need little other than a theory of the self-interested responses to market incentives. Since control of the environment requires influencing the mass of small decisions, as well as a few large ones, the appeal to self-interest is the only currently known way to induce the required behaviour through voluntary actions.

3. *Some environmentalists have the view that resources such as clean air and pure water are above mere monetary calculation and should thus be treated in special ways.* The economist can point out that the use of this view to justify departing from market-based solutions ensures that measured material living standards will be lowered. If that is the understood and accepted price of regarding resources as special entities, then so be it!

given machine and may not be able to find out easily whether there are toxic chemicals in the workplace.

HEALTH AND SAFETY INFORMATION AS A PUBLIC GOOD

In Chapter 18, we saw that information is likely to be underproduced in private markets because many kinds of information are *public goods*. Once the flammability of different materials that are used in children's pajamas is known, making the information available to interested parents can be done at negligible marginal cost. A private firm that develops the information would be unable to recoup its investment. Thus unless the government intervenes, product information would tend to be either unavailable or available only at inefficiently high prices. Most economists would agree that information about safety in the workplace and product safety is a public good; this provides a rationale for the government either to produce such information or to require that private firms produce it.[2]

Is Good Information Enough?

In practice, most health and safety regulation goes well beyond the simple provision of information. Rather, firms are required to meet standards of workplace and product safety. Many economists have argued that, given good information, private markets will ensure efficient levels of workplace safety. To evaluate this argument, we present here a very simple example of what might happen if there were no legislated standards but everyone had accurate information about safety risks.

Consider a worker who can take a job at either Firm A or Firm B. Suppose that the worker knows that accidents at Firm A will lead the typical worker to miss two weeks of work per year, whereas the average time lost to injury at firm B is one week per year. No compensation is paid for the time spent at home due to injury. To keep the example simple, suppose also that lost pay is the only cost of accidents that is borne by workers. Equilibrium in the labour market can occur only if workers at Firm A have a higher wage than workers at Firm B. Suppose that full-time work at both firms is 50 weeks per year. Workers at Firm A can expect to be laid up and unable to work for an average of one week per year more than those at Firm B. They will thus require a wage that is 50/49 times the wage paid to workers at Firm B (assuming that they get no pleasure from spending a week at home in bed).

The result in this example that the wage at the less-safe Firm A is higher than the wage at the more-safe Firm B is simply an application of the idea of equilibrium wage differentials, first introduced in Chapter 15.

Notice that in this example, all that is required for equilibrium to occur is that the workers know the probability of accidents at each firm and that markets respond to conditions of demand and supply. No government standard needs to be set. Rather, workers who work at the firm that is less safe will demand a compensating wage differential in order to work there. Thus the greater the chance of an accident at work, the higher the wages that a firm must pay. This is illustrated by the upward-sloping curve shown in Figure 19-5. From the perspective of the employer, the curve represents the marginal wage cost (per worker) of *increasing* the probability of accidents. As accidents become more likely (moving along the horizontal axis), the firm must pay higher wages to attract workers.

The firm also has a marginal benefit of increasing the probability of accidents. That is, if improving work-place safety requires an expenditure of real resources (such as improved lighting or more frequent clean-up), then *increasing* the probability of accidents is associated with a *saving* of real resources, and this saving of resources is the marginal benefit to the firm. Since the costs of making marginal improvements in work-place safety are higher when the workplace is already quite safe, the marginal benefit of *less safety* is higher when the workplace is less safe. Thus the firm's marginal benefit curve in Figure 19-5 is downward sloping.

In equilibrium, firms will choose a level of safety such that the savings in nonwage costs of reducing safety a little bit is just equal to the increase in the wages that the firm would have to pay. Notice that the optimal rate of accidents, much like the optimal level of pollution, is not zero. Rather, it depends on the cost of reducing the level of accidents.

In the simplified world of Figure 19-5, there is no need for safety standards; if workers are perfectly informed about the risk of accidents (and about the costs that they would bear when accidents occur) and firms minimize costs, the private market will generate the allocatively efficient solution. This argument also can be extended to product safety, given the strong assumption that consumers are perfectly informed about the risks inherent in consuming the products that they buy.

With perfect information, private markets will produce allocatively efficient levels of occupational and product safety.

---

[2]People who do not agree would rely on the legal system to compel private producers and employers to develop the information. If someone is hurt by an unsafe product, the person can sue the manufacturer for damages. If the manufacturer has provided accurate information about the risks inherent in using the product, such as warning labels on medicines, the consumer's chance of winning the lawsuit is much reduced. Thus the manufacturer has an interest in developing accurate information. A similar case can be made regarding worker health and safety. In practice, however, many lawsuits of this kind are defended on the grounds that manufacturers had no knowledge of or reason to be concerned about their products' hazards. That such defenses often succeed suggests that there is an incentive to fail to develop relevant information about health and safety.

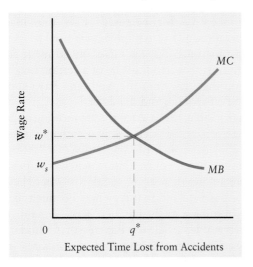

FIGURE 19-5
The Market for Occupational Safety

Competition in the labour market can induce firms to provide workplace safety. Suppose that a perfectly safe workplace would have to pay a wage of only w_s. As the expected time lost because of accidents increases, the required wage rises to compensate workers for the risk of injury. The curve that shows the higher wages is labeled MC because it gives the marginal cost to the firm per worker of letting the workplace become less safe.

The marginal benefit to the firm of reducing safety is given by the MB curve, which shows the savings per worker that the firm can obtain by reducing safety-related expenditures. At the axis, time that is lost through accidents is zero; the workplace is perfectly safe. The MB curve starts very high because the cost of making an already very safe workplace perfectly safe is likely to be very high. Thus reducing safety by a small amount from perfect safety would sharply reduce the firm's costs.

Where the two curves intersect, the marginal cost of making the workplace safer is just equal to the marginal benefit from doing so. To the left of q^*, reducing safety in the workplace saves MB and costs only MC.

Given that the MC curve is derived from the preferences of workers who are well informed about workplace risks, the market solution of q^* and w^* will be cost-minimizing for the firm and allocatively efficient.

A Role for Government

There are two main arguments for government intervention to promote health and safety. One relies on the presence of *imperfect information*. The other is based on *paternalism*.

Imperfect Information. Perfect information may be impossible to obtain or to evaluate. Our example of Firm A and Firm B could work quite well for, say, an experienced machinist who is comparing two machine shops. Such a worker will have a good sense of what can be expected on the shop floor and may be able to estimate the chances of injury quite accurately. If the government requires all firms to publish their accident histories every year, the worker can make an informed choice. Such a choice may be impossible, however, when the cause of harm in the workplace is a chemical that might cause cancer. Evaluation of carcinogens often takes many years; there is likely to be uncertainty in the medical literature; and it is very likely that the typical worker will have a difficult time interpreting the information, even if it is made easily available.

Information about safety risks in offices is also unlikely to be available, at least in some cases. Most white-collar workers have no idea what their buildings are made of, how quickly the buildings would burn, or what kind of emergency lighting would be available in case of a fire. Further, it would not be easy for them to decode the blueprints of different buildings to make informed choices about fire safety.

Similar problems arise with product safety. The typical automobile driver is not able to make informed choices about the benefits of collapsing steering columns, reinforced door panels, or antilock braking systems. A complete maintenance report on each airplane that you fly on would probably be of little help to you in assessing the safety of the airplane. Less dramatically, it would be prohibitively expensive for the government to develop accident data for every consumer product and then to let consumers sift through the information as they decided what to buy.

Safety standards can free workers and consumers from attempting difficult calculations that they are ill-equipped to make. When information is costly or impossible to process, standards can enhance efficiency.

Paternalism. One of the most cost-effective regulations in existence involves collapsing steering columns in automobiles. (The idea is that in the event of a front-end collision, the steering column breaks rather than impaling the driver.) According to one estimate, the protection afforded by the collapsing steering column saves about 1,300 lives per year at a total cost of $188.5 million—this implies a cost *per saved life* of $145,000. On pure efficiency grounds, matters might be further improved if automobile manufacturers offered the collapsing steering column as an option and were required to provide data on the hazards of noncollapsing steering columns. Only very ardent proponents of laissez faire would argue for such a policy.

Another safety regulation requires that children's sleepwear meet a nonflammability standard. (The standard requires that the fabric not burst into flame when it is lit.) This regulation is less cost-effective than the requirement of collapsing steering columns. The cost per life saved is estimated to be about $1.9 million. Still, few people would wish to permit parents to choose flammable pajamas at somewhat lower cost. It is hard to think of a government regulation that is more literally paternalistic!

HEALTH AND SAFETY REGULATION IN PRACTICE

In Chapter 18, we noted that even when there is market failure, the case for government intervention is weakened by the possibility of government failure. Perhaps the most widely cited examples of government failure arise in the area of health and safety regulation. A notorious example of (temporary) regulatory failure is the short-lived ban on saccharin. Saccharin was banned when huge doses were shown to cause cancer in rats. When the required doses were seen to exceed anything humans were likely to take, the ban was lifted.

Assessing the risk that a product will cause cancer can be extremely difficult, and scientists' estimates of the risk often changes with new information. For example, dioxin, which was once believed to be among the most toxic of substances produced by industry, is now widely believed to be much less dangerous. At the same time, many scientists are coming to believe that electric blankets may increase the risk of cancer. Uncertainty about the actual risks engendered by the use of different products greatly increases the difficulty of health and safety regulation and increases the economic cost of regulation as well. If regulatory standards and rules could be expected to stay fixed, businesses could plan and act accordingly. However, new scientific evidence often leads to changes in regulation, which can require that firms change their techniques and their products, adding to the average cost of doing business. There is no obvious solution to this problem.

As with pollution, health and safety regulators often take an engineering approach to their task. Rather than specifying a particular outcome or providing incentives for increased safety, they mandate that certain kinds of equipment be used to perform certain functions. For example, government regulation requires that handrails be of a certain height and a certain distance from the wall, and have supports of specified spacing and diameter.

In principle, the case for the engineering approach may be stronger for safety regulation than it is for pollution control because the alternative of a "safety tax" is generally not feasible. Unfortunately, the problems inherent in all engineering standards—that they may become obsolete and that they may be much more effective in some settings than in others—remain. To the extent possible, efficiency dictates that standards be expressed in terms of *required performance* rather than *required design and materials*. The reason for this is that it provides an incentive for firms to find inexpensive ways of meeting the standards, thereby reducing the cost of complying with them.

BENEFIT-COST ANALYSIS OF SOCIAL REGULATION

The social purpose of health, safety, and pollution regulation is obvious. No one wants unsafe products, hazardous workplaces, and ugly or dangerous environments. However, even for as wealthy a society as Canada in the 1990s, the goals of health, safety, and a clean environment cannot be absolute ones. There is no such thing as a completely safe workplace or product; it is impossible to establish that a prescription drug can never be harmful, and it is difficult to think of any human activity that does not generate some amount of pollution. Given that these problems will always be with us to some degree, the relevant question is, *To what degree?* Economics can help provide an answer by evaluating costs as well as benefits—a recurring theme of this chapter and this book.

For economic efficiency, environmental, health, and safety risks should be reduced to the point where the marginal social cost of further reduction is just equal to the marginal social benefit of further reduction.

Many critics of the economic approach to social regulation rightly point out that these costs and benefits are often very difficult to measure. True as this may be in certain cases, the logic of the benefit-cost criterion still holds. Thus unless public policies attempt to equate marginal benefits and marginal costs, scarce social resources will be wasted and we will get fewer positive results than could be obtained from the resources that are used.

Cost-effectiveness analysis is a procedure that is much easier to perform than cost-benefit analysis. In cost-effectiveness analysis, the analyst holds constant the *outputs* of a policy and looks for the cheapest (most cost-effective) way of pursuing those outputs. Such analysis is particularly useful when it is difficult to measure the value of outputs. A prominent example involves the cost of saving lives. We do not presume to put a dollar value on a human life. Cost-effectiveness analysis, however, tells us that in designing programs to save human lives, we should implement programs that do so at lowest cost first. If we do not, we will be wasting resources that could be devoted to saving lives and thus will be saving fewer lives than we could.

A study of regulations designed to save lives reveals an extraordinary range in the cost per life saved of actual and proposed regulations. The most cost-effective is the collapsing steering column, at $145,000 per life. The least cost-effective regulation in place at the time of the study involved the use of DES in cattle feed and was calculated at $190 million per life saved, over 1,000 times as much.[3] We do not need to put a specific value on human life to know that there are thousands of ways to spend $190 million and save more than one life. Consider, for example, the hiring of crossing guards who would work during rush hours, policing the most traveled street corners that do not have crossing guards. Assuming a salary of $19,000 per year per guard (which is a part-time job), 10,000 such guards could be hired per year. They would surely save more than one life. Moreover, researchers have identified numerous examples in which the cost of life-saving interventions is nearly zero; examples include windshields with adhesive bonding rather than rubber gaskets, elimination of flammable fabrics in children's sleepwear, and immunization of children for measles, mumps, and rubella. At the other end of the spectrum, however, a number of interventions such as radionuclide emission control at coal-fired indus-

trial boilers, sickle-cell screening for all newborns, and control of benzene emission at rubber tire manufacturing plants are estimated to cost more than $1 million per life-year saved.[4]

The rationale for seeking efficiency in social regulation comes from the same source as the rationale for seeking efficiency in other areas. The more efficiently the goals of social regulation are pursued, the more resources will be available to pursue other things of value, and the more benefits can be achieved for any given amount of resource use.

REGULATORY REFORM

Growing concerns about a variety of perceived problems with Canada's regulatory structure—including obsolescence in the face of rapid changes in technology and world markets, significant compliance costs, and inefficiencies in the regulatory process—have led to a number of developments in Canada.[5] (There have been similar developments in the United States, Europe, and Japan.) We have already encountered the deregulation trend in Chapter 13 in the context of competition policy, but the current debate and trend concerning regulation of the economy extends beyond the direct regulation of industry.

Several years ago, the now-disbanded Economic Council of Canada published two major reports of the regulatory process, and included a number of specific recommendations. In one report, the Council proposed that an extensive consultative process be part of any major government attempt at regulatory change, that any major new regulatory proposals be subjected to formal benefit-cost analysis, and that the government review existing regulations and operations of regulatory agencies on a regular basis.

In the other report, the Council made proposals that touched on a wide range of regulated activities—trucking, airlines, telecommunications, agriculture, occupational health and safety, and the environment. The general thrust of its proposals was to "streamline the regulatory process and where possible to reduce the extent of regulation." Increased

---

[3]John F. Morral III, "A Review of the Record", *Regulation*, November–December 1986, pp. 25–34.

[4]Tammy Tengs et al., "Five-Hundred Life-saving Interventions and Their Cost-effectiveness", self-published manuscript, 1994.

[5]This section draws on the discussion by Professor John Strick of the University of Windsor, *The Economics of Government Regulation. Theory and Canadian Practice* (Toronto: Thompson, 1990).

competition and increased application of market forces and financial incentives were also stressed.

In the mid 1980s, the Canadian government took up this theme of regulatory reform and announced its Regulatory Reform Strategy. Although it did not endorse comprehensive deregulation, the government committed itself not only to limit the proliferation of new regulations but also "to 'regulate smarter' through greater efficiency, greater accountability, and greater sensitivity to those affected by federal regulations." The strategy invoked a number of principles, including

- Recognition of the importance of markets

- Continued use of regulation to achieve social and economic objectives

- Use of benefit-cost analysis to screen new initiatives

- Increased public access and participation in the process

Many of the new procedures found their way into practice, and regulatory hearings have become a regular part of the public policy landscape. Whether the new procedures have in fact met the stated objectives is not yet clear; many critics argue that the new processes, though open, are inefficient. For example, the hearings that finally ended Bell Canada's monopoly on long-distance phone service lasted over 18 months and cost close to $100 million.

Most economists would support the principles of the Regulatory Reform Strategy. Even if it is fully adopted, however, difficult social choices and difficult technical problems, of both measurement and program design, will remain. Moreover, when health, life, and safety are at stake, there are many who will never be comfortable with the results of decentralized decision making, no matter how well-informed the parties to private transactions may be. The desire to protect people from the negative consequences of their actions extends well beyond an interest in internalizing externalities or providing efficient levels of information.

Economic analysis can help society to examine the costs and the consequences of social regulation. Most important, it can help regulators to achieve desired consequences at minimum cost and thus reduce the level of government failure. It can help us to decide *how best* to intervene in the interest of health and safety, but it cannot tell us *how much* we should intervene.

SUMMARY

A. THE ECONOMICS OF POLLUTION CONTROL

- Almost all economic activity is subject to at least some government regulation. Government regulation, of some form or another, is used to deal with every type of market failure—public goods, externalities, natural monopoly problems, information asymmetries, and social values.

- Economic regulation typically refers to the regulation of natural monopoly, which was discussed in Chapter 13. Social regulation is the regulation of economic behaviour to advance social goals where neither competition nor economic regulation can be expected to do the job.

- Most pollution problems can be analyzed as negative externalities. Polluting firms and households going about their daily business do harm to the environment and fail to take account of the costs that they impose on others.

- The allocatively efficient level of pollution in any activity is generally not zero; it is the level where the marginal cost of further pollution reduction is just equal to the marginal damage done by a unit of pollution. If a firm or a household faces incentives that cause it to internalize fully the costs that pollution imposes, it will choose the allocatively efficient level of pollution.

- Pollution can be regulated either directly or indirectly. Direct controls are used most often. Direct controls are often inefficient because they require that all polluters meet the same standard regardless of the benefits and costs of doing so. Indirect controls, such as taxes on emissions, are more efficient; ideally, they cause firms to internalize perfectly the pollution externality. Tradable emissions permits could have the same effect as taxes without requiring regulators to know as much about the technology of pollution abatement.

B. REGULATION FOR HEALTH AND SAFETY

- Health and safety regulation covers workplace health and safety and product safety. Some economists have argued that regulation of this kind is unnecessary be-cause if people are well informed about health and safety risks, the level of resources devoted to safety and health will be allocatively efficient.

- Information about health and safety risks is often difficult to obtain or to evaluate. Society may also choose not to permit people to face certain kinds of risks. In either of these cases, health and safety regulation addresses a real market failure. Government failure is common in the areas of health and safety regulation.

C. BENEFIT-COST ANALYSIS OF SOCIAL REFULATION

- Cost-effectiveness analysis is a method of evaluating regulations when the benefits are hard to measure. It is particularly helpful for evaluating regulations that are designed to save lives, where the most cost-effective regulation is the one that saves the most lives per dollar of cost.
- Increased use of benefit-cost and cost-effectiveness analysis could reduce the social costs imposed by social regulation. Alternatively, holding social cost constant, it could increase the benefits from social regulation.

KEY CONCEPTS

Costs and benefits of pollution abatement

The efficient level of pollution

Direct pollution controls

Emissions taxes and tradable emissions permits

Regulatory failure

Cost-effectiveness analysis

Regulatory reform

DISCUSSION QUESTIONS

1. Many occupations are licensed, either by governments or by professional organizations (such as provincial engineering associations, which are run by professional engineers). Are economists licensed? Should they be? Why or why not?

2. "Pollution is wrong. When a corporation pollutes, it commits assault on the citizens of the country, and it should be punished." Comment on this statement in light of the discussion in this chapter.

3. Assume that the following statements are true. What do they imply about the argument that health and safety regulations are necessary to promote economic efficiency?

   a. Welders who work on the upper stories of unfinished skyscrapers are paid more than welders who work only indoors.
   b. Following a commercial airplane crash, the stock market value of the airline company tends to fall.
   c. Within a city, housing of a given structural quality tends to sell for less, the greater the health risk posed by air quality in the neighbourhood.
   d. For decades, asbestos was widely used as insulation. Installers of asbestos insulation routinely

breathed asbestos fibre in concentrations that are now known to be potentially lethal. For some years, asbestos producers were aware that asbestos was dangerous but did not share this information with installers.
   e. Until the mid 1980s, the upholstery in airline seats emitted lethal fumes when the seats were burning.

4. Consider the following (alleged) facts about pollution control and indicate what influence they might have on policy determination.

   a. The cost of meeting government pollution requirements is about $300 per person per year.
   b. More than one-third of the world's known oil supplies lie under the ocean floor, and there is no known blowout-proof method of recovery.
   c. Sulfur-removal requirements and strip-mining regulations have led to the tripling of the cost of a ton of coal used in generating electricity.
   d. Every million dollars that is spent on pollution control creates 47 new jobs in the economy.

5. Suppose you were given the job of drafting a law to regulate water pollution over the entire length of some river.

a. How would you determine how much total pollution to permit?

b. What control mechanism would you use to regulate emissions into the river? Why?

c. Would you impose the same rules on cities as on farms?

d. Would your answer to a, b, or c depend on the quality of information that would be available to you? How and why?

6. Under current regulations, cleaning up all known toxic waste sites in the United States would cost between $300 billion and $700 billion. Yet according to the *New York Times,* "Virtually all of the risk to human health, most analysts agree, could be eliminated for a tiny fraction of these sums." The same article notes that many experts argue that once dangerous sites are identified, "the cleanup should be carefully aimed at saving lives rather than restoring land to preindustrial condition." In one site, the former goal could be achieved for $71,000; the latter would cost over $13 million. How would you frame a benefit-cost analysis of different strategies for cleaning up toxic waste?

7. The text presents several values of regulation per human life saved, ranging from $145,000 to $190 million. What do you think is the value of a statistical human life? Are there ever circumstances in which we would be willing to trade one group's lives for another's lives—or for another's comfort?

8. The federal government has imposed many regulations aimed at reducing the pollution which is generated by driving. The more familiar regulations are direct—catalytic converters, fuel efficiency, and the like. Given the discussion in the chapter, why do you think the government opted for such direct controls? Can you think of any indirect controls currently in use to reduce automobile pollution?

9. The federal government has a very rigorous approval process for all drugs introduced into the Canadian market. Drug makers are required to demonstrate safety and effectiveness through a process of animal and human trials that can take as long as 10 years. Is it efficient to have the same approval process for all drugs? Explain your answer.

CHAPTER 20

TAXATION AND PUBLIC EXPENDITURE

PUBLIC VERSUS PRIVATE SECTOR
SCOPE OF GOVERNMENT ACTIVITY
EQUITY AND EFFICIENCY
EVOLUTION OF POLICY

In Chapter 19, we saw some of the reasons why the scope of government is so extensive. Taxation is needed to raise money for public spending, and it can also play a policy role in its own right. Taxes can affect the distribution of income—some people get taxed more than others. Moreover, by taxing some activities heavily and others lightly or not at all, the tax system can influence the allocation of resources. In some cases, tax policy is carefully designed with such effects in mind; in other cases, the effects are unintentional by-products of policies pursued for other purposes.

By far the largest item on which Canadian governments spend—both federally and provincially—is on social programs. For the past few years, Canada's social programs have been under significant pressure for reform, the pressure coming both from the governments' tight fiscal situation and from an overall desire to reconstruct the social programs in ways that will be both more efficient and more fair. Coincident with these pressures to reform Canada's social programs has been pressure for the devolution of power from the federal government to the provincial governments.

In this chapter, we examine the various sources of government tax revenues and the various types of government expenditures. We ask how taxation and public expenditure affect the allocation of resources and the distribution of income, and to what extent they are effective tools of public policy. We begin with a discussion of taxation in Canada. We then examine the basis on which one would evaluate a tax system, emphasizing the distinction between equity and efficiency. The types of public expenditures in Canada are then examined along with the important concept of "fiscal federalism." The five pillars of Canadian social policy are then described, as are some of the current pressures for reform of social programs. Finally, we conclude this chapter with a discussion of evaluating the overall role of government.

Taxation in Canada

There is a bewildering array of taxes in Canada today. These are levied at the federal, provincial, and local levels. Some are highly visible, such as income taxes and the Goods and Services Tax (GST). Others are all but invisible to most people because they do not show up on income tax forms or on receipts for purchases. For example, there are special taxes levied on the sales of alcohol, cigarettes, and gasoline, but these taxes are levied directly on the producers (rather than the retailers) of these goods. People and firms are taxed on what they earn, on what they spend, and on what they own. Not only are taxes numerous, but taken together they raise a tremendous amount of revenue. Canada is not alone in the significance of government taxation. Table 20-1 shows for several countries in 1993 the total tax revenues as a fraction of Gross Domestic Product. At the top of the list is Denmark, which collects taxes equal to 50 percent of GDP; at the bottom is Turkey, collecting only 23 percent of GDP in tax revenue. Canada lies roughly in the middle, with total tax revenue equal to 36 percent of GDP.

SOME DEFINITIONS

Before discussing some details about the Canadian tax system, we examine two general concepts—*tax expenditures*, and the *progressivity* of taxes.

Tax Expenditures

Sometimes taxes are used in ways that are similar to spending programs. For example, one way to deal with polluted rivers is to spend public funds to clean them up. An alternative, as we saw in Chapter 19, is to use taxes to penalize polluters or to give tax concessions to firms that install pollution-abating devices. Tax concessions that seek to induce market responses are called **tax expenditures**—tax revenue forgone to achieve purposes that the government believes are desirable.

The difference between a tax expenditure and an ordinary budgetary expenditure is that a tax expenditure represents *a reduction in tax revenue* whereas an ordinary expenditure represents *an increase in spending*. Because tax expenditures represent foregone earnings for the government, they are considerably less visible than actual budgetary expenditures. They therefore usually receive little scrutiny from Parliament or the public. But this does not mean that they are small or unimportant. On the contrary, tax expenditures are very significant in the current Canadian economy. Table 20-2 gives some examples of federal personal income tax expenditures. As is clear from the table, specific tax expenditures range in value from a few million to many billion dollars per year.

TABLE 20-1
International Comparison of Government
Tax Revenues, 1993

Country	Total Tax Revenue as Percent of GDP
Denmark	50.0
Sweden	49.5
Netherlands	48.2
Finland	46.8
Norway	45.8
Belgium	45.7
France	44.0
Austria	43.4
Italy	43.2
Germany	39.7
Ireland	37.1
Canada	36.1
New Zealand	35.6
Spain	34.7
United Kingdom	34.4
Switzerland	32.5
Iceland	32.2
Portugal	31.1
United States	30.0
Japan	29.4[a]
Turkey	22.7

Canada lies roughly in the middle of other developed countries in terms of total tax revenue as a share of GDP. The figures reflect total tax revenues by all levels of government, including mandatory contributions to public pension plans. Of those countries shown in the table, Denmark has the highest tax burden, at 50 percent of GDP; Turkey has the lowest, at under 23 percent of GDP.

[a]Data for Japan is for 1992.

(*Source:* David Perry, "Fiscal Figures", *Canadian Tax Journal* 1994.)

TABLE 20-2
Some Federal Personal Income Tax Expenditures for 1992

Nature of Tax Expenditure	Millions of Dollars
Nontaxation of lottery and gambling winnings	900
Deductions for clergy residence	50
Tuition fee credit	155
Northern residents deduction	235
Investment tax credit	58
Nontaxation of employer-paid health and dental benefits	1,125
Nontaxation of employer-paid premiums for life insurance	160
Deductions for contributions to RRSPs	3,685
Nontaxation of investment income inside RRSPs	2,755
Deductions for contributions to employer-sponsored pension plans	4,990
Nontaxation of investment income inside employer-sponsored pension plans	7,690
Nontaxation of capital gains on principal residences	8,955
Charitable donations credit	865
Child-care expense deductions	315
Subtotal	31,938
Other personal income-tax expenditures	32,121
Total personal income-tax expenditures	64,059

There is a wide variety of tax expenditures, ranging in size from a few million dollars to several billion dollars per year. The table shows some selected personal income tax expenditures for the federal government. Each number represents tax revenue that is not earned due to the presence of some exemption or deduction in the federal personal income-tax system. For example, if the federal government did not permit tuition fees to be tax deductible, its personal income-tax revenues in 1992 would have been $155 million higher. Note that the total excludes tax expenditures that arise out of federal-provincial tax-sharing arrangements.

(*Source: Government of Canada Tax Expenditures,* December 1994.)

Progressivity

When the government taxes one group in society more heavily than it taxes another, it influences the distribution of income. The effect of taxes on the distribution of income can be summarized in terms of *progressivity*. A **progressive tax** takes a larger percentage of income from high-income people than it does from low-income people. A **proportional tax** takes amounts of money from people in direct proportion to their income—for example, every individual pays 10 percent of their income in taxes. A **regressive tax** takes a larger percentage of income from people the lower their income.

Note that the progressivity or regressivity of a tax is expressed in terms of *shares* of income rather than absolute dollar amounts. So, a tax which collects $1000 from each individual clearly collects the same dollar amount from everybody, though it collects a higher share of income from low-income people than from higher-income people. A tax of this type—often called a **poll tax** or a *lump-sum tax*—is therefore a regressive tax.

Since a progressive tax takes a larger share of income from high-income people than it does from low-income people, progressive taxes reduce the inequality

TABLE 20-3

Taxes as a Percentage of Canadian GDP and Their Division Among Levels of Government, 1992

	Taxes as Percentage of GDP	Percentage of Taxes Divided	
		Federal	Provincial/Local
Personal income taxes	15.0	62.8	37.2
Corporate income taxes	2.0	65.0	35.0
Property taxes	4.0	—	100.0
General sales taxes	5.2	47.9	52.1
Excise taxes			
(fuel, alcohol, and cigarettes)	2.1	46.4	53.6
Import duties	0.6	100.0	—
Health and social insurance levies	3.6	62.6	37.4
Other taxes	2.3	15.8	84.2
Total Taxes	34.8		

Taxes on personal income raise the most revenue, two thirds of which goes to the federal government. The first column shows the percentage of Canadian GDP taken by various taxes. The next two columns show the percentage division of the revenues from each tax going to each level of government.

(*Source: The National Finances 1994,* The Canadian Tax Foundation.)

of income. A regressive tax increases the inequality of income.

THE CANADIAN TAX SYSTEM

Taxes are collected by the federal government, by each of the provinces, and by thousands of cities, townships, and villages. The federal government collects about as much revenue as all other governments put together. The provinces, in turn, collect about four times as much as local governments. The federal government gets over 50 percent of its revenues from taxes paid directly by individuals and corporations and over 20 percent from taxes collected on the sale of goods and services (mainly the GST). The provinces get just over 40 percent from income taxes and about 35 percent from sales taxes.[1] The municipalities rely almost exclusively on property taxes for their tax revenues. The diversity and yield of various taxes are shown in Table 20-3.

Personal Income Taxes

Personal income taxes are paid directly to the government by individuals. The amount of tax any individual pays is the result of a fairly complicated series of calculations. All types of income are included in what is called total income, although certain types of income qualify for total or partial exemption. Then a number of allowable deductions are subtracted from total income to determine taxable income. Once taxable income is calculated, the amount of tax payable is then calculated by applying different tax rates to different levels of income. There are three federal personal income tax rates, each applying within what is called a tax bracket. In 1996, the three **tax brackets** were roughly $0–$28,000, $28,000–$56,000, and greater than $56,000. The federal tax rates in these brackets were 17 percent, 26 percent, and 29 percent, respectively.

To see how this system of differential tax rates and tax brackets operates, consider an individual who has a taxable income of $70,000. To the federal government, she pays at a rate of 17 percent on the first $28,000 ($4,760), at a rate of 26 percent on the next $28,000 ($7,280), and at a rate of 29 percent on all income *above* $56,000 (0.29 × $14,000 = $4,060). Her total federal income tax payable is thus equal to $16,100.

Average Versus Marginal Tax Rates. This brings us to the important distinction between an individual's *average tax rate* and *marginal tax rate*. The **average tax rate** paid by a taxpayer is his or her total income tax payment divided by total income. In the previous example, the average tax rate is 23 percent ($16,100/$70,000 = 0.23). The taxpayer's **marginal tax rate** is the amount of tax he or she would pay on

---

[1]Each of the lower levels of government also receives revenue in the form of transfers from more senior governments. We examine such transfer payments shortly.

an additional dollar of income—for this individual, 29 percent since she is in the highest tax bracket.

Provincial Taxation.   The three federal personal income-tax rates do not represent the complete taxation of personal income in Canada, for two reasons. First, both the federal and many provincial governments have added more progressivity to the personal income tax by levying surcharges that kick in at various higher levels of income.

Second, the provincial governments also tax personal income. Quebec runs its own income-tax system, whereas the other nine provinces simply use the federal tax base (and federally distributed tax forms) and essentially "top up" federal taxes. Except for Quebec, taxpayers pay a single amount to Revenue Canada, which then distributes the total between the federal government and each province according to the amount collected from residents of that province.

Table 20-4 shows the marginal income-tax rates paid by a single taxpayer at various income levels and in each province. The figures vary across provinces because different provincial rates are added onto the common federal rate. Average tax rates rise continually with income as more and more income becomes subject to the top marginal tax rate. Currently in most provinces an average tax rate of 40 percent is reached when income is about $100,000. As can be seen from the table, the combined marginal tax rate rises as income rises; this rising marginal tax rate contributes to the progressivity of the income tax system.

The 1987 Reforms.   Many of the elements of the current personal income tax system date from a major federal reform which occurred in 1987. The theme of that reform was to broaden the tax base by eliminating a number of exemptions and deductions and to lower marginal tax rates. The new system also reduced the number of tax brackets from ten to the current three.

Although the changes introduced in 1987 were substantial and were intended to be part of a comprehensive reform of the tax system, the personal income-tax system continues to change. A special levy has been introduced on high-income earners, intended to "claw back" social benefits such as family allowances. Also, both federal and provincial governments have introduced temporary surtaxes on medium and high incomes to help deal with growing fiscal deficits. As of 1995, these surtaxes had pushed the top marginal rate above 50 percent in all provinces except Alberta.

The 1987 reforms simplified the income-tax system, removed loopholes and broadened the tax base. The subsequent levying of surtaxes, however, made the tax system more complex and significantly increased the top marginal tax rates. These developments run counter to the principles that guided the 1987 reforms. They also raise the question of how high tax rates can become without causing major shrinkages in the tax base as some people emigrate, some move to the underground economy, and some choose leisure over work.

TABLE 20-4
Combined Marginal Personal Income Tax Rates for a Single Taxpayer in Selected Provinces, 1994

Province	\$10,000	\$25,000	\$50,000	\$75,000	\$100,000
Newfoundland	25.6	27.6	44.7	51.3	51.3
PEI	24.1	26.1	42.3	48.6	50.3
Nova Scotia	24.1	26.1	42.3	52.0	53.8
New Brunswick	24.8	26.8	43.4	49.9	51.4
Quebec	30.1	36.2	48.2	52.9	52.9
Ontario	42.4	25.8	41.9	53.2	53.2
Manitoba	27.9	26.9	44.3	50.4	50.4
Saskatchewan	30.5	27.5	45.5	51.9	51.9
Alberta	26.2	24.3	40.1	46.1	46.1
British Columbia	22.9	24.9	40.4	51.1	54.2

Tax rates vary across provinces due to different provincial add-ons and surtaxes. These rates, which include federal and provincial surtaxes, have been creeping up over the last few years. By 1994, the combined maximum marginal rate exceeded 50 percent in all but one province (Alberta) and approached 55 percent in some.

(*Source: The National Finances 1994*, Canadian Tax Foundation.)

Corporate Taxes

The federal corporate income tax is, for practical purposes, a flat-rate tax on profits as defined by the taxing authorities—which includes the return on capital as well as economic profits. In 1995, the rate was 28 percent.

As with the personal income tax, the 1987 reforms not only lowered tax rates but also broadened the tax base, and on the whole, the changes tended to raise taxes paid by corporations. The broadening of the tax base was accomplished primarily by eliminating tax concessions, called investment tax credits, that had been used to encourage investment.

Recently the British Columbia government instituted a corporate wealth tax. This is an annual levy on the value of each firm's assets. It is paid whether the firm makes profits or losses. Such corporate wealth taxes are almost unknown in other industrialized countries, and their introduction in British Columbia was bitterly criticized by the business community and would-be foreign investors, especially from Southeast Asia.

Excise and Sales Taxes

An excise tax is levied on a particular commodity. In many countries, commodities such as tobacco, alcohol, and gasoline are singled out for high rates of excise taxation. Because these commodities usually account for a much greater proportion of the expenditure of lower-income than higher-income groups, the excise taxes on them are regressive.

A sales tax applies to the sale of all or most goods and services. All provinces except Alberta impose a retail sales tax. Such a tax is mildly regressive, because poorer families tend to spend a larger proportion of their incomes than richer families. For example, suppose there is a 7 percent comprehensive sales tax. A family that earns $25,000 per year and saves nothing will pay 7 percent of its income on sales taxes; a family that earns $70,000 per year and saves $10,000 will pay 6 percent.

Both excise and sales taxes are often referred to as "indirect" taxes to contrast them with income taxes, which are levied directly on the income of individuals or firms.

The Goods and Services Tax. Since 1991, Canada has had a country-wide tax which applies at the same rate (7 percent) to the sale of all goods and services (with a few exceptions, such as basic groceries). The Goods and Services Tax (GST) was introduced—despite enormous political controversy—for a number of reasons. First, it followed the modern trend in taxing expenditure rather than income. One problem with taxing income is that interest earnings from accumulated savings get counted as income and thus get taxed. Income taxes therefore discourage saving by lowering the after-tax rate of return to saving. In contrast, the GST only applies to the value of expenditure. Since the GST does not tax income (and therefore does not tax interest income) it does not discourage saving.

Second, the GST does not distort the relative prices of goods and services because it is applied at the same rate to all goods and services; in contrast, the old Manufacturers Sales Tax (MST) which the GST replaced applied only to goods and thus raised the price of goods relative to services. Third, it followed the trend in almost all other developed nations (except the United States), which levy similar taxes; they are called *value added taxes* (VAT) in Europe.

In practice, the GST works by taxing a firm on the gross value of its output and then allowing a tax credit equal to the taxes paid on the inputs that were produced by other firms. Effectively, this taxes each firm's contribution to the value of final output—its value added. The result is the same as if each good and service bore a 7 percent tax when it was sold to its final user. An example of the operation of the GST for the case of the stages leading from the mining of iron ore to the manufacture of a washing machine is illustrated in Figure 20-1.

As is clear from the figure, the GST is a *multistage* tax, applying at each stage of the production process. One advantage of using a multistage tax is that it reduces *tax cascading,* which is the term used to describe the fact that under the MST some commodities effectively got taxed more than once. For example, consider again the case of the washing machine in Figure 20-1. If sales taxes were levied on all transactions, with no offsetting tax credits applied to inputs in the manufacturing process, the ore would be taxed three times: when it was sold to the steel maker, when the steel was sold to the appliance manufacturer, and when the appliance was sold to the consumer. Similarly, the steel would be taxed twice. The GST eliminates this cascading. Once the tax on the ore is collected when it is sold to the steel maker, its value is not taxed again, since further purchasers are given a tax credit for the tax embodied in their purchases.

The elimination of tax cascading is especially important when considering investment and international trade. When a firm invests in a new machine

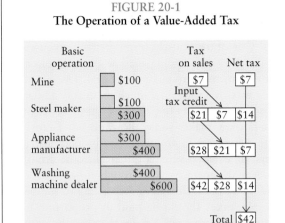

FIGURE 20-1
The Operation of a Value-Added Tax

A tax on value added is the same as a tax on the value of total output produced by a firm with a credit allowed for the tax paid to other firms from which it has purchased produced inputs. The example is for the stages involved as iron ore is mined and then sold to a steel maker, the steel then sold to an appliance manufacturer, and the washing machine sold to a retailer and then to a consumer. The example makes the simplifying assumption that no produced inputs are used in the mining operation (so that the value of the iron ore is all value added); at all further stages, however, the use of produced inputs makes the firm's value added less than the value of final output at that stage. The steel maker's value added is $200, and its tax is thus $14; $21 on the total value of its output less the $7 credit on the taxes already paid by the mine on the value of the iron ore. Total taxes paid equal $42, which is 7 percent of the $600 value of the final product; each firm pays 7 percent of its share in creating that $600 value.

or builds a new plant, many of its purchases will be subject to sales tax. Under a single-stage tax, this is the end of the story, and the sales tax clearly raises the cost of investment to the firm. With a multistage tax, the firm gets a credit for the taxes already paid on its purchases of goods and machines. This reduces the cost of investment to the firm.

In spite of its being an improvement over the MST, the GST proved to be extremely unpopular, partly because most Canadians were unaware of the MST, and its deficiencies. Unlike provincial sales taxes, the MST was "invisible"; it was applied before the retail transaction, and hence its presence was hidden in retail selling prices. Much of the opposition to the GST came from small business, farmers, fisher-

men, and professionals, who feared the burden of record keeping and paperwork that such a complicated system entails. Others feared that once the GST was introduced, governments could easily raise more revenue by increasing the GST rate.

Being a tax applied to expenditure rather than income, the GST taken alone would be mildly regressive, because the proportion of income saved, and hence not taxed, rises with income. This characteristic was avoided by exempting food and, more importantly, giving low- and middle-income people a refundable tax credit, which for the poor exceeds the value of GST that they would pay even if they spent all of their incomes on taxable commodities.

Property Taxes

The property tax is the most important Canadian tax that is based on wealth, and it an important source of revenue for municipalities. It is different from any other important tax because it is not related directly to a current transaction. In contrast, income taxes are levied on the current payment to a factor of production (income) and sales taxes are levied on the value of a currently purchased good or service.

Taxing the value of existing property creates two problems. First, someone has to assess what the property is worth. Because the assessment is only an estimate, it is always subject to challenge. Second, sometimes owners of valuable property have low *incomes* (though considerable wealth) and thus have difficulty paying the tax.

The progressivity of the property tax has been studied extensively. It is obvious that the rich typically live in more expensive houses than the poor, and thus pay more in property taxes. But this does not mean that the rich pay more property taxes *as a fraction of their income* than the poor. Thus it is not readily apparent that property taxes are progressive. Indeed, most studies have shown that the proportion of income spent on housing tends to decrease with income. This suggests, therefore, that the property tax tends to be mildly regressive in its overall effect.

EVALUATING THE TAX SYSTEM

To evaluate the *tax system* (as opposed to a specific tax within the system), the important question is this: Holding constant the amount of revenue to be raised, what makes one tax system better or worse than another? Economists deal with this question by considering two aspects of taxation—equity and efficiency. We deal with equity first.

TAXATION AND EQUITY

Debate about income distribution and tax policy usually involves the important but hard-to-define concepts of *equality* and *equity*.

Equality Versus Equity

To tax everyone *equally* can mean several things. It might mean that everyone should pay the same amount—as would be the case with a lump-sum tax. But this would clearly be much harder on the unemployed worker than on the heiress. It might mean that everyone should pay the same proportion of income—say, a flat 20 percent, whether rich or poor, living alone or supporting eight children, healthy or suffering from a costly-to-treat disease. It might mean that each should pay an amount of tax such that everyone's income after taxes is the same—which would remove any incentive to earn an above-average income. Or it might mean none of these things.

Unlike equality, *equity* (or fairness) is a normative concept; what one group thinks is fair may seem outrageous to another. Two principles can be helpful in assessing equity in taxation: equity according to *ability to pay,* and equity according to *benefits received.*

The Ability-to-Pay Principle. Most people view an equitable tax system as being based on people's ability to pay taxes. In considering equity that is based on ability to pay, two concepts need to be distinguished.

Vertical equity concerns equity *across* income groups; it focuses on comparisons between individuals or families with different levels of income. The concept of vertical equity is central to discussions of the progressivity of taxation. Proponents of progressive taxation argue as follows. First, taxes should be based on ability to pay. Second, the greater one's income, the greater the percentage of income that is available for goods and services beyond the bare necessities. It follows, therefore, that the greater one's income, the greater the proportion of income that is available to pay taxes. Thus an ability-to-pay standard of vertical equity requires progressive taxation.

Horizontal equity concerns equity *within* a given income group; it is concerned with establishing just who should be considered equal to whom in terms of ability to pay taxes. Two households with the same in-

come may have different numbers of children to support. One of the households may have greater dental expenses, leaving less for life's necessities and for taxes. One of the households may incur expenses that are necessary for earning income (e.g., requirements to buy uniforms or to pay union dues). There is no objective way to decide how much these and similar factors affect the ability to pay taxes. In practice, the income-tax law makes some allowance for factors that create differences in ability to pay by permitting taxpayers to exempt some of their income from tax. However, the corrections are rough at best.

The Benefit Principle. According to the benefit principle, taxes should be paid in proportion to the benefits that taxpayers derive from public expenditure.[2] From this perspective, the ideal taxes are *user charges,* such as those that would be charged if private firms provided the government services.

The benefit principle is the basis for the gasoline tax, since gasoline usage is closely related to the services obtained from using public roads. There is also a special airline ticket excise tax that is used for airport operations, air traffic control, and airport security. Although there are other examples, especially at the local level, the benefit principle has historically played only a minor role in the design of the Canadian tax system. But its use is growing in Canada and elsewhere as governments seek new ways to finance many of their expenditures.

How Progressive Is the Canadian Tax System?

Although most public controversy over tax equity stresses the progressivity or regressivity of particular taxes, what matters in the end is the overall progressivity of the *entire tax system*. For a modern government to raise sufficient funds, many taxes must be used. We have already discussed personal and corporate income taxes, excise and provincial sales taxes, the Canada-wide GST, and municipal property taxes. Not all of them are equally progressive in design and each one has its own loopholes and anomalies. So, how high-, middle- and low-income people are taxed relative to each other depends on how the entire tax system impacts on each group.

---

[2]It is difficult to see how the benefit principle could be applied to many of the most important categories of government spending. Who gets how much benefit from national defense or from interest on the public debt? It is even more difficult to imagine applying the benefit principle to programs that redistribute income.

Assessing how the entire tax system affects the distribution of income is complicated by two factors. First, the progressivity of the system depends on the mix of the different taxes. Federal taxes tend to be somewhat progressive; the progressivity of the income-tax system and the use of a low-income tax credit more than offset the regressivity of the federal GST. Provincial and municipal governments rely heavily on property and sales taxes and thus have tax systems that are probably slightly regressive.

Second, income from different sources is taxed at different rates. For example, in the federal personal income tax, income from royalties on oil wells is taxed less than income from royalties on books, and profits from sales of assets (capital gains) are taxed less than wages and salaries. To evaluate progressivity, therefore, one needs to know the way in which different *levels* of income are related with different *sources* of income. For example, is wage income more important than capital-gain income for high-income people *relative to* low-income people?

Many economists have concluded that the Canadian tax system has very little overall effect on the distribution of income, except for very low- and very high-income persons. The tax system tends to be roughly proportional for middle-income classes and mildly progressive for low- and high-income persons. Thus the overall tax system is essentially redistributing income from high-income people to low-income people, and doing very little redistribution among the middle-income people. (Look back to Table 15-3 in Chapter 15 to see the pre-tax and post-tax distribution of family income in Canada. That table shows that income is essentially redistributed from the richest one-fifth of the families to the poorest two-fifths of the families, leaving the middle-income families largely unaffected.) Mainly what it is doing therefore is raising revenue to finance government spending rather than effecting major income redistributions.

TAXATION AND EFFICIENCY

The tax system influences the allocation of resources by altering such things as the relative prices of various goods and factors and the relative profitability of various industries.

Although it is theoretically possible to design a neutral tax system—one that leaves all relative prices unchanged—the conditions are too complex to be met in practice. As a result, any actual tax system, including Canada's, does alter the allocation of resources. The taxes change the relationship between prices and marginal costs and shift consumption and production toward goods and services that are taxed relatively lightly and away from those that are taxed more heavily. Usually, this alteration of free-market outcomes causes allocative inefficiency. In a world without taxes (and without other market imperfections), prices would equal marginal costs, and society's resources could be allocated efficiently.

Of course, in a world without taxes, there would be other problems—it would be impossible to pay for any government programs or public goods desired by society. In practise, then, the relevant objective for tax policy is to design a tax system that minimizes inefficiency, *holding constant the amount of revenue to be raised*. In designing such a tax system, a natural place to start would be with taxes that both raise revenue and enhance efficiency. An example of such a tax is the emissions tax that we discussed in Chapter 19. When taxes are imposed on negative externalities, marginal social benefit is moved closer to marginal social cost, *and* government revenue is raised. Unfortunately, such taxes cannot raise nearly enough revenue to finance all of government expenditure.

The Burdens of Taxation

In the absence of externalities, a tax normally does two things. It takes money from the taxpayers, and it changes their behaviour. Taxpayers are typically made worse off by both. Economists call the revenue collected the **direct burden** of the tax. The additional cost that result from the induced changes in behaviour is called the **excess burden.**

The excess burden of a tax is the amount of money that the taxpayers would have to be given, over and above the tax paid, in order to be just as well off as they would be without the tax. The excess burden reflects the allocative inefficiency of the tax.

An example will illustrate this important distinction. Suppose that your provincial government imposes a $2 excise tax on the purchase of compact discs. Suppose further that you are a serious music lover and that this tax does not change your quantity demanded of CDs—that is, your demand for them is perfectly inelastic and hence you continue to buy your usual five CDs per month. In this case, you pay $10 in taxes per month, and you therefore have to reduce your consumption of other goods by $10 per month.

In this special case, the burden on you is not reflected by the change in your consumption of CDs (because there is no change), but rather by the change in your overall purchasing power. That is, if you were to be given an additional $10 a month in income, you would be exactly as well off as you were before the tax was imposed. Thus the total burden on you is equal to the direct burden, $10 a month; there is no excess burden of this tax. The absence of any excess burden from this tax is just another way of saying that there is no allocative inefficiency; the cost of raising $10 a month for the province is just the $10 a month that you pay in taxes. In this case, the tax is *purely* a redistribution of resources from you to the government.

Now suppose that a friend of yours is also a music lover but is not quite so dedicated. The tax leads her to cut back on her consumption of CDs from two per month to none. In this case, your friend pays no taxes and therefore experiences no reduction in her overall purchasing power. The direct burden of the tax is therefore zero. However, your friend *is* worse off as a result of this tax—she has given up the satisfaction that she would have derived from two new CDs per month. She would have to be given some amount of money greater than zero (exactly her consumer surplus from buying two untaxed CDs per month) in order to make her as well off as she was before the tax was imposed. In this case, the direct burden is zero (because no tax is paid) but there *is* an excess burden. The excess burden is equal to her loss in consumer surplus from the CDs that she no longer enjoys.

When a tax is imposed, some people behave like the music buff and do not change their consumption of the taxed good at all, others cease consuming the taxed good altogether, and most simply reduce their consumption. There will be an excess burden for those in the latter two groups. This means that the revenue collected will understate the total cost to taxpayers of generating that revenue. Since our exercise in judging the efficiency of a tax system is to hold constant the total revenue raised, and thus to hold constant the direct burden generated by the tax system, *an efficient tax system will be one that minimizes the amount of excess burden.*

As the example above shows, the excess burden is minimized when taxes are imposed on goods with the lowest price elasticities of demand; the extreme case is illustrated by the music fan, whose price elasticity of demand is zero. A good with perfectly inelastic demand (one that has a vertical de-

mand curve) can be taxed with no excess burden at all. Unfortunately, many of life's necessities (such as food) have very price inelastic demand curves, so a tax system that taxed only goods that had inelastic demand curves would prove to be very regressive. This example illustrates an important general point:

Efficiency and equity are often competing goals in the design of tax systems. Improving efficiency often reduces equity; improving equity often reduces efficiency.

Supply-Side Effects of Taxation

In principle, income taxes can be so high that reducing the tax rate would actually *increase* tax revenue. This is the idea behind the **Laffer curve** shown in Figure 20-2. Its essential feature is that income tax revenues reach a maximum at some income tax rate well below 100 percent.

The reasoning behind the general shape of the Laffer curve is as follows. At a zero tax rate, no revenue would be collected. As rates are raised above zero, some revenue will be gained. But as rates approach 100 percent, revenue will again fall to zero because no one will bother to earn income if they

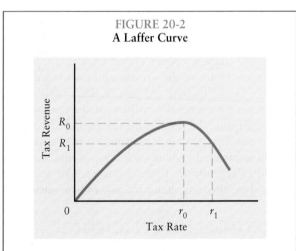

FIGURE 20-2
A Laffer Curve

Increases in tax rates beyond some level will decrease rather than increase tax revenues. The curve relates the government's tax revenue to the tax rate. As drawn, revenue reaches a maximum level of R_0 at the tax rate r_0. If the tax rate were r_1, then *reducing* it to r_0 would increase the government's tax revenue from R_1 to R_0.

know that it must all be paid to the government in taxes. It follows that there must be *some* tax rate, greater than zero and less than 100 percent, at which tax revenue reaches a maximum. Tax rates above that revenue-maximizing rate will actually generate less tax revenue.

The shape of the Laffer curve can be better understood by thinking about the income and the substitution effects of an increase in the tax rate. An increase in the income tax rate makes each additional dollar earned less valuable to the individual and this leads the individual to earn less income by working less hard—this is the substitution effect of the increase in the tax rate. But the increase in the tax rate also produces an income effect—by lowering after-tax income, the individual is led to consume less leisure and work harder, thus earning more income. Which effect dominates as tax rates rise? In general, we don't know. Individuals may choose to earn less or they may choose to earn more as tax rates increase. But since individuals will choose to earn *no income* when tax rates are 100 percent, we know that as tax rates continue to rise higher and higher toward 100 percent, the substitution effect eventually dominates.

Figure 20-2 is drawn under the assumption that there is a steady increase in tax revenue as tax rates rise to r_0, and a steady decrease in tax revenues as tax rates continue to rise toward 100 percent. This particular shape—with a single peak in tax revenues—is not necessary. It is possible that as the tax rate rises from zero to 100 percent, the income and substitution effects combine to produce a tax-revenue curve that has many peaks; this would be unusual but it is not impossible. But this is largely beside the point. The key point is that there is *some* tax rate like r_0 that maximizes total tax revenue. And as long as this is true, then tax rates both above and below r_0 will raise less tax revenue than is raised at r_0.

Just where this maximum occurs—whether at average tax rates closer to 40 or to 70 percent—is currently unknown for either corporate or personal income taxes. Also, there will be a separate Laffer curve for each type of tax. The curve does, however, provide an important warning: Governments cannot increase their tax revenues to any desired level simply by increasing their tax rates. Sooner or later, further increases in the rates will reduce economic activity so much that total tax revenues will fall.

A PROPOSAL TO INCREASE EQUITY AND EFFICIENCY

We saw above that most people's view of an equitable tax system is based on the notion of progressivity. Furthermore, the evidence seems to suggest that the Canadian tax system is roughly proportional for middle-income people and only mildy progressive for high-income and low-income people. This explains why many people would probably be in favour of an increase in the progressivity of the Canadian tax system.

On the other hand, we have also discussed some of the efficiency losses associated with taxation. In particular, the Laffer curve illustrates the important income-reducing effects of taxation—the higher is the tax rate on income, the less incentive individuals have to earn an extra dollar of income. It is important to note here that the disincentive effects from taxation relate to the *marginal tax rate* rather than the average tax rate; your decision to work an *extra* hour depends on the rate at which that *extra*—or marginal—income would be taxed. Concern over these disincentive effects of taxation have lead many people to support reforms in the tax system that reduce marginal income tax rates. Indeed, many of the 1987 reforms that we referred to above were driven by these concerns.[3]

Can more progressivity and lower marginal tax rates be achieved simultaneously? It would appear that there is some trade off between the two goals, especially since we saw in Table 20-4 that it is marginal tax rates *rising with income* which generates much of the progressivity of the Canadian tax system. Many economists, however, have proposed a major reform to the income tax system which combines the benefits of a progressive tax system with *constant* marginal income tax rates. For a more detailed discussion of such a proposal—the Negative Income Tax—see Application 20-1.

---

[3]Such concern over high marginal tax rates has led some people to accept the roughly proportional nature of the tax system, but to look to the system of government *expenditures* to give progressivity to the *entire range* of government activity.

THE NEGATIVE INCOME TAX

A tax is negative when the government pays the taxpayer rather than the other way around. The so-called **negative income tax (NIT)** is designed to increase progressivity by making taxes negative at very low incomes. Such a tax would extend progressivity to the very lowest incomes, and thus help to combat poverty. Furthermore, the NIT achieves its progressivity *without* a schedule of marginal income-tax rates that rise with income, and thus potentially avoids some of the extreme supply-side effects that are caused by very high marginal tax rates.

Many versions of the NIT have been proposed; the one described here illustrates the basic idea. The underlying principle is that a family of a given size should be *guaranteed* a minimum annual income. The tax system must be designed, however, to guarantee this income without eliminating the household's incentive to be self-supporting.

As an example (illustrated in the figure), consider a system in which each household is guaranteed a minimum annual income of $10,000 and the marginal tax rate is 40 percent. Money can be thought of as flowing in two directions; the government gives every household $10,000, and then every household remits 40 percent of any *earned* income back to the government. The *break-even* level of income in this example is $25,000. All households earning less than $25,000 pay *negative*

taxes overall; they receive more money from the government than they remit in taxes. Households earning exactly $25,000 pay no taxes—their $10,000 from the government exactly equals the taxes they remit to the government on their earned income. All households earning more than $25,000 pay more than $10,000 in taxes and so they are paying *positive* taxes overall.

The figure shows the operation of this scheme by relating earned income on the horizontal axis to after-tax income on the vertical axis. The 45° line shows what after-tax income would be if there were no taxes. The heavy line shows the operation of the negative income tax. It starts at the guaranteed annual income of $10,000, rises by 60 cents for every one dollar increase in earned income, and crosses the 45° line at the break-even level of income, $25,000. The vertical distance between the two lines shows the net transfers between the household and the government: Below the break-even level, the government makes a net transfer to the household; above the break-even level, the household makes a net transfer to the government.

Note that the NIT is a progressive tax, despite the *constant* marginal income tax rate. To see this, note that a household's *average* tax rate is equal to the total taxes paid divided by total earned income. If I_E is earned income, then the average tax rate is

PUBLIC EXPENDITURE IN CANADA

In recent years, spending by the consolidated public sector—which includes federal, provincial, and municipal governments—has equaled about 45 percent of Canadian GDP. Table 20-5 gives the distribution of consolidated government spending across a number of major *functions*. As can be seen, health care, education, and social welfare are the largest items; collectively, they make up half the total. Spending on transportation and communication makes up 4.6 percent of the total. Interest on the public debt—a category of spending that has received considerable attention in recent years—represents 18.2 percent of total expenditure. The remaining

27 percent covers everything else, from police protection and sanitation to general administration of government and scientific research. About 40 percent of combined public expenditure is made by the federal government.

TYPES OF GOVERNMENT EXPENDITURE

Table 20-6 classifies federal and provincial government expenditure by type. For each level of government, total expenditures are equal to the sum of program expenditures and debt service payments; program expenditures include purchases of goods and services and various transfer payments.

Figure 20-3 shows the changing importance of different types of federal government spending.

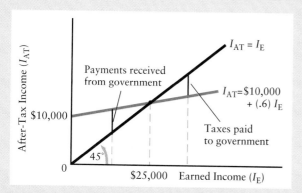

$$\text{Average Tax Rate} = \frac{(0.40) \times I_E - \$10,000}{I_E}$$

$$= (0.40) - \frac{\$10,000}{I_E}$$

Thus the average tax rate for the household rises as earned income rises, but the average tax rate is *always less* than the marginal tax rate (40 percent). That the average tax rate rises with earned income means that higher-income households pay a larger fraction of their income in taxes than is paid by lower-income households—that is, the negative income tax is progressive. For example, a household with earned income of \$30,000 would pay total taxes of \$2,000 (\$12,000 − \$10,000), for an average tax rate of 6.67 percent. A household with earned income of \$60,000 would pay total taxes of \$14,000 (\$24,000 − \$10,000), for an average tax rate of 23.3 percent.

Supporters of the negative income tax believe that it would be an effective tool for reducing poverty. The NIT provides a minimum level of income as a matter of right, not of charity, and it does so without removing the work incentives for people who are eligible for payments; every dollar earned adds to the after-tax income of the family.

One step toward the NIT was taken with the 1987 reforms to the personal income tax. In those reforms, many personal *exemptions* were replaced with *tax credits*. An exemption reduces an individual's tax base relative to earned income, whereas a tax credit reduces taxes payable by the amount of the credit. At present, however, the tax credit is not *refundable*—this means that the credit can be used to reduce taxes payable to zero, but *cannot* be used to reduce taxes payable to a negative number. Thus if an individual has taxes payable equal to \$5,000 and then receives a \$6000 tax credit, total taxes payable fall only to zero—any remaining credit (\$1,000) cannot be claimed back from the government. If the tax credit were fully *refundable*, however, someone whose taxes on earned income were less than the tax credit would receive the difference from the government. This would be a negative income tax. Many advocates of the NIT argue that the government should take the next step of making the personal tax credits fully refundable, thus bringing the Canadian personal income tax system closer to the pure negative income tax.

Federal government purchases of goods and services have been declining steadily over the past forty years. In the early 1950s, roughly 50 percent of federal spending was purchases of goods and services; by 1995, the share was below 20 percent. In contrast, federal transfers to individuals have been gradually increasing, from about 20 percent of federal spending in the early 1950s to about 35 percent in 1995.

Two other spending categories of federal spending are shown in Figure 20-3. First, the federal government makes transfers to provincial and municipal governments (which we explore in detail later in this chapter). These transfers increased steadily from 5 percent of federal spending in the early 1950s to a high of 25 percent in 1971. Since then, these transfers have fallen to about 18 percent of federal spend-

ing, where they are now. The final category of federal spending, which has received considerable attention in the past decade, is the payments made to service the outstanding stock of government debt—these are called *debt service* payments. In the mid 1950s, debt service amounted to about 10 percent of federal spending. But with the arrival of large budget deficits beginning in the early 1970s, the stock of debt began increasing quickly, pushing debt service payments up to about 28 percent of federal spending in 1990. Over the past few years, however, there has been a modest decline in the share of federal spending devoted to debt service (though there has been an increase in the share of provincial government spending on debt service). This recent decline in the share of federal spending on debt service

TABLE 20-5
Expenditures of Combined Governments by Function, 1994

Category	Expenditures (billions of dollars)	Percentage of total	Average annual rate of growth 1984–1994 (%)
Health	47.8	13.5	7.3
Social services	85.6	24.1	7.8
Education	44.4	12.5	6.1
Interest on public debt	64.7	18.2	8.6
Transportation & Communication	16.3	4.6	3.4
All other	95.8	27.1	4.6
Total	354.6	100.0	6.4

Health, social services, and debt service charges were the fastest growing categories of combined government expenditure from 1984 to 1994. The table shows combined expenditures for federal, provincial, and municipal governments. The category "All other" includes sanitation and waste removal, natural resources, general government, police and fire protection, recreation, and cultural activities.

(*Source*: Statistics Canada, CANSIM database.)

has been due largely to a reduction in interest rates since the early 1990s, despite the continued rise in the stock of debt until the mid 1990s.

Provision of Goods and Services

As Table 20-6 indicates, about 20 percent of federal and 30 percent of provincial government spending is for the purchase of goods and services. Among these are defense, transportation facilities, education, and municipal services. In these activities, the government acts in much the same way a firm acts, using factors of production to produce outputs. By and large, these are outputs of public goods, goods with

strong externalities, or services whose benefits are not marketable. Public-opinion polls show that the majority of Canadians support public provision of such services as basic education, hospital care, and medical care. Nonetheless, rising costs of such services are becoming a serious problem, forcing the various governments to re-think the level of government provision that is deemed to be appropriate.

Transfer payments

Transfer payments are defined as payments that do not arise out of the production or sale of goods and services. They include welfare, unemployment insurance,

TABLE 20-6
Federal and Provincial Expenditures by Type, 1993

	Federal		Provincial	
	billion $	percentage of total	billion $	percentage of total
Purchases of goods and services	33.3	19.9	49.7	30.3
Transfers to persons	56.6	33.8	34.6	21.1
Transfers to businesses	4.7	2.8	5.7	3.4
Transfers to other levels of government	31.2	18.6	50.9	31.0
Other transfers	3.4	2.0	0.8	0.5
Interest on public debt	38.3	22.9	22.4	13.7
Total	167.5	100.0	164.1	100.0

Purchases of goods and services constitute about 20 percent of federal government expenditures and about 30 percent of provincial government expenditures. The table shows total expenditures by type for the federal and provincial governments. Transfer payments constitute the majority of expenditures. For the federal government, transfers to persons plus interest on the debt account for about 57 percent of its total expenditures, while transfers to governments (mostly the provinces) account for another 20 percent. For the provinces, transfers to municipalities account for 32 percent of total expenditures (excluding hospitals).

(*Source*: Statistics Canada, 13-001.)

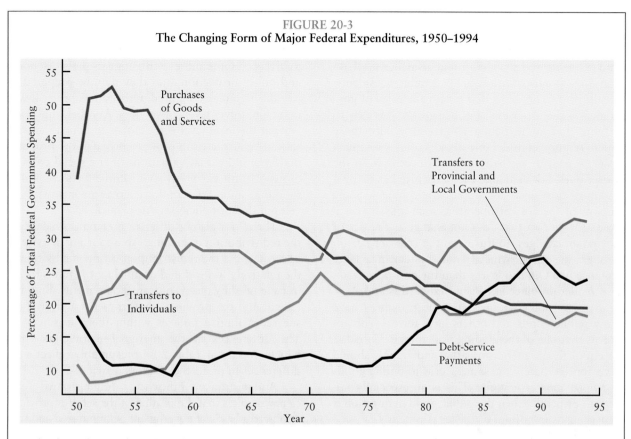

FIGURE 20-3
The Changing Form of Major Federal Expenditures, 1950–1994

Federal purchases of goods and services have declined dramatically in importance over the past 45 years, whereas debt-service payments have increased in importance. Transfers to individuals have gradually increased from about 20 percent of federal spending in the 1950s to about 35 percent today. Transfer payments to provinces are currently around 18 percent of federal spending.

(Source: Statistics Canada, *National Income and Expenditure Accounts)*

and Canada Pension Plan (CPP) payments, and intergovernmental transfers—that is, transfers from one level of government to another. Transfers are also made by provincial and municipal governments.

Although federal government purchases of goods and services are large (about $35 billion in 1995), they have remained roughly constant in *real* terms since the early 1960s. They have been overtaken by transfer payments as the largest form of federal government expenditure.

FISCAL FEDERALISM

Canada is a federal state with governing powers divided between the central authority and the ten provinces and three territories. Municipalities provide a third level of government, whose powers are determined by the provincial legislatures. Understanding the fiscal interaction of the various levels of govern-

ment is central to understanding the nature of government expenditure in Canada. In this section, we examine the concept of *fiscal federalism;* in the next section we examine how fiscal federalism affects the operation of Canada's social programs.

The Logic of Fiscal Federalism

The essence of fiscal federalism is the recognition that Canada is a country with many different fiscal authorities (federal, provincial, and municipal governments) that need a certain amount of coordination to be responsive to the needs and desires of the citizens—who are free to move from one area to another. We discuss four motivations for fiscal federalism: *revenue sources versus revenue needs; geographic externalities; regional preferences; and administrative efficiency.*

Revenue Sources Versus Revenue Needs. One obvious fact about Canada is that the provinces vary in population and income and thus correspondingly vary in the size of their tax bases. For example, Prince Edward Island has only a few hundred thousand residents and thus has a much smaller tax base than does Ontario, with roughly 9 million residents. Recall from Chapter 18 that one of the roles of government is the provision of public goods. It is easy to imagine that some public goods—especially those which require considerable fixed costs—are much easier to provide in the richer provinces than in the poorer ones. For example, each province has its own system of provincial laws, courts, and judges. Some amount of the cost of operating such a system is a fixed cost—a cost that does not change as the *size* of the system changes. In this case, the cost *per person* of operating the provincial court system in a large province like Ontario is less than the cost *per person* in a smaller province like Prince Edward Island.

So why don't we just let some provinces have many public goods and others have fewer? The answer is that one of the guiding principles in Canada's system of fiscal federalism is that individuals should have approximately the same access to public goods *no matter where they live.* This is an especially important principle when the public good in question is something as important as the legal system.

Since revenue sources do not always match revenue needs at each level, and since there are typically significant fixed costs associated with the provision of public goods, *intergovernmental transfers* are required (as shown in Table 20-6). This is the underlying motivation behind Canada's system of equalization payments, which transfers resources from the richer provinces to the poorer ones. We examine this shortly.

Geographic Extent of Externalities. Because the government of a province or a municipality is unlikely to be responsive to the needs of citizens outside its jurisdiction, public services that involve *geographic spillovers* may not be provided adequately unless responsibility for them is delegated to a higher level of government. For example, national defense is normally delegated to the central government for this reason. Control of pollution is another obvious case, since contamination of air and water often literally spills over provincial and municipal boundaries. At the other extreme is fire protection. If fire protection is to be effective, it is necessary that there be fire stations serving small geographic areas. Accordingly, responsibility for fire stations lies with municipal governments.

Regional Differences in Preferences. The delegation of some functions to lower levels of government may provide a political process that is more responsive to regional differences in preferences for public versus private goods. Some people may prefer to live in communities with higher-quality schools and police protection, and they may be prepared to pay the high taxes required. Others may prefer lower taxes and lower levels of services. Another important issue at the local level is the extent to which industry should be attracted in order to broaden the property tax base; individual valuations of the social costs in terms of aesthetic or environmental effects are bound to differ, and different local governments will develop different policies in this regard.

There may also be different preferences regarding the redistribution of income. An important activity of government is the redistribution of income by taxing the relatively well-off and channeling the funds to citizens in need by means of transfer payments. Both the federal and the provincial governments actively pursue redistributive policies within their jurisdictions. The differences in the marginal income-tax rates which we saw in Table 20-4 presumably reflect such differences in preferences across provinces.

Administrative Efficiency. Administrative efficiency requires that duplication of the services provided at different levels of government be minimized and that related programs be coordinated. On the revenue side, it is desirable that a particular tax be collected by only one level of government. This consideration has led to the negotiation of federal-provincial tax agreements that provide for efficient tax collection and revenue sharing.

The foregoing discussion suggests two central ideas for a system of fiscal federalism to be effective. First, the various fiscal authorities need to be *coordinated,* at least in the sense that there are well-defined responsibilties. Thus national defense is the sole responsibility of the federal government whereas fire protection is the sole responsibility of municipal governments. In the absence of such coordination, there would be a considerable waste of resources as the various fiscal authorities duplicated tasks.

The second central idea is that an effective system of fiscal federalism needs a mechanism to make *intergovernmental transfers*. This is especially true if there are considerable fixed costs involved in the provision of public goods. We explore the types of Canadian intergovernmental transfers in detail in the next subsection.

Intergovernmental Transfers

The scope and nature of intergovernmental grants have changed dramatically over the years. Measured in constant 1994 dollars, federal transfers to provincial governments expanded from $1.38 billion in 1950 to over $30 billion in 1994. This represented an increase from 6.8 percent to 19 percent of federal revenues; for the provincial governments, federal transfers as a share of their revenues increased, on average, from 20 percent to over 35 percent.

Over the past few years, the system of intergovernmental transfers in Canada has undergone substantial reform. One major part of this reform was the creation in 1996 of the *Canada Health and Social Transfer (CHST)*. Before examining the CHST it is useful to examine briefly the system of intergovernmental transfers in place immediately preceding this reform. Four central programs comprised the system of intergovernmental transfers until 1996: *equalization payments, revenue sharing, Established Programs Financing (EPF)*, and *Canada Assistance Plan (CAP)*. The equalization and revenue-sharing programs exist today; the EPF and CAP ended with the creation of the CHST in 1996.

Equalization Payments.   With the object of ensuring that citizens in all regions of the country have access to a reasonable level of public services, **equalization payments** are made out of federal government general revenues to provinces with below-average tax capacity. Though this is not explicitly a revenue-sharing program (provinces with above-average tax capacity do not pay in), the richer provinces (typically British Columbia, Alberta, and Ontario) are, in effect, transferring resources via the federal government to the poorer provinces. The equalization payments are calculated by a complicated formula that involves, at last count, 29 revenue sources.

Equalization payments are a relatively new phenomenon in Canada, but they have exhibited rapid growth. From their inception with the 1957 Tax-Sharing Act to the time of the 1977 Fiscal Arrangements Act to their formal inclusion in the Constitution Act of 1982, they have expanded considerably. Equalization payments for the 1992–1993 fiscal year were $307 per person, making a total of about $9 billion.

Revenue Sharing. Since the 1940s, most provinces have maintained **tax-rental arrangements,** whereby the federal government collects income taxes and makes a per capita payment to the provinces for that right. In 1995, with the exception of the Quebec personal income tax and the Ontario and Quebec corporate levies, all income taxes in Canada were collected by the federal government.

Outside Quebec, the provincial income tax is calculated as a percentage of the federal tax payable at rates determined by the individual provinces. Federal income-tax rates are set at levels that allow substantial "tax room" to the provinces. That is, by keeping the federal income-tax rates relatively low (17 percent, 26 percent, or 29 percent), the provinces can still raise considerable revenue by taxing income (without extreme supply-side effects such as those discussed in Figure 20-2). A similar arrangement applies to the corporate income tax. The effect of these measures can be thought of in terms of the "value of tax points." Tax points reflect the taxes levied by the provinces, collected by the federal government, and then returned to the provinces as a transfer.

Established Programs Financing (EPF). Until 1996, federal financing of health care and postsecondary education was referred to as *established programs financing* (to indicate that the existence of these programs was not conditional on federal involvement). Because federal contributions were independent of the costs of the programs, the federal government could control its own contribution. The provinces benefited from such autonomy, for they were not constrained by narrowly defined federal program conditions. In the early 1990s, transfers for EPF (cash plus tax points) made up over one half of the total federal transfers to provinces.

Canada Assistance Plan (CAP). Under this program, which also ended in the 1996 reforms, the federal government paid half of the costs of the provincial welfare programs, including half the associated administrative costs. Uniformity of the various provincial welfare programs was not a requirement. The provinces could design and administer their own programs but then only needed to meet one-half of the cost themselves. These programs also covered road building, vocational schools, and assistance to needy seniors, the disabled, and unemployed persons not eligible for unemployment insurance.

National Standards

Although it is common to hear people talk as if the federal-provincial transfers established *national standards* for the provision of health care or education, neither the CAP nor the EPF actually had such standards. Support levels under the Canada Assistance Plan varied widely across provinces, reflecting the fact the the CAP was simply a way of sharing the costs of *provincially* designed and administered programs. No conditions were set in relation to the transfers linked to postsecondary education. In health care, the only national standards were general principles such as portability among provinces and universality. No federal authority could complain about an alleged inadequacy in some province's health care system. The only rule was that whatever was provided by a province must be universally available within that province.[4]

Financial Cutbacks

As we said above, the system of intergovernmental transfers was in the midst of major reform as recently as the spring of 1996. Thus the four programs just described do not describe the *current* system of transfers—they describe the system that was in place from the mid 1970s to the spring of 1996. To understand the pressure for the most recent reforms, we have to go back to the mid 1970s.

In every year since the mid 1970s, the federal government has had a budget deficit. By the mid 1980s, the annual deficit had reached $30 billion and was projected to rise even further. Furthermore, the stock of debt (the accumulated past deficits) had reached the point where debt-service payments were becoming onerous, and were placing severe constraints on the government's plans for program spending. In that atmosphere of fiscal concern, the federal government began to look for every possible avenue of expenditure reduction. Not surprisingly, the intergovernmental transfer system came under close scrutiny.

Financial cutbacks affected all major areas of the system. A ceiling was placed on equalization payments so that they could not grow faster than the GDP. In 1987, the ceiling began to have an effect, reducing equalization payments by about $3 billion from what they otherwise would have been over the next three years.

The EPF programs were first "capped" in 1983. The growth in EPF transfers (cash plus tax points) was reduced successively from the rate of GDP growth to GDP growth minus first one, then two, then three percentage points. Finally in 1989–1990, the EPF transfers were fixed in nominal dollar terms. The CAP was also "capped." Beginning in 1990, the rule was that payments under the CAP to provinces *not receiving equalization payments* (typically the "rich" provinces

of B.C., Alberta, and Ontario) could not increase by more than 5 percent per year. This was a particularly severe blow to Ontario, which lost $1.1 billion of CAP payments in the 1991–1992 fiscal year alone.

Writing in 1993, Queen's University professor Peter Leslie said:

> It is quite clear that the present pattern of fiscal arrangements cannot be sustained for long. They are already set to self-destruct. The problem is most obvious in the case of EPF. As the federal government's cash contribution to health care and postsecondary education dwindles, its ability to exercise any policy influence in these areas will also disappear. Opinions on the subject will vary on whether the removal is desirable or not. However, there is no doubt that when it happens—as it will if EPF is allowed to phase itself out—a major feature of Canadian federalism will be phased out with it.[5]

Professor Leslie's prediction that the fiscal arrangements in place in 1993 could not be sustained for long turned out to be true. The tight financial position in which the federal government found itself in the early 1990s forced changes in the size and the nature of federal transfer payments to provinces. In its budget of 1995, the federal government announced the creation of the *Canada Health and Social Transfer (CHST)* to be implemented in spring of 1996. The CHST is a "block transfer" that rolls together the transfers previously made under the Established Program Financing (EPF) and Canada Assistance Plan (CAP). With the new CHST, the federal government gives a lump sum to each province (depending on the number of residents) which the provincial government can then use to fund post-secondary education, health care, and income-support programs.

There are benefits to both federal and provincial governments with the CHST. The federal government now focusses on a single lump-sum transfer to the province. The provincial governments, though still receiving considerable transfers from the federal government, have much more freedom in how that money is spent—the CHST is money with "no strings attached." As the new CHST settles into place, and the federal government decides on the appropriate size of lump-sum transfer to make under the CHST, there will inevitably be an effect on the nature and generosity of

---

[4]In recent years, the federal government has threatened to remove funding to those provinces permitting physicians to "extra bill" for health services. The federal government has interpreted such extra billing as a movement away from universality and toward a two-tier health system.

[5]Peter Leslie, "The Fiscal Crisis of Canadian Federalism", in *A Partnership in Trouble*, C. D. Howe Institute (Toronto, 1993).

provincially designed social programs. It is to the various social programs in Canada that we now turn.

CANADIAN SOCIAL POLICY

Canada has a wide variety of social programs, from unemployment insurance and the Canada Pension Plan to the systems of publicly provided health care and heavily subsidized post-secondary education. Canadian governments—both federal and provincial—have been urged to reexamine and redesign these programs with the twin objectives of improving the benefits delivered to the intended beneficiaries and reducing costs wherever possible. In the midst of such reform-minded governments, it is not surprising that controversies over Canada's social programs have been major news items in recent years. Indeed, these contoversies will likely continue well into the future.

Given the concern over government budget deficits in the past 15 years, it is natural that such a large category of spending should come under scrutiny. Assessing program effectiveness and evaluating proposals for the reform of Canada's social policies are not, however, simple matters. One-line evaluations, such as "Nothing needs to be changed" or "The whole system needs to be swept away," are too simplistic but all too common.

THE BASIC SETTING

Spending by all levels of government on social programs has grown dramatically over the past 40 years. Table 20-5 shows that in 1994 combined government expenditures on health, education, and social services equalled $178 billion, just over 50 percent of total government expenditures. In addition to the upward trend in spending on social programs, there has been a steady increase in the relative importance of spending by the provincial governments; their share of spending on social programs has grown from just over 5 percent in 1950 to about 25 percent in 1995.

The Variety of Social Programs

Some social programs are universal, in the sense that they pay benefits to anyone meeting only such minimal requirements as age or residence. These are referred to as **demogrants**. Other programs are selective, in the sense that they pay benefits only to people who qualify by meeting specific conditions, such as by having young children or being unemployed. When these conditions are related to the individual's income, the term **income-tested** (or *income-related*) **benefits** is used. Some benefits are taxable, so that the after-tax benefits decline as income rises; others are not taxable, so after-tax benefits are independent of income. Some benefits are expenditure programs (including direct transfers to persons), while others are delivered through the tax system in the form of tax expenditures (see Table 20-2 for some examples). Some programs are administered by the federal government, some by the provincial governments, and still others by the municipalities.

The Federal-Provincial Perspective

Canada's constitution originally granted all authority in social policy to the provinces. As social policy became increasingly important, agreements between the two levels of government gave the federal government responsibility for a large amount of social spending. In some cases, this involves direct federal spending, as with the Old Age Security (OAS) program, and in other cases it involves transferring funds to the provincial governments, as with the Canada Health and Social Transfer (CHST). Thus some federal payments to provinces are distributed directly to individuals; others are used by the provinces to finance various expenditures.

Understanding Canada's social programs, therefore, requires an understanding of federal-provincial relations, together with recognizing some of the important differences across regions. We make four points in this regard.

Federal Transfers. As we have already observed, a large amount of federal spending is in the form of transfer payments to the provinces. Though some transfer payments are nominally earmarked for specific purposes, the provinces are not required to match their spending changes in these areas to changes in federal transfers received. In recent years, growth in provincial spending in these areas, particularly education, has often been less than the growth in transfers from the federal government. Hence to analyse the efficacy of social programs in these areas, it is not sufficient to focus only on federal transfers. Further, since provinces typically allocate over 60 percent of their spending to social policy, any dramatic change in provincial spending would also represent a significant change in total national spending.

Regional Pressures. Canada's regional pressures play a major role in shaping federal-provincial fiscal relations. Equalization payments, discussed in the previous section, are relevant here. Although they are not considered part of federal social spending, they are a transfer to the provinces whose explicit purpose is to compensate for any shortfall in the fiscal capacity of the relatively poorer provinces to provide a minimum level of government services.

Financial Cutbacks. Under intense pressure over the past decade to reduce its budget deficit, the federal government has been capping, and sometimes reducing, its transfers to the provinces. The extent of these changes is such that the whole concept of fiscal federalism is being eroded and may slowly disappear. As the federal contributions are reduced, provincial autonomy is increased. Some see this as a major loss of national commonality, others as an important and beneficial step toward much-needed decentralization.

The Need for Coordination. Since the multitude of federal and provincial social programs overlap in their effects, any program change made by one level of government will have one effect if it is offset by the other level and another effect if it is not offset. For example, when in its 1985 budget the federal government enriched the child tax credit to increase the after-tax income of very poor families with children, a number of provinces reacted by cutting back on their welfare programs. In those provinces, benefits delivered to the poor were not changed in aggregate, but the burden of financing those benefits was shifted to the federal government, and the distribution of benefits was shifted from families without children to those with children.

These observations suggest an important lesson relating to the potential reform of Canada's social programs:

Reform of Canadian social policy is more effective when changes are coordinated and sweeping rather than piecemeal. The inherent difficulties of such coordination are aggravated by Canada's adversarial political system and by the often stormy nature of federal-provincial relations in Canada.

We first wrote the above colour passage in 1987, and events since then only serve to underline the central message. Every independent body that has studied Canadian social policy has called for major reforms to allow the system to continue to do its job at a cost the tax system can bear; every attempt at reform by the federal government (first Conservative, then Liberal) has met with strong resistance from the opposition parties and the provinces.

FIVE PILLARS OF CANADIAN SOCIAL POLICY

We now turn to a brief description of the five pillars of Canadian social policy: education, health care, income support, unemployment insurance, and retirement benefits. Each of these pillars, at various points in recent years, have been the focus of attention as financially strapped governments have explored new ways to provide what many perceive as vital social services.

Education and Training

Public education, one of the earliest types of social expenditure in Canada, remains one of the most important. It has been supplemented over the years by numerous other programs aimed at developing human resources.

Basic Education. Primary and secondary schools teach literacy and numeracy. These basic skills are needed in order to acquire further marketable skills. Canada has one of the world's highest per capita expenditures on basic education, yet Canadian students do relatively poorly on international comparisons that use standardized tests. Studies show that many Canadian adults (some estimates say as many as one-quarter) are functional illiterates—people who cannot comprehend simple written instructions well enough to carry them out. One educational target should be to reduce illiteracy and innumeracy, deficiencies that are lifetime handicaps.

Basic education is supplemented by further education and training. This occurs in technical schools, colleges and universities, as well as in the workplace. At the beginning of the 1990s, the federal government operated about a dozen nonuniversity job creation and training programs, enrolling nearly half a million people and costing nearly $2 billion. Although few doubt that these schemes are of great value, the critics have noted many deficiencies in the programs and recommended major changes.

Postsecondary Education. Postsecondary education is a provincial responsibility in Canada. As discussed earlier in this chapter, until 1996 the federal government made large payments to the provinces for postsecondary education as part of Established Programs Financing (EPF)—in the early 1990s the annual transfer for post secondary education was about $1.5 billion. Since 1996, federal transfers for postsecondary education have been contained in the Canada Health and Social Transfer (CHST).

In Canada, all universities are public institutions, and university education is heavily subsidized by government, with tuition fees accounting for only about 15 percent of total costs. Two arguments can be advanced for subsidizing higher education; one is an efficiency argument, and the other concerns equity. The efficiency argument is based on the claim that there are positive externalities from higher education—that is, that the country as a whole benefits when a student receives higher education. In many cases these externalities cannot be internalized by the students receiving the education, so, left to their own maximizing decisions, students who had to pay the whole cost of their education would choose less than is socially optimal. The equity argument is that if students were forced to pay anything like the full cost of the services they receive, a university education would become prohibitively expensive to low- and even middle-income families. Government subsidies help provide training according to ability rather than according to income.

Arguments to reduce the subsidy to higher education, and thus to finance a larger fraction of the costs of running universities from tuition fees, start with the observation that the value of many kinds of education is internalized and recaptured in higher incomes earned by the recipients later in their life. This is particularly true of professional training in such fields as law, medicine, dentistry, management, and computer science. Yet students in these fields typically pay a smaller part of their real education costs than students in the arts, where the argument for externalities is greatest. Also, subsidized education does represent a significant income transfer from taxpayers to students, even though the average taxpayer may have a lower income than the average student can expect to earn in the future.

People who worry about the equity issue in this context often argue for a system of student loans (which currently exist in Canada), whereby more of the cost of education would be recouped from the students themselves later in their lifetimes. People opposed to loans argue, among other things, that loans will discourage children in lower-income families from continuing on to higher education because, from the vantage point of their family's current low income, the liability to be taken on by the student will seem enormous.

Health Care

Taking federal and provincial payments into account, Canada's public health-care system is the country's single most expensive social program. In 1994, government expenditures on health care accounted for about 7.5 percent of Canadian GDP; private spending on health care brought total (private plus public) expenditures up to 10.1 percent of GDP. This is the second highest proportion of GDP so devoted in all the advanced industrial countries. The annual cost of the part of health care that is paid for by government amounted in that year to over $2,500 for every man, woman, and child in the country. It has also been rising rapidly in recent years.

"Cost containment" in the health-care sector has become a priority for most provincial governments and the debate currently rages over what reforms are practicable and acceptable. Hospital and bed closures, and growing queues for non-critical treatments, are part of the daily news. Most observers agree that some type of expenditure-controlling reform is urgently needed. Unfortunately, agreement stops here.

Fee for Service. One major possibility of cost containment is to move away from the present system of "fee for service." In the system used in most of Canada, the physician and the hospital charge a prescribed fee for each service that is performed. Since under any provincial health scheme, the doctor's and hospital's collection rate is 100 percent, there is no reason for the provider of health services to economize on those services. Indeed, much research shows that the rate of elective surgery—operations that are not necessary for survival but may be useful—rises with the ratio of physicians to the population. In areas where there are many physicians, the typical physician has time on his or her hands, and the rate of elective surgery goes up. In areas where doctors are in short supply, much less elective surgery is performed.

This illustrates a general point. The case for the free market is strongest when consumers are the best judges of their own needs. The case for market efficiency is greatly weakened when suppliers, such as physicians, can influence the demand for the product they supply. Thus in the many cases where judgment is needed to decide among several courses of action, all of which have something to recommend them, the evidence is that doctors often create their own demand. This does not imply dishonesty on the part of doctors, merely that where judgment calls must be made, the amount of spare time available to doctors will influence their decisions.

Health Maintenance Organizations. Health maintenance organizations (HMOs) provide a possi-

---

EXTENSION 20-1

POVERTY IN CANADA

What is poverty, and whom does it affect? One definition says that one lives in poverty if one is poorer than most of one's fellow citizens. Since there will always be a bottom 10 percent of any income distribution who are poorer than the remaining 90 percent, poverty in this sense will always be with us. If a completely relative definition is not very revealing, neither is an unchanging absolute definition. The living standards of Canadians who are today regarded as poor would have looked more than adequate to Canadians of 100 years ago and would look princely to citizens of many countries even today.

To meet both of these concerns, economists define poverty as some given level of income, rather than just in relative terms, but they also recognize that as average living standards rise over time, so will our ideas of what constitutes poverty.

Statistics Canada defines the **poverty line** as the level of income at which a household spends on average more than 54.7 percent of its income on the three basic necessities of food, shelter, and clothing. For a family of four, the Canadian poverty line in 1994 ranged from $21,472 in rural areas to $31,071 in the largest cities. Although $30,000 may buy enough food, shelter, and clothing for a family of four to get by, it does not provide enough money for the full range of commodities that most of us take for granted, such as having a refrigerator, a TV set that works, constant hot water, and an occasional night out for dinner or a movie. Many of the poor are understandably upset that they are outsiders looking in on the comfortable way of life shown in ads and on television.

WHO ARE THE POOR?

According to the criterion just outlined, 13.5 percent of Canadian families were living in poverty in 1994.

There are poor among all ages, races, and educational levels, employed as well as unemployed. Yet some groups have much higher incidences of poverty than others. For example, the table shows that you are more likely to be poor if you live in Quebec, if you are a member of a large family, or if you live in a large city.

But poverty is by no means restricted to these groups. More than half the poor families live in urban areas, live in Ontario and the western provinces, have no more than one child, and are headed by persons of working age. Furthermore, about one quarter of those in poverty work full time (the so-called working poor), and over half work at least part time. These facts help to dispose of two superficial caricatures: the slothful father who feigns a disability because he is too lazy to do an honest day's work and the family with so many children that an ordinary decent wage is spread so thin that the entire household is reduced to poverty. Individual households that come close to these extremes can be found, but most poor households do not.

CAN ECONOMIC GROWTH SOLVE THE PROBLEM?

Between 1969 and 1994, the proportion of Canadians living in poverty fell by 35 percent. In part this reflected a variety of government initiatives of the sort discussed in this chapter. But in large mea-

---

ble way around this problem. Large hospitals and large groups of doctors work on what is called a *capitation* basis. This means that the HMO is paid an annual fee for each person registered with it. Since payment is on a per capita basis rather than on a services-rendered basis, there is no incentive to prescribe more care than is needed. Furthermore, to the extent that an individual registers with the same HMO for several years, there is little incentive for the HMO to scimp on necessary services, because scimping today (by ignoring a problem, for example) may

mean that much more is spent in the future (to correct the problem after it has gotten worse). Thus one big advantage of HMOs is that each HMO has the incentive to keep its clients healthly *and* to keep costs down. The HMO at Sault Ste. Marie, pioneered by the steelworkers' union and their employers, was an early and successful Canadian example of such an organization.

The Alberta Reforms.   One of the hot spots for debate over reform of the health-care system in recent years has been Alberta. In the early 1990s, sure, it resulted from the growth in average income, which has always been the greatest source of relief from poverty.

It would be a mistake, however, to expect growth to eliminate all poverty. The source of to-day's poverty problem is no longer low average income but particular groups who are left behind in the general rise in living standards caused by economic growth. It is little consolation—indeed, it must add to the gall—that they are poor in an increasingly affluent society.

There is no single answer to the question of what causes poverty in the midst of plenty. It is partly a result of mental and physical handicaps, partly of low motivation, partly of the raw deal that fate gives to some, partly the result of changing market conditions when industries and occupations can no longer prosper, partly a result of unwillingness or inability to invest in the kind of human capital that does pay off in the long run, and partly the result of the market's valuing the particular abilities an individual does have at such a low price that even in good health and with full-time employment the income that can be earned leaves that person below the poverty line.

Just as there is no single reason for poverty, there is no single cure. Many of the social programs outlined in this chapter attempt to get at various causes. If poverty has fallen over the decades in Canada, the two main reasons are economic growth and social programs that seek to provide assistance for those who cannot help themselves and to assist those who can to learn to do so.

Incidence of Poverty Among Canadian Families by Selected Characteristics, 1994

Characteristics	Percentage of families falling below the poverty line
All families	13.5
Place of residence	
Metropolitan	16.0
Other urban	12.3
Rural	9.2
Region	
Atlantic	14.4
Quebec	16.4
Ontario	11.7
Prairies	13.2
British Columbia	12.6
Number of children under 16 years of age	
0	9.0
1	20.1
2	16.4
3 or more	24.5
Age of head of family	
Under 25	44.4
25–54	13.5
55–64	13.0
65 and over	7.1
Sex of head of family	
Male	9.7
Female	40.9
Employment status of head of family	
In labour force	9.7
Not in labour force	23.6

Source: Statistics Canada, 13-207.

Premier Ralph Klein brought health care in Alberta onto the centre stage of policy reform. Regional health boards were established in the hope that decentralized decisions concerning resource allocation would be superior to those made by a centralized provinical health ministry. Each health board decides which hospitals in its region will remain open and which will close, which will have emergency wards and which will not, which will conduct heart transplants and which will not. The regional health boards receive their funds directly from the provin-cial government and disperse the money according to its plans for health care in the region.

Not surprisingly, there have been competing views on the value of the Alberta reforms. Many people associated with the provision of health care (e.g., doctors and nurses) were opposed to the rationalization and consolidation of hospital services, not least because some of them lost their jobs. On the other hand, many people across the province viewed the reforms as a sensible slimming of a social program that had become too fat over the years. By early 1996, the basic designs of the system were in place; but it will take a few years before a complete evaluation of the reforms is possible.

Income Support Programs

Canada has various programs that provide assistance for people in financial need—these programs constitute what is often called the "social safety net." The overriding objective of this safety net is to reduce poverty. Though nothing like the serious problem it was in Canada's past and still is in many other countries, poverty remains a matter of real concern to Canadian policy makers. One cause for concern is that most of the poverty that can be eliminated by economic growth may have already been eliminated, implying that much of the remaining poverty may represent the "hard core" that will persist no matter how wealthy the society (on average) becomes and can only be alleviated by active public policy. See Extension 20-1 for a more detailed discussion of poverty in Canada.

The variety of income-support programs can be divided into three groups. The first is designed to provide income assistance to those individuals whose incomes are deemed to be too low to provide an adequate standard of living. The second is designed to assist specifically those individuals who are in financial need because of temporary job loss—unemployment insurance. The third is designed to provide income assistance specifically to the elderly. In this subsection, we examine the first group. The next two subsections discuss unemployment insurance and elderly benefits, respectively.

Social Assistance.   Social assistance for individuals below retirement age, usually called *welfare,* is mainly a provincial responsibility in Canada. The details of the programs vary considerably across the provinces even though they are partly financed by transfers received from the federal government. Until 1996, the federal government contributed (under the CAP) to the provincial welfare programs. Until 1990, the federal contribution was equal to one-half of the cost of the program, but starting in 1990 the higher-income provinces had the federal government's contribution limited to an increase of 5 percent per year. In 1996, the federal government initiated the Canada Health and Social Transfer (CHST) which folded together transfers previously made under the EPF and CAP into a single lump-sum transfer (based on the number of residents in the province). The changes in the form of federal funding have put strong pressures on the provincial governments to al-

ter their systems—for better or worse. This is especially true of the CHST—since the cost of the welfare program is no longer directly shared with the federal government, each provincial government has an increased incentive to reduce costs.

Suggested reforms to social assistance take two main forms. First, most economists advocate reforms of the tax-and-transfer system in an effort to reduce what are called *poverty traps.* **Poverty traps,** which are common, occur whenever the tax-and-transfer system results in individuals having very little incentive to increase their pre-tax income (by accepting a job, for example) because such an increase in their pre-tax income would make them ineligible for some benefits (such as welfare) and might even make them worse off overall. The presence of such poverty traps reflects a tax-and-transfer system that has been modified in many small steps over many years, the result of which is a plethora of programs often working at cross purposes. The elimination of such poverty traps requires that the tax-and-transfer system be examined in its entirety rather than on a piecemeal basis.

The second type of reform is designed to provide positive incentives to self-help by increasing benefits for recipients who accept work or training for work. A related (and quite contentious) proposal is referred to as *workfare*—the idea that welfare recipients should be required to put in some sort of work in order to be eligible for welfare benefits.[6]

Child Benefits.   The support system for families with children has been evolving quite rapidly over the years. Prior to the last change in 1993, the system was a combination of universal family allowance payments and tax credits. In 1993, universality was eliminated. A Child Tax Benefit is now paid according to the number of children in the family and varies according to family income, reaching zero at an income of $60,000.

The reforms to the child benefits system no doubt points the direction to be taken by many other welfare reforms to come. Indeed, it is probable that no part of the system has settled into its final new shape. Further changes can be expected until the whole system of social expenditures has been rethought from top to bottom.

---

[6]For a wide-ranging discussion of the issues involved in workfare, see John Richards and William Watson (eds.), *Helping the Poor: A Qualified Case for Workfare,* C. D. Howe Institute (Social Policy Challenge No. 5), Toronto, 1995.

Unemployment Insurance

Unemployment insurance (UI) is the single most costly program administered by the federal government, accounting for over $17.5 billion of payments in 1993–1994. Just looking at the federal *spending* on UI, however, is misleading because the program is more-or-less self financing, at least over the duration of the average business cycle (5–6 years). Employers and employees remit UI premiums to the government equal to a small percentage of wages and salaries—these premiums then finance the UI payments to unemployed workers who qualify for the benefits. In boom times, when there is little unemployment, the UI premiums exceed the UI benefits; in times of high unemployment, the benefits exceed the premiums.[7]

Originally instituted in 1940 as an insurance scheme against temporary bouts of unemployment, it was extended in scope and generosity by changes instituted in the 1970s. Many studies of the UI system over the last decade have concluded that the system has become overburdened by being used for too many, often conflicting objectives. It should, they argued, be returned to its prime objective of providing insurance against temporary bouts of involuntary unemployment, and other schemes should be used to achieve other objectives. Supporters of the system have fiercely resisted all suggested changes.

UI gives incentives to remain in seasonal jobs and in areas with poor employment prospects and to take UI-financed holidays. Saying that the UI system encourages behaviour that increases unemployment and reduces regional mobility does not say that the unemployed themselves are responsible for the "abuses" of the system that lead to these results. The responsibility lies with the people who designed the incentives and those who strive to preserve them. It is they who can alter the system to make it deliver the intended benefits with fewer incentives for undesired behaviour.

A number of changes have been made during the 1990s. Some respond to the criticisms noted above. For example, rules for qualifying to receive benefits have been tightened, and extended coverage and additional assistance provided for individuals attending approved training courses. Other changes worked in the opposite direction, by expanding coverage into areas some critics had argued were better handled outside of the UI program (for example, expanded parental and sickness benefits).

Retirement Benefits

Canada's present youthful age structure may make us think we are richer as a nation than we actually are. When only a small fraction of the population is retired, it is easy to be generous to them, because the burden is spread over so many working persons. However, generous schemes may become difficult to honour when a large proportion of the population is retired, as it will be early in the twenty-first century. Over the coming decades, a larger and larger fraction of Canadians will be retired, and the working people who will be directly or indirectly supporting the retired will constitute a smaller and smaller fraction of the population.

There are essentially three components of the system of benefits for the elderly. These are the Canada Pension Plan (CPP), retirement income support programs such as Old Age Security (OAS) and Guaranteed Income Supplement (GIS), and tax-assisted saving plans.

The Canada Pension Plan (CPP). The CPP provides a basic level of retirement income for all Canadians who have contributed to it over their working lives. (A separate but similar scheme exists in Quebec, the Quebec Pension Plan or QPP.) Unlike some private programs, the pension provided by the CPP is portable—changing jobs does not cause any loss of eligibility.

The most important concern about the CPP is that it subsidizes the generation currently receiving pensions. Contribution rates were very low when these people were young, and as a result they will receive pensions more than five times as large as what their contributions would actually have bought. This makes the plan a very good deal for those presently retired, but it means that any increase in future benefits will have to be paid for on top of the existing subsidy to those already retired. To make the scheme self-supporting, the government would have to more than double the CPP contribution rates over the next twenty years.

Such proposed increases in the contribution rates (with no scheduled increases in the benefits), however, make the Canada Pension Plan a "poor investment" for the current younger generations, because the rate of return that the young will effectively earn on their contributions will be less than what they could earn on alternative investments. This situation naturally leads

[7]In 1996, the name of the program was formally changed to Employment Insurance (EI). In this textbook, however, we continue to use the acronym "UI" because of its familiarity.

to calls for a complete overhaul—and perhaps even the elimination—of the current system of public pensions.[8]

Retirement Income Support Programs.   The existing public benefits system for the elderly is in many ways analogous to the child benefits system. There are three parts to the system. First, a universal benefit called the Old Age Security (OAS) program, acts much like the family allowance. Under the OAS program, the government sends out monthly benefit cheques to each Canadian over the qualifying age of 65. Since 1989, however, OAS payments to relatively wealthy individuals have been recaptured by means of a tax "clawback."

Second, in calculating the personal nonrefundable tax credit, provisions available to the elderly serve to reduce their taxes payable. These include a credit available to anyone 65 or older and a pension income credit that offsets the taxes due on the first $1,000 of pension income.

Third, an income-tested program, called the Guaranteed Income Supplement (GIS), provides benefits targeted to the low-income elderly. (In some provinces this is supplemented by further targeted assistance.) The GIS provides for most of the progressivity that arises in the elderly benefits system.

Tax-Assisted Saving Plans.   The CPP, OAS, and GIS are programs which involve direct spending on the part of the government. But the government has also introduced programs that require no direct government spending but instead rely on *tax expenditures* (i.e., tax reductions). These tax expenditures are designed to provide incentives for individuals to save more for their retirement. There are essentially two types of programs. The first is through Registered Retirement Savings Plans (RRSPs) and the second is through employer-sponsored Registered Pension Plans (RPPs).

RRSPs provide an incentive for individuals to provide for their own retirement, either because they are not covered by a company plan or because they wish to supplement their company plan. Funds contributed are deductible from taxable income but become fully taxable when they are withdrawn. It is thus a tax deferral plan, and as such it is more valuable the higher one's current taxable income and the lower one's expected future income.

Individuals without RRSPs may still receive some tax assistance for saving if their employer has a Registered Pension Plan. In this case, contributions to the company pension plan (which are often mandatory and are withdrawn directly from the regular paycheque) are tax deductible in a manner similar to an RRSP contribution.

The program of RRSPs and RPPs does not require direct expenditures from either the federal or provincial governments, but because of the tax-deductability of contributions, these plans represent a significant amount of foregone tax revenue. From Table 20-2, the total tax expenditures associated with RRSPs and RPPs in 1992 was $13.6 billion, and this is for the federal government only. The combined federal and provincial tax expenditures would be approximately $20 billion for 1992.

A FINAL WORD

We have seen that Canada's social policy is made up of a complex system of benefits and tax expenditures. While there is no doubt that many of its goals are achieved, there is also no doubt that the system is under increasing pressure for a massive and integrated set of reforms. As the problems of large government deficits continue, many who support the system argue that it must be reformed to become more focused on those in need. They argue that, failing such reform, across-the-board massive reductions may be forced on governments who are being pressed by unsustainably high levels of debt to make major cuts in their deficits.

Reforming the system, however, is unpopular. When the Ontario government in 1995 reduced welfare payments in that province by 22 percent, there was public outcry. When Alberta instituted its reforms of the health-care system in 1994–1995, there was public outcry. When the federal government in 1995–1996 proposed changes to the unemployment insurance system, especially to reduce the generosity of the program to seasonal workers, there was public outcry.

It is no surprise that reform is unpopular. People who run the risk of losing some net benefits tend to be very vocal and to find ready political champions. Other opponents of reform fear that any changes will begin a process of eroding the whole social policy system, which many regard as one of Canada's outstanding accomplishments. It remains to be seen whether any Canadian government will attempt a major and comprehensive overhaul of the system— an overhaul that many observers feel would make the system fairer, less costly, yet more effective, but

---

[8]See, for example, William Robson, *Putting Some Gold in the Golden Years: Fixing the Canada Pension Plan,* C. D. Howe Institute, Commentary No. 76, January 1996.

which others feel would be the beginning of the end of Canada as a "caring society."

EVALUATING THE ROLE OF GOVERNMENT

Almost everyone would agree that the government has a major role to play in the economy because of the many sources of possible market failure. Yet there is no consensus that the present level and role of government intervention is the correct one.

PUBLIC VERSUS PRIVATE SECTOR

When the government raises money by taxation and spends it on an activity, it increases the spending of the public sector and decreases that of the private sector. Since the public sector and the private sector spend on different things, the government is changing the allocation of resources. Is that good or bad? How do we know if the country has the "right" balance between the public and private sectors? Should there be more schools and fewer houses or more houses and fewer schools?

For all goods that are produced and sold on the market, consumers' demand has a significant influence on the relative prices and quantities produced and thus on the allocation of the nation's resources. But no market provides relative prices for private houses versus public schools; thus, the choice between allowing money to be spent in the private sector and allowing it to be spent for public goods is a matter to be decided by Parliament and other legislative bodies.

John Kenneth Galbraith's bestseller, *The Affluent Society,* proclaimed that a correct assignment of marginal utilities would show them to be higher for an extra dollar's worth of public parks, clean water, and education than for an extra dollar's worth of television sets, shampoo, or automobiles. In Galbraith's view, the political process often fails to translate preferences for public goods into effective action; thus more resources are devoted to the private sector and fewer to the public sector than would be the case if the political mechanism were as effective as the market.

The alternative view has many supporters, who agree with Nobel Laureate James Buchanan that society has already reached a point where the value of the *marginal* dollar spent by government is less than the value of that dollar left in the hands of households or firms. These people argue that because bureaucrats are spending other people's money, they care very little about a few million or billion dollars here or there. They have only a weak sense of the opportunity cost of public expenditure and, thus, tend to spend beyond the point where marginal benefits equal marginal costs.

SCOPE OF GOVERNMENT ACTIVITY

One of the most difficult problems for the student of the Canadian economic system is to maintain the appropriate perspective about the scope of government activity in the market economy. On the one hand, there are literally tens of thousands of laws, regulations, and policies that affect firms and households. Many people believe that a general reduction in the role of government—fewer regulations as well as fewer crown corporations—is both possible and desirable. On the other hand, private decision makers still have an enormous amount of discretion about what they do and how they do it.

One pitfall is to become so impressed (or obsessed) with the many ways in which government activity impinges on the individual that one fails to see that these only make changes—sometimes large, but often small—in market signals in a system that basically leaves individuals free to make their own decisions. It is in the private sector that most individuals choose their occupations, earn their living, spend their incomes, and live their lives. In this sector too, firms are formed, choose products, live, grow, and sometimes die.

A different pitfall is to fail to see that a significant share of the taxes paid by the private sector is used to buy goods and services that add to the welfare of individuals. By and large, the public sector complements the private sector, doing things the private sector would leave undone or would do differently. For example, Canadians pay taxes which are used to finance expenditures on health and education. But certainly Canadians would continue to use hospitals and attend schools even if the various levels of government did not provide these goods, and instead left more money in peoples' pockets. Thus in many cases the government is levying taxes to raise money to finance goods that people would have purchased anyway. To recognize that we often benefit directly from public expenditure in no way denies that there is often waste, and sometimes worse, in public expenditure.

Yet another pitfall is failing to recognize that the public and private sectors compete in the sense that both make claims on the resources of the economy. Government activities are not without opportunity costs, except in those very rare circumstances in which they use resources that have no alternative use.

EQUITY AND EFFICIENCY

A related pitfall is to believe that the government's alleged inability to improve efficiency also implies an inability to improve equity. Throughout the world, governments are placing more reliance on markets in order to improve allocative efficiency and prospects for growth. Accepting the market for efficiency reasons does not, however, require accepting an increase in the hardships borne by the poor. Promoting social justice through government interventions directed at equity is compatible with promoting allocative efficiency, provided that appropriate means are carefully chosen.

EVOLUTION OF POLICY

Public policies in operation at any time are not the result of a single master plan that specifies precisely where and how the public sector shall seek to complement or interfere with the workings of the market mechanism. Rather, as individual problems arise, governments attempt to meet them by passing appropriate legislation to deal with the problem. These laws stay on the books, and some become obsolete and unenforceable. This is generally true of systems of law.

Many anomalies exist in our economic policies; for example, laws designed to support the incomes of small farmers have created some agricultural millionaires, and commissions created to ensure competition between firms often end up creating and protecting monopolies. Neither individual policies nor whole programs are above criticism.

In a society that elects its policy makers at regular intervals, however, the majority view on the amount and type of government intervention that is desirable will have some considerable influence on the amount of intervention that actually occurs. Fundamentally, a free-market system is retained because it is valued for its lack of coercion and its ability to do much of the allocating of society's resources better than any known alternative. But we are not mesmerized by it; we feel free to intervene in pursuit of a better world in which to live. We also recognize, however, that sometimes intervention has proved ineffective or even counterproductive.

SUMMARY

A. TAXATION IN CANADA

- Although the main purpose of the tax system is to raise revenue, tax policy is potentially a powerful device for income redistribution because the progressivity of different kinds of taxes varies greatly. An important part of the Canadian tax system is based on tax expenditures—provisions in the tax law that provide favourable tax treatment for certain economic behaviour.
- The most important taxes in Canada are the personal income tax, the corporate income tax, excise and sales taxes (including the nation-wide GST), and property taxes.

B. EVALUATING THE TAX SYSTEM

- Evaluating the tax system involves evaluating the efficiency and progressivity of the entire system, rather than of individual taxes within the system. For a given amount of revenue to be raised, efficiency and progressivity can be altered by changing the mix of the various taxes used.
- The total Canadian tax structure is roughly proportional, except for very low-income and very high-income groups (where it is mildly progressive).
- There are potentially important supply-side effects of taxation, as represented by a Laffer curve. A rise in the tax rate initially raises total tax revenue; after some point, however, further increases in the tax rate eliminate the incentive to produce taxable income, and so total tax revenue falls. Governments thus cannot always raise tax revenues by raising tax rates.

C. PUBLIC EXPENDITURE IN CANADA

- A large part of public expenditure is for the provision of goods and services. Other types of expenditures, including subsidies, transfer payments to individuals, and intergovernmental transfers, have increased sharply from the 1950s.

- Fiscal federalism is the idea that the various fiscal authorities should be coordinated in their spending plans and should have a mechanism for transfers between the various levels of government. Understanding the relationship between the federal government and the various provincial governments is of utmost importance in understanding many of Canada's most important government spending programs.

D. CANADIAN SOCIAL POLICY

- The five pillars of Canadian social policy are:

    1. Education
    2. Health care
    3. Income support programs (welfare and child benefits)
    4. Unemployment insurance
    5. Retirement benefits (CPP, GIS, OAS, and tax-assisted saving plans)

- Canadian governments have been urged to reexamine and redesign most social programs with the twin goals of improving their ability to deliver benefits and reducing costs.

E. EVALUATING THE ROLE OF GOVERNMENT

- When evaluating the overall role of government in the economy, we should keep four basic issues in mind:

    1. What is the appropriate mix between public goods and private goods?
    2. Much government activity is directed to providing goods and services that add directly to the welfare of the private sector (health and education, for example).
    3. The alleged inability of the government to improve the efficiency of the economy does not necessarily mean that it is also unable to improve equity.
    4. We should continually reevaluate existing programs; some that were needed in the past may no longer be needed; others may have unintended and undesirable side effects.

KEY CONCEPTS

Tax expenditures	Vertical and horizontal equity	Fiscal federalism
Progressive, proportional, and regressive taxes	Laffer curve	Intergovernmental transfers
	Transfer payments to individuals	Canadian social policy

DISCUSSION QUESTIONS

1. The Canadian taxpayer faces dozens of different taxes with different incidences, different progressivities, and different methods of collection. Discuss the case for and against a single taxing authority that would share the revenue with all levels of government. Why don't governments use a single tax source with the desired amount of progressivity built into it?

2. Consider a change in the tax law that lowers every taxpayer's marginal tax rate, with the maximum rate dropping from 50 percent to 33 percent, but with an increase in the tax base that leaves total tax revenue unchanged.

    a. Is it possible that everyone's average tax rate will fall?
    b. Is it possible that everyone's tax bill will fall?
    c. Suppose that charitable contributions to universities and colleges are tax deductible under the original tax law but not under the revised one. Would

   you predict that such contributions would increase, decrease, or remain the same?

    d. If such contributions are fully deductible under both the original and revised tax laws, would the amount of such contributions be expected to increase, decrease, or remain the same?
    e. Consider now taxpayers whose marginal tax rate falls from 50 percent to 33 percent and whose tax bills are less after the revision. Repeat the question in *d*.

3. Until recently in Canada, each individual had a lifetime $100,000 exemption for capital gains income, and subsequent capital gains were taxed at three-quarters the rates applicable to other income. Who were the likely beneficiaries of this policy? What were the likely effects on the distribution of income and the allocation of resources? Can you think of both equity and efficiency arguments supporting the elimination of such an exemption?

4. "Taxes on tobacco and alcohol are nearly perfect taxes. They raise lots of revenue and discourage smoking and drinking." In this statement, to what extent are the two effects inconsistent? How is the incidence of an excise tax related to the extent to which it discourages use of the product?

5. Suppose that it is agreed to spend $1 billion in programs to provide the poor with housing, better clothing, more food, and better health services.

   a. Argue the case for and against assistance of this kind rather than giving the money to the poor to spend as they think best.

   b. Should federal transfers to the provinces be conditional grants or grants with no strings attached? Is this the same issue raised in *a* or is it a different one?

6. Medical and health costs were 4.5 percent of GDP in 1950 and over 10 percent in 1993. Is 10 percent necessarily too much? Is it necessarily a sign that we are providing better health care? How might an economist think about what is the right percentage of GDP to devote to medical care?

7. Is the tax deduction allowed for RRSPs progressive or regressive (or neither)?

PART ELEVEN

INTERNATIONAL ECONOMICS

Does a country always benefit from free trade? If so, why do so many people appear to believe the opposite? Can government policy influence a country's pattern of comparative advantage? What is "dumping," and who, if anyone, is hurt by it? What is "trade creation" and "trade diversion," and how does this relate to NAFTA? How is Canada's exchange rate determined? Is Canada's current account deficit a problem, or does it merely reflect strong growth domestically? How is the conduct of macroeconomic policy altered in an open economy? Does international capital mobility make monetary and fiscal policy more or less effective? Is there any connection between the government's budget deficit and the country's current account deficit? These are the sorts of questions you will be able to answer after reading the final four chapters of this book.*

Chapter 35 explores the *gains from trade,* and how these gains are based on the important concept of *comparative advantage.* You will learn the reasons why a country might have a *comparative advantage* in a particular product, and how some government policies can have the effect of changing a country's pattern of comparative advantage. You will also be introduced to a country's *terms of trade,* the relative prices at which a country trades with the rest of the world.

In Chapter 36, the focus is on *trade policy.* You will learn about the case for *free trade* as well as the case for *protectionism* (you will also encounter some common but fallacious arguments for protectionism). We then examine some *methods of protection,* such as *tariffs, quotas,* and *nontariff barriers.* The Chapter then examines current trade policy in Canada, with an obvious emphasis on the North American Free Trade Agreement.

Chapter 37 introduces you to the *exchange rate* and the *balance of payments.* You will learn about the *foreign exchange market* and about why the balance of payments *always balances.* The important distinction between *fixed exchange rates* and *flexible exchange rates* will be discussed in detail, and you will understand the kinds of events that lead to an *appreciation* or a *depreciation* of the Canadian dollar.

In Chapter 38, the emphasis is on the conduct of macroeconomic policy in an open economy. You will learn why *international capital mobility* is so important to the conduct of policy. You will also see that there is indeed a close connection between the government's budget deficit and the country's current account deficit—the so-called *twin deficits.* Finally, the chapter ends with a discussion of how exchange rates and capital mobility have entered into the past two decades of monetary policy.

---

*Chapters 37 and 38 do not appear in *Microeconomics.*

CHAPTER 35

THE GAINS FROM INTERNATIONAL TRADE

Canadian consumers buy cars from Germany, Germans take holidays in Italy, Italians buy spices from Africa, Africans import oil from Kuwait, Kuwaitis buy Japanese cameras, and the Japanese buy Canadian lumber. *International trade* refers to exchanges of goods and services that take place across international boundaries.

The founders of modern economics were concerned with foreign trade problems. The great eighteenth-century British philosopher and economist David Hume (1711–1776), one of the first to work out the theory of the price system as a control mechanism, developed his concepts mainly in terms of prices in foreign trade. Adam Smith (1723–1790) in his *Wealth of Nations* attacked government restriction of trade. David Ricardo (1772–1823) developed the basic theory of the gains from trade that is studied in this chapter. The repeal of the Corn Laws—tariffs on the importation of grains into the United Kingdom—and the transformation of that country during the nineteenth century from a country of high tariffs to one of complete free trade were to some extent the result of agitation by economists whose theories of the gains from international trade led them to condemn all tariffs.

In this chapter, we inquire into the gains to living standards that result from trade. We find that the source of the gains from trade lies in differing cost conditions among geographical regions. World income is maximized when countries specialize in the products in which they have the lowest opportunity costs of production. These costs are partly determined by natural endowments, geographical and climatic conditions, partly by public policy, and partly by historical accident. We then go on to discuss the terms on which trade takes place—which refers to the amount that must be exported to obtain a given amount of imports.

Sources of the gains from trade

First, we need to define a few terms. An economy that engages in international trade is called an **open economy;** one that does not is called a **closed economy.** A situation in which a country does no foreign trade is called one of **autarky.** The advantages realized as a result of trade are called the **gains from trade.**

The source of such gains is most easily visualized by considering the differences between a world with trade and a world without it. Although politicians often regard foreign trade differently from domestic trade, economists from Adam Smith on have argued that the causes and consequences of international trade are simply an extension of the principles governing domestic trade. What is the advantage of trade among individuals, among groups, among regions, or among countries?

INTERPERSONAL, INTERREGIONAL, AND INTERNATIONAL TRADE

To begin, consider trade among individuals. Without trade, each person would have to be self-sufficient; each would have to produce all the food, clothing, shelter, medical services, entertainment, and luxuries that he or she consumed. A world of individual self-sufficiency would be a world with extremely low living standards.

Trade among individuals allows people to specialize in activities they can do well and to buy from others the goods and services they cannot easily produce. A good doctor who is a bad carpenter can provide medical services not only for his or her own family but also for an excellent carpenter without the training or the ability to practice medicine. Thus trade and specialization are intimately connected. Without trade, everyone must be self-sufficient; with trade, each person can specialize in what he or she does well and satisfy other needs by trading.

The same principles apply to regions. Without interregional trade, each region would be forced to be self-sufficient. With trade, each region can specialize in producing products for which it has some natural or acquired advantage. Plains regions can specialize in growing grain, mountain regions in mining and forest products, and regions with abundant power in manufacturing. Cool regions can produce wheat and other crops that thrive in temperate climates, and hot regions can grow such tropical crops as bananas, sugarcane, and coffee. The living standards of the inhabitants of all regions will be higher when each region specializes in products in which it has some natural or acquired advantage and obtains other products by trade than when all regions seek to be self-sufficient.

This same basic principle also applies to nations. A national boundary seldom delimits an area that is naturally self-sufficient. Nations, like regions or persons, can gain from specialization. More of the goods in which production is specialized are produced than residents wish to consume, while less domestic production of other goods that residents desire is available.

International trade is necessary to achieve the gains that international specialization makes possible.

This discussion suggests one important possible gain from trade.

With trade, each individual, region, or nation is able to concentrate on producing goods and services that it produces efficiently while trading to obtain goods and services that it does not produce efficiently.

Specialization and trade go hand in hand because there is no motivation to achieve the gains from specialization without being able to trade the goods produced for goods desired. Economists use the term *gains from trade* to embrace the results of both.

We will examine two sources of the gains from trade. The first is differences among regions of the world in climate and resource endowment that lead to advantages in producing certain goods and disadvantages in producing others. These gains occur even though each country's costs of production are unchanged by the existence of trade. The second source is the reduction in each country's costs of production that results from the greater production that specialization brings.

GAINS FROM SPECIALIZATION WITH GIVEN COSTS

To focus on differences in countries' conditions of production, suppose that there are no advantages arising from either economies of large-scale production or cost reductions that are the consequence of learning new skills. In these circumstances, what leads to gains from trade? To examine this question, we shall use an example involving only two countries and two products, but the general principles also apply when there are many countries and many products. This discussion provides an elaboration of the points made in Extension 3-1 in Chapter 3 on comparative and absolute advantage.

A Special Case: Absolute Advantage

The gains from trade are clear when there is a simple situation involving absolute advantage. **Absolute advantage** involves comparing the quantities of a specific product that can be produced using the same quantity of resources in two different regions. One region is said to have an absolute advantage over another in the production of product X when an equal quantity of resources can produce more X in the first region than in the second.

Suppose that region A has an absolute advantage over region B in one product, while region B has an absolute advantage over region A in another. This is a case of *reciprocal absolute advantage:* Each country has an absolute advantage in one product. In such a situation, the total production of both regions can be increased (relative to a situation of self-sufficiency) if each specializes in the product in which it has the absolute advantage.

Table 35-1 provides a simple example, using hypothetical data for wheat and cloth production in Canada and in England. In the example, total world production of both wheat and cloth increases when each country produces more of the good in which it has an absolute advantage. As a result, more wheat and more cloth are obtained for the same use of resources.

These gains from *specialization* make the gains from *trade* possible. England will now be producing more cloth and Canada more wheat than when they were self-sufficient. Thus Canada will be producing more wheat and less cloth than Canadian consumers wish to buy, and England will be producing more cloth and less wheat than English consumers wish to buy. If consumers in both countries are to get cloth and wheat in the desired proportions, England must export cloth to Canada and import wheat from Canada.

A First General Statement: Comparative Advantage

When each country has an absolute advantage over the other in a product, the gains from trade are obvi-

TABLE 35-1
Gains from Specialization with Absolute Advantage

Part A: Amounts of wheat and cloth that can be produced with 1 unit of resources in Canada and England

	Wheat (bushels)	Cloth (metres)
Canada	10	6
England	5	10

Part B: Changes resulting from the transfer of 1 unit of Canadian resources into wheat and 1 unit of English resources into cloth

	Wheat (bushels)	Cloth (metres)
Canada	+10	−6
England	−5	+10
World	+5	+4

When there is a reciprocal absolute advantage, specialization makes it possible to produce more of both commodities. Part A shows the production of wheat and cloth that can be achieved in each country by using 1 unit of resources. Canada can produce 10 bushels of wheat or 6 metres of cloth; England can produce 5 bushels of wheat or 10 metres of cloth. Canada has an absolute advantage in producing wheat, England in producing cloth. Part B shows the changes in production caused by moving 1 unit of resources out of cloth and into wheat production in Canada and moving 1 unit of resources in the opposite direction in England. There is an increase in world production of 5 bushels of wheat and 4 metres of cloth; worldwide, there are gains from specialization. In this example, the more resources are transferred into wheat production in Canada and into cloth production in England, the larger the gains will be.

ous. But what if Canada can produce both wheat and cloth more efficiently than England? In essence, this was David Ricardo's question, posed nearly two centuries ago. His answer underlies the theory of comparative advantage and is still accepted by economists as a valid statement of the potential gains from trade.

To start with, suppose that Canadian efficiency increases 10-fold above the levels recorded in the previous example, so that a unit of Canadian resources can produce either 100 bushels of wheat or 60 metres of cloth. English efficiency remains unchanged (see Table 35-2). It might appear that Canada, which is now better than England at producing both wheat and cloth, has nothing to gain by trading with such an inefficient foreign country. But this is wrong. That it *does* have something to gain is shown in Table 35-2. Even though Canada is 10 times as efficient as in the situation of Table 35-1, it is still possible to increase world production of both wheat and cloth by having Canada produce more wheat and less cloth and England produce more cloth and less wheat.

TABLE 35-2
Gains from Specialization with Comparative Advantage

Part A: Amounts of wheat and cloth that can be produced with 1 unit of resources in Canada and England

	Wheat (bushels)	Cloth (metres)
Canada	100	60
England	5	10

Part B: Changes resulting from the transfer of one-tenth of 1 unit of Canadian resources into wheat and 1 unit of English resources into cloth

	Wheat (bushels)	Cloth (metres)
Canada	+10	−6
England	−5	+10
World	+5	+4

When there is comparative advantage, specialization makes it possible to produce more of both commodities. The productivity of English resources is left unchanged from Table 35-1; that of Canadian resources is increased 10-fold. England no longer has an absolute advantage in producing either commodity. Total production of both commodities can nonetheless be increased by specialization. Moving one-tenth of 1 unit of Canadian resources out of cloth and into wheat and moving 1 unit of resources in the opposite direction in England causes world production of wheat to rise by 5 bushels and cloth by 4 metres.

What is the source of this gain? Although Canada has an absolute advantage over England in the production of both wheat and cloth, the *margin* of advantage differs in the two products. Canada can produce 20 times as much wheat as England by using the same quantity of resources but only 6 times as much cloth. Canada is said to have a *comparative advantage* in the production of wheat (and a comparative disadvantage in the production of the cloth). This statement implies another: England has a comparative advantage in the production of cloth and a comparative disadvantage in the production of wheat.

One of the theory's key propositions is this:

The gains from specialization and trade depend on the pattern of comparative, not absolute, advantage.

A comparison of Tables 35-1 and 35-2 refutes the notion that the absolute *levels* of efficiency of two regions determine the gains from specialization. The key is that the margin of advantage one region has over the other must differ between products. Total world production can then be increased if each region specializes in producing the product in which it has a comparative advantage.

Comparative advantage is necessary as well as sufficient for gains from trade. This means that *if* there is comparative advantage then there *are* gains from trade; it also means that if there is *no* comparative advantage then there are *no* gains from trade. This is illustrated in Table 35-3, showing Canada with an absolute advantage in both products and neither country with a comparative advantage over the other in the production of either product. Canada is 10 times as efficient as England in the production of wheat and in the production of cloth. Now there is no way to increase the production of *both* wheat and cloth by reallocating resources within Canada and within England. Part B of the table provides one example of a resource shift that illustrates this. *Absolute advantage without comparative advantage does not lead to gains from trade.*

A Second General Statement: Opportunity Costs

Much of the foregoing argument has used the concept of a unit of resources. It assumes that units of resources can be equated across countries so that statements such as "Canada can produce 10 times as much wheat with the same quantity of resources as England" are meaningful. Measurement of the real resource cost of producing products poses many difficulties. If, for example, England uses land, labour, and capital in proportions different from those used in Canada, it may not be clear which country gets more output per unit of resource input. Fortunately, the proposition about the gains from trade can be restated without reference to so fuzzy a concept as units of resources.

To do this, go back to the examples of Tables 35-1 and 35-2. Calculate the *opportunity cost* of wheat and cloth in the two countries. When resources are fully employed (so that production takes place on the country's production possibilities frontier), the only way to produce more of one product is to produce less of the other product. Table 35-1 shows that a unit of resources in Canada can produce 10 bushels of wheat *or* 6 metres of cloth. From this it follows that the opportunity cost of producing a unit of wheat is 0.60 units of cloth, while the opportunity cost of producing a unit of cloth is 1.67 units of wheat. These data are summarized in Table 35-4. The table also shows that in England, the opportunity cost of a unit of wheat is 2 units of cloth, while the opportunity cost of a unit of cloth is 0.50 units of wheat. Table 35-2 (which shows the same pattern of *comparative* advantage as Table 35-1) also gives rise to the opportunity costs in Table 35-4.

TABLE 35-3
Absence of Gains from Specialization When There Is No Comparative Advantage

Part A: Amounts of wheat and cloth that can be produced with 1 unit of resources in Canada and England

	Wheat (bushels)	Cloth (metres)
Canada	100	60
England	10	6

Part B: Changes resulting from the transfer of 1 unit of Canadian resources into wheat and 10 units of English resources into cloth

	Wheat (bushels)	Cloth (metres)
Canada	+100	−60
England	−100	+60
World	0	0

Where there is no comparative advantage, no reallocation of resources within each country can increase the production of both commodities. In this example, Canada has the same absolute advantage over England in each commodity (10-fold). There is no comparative advantage, and world production cannot be increased by reallocating resources in both countries. Therefore, specialization does not increase total output.

The sacrifice of cloth involved in producing wheat is much lower in Canada than it is in England. World wheat production can be increased if Canada rather than England produces it. Looking at cloth production, we can see that the loss of wheat involved in producing one unit of cloth is lower in England than in Canada. England is the lower-cost (that is, lower opportunity cost) producer of cloth. World cloth production can therefore be increased if England rather than Canada produces it. This situation is shown in Table 35-5.

The gains from trade arise from differing opportunity costs in the two countries.

Although Table 35-4 was calculated from Table 35-1 (or Table 35-2), we do not need to be able to compare real resource costs to calculate comparative advantages. The existence of a production possibility boundary implies opportunity costs, and the existence of different opportunity costs implies comparative advantages and disadvantages.

The conclusions about the gains from trade arising from international differences in opportunity costs may be summarized as follows:

1. Country A has a comparative advantage over country B in producing a product when the opportunity cost of production in country A is

TABLE 35-4
Opportunity Cost of Wheat and Cloth in Canada and England

	Wheat (bushels)	Cloth (metres)
Canada	0.60 metres cloth	1.67 bushels wheat
England	2.00 metres cloth	0.50 bushels wheat

Comparative advantages can be expressed in terms of opportunity costs that differ between countries. These opportunity costs can be obtained from Table 35-1 or Table 35-2. The English opportunity cost of 1 unit of wheat is obtained by dividing the cloth output of 1 unit of English resources by the wheat output. The result shows that 2 metres of cloth must be sacrificed for every extra unit of wheat produced by transferring English resources out of cloth production and into wheat. The other three cost figures are obtained in a similar manner.

lower. This implies, however, that it has a comparative *dis*advantage in the other product.

2. Opportunity costs depend on the relative costs of producing two products, not on absolute costs. (Notice that the examples in Tables 35-1 and 35-2 each give rise to the opportunity costs in Table 35-4.)

3. When opportunity costs are the same in all countries, there is no comparative advantage and there is no possibility of gains from specialization and trade. (You can illustrate this for yourself by calculating the opportunity costs implied by the data in Table 35-3.)

4. When opportunity costs differ in any two countries and both countries are producing both products, it is always possible to increase production of both products by a suitable reallocation of resources within each country. (This proposition is illustrated in Table 35-5.)

GAINS FROM TRADE WITH VARIABLE COSTS

So far, we have assumed that unit costs are the same whatever the scale of output, and we have seen that there are gains from specialization and trade as long as there are interregional differences in opportunity costs. If costs vary with the level of output, or as experience is acquired via specialization, *additional* sources of gain are possible.

Scale and Imperfect Competition

Real production costs, measured in terms of resources used, generally fall as the scale of output increases.

TABLE 35-5
Gains from Specialization with Differing Opportunity Costs

Changes resulting from each country's producing 1 more unit of a commodity in which it has the lower opportunity cost

	Wheat (bushels)	Cloth (metres)
Canada	+1.0	−0.6
England	−0.5	+1.0
World	+0.5	+0.4

Whenever opportunity costs differ between countries, specialization can increase the production of both commodities. These calculations show that there are gains from specialization, given the opportunity costs of Table 35-4. To produce 1 more bushel of wheat, Canada must sacrifice 0.6 metres of cloth. To produce 1 more metre of cloth, England must sacrifice 0.5 bushels of wheat. Making both changes raises world production of both wheat and cloth.

The larger the scale of operations, the more efficiently large-scale machinery can be used and the more a detailed division of tasks among workers is possible. Small countries such as Switzerland, Belgium, and Israel whose domestic markets are not large enough to exploit economies of scale would find it prohibitively expensive to become self-sufficient by producing a little bit of everything at very high cost.

Trade allows small countries to specialize and produce a few products at high enough levels of output to reap the available economies of scale.

Very large countries, such as the United States, have markets large enough to allow the production of most items at home at a scale of output great enough to obtain the available economies of scale. For them, the gains from trade arise mainly from specializing in products in which they have a comparative advantage. Yet even for such countries, a broadening of their markets permits achieving scale economies in subproduct lines, such as specialty steels or blue jeans.

One of the important lessons learned from patterns of world trade since World War II has concerned imperfect competition and product differentiation. Virtually all of today's manufactured consumer goods are produced in a vast array of differentiated product lines. In some industries, many firms produce this array; in others, only a few firms

produce the entire array. In either case, they do not exhaust all available economies of scale. (Students who have studied microeconomics may recall this from Chapter 12.) This means that an increase in the size of the market, even in an economy as large as the United States, may allow the exploitation of some previously unexploited scale economies in individual product lines.

These possibilities were first dramatically illustrated when the European Common Market (now known as the European Union or EU) was set up in the late 1950s. Economists had expected that specialization would occur according to the theory of comparative advantage, with one country specializing in cars, another in refrigerators, another in fashion clothes, another in shoes, and so on. This is not the way it worked out. Instead, much of the vast growth of trade was in *intra-industry* trade. Today, one can buy French, English, Italian, and German fashion goods, cars, shoes, appliances, and a host of other products in London, Paris, Bonn, and Rome. Ships loaded with Swedish furniture bound for London pass ships loaded with English furniture bound for Stockholm, and so on.

What free European trade did was to allow a proliferation of differentiated products, with different countries each specializing in different subproduct lines. Consumers have shown by their expenditures that they value this enormous increase in the range of choice among differentiated products. As Asian countries have expanded into North American and European markets with textiles, cars, and electronic goods, North American and European manufacturers have increasingly specialized their production and now export textiles, cars, and electronic equipment to Japan even while importing similar but differentiated products from Japan.

Learning by Doing

The discussion so far has assumed that costs vary only with the *level* of output. But they may also vary with the *accumulated experience* in producing a product over time.

Early economists placed great importance on a concept that we now call *learning by doing*. They believed that as countries gained experience in particular tasks, workers and managers would become more efficient in performing them. As people acquire expertise, costs tend to fall. There is substantial evidence that such learning by doing does occur. It is

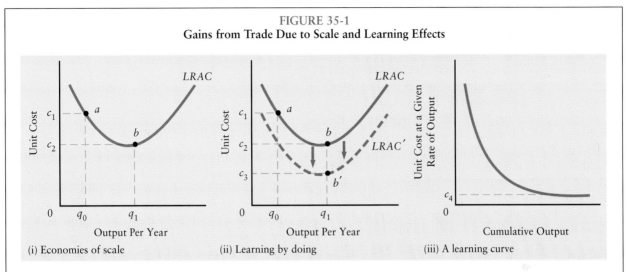

FIGURE 35-1
Gains from Trade Due to Scale and Learning Effects

(i) Economies of scale   (ii) Learning by doing   (iii) A learning curve

Specialization may lead to gains from trade by permitting economies of larger-scale output, by leading to downward shifts of cost curves, or both. Consider a country that wishes to consume the quantity q_0. Suppose that it can produce that quantity at an average cost per unit of c_1. Suppose further that the country has a comparative advantage in producing this product and can export the quantity $q_0 q_1$ if it produces q_1. This may lead to cost savings in two ways.

As shown in part (i), the increased level of production of q_1 compared to q_0 permits it to *move along* its cost curve from a to b, thereby reducing costs per unit to c_2. This is an economy of scale.

As shown in part (ii), as workers and management become more experienced, they may discover means of increasing productivity that lead to a downward shift of the cost curve. This is learning by doing. The downward *shift*, shown by the arrows, lowers the cost of producing every unit of output. At output q_1, costs per unit fall to c_3. The movement from a to b' incorporates both economies of scale and learning by doing.

Part (iii) shows a **learning curve,** which is another way of showing the effects of learning by doing. This curve shows the relation between the costs of producing a given output *per period* and the total accumulated output over the whole time during which production has taken place. Growing experience with making the product causes costs to fall as more and more is produced. When all learning possibilities have been exploited, costs reach a minimum level, shown by c_4 in the figure.

particularly important in many of today's knowledge-intensive high-tech industries.

The distinction between this phenomenon and the gains from economies of scale is illustrated in Figure 35-1. It is one more example of the difference between a movement along a curve and a shift of the curve.

Recognition of the opportunities for learning by doing leads to an important implication: Policymakers need not accept *current* comparative advantages as given. Through such means as education and tax incentives, they can seek to develop new comparative advantages.[1] Moreover, countries

cannot complacently assume that their existing comparative advantages will persist. Misguided education policies, the wrong tax incentives, or policies that discourage risk taking can lead to the rapid erosion of a country's comparative advantage in particular products. So, too, can developments in other countries.

SOURCES OF COMPARATIVE ADVANTAGE

We have seen that comparative advantage is the source of the gains from trade. But why do comparative advantages exist? Since a country's comparative advantage depends on its opportunity costs, we could also ask: Why do different countries have different opportunity costs?

---

[1]Of course, they can also foolishly use such policies to develop industries in which they do not have and will never achieve comparative advantages.

Different Factor Endowments

What has become the traditional answer to this question was provided early in the twentieth century by two great Swedish economists, Eli Heckscher and Bertil Ohlin, the latter subsequently being awarded the Nobel Prize in economics for his work in the theory of international trade. Their explanation for international cost differences is now incorporated in the so-called Heckscher-Ohlin model. According to their theory, the international cost differences that form the basis for comparative advantage arise because factor endowments differ across countries.

To see how this works, consider the prices for various types of goods in countries *in the absence of trade*. A country that is well endowed with fertile land but has a small population (like large parts of Canada) will find that land is cheap but labour is expensive. It will therefore produce land-intensive agricultural goods cheaply and labour-intensive goods, such as machine tools, only at high cost. The reverse will be true for a second country that is small in size but possesses abundant and efficient labour (like Japan). As a result, the first country will have a comparative advantage in agricultural production and the second in goods that use much labour and little land. Another country that is unusually well endowed with energy will have low energy prices. It will thus have a comparative advantage in such energy-intensive goods as chemicals and aluminium.

According to the Heckscher-Ohlin theory, countries have comparative advantages in the production of products that are intensive in the use of the factors of production with which they are abundantly endowed.

This is often called the *factor endowment theory of comparative advantage.*

Different Climates

Modern research suggests that this theory has considerable power to explain comparative advantage but that it does not provide the whole explanation. One obvious additional influence comes from all those natural factors that can be called *climate* in the broadest sense. If you combine land, labour, and capital in the same way in Nicaragua and in Iceland, you will not get the same output of most agricultural goods. Sunshine, rainfall, and average temperature also matter. If you seek to work with wool or cotton in dry and damp climates, you will get different results. (You can, of course, artificially create any climate you wish in a factory, but it costs money to create what is freely provided elsewhere.)

Climate, interpreted in the broadest sense, affects comparative advantage.[2]

Acquired Comparative Advantage

There is today a competing view. In extreme form, it says that comparative advantages exist but are typically *acquired*, not nature-given, and can change. This view of comparative advantage is *dynamic* rather than static. New industries are seen to depend more on human capital than on fixed physical capital or natural resources. The skills of a computer designer, a videogame programmer, a sound mix technician, or a rock star are acquired by education and on-the-job training. Natural endowments of energy and raw materials cannot account for the leadership in computer technology of Silicon Valley in California, for Britain's prominence in modern pop music or Canada's prominence in communications technology. When countries find their former dominance (based on comparative advantage) in such smokestack industries as cars and steel declining, their firms need not sit idly by. Instead, they can begin to adapt by developing new areas of comparative advantage.

Contrasts

This modern view is in sharp contrast with the traditional assumption that cost structures based largely on a country's natural endowments lead to a given pattern of international comparative advantage. The traditional view suggests that a government interested in maximizing its citizens' material standard of living should encourage specialization of production in goods where it currently has a comparative advantage. If all countries follow this advice, the theory predicts, each will be specialized in a relatively narrow range of distinct products. The British will produce engineering products, Canadians will be producers of resource-based primary products,

---

[2]Of course, if we consider "warm weather" a factor of production, then we could simply say that countries like Nicaragua are better endowed with that factor than countries like Iceland. In this sense, explanations of comparative advantage based on different climates are really just a special case of explanations based on factor endowments.

Americans will be farmers and factory workers, Central Americans will be banana growers, and so on.

There are surely elements of truth in both extreme views. It would be unwise to neglect resource endowments, climate, culture, social patterns, and institutional arrangements. But it would also be unwise to assume that all of them were innate and immutable.

To some extent, these views are reconciled by the theory of human capital which is a topic we discussed in Microeconomics. Comparative advantages that depend on human capital are consistent with traditional Heckscher-Ohlin theory. The difference is that this type of capital is acquired through conscious decisions relating to such matters as education and technical training.

IS COMPARATIVE ADVANTAGE OBSOLETE?

In the debate preceding the signing of both the Canada-U.S. Free Trade Agreement and the North American Free Trade Agreement (NAFTA), some opponents argued that the agreements relied on an outdated view of the gains from trade based on comparative advantage. The theory of comparative advantage was said to have been made obsolete by the new theories that we have just discussed.

In spite of such assertions, comparative advantage remains an important economic concept. At any one time, the operation of the price system will result in trade that follows the current pattern of comparative advantage. This is because comparative advantage is reflected in international relative prices, and these relative prices determine what goods a country will import and what it will export. For example, if Canadian costs of producing steel are particularly low relative to other Canadian costs, Canada's price of steel will be low by international standards, and steel will be a Canadian export (which it is). If Canada's costs of producing textiles are particularly high relative to other Canadian costs, Canada's price of textiles will be high by international standards, and Canada will import textiles (which it does). So there is no reason to change the view that Ricardo long ago expounded: *Current comparative advantage is a major determinant of trade under free-market conditions.*

What has changed, however, is economists' views about the *determinants* of comparative advantage. It now seems that current comparative advantage may be more open to change by private entrepreneurial ac-

tivities and by government policy than used to be thought. Thus what is obsolete is the belief that a country's current pattern of comparative advantage, and hence its current pattern of imports and exports, must be accepted as given and unchangeable.

The theory that comparative advantage determines trade flows is not obsolete, but the theory that comparative advantage is completely determined by forces beyond the reach of public policy has been discredited.

It is one thing to observe that it is *possible* for governments to influence a country's pattern of comparative advantage. It is quite another to conclude that it is *advisable* for them to try. The case in support of a specific government intervention requires that (1) there is scope for governments to improve on the results achieved by the free market, (2) the costs of the intervention be less than the value of the improvement to be achieved, and (3) governments will actually be able to carry out the required interventionist policies (without, for example, being sidetracked by considerations of electoral advantage).

THE TERMS OF TRADE

So far, we have seen that world production can be increased when countries specialize in the production of the products in which they have a comparative advantage and then trade with one another. We now ask, how will these gains from specialization and trade be shared among countries? The division of the gain depends on what is called the **terms of trade,** which relates to the quantity of imported goods that can be obtained per unit of goods exported. They are measured by the ratio of the price of exports to the price of imports.

A rise in the price of imported goods, with the price of exports unchanged, indicates a *fall in the terms of trade;* it will now take more exports to buy the same quantity of imports. Similarly, a rise in the price of exported goods, with the price of imports unchanged, indicates a *rise in the terms of trade;* it will now take fewer exports to buy the same quantity of imports. Thus the ratio of these prices measures the amount of imports that can be obtained per unit of goods exported.

In the example of Table 35-4, the Canadian domestic opportunity cost of 1 unit of cloth is 1.67 bushels of wheat. If Canadian resources are transferred from wheat to cloth, 1.67 bushels of wheat are given up for every metre of cloth. But if Canada could obtain its

THE GAINS FROM TRADE ILLUSTRATED GRAPHICALLY

International trade leads to an expansion of the set of goods that can be consumed in the economy in two ways:

1. by allowing the bundle of goods consumed to differ from the bundle produced; and,

2. by permitting a profitable change in the pattern of production.

Without international trade, the bundle of goods produced is the bundle consumed. With international trade, the consumption and production bundles can be altered independently to reflect the relative values placed on goods by international markets.

The graphical demonstration of the gains from trade proceeds in two stages.

STAGE 1: FIXED PRODUCTION

In each part of the figure, the black curve is the economy's production possibility boundary. If there is no international trade, the economy must consume the same bundle of goods that it produces. Thus the production possibility boundary is also the consumption possibility boundary. Suppose that the economy produces, and consumes, at point a, with x_1 of good X and y_1 of good Y, as in part (i) of the figure.

Next suppose that with production point a, good Y can be exchanged for good X internationally. The consumption possibilities are now shown by the line tt drawn through point a. The slope of tt indicates the quantity of Y that exchanges for a unit of X on the international market—the terms of trade.

Although production is fixed at point a, consumption can now be anywhere on the line tt. For example, the consumption point could be at b. This could be achieved by exporting y_2y_1 units of Y and importing x_1x_2 units of X. Because point b (and all others on line tt to the right of a) lies outside the production possibility boundary, there are potential gains from trade. Consumers are no longer limited by their own country's production possibilities. Let us suppose that they prefer point b to point a. They have achieved a gain from trade by being allowed to exchange some of their production of good Y for some quantity of good X and thus to consume more of good X than is produced at home.

STAGE 2: VARIABLE PRODUCTION

There is a further opportunity for the expansion of the country's consumption possibilities: With trade, the production bundle may be profitably altered in response to international prices. The country may pro-

cloth on more favourable terms by trading, then there would be gains to producing and exporting wheat in order to pay for the imports of cloth. Suppose, for example, that international prices were such that 1 bushel of wheat exchanged for (was equal in value to) 1 metre of cloth. At those terms of trade, Canada could obtain 1 metre of cloth for every bushel of wheat exported. It would get more cloth per unit of wheat exported than it could obtain by moving resources out of wheat into cloth production at home. These terms of trade would thus favour specializing in the production of wheat and trading it for cloth on international markets.

Similarly, in the example of Table 35-4, English consumers would gain if they could obtain wheat abroad at any terms of trade more favourable than 2 metres of cloth sacrificed. If the terms of trade permitted

the exchange of 1 bushel of wheat for 1 metre of cloth, the terms of trade would favour England's obtaining its wheat by exporting cloth rather than producing it at home: a unit of wheat would then cost 2 units of cloth sacrificed when produced at home compared to only 1 unit of cloth when obtained through trade.

In this example, both Canada and England gain from trade. Each can obtain units of the product in which it has a comparative disadvantage at a lower opportunity cost through international trade than through domestic production. The way in which the terms of trade interact with the gains from trade is illustrated graphically in Extension 35-1.

Because actual international trade involves many countries and many products, a country's terms of trade are computed as an index number:

duce the bundle of goods that is most valuable in world markets. That is represented by the bundle *d* in part (ii). The consumption possibility set is shifted to the line *t'*t'* by changing production from *a* to *d* and thereby increasing the country's degree of specialization in good *Y*. For every point on the original consumption possibility set *tt*, there are points on the new set *t'*t'* that allow more consumption of both goods—for example, compare points *b* and *f*. Notice also that except at the zero-trade point *d*, the new consumption

possibility set lies *everywhere above the production possibility curve*.

The benefits of moving from a no-trade position, such as *a*, to a trading position such as *b* or *f* are the *gains from trade* to the country. When the production of good *Y* is increased and the production of good *X* decreased, the country is able to move to a point such as *f* by producing more of good *Y*, in which the country has a comparative advantage, and trading the additional production for good *X*.

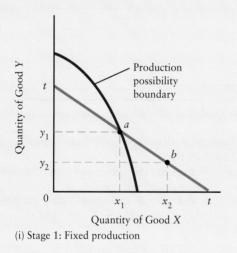

(i) Stage 1: Fixed production

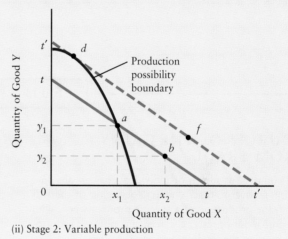

(ii) Stage 2: Variable production

$$\text{Terms of Trade} = \frac{\text{Index of Export Prices}}{\text{Index of Import Prices}} \times 100$$

A rise in the index is referred to as a *favourable* change in a country's terms of trade (sometimes called a terms of trade *improvement*). A favourable change means that more can be imported per unit of goods exported than previously. For example, if the export price index rises from 100 to 120 while the import price index rises from 100 to 110, the terms-of-trade index rises from 100 to 109. At the new terms of trade, a unit of exports will buy 9 percent more imports than at the old terms.

A decrease in the index of the terms of trade, called an *unfavourable* change (or a terms of trade *deterioration*), means that the country can import

less in return for any given amount of exports, or, equivalently, it must export more to pay for any given amount of imports. For example, the sharp rise in oil prices in the 1970s led to large unfavourable shifts in the terms of trade of oil-importing countries. When oil prices fell sharply in the mid 1980s, the terms of trade of oil-importing countries changed favourably. The converse was true for oil-exporting countries.

Canada's terms of trade since 1970 are shown in Figure 35-2. As is clear, the terms of trade are quite variable, reflecting cyclical changes in the relative prices of different products. Also clear from the figure is that Canada's terms of trade have displayed a long-term improvement over the past 25 years.

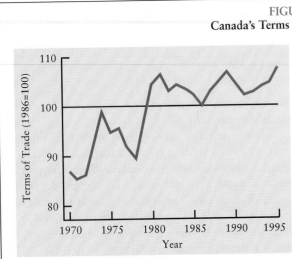

FIGURE 35-2
Canada's Terms of Trade, 1970–1995

Canada's terms of trade have been quite variable over the past 25 years, but they have also displayed a long-term improvement. The data shown is Canada's terms of trade—the ratio of an index of Canadian export prices to an index of Canadian import prices. As the relative prices of lumber, oil, wheat, electronic equipment, textiles, fruit, and other products change, the terms of trade naturally change. For Canada, however, there has also been a trend improvement in the terms of trade over the past 25 years.

(*Source: Economic Reference Tables*, Department of Finance, August 1995.)

SUMMARY

A. SOURCES OF THE GAINS FROM TRADE

- One country (or region or individual) has an absolute advantage over another country (or region or individual) in the production of a specific product when, with the same input of resources in each country, it can produce more of the product than can the other.

- Comparative advantage is the relative advantage one country enjoys over another in the production of various products. It occurs whenever countries have different opportunity costs of producing particular goods. World production of all products can be increased if each country transfers resources into the production of the products in which it has a comparative advantage.

- In a situation of reciprocal *absolute* advantage, the total production of both products will be raised if each country specializes in the production of the product in which it has the absolute advantage. However, the gains from trade do not require absolute advantage on the part of each country, only comparative advantage.

- The most important proposition in the theory of the gains from trade is that trade allows all countries to obtain the goods in which they do not have a comparative advantage at a lower opportunity cost than they would face if they were to produce all products for themselves; this allows all countries to have more of

all products than they could have if they tried to be self-sufficient.

- As well as gaining the advantages of specialization arising from comparative advantage, a nation that engages in trade and specialization may realize the benefits of economies of large-scale production and of learning by doing.

- Classical theory regarded comparative advantage as largely determined by natural resource endowments that are difficult to change. Economists now believe that some comparative advantages can be acquired and consequently can be changed. A country may, in this view, influence its role in world production and trade. Successful intervention leads to a country's acquiring a comparative advantage; unsuccessful intervention fails to develop such an advantage.

B. THE TERMS OF TRADE

- The terms of trade refer to the ratio of the prices of goods exported to the prices of those imported. This determines the quantity of imports that can be obtained per unit of exports. The terms of trade determine how the gains from trade are shared.

- A favourable change in the terms of trade—a rise in export prices relative to import prices—means that a country can acquire more imports per unit of exports, and vice versa.

Interpersonal, interregional, and international specialization

Absolute advantage and comparative advantage

Opportunity cost and comparative advantage

The gains from trade: specialization, scale economies, and learning by doing

The sources of comparative advantage

Factor endowments

Acquired comparative advantage

The terms of trade

1. Adam Smith saw a close connection between the wealth of a nation and its willingness "freely to engage" in foreign trade. What is the connection?

2. One critic of the North American Free Trade Agreement argued that "it can't be in our interest to sign this deal; Mexico gains too much from it." What does the theory of the gains from trade have to say about that criticism?

3. Canada, the United States, and Mexico are clearly separate countries. Does this fact imply a lower standard of living in each of the three countries compared to the situation where they are united into a single new country? If Quebec were to separate from the rest of Canada, would this fact alone mean that Quebec and (the new) Canada would have a lower standard of living (ignoring the costs of upheaval that would be associated with the actual separation)?

4. One product innovation that appears imminent is the electric car. However, development costs are high, and economies of scale and learning by doing are both likely to be operative. As a result, there will be a substantial competitive advantage for those who develop a marketable product early. What implications might this have for government policies toward North American automobile manufacturers' activities in this area? Should the Canadian or U.S. governments encourage joint efforts by Chrysler, Ford, and GM, even if this appears to lessen competition between them?

5. Studies of Canadian trade patterns have shown that industries with high wages are among the largest and fastest-growing export sectors. Does this contradict the principle of comparative advantage?

6. Predict what each of the following events would do to the terms of trade of the importing country and the exporting country, other things being equal.

   a. A blight destroys a large part of the coffee beans produced in the world.

   b. The Koreans cut the price of the steel they sell to Canada.

   c. General inflation of 10 percent occurs around the world.

   d. Violation of OPEC output quotas leads to a sharp fall in the price of oil.

7. Heavy Canadian borrowing abroad has several times led to a high value of the dollar and thus a rise in the ratio of export prices to import prices. Although this is called a favourable change in the terms of trade, are there any reasons why it may not have been a good thing for the Canadian economy?

8. Suppose that the situation described in the accompanying table exists. Assume that there are no tariffs and no government intervention and that labour is the only factor of production. Let X take different values—say, $10, $20, $40, and $60. In each case, in what direction will trade have to flow in order for the gains from trade to be exploited?

| | Labour cost of producing 1 unit of | |
Country	Artichokes	Bathtubs
Inland	$20	$40
Outland	$15	$X

9. Suppose the following table shows the production of wheat and corn in Brazil and Mexico assuming no trade between the countries.

	Brazil	Mexico
Wheat	90 bushels per acre	50 bushels per acre
Corn	30 bushels per acre	20 bushels per acre

   a. Which country, Brazil or Mexico, maintains an absolute advantage in the production of wheat? Of corn?

   b. Which country, Brazil or Mexico, maintains a comparative advantage in the production of wheat? Of corn?

   c. Assuming constant returns to scale, draw the appropriate production possibilities curve for each country. In the absence of trade, assume each country has exactly 1 million acres of farmland and devotes exactly half towards the production of each commodity. How much of each commodity does each country produce without trade?

   d. Give an example (using specific figures) of how specialization and trade could benefit both countries.

10. Are there always benefits to specialization and trade? When are the benefits greatest? Under what situations are there *no* benefits from specialization and trade?

TRADE POLICY

Conducting business in a foreign country is not always easy. Differences in language, in local laws and customs, and in currency often complicate transactions. Our concern in this chapter, however, is not with these complications but with government policy toward international trade and related matters, which is called **trade policy** or **commercial policy**. At one extreme is a policy of free trade, which means an absence of any form of government interference with the free flow of international trade. Any departure from free trade designed to protect domestic industries from foreign competition is called **protectionism.**

This chapter begins by restating the case for free trade and then goes on to study various valid and invalid arguments that are commonly advanced for some degree of protectionism. After that, we study the many modern institutions designed to foster freer trade on either a global or a regional basis. We conclude by studying one such institution that is of central importance to Canada—the North American Free Trade Agreement (NAFTA).

THE THEORY OF TRADE POLICY

Today, most governments accept that a relatively free flow of international trade is desirable for the health of their individual economies. But heated debates still occur over trade policy. Should a country permit the completely free flow of international trade, or should it seek to protect some of its local producers from some of the foreign competition that they face? If some protection is desired, should it be achieved by tariffs or by nontariff barriers? **Tariffs** are taxes designed to raise the price of foreign goods. **Nontariff barriers (NTBs)** are devices other than tariffs that are designed to reduce the flow of imports; examples are quotas and customs procedures that are deliberately more cumbersome than necessary.

THE CASE FOR FREE TRADE

The case for free trade was presented in Chapter 35. Comparative advantages arise whenever countries have different opportunity costs. Free trade allows all countries to specialize in producing products in which they have a comparative advantage. This in turn maximizes world production and hence maximizes average world living standards (as reflected by the world's per capita GDP).

Free trade does not necessarily make everyone better off than they would be in its absence. For example, reducing an existing tariff often results in individual groups receiving a smaller share of a larger world output so that they lose even though the average person gains. If we ask whether it is *possible* for free trade to improve everyone's living standards, the answer is "yes." But if we ask whether free trade always does so, the answer is "not necessarily."

There is abundant evidence that significant differences in opportunity costs do exist and that large gains are realized from international trade because of these differences.

What needs explanation is the fact that trade is not wholly free. Why do tariffs and other barriers to trade continue to exist two centuries after Adam Smith and David Ricardo stated the case for free trade? Is there a valid case for some protectionism?

THE CASE FOR PROTECTIONISM

Two kinds of arguments for protection are commonly offered. The first concerns national objectives *other than* maximizing total income; the second concerns the desire to increase one country's national income, possibly at the expense of the national incomes of other countries.

Objectives Other than Maximizing National Income

It is possible to believe that a country's national income is maximized with free trade and yet rationally oppose free trade because of a concern with other policy objectives.

Noneconomic Advantages of Diversification. Comparative advantage might dictate that a small country should specialize in producing a narrow range of products. The government might decide, however, that there are distinct social advantages in encouraging a more diverse economy. Citizens would be given a wider range of occupations, and the social and psychological advantages of diversification may more than compensate for a reduction in per capita output below what they would be with complete specialization of production according to comparative advantage.

Risks of Specialization. For a very small country, specializing in the production of only a few products—though dictated by comparative advantage—might involve risks that the country does not wish to take. One such risk is that technological advances may render its basic product obsolete. Everyone understands this risk, but there is debate about what governments can do about it. The pro-tariff argument is that the government can encourage a more diversified economy by protecting industries that otherwise could not compete. Opponents argue that governments, being naturally influenced by political motives are poor judges of which industries can be protected in order to produce diversification at a reasonable cost.

National Defence. Another reason for protectionism concerns national defence. It is argued, for example, that the United States needs an experienced commercial shipping industry in case of war and that this industry should be fostered by protectionist policies even though it is less efficient than the foreign competition. Current U.S. policy does this by forbidding foreign ships from transporting cargo between any two U.S. ports. Opponents of this measure argue that it has little to do with national security and much to do with increasing the incomes of ship owners and their crews at the expense of all those who use those ships.

Protection of Specific Groups.   Although free trade—and specialization according to comparative advantage—will maximize per capita GDP over the whole economy, some specific groups may have higher incomes under protection than under free trade. An obvious example is a firm or an industry that is given monopoly power when tariffs are used to restrict foreign competition. If a small group of firms and their employees find their incomes increased by a substantial amount when they get tariff protection, they may not be concerned that income for everyone else in the economy falls by a small amount. They get a much larger share of a slightly smaller total income and end up better off. If they gain from the trade restrictions, they will lose from free trade.

A similar argument can apply to larger groups. Consider the ratio of skilled workers to unskilled workers. There are plenty of both types throughout the world. Compared to much of the rest of the world, however, Canada has more skilled and fewer unskilled people. When trade is expanded because of a reduction in tariffs, Canada will tend to export goods made by its abundant skilled workers and import goods made by unskilled workers. (This is the basic prediction of the *factor endowment theory* of comparative advantage that we discussed in Chapter 35.) Because Canada is now exporting more goods made by skilled labour, the demand for such labour rises. Because Canada is now importing more goods made by unskilled labour, the demand for such labour falls. This specialization according to comparative advantage raises average Canadian living standards, but it will also tend to raise the wages of skilled Canadian workers relative to the wages of unskilled Canadian workers.

If increasing trade has these effects, then reducing trade by raising trade barriers can have the opposite effects. Raising trade barriers may raise the relative wages of unskilled Canadian workers, giving them a larger share of a smaller total GDP. The conclusion is that trade restrictions can improve the *relative* earnings of one group whenever the restrictions increase the demand for that group's services. This is done, however, at the expense of a reduction in *overall* national income and hence the country's average living standards.

This analysis is important because it reveals both the grain of truth and the dangers that lie behind the resistance to reductions in trade restrictions on the part of some labour groups and some organizations whose main concern is with the poor.

What is the conclusion from the foregoing discussion? Other things being equal, most people prefer more income to less. However, economists cannot say that it is irrational for a society to sacrifice some income to achieve other goals. But economists can do three things when presented with such arguments for adopting protectionist measures. First, they can ask if the proposed measures really do achieve the ends suggested. Second, they can calculate the cost of the measures in terms of lowered living standards. Third, they can see if there are alternative means of achieving the stated goals at lower cost in terms of lost national income.

Maximizing One Country's National Income

Next we consider several arguments for the use of tariffs when the objective is to make a country's national income as large as possible.

To Alter the Terms of Trade.   Tariffs can be used to change the terms of trade in favour of a country that makes up a large fraction of the world demand for some product that it imports. By restricting its demand for that product through a tariff, it can force down the price that foreign exporters receive for that product. The price paid by domestic consumers will probably rise but as long as the increase is less than the tariff, foreign suppliers will receive less per unit. For example, a 20 percent U.S. tariff on the import of Canadian softwood lumber or natural gas might raise the price paid by U.S. consumers by 12 percent and lower the price received by Canadian suppliers by 8 percent (the difference between the two prices being received by the U.S. treasury).

Imposing tariffs to alter the terms of trade reduces world output. It can, however, make it possible for a single country to gain because its gets a sufficiently larger share of the smaller world output. However, if foreign countries retaliate by raising their trade restrictions, the ensuing trade war can easily leave every country with a reduced national income.

In many modern cases, the U.S. has left the exporting country to apply its own export-restricting measures. The effect of such export restrictions, as we shall see later in this chapter, is to turn the terms of trade in favour of the exporting country at the expense of the importing one.

To Protect Against "Unfair" Actions by Foreign Firms and Governments. Tariffs are used to prevent foreign industries from harming domestic industries by employing predatory practices. Two common practices are subsidies paid by foreign governments to their exporters and price discrimination by foreign firms, which is called *dumping* when it is done across international borders. These practices are typically countered by levying tariffs called *countervailing duties* and *antidumping duties*. The circumstances under which dumping and foreign subsidization provide a valid argument for such tariffs are considered in detail later in this chapter.

To Protect Infant Industries. The oldest valid argument for protectionism as a means of raising living standards concerns economies of scale. It is usually called the **infant industry argument.** An infant industry is nothing more than a new, small industry. If such an industry has large economies of scale, costs will be high when the industry is small but will fall as the industry grows. In such industries, the country first in the field has a tremendous advantage. A newly developing country may find that in the early stages of development, its industries are unable to compete with established foreign rivals. A trade restriction may protect these industries from foreign competition while they grow up. When they are large enough, they will be able to produce as cheaply as foreign rivals and thus be able to compete without protection.

Most of the now industrialized countries developed their industries initially under quite heavy tariff protection. This group included Canada, the United States, Germany, and South Korea. Once the industrial sector was well developed, all of these countries moved to reduce their levels of protection moving a long way toward freer trade.

To Encourage Learning by Doing. Learning by doing, which we discussed in Chapter 35, suggests that the pattern of comparative advantage can be changed. If a country learns enough by producing products for which it currently has a comparative *dis*advantage, it may gain in the long run by specializing in those products, developing a comparative advantage as the learning process lowers their costs.

Learning by doing is an example of what in Chapter 35 we called dynamic comparative advantage. The success of such *newly industrializing countries (NICs)* as Hong Kong, South Korea, Singapore, Taiwan, Indonesia, and Thailand seemed to many observers to be based on acquired skills and government policies that created favourable business conditions. This gave rise to the theory that comparative advantages can change and that they can be developed by suitable government policies, which can, however, take many forms other than restricting trade.

Some countries have succeeded in developing strong comparative advantages in targeted industries, but others have failed. One reason such policies sometimes fail is that protecting local industries from foreign competition may make the industries unadaptive and complacent. Another reason is the difficulty of identifying the industries that will be able to succeed in the long run. All too often, the protected infant grows up to be a weakling requiring permanent protection for its continued existence. Or else the rate of learning is slower than for similar industries in countries that do not provide protection from the chill winds of international competition. In these instances, the anticipated comparative advantage never materializes. One way of accomplishing these goals without the risk of protecting failures is to give other forms of assistance to the industries but insist that they compete in international markets from the outset. This assists industries without insulating them from the need to be internationally competitive.

To Create or Exploit a Strategic Trade Advantage. A major new argument for tariffs or other trade restrictions is to create a strategic advantage in producing or marketing some new product that is expected to generate pure profits. To the extent that all lines of production earn normal profits, there is no reason to produce goods other than ones for which a country has a comparative advantage. Some goods, however, are produced in industries containing a few large firms where economies of scale provide a natural barrier to entry. Firms in these industries can earn high profits even over long periods of time. If protection of the domestic market can increase the chance that one of the protected domestic firms will become established and thus earn high profits, the protection may pay off. This is the general idea behind the modern concept of *strategic trade policy,* and it is treated in more detail in the next section.

Strategic Trade Policy

In the past dozen or so years, another group of arguments *against* free trade have evolved; these arguments are based on the existence of imperfect competition and increasing returns to scale that arise from the presence of high fixed costs.

Implications of High Fixed Costs. Many of today's high-tech industries have large fixed costs of product development. For a new generation of civilian aircraft, silicon chips, computers, artificial intelligence machines, and genetically engineered food products, a very high proportion of each producer's total costs goes to product development. These are fixed costs of entering the market, and they must be incurred before a single unit of output can be sold.

In such industries, the actual costs of producing each unit of an already developed product may be quite small. Even if average variable costs are constant, the large fixed development costs mean that the average total cost curve has a significant negative slope over a large range of output. It follows that the price at which a firm can expect to recover its total cost is negatively related to its expected volume of sales—the larger its sales, the lower the price that it can charge and still cover its full costs.

In such industries, a large number of firms, each of which has a relatively small output, could not cover their fixed costs. However, a small number of firms, each of which has a high output, could do so. Furthermore, it is possible for these firms to make large profits, whereas the entry of one more firm would cause everyone to suffer losses. In this case, the first firms that become established in the market will control it and will earn the profits.[1]

The production of full-sized commercial jets provides an example of an industry that possesses many of these characteristics. The development costs of a new generation of jet aircraft have increased with each new generation. If the aircraft manufacturers are to recover these costs, each of them must have large sales. Thus the number of firms that the market can support has diminished steadily until today there is room in the world aircraft industry for only two or three firms producing a full range of commercial jets.

Argument for Protection. The characteristics just listed are sometimes used to provide arguments for protecting such industries. Suppose, for example, that there is room in the aircraft industry for only three major producers of the next round of passenger jets. If a government subsidizes a domestic firm, this firm may become one of the three that succeed. In this case, the profits that are subsequently earned may more than repay the cost of the subsidy. Furthermore, another country's firm, which was not subsidized, may have been just as good as the three that succeeded. Without the subsidy, however, this firm may lose out in the battle to establish itself as one of the three surviving firms in the market. Having lost this one battle, it loses its entire fight for existence.

This example is not unlike the story of Airbus, a European producer of commercial jet aircraft. Airbus received many direct subsidies (and they charge that their main competitor, Boeing, received many indirect ones). Whatever the merits of the argument, several things are clear: The civilian jet aircraft industry remains profitable, there is room for only two or three major producers, and one of these would not have been Airbus if it had not been for substantial government assistance. (It is not clear, however, if profits earned by Airbus will ever cover the enormous subsidies paid by governments during earlier stages of design and production.)

Debate over Strategic Trade Policy. Airbus provides an example where strategic trade policy was successful in permitting a group of countries to succeed in an industry with high worldwide profits. (Whether Airbus can compete without subsidies, in the long run, remains to be seen.) The Japanese automobile industry is another example. It was protected from foreign competition all through its early stages of development in the 1950s and 1960s. In the 1980s it had reached such levels of technological efficiency that it went on to become a serious competitive threat to European and North American automobile producers.

High-definition television (HDTV) is an example of the failure of such a policy. During the 1980s, the Japanese government provided extensive subsidies to the development of HDTV (which, when it is introduced, will have much higher video quality than current television). The U.S. government did not provide such subsidies, despite widespread concern from the U.S. electronics industry that it would lose out to Japan in an important market. As it happened, however, a number of U.S. firms, acting on their own, developed a technique for HDTV that is superior to the subsidized Japanese version, and the U.S. standard

---

[1]The reason for this is found in the indivisibility of product development costs. For example, if $500 million is required to develop a marketable product, a firm that spends only $300 million gets nothing. To see why this creates the potential for profits, suppose that the market is large enough for the product to be sold at a price that would cover variable costs of production and also pay the opportunity costs of $1.25 billion worth of capital. Further suppose that the capital required for actual production is negligible. In this case, two firms with a total of $1 billion of capital invested in development costs will enter the market and earn large profits. However, if a third firm entered, making the industry's total invested capital $1.5 billion, all three firms would incur losses.

for HDTV is generally expected to dominate the global market.

Just as the Airbus story seems to support proponents of strategic trade policy, the HDTV story seems to support the opponents. Opponents argue that strategic trade policy is nothing more than a modern version of age-old and faulty justifications for tariff protection. Once all countries try to be strategic, they will all waste vast sums trying to break into industries in which there is no room for most of them. Domestic consumers would benefit most, they say, if their governments let other countries engage in this game. Consumers could then buy the cheap, subsidized foreign products and export traditional non-subsidized products in return. The opponents of strategic trade policy also argue that democratic governments that enter the game of picking and backing winners are likely to make more bad choices than good ones. One bad choice, with all of its massive development costs written off, would require that many good choices also be made in order to make the equivalent in profits that would allow taxpayers to break even overall.

The Importance of International Competition. In today's world, a country's products must stand up to international competition if they are to survive. Over time, this requires that they hold their own in competition for successful innovations. Over even so short a period as a decade, firms that do not develop new products and new production methods fall seriously behind their competitors in many industries. Using case studies covering many countries, economists such as Michael Porter of Harvard University have shown that almost all firms that succeed in holding their own in competition based on innovation operate in highly competitive environments. Protection, by reducing competition from foreign firms, reduces the incentive for industries to fight to succeed internationally. If any one country adopts high tariffs unilaterally, its domestic industries will become less competitive. Secure in its home market because of the tariff wall, its protected industries are likely to become less and less competitive in the international market. As the gap between domestic and foreign industries widens, any tariff wall will provide less and less protection. Eventually, the domestic industries will succumb to the foreign competition. Meanwhile, domestic living standards will fall relative to foreign ones as an increasing productivity gap opens between domestic protected industries and foreign, internationally oriented ones.

Although restrictive policies have sometimes been pursued following a rational assessment of the approximate cost, it is hard to avoid the conclusion that more often than not, such policies are often pursued for political objectives or on fallacious economic grounds, with little appreciation of the actual costs involved. The very high tariffs in Canada and the United States during the 1920s and 1930s are a conspicuous example. The current pressure on the governments of Canada, the United States, and the EU to "do something" about the competition from Japan, Korea, and other Pacific Rim countries may well be another.

FALLACIOUS ARGUMENTS FOR PROTECTIONISM

We have seen that there are generally gains from trade, although trade does not necessarily make everyone in a country better off. We have also seen that there are some situations in which there are valid arguments for restricting trade. For every valid argument, however, there are many fallacious arguments—many of these are based, directly or indirectly, on the misconception that in every transaction there is a winner and a loser. Here we review a few such arguments that are frequently advanced in political debates concerning international trade.

Keep the Money at Home

This argument says that if I buy a foreign good, I have the good and the foreigner has the money, whereas if I buy the same good locally, I have the good and our country has the money, too. This argument is based on a common misconception. It assumes that domestic money actually goes abroad physically when imports are purchased and that trade flows only in one direction. But when Canadian importers purchase Japanese goods, they do not send dollars abroad. They (or their financial agents) buy Japanese yen and use them to pay the Japanese manufacturers. They purchase the yen on the foreign exchange market by giving up dollars to someone who wishes to use them for expenditure in Canada. Even if the money did go abroad physically—that is, if a Japanese firm accepted a shipload of Canadian $100 bills—it would be because that firm (or someone to whom it could sell the dollars) wanted them to spend in the only country where they are legal tender—Canada.

Canadian currency, or any other national currency, ultimately does no one any good except as purchasing power. It would be miraculous if Canadian money could be exported in return for real goods. After all, the Bank of Canada has the power to create as much new Canadian money as it wishes (at almost zero direct cost). It is only because Canadian money can buy Canadian products and Canadian assets that others want it.

Protect Against Low-Wage Foreign Labour

This argument says that the products of low-wage countries will drive Canadian products from the market, and the high Canadian standard of living will be dragged down to that of its poorer trading partners. Arguments of this sort have swayed many voters over the years.

As a prelude to considering them, stop and think what the argument would imply if taken out of the international context and put into a local one, where the same principles govern the gains from trade. Is it really impossible for a rich person to gain by trading with a poor person? Would the local millionaire be better off if she did all her own typing, gardening, and cooking? No one believes that a rich person gains nothing by trading with those who are less rich.

Why, then, must a rich group of people lose when they trade with a poor group? "Well," some may say, "the poor group will price its goods too cheaply." Does anyone believe that consumers lose from buying in discount houses or supermarkets just because the prices are lower there than at the old-fashioned corner store? Consumers gain when they can buy the same goods at a lower price. If the Mexicans pay low wages and sell their goods cheaply, Mexican labour may suffer, but Canadians will gain by obtaining imports at a low cost in terms of the goods that must be exported in return. The cheaper our imports are, the better off we are in terms of the goods and services available for domestic consumption.

The gains from trade depend on comparative, not absolute, advantages. World production is higher when any two countries specialize in the production of the goods for which they each have comparative advantages than when they both try to be self-sufficient.

Might it not be possible, however, that Mexico will undersell Canada in all lines of production and thus appropriate all the gains for itself, leaving Canada no better off, or even worse off, than if it had no trade with Mexico? The answer is no. The reason for this depends on the behaviour of exchange rates, which are discussed in Chapter 37. As we shall see in that chapter, equality of demand and supply in foreign exchange markets ensures that trade flows in both directions. In the meantime, the reason a coun-

try cannot import for long without exporting may be stated intuitively as follows: Imports can be obtained only by spending the currency of the country that makes the imports. Claims to this currency can be obtained only by exporting goods and services or by borrowing. Consequently, lending and borrowing aside, imports must equal exports. All trade must be in two directions; we can buy only if we can also sell.

In the long run, trade cannot hurt a country by causing it to import without exporting.

Trade, then, always provides scope for international specialization, with each country producing and exporting the goods for which it has a comparative advantage and importing the goods for which it does not.

Exports are Good; Imports are Bad

Exports create domestic income; imports create income for foreigners. Thus, other things being equal, exports tend to increase our total national income, and imports tend to reduce it. Surely, then, it is desirable to encourage exports by subsidizing them and to discourage imports by taxing them. This is an appealing argument, but it is incorrect.

Exports raise national income by adding to the value of domestic output, but they do not add to the value of domestic consumption. In fact, exports are goods produced at home and consumed abroad, while imports are goods produced abroad and consumed at home.

The standard of living in a country depends on the goods and services available for consumption, not on what is produced.

If exports really were "good" and imports really were "bad," then a fully employed economy that managed to increase exports without a corresponding increase in imports ought to be better off. Such a change, however, would result in a reduction in current standards of living because when more goods are sent abroad but no more are brought in from abroad, the total goods available for domestic consumption must fall.

The living standards of a country depend on the goods and services consumed in that country. The importance of exports is that they provide the resources required to purchase imports, either now or in the future.

Create Domestic Jobs

It is sometimes said that an economy with substantial unemployment, such as Canada during much of the

1990s, provides an exception to the case for freer trade. Suppose that tariffs or import quotas cut the imports of Japanese cars, Korean textiles, German kitchen equipment, and Polish vodka. Surely, the argument maintains, this will create more employment in Canadian industries producing similar products. This may be true—but it will *reduce* employment in other industries.

The Japanese, Koreans, Germans, and Poles can buy from Canada only if they earn Canadian dollars by selling things to Canada (or by borrowing dollars from Canada).[2] The decline in their sales of cars, textiles, kitchen equipment, and vodka will decrease their purchases of Canadian lumber, cars, software, banking services, and holidays in Canada. Jobs will be lost in Canadian export industries and gained in industries that formerly faced competition from imports. The major long-term effect is that the same total of employment will merely be redistributed among industries. In the process, living standards will be reduced because employment expands in inefficient import-competing industries and contracts in efficient exporting industries.

Protection is an ineffective way to increase employment or reduce unemployment. It does, however, lead to a redistribution of a given amount of employment.

METHODS OF PROTECTION

We have now studied some of the many reasons why governments may wish to provide some protection to their domestic industries. Our next task is to see how they do it. What are the tools that provide protection?

Two main types of protectionist policy are illustrated in Figure 36-1. Both cause the price of the imported good to rise and its quantity demanded to fall. They differ, however, in how they achieve these results. The caption to the figure analyzes these two types of policy.

POLICIES THAT DIRECTLY RAISE PRICES

The first type of protectionist policy directly raises the price of the imported product. A tariff, also often called an import duty, is the most common policy of

this type. Other such policies are any rules or regulations that fulfill three conditions: They are costly to comply with; they do not apply to competing, domestically produced products; and they are more than is required to meet any legitimate purpose other than restricting trade.

As shown in part (i) of Figure 36-1, tariffs affect both foreign and domestic producers, as well as domestic consumers. The initial effect is to raise the domestic price of the imported product above its world price by the amount of the tariff. Imports fall. As a result, foreign producers sell less and so must transfer resources to other lines of production. The price received on domestically produced units rises, as does the quantity produced domestically. On both counts, domestic producers earn more. However, the cost of producing the extra production at home exceeds the price at which it could be purchased on the world market. Thus the benefit to domestic producers comes at the expense of domestic consumers. Indeed, domestic consumers lose on two counts: First, they consume less of the product because its price rises, and second, they pay a higher price for the amount that they do consume. This extra spending ends up in two places: The extra that is paid on all units produced at home goes to domestic producers, and the extra that is paid on units still imported goes to the government as tariff revenue.

POLICIES THAT DIRECTLY LOWER QUANTITIES

The second type of protectionist policy directly restricts the quantity of an imported product. A common example is the **import quota,** by which the importing country sets a maximum of the quantity of some product that may be imported each year.

A relatively new measure that is becoming increasingly popular is the **voluntary export restriction (VER),** an agreement by an exporting country to limit the amount of a product that it sells to the importing country.

Canada, the United States, and the European Union have used VERs extensively, and the EU makes frequent use of import quotas. Japan has been pressured into negotiating several VERs with Canada, the United States, and the EU in order to limit sales of some of the Japanese goods that have had the most success in international competition. For example, in 1983, the United States and Canada negotiated VERs whereby the Japanese government agreed to restrict total sales of

---

[2]They can also get dollars by selling to other countries and then using their currencies to buy Canadian dollars. But this only complicates the transaction; it does not change its fundamental nature. Other countries must have earned the dollars by selling goods to Canada or borrowing from Canada.

FIGURE 36-1
Methods of Protecting Domestic Producers

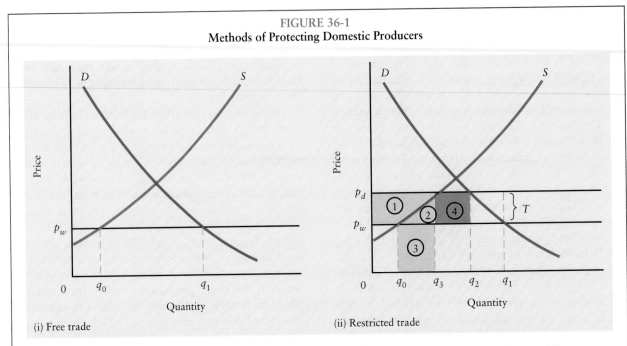

(i) Free trade

(ii) Restricted trade

The same reduction in imports and increase in domestic production can be achieved by using either a tariff or a quantity restriction. In both parts of the figure, D and S are the domestic demand and supply curves, respectively, and p_w is the world price of some product that is both produced at home and imported.

Part (i) of the figure shows the situation under free trade. Domestic consumption is q_1, domestic production is q_0, and imports are q_0q_1.

Part (ii) shows what happens when protectionist policies restrict imports to the amount q_3q_2. When this is done by levying a tariff of T per unit, the price in the domestic market rises by the full amount of the tariff to p_d. Consumers reduce consumption from q_1 to q_2 and pay an extra amount, shown by the shaded areas 1, 2, and 4, for the q_2 that they now purchase. Domestic production rises from q_0 to q_3. Because domestic producers receive the domestic price, their receipts rise by the three light-shaded areas, labelled 1, 2, and 3. Area 3 is revenue that was previously earned by foreign producers under free trade, while areas 1 and 2 are now paid by domestic consumers because of the higher prices they now face. Foreign suppliers of the imported good continue to receive the world price, so the government receives as tariff revenue the extra amount paid by consumers for the $q_3 q_2$ units that are still imported (shown by the dark shaded area, 4).

When the same result is accomplished by a quantity restriction, the government—through either a quota or a voluntary export restriction (VER)—reduces imports to q_3q_2. This drives the domestic market price up to p_d and has the same effect on domestic producers and consumers as the tariff. Since the government has merely restricted the quantity of imports, both foreign and domestic suppliers get the higher price in the domestic market. Thus foreign suppliers now receive the extra amount paid by domestic consumers (represented by the shaded area labelled 4) for the units that are still imported.

Japanese cars to these two countries for three years. When the agreements ran out in 1986, the Japanese continued to restrict their automobile sales by unilateral voluntary action, which they still do over ten years later. This episode is further considered in Application 36-1.

At one time or another, most of the rapidly growing countries of Asia have seen the United States place quantitative restrictions on the sales of some of their products that were most successful in penetrating the U.S. market.

NOMINAL AND EFFECTIVE TARIFF RATES

The tariff rate charged on each product, called the **nominal tariff rate,** does not necessarily show the degree of protection given to that product. Nominal rates frequently understate the degree of protection offered to domestic manufacturing industries, and a better measure is provided by what is called the **effective tariff rate.**

Nominal and effective tariff rates differ whenever imported raw materials or semifinished goods carry a different tariff rate than imports of the final goods that embody these intermediate products.

To illustrate this important point, consider an example drawn from Canadian-U.S. trade before these countries' free trade agreement began eliminating tariffs. Office furniture was manufactured in both the United States and Canada using Canadian wood. There was no tariff applied to the wood entering the United States, but the manufactured furniture was subject to a 10 percent tariff. When the product was manufactured in Canada, the raw material accounted for half the cost of the final product, and the other half was value added by Canadian manufacturers. Because of the 10 percent tariff, a unit of output that cost $100 to produce in Canada sold in the United States for $110 (in Canadian dollars).

Now consider the position of a U.S. manufacturer who was less efficient than its Canadian competitor. Say that the U.S. firm's production costs were 20 percent higher than those of the Canadian firm. Thus to produce one unit of output, the raw material cost the U.S. firm $50, but its other costs—including the opportunity costs of its capital—were $60 (i.e., 20 percent higher than the Canadian manufacturer's costs of $50). This gave the U.S. firm a final price of $110, which was just low enough to compete against the tariff-burdened Canadian import.

In this example, a U.S. tariff of 10 percent on the value of the final product is sufficient to protect a U.S. firm that is 20 percent less efficient than its Canadian competitor. To measure this effect, the effective tariff rate expresses the tariff as a percentage of the *value added* by the exporting industry in question. Thus the effective U.S. tariff rate on the Canadian furniture in our example is 20 percent, whereas the nominal tariff rate on furniture is only 10 percent.

TRADE-REMEDY LAWS AND NONTARIFF BARRIERS

As tariffs were lowered over the years since 1947, countries that wished to protect domestic industries began using, and often abusing, a series of trade restrictions that came to be known as nontariff barriers (NTBs). The original purpose of some of these was to remedy certain legitimate problems that arise in international trade, and for this reason, they are often called *trade-remedy laws*. All too often, how-

ever, they are misused to become potent means of simple protectionism.

The Escape Clause

One procedure that can be used as an NTB is the so-called escape clause action. A rapid surge of some imports may threaten the existence of domestic producers. These producers may then be given temporary relief to allow them time to adjust. This is done by raising tariff rates on the product in question above those set by international agreements. The trouble is that, once imposed, these "temporary" measures are hard to eliminate.

Dumping

Selling a product in a foreign country at a lower price than in the domestic market is known as **dumping**. Dumping is a form of price discrimination studied in the theory of monopoly. Most governments have antidumping duties designed to protect their own industries against what is viewed as unfair foreign pricing practices.

Dumping, if it lasts indefinitely, can be a gift to the receiving country. Its consumers get goods from abroad at less than their full cost of production. Dumping is more often a temporary measure, designed to get rid of unwanted surpluses, or a predatory attempt to drive competitors out of business. In either case, domestic producers complain about unfair foreign competition. In both cases, it is accepted international practice to levy antidumping duties on foreign imports. These duties are designed to eliminate the discriminatory elements in their prices.

Unfortunately, antidumping laws have been evolving over the past three decades in ways that allow antidumping duties to become barriers to trade and competition rather than to provide redress for unfair trading practices. Several features of the antidumping system that is now in effect in many countries make it highly protectionist.

First, any price discrimination is classified as dumping and is subject to penalties. Thus prices in the producer's domestic market become, in effect, minimum prices below which no sales can be made in foreign markets, whatever the circumstances in the domestic and foreign markets.

Second, following a change in the U.S. law in the early 1970s, many countries' laws now calculate the "margin of dumping" as the difference between the price that is charged in that country's market and the

---

APPLICATION 36-1

IMPORT RESTRICTIONS ON JAPANESE CARS: TARIFFS OR QUOTAS?

Voluntary export restrictions (VERs) have been commonly used by the European Union, Canada, and the United States to limit Japanese imports in key industries where the Japanese have a strong competitive advantage, such as cars and electronics. The Japanese have agreed to such arrangements because for any given volume of trade restrictions, they are far more profitable to the Japanese than most alternative arrangements.

People who are strong supporters of free trade criticize such arrangements, which certainly shield several North American and European industries from intense Japanese competition and greatly raise the price of the affected products to North American and European consumers and producers who use such goods.

The issue raised in this box concerns alternative methods of restricting the import of Japanese cars into Canada. Given that trade is to be restricted, what does economic theory predict to be the relative merits of VERs and tariffs? In both cases, imports are restricted, and the resulting scarcity supports a higher market price. With a tariff, the extra market value is appropriated by the Canadian government. With a VER, the extra market value accrues to the goods' suppliers—in this case, the Japanese car makers and their Canadian retailers.

Both cases are illustrated in the accompanying figure. We assume that the Canadian market provides a small enough part of total Japanese car sales to leave the Japanese willing to supply all the cars that are demanded in Canada at their fixed list price. This is the price p_0 in both parts of the figure. Given the Canadian demand curve for Japanese cars, D, there are q_0 cars sold before restrictions are imposed.

In part (i), Canada places a tariff of T per unit on Japanese cars, raising their price in Canada to p_1 and lowering sales to q_1. Suppliers' revenue is shown by the light shaded area. Government tariff revenue is shown by the dark shaded area. In part (ii), a VER of q_1 is negotiated, making the supply curve of Japanese cars vertical at q_1. The market-clearing price is p_1. The suppliers' revenue is the whole shaded area ($p_1 \times q_1$). In both cases, the shortage of Japanese cars drives up their price, creating a substantial margin over costs. Under a tariff, the Canadian government captures the margin. Under a VER policy, however, the margin accrues to the Japanese manufacturers.

Although this is a simplified picture, it captures the essence of what actually happened between 1983 and 1986 when the Japanese agreed to restrict their sales of cars in Canada and the United States. First, while sellers of North American cars were keeping prices as low as possible, and sometimes offering rebates on slow-selling models, Japanese cars were listed at healthy profit margins. Second, while it was always possible for the buyer of a North American car to negotiate a good discount off the list price, Japanese cars usually sold for their full list price.

---

foreign producers' "full allocated cost" (average total cost). This means that when there is global excess capacity in some industry so that the profit-maximizing price for all producers is below average total cost (but above average variable cost), foreign producers can be convicted of dumping. This gives domestic producers enormous protection whenever the market price falls temporarily below average total cost.

Third, law in the United States (but not in all other countries) places the onus of proof on the accused. Facing a charge of dumping, a foreign producer must prove within the short time that is allowed for such a defence that the charge is unfounded.

Fourth, U.S. antidumping duties are imposed with no time limit, so they often persist long after foreign firms have altered the prices that gave rise to them. The United States, and to a lesser extent Canada and the EU, have been world leaders in turning antidumping policies increasingly into trade barriers. Unfortunately, more and more of the world's trading countries are copying U.S. law, and U.S. and Canadian exporters are finding themselves increasingly subjected to the kinds

Third, because Japanese manufacturers were not allowed to supply all of the cars that they could sell in Canada, they had to choose which types of cars to supply. Not surprisingly, they tended to satisfy fully the demand for their more expensive cars, which have higher profit margins. This change in the "product mix" of Japanese cars exported to North America raised the average profit per car exported.

The VERs were thus costly to North American consumers and profitable to Japanese auto manufacturers. It has been estimated that North American consumers paid about $150,000 (U.S.) per year for each

job that was saved in the North American automobile industry and that most of this went to Japanese producers! (This cost to consumers per job saved is typical of what is found in many industries where VERs or their equivalents have been used.) Of course, this amount is spread over a great many consumers, so each does not notice the amount of his or her contribution. Nonetheless, $150,000 per year could do a lot of things, including fully retraining the workers and subsidizing their transfer to industries and areas where they could produce things that could be sold on free markets without government protection.

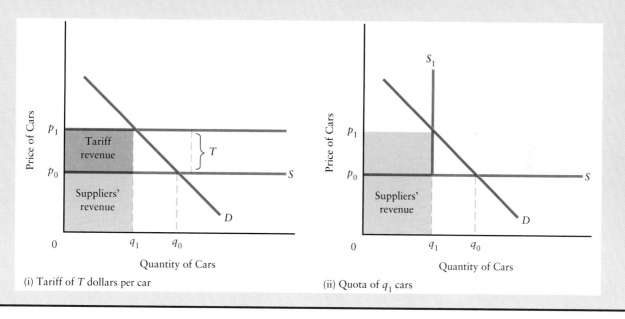

(i) Tariff of *T* dollars per car

(ii) Quota of q_1 cars

of antidumping duties formerly used mainly by the United States, Canada, and the EU.

Countervailing Duties

Countervailing duties, which are commonly used by the U.S. government but much less so elsewhere, provide another case in which a trade relief measure can sometimes become a covert NTB. The countervailing duty is designed to act, not as a tariff barrier, but rather as a means of creating a "level playing field" on which fair international competition can take place. Privately

owned domestic firms rightly complain that they cannot compete against the seemingly bottomless purses of foreign governments. Subsidized foreign exports can be sold indefinitely at prices that would produce losses in the absence of the subsidy. The original object of countervailing duties was to counteract the effect on price of the presence of such foreign subsidies.

If a domestic firm suspects the existence of such a subsidy and registers a complaint, its government is required to make an investigation. For a countervailing duty to be levied, the investigation must determine, first, that the foreign subsidy to the specific industry in question does exist and, second, that it is large enough to cause significant injury to competing domestic firms. (A similar determination by domestic authorities is required before antidumping duties are imposed.)

There is no doubt that countervailing duties have sometimes been used to remove the effects of "unfair" competition that are caused by foreign subsidies. Many governments complain, however, that U.S. countervailing duties are often used as thinly disguised barriers to trade. At the early stages of the development of countervailing duties, only subsidies whose prime effect was to distort trade were possible objects of countervailing duties. Even then, however, the existence of equivalent domestic subsidies was not taken into account when decisions were made to put countervailing duties on subsidized imports. Thus the United States levies some countervailing duties against foreign goods even though the foreign subsidy is less than the domestic subsidy. This does not create a level playing field.

Over time, the type of subsidy that is subject to countervailing duties has evolved until almost any government program that affects industry now risks becoming the object of a countervailing duty. Because all governments, including most U.S. state governments, have programs that provide direct or indirect assistance to industry, the potential for the use of countervailing duties as thinly disguised trade barriers is enormous.

CURRENT TRADE POLICY

In the remainder of the chapter, we discuss trade policy in practice. We start with the many international agreements that govern current trade policies and then look in a little more detail at the NAFTA.

Before 1947, any country was free to impose tariffs on its imports. However, when one country increased its tariffs, the action often triggered retaliatory actions by its trading partners. The 1930s saw a high-water mark of world protectionism as each country sought to raise its employment and national income by raising its tariffs. The end result was lowered efficiency, less trade, but no more employment or income. Since the end of World War II, much effort has been devoted to reducing tariff barriers, both on a multilateral and on a regional basis.

THE GENERAL AGREEMENT ON TARIFFS AND TRADE (GATT)

One of the most notable achievements of the post-World War II era was the creation of the General Agreement on Tariffs and Trade (GATT). The principle of the GATT is that each member country agrees not to make unilateral tariff increases. This prevents the outbreak of tariff wars in which countries raise tariffs to protect particular domestic industries and to retaliate against other countries' tariff increases. The last such round of mutually destructive tariff wars occurred in the 1920s and 1930s. The GATT countries, which numbered 117 in 1996, also meet periodically to negotiate on matters affecting foreign trade and related matters and to agree on across-the-board tariff cuts.

The three most recently completed rounds of GATT agreements, the Kennedy Round (completed in 1967), the Tokyo Round (completed in 1979), and the Uruguay Round (completed in 1994), have each agreed to reduce world tariffs substantially, the first two by about one-third each and the last by about 40 percent.

The Uruguay Round agreement was the culmination of years of negotiation. The agreement created a new body, the World Trade Organization (WTO), to replace the GATT. It also created a new legal structure for multilateral trading under which all members have equal mutual rights and obligations. Until the WTO was formed, developing countries that were in the GATT enjoyed all the GATT rights but were exempt from most of its obligations to liberalize trade—obligations that applied only to the developed countries. Now, however, all such special treatments are to be phased out over the seven years ending in 2002. There is also a new dispute settlement mechanism with much more power to reach and enforce effective rulings over nontariff barriers than existed in the past.

The Multifiber Agreement, which greatly restricts the ability of developing countries to export textiles in which they have a major comparative advantage, is to be phased out over 10 years. There are much stronger rules for trade in services, the protection of foreign investment, and intellectual property. There is also a much improved mechanism for settling disputes about alleged infractions of WTO agreements.

From the point of view of most of the world's countries, the big failure of these talks was in not getting a major liberalization of trade in agricultural goods. Such an agreement was resisted by the EU and Canada. The EU has a scheme called the Common Agricultural Policy (CAP) which provides general support for most of its agricultural products. The CAP has made Europe self-sufficient in many agricultural products that it used to import from developing nations and it also creates large surpluses which the EU sells abroad at heavily subsidized prices. This causes major harm to agricultural producers in less developed countries whose governments are too poor to compete with the EU in a subsidy war.

Canada, which has free trade in many agricultural commodities, was concerned to maintain its supply management over a number of industries including poultry, eggs, and diary products. These schemes, which we described in Chapter 6, are administered by the provinces who restrict domestic production and thus push domestic prices well above world levels. The federal government made them possible by imposing quotas on imports of these products at the national level.

Canada, the EU, and a number of other countries that lavishly protect some or all of their domestic agricultural producers, were finally forced to agree to a plan to end all import quotas on agricultural products. In a process called "tariffication" these quotas have been replaced by "tariff equivalents," which are tariffs that restrict trade by the same amount as the quotas did. Canadian tariff equivalents are as high as several hundred percent in some products, showing just how restrictive the Canadian policy is. The hope among countries which are pushing for freer trade in agricultural commodities is that pressure will build to reduce these very high tariffs over the next few decades. As we shall see later in this chapter, the tariffication caused more immediate problems for Canada.

All in all, however, the successful completion of the Uruguay Round represented a major victory for the supporters of a strong, rule-based, multilateral trading system.

TYPES OF REGIONAL AGREEMENTS

Regional agreements seek to liberalize trade over a much smaller group of countries than the WTO membership. Three standard forms of regional trade-liberalizing agreements are *free trade areas, customs unions,* and *common markets.*

A **free trade area** (**FTA**) is the least comprehensive of the three. It allows for tariff-free trade among the member countries, but it leaves each member free to levy its own trade policy with respect to other countries. As a result, members must maintain customs points at their common borders to make sure that imports into the free trade area do not all enter through the member that is levying the lowest tariff on each item. They must also agree on rules of origin to establish when a good is made in a member country and hence is able to pass tariff-free across their borders and when it is imported from outside the FTA and hence is subject to tariffs when it crosses borders within the FTA.

A **customs union** is a free trade area plus an agreement to establish a common trade policy with the rest of the world. Because they have a common trade policy, the members need neither customs controls on goods moving among themselves nor rules of origin. Once a good has entered any member country it has met the common rules and regulations and paid the common tariff and so it may henceforth be treated the same as a good that is produced within the union.

A **common market** is a customs union that also has free movement of labour and capital among its members. The European Union is by far the most successful example of a common market.

TRADE CREATION AND TRADE DIVERSION

A major effect of regional trade liberalization is to reallocate resources. Economists divide these effects into two categories, *trade creation* and *trade diversion*.

Trade creation occurs when producers in one member country find that they can export to another member country as a result of the elimination of the tariffs. For example, as the Canada-U.S. free trade agreement eliminated most cross-border tariffs, some U.S. firms found that they could undersell their Canadian competitors in some product lines, and some Canadian firms found that they could undersell their U.S. competitors in other product lines. As a result, specialization occurred, and new international trade developed. This trade, which is based on (natural or acquired) comparative advantage, is illustrated in Table 36-1.

Trade creation represents efficient specialization according to comparative advantage.

Trade diversion occurs when exporters in one member country replace foreign exporters as suppliers to another member country. For example, trade diversion occurs when U.S. firms find that they can undersell competitors from the rest of the world in the Canadian market, not because they are the cheapest source of supply, but because their tariff-free prices are lower than the tariff-burdened prices of imports from other countries. This effect is a gain to Canadian firms but a loss to Canada overall, which now has to export more goods for any given amount of imports than before the trade diversion occurred. Similarly, trade diversion occurs when Canadian producers win out over

TABLE 36-1
Trade Creation and Trade Diversion

Producing Country	Canadian Delivered Price Without Tariffs (dollars)	Canadian Delivered Price with a 10 percent Tariff (dollars)
Trade creation		
Canada	40.00	40.00
United States	37.00	40.70
Trade diversion		
Taiwan	20.00	22.00
United States	21.50	23.65

Regional tariff reductions can cause trade creation and trade diversion. The table gives two cases. In the first case, a U.S. good, which could be sold for $37.00 in Canada, has its price increased to $40.70 by a 10 percent Canadian tariff. The Canadian industry, which can sell the good for $40.00 with or without a tariff on imports, is protected against the more efficient U.S. producer. When the tariff is removed by the Canada-U.S. free trade agreement, the U.S. good wins the market by selling at $37.00. Trade is created between Canada and the United States by eliminating the inefficient Canadian production solely for a protected home market.

In the second case, Taiwan can undersell the U.S. in the Canadian market for another product when neither is subject to a tariff (column 1) and when both are subject to a 10 percent tariff (column 2). But after the Canada-U.S. free trade agreement, the U.S. good enters Canada tariff-free and sells for $21.50, whereas the Taiwanese good, which is still subject to the Canadian tariff, continues to sell for $22.00. The U.S. good wins the market, and Canadian trade is diverted from Taiwan to the U.S. even though Taiwan is the lower-cost supplier (excluding the tariff).

competitors from the rest of the world in the U.S. market because they are not subject to a tariff in that market while their nonmember competitors are. This effect benefits Canadian firms at the expense of U.S. consumers. Table 36-1 also illustrates trade diversion.

From the global perspective, trade diversion represents an inefficient use of resources.

THE HISTORY OF FREE TRADE AREAS

The first important free trade area in the modern era was the European Free Trade Association (EFTA). It was formed in 1960 by a group of European countries that were unwilling to join the European Common Market (the forerunner of the European Union) because of its all-embracing character. Not wanting to be left out of the gains from trade, they formed an association whose sole purpose was tariff removal. First, they removed all tariffs on trade among themselves. Then each country signed a free-trade-area agreement with the EU. This made the EU-EFTA market the largest tariff-free market in the world (over 300 million people). In recent years almost all of the EFTA countries have entered the EU.

In 1988, a sweeping agreement was signed between Canada and the United States, instituting free trade on almost all goods and most nongovernment services and covering what is the world's largest flow of international trade between any two countries. In 1993, this agreement was extended into the North American Free Trade Agreement (NAFTA) by renegotiating the Canada-U.S. agreement to include Mexico. Provision is made within the NAFTA for the accession of other countries with the hope that it may eventually evolve into a Western Hemispheric Free Trade Area (WHFTA) by taking in most, or even all, of the countries of South and Central America. The first accession was to have been Chile. But at the beginning of 1996, the negotiations for its entry into NAFTA were being held up by domestic political considerations in the United States.

Australia and New Zealand have also entered into an association that removes restrictions on trade in goods and services between their two countries. The countries of Latin America have been experimenting with free trade areas for many decades. Most earlier attempts failed, but in the past few years, more durable FTAs seem to have been formed, the most successful of which is Mercosur, which includes Argentina, Brazil, Uruguay, and Paraguay. Whether these will remain stand-alone agreements or evolve into a WHFTA remains to be seen.

THE NORTH AMERICAN FREE TRADE AGREEMENT (NAFTA)

The NAFTA is merely an extension of the Canada-U.S. free trade agreement with some important improvements based on the experience of the earlier agreement. It is a free trade area and not a customs union; each country retains its own external trade policy, and rules of origin are needed to determine when a good is made within the NAFTA and so allowed to move freely among the members. We now look in detail at various aspects of the NAFTA.

National Treatment

The fundamental principle that guides the NAFTA is the principle of *national treatment*. This means that countries are free to establish any laws they wish and that these can differ as much as desired among member countries, with the sole proviso that these laws must not discriminate on the basis of nationality. So the United States can have tough environmental laws or standards for particular goods, but it must enforce these equally on Canadian, Mexican, and U.S. firms and on domestically produced and imported goods. The idea of national treatment is to allow a maximum of policy independence while preventing national policies from being used as barriers to trade and investment. This principle of maximizing policy independence subject to removing trade barriers is opposite to the EU's philosophy, which seeks to harmonize as many policies as possible in order to create an all-encompassing economic union.[3]

Other Major Provisions

First, all tariffs on trade between the United States and Canada are to be eliminated by 1999. Canada-Mexico and Mexico-U.S. tariffs are to be phased out over a 15-year period that started in 1994. Also, a number of nontariff barriers are eliminated or circumscribed.

Second, the agreement guarantees national treatment to foreign investment once it enters a country while permitting each country to screen a substantial amount of inbound foreign investment before it enters.

Third, all existing measures that restrict trade and investment that are not explicitly removed are "grandfathered," a term referring to the continuation of a practice that predates the agreement and would have been prohibited by the terms of the agreement were it not specifically exempted. This is probably the single most important departure from free trade under the NAFTA. Under it, a large collection of restrictive measures in each of the three countries are given indefinite life. An alternative would have been to "sunset" all of these provisions by negotiating dates at which each would be eliminated. From the point of view of long-term trade liberalization, even a 50-year extension would have been preferable to an indefinite exemption.

Fourth, a few goods remain subject to serious nontariff trade restrictions. In Canada, the main examples are supply-managed agricultural products, beer, textiles, and the cultural industries. Restrictions for the Canadian supply-managed agricultural products may be short-lived because of their tariffication under the Uruguay round of GATT. Textile restriction comes under the Multifiber Agreement which is

being phased out over a 15-year period under the Uruguay round. So beer and culture are the only Canadian restrictions that seem secure at the moment. In the U.S., textiles, shipping between U.S. ports, and banking were shielded from free trade in good and services.

Fifth, trade in most nongovernmental services is liberalized by giving service firms the right of establishment in all member countries and the privilege of national treatment. There is also a limited opening of the markets in financial services to entry from firms based in the NAFTA countries.

Finally, a significant minority of government procurement is opened to cross-border bids.

Dispute Settlement

From Canada's point of view, by far the biggest setback in the negotiations for the Canada-U.S. FTA was the failure to obtain agreement on a common regime for countervailing and antidumping duties. In view of that failure, no significant attempt was made to deal with this issue in the NAFTA negotiations. The U.S. Congress has been unwilling to abandon the unilateral use of these powerful weapons.

In the absence of such a multilateral regime, a dispute settlement mechanism was put in place. Under it, the domestic determinations that are required for the levying of antidumping and countervailing duties are subject to review by a panel of Canadians, Americans, and Mexicans. This international review replaces appeal through the domestic courts. Panels are empowered to uphold the domestic determinations or refer the decision to the domestic authority—which in effect is a binding order for a new investigation. The referral can be repeated until the panel is satisfied that the domestic laws have been correctly and fairly applied.

This is pathbreaking: For the first time in its history, the United States has agreed to submit the administration of its domestic laws to binding scrutiny by an international panel that often contains a majority of foreigners.

Results

The Canada-U.S. FTA aroused a great debate in Canada. Supporters looked for major increases in the security of existing trade from U.S. protectionist attacks and for a growth of new trade. Detractors predicted a flight of firms to the U.S., the loss of Canadian competitiveness, and even the loss of Canada's political independence.

---

[3]This principle was qualified to some extent by the negotiation, after the main treaty was signed, of a side agreement between the United States and Mexico establishing minimum standards of environmental protection in Mexico.

CANADA-U.S. TRADE DISPUTES

Although more than 95 percent of Canada-U.S. trade in goods and services passes between the two countries without dispute or hindrance, some items have been beset by persistent disputes. Here is a brief discussion of three of the most important.

SOFTWOOD LUMBER

Canada exports large amounts of softwood lumber to the United States. And U.S. producers have persistently claimed that Canadian Provincial government policies provide a concealed subsidy which should be evened out with a countervailing duty. The main bone of contention is *stumpage,* which is the royalty that governments charge the logging companies for cutting timber on government-owned land. In the U.S., stumpage fees are set by open auction. In Canada, the fees are set in private negotiations between logging companies and the government. U.S. critics argue that the much lower Canadian stumpage fees that emerge from this process are a subsidy from the government to its powerful friends in the lumber industry. Canadians argue that the higher U.S. stumpage fees reflect the higher services that U.S. government provides for their lumber companies by way of infrastructure that Canadian lumber companies must provide for themselves.

Just before the Canada-U.S. FTA was finalized, the Canadian government imposed an export tax on lumber going to the U.S. to forestall the imposition of a U.S. countervailing duty. When this tax expired, Canada did not renew it and the U.S. imposed a countervailing duty. Two dispute settlement panels found in Canada's favour, but largely on the grounds of narrow technicalities. The U.S. then changed its laws to remove what they saw as the loopholes that the Canadians had used. In 1996, under the threat of another countervailing duty, the Canadian government left negotiations to the provinces who reached separate accommodations with the U.S. authorities to use taxes to limit exports to current levels.

Who wins and who loses? The restriction raised prices in the U.S. market making U.S. users of lumber clear losers, and U.S. lumber producers clear winners. The effect on the Canadian lumber industry depends on the elasticity of demand for Canadian lumber in the U.S. market. Providing that U.S. demand is sufficiently inelastic, Canadian lumber producers are winners—just as the Japanese car producers were winners from their voluntary export restrictions to the North American market.

SUPPLY-MANAGED AGRICULTURAL INDUSTRIES

We have seen that supply management by the Canadian provinces in the poultry and dairy indus-

During this great debate, the official opposition, the Liberal party, opposed the agreement. Later, when the NAFTA was negotiated, they advocated major renegotiation of that agreement before it was approved. In 1993, after the NAFTA had been negotiated, but before the enabling legislation had been passed, the Liberals won a massive electoral victory over the Conservatives who had negotiated both the Canada-U.S. FTA and the NAFTA. After only a short time, however, the new Liberal government announced that it would approve the NAFTA exactly as the Conservatives had negotiated it and would

make no attempt to withdraw from the Canada-U.S. FTA. Political debate then ended. When the major party to oppose the agreements accepted them as soon as it came into power, both agreements ceased to be major political issues.

By and large, both the Canada-U.S. FTA and NAFTA agreements have worked out just about as expected by their supporters—although it is still too early to determine their very long-term effects. Industry has clearly restructured in the direction of export orientation in all three countries. All three countries are importing more from and exporting tries substantially raises the prices paid by Canadian consumers. For years, the federal government had supported these policies by imposing import quotas on the managed products, without which their prices would be driven down to world levels. The federal government successfully negotiated exemptions for these quotas under the Canada-U.S. FTA. In the Uruguay round of GATT negotiations despite spirited resistance, the federal government was forced to agree to "tariffication" of these quotas. The U.S. then took the position that although the quotas had been exempt under the FTA, their tariff equivalents were not. After all, the U.S. argued, all tariffs without exception are to be removed by 1999 under the FTA. At the time of writing, the debate continues without an obvious resolution.

Who wins and who loses? Although it would be a political victory for the U.S. if Canada were forced to remove the massive tariffs currently levied on supply-managed agricultural products, it would also be a clear victory for Canadian consumers who pay much more than world prices for these protected products.

CULTURAL INDUSTRIES

Canada has always sought to support its magazines, book sellers, film distributors, and other cultural industries from U.S. competition. Although there was never any pressure to prevent governments on both sides of the border from subsidizing the performing arts, such as music and drama, protection of the cultural industries more widely defined was a serious bone of contention during the FTA negotiations. In the end, Canada got exemption for all of its broadly defined cultural industries.

Who wins and who loses? The Canadian exemption for its cultural industries was a mixed blessing because, unlike business, professional and trades persons, Canadian performing artists did not obtain the right extended under the FTA's "temporary access" provision to enter the U.S. on temporary visas to do specific jobs for up to two years. These would have been available to performing artists had it not been for the blanket exemption of the Canadian cultural industries. The clear winners were the owners of Canadian magazines and other Canadian-made cultural products that would otherwise have had to compete with U.S. products in the Canadian market.

The U.S. continues to be highly critical of Canadian cultural protectionism. The Canadian government replies that, without this protection, Canada-only publications could not compete with U.S. products which had already covered their fixed cost in the U.S. market and were then marginally adapted to the Canadian market.

This is a debate which will very probably go on for years if not decades.

more to each other. This is particularly true between Canada and the United States, where the great majority of tariffs have already been removed (some at the outset in 1989, some over a 5-year period ending in 1994, and the rest over a 10-year period which will end in 1999). As the theory of trade predicts, specialization has occurred in many areas, resulting in more U.S. imports of some product lines from Canada and more U.S. exports of other goods to Canada. Total trade—in both directions—increased sharply between the United States and Mexico during the first two years of NAFTA; it also increased, although much less sharply, between Canada and Mexico.

It is hard to say how much trade diversion there will be. The greatest potential is with Mexico, which competes in the U.S. and Canadian markets with a large number of products produced in other low-wage countries. South-East Asian exporters to the United States and Canada have been worried that Mexico would capture some of their markets by virtue of having tariff-free access denied to their goods. Most estimates predict, however, that trade creation will dominate over trade diversion.

Foreign investment has increased, particularly in Canada and Mexico, although it will be years before the magnitude of the induced increase in foreign investment can be reasonably estimated. A recent government report estimated that the bulk of the new jobs created in Canada over the next several years would be created by foreign rather than domestic investment. This made the fears of a NAFTA-induced flight of foreign capital from Canada look ill founded.

Most transitional difficulties were initially felt in each country's import-competing industries, which is what theory predicts. An agreement such as the NAFTA brings its advantages by encouraging a movement of resources out of protected but inefficient import-competing industries, which decline, and into efficient export industries, which expand because they have better access to the markets of other members countries. Southern Ontario and parts of Quebec had major problems as some traditional exports fell and resources had to be moved to sectors where trade was expanding. Eight years after the agreement however, Southern Ontario was booming again and its most profitable sectors were those that exported to the United States. Taking the 40 industries that account for virtually all of Ontario's foreign trade, exports to the U.S. were up in all but two (while exports to the rest of the world expanded significantly in only about 10). Similarly with imports: they increased in all but seven categories, all of which were relatively insignificant in total trade.

Finally, the dispute settlement mechanism seems to have worked well. A large number of disputes have arisen and have been referred to panels. Panel members have usually reacted as professionals rather than as nationals. Most cases have been decided on their merits with Canada winning significantly more than half the cases, the rest of the decisions being in favour of the United States. Allegations that decisions were reached on national rather than professional grounds have only been seriously raised in one case. There, the single U.S. panellist asserted forcibly that the two Canadian panellists acted in a prejudicial manner.

Nonetheless, as Application 36-2 shows, several long-term disputes still disturb the generally tranquil state of trading relations between Canada and the U.S.

THE FUTURE OF CANADIAN TRADE POLICY

Although the United States has been one of the staunchest defenders of the free-market system, many American voices have recently advocated moves that would reduce the influence of market forces on international trade and increase the degree of government control over that trade. It is ironic to see enthusiasm for state-managed trade growing in the United States just as the former Socialist countries of Eastern Europe have at last agreed that free markets are better regulators of economic activity than any government. The strength of the movement toward managed trade will become clearer during the next 5 or 10 years.

The Canadian government opposes these non-market pushes coming from the United States. As a small trading nation with about a third of its total GDP accounted for by international trade in goods and services, trade policy will always be at the centre of any Canadian government's policy. Whatever they have said while in opposition, no Canadian government in modern times has departed from the policy of liberalizing trade and, more recently, of liberalizing investment flows as well.

The breakup of the world into a set of trading blocks that did more and more trade within the block and less and less with outside countries would be to the disadvantage of most countries, particularly the smaller ones. Bilateral bargaining between groups of nations tend to involve large countries while leaving the smaller ones on the sidelines. For these reasons, among many others, Canada as a small trading nation has an enormous stake in the preservation of the liberalized multilateral trading regime.

Such high stakes ensure that Canadian policy makers will regard the WTO as Canada's best friend in pushing for more liberalized international trade and as its best defence against protectionist pressures (as they earlier regarded its predecessor the GATT). Regional agreements are seen as supplements rather than as alternatives to the multilateralism of the WTO. The Canada-U.S. FTA and the NAFTA give Canada increased access to what is by far its largest market and shields that access to a great extent from protectionist sentiments in the United States.

Canada prospers or suffers as its trading sector prospers or suffers. For this reason, maintaining a healthy trading sector will remain, as it has been for decades, a prime concern of Canadian policy markers, who wish to maintain and enhance the country's material prosperity.

A. THE THEORY OF TRADE POLICY

- The case for free trade is that world output of all products can be higher under free trade than when protectionism restricts regional specialization.
- Protection can be urged as a means to ends other than maximizing world living standards. Examples of such ends are to produce a diversified economy, to reduce fluctuations in national income, to retain distinctive national traditions, and to improve national defence.
- Protection can also be urged on the grounds that it may lead to higher living standards for the protectionist country than a policy of free trade would. Such a result might come about by using a monopoly position to influence the terms of trade or by developing a dynamic comparative advantage by allowing inexperienced or uneconomically small industries to become efficient enough to compete with foreign industries.
- A recent argument for protection is to operate a strategic trade policy whereby a country attracts firms in oligopolistic industries that, due to scale economies, can earn large profits even in the long run.
- Some fallacious protectionist arguments are that (a) mutually advantageous trade is impossible because one trader's gain must always be the other's loss; (b) buying abroad sends our money abroad, while buying at home keeps our money at home; (c) our high-paid workers must be protected against the competition from low-paid foreign workers; and (d) imports are to be discouraged because they lower national income and cause unemployment.

B. METHODS OF PROTECTION

- Trade can be restricted either by policies that directly raise prices such as tariffs or that operate in the first instance on quantities such as import quotas and voluntary export restrictions.
- As tariff barriers have been reduced over the years, they have been replaced in part by nontariff barriers. The two most important are antidumping and countervailing duties which, although they can provide legitimate restraints on unfair trading practices, are also used as serious nontariff barriers to trade.

C. CURRENT TRADE POLICY

- The General Agreement on Tariffs and Trade under which countries agree to reduce trade barriers through multilateral negotiations and not to raise them unilaterally, has greatly reduced world tariffs since its inception in 1947. At the end of the Uruguay round, the GATT was succeeded by the World Trade Organization (WTO).
- Regional trade-liberalizing agreements such as free trade areas and common markets bring efficiency gains through trade creation and efficiency losses through trade diversion.
- The NAFTA is the world's largest and most successful free trade area, and the European Union is the world's largest and most successful common market.

Free trade and protectionism
Tariffs and nontariff barriers
Voluntary export restrictions (VERs)
Countervailing and antidumping duties
The General Agreement on Tariffs and
 Trade (GATT)

The World Trade Organization (WTO)
Common markets, customs unions,
 and free trade areas
Trade creation and trade diversion

The North American Free Trade
 Agreement (NAFTA)

1. Some Canadians opposed Canada's entry into NAFTA on the grounds that Canadian firms could not compete with the goods produced by cheap Mexican labour, which at the current exchange rate is earning less than $2 per hour in Mexico's highest wage sectors. Comment on the following points in relation to the above worries:

   a. Many Mexican goods entered Canada tariff-free before the NAFTA, and where they did not, the average Canadian tariff was about 10 percent.
   b. "Mexicans are the most expensive cheap labour I have ever encountered"—statement by the owner of a Canadian firm who is moving back from Mexico to Canada.

c. The theory of the gains from trade says that a high-productivity, high-wage country can gain from trading with a low-wage, low-productivity country.

d. International equilibrium could not be one in which Mexico undersold all Canadian-made goods in the Canadian market.

e. Technological change is rapidly reducing labour costs as a proportion of total costs in many products; in many industries that use high-tech production methods this proportion is already well below 20 percent.

2. Many Canadian opponents of the Canada-U.S. FTA and the NAFTA worried that it would cause an exodus of Canadian-based firms to the U.S. or Mexico. Suppose you are advising a foreign firm that is considering locating in one of the NAFTA countries to serve the North American market. Rank the following arrangements as to the attraction they offer for Canada as a location for this foreign investment (other things being equal). Which were within the control of Canadian policy makers and which beyond their control?

a. There are no regional trade-liberalizing agreements between any of the three countries (the status quo as of 1985).

b. The only agreement is the Canada-U.S. FTA (the status quo in 1990).

c. The U.S. has separate agreements with Canada and Mexico (which would have happened if Canada had stayed out of NAFTA).

d. The only agreement is a bilateral one between the U.S. and Mexico (which would have happened if Canada had cancelled the Canada-U.S. FTA and kept out of the NAFTA).

e. There is a single NAFTA agreement between the three countries (the status quo as of 1996).

3. Should Canada and the U.S. trade with countries with poor human rights records? If trade with China is severely restricted because of its lack of respect for human rights, who will be the gainers and who the losers? Argue the cases that this policy will help, and that it will hinder, human rights progress in China.

4. It has been calculated that the voluntary export agreement to reduce the import of Japanese cars into the North American market cost North American consumers $150,000 per job saved in North American automobile firms. Do consumers pay the cost? Who benefits? What alternatives are there to protecting jobs in the auto industry?

5. "What unfair trade has done to an American community" was the headline of a recent full-page ad in the *New York Times*. The ad claimed that subsidized and "dumped" steel imports from unstated foreign countries were unfairly driving U.S. steel plants out of business. Although not specifically mentioned in the article, Canadian steel companies were at the time facing antidumping duties on their sales to the United States. What foreign practices might justify this claim? What apparent dumping might represent perfectly fair competition? What U.S. legislation or other practices could provide relief, whether justified or not, to the U.S. firms?

6. What are some of the things that would happen if all countries tried to increase their domestic employment by imposing major restrictions on all imports?

7. "U.S. consumer is seen as big loser in new restraints on imported steel," said a recent *Wall Street Journal* headline. The big gainers from the quota limitations on imported steel were predicted to be U.S. producers, who would sell more, and foreign producers, who would sell less but at a higher price; the big losers would be U.S. consumers. Explain carefully why each of these groups might gain or lose.

8. Suppose Canada and the United States had imposed prohibitive tariffs on all imported cars over the past three decades. How do you think this would have affected the North American automobile industry? The Canadian and U.S. public? The kinds of cars produced by North American manufacturers?

9. Import quotas and voluntary export agreements are often used instead of tariffs. What real difference, if any, is there between quotas, voluntary export restrictions (VERs), and tariffs? Explain why lobbyists for some import-competing industries (cheese, milk, shoes) support import quotas while lobbyists for others (pizza manufacturers, soft drink manufacturers, retail stores) oppose them. Would you expect labour unions to support or oppose quotas?

10. Over the past several years, many foreign automobile producers have built production and assembly facilities in Canada and in the United States. What are some advantages and disadvantages associated with shifting production from, for example, Japan to Canada? Will these cars still be considered "imports"? What is beginning to happen to the definitions of "foreign made" and "domestic made"?

MATHEMATICAL NOTES

1. The rule of 72 is an approximation, derived from the mathematics of compound interest. Any variable X with an initial value of X_0 will have the value $X_t = X_0 e^{rt}$ after t years at a continuous growth rate of r percent per year. Doubling the value of X requires $X_t/X_0 = 2$, and this requires $r \cdot t = 0.69$. A "rule of 69" would thus be correct for continuous growth. The rule of 72 was developed in the context of compound interest, and if interest is compounded only once a year, the product of r times t for X to double is approximately 0.72.

2. Because one cannot divide by zero, the ratio $\Delta Y/\Delta X$ cannot be evaluated when $\Delta X = 0$. However, as ΔX *approaches* zero, the ratio $\Delta Y/\Delta X$ increases without limit:

$$\lim_{\Delta X \to 0} \frac{\Delta Y}{\Delta X} = \infty$$

3. Many variables affect the quantity demanded. Using functional notation, the argument of the next several pages of the text can be anticipated. Let Q^D represent the quantity of a commodity demanded and

$$T, \overline{Y}, N, \hat{Y}, p, p_j$$

represent, respectively, tastes, average household income, population, income distribution, the commodity's own price, and the price of the jth other commodity.

The demand function is

$$Q^D = D(T, \overline{Y}, N, \hat{Y}, p, p_j), \qquad j = 1, 2, \ldots, n$$

The demand schedule or curve is given by

$$Q^D = d(p) \Big|_{T, \overline{Y}, N, \hat{Y}, p_j}$$

where the notation means that the variables to the right of the vertical line are held constant.

This function is correctly described as the demand function with respect to price, all other variables being held constant. This function, often written concisely as $q = d(p)$, shifts in response to changes in other variables. Consider average income: if, as is usually hypothesized, $\partial Q^D/\partial \overline{Y} > 0$, then increases in average income shift $q = d(p)$ rightward and decreases in average income shift $q = d(p)$ leftward. Changes in other variables likewise shift this function in the direction implied by the relationship of that variable to the quantity demanded.

4. Quantity demanded is a simple and straightforward but frequently misunderstood concept in everyday use, but it has a clear mathematical meaning. It refers to the dependent variable in the demand function from note 3:

$$Q^D = D(T, \overline{Y}, N, \hat{Y}, p, p_j)$$

It takes on a specific value whenever a specific value is assigned to each of the independent variables. The value of Q^D changes whenever the value of any independent variable is changed. Q^D could change, for example, as a result of a *ceteris paribus* change in any one price, in average income, in the distribution of income, in tastes, or in population. It could also change as a result of the net effect of changes in all of the independent variables occurring at once. Thus a change in the price of a commodity is a sufficient reason for a change in Q^D but not a necessary reason.

Some textbooks reserve the term *change in quantity demanded* for a movement along a demand curve, that is, a change in Q^D as a result only of a change in p. They then use other words for a change in Q^D caused by a change in the other variables in the demand function. This usage is potentially confusing because it gives the single variable Q^D more than one name.

Our usage, which corresponds to that in more advanced treatments, avoids this confusion. We call Q^D *quantity demanded* and refer to any change in Q^D as a *change in quantity demanded*. In this usage it is correct to say that a movement along a demand curve is a change in quantity demanded, but it is incorrect to say that a change in quantity demanded can occur *only because of* a movement along a demand curve (because Q^D can change for other reasons, for example, a *ceteris paribus* change in average household income).

5. Similar to the way we treated quantity demanded in note 3, let Q^S represent the quantity of a commodity supplied and

$$C, X, p, w_i$$

represent, respectively, producers' goals, technology, the product's price, and the price of the *i*th input.

The supply function is

$$Q^S = S(C, X, p, w_i), \qquad i = 1, 2, \ldots, m$$

The supply schedule or curve is given by

$$Q^S = s(p) \Big|_{C, X, w_i}$$

This is the supply function with respect to price, all other variables being held constant. This function, often written concisely as $q = s(p)$, shifts in response to changes in other variables.

6. Equilibrium occurs where $Q^D = Q^S$. For *specified values of all other variables*, this requires that

$$d(p) = s(p) \qquad [6.1]$$

Equation 6.1 defines an equilibrium value of p; hence, although p is an *independent* or *exogenous* variable in each of the supply and demand functions, it is an *endogenous* variable in the economic model that imposes the equilibrium condition expressed in Equation 6.1. Price is endoge-

nous because it is assumed to adjust to bring about equality between quantity demanded and quantity supplied. Equilibrium quantity, also an endogenous variable, is determined by substituting the equilibrium price into either $d(p)$ or $s(p)$.

Graphically, Equation 6.1 is satisfied only at the point where the demand and supply curves intersect. Thus supply and demand curves are said to determine the equilibrium values of the endogenous variables, price and quantity. A shift in any of the independent variables held constant in the d and s functions will shift the demand or supply curves and lead to different equilibrium values for price and quantity.

7. The definition in the text uses finite changes and is called *arc elasticity*. The parallel definition using derivatives is

$$\eta = \frac{dq}{dp} \cdot \frac{p}{q}$$

and is called *point elasticity*. Further discussion appears in the Appendix to Chapter 5.

8. The propositions in the text are proved as follows. Letting TR stand for total revenue, we can write

$$TR = p \cdot q$$

It follows that the change in total revenue is

$$dTR = q \cdot dp + p \cdot dq \qquad [8.1]$$

(Recall that total revenue of the firm and total expenditure by consumers are identical, so the following applies equally to total expenditure.) Multiplying and dividing both terms on the right-hand side of Equation 8.1 by $p \cdot q$ yields

$$dTR = \left[\frac{dp}{p} + \frac{dq}{q} \right] \cdot (p \cdot q)$$

Because dp and dq are opposite in sign as we move along the demand curve, dTR will have the same sign as the term in brackets on the right-hand side that dominates—that is, on which percentage change is largest.

A second way of arranging Equation 8.1 is to divide both sides by dp to get

$$\frac{dTR}{dp} = q + p \cdot \frac{dq}{dp} \qquad [8.2]$$

From the definition of point elasticity in note 7, however,

$$q \cdot \eta = p \cdot \frac{dq}{dp} \qquad [8.3]$$

which we can substitute into Equation 8.1 to obtain

$$\frac{dTR}{dp} = q + q \cdot \eta = q \cdot (1 + \eta) \qquad [8.4]$$

Because η is a negative number, the sign of the right-hand side of Equation 8.4 is negative if the absolute value of η exceeds unity (elastic demand) and positive if it is less than unity (inelastic demand).

Total revenue is maximized when dTR/dp is equal to zero. As can be seen from Equation 8.4, this occurs when elasticity is equal to -1.

9. The axis reversal arose in the following way. Alfred Marshall (1842–1924) theorized in terms of "demand price" and "supply price," these being the prices that would lead to a given quantity being demanded or supplied. Thus

$$p^d = d(q) \qquad [9.1]$$
$$p^s = s(q) \qquad [9.2]$$

and the condition of equilibrium is

$$d(q) = s(q)$$

When graphing the behavioural relationships expressed in Equations 9.1 and 9.2, Marshall naturally put the independent variable, q, on the horizontal axis.

Leon Walras (1834–1910), whose formulation of the working of a competitive market has become the accepted one, focused on quantity demanded and quantity supplied *at a given price*. Thus

$$q^d = d(p)$$
$$q^s = s(p)$$

and the condition of equilibrium is

$$d(p) = s(p)$$

Walras did not use graphical representation. Had he done so, he would surely have placed p (his independent variable) on the horizontal axis.

Marshall, among his other influences on later generations of economists, was the great popularizer of graphical analysis in economics. Today, we use his graphs, even for Walras's analysis. The axis reversal is thus one of those historical accidents that seem odd to people who did not live through the "perfectly natural" sequence of steps that produced it.

10. The distinction made between an incremental change and a marginal change is the distinction for the function $Y = Y(X)$ between $\Delta Y/\Delta X$ and the derivative dY/dX. The latter is the limit of the former as ΔX approaches zero. Precisely this sort of difference underlies the distinction between arc and point elasticity, and we shall meet it repeatedly—in this chapter in reference to marginal and incremental *utility* and in later chapters with respect to such concepts as marginal and incremental *product, cost,* and *revenue*. Where Y is a function of more than one variable—for example, $Y = f(X,Z)$—the marginal relationship between Y and X is the partial derivative $\partial Y/\partial X$ rather than the total derivative, dY/dX.

11. The hypothesis of diminishing marginal utility requires that we can measure utility of consumption by a function

$$U = U(X_1, X_2, \ldots, X_n)$$

where $X_1, \ldots, X_n$ are quantities of the n goods consumed by a household. It really embodies two utility hypotheses: first,

$$\partial U/\partial X_i > 0$$

which says that the consumer can get more utility by increasing consumption of the commodity; second,

$$\partial^2 U/\partial X_i^2 < 0$$

which says that the marginal utility of additional consumption of some good declines as the amount of that good consumed increases.

12. Because the slope of the indifference curve is negative, it is the absolute value of the slope that declines as one moves downward to the right along the curve. The algebraic value, of course, increases. The phrase *diminishing marginal rate of substitution* thus refers to the absolute, not the algebraic, value of the slope.

13. The relationship between the slope of the budget line and relative prices can be seen as follows. In the two-commodity example, a change in expenditure (ΔE) is given by the equation

$$\Delta E = p_C \cdot \Delta C + p_F \cdot \Delta F \qquad [13.1]$$

Expenditure is constant for all combinations of F and C that lie on the same budget line. Thus along such a line we have $\Delta E = 0$. This implies

$$p_C \cdot \Delta C + p_F \cdot \Delta F = 0 \qquad [13.2]$$

and thus

$$-\Delta C/\Delta F = p_F/p_C \qquad [13.3]$$

The ratio $-\Delta C/\Delta F$ is the slope of the budget line. It is negative because, with a fixed budget, one must consume less C in order to consume more F. In other words, Equation 13.3 says that the negative of the slope of the budget line is the ratio of the absolute prices (i.e., the relative price). Although prices do not show directly in Figure 7A-3, they are implicit in the budget line: Its slope depends solely on the relative price, while its position, given a fixed money income, depends on the absolute prices of the two goods.

14. *Marginal product,* as defined in the text, is really *incremental* product. More advanced treatments distinguish between this notion and marginal product as the limit of the ratio as ΔL approaches zero. Marginal product thus measures the rate at which total product is changing as one factor is varied and is the partial derivative of the total product with respect to the variable factor. In symbols,

$$MP = \frac{\partial TP}{\partial L}$$

15. We have referred specifically both to diminishing *marginal* product and to diminishing *average* product. In most cases, eventually diminishing marginal product implies eventually diminishing average product. This is, however, not necessary, as the accompanying figure shows.

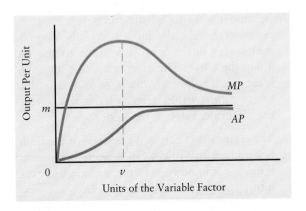

Units of the Variable Factor

In this case, marginal product diminishes after v units of the variable factor are employed. Because marginal product falls toward, but never quite reaches, a value of m, average product rises continually toward, but never quite reaches, the same value.

16. Let q be the quantity of output and L the quantity of the variable factor. In the short run,

$$TP = q = f(L) \qquad [16.1]$$

We now define

$$AP = \frac{q}{L} = \frac{f(L)}{L} \qquad [16.2]$$

$$MP = \frac{dq}{dL} \qquad [16.3]$$

We are concerned with the relationship between these two. Where average product is rising, at a maximum, or falling is determined by its derivative with respect to L:

$$\frac{d(q/L)}{dL} = \frac{L \cdot (dq/dL) - q}{L^2} \qquad [16.4]$$

This may be rewritten

$$\frac{1}{L} \cdot \left[\frac{dq}{dL} - \frac{q}{L}\right] = \frac{1}{L} \cdot (MP - AP) \qquad [16.5]$$

Clearly, when MP is greater than AP, the expression in Equation 16.5 is positive and thus AP is rising. When MP is less than AP, AP is falling. When they are equal, AP is neither rising nor falling.

17. The text defines *incremental cost.* Strictly, marginal cost is the rate of change of total cost with respect to output, q. Thus

$$MC = \frac{dTC}{dq}$$

From the definitions, $TC = TFC + TVC$. Fixed costs are not a function of output. Thus we may write $TC = Z + f(q)$, where $f(q)$ is total variable costs and Z is a constant. From this we see that $MC = df(q)/dq$. MC is thus independent of the size of the fixed costs.

18. This point is easily seen if a little algebra is used:

$$AVC = \frac{TVC}{q}$$

but note that $TVC = L \cdot w$ and $q = AP \cdot L$, where L is the quantity of the variable factor used and w is its cost per unit. Therefore,

$$AVC = \frac{L \cdot w}{AP \cdot L} = \frac{w}{AP}$$

Because w is a constant, it follows that AVC and AP vary inversely with each other, and when AP is at its maximum value, AVC must be at its minimum value.

19. A little elementary calculus will prove the point:

$$MC = \frac{dTC}{dq} = \frac{dTVC}{dq} = \frac{d(L \cdot w)}{dq}$$

If w does not vary with output,

$$MC = \frac{dL}{dq} \cdot w$$

However, referring to note 16 (Equation 16.3), we see that

$$\frac{dL}{dq} = \frac{1}{MP}$$

Thus

$$MC = \frac{w}{MP}$$

Because w is fixed, MC varies negatively with MP. When MP is at a maximum, MC is at a minimum.

20. As we saw in note 17, $MC = dTVC/dq$. If we take the integral of MC from zero to q_0, we get

$$\int_0^{q_0} MC \, dq = TVC(q_0) + Z$$

The first term is the area under the marginal cost curve; the constant of integration, Z, is fixed cost.

21. Strictly speaking, the marginal rate of substitution refers to the slope of the tangent to the isoquant at a particular point, whereas the calculations in Table 9A-1 refer to the average rate of substitution between two distinct points on the isoquant. Assume a production function

$$Q = Q(K,L) \qquad [21.1]$$

Isoquants are given by the function

$$K = I(L, \overline{Q}) \qquad [21.2]$$

derived from Equation 21.1 by expressing K as an explicit function of L and Q. A single isoquant relates to a particular level of output, Q. Define Q_K and Q_L as an alternative, more compact notation for $\partial Q / \partial K$ and $\partial Q / \partial L$, the marginal products of capital and labour. Also, let Q_{KK} and Q_{LL} stand for $\partial^2 Q / \partial K^2$ and $\partial^2 Q / \partial L^2$, respectively. To obtain the slope of the isoquant, totally differentiate Equation 21.1 to obtain

$$dQ = Q_K \cdot dK + Q_L \cdot dL$$

Then, because we are moving along a single isoquant, set $dQ = 0$ to obtain

$$\frac{dK}{dL} = -\frac{Q_L}{Q_K} = MRS$$

Diminishing marginal productivity implies $Q_{LL} < 0$ and $Q_{KK} < 0$, and hence, as we move down the isoquant of Figure 9A-1, Q_K is rising and Q_L is falling, so the absolute value of MRS is diminishing. This is called the *hypothesis of a diminishing marginal rate of substitution*.

22. Formally, the problem is to maximize

$$Q = Q(K,L)$$

subject to the constraint

$$p_K \cdot K + p_L \cdot L = C$$

To do this, form the Lagrangean,

$$\mathcal{L} = Q(K, L) - \lambda(p_K \cdot K + p_L \cdot L - C)$$

The first-order conditions for finding the saddle point on this function are

$$Q_K = \lambda \cdot p_K \qquad [22.1]$$

$$Q_L = \lambda \cdot p_L \qquad [22.2]$$

$$p_K \cdot K + p_L \cdot L = C \qquad [22.3]$$

Dividing Equation 22.1 by Equation 22.2 yields

$$\frac{Q_K}{Q_L} = \frac{p_K}{p_L}$$

That is, the ratio of the marginal products, which is -1 times the MRS, is equal to the ratio of the prices, which is -1 times the slope of the isocost line.

23. Marginal revenue is mathematically the derivative of total revenue with respect to output, dTR/dq. Incremental revenue is $\Delta TR / \Delta q$.

However, the term *marginal revenue* is used loosely to refer to both concepts.

24. For notes 24 through 26, it is helpful first to define some terms. Let

$$\pi_n = TR_n - TC_n$$

where π_n is the profit when n units are sold.

If the firm is maximizing its profits by producing n units, it is necessary that the profits at output q_n be at least as large as the profits at output zero. If the firm is maximizing its profits at output n, then

$$\pi_n \geq \pi_0 \qquad [24.1]$$

The condition says that profits from producing must be greater than profits from not producing. Condition 24.1 can be rewritten as

$$TR_n - TVC_n - TFC_n \\ \geq TR_0 - TVC_0 - TFC_0 \qquad [24.2]$$

However, note that by definition

$$TR_0 = 0 \qquad [24.3]$$
$$TVC_0 = 0 \qquad [24.4]$$
$$TFC_n = TFC_0 = Z \qquad [24.5]$$

where Z is a constant. By substituting Equations 24.3, 24.4, and 24.5 into Condition 24.2, we get

$$TR_n - TVC_n \geq 0$$

from which we obtain

$$TR_n \geq TVC_n$$

This proves Rule 1.

On a per-unit basis, it becomes

$$\frac{TR_n}{q_n} \geq \frac{TVC_n}{q_n} \qquad [24.6]$$

where q_n is the number of units produced.

Because $TR_n = q_n \cdot p_n$, where p_n is the price when n units are sold, Equation 24.6 may be rewritten as

$$p_n \geq AVC_n$$

25. Using elementary calculus, we may prove Rule 2.

$$\pi_n = TR_n - TC_n$$

each of which is a function of output q. To maximize π, it is necessary that

$$\frac{d\pi}{dq} = 0 \qquad [25.1]$$

and that

$$\frac{d^2\pi}{dq^2} < 0 \qquad [25.2]$$

From the definitions,

$$\frac{d\pi}{dq} = \frac{dTR}{dq} - \frac{dTC}{dq} = MR - MC \quad [25.3]$$

From Equations 25.1 and 25.3, a necessary condition for attaining maximum π is $MR - MC = 0$, or $MR = MC$, as is required by Rule 2.

26. To prove that for a negatively sloped demand curve, marginal revenue is less than price, let $p = p(q)$. Then

$$TR = p \cdot q = p(q) \cdot q$$

$$MR = \frac{dTR}{dq} = q \cdot \frac{dp}{dq} + p$$

For a negatively sloped demand curve, dp/dq is negative, and thus MR is less than price for positive values of q.

27. The equation for a downward-sloping straight-line demand curve with price on the vertical axis is

$$p = a - b \cdot q$$

where $-b$ is the slope of the demand curve. Total revenue is price times quantity:

$$TR = p \cdot q = a \cdot q - b \cdot q^2$$

Marginal revenue is

$$MR = \frac{dTR}{dq} = a - 2 \cdot b \cdot q$$

Thus the MR curve and the demand curve are both straight lines, and the (absolute value of the) slope of the MR curve ($2b$) is twice that of the demand curve (b).

28. A monopolist, selling in two or more markets, will set its marginal cost equal to marginal revenue in each market. Thus the condition

$$MC = MR_1 = MR_2$$

is a profit-maximizing condition for a monopolist that is selling in two markets. In general, equal marginal revenues will mean unequal prices because the ratio of price to marginal revenue is a function of elasticity of demand: The higher the elasticity, the lower the ratio. Thus equal marginal revenues imply a higher price in the market with the less elastic demand.

29. The marginal revenue produced by the factor involves two elements: first, the additional output that an extra unit of the factor makes possible and, second, the change in price of the product that the extra output causes. Let Q be output, R revenue, and L the number of units of labour hired. The contribution to revenue of additional labour is $\partial R/\partial L$. This, in turn, depends on the contribution of the extra labour to output $\partial Q/\partial L$ (the marginal product of the factor) and $\partial R/\partial Q$ (the firm's marginal revenue from the extra output). Thus

$$\frac{\partial R}{\partial L} = \frac{\partial Q}{\partial L} \cdot \frac{\partial R}{\partial Q}$$

We define the left-hand side as marginal revenue product, *MRP*. Thus

$$MRP = MP \cdot MR$$

30. The proposition that the marginal labour cost is above the average labour cost when the average is rising is essentially the same proposition proved in note 16. Nevertheless, let us do it again, using elementary calculus.

The quantity of labour depends on the wage rate: $L = f(w)$. Total labour cost is $w \cdot L$. Marginal cost of labour is

$$\frac{d(w \cdot L)}{dL} = w + L \cdot \frac{dw}{dL}$$

Rewrite this as

$$MC = AC + L \cdot \frac{dw}{dL}$$

As long as the supply curve slopes upward, $dw/dL > 0$; therefore, $MC > AC$.

31. In general, for any growth rate per unit of time, g, and starting value, P_0, the price level at time t, P_t, will be $P_0(1 + g)^t$. This is the formula for *compound* growth at rate g per unit of time. For small

values of g, $(1 + g)^t$ will be very close to $(1 + tg)$. But as g gets larger, so does the difference. For example, if prices are growing at 2 percent per month, the annual growth will be $(1.02)^{12} = 1.268$, yielding a growth rate of 26.8 percent per year. This is considerably more than 24 percent, which is just the monthly rate times 12. Generally, annual rates of growth are calculated by compounding rates of growth that are measured over shorter or longer periods than one year.

32. In the text, we define *MPC* as an incremental ratio. For mathematical treatment, it is sometimes convenient to define all marginal concepts as derivatives: $MPC = dC/dY_D$, $MPS = dS/dY_D$, and so on.

33. The basic relationship is

$$Y_D = C + S$$

Dividing through by Y_D yields

$$\frac{Y_D}{Y_D} = \frac{C}{Y_D} + \frac{S}{Y_D}$$

and thus

$$1 = APC + APS$$

Next, take the first difference of the basic relationship to get

$$\Delta Y_D = \Delta C + \Delta S$$

Dividing through by ΔY_D gives

$$\frac{\Delta Y_D}{\Delta Y_D} = \frac{\Delta C}{\Delta Y_D} + \frac{\Delta S}{\Delta Y_D}$$

and thus

$$1 = MPC + MPS$$

34. The total expenditure over all rounds is the sum of an infinite series. If we let A stand for autonomous expenditure and z for the marginal propensity to spend, the change in autonomous expenditure is ΔA in the first round, $z \cdot \Delta A$ in the second, $z^2 \cdot \Delta A)$ in the third, and so on. This can be written as

$$\Delta A \cdot (1 + z + z^2 + \ldots + z^n)$$

If z is less than 1, the series in parentheses converges to $1/(1 - z)$ as n approaches infinity. The total change in expenditure is thus $\Delta A/(1 - z)$. In the example in the box, $z = 0.80$; therefore, the change in total expenditure is five times ΔA.

35. This involves using functions of functions. We have $C = C(Y_D)$ and $Y_D = f(Y)$. So, by substitution, $C = C[f(Y)]$. In the linear expressions that are used in the text, $C = a + bY_D$, where b is the marginal propensity to consume. $Y_D = hY$, so $C = a + bhY$, where bh is thus the marginal response of C to a change in Y.

36. This is easily proved. The banking system wants sufficient deposits (D) to establish the target ratio (v) of deposits to reserves (R). This gives $R/D = v$. Any change in D of size ΔD has to be accompanied by a change in R of ΔR of sufficient size to restore v. Thus $\Delta R/\Delta D = v$, so $\Delta D = \Delta R/v$, and $\Delta D/\Delta R = 1/v$. This can be shown also in terms of the deposits created by the sequence in Table 27-7. Let v be the reserve ratio and $e = 1 - v$ be the excess reserves per dollar of new deposits. If X dollars are initially deposited in the system, the successive rounds of new deposits will be $X, eX, e^2X, e^3X, \ldots$. The series

$$X + eX + e^2X + e^3X + \ldots$$
$$= X \cdot [1 + e + e^2 + e^3 + \ldots]$$

has a limit

$$X \cdot \frac{1}{1 - e} = X \cdot \frac{1}{1 - (1 - v)} = \frac{X}{v}$$

This is the total new deposits created by an injection of $\$X$ of new reserves into the banking system. For example, when $v = 0.20$, an injection of $\$100$ into the system will lead to an overall increase in deposits of $\$500$.

37. Suppose that the public wishes to hold a fraction, c, of deposits in cash, C. Now suppose that X dollars are injected into the system. Ultimately, this money will be held either as reserves by the banking system or as cash by the public. Thus we have

$$\Delta C + \Delta R = X$$

From the banking system's reserve behaviour, we have $\Delta R = v \cdot \Delta D$, and from the public's cash behaviour, we have $\Delta C = c \cdot \Delta D$. Substituting into the above equation, we get the result that

$$\Delta D = \frac{X}{v + c}$$

From this we can also relate the change in reserves and the change in cash holdings to the initial injection:

$$\Delta R = \frac{v}{v + c} \cdot X$$

$$\Delta C = \frac{c}{v + c} \cdot X$$

For example, when $v = 0.20$ and $c = 0.05$, an injection of $\$100$ will lead to an increase in reserves of $\$80$, an increase in cash in the hands of the public of $\$20$, and an increase in deposits of $\$400$.

38. The argument is simply as follows, where prime marks stand for first derivatives:

$$M^D = F_1(T), \qquad F_1' > 0$$
$$T = F_2(Y), \qquad F_2' > 0$$

Therefore,

$$M^D = F_1(F_2(Y)), \text{ or}$$
$$M^D = H(Y), \qquad H' > 0$$

where H is the function of the function combining F_1 and F_2.

39. Let $L(Y, r)$ give the real demand for money measured in purchasing power units. Let M be the supply of money measured in nominal units and P an index of the price level, so that M/P is the real supply of money. Now the equilibrium condition requiring equality between the demand for money and the supply of money can be expressed in real terms as

$$L(Y, r) = \frac{M}{P} \qquad [39.1]$$

or in nominal terms by multiplying through by P,

$$P \cdot L(Y, r) = M \qquad [39.2]$$

In Equation 39.1, a rise in P disturbs equilibrium by lowering M/P, and in Equation 39.2, it disturbs equilibrium by raising $P \cdot L(Y, r)$.

40. The relations involved here are discussed in note 1.

41. The time taken to break even is a function of the *difference* in growth rates, not their *levels*. Thus had 4 percent and 5 percent or 5 percent and 6 percent been used in the example, it still would have taken the same number of years. To see this quickly, recognize that we are interested in the ratio of two growth paths:

$$\frac{e^{r_1 t}}{e^{r_2 t}} = e^{(r_1 - r_2)t}$$

42. A simple example of a production function is GDP $= z(LK)^{1/2}$. This equation says that to find the amount of GDP produced, multiply the amount of labour by the amount of capital, take the square root, and multiply the result by the constant z. This production function has positive but diminishing returns to either factor. This can be seen by evaluating the first and second partial derivatives and showing the first derivatives to be positive and the second derivatives to be negative.

For example,

$$\frac{\partial \text{GDP}}{\partial K} = \frac{z \cdot L^{1/2}}{2 \cdot K^{1/2}} > 0$$

and

$$\frac{\partial^2 \text{GDP}}{\partial K^2} = -\frac{z \cdot L^{1/2}}{2 \cdot K^{3/2}} < 0$$

The production function also displays constant returns to scale, as can be seen by multiplying both L and K by the same constant, θ, and seeing that this multiplies the whole value of GDP by θ:

$$z(\theta L \cdot \theta K)^{1/2} = z(\theta^2 \cdot LK)^{1/2} = \theta z(LK)^{1/2} = \theta \cdot \text{GDP}$$

43. The values are derived from the production function,

$$\text{output} = 4(KL)^{1/2}$$

in which both factors have the same average and marginal products.

GLOSSARY

absolute advantage The situation that exists when a given amount of resources can produce more of some commodity in one country than in another.

absolute price The amount of money that must be spent to acquire one unit of a commodity. Also called *money price*.

acceleration hypothesis The hypothesis that when national income is held above potential, the persistent inflationary gap will cause inflation to accelerate, and when national income is held below potential, the persistent recessionary gap will cause inflation to decelerate.

adjustable peg system A system in which exchange rates are fixed in the short term but are occasionally changed in response to persistent payments imbalances.

administered price A price set by the conscious decision of the seller rather than by impersonal market forces.

adverse selection Self-selection, within a single risk category, of persons of above-average risk.

AE See *aggregate expenditure*.

agents Decision makers, including households, firms, and government bodies.

aggregate demand Total desired purchases by all the buyers of an economy's output.

aggregate demand (AD) curve A curve showing the combinations of real national income and the price level that makes aggregate desired expenditure equal to national income; the curve thus relates the price level to the total amount of output that will be demanded.

aggregate demand shock Any event that causes a shift in the aggregate demand curve.

aggregate expenditure (AE) Total desired expenditure on final output of the economy;

$$AE = C + I + G + (X - IM),$$

representing the four major components of aggregate desired expenditure.

aggregate expenditure (AE) function The function that relates aggregate desired expenditure to actual national income.

aggregate production function The relation between the total amount of each factor of production employed in the nation and the nation's total output, its GDP.

aggregate supply Total desired sales by all the producers of an economy's output.

aggregate supply (AS) curve See *short-run aggregate supply curve* and *long-run aggregate supply curve*.

aggregate supply shock Any event that causes a shift in the aggregate supply curve.

allocative efficiency A situation in which no reorganization of production or consumption could make everyone better off (or, as it is sometimes stated, make at least one person better off while making no one worse off).

appreciation A rise in the external value of the domestic currency in terms of foreign currencies; a fall in the exchange rate.

a priori Literally, "at a prior time" or "in advance"; that which is prior to actual experience.

arc elasticity A measure of the responsiveness of quantity to a change in price over an interval of the demand curve. It is usually defined by the formula

$$\eta = \frac{\Delta q/q}{\Delta p/q}$$

An alternative formula often used where computations are involved is

$$\eta = \frac{(q_2 - q_1)/(q_2 + q_1)}{(p_2 - p_1)/(p_2 + p_1)}$$

where p_1 and q_1 are the original price and quantity and p_2 and q_2 are the new price and quantity. With negatively sloped demand curves, elasticity is a negative number. The above expressions are therefore usually multiplied by -1 to make measured elasticity positive.

autarky A situation in which a country engages in no foreign trade.

automatic fiscal stabilizers Actions that automatically lessen the magnitude of the fluctuations in national income caused by changes in autonomous expenditures.

autonomous expenditure   Elements of expenditure that do not vary systematically with national income or the interest rate, but are determined by forces outside of the theory.

average cost (AC)   See *average total cost.*

average fixed cost (AFC)   Total fixed costs divided by the number of units of output.

average product (AP)   Total product divided by the number of units of the variable factor used in its production.

average propensity to consume (APC)   The proportion of income devoted to consumption; total consumption expenditure divided by total disposable income ($APC = C/Y_D$).

average propensity to save (APS)   The proportion of disposable income devoted to saving; total saving divided by total disposable income ($APS = S/Y_D$).

average revenue (AR)   Total revenue divided by quantity sold; this is the market price when all units are sold at one price.

average tax rate   The ratio of total taxes paid to total income earned.

average total cost (ATC)   Total cost of producing a given output divided by the number of units of output; it can also be calculated as the sum of average fixed costs and average variable costs. Also called *cost per unit, unit cost, average cost.*

average variable cost (AVC)   Total variable costs divided by the number of units of output.

balanced budget   A situation in which current revenue is exactly equal to current expenditures.

balanced budget multiplier   The change in equilibrium national income divided by the tax-financed change in government expenditure that brought it about.

balance-of-payments accounts   A summary record of a country's transactions with the rest of the world, including the buying and selling of goods, services, and assets.

balance of trade   The difference between the value of exports and the value of imports of goods and services.

bank notes   Paper money issued by commercial banks.

bank rate   The rate of interest at which the Bank of Canada makes loans to the chartered banks.

barter   A system in which goods and services are traded directly for other goods and services.

beggar-my-neighbour policies   Policies designed to increase a country's prosperity at the expense of reducing prosperity in other countries.

benefit-cost analysis   A technique for evaluating government policies. The sum of the opportunity cost to all parties is compared with the value of the benefits to all parties.

black market   A situation in which goods are sold illegally at prices that violate a legal price control.

bond   A debt instrument carrying a specified amount and schedule of interest payments and (usually) a date for redemption of its face value.

break-even price   The price at which a firm is just able to cover all of its costs, including the opportunity cost of capital.

budget balance   The difference between total government revenue and total government expenditure.

budget deficit   Any shortfall of current revenue below current expenditure.

budget deficit function   A relationship which plots the government's budget deficit as a function of the level of national income.

budget line   Graphical representation of all combinations of commodities (or factors) that a household (or firm) may obtain if it spends a specified amount of money at fixed prices of the commodities (or factors). In the theory of the firm, this is usually called an *isocost line.*

budget surplus   Any excess of current revenue over current expenditure.

business cycle   Fluctuations of national income around its trend value, after seasonal fluctuations have been removed, that follow a wavelike pattern.

C See *consumption expenditure.*

capacity   The level of output that corresponds to the firm's minimum short-run average total cost.

capital   A factor of production consisting of all manufactured aids to further production, including plant, equipment, and inventories.

capital account   A part of the balance-of-payments accounts that records payments and receipts arising from the import and export of long-term and short-term financial capital.

capital consumption allowance   See *depreciation.*

capital-labour ratio   A measure of the amount of capital per worker.

capital-service account   In the balance of payments, this account records the payments and receipts that represent income on assets (such as interest and dividends).

capital stock   The aggregate quantity of capital goods.

cartel   An organization of producers who agree to act as a single seller in order to maximize joint profits.

central bank   A bank that acts as banker to the commercial banking system and often to the government as well. In the modern world, usually a government-owned and operated institution that controls the banking system and is the sole money-issuing authority.

centrally planned economy   See *command economy.*

ceteris paribus   Literally, "other things being equal"; usually used in economics to indicate that all variables except the ones specified are assumed not to change.

change in demand   A change in the quantity demanded at each possible price of the commodity, represented by a shift in the whole demand curve.

change in quantity demanded   A change in the specific quantity bought, represented by a change from one point on a demand curve to another point, either on the original demand curve or on a new one.

change in quantity supplied   A change in the specific quantity supplied, represented by a change from one point on a supply curve to another point, either on the original supply curve or on a new one.

change in supply   A change in the quantity supplied at each possible price of the commodity, represented by a shift in the whole supply curve.

Classical dichotomy   The view that national income is determined only by the real sector of the economy and that changes in the money supply lead only to changes in the price level.

clearing house   An institution where interbank indebtedness, arising from the transfer of cheques between banks, is computed and offset and net amounts owing are calculated.

closed economy   An economy that has no foreign trade.

Coase theorem   The idea (originally put forward by Ronald Coase) that as long as property rights are clearly assigned, externalities need not result in allocative inefficiency.

collective bargaining   The process by which unions and employers arrive at and enforce agreements.

collusion   An agreement among sellers to act jointly in their common interest, for example, by agreeing to raise prices. Collusion may be overt or covert, explicit, or tacit.

combine laws   Laws that prevent firms either from combining into one unit or from cooperating so as to behave monopolistically.

command economy   An economy in which the decisions of the government (as distinct from households and firms) exert the major influence over the allocation of resources.

commercial bank   A privately owned, profit-seeking institution that provides a variety of financial services, such as accepting deposits from customers and making loans and other investments.

commercial policy   See *trade policy*.

common market   A customs union with the added provision that factors of production can move freely among the members.

comparative advantage   The ability of one nation (region or individual) to produce a commodity at a lesser opportunity cost than another nation (region or individual).

comparative statics   The derivation of predictions by analyzing the effect of a change in some exogenous variable on the equilibrium position.

competition policy   Policy designed to prohibit the acquisition and exercise of monopoly power by business firms.

complements   Commodities that tend to be used jointly. The degree of complementarity of any two goods is measured by the size of the negative cross elasticity between the two goods.

concentration ratio   The fraction of total market sales (or some other measure of market occupancy) controlled by a specified number of the industry's largest firms, four-firm and eight-firm concentration ratios being most frequently used.

constant-cost industry   An industry in which costs of the most efficient size firm remain constant as the entire industry expands or contracts in the long run.

constant returns (to scale)   A situation in which output increases in proportion to inputs as the scale of production is increased. A firm in this situation, and facing fixed factor prices, is a *constant-cost firm*.

Consumer Price Index (CPI)   A measure of the average prices of goods commonly bought by households.

consumer surplus   The difference between the total value that consumers place on all units consumed of a commodity and the payment that they must make to purchase that amount of the commodity.

consumption   The act of using commodities, either goods or services, to satisfy wants.

consumption expenditure   In macroeconomics, household expenditure on all goods and services. Represented by the symbol C as one of the four components of aggregate expenditure.

consumption function   The relationship between total desired consumption expenditure and all the variables that determine it; in the simplest cases, the relationship between consumption expenditure and disposable income and consumption expenditure and national income.

contestable market   A market in which there are no sunk costs of entry or exit so that potential entry may hold profits of existing firms to low levels—zero in the case of perfect contestability.

cooperative outcome   A situation in which existing firms cooperate to maximize their joint profits.

corporation   A form of business organization in which the firm has a legal existence separate from that of the owners, and ownership and financial responsibility are divided, limited, and shared among any number of individual and institutional shareholders.

cost   To a producing firm, the value of inputs used to produce output.

cost-effectiveness analysis   Analysis of program costs with the purpose of finding the least-cost way to achieve a given result. See also *benefit-cost analysis*.

cost minimization   An implication of profit maximization that firms choose the method that produces specific output at the lowest attainable cost.

CPI   See *Consumer Price Index*.

cross elasticity of demand   (η_{XY}) A measure of the responsiveness of the quantity of one commodity demanded to changes in the price of another commodity:

$$\eta_{XY} = \frac{\text{percentage change in quantity demanded of good } X}{\text{percentage change in price of good } Y}$$

cross-sectional data   A set of measurements or observations made at the same time across several different units (such as households, firms, or countries).

crowding out   The offsetting reduction in private expenditure caused by the rise in interest rates that follows an expansionary fiscal policy.

crown corporations   Business concerns owned by the government.

current account   A part of the balance-of-payments accounts that records payments and receipts arising from trade in goods and services and from interest and dividends that are earned by capital owned in one country and invested in another.

current-dollar GDP   Gross domestic product valued in prices prevailing at the time of measurement; year-to-year changes in current-dollar GDP reflect changes both in quantities produced and in market prices. Also called *nominal GDP*.

current-dollar national income   See *nominal national income*.

customs union   A group of countries who agree to have free trade among themselves and a common set of barriers against imports from the rest of the world.

cyclical unemployment   Unemployment in excess of frictional and structural unemployment; it is due to a shortfall of actual national income below potential national income. Sometimes called *deficient-demand unemployment*.

cyclically adjusted deficit (CAD)   An estimate of the government budget deficit (expenditure minus tax revenue), not as it actually is but as it would be if national income were at its potential level.

debt   Money owed to one's creditors; from a firm's point of view, the portion of its money capital that is borrowed rather than subscribed by shareholders.

debt-service payments   Payments which represent the interest owed on a current stock of debt.

decision lag   The period of time between perceiving some problem and reaching a decision on what to do about it.

declining-cost industry   An industry in which costs of the most efficient size firm decline as the entire industry expands (or rise as the entire industry contracts) in the long run.

decreasing returns (to scale)   A situation in which output increases less than in proportion to inputs as the scale of a firm's production increases. A firm in this situation, with fixed factor prices, is an *increasing-cost firm*.

deflation   A situation in which there is a reduction in the general price level—the rate of inflation is negative.

demand   The entire relationship between the quantity of a commodity that buyers wish to purchase (per period of time) and the price of that commodity, other things being equal.

demand curve   The graphical representation of the relationship between the quantity of a commodity that buyers wish to purchase (per period of time) and the price of that commodity, other things being equal.

demand for money   The total amount of money balances that the public wishes to hold for all purposes.

demand for money function   See *liquidity preference function*.

demand inflation   Inflation arising from excess aggregate demand, that is, when national income exceeds potential income.

demand schedule   A table showing the relationship between the quantity of a commodity that buyers wish to purchase (per period of time) and the price of that commodity, other things being equal.

demogrants   Social benefits paid to anyone meeting only minimal requirements such as age or residence; in particular, *not* income-tested.

deposit money   Money held by the public in the form of demand deposits with commercial banks.

depreciation   (1) A fall in the external value of domestic currency in terms of foreign currency; that is, a rise in the exchange rate. (2) An estimate of the amount by which the capital stock is depleted through its contribution to current production. Also called *capital consumption allowance*.

depression   A persistent period of very low economic activity with very high unemployment and high excess capacity.

derived demand   The demand for a factor of production that results from the demand for the products that it is used to make.

developed countries   The higher-income countries of the world, including the United States, Canada, Western Europe, Japan, Australia, and South Africa.

developing countries   The lower-income countries of the world, most of which are in Africa, Asia, and Latin America. Also called *underdeveloped countries* or *less-developed countries*.

differentiated product   A group of commodities that are similar enough to be called the same product but dissimilar enough so that all of them do not have to be sold at the same price.

diminishing marginal rate of substitution   The hypothesis that the marginal rate of substitution changes systematically as the amounts of two commodities being consumed vary.

direct burden   Amount of money for a tax that is collected from taxpayers.

direct investment   See *foreign direct investment*.

discouraged workers   People who would like to work but have ceased looking for a job and hence have withdrawn from the labour force because they believe that no jobs are available for them.

discretionary fiscal policy   Fiscal policy that is a conscious response (not according to any predetermined rule) to each particular state of the economy as it arises.

disequilibrium The situation of a market in which there is excess demand or excess supply.

disequilibrium price A price at which quantity demanded does not equal quantity supplied.

disposable personal income *(Y_D)* GNP minus any part of it not actually paid to households minus personal income taxes paid by households plus transfer payments to households; personal income minus personal income taxes.

dividends Profits paid out to shareholders of a corporation. Sometimes called *distributed profits.*

division of labour The breaking up of a production process into a series of specialized tasks, each done by a different worker.

double counting In national income accounting, adding up the total outputs of all the sectors in the economy so that the value of intermediate goods is counted in the sector that produces them and every time they are purchased as an input by another sector.

dumping In international trade, the practice of selling a commodity at a lower price in the export market than in the domestic market for reasons unrelated to differences in costs of servicing the two markets.

duopoly An industry that contains only two firms.

durable good A good that yields its services over an extended period of time.

economic efficiency See *allocative efficiency* and *productive efficiency.*

economic growth Increases in real potential GDP.

economic profits or losses The difference between the revenues received from the sale of output and the opportunity cost of the inputs used to make the output. Negative economic profits are economic losses. Also called *pure profits* or *pure losses,* or simply *profits* or *losses.*

economic rent The surplus of total earnings over what must be paid to prevent a factor from moving to another use.

economies of scale Reduction of average total costs resulting from an expansion in the scale of a firm's operations so that more of all inputs are being used.

economies of scope Economies achieved by a firm that is large enough to engage efficiently in multiproduct production and associated large-scale distribution, advertising, and purchasing.

economy A set of interrelated production and consumption activities.

effective tariff rate The tax charged on any imported commodity expressed as a percentage of the value added by the exporting industry.

efficiency wage A wage paid to a worker that exceeds the minimum required in order to induce him to work for the firm. This is profitable for the firm if the higher wage increases the worker's productivity.

elastic demand The situation in which, for a given percentage change in price, there is a greater percentage change in quantity demanded; elasticity greater than unity.

elasticity of demand (η) A measure of the responsiveness of quantity of a commodity demanded to a change in its market price:

$$\eta = \frac{\text{percentage change in quantity demanded}}{\text{percentage change in price}}$$

With negatively sloped demand curves, elasticity is a negative number. The above expression is therefore usually multiplied by -1 to make measured elasticity positive. Also called *demand elasticity* and *price elasticity.*

elasticity of supply (η_S) A measure of the responsiveness of the quantity of a commodity supplied to a change in its market price:

$$\eta_S = \frac{\text{percentage change in quantity supplied}}{\text{percentage change in price}}$$

embodied technical change Technical change that is intrinsic to the particular capital goods in use and hence can be used only when new capital, embodying the new techniques, is built.

employment The number of adult workers (15 years of age and older) who hold jobs.

endogenous variable A variable that is explained within a theory. Sometimes called an *induced variable* or a *dependent variable.*

ends The goals that one seeks to attain.

entry barrier Any natural barrier to the entry of new firms into an industry, such as a large minimum efficient scale for firms, or any firm-created barrier, such as a patent.

envelope Any curve that encloses, by being tangent to, a series of other curves. In particular, the envelope cost curve is the *LRAC* curve, which encloses the *SRATC* curves by being tangent to each without cutting any of them.

equalization payments Transfers of tax revenues from the federal government to the low-income provinces to compensate them for their lower per capita tax yields.

equilibrium condition A condition that must be fulfilled if some market or sector of the economy, or the whole economy, is to be in equilibrium.

equilibrium differential A difference in factor prices that persists in equilibrium, with no tendency for it to change.

equilibrium price The price at which quantity demanded equals quantity supplied.

equity capital Funds provided by the owners of a firm, the return on which depends on the firm's profits.

excess burden The value to taxpayers of the changes in behaviour that are induced by taxes; the amount that taxpayers would be willing to pay, over and above the direct burden of taxes, to abolish the taxes.

excess capacity   The amount by which actual output falls short of capacity output (which is the output that corresponds to the minimum short-run average total cost).

excess-capacity theorem   The property of long-run equilibrium in monopolistic competition that firms produce on the falling portion of their average total cost curves so that they have excess capacity measured by the gap between present output and the output that coincides with minimum average total cost.

excess demand   A situation in which, at the given price, quantity demanded exceeds quantity supplied.

excess reserves   Reserves held by a commercial bank in excess of its target reserves.

excess supply   A situation in which, at the given price, quantity supplied exceeds quantity demanded.

exchange rate   The number of units of domestic currency required to purchase one unit of foreign currency.

excise tax   A tax on the sale of a particular commodity; may be a specific tax (fixed tax per unit of commodity) or an ad valorem tax (fixed percentage of the value of the commodity).

execution lag   The time that it takes to put policies in place after a decision has been made.

exogenous variable   A variable that influences endogenous variables but is itself determined by factors outside the theory. Sometimes called an *autonomous variable* or an *independent variable*.

expectational inflation   Inflation that occurs because decision makers raise prices (so as to keep their relative prices constant) in the expectation that the price level is going to rise.

expectations-augmented Phillips curve   The relationship between unemployment and the rate of increase of money wages or between national income and the rate of inflation that arises when the demand and expectations components of inflation are combined.

exports   The value of all goods and services sold to firms, households, and governments in other countries.

external economies of scale   Scale economies that cause the firm's costs to fall as industry output rises but are external to the firm and so cannot be obtained by the firm's increasing its own output.

external value of the dollar   The value of the dollar expressed in terms of foreign currencies; a rise in the dollar's external value is reflected by a fall in the exchange rate. See *exchange rate.*

externality   An effect, either good or bad, on parties not directly involved in the production or use of a commodity. Also called *third-party effects.*

factor markets   Markets in which the services of factors of production are sold.

factor mobility   The ease with which factors can be transferred between uses.

factors of production   Resources used to produce goods and services; frequently divided into the basic categories of land, labour, and capital.

fiat money   Paper money or coinage that is neither backed by nor convertible into anything else but is decreed by the government to be accepted as legal tender and is generally accepted in exchange for goods and services and for the discharge of debts.

final demand   Demand for the economy's final output.

final goods   Goods that are not used as inputs by other firms but are produced to be sold for consumption, investment, government, or exports during the period under consideration.

financial capital   Money that a firm raises to carry on its business, including both equity capital and debt. Also called *money capital.*

fine tuning   The attempt to maintain national income at its full-employment level by means of frequent changes in fiscal or monetary policy.

firm   A unit that employs factors of production to produce goods and services.

fiscal policy   The use of the government's tax and spending policies in an effort to influence the behaviour of GDP.

fixed exchange rate   An exchange rate that is maintained within a small range around its publicly stated par value by the intervention of a country's central bank in foreign market operations.

fixed factor   An input that cannot be increased beyond a given amount in the short run.

fixed investment   Investment in plant and equipment. Also called *business fixed investment.*

flexible exchange rate   An exchange rate that is left free to be determined by the forces of demand and supply on the free market, with no intervention by the monetary authorities.

foreign direct investment (FDI)   Nonresident investment in the form of a takeover or capital investment in a domestic branch plant or subsidiary corporation in which the investor has voting control. Also called *direct investment.*

foreign exchange   Actual foreign currencies or various claims on them, such as bank balances or promises to pay, that are traded on the foreign exchange market.

foreign exchange market   The market where different national currencies, or claims to these currencies, are traded.

45° line   In macroeconomics, the line that graphs the equilibrium condition that desired aggregate expenditure equals actual national income, $AE = Y$.

fractional-reserve system   A banking system in which commercial banks keep only a fraction of their deposits in cash or on deposit with the central bank.

free good   A commodity for which the quantity supplied exceeds the quantity demanded at a price of zero; therefore, a good that does not command a positive price in a market economy.

free-market economy   An economy in which the decisions of individual households and firms (as distinct from the government) exert the major influence over the allocation of resources.

free trade   The absence of any form of government intervention in international trade, which implies that imports and exports are not subject to special taxes or restrictions levied merely because of their status as "imports" or "exports."

free trade area (FTA)   An agreement among two or more countries to abolish tariffs on all or most of the trade among themselves while each remains free to set its own tariffs against other countries.

frictional unemployment   Unemployment caused by the time that is taken for labour to move from one job to another.

full employment   Employment that is sufficient to produce the economy's potential output; at full employment, all remaining unemployment is frictional and structural.

function   Loosely, an expression of a relationship between two or more variables. Precisely, Y is a function of the variables $X_1, \ldots, X_n$ if, for every set of values of the variables $X_1, \ldots, X_n$, there is associated a unique value of the variable Y.

functional distribution of income   The distribution of national income among the major factors of production.

G See *government purchases*.

gains from trade   The increased output due to the specialization according to comparative advantage that is made possible by trade.

game theory   The theory that studies rational decision making in situations in which one must anticipate the reactions of one's competitors to the moves that one makes.

Giffen good   An inferior good for which the negative income effect outweighs the substitution effect so that the demand curve is positively sloped.

goods   Tangible commodities, such as cars or shoes.

goods markets   Markets in which outputs of goods and services are sold. Also called *product markets*.

government   All public officials, agencies, and other organizations belonging to or under the control of local, provincial, or federal governments.

government purchases   All government expenditure on currently produced goods and services, exclusive of government transfer payments. Represented by the symbol G as one of the four components of aggregate expenditure.

Gresham's law   The theory that "bad," or debased, money drives "good," or undebased, money out of circulation because people keep the good money for other purposes and use the bad money for transactions.

gross domestic product (GDP)   National income as measured by the output approach; equal to the sum of all values added in the economy or, what is the same thing, the values of all final goods produced in the economy. It can be valued at current prices to get *nominal GDP* or it can be valued at base-year prices to get *real GDP*, which is also called *GDP at constant prices*.

gross investment   The total value of all investment goods produced in the economy during a stated period of time.

gross national product (GNP)   The value of total incomes earned by domestically based producers and factors of production.

gross tuning   The use of macroeconomic policy to stabilize the economy such that large deviations from full employment do not occur for extended periods of time.

homogeneous product   In the eyes of purchasers, a product every unit of which is identical to every other unit.

Hotelling's rule   Determines the optimal rate of extraction of a nonrenewable resource as one such that the price rises at a rate equal to the interest rate.

household   All of the people who live under one roof and who make joint financial decisions or are subject to others making decisions for them.

human capital   The capitalized value of productive investments in persons; usually refers to value derived from expenditures on education, training, and health improvements.

I See *investment expenditure*.

IM See *imports*.

implicit GDP deflator   An index number derived by dividing GDP, measured in current dollars, by GDP, measured in constant dollars, and multiplying by 100. In effect, a price index, with current-year quantity weights, measuring the average change in price of all the items in the GDP.

import quota   A limit set by the government on the quantity of a foreign commodity that may be shipped into that country in a given time period.

imports   The value of all goods and services purchased from firms, households, or governments in other countries.

imputed costs   The costs of using factors of production already owned by the firm, measured by the earnings they could have received in their best alternative use.

income-consumption line   (1) A curve showing the relationship for a commodity between quantity demanded and income, *ceteris paribus*. (2) A curve drawn on an indifference curve diagram and connecting the points of tangency between a set of indifference curves and a set of parallel budget lines, showing how the consumption bundle changes as income changes, with relative prices being held constant.

income effect   The effect on quantity demanded of a change in real income, holding relative prices constant.

income elasticity of demand (η_Y)   A measure of the responsiveness of quantity demanded to a change in income:

$$\eta_Y = \frac{\text{percentage change in quantity demanded}}{\text{percentage change in income}}$$

incomes policy   Any direct intervention by the government to influence wage and price formation.

income-tested benefits   Social benefits paid to recipients who qualify because their income is less than some critical level.

increasing-cost industry   An industry in which costs of the most efficient size firm rise as the entire industry expands (or fall as the entire industry contracts) in the long run.

increasing returns (to scale)   A situation in which output increases more than in proportion to inputs as the scale of a firm's production increases. A firm in this situation, with fixed factor prices, is a *decreasing-cost firm*.

incremental cost   See *marginal cost*.

incremental product   See *marginal product*.

incremental revenue   See *marginal revenue*.

indexation   Automatic change in any money payment in proportion to the change in the price level.

index number   An average that measures change over time of such variables as the price level and industrial production; conventionally expressed as a percentage relative to a base period, which is assigned the value 100.

indifference curve   A curve showing all combinations of two commodities that give the household equal utility and between which the household is thus indifferent.

indifference map   A set of indifference curves based on a given set of household preferences.

induced expenditure   Elements of expenditure that are explained by variables within the theory. In the aggregate desired expenditure function, it is any component of expenditure that is related to national income. Also called *endogenous expenditure*.

industry   A group of firms that produce a single product or group of related products.

inelastic demand   The situation in which, for a given percentage change in price, there is a smaller percentage change in quantity demanded; elasticity less than one.

infant industry argument   The argument that new domestic industries with potential for economies of scale or learning by doing need to be protected from competition from established, low-cost foreign producers so that they can grow large enough to achieve costs as low as those of foreign producers.

inferior good   A good for which quantity demanded falls as income rises—its income elasticity is negative.

inflation   A rise in the average level of all prices.

inflationary gap   A situation in which actual national income exceeds potential income.

infrastructure   The basic installations and facilities (especially transportation and communications systems) on which the commerce of a community depends.

injections   Income earned by domestic firms that does not arise out of the spending of domestic households and income earned by domestic households that does not arise out of the spending of domestic firms.

innovation   The introduction of an invention into methods of production.

inputs   Intermediate products and factor services that are used in the process of production.

interest   The payment for the use of borrowed money.

interest rate   The price paid per dollar borrowed per period of time, expressed either as a proportion (e.g., 0.06) or as a percentage (e.g., 6 percent). Also called the *nominal interest rate* to distinguish it from the *real interest rate*.

intermediate products   All outputs that are used as inputs by other producers in a further stage of production.

intermediate targets   Variables that the government cannot control directly and does not seek to control ultimately, yet that have an important influence on policy variables.

internal economies of scale   Scale economies that result from the firm's own actions and hence are available to it by raising its own output.

internal value of the dollar   The purchasing power of the dollar measured in terms of domestic goods and services; changes in the internal value of the dollar are measured by changes in an index of Canadian prices (such as the consumer price index).

internalization   A process that results in a producer or consumer taking account of a previously external effect.

invention   The creation of something new, such as a production technique or a product.

inventories   Stocks of raw materials, goods in process, and finished goods held by firms to mitigate the effect of short-term fluctuations in production or sales.

investment expenditure   Expenditure on the production of goods not for present consumption.

investment goods   Goods that are produced not for present consumption, such as capital goods, inventories, and residential housing.

involuntary unemployment   Unemployment due to the inability of qualified persons who are seeking work to find jobs at the going wage rate.

isoquant   A curve showing all technologically efficient factor combinations for producing a specified amount of output.

isoquant map   A series of isoquants from the same production function, each isoquant relating to a specific level of output.

Keynesians   Economists who tend to believe (following the views of John Maynard Keynes) that during recessions, expansionary fiscal policy is more effective than expansionary monetary policy in raising national income.

Keynesian short-run aggregate supply curve   A horizontal aggregate supply curve indicating that when national income is below potential, changes in national income can occur with little or no accompanying change in prices.

labour A factor of production consisting of all physical and mental efforts provided by people.

labour force The total number of persons employed in both civilian and military jobs, plus the number of persons who are unemployed.

labour-force participation rate The percentage of the population of working age that is actually in the labour force (either working or seeking work).

labour union See *union*.

Laffer curve A relationship between the revenue yield of a tax and the tax rate imposed. Named after its originator, Arthur Laffer.

laissez faire Literally, "let do"; a policy advocating the minimization of government intervention in a market economy.

land A factor of production consisting of all gifts of nature, including raw materials and land, as understood in ordinary speech.

law of diminishing returns The hypothesis that if increasing quantities of a variable factor are applied to a given quantity of fixed factors, the marginal product and average product of the variable factor will eventually decrease.

learning curve A curve showing how a firm's costs of producing at a given rate of output fall as the total amount produced increases over time as a result of accumulated learning.

legal tender Anything that by law must be accepted for the purchase of goods and services or in discharge of a debt.

less-developed countries (LDCs) See *developing countries*.

limited liability The limitation of the financial responsibility of an owner (shareholder) of a corporation to the amount of money that the shareholder has actually invested in the firm by purchasing its shares.

limited partnership A form of business organization in which the firm has two classes of owners: general partners, who take part in managing the firm and are personally liable for all of the firm's actions and debts, and limited partners, who take no part in the management of the firm and risk only the money that they have invested.

liquidity preference (LP) function The function that relates the demand for money to the rate of interest. Also called the *demand for money function*.

logarithmic scale A scale in which equal proportional changes are shown as equal distances (for example, 1 cm may always represent doubling of a variable, whether from 3 to 6 or 50 to 100). Also called log scale, ratio scale.

long run A period of time in which all inputs may be varied but the basic technology of production cannot be changed.

long-run aggregate supply (LRAS) curve A curve showing the relationship between the price level and the total quantity of output supplied when all markets have fully adjusted to the existing price level; a vertical line at $Y = Y^*$.

long-run average cost (LRAC) curve The curve showing the lowest possible cost of producing each level of output when all inputs can be varied.

long-run industry supply (LRS) curve A curve showing the relationship between the market price and the quantity supplied by a competitive industry when all the firms in that industry are at the minimum of their *LRAC* curves.

Lorenz curve A graph showing the extent of departure from equality of income distribution.

M1 Currency plus demand deposits plus other chequable deposits.

M2 M1 plus saving deposits at the chartered banks.

M2+ M2 plus deposits held at institutions that are *not* chartered banks.

macroeconomics The study of the determination of economic aggregates, such as total output, total employment, the price level, and the rate of economic growth.

managed float A situation in which the central bank intervenes in the foreign exchange market to smooth out some of the large, short-term fluctuations in a country's exchange rate, while still leaving the market to determine the exchange rate in the longer term.

marginal cost (MC) The increase in total cost resulting from raising the rate of production by one unit. Mathematically, the rate of change of cost with respect to output. Also called *incremental cost*.

marginal-cost pricing Setting price equal to marginal cost so that buyers are just willing to pay for the last unit bought the amount that it cost to make that unit.

marginal efficiency of capital (MEC) The rate of return on one additional unit of physical capital.

marginal efficiency of investment (MEI) function The function that relates the quantity of desired investment to the rate of interest.

marginal physical product (MPP) See *marginal product*.

marginal product (MP) The change in quantity of total output that results from using one unit more of a variable factor. Mathematically, the rate of change of output with respect to the quantity of the variable factor. Also called *incremental product* and *marginal physical product (MPP)*.

marginal propensity to consume (MPC) The change in consumption divided by the change in disposable income that brought it about; mathematically, the rate of change of consumption with respect to disposable income ($MPC = \Delta C/\Delta Y_D$).

marginal propensity not to spend The fraction of any increment to national income that is not spent on domestic production (1 minus the marginal propensity to spend; that is, $1 - \Delta AE/\Delta Y$).

marginal propensity to save (MPS) The change in total desired saving divided by the change in disposable income that brought it about ($\Delta S/\Delta Y_D$).

marginal propensity to spend The fraction of any increment to national income that is spent on domestic production; measured by the change in aggregate expenditure divided by the change in national income ($\Delta AE/\Delta Y$).

marginal rate of substitution (MRS) (1) In consumption, the slope of an indifference curve, showing how much more of one commodity must be provided to compensate for the giving up of one unit of another commodity if the level of satisfaction is to be held constant. (2) In production, the slope of an isoquant, showing how much more of one factor of production must be used to compensate for the use of one less unit of another factor of production if production is to be held constant.

marginal revenue (MR) The change in a firm's total revenue resulting from a change in its rate of sales by one unit. Mathematically, the rate of change of revenue with respect to output. Also called *incremental revenue*.

marginal revenue product (MRP) The addition of revenue attributable to the last unit of a variable factor ($MRP = MP \times MR$). Mathematically, the rate of change of revenue with respect to quantity of the variable factor.

marginal tax rate The fraction of an additional dollar of income that is paid in taxes.

marginal utility The additional satisfaction obtained by a consumer from consuming one unit more of a good or service; mathematically, the rate of change of utility with respect to consumption.

market Any situation in which buyers and sellers can negotiate the exchange of goods or services.

market-clearing price The price at which quantity demanded equals quantity supplied so that there are neither unsatisfied buyers nor unsatisfied sellers; the *equilibrium price*.

market economy See *free-market economy*.

market failure Failure of the unregulated market system to achieve allocative efficiency or social goals because of externalities, market impediments, or market imperfections.

market for corporate control An interpretation of conglomerate mergers, leveraged buyouts, and hostile takeovers as mechanisms that place the firm in the hands of the parties who value it most.

market sector The portion of an economy in which commodities are bought and sold and in which producers must cover their costs from sales revenue.

market structure All features of a market that affect the behaviour and performance of firms in that market, such as the number and size of sellers, the extent of knowledge about one another's actions, the degree of freedom of entry, and the degree of product differentiation.

means The methods of achieving one's goals.

median The value within any set of data at which half of the observations are greater and half are less. Thus half of a population earns income above the median income, and half earns income below the median.

medium of exchange Anything that is generally acceptable in return for goods and services sold.

merger The purchase of either the physical assets or the controlling share of ownership of one firm by another. In a *horizontal merger,* both firms are in the same line of business; in a *vertical merger,* one firm is a supplier of the other; if the two are in unrelated industries, it is a *conglomerate merger.*

microeconomics The study of the allocation of resources and the distribution of income as they are affected by the workings of the price system and by government policies.

minimum efficient scale (MES) The smallest output at which long-run average cost reaches its minimum; all available economies of scale in production and/or distribution have been realized at this point.

minimum wages Legally specified minimum rate of pay for labour in covered occupations.

mixed economy An economy in which some decisions about the allocation of resources are made by firms and households and some by the government.

Monetarists Economists who stress monetary causes of cyclical fluctuations and inflation.

monetary base The sum of currency in circulation plus reserves of the commercial banks; equal to the monetary liabilities of the central bank.

monetary equilibrium A situation in which the demand for money equals the supply of money.

monetary policy The central bank's attempt to influence the economy by changing the level of reserves in the banking system.

money A medium of exchange that can also serve as a store of value and a unit of account.

money capital See *financial capital.*

money income Income measured in monetary units per period of time. Also called *nominal income.*

money market deposit account (MMDA) A chequable deposit account at a nonbank financial institution that earns a relatively high interest rate.

money market mutual fund (MMMF) A liquid financial instrument that earns a high yield and is chequable but is subject to transaction restrictions.

money rate of interest See *interest rate.*

money substitute Something that serves as a temporary medium of exchange but is not a store of value.

money supply The total quantity of money in an economy at a point in time. Also called the *supply of money.*

monopolist A firm that is the only seller in a market.

monopolistic competition   Market structure of an industry in which there are many firms and freedom of entry and exit but in which each firm has a product somewhat differentiated from the others, giving it some control over its price.

monopoly   A market containing a single firm.

monopsony   A market situation in which there is a single buyer.

moral hazard   A situation in which an individual or a firm takes advantage of special knowledge while engaging in socially uneconomic behaviour.

multilateral balance of payments   The balance of payments between one country and the rest of the world taken as a whole.

multinational enterprises (MNEs)   See *transnational corporation.*

multiplier   The ratio of the change in equilibrium national income to the change in autonomous expenditure that brought it about.

NAIRU   Short for *nonaccelerating inflation rate of unemployment*. The rate of unemployment associated with potential national income and at which a steady, nonaccelerating or nondecelerating inflation can be sustained indefinitely. Also called the *natural rate of unemployment*.

Nash equilibrium   An equilibrium that results when each firm in an industry is currently doing the best that it can, given the current behaviour of the other firms in the industry.

national asset formation   The sum of investment and net exports.

national income   The value of total output (in a given period of time) and of the income that is generated by the production of that output.

national saving   The sum of public saving and private saving; all national income that is not spent on government purchases or private consumption.

natural monopoly   An industry characterized by economies of scale sufficiently large that one firm can most efficiently supply the entire market demand.

natural rate of unemployment   See *NAIRU.*

natural scale   A scale in which equal absolute amounts are represented by equal distances.

near money   Liquid assets that are easily convertible into money without risk of significant loss of value and can be used as short-term stores of purchasing power but are not themselves media of exchange.

negative income tax (NIT)   A tax system in which households with income below some critical level receive payments from the government that are based on the amount by which their income is less than the critical level.

net domestic product   Gross domestic product less capital consumed in the production of GDP.

net exports   The value of total exports minus the value of total imports. Represented by the expression X-IM as a component of aggregate expenditure, where X is total exports and IM is total imports. Net exports is denoted by the symbol NX.

net investment   Gross investment minus replacement investment.

net taxes   Total tax revenue minus transfer payments, denoted T.

neutrality of money   The doctrine that the money supply affects only the absolute level of prices and has no effect on relative prices and hence no effect on the allocation of resources or the distribution of income.

New Classical economics   An approach to explaining macroeconomic fluctuations in which fluctuations in economic activity are explained by shocks to technology and tastes rather than to markets that fail to clear.

newly industrialized countries (NICs)   Countries that have industrialized and grown rapidly over the past 40 years to achieve per capita incomes roughly half of those achieved in Canada or the United States.

nominal interest rate   See *interest rate.*

nominal national income   Total national income measured in dollars; the money value of national income. Also called *current-dollar national income.*

nominal tariff rate   The tax charged on any imported commodity.

noncooperative outcome   An industry outcome reached when firms calculate their own best policy without considering competitor's reactions.

nonmarket sector   The portion of the economy in which goods are provided freely so that producers must cover their costs from sources other than sales revenue.

nonrenewable resource   Any productive resource that is available as a fixed stock that cannot be replaced once it is used. Also called an *exhaustible resource.*

nonstrategic behaviour   Behaviour that does not take account of the reactions of rivals to one's own behaviour.

nontariff barriers (NTBs)   Restrictions other than tariffs designed to reduce the flow of imported goods.

normal good   A good for which quantity demanded rises as income rises—its income elasticity is positive.

normal profits   The opportunity cost of capital and risk taking just necessary to keep the owners in the industry. Normal profits are usually included in what economists (but not businesspersons) call *total costs.*

normative statement   A statement about what ought to be as opposed to what actually is. See also *positive statement.*

NX See *net exports.*

oligopoly   An industry that contains two or more firms, at least one of which produces a significant portion of the industry's total output.

open economy   An economy that engages in international trade.

open-market operations   The purchase and sale of securities (usually short-term government securities) on the open market by the central bank.

opportunity cost   The cost of using resources for a certain purpose, measured by the benefit given up by not using them in their best alternative use.

output gap   Actual national income minus potential national income. Also called the *GDP gap*.

outputs   The goods and services that result from the process of production.

overnight rate   The interest rate that commercial banks charge each other for very-short-term loans.

partnership   A form of business organization in which the firm has two or more joint owners, each of whom takes part in the management of the firm and is personally responsible for all of the firm's actions and debts.

paternalism   Intervention in the free choices of individuals by others (including governments) to protect them against their own ignorance or folly.

pay equity   A government policy designed to eliminate the wage differentials between workers in different jobs who nonetheless appear to have similar levels of skills and responsibilities.

per capita output   GDP divided by total population.

perfect competition   A market structure in which all firms in an industry are price takers and in which there is freedom of entry into and exit from the industry.

personal income   Income of individuals before allowance for personal income taxes on that income.

Phillips curve   Originally, a relationship between the percentage of the labour force unemployed and the rate of change of money wages. Now often drawn as a relationship between actual national income and the rate of price inflation.

physical capital   See *real capital*.

point elasticity   A measure of the responsiveness of quantity to a change in price at a particular point on the demand curve. The formula for point elasticity of demand is

$$\eta = \frac{dq}{dp} \cdot \frac{p}{q}$$

With negatively sloped demand curves, elasticity is a negative number. The above expression is usually multiplied by -1 to make elasticity positive.

point of diminishing average productivity   The level of factor use at which average product reaches a maximum.

point of diminishing marginal productivity   The level of factor use at which marginal product reaches a maximum.

policy instruments   The variables that the government can control directly to achieve its policy objectives.

policy variables   The variables that the government seeks to control, such as real national income and the price level.

poll tax   A tax that takes the same absolute amount from each person, independent of the level of their income. Also called a *lump-sum tax*.

portfolio investment   Foreign investment in bonds or a minority holding of shares that does not involve legal control.

positive statement   A statement about what actually is (was or will be), as opposed to what ought to be. See also *normative statement*.

potential income (Y^*)   The real gross domestic product that the economy could produce if its productive resources were fully employed at their normal levels of utilization. Also called *potential GDP*.

poverty line   The official government estimate of the annual family income that is required to maintain a minimum adequate standard of living.

poverty trap   Occurs whenever individuals have little incentive to increase their pre-tax income because the resulting loss of benefits makes them worse off.

precautionary balances   Money balances held for protection against the uncertainty of the timing of cash flows.

present value *(PV)*   The value now of one or more payments to be received in the future; often referred to as the *discounted present value* of future payments.

price ceiling   A government-imposed maximum permissible price at which a commodity may be sold.

price-consumption line   A line connecting the points of tangency between a set of indifference curves and a set of budget lines where one absolute price is fixed and the other varies, money income being held constant.

price controls   Government policies that attempt to hold the price in a particular market at a disequilibrium value.

price discrimination   The sale by one firm of different units of a commodity at two or more different prices for reasons not associated with differences in cost.

price elasticity of demand   See *elasticity of demand*.

price floor   A government-imposed minimum permissible price at which a commodity may be sold.

price index   A number that shows the average of some group of prices, expressed as a percentage of the average in some base period. Price indexes are used to measure the price level at a given time relative to a base period.

price level   The average level of all prices in the economy, usually expressed as an index number.

price maker   A firm that administers its prices. See *administered price*.

price taker   A firm that can alter its rate of production and sales without significantly affecting the market price of its product.

price theory   The theory of how prices are determined; competitive price theory concerns the determination of prices in competitive markets by the interaction of demand and supply.

primary budget deficit The difference between the government's overall budget deficit and its debt-service payments.

principal-agent problem The problem of resource allocation that arises because contracts that will induce agents to act in their principals' best interests are generally impossible to write or too costly to monitor.

principle of substitution The principle that methods of production will change if relative prices of inputs change, with relatively more of the cheaper input and relatively less of the more expensive input being used.

private cost The value of the best alternative use of resources used in production as valued by the producer.

private saving Saving on the part of households—the part of disposable income that is not spent on current consumption.

private sector The portion of an economy in which goods and services are produced by nongovernmental units, such as firms and households.

procyclical Moving in the same direction as the business cycle—up in booms and down in slumps.

producer surplus The difference between the total amount that producers receive for all units sold of a commodity and the total variable cost of producing the commodity.

product differentiation The existence of similar but not identical products sold by a single industry, such as the breakfast food or automobile industry. See *differentiated product*.

production The act of making commodities—either goods or services.

production function A functional relation showing the maximum output that can be produced by each and every combination of inputs.

production possibility boundary A curve that shows which alternative combinations of commodities can just be attained if all available resources are used; it is thus the boundary between attainable and unattainable output combinations. Also called *production possibility curve*.

production possibility curve See *production possibility boundary*.

productive efficiency Production of any output at the lowest attainable cost for that level of output.

productivity Output produced per unit of some input; frequently used to refer to labour productivity, measured by total output divided by the amount of labour used.

product markets Markets in which goods and services are sold. Also called *goods markets*.

profit (1) In ordinary usage, the difference between the value of outputs and the value of inputs. (2) In microeconomics, the difference between revenues received from the sale of goods and the value of inputs, which includes the opportunity cost of capital, so that profits are *economic profits*. (3) In macroeconomics, profits exclude interest on borrowed capital but do not exclude the return on owner's capital.

progressive tax A tax that takes a larger percentage of income the higher the level of income.

proportional tax A tax that takes a constant percentage of income at all levels of income and is thus neither progressive nor regressive.

protectionism Any government policy that interferes with free trade in order to give some protection to domestic industries against foreign competition.

proxy An order from a shareholder that transfers the right to vote to a nominee, usually an existing member of the board of the firm.

public goods Goods or services that, if they provide benefits to anyone, can, at little or no additional cost, provide benefits to a large group of people, possibly everyone in the country. Also called *collective consumption goods*.

public saving Saving on the part of governments. Public saving is exactly equal to government budget surpluses, or government revenues less government expenditures.

public sector The portion of an economy in which goods and services are produced by the government or by government-owned agencies and firms.

purchasing power of money The amount of goods and services that can be purchased with a unit of money. The purchasing power of money varies inversely with the price level.

purchasing power parity (PPP) The theory that over the long term, the exchange rate between two currencies adjusts to reflect relative price levels (relative purchasing power).

quantity demanded The amount of a commodity that households wish to purchase in some time period.

quantity supplied The amount of a commodity that producers wish to sell in some time period.

rate of inflation The percentage rate of increase in some price index from one period to another.

rate of return The ratio of net profits earned by a firm to total invested capital.

rational expectations The theory that people understand how the economy works and learn quickly from their mistakes so that even though random errors may be made, systematic and persistent errors are not.

ratio scale See *logarithmic scale*.

real capital The physical assets that a firm uses to conduct its business, composed of plant, equipment, and inventories. Also called *physical capital*.

real income Income expressed in terms of the purchasing power of money income, that is, the quantity of goods and services that can be purchased with the money income. It can be calculated as money income deflated by a price index.

real interest rate   The money rate of interest corrected for the change in the purchasing power of money by subtracting the inflation rate.

real national income   National income measured in constant dollars so that it changes only when quantities change.

recession   A downturn in the level of economic activity. Often defined precisely as two consecutive quarters in which real GDP falls.

recessionary gap   A negative output gap; that is, a situation in which actual national income is less than potential income. Also called a *deflationary gap*.

regressive tax   A tax that takes a lower percentage of income the higher the level of income.

relative price   The ratio of the money price of one commodity to the money price of another commodity; that is, a ratio of two absolute prices.

renewable resources   Productive resources that can be replaced as they are used up, as with physical capital; distinguished from nonrenewable resources, which are available in a fixed stock that can be depleted but not replaced.

rent seeking   Behaviour whereby private firms and individuals try to use the powers of the government to enhance their own economic well-being.

replacement investment   The amount of investment that is needed to maintain the existing capital stock intact.

required reserves   The reserves that a bank must, by law, keep either in currency or in deposits with the central bank.

reserve ratio   The fraction of its deposits that a commercial bank holds as reserves in the form of cash or deposits with a central bank.

resource allocation   The allocation of an economy's scarce resources of land, labour, and capital among alternative uses.

retained earnings   See *undistributed profits*.

Ricardian equivalence   The proposition that the method of financing government spending (taxes or borrowing) has no effect on national saving because private saving will just offset any government dissaving. Hence, if the government raises its current deficit, private agents will save enough to cover the future taxes required to repay the increased debt, leaving national saving and *AD* unchanged.

satisficing   A hypothesized objective of firms to achieve levels of performance deemed satisfactory rather than to maximize some objective.

saving   All disposable income that is not consumed. See *private saving*, *public saving*, and *national saving*.

scarce good   A commodity for which the quantity demanded exceeds the quantity supplied at a price of zero; therefore, a good that commands a positive price in a market economy.

scatter diagram   A graph of statistical observations of paired values of two variables, one measured on the horizontal and the other on the vertical axis. Each point on the coordinate grid represents the values of the variables for a particular unit of observation.

search unemployment   Unemployment caused by people continuing to search for a good job rather than accepting the first job that they come across after they become unemployed.

sectors   Parts of an economy (such as the agricultural or manufacturing sectors).

sellers' preferences   Allocation of commodities in excess demand by decisions of the sellers.

services   Intangible commodities, such as haircuts or medical care.

shareholders   See *stockholders*.

short run   A period of time in which the quantity of some inputs cannot be increased beyond the fixed amount that is available.

short-run aggregate supply (*SRAS*) curve   A curve showing the relation between the price level and the quantity of output supplied on the assumption that all factor prices are held constant.

short-run equilibrium   Generally, equilibrium subject to fixed factors or other things that cannot change over the time period being considered. For a competitive industry, the price and output at which industry demand equals short-run industry supply, and all firms are maximizing their profits. Either profits or losses for individual firms are possible.

short-run supply curve   A curve showing the relationship between quantity supplied and market price, with one or more fixed factors; it is the horizontal sum of marginal cost curves (above the level of average variable costs) of all firms in a perfectly competitive industry.

shut-down price   The price that is equal to a firm's average variable costs. At prices below this, a profit-maximizing firm will produce no output.

simple multiplier   The ratio of the change in equilibrium national income to the change in autonomous expenditure that brought it about, calculated for a constant price level.

single proprietorship   A form of business organization in which the firm has one owner who makes all the decisions and is personally responsible for all of the firm's actions and debts.

size distribution of income   The distribution of income among households, without regard to source of income or social class of households.

slope   The ratio of the vertical change to the horizontal change between two points on a curve.

social benefit   The contribution that an activity makes to society's welfare.

social cost The value of the best alternative use of resources available to society as valued by society. Also called *social opportunity cost*.

social regulation The regulation of economic behaviour to advance social goals when competition and economic regulation will fail to achieve those goals.

special drawing rights (SDRs) Financial liabilities of the International Monetary Fund, held in a special account generated by contributions of member countries. Members can use SDRs to maintain supplies of convertible currencies when these are needed to support foreign exchange trades.

specialization of labour The specialization of individual workers in the production of particular goods and services, rather than producing everything that they consume.

speculative balances Money balances held as a hedge against the uncertainty of the prices of other financial assets.

stabilization policy Any policy designed to reduce the economy's cyclical fluctuations and thereby to stabilize national income at a desired level.

stagflation The coexistence of high rates of unemployment with high, and sometimes rising, rates of inflation.

stockholders The owners of a corporation who have supplied money to the firm by purchasing its shares. Also called *shareholders*.

stock market An organized market where stocks and bonds are bought and sold. Also called *securities market*.

strategic behaviour Behaviour designed to take account of the reactions of one's rivals to one's own behaviour.

structural unemployment Unemployment due to a mismatch between characteristics required by available jobs and characteristics possessed by the unemployed labour.

substitute Any good that can be used in place of another good to satisfy similar needs or desires. The degree of substitutability is measured by the magnitude of the positive cross elasticity between the two goods.

substitution effect A change in the quantity of a good demanded resulting from a change in its relative price (while holding constant real income).

supply The entire relationship between the quantity of some commodity that producers wish to sell (per period of time) and the price of that commodity, other things being equal.

supply curve The graphical representation of the relationship between the quantity of some commodity that producers wish to sell (per period of time) and the price of that commodity, other things being equal.

supply inflation A rise in the price level originating from increases in costs that are not caused by excess demand in the domestic markets for factors of production.

supply of labour The total number of hours of work that the population is willing to supply. Also called the *supply of effort*.

supply of money See *money supply*.

supply schedule A table showing the relationship between the quantity of some commodity that producers wish to sell (per period of time) and the price of that commodity, other things being equal.

tacit collusion Collusion that takes place with no explicit agreements. See *collusion*.

takeover The purchase of one firm by another.

takeover bid See *tender offer*.

target reserve ratio The fraction of its deposits that a commercial bank wants to hold as reserves.

tariff A tax applied on imports.

tax bracket A range of income for which there is a constant marginal tax rate.

tax expenditures Tax provisions, such as exemptions and deductions from taxable income and tax credits, that are designed to induce market responses considered to be desirable. They are called expenditures because they have the same effect as directly spending money to induce the desired behaviour.

tax incidence The location of the burden of a tax; that is, the identity of the ultimate bearer of the tax.

tax-related incomes policy (TIP) Tax incentives for labour and management to encourage them to conform to wage and price guidelines.

tax-rental arrangements An agreement by which the federal government makes a per capita payment to the provinces for the right to collect income taxes.

technological change Any change in the available techniques of production.

tender offer A time-limited offer to buy some or all of the outstanding common stock of a corporation from its stockholders at a specified price per share in an attempt to gain control of the corporation. Also called *takeover bid*.

term See *term to maturity*.

term deposit An interest-earning bank deposit, legally subject to notice before withdrawal (in practice, the notice requirement is not normally enforced) and until recently not transferable by cheque. Also called *savings deposit* and *time deposit*.

terms of trade The ratio of the average price of a country's exports to the average price of its imports, both averages usually being measured by index numbers; it is the quantity of imported goods that can be obtained per unit of goods exported.

term to maturity The period of time from the present to the redemption date of a bond. Also called simply the *term*.

time-series data A set of measurements or observations made repeatedly at successive periods (or moments) of time.

total cost (TC) The total cost to the firm of producing any given level of output; it can be divided into *total fixed costs* and *total variable costs*.

total fixed cost *(TFC)* All costs of production that do not vary with level of output.

total product *(TP)* Total amount produced by a firm during some time period.

total revenue *(TR)* Total receipts from the sale of a product; price times quantity.

total utility The total satisfaction resulting from the consumption of a given commodity or group of commodities by a consumer in a period of time.

total variable cost *(TVC)* Total costs of production that vary directly with level of output.

tradable emission permits Government-granted rights to emit specific amounts of specified pollutants that private firms may buy and sell among themselves.

trade balance See *balance of trade.*

trade creation A consequence of reduced trade barriers among a set of countries (typically signatories to a free trade agreement) whereby trade within the group is increased and trade with the rest of the world remains roughly constant. Thus the increase in trade among group members is an increase in total world trade.

trade diversion A consequence of reduced trade barriers among a set of countries whereby trade within the group replaces trade that used to take place with countries outside the group.

trade policy A government's policy involving restrictions placed on international trade. Also called *commercial policy.*

trade union See *union.* Also called *labour union.*

transactions balances Money balances held to finance payments because payments and receipts are not perfectly synchronized.

transactions costs Costs incurred in effecting market transactions (such as negotiation costs, billing costs, and bad debts).

transfer payment A payment to a private person or institution that does not arise out of current productive activity; typically made by governments, as in welfare payments, but also made by businesses and private individuals in the form of charitable contributions.

transmission mechanism The channels by which a change in the demand or supply of money leads to a shift of the aggregate demand curve.

transnational corporations *(TNCs)* Firms that have operations in more than one country. Also called *multinational enterprises (MNEs).*

treasury bill The conventional form of short-term government debt. A promise to pay a certain sum of money at a specified time in the future (usually 90 days to 1 year from date of issue).

two-part tariff A method of charging for a good or a service, usually a utility such as electricity, in which the consumer pays a flat access fee and a specified amount per unit purchased.

U See *unemployment.*

undistributed profits Earnings of a firm that are not distributed to shareholders as dividends but are retained by the firm. Also called *retained earnings.*

unemployment The number of persons 15 years of age and older who are not employed and are actively searching for a job, denoted *U.*

unemployment rate Unemployment expressed as a percentage of the labour force.

union An association of workers authorized to represent them in bargaining with employers. Also called *trade union* and *labour union.*

unit cost Cost per unit of output, equal to total cost divided by total output. Also called *average total cost.*

utility The satisfaction that a consumer receives from consuming some good or service.

value added The value of a firm's output minus the value of the inputs that it purchases from other firms.

variable Any well-defined item, such as the price of a commodity or its quantity, that can take on various specific values.

variable factor An input that can be varied by any desired amount in the short run.

very-long run A period of time that is long enough for the technological possibilities available to a firm to change.

voluntary export restriction *(VER)* An agreement by an exporting country to limit the amount of a good exported to another country.

wage and price controls Direct government intervention into wage and price formation with legal power to enforce the government's decisions on wages and prices.

wealth The sum of all assets minus liabilities.

withdrawals Income earned by households and not passed on to firms in return for goods and services purchased, and income earned by firms and not passed on to households in return for factor services purchased.

X See *exports.*

TIME LINE OF GREAT ECONOMISTS

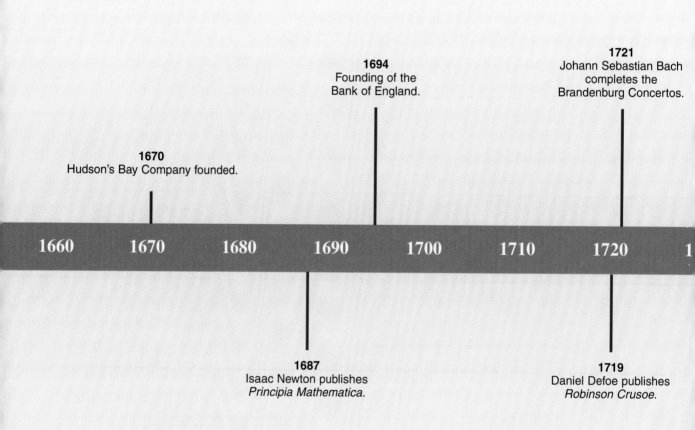

1721
Johann Sebastian Bach
completes the
Brandenburg Concertos.

1694
Founding of the
Bank of England.

1670
Hudson's Bay Company founded.

1660 1670 1680 1690 1700 1710 1720 1

1687
Isaac Newton publishes
Principia Mathematica.

1719
Daniel Defoe publishes
Robinson Crusoe.

Adam Smith (1723–1790)

Adam Smith was born in Kircaldy, Scotland and was raised by his mother alone, as his father had died before his birth. His intellectual promise was discovered early and Smith was sent to study at Oxford, after which he returned to Scotland, obtaining an appointment as professor of moral philosophy. Smith became one of the leading philosophers of his day and lectured on natural theology, ethics, jurisprudence, and political economy to students who travelled from as far as Russia to hear his lectures.

In 1759, Smith published *The Theory of Moral Sentiments,* his attempt to identify the origins of moral judgment. It is here that Smith writes of the motivation of self-interest and of the morality which holds it in abeyance. After its publication, Smith left his post at the university to embark on a grand European tour as a tutor to a young aristocrat. He returned to Scotland in 1766 and lived the remainder of his life in scholarly retirement. During this time Smith wrote *An Inquiry into the Nature and Causes of The Wealth of Nations* (1776), which was to become the foundation for much of modern economics and which continues to be reprinted today.

The three main features of Smith's analysis are the division of labour, the analysis of price and allocation, and the nature of economic growth. Smith was able to incorporate these concepts into a framework for analyzing the economic questions of income growth, value, and distribution. This intellectual contribution to economic thought was made at a time when national outputs of Great Britain and Europe were increasing and the industrial revolution was in its early stages. Smith's idea of a self-regulating economy operating within a market system was a new one in the mid-eighteenth century and propelled economic inquiry onto an entirely new path.

Smith's work also marked the beginning of what is called the Classical period in economic thought, which continued for the next 75 years. This school of thought was centred on the principles of natural liberty (laissez-faire) and the importance of economic growth as a means of bettering the conditions of human existence.

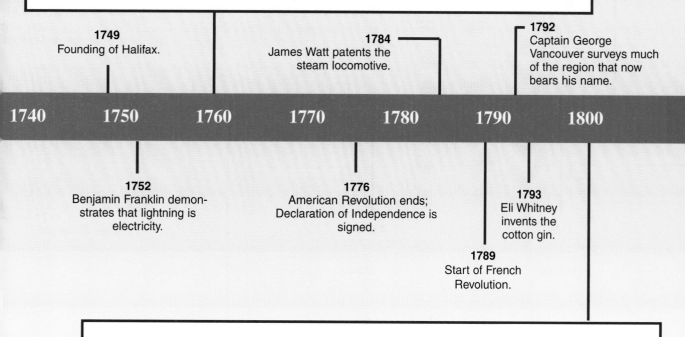

1749
Founding of Halifax.

1784
James Watt patents the steam locomotive.

1792
Captain George Vancouver surveys much of the region that now bears his name.

1740   1750   1760   1770   1780   1790   1800

1752
Benjamin Franklin demonstrates that lightning is electricity.

1776
American Revolution ends; Declaration of Independence is signed.

1793
Eli Whitney invents the cotton gin.

1789
Start of French Revolution.

Thomas Malthus (1766–1834)

Thomas Malthus was born into a reasonably well-to-do English family. He was educated at Cambridge and from 1805 until his death he held the first British professorship of political economy in the East India Company's college at Haileybury. In 1798 he published *An Essay on the Principle of Population as it Affects the Future Improvement of Society,* which was revised many times in subsequent years until finally he published *A Summary View of the Principle of Population* in 1830.

It is these essays on population for which Malthus is best known. His first proposition was that population, when unchecked, would increase in a geometric progression such that the population would double every twenty-five years. His second proposition was that the means of subsistence (i.e., the food supply) cannot possibly increase faster than in arithmetic progression (increasing by a given number of units every year). The result would be population growth eventually outstripping food production, and thus abject poverty and suffering for the majority of people in every society.

Malthus's population theory had tremendous intellectual influence at the time and became an integral part of the Classical theory of income distribution. However, it is no longer taken as a good description of current or past trends.

David Ricardo (1772–1823)

David Ricardo was born in London to parents who had immigrated from the Netherlands. Ricardo's father was very successful in money markets and Ricardo himself had earned enough money on the stock exchange that he was very wealthy before he was thirty. He had little formal education, but after reading Adam Smith's *The Wealth of Nations* in 1799, he chose to divide his time between studying and writing about political economy and increasing his own personal wealth.

Ricardo's place in the history of economics was assured by his achievement in constructing an abstract model of how capitalism worked. He built an analytic "system" using deductive reasoning that characterizes economic theorizing to the present day. The three critical principles in Ricardo's system were (1) the theory of rent, (2) Thomas Malthus's population principle, and (3) the wages-fund doctrine. Ricardo published *The Principles of Political Economy and Taxation* in 1817, which dominated Classical economics for the following half-century.

Ricardo also contributed the concept of comparative advantage to the study of international trade. Ricardo's theories regarding the gains from trade had some influence on the repeal of the British Corn Laws in 1846—tariffs on the importation of grains into Great Britain—and the subsequent transformation of that country during the nineteenth century from a country of high tariffs to one of completely free trade.

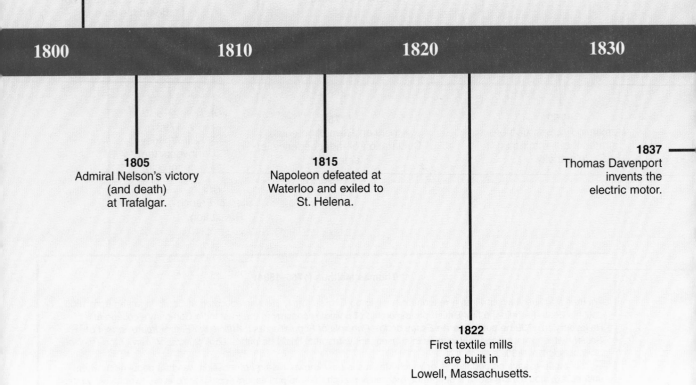

1837
Rebellions in
Upper and
Lower Canada

1800   **1810**   **1820**   **1830**

1805
Admiral Nelson's victory
(and death)
at Trafalgar.

1815
Napoleon defeated at
Waterloo and exiled to
St. Helena.

1837
Thomas Davenport
invents the
electric motor.

1822
First textile mills
are built in
Lowell, Massachusetts.

Karl Marx (1818–1883)

Karl Marx was born in Trier, Germany (then part of Prussia) and studied law, history, and philosophy at the universities of Bonn, Berlin, and Jena. Marx travelled between Prussia, Paris, and Brussels where he worked at various jobs until finally settling in London in 1849 where he lived the remainder of his life. Most of his time was spent in the mainly unpaid pursuits of writing and studying economics in the library of the British Museum. Marx's contributions to economics are intricately bound to his views of history and society. *The Communist Manifesto* was published with Friedrich Engels in 1848, his *Critique of Political Economy* in 1859 and in 1867 the first volume of *Das Kapital*. (The remaining volumes, edited by Engels, were published after Marx's death.)

For Marx, capitalism was a stage in an evolutionary process from a primitive agricultural economy toward an inevitable elimination of private property and the class structure. Marx's "labour theory of value" held the central place in his economic thought, whereby the quantity of labour used in the manufacture of a product determined its value. He believed that the worker provided "surplus value" to the capitalist. The capitalist would then use the profit arising from this surplus value to reinvest in plant and machinery. Through time, more would be spent on plant and machinery than for wages, which would lead to lower profits (since profits only arose from the surplus value from labour) and a resulting squeeze in the real income of workers. Marx believed that in the capitalists' effort to maintain profits in this unstable system, there would emerge a "reserve army of the unemployed." The resulting class conflict would become increasingly acute until revolution by the workers would overthrow capitalism.

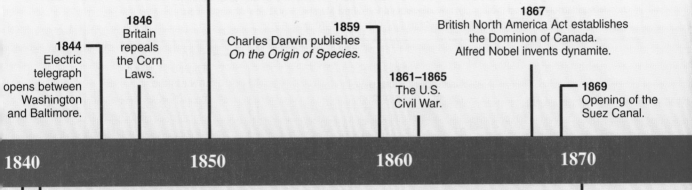

1844 Electric telegraph opens between Washington and Baltimore.

1846 Britain repeals the Corn Laws.

1859 Charles Darwin publishes *On the Origin of Species.*

1861–1865 The U.S. Civil War.

1867 British North America Act establishes the Dominion of Canada. Alfred Nobel invents dynamite.

1869 Opening of the Suez Canal.

1840   1850   1860   1870

1840 Act of Union unites Upper and Lower Canada.

John Stuart Mill (1806–1873)

John Stuart Mill was born in London and was the son of James Mill, a prominent British historian, economist and philosopher. By the age of twelve he was acquainted with the major economics works of the day and at thirteen he was correcting the proofs of his father's book, *Elements of Political Economy.* J. S. Mill spent most of his life working at the East India Company—his extraordinarily prolific writing career was conducted entirely as an aside. In 1848 he published his *Principles of Political Economy,* which updated the principles found in Adam Smith's *The Wealth of Nations* and which remained the basic textbook for students of economics until the end of the 19th century. In *Principles,* Mill made an important contribution to the economics discipline by distinguishing between the economics of production and of distribution. He was able to point out that economic laws had nothing to do with the distribution of wealth, which was a societal matter, but had everything to do with production.

Previous to Mill's *Principles* was his *A System of Logic* (1843), which was the century's most influential text on logic and the theory of knowledge. His essays on ethics, contemporary culture, and freedom of speech, such as *Utilitarianism* and *On Liberty,* are still widely studied today.

Leon Walras (1834–1910)

Leon Walras was born in France, and was the son of an economist. After being trained inauspiciously in engineering and performing poorly in mathematics, Walras spent some time pursuing other endeavours, such as novel writing and working for the railway. Eventually he promised his father he would study economics and by 1870 he was given a professorship in economics in the Faculty of Law at the University of Lausanne in Switzerland. Once there, Walras began the feverish activity that eventually led to his important contributions to economic theory.

In the 1870s, Walras was one of three economists to put forward the marginal utility theory of value (simultaneously with William Stanley Jevons of England and Carl Menger of Austria). Further, he constructed a mathematical model of general equilibrium using a system of simultaneous equations which he used to argue that equilibrium prices and quantities are uniquely determined. Central to general equilibrium analysis is the notion that the prices and quantities of all commodities are determined simultaneously because the whole system is interdependent. Walras's most important work was *Elements of Pure Economics* published in 1874. In addition to all of Walras's other accomplishments in economics (and despite his early poor performance in mathematics!), we today regard him as the founder of mathematical economics.

Leon Walras and Alfred Marshall are regarded by many economists to be the two most important economic theorists who ever lived. Much of the framework of economic theory studied today is either Walrasian or Marshallian in character.

Carl Menger (1840–1921)

Carl Menger was born in Galicia (then part of Austria) and he came from a family of Austrian civil servants and army officers. After studying law in Prague and Vienna, he turned to economics and in 1871 published *Grundsatze der Volkswirtschaftslehre* (translated as *Principles of Economics*) for which he became famous. He held a professorship at the University of Vienna until 1903. Menger was the founder of a school of thought known as the "Austrian School," which effectively displaced the German historical method on the continent and which survives today as an alternative to mainstream Neoclassical economics.

Menger was one of three economists in the 1870s who independently put forward a theory of value based on marginal utility. Prior to what economists now call the "marginal revolution," value was thought to be derived solely from the inputs of labour and capital. Menger developed the marginal utility theory of value in which the value of any good is determined by individuals' subjective evaluations of that good. According to Menger, a good has some value if it has the ability to satisfy some human want or desire, and *utility* is the capacity of the good to do so. Menger went on to develop the idea that the individual will maximize total utility at the point where the last unit of each good consumed provides equal utility—that is, where marginal utilities are equal.

Menger's emphasis on the marginal utility theory of value led him to focus on consumption rather than production as the determinant of price. That is, Menger focused only on the demand for goods and largely ignored the supply. It would remain for Alfred Marshall and Leon Walras to combine demand and supply for a more complete picture of price determination.

1885
The last spike is driven on the Canadian Pacific Railway.

1880
Thomas Edison invents the electric light bulb.

1876
Alexander Graham Bell invents the telephone.

1870	1875	1880	1885

Alfred Marshall (1842–1924)

Alfred Marshall was born in Clapham, England, the son of a bank cashier, and was descended from a long line of clerics. Marshall's father, despite intense effort, was unable to steer the young Marshall into the church. Instead, Marshall followed his passion for mathematics at Cambridge and chose economics as a field of study after reading J. S. Mill's *Principles of Political Economy*. His career was then spent mainly at Cambridge where he taught economics to John Maynard Keynes, Arthur Pigou, Joan Robinson and countless other British theorists in the "Cambridge tradition." His *Principles of Economics,* published in 1890, replaced Mill's *Principles* as the dominant economics textbook of English-speaking universities.

Marshall institutionalized modern marginal analysis, the basic concepts of supply and demand, and perhaps most importantly the notion of economic equilibrium resulting from the interaction of supply and demand. He also pioneered partial equilibrium analysis—examining the forces of supply and demand in a particular market provided that all other influences can be excluded, *ceteris paribus*.

Although many of the ideas had been put forward by previous writers, Marshall was able to synthesize the previous analyses of utility and cost and present a thorough and complete statement of the laws of demand and supply. Marshall refined and developed microeconomic theory to such a degree that much of what he wrote would be familiar to students of this textbook today.

It is also interesting to note that although Alfred Marshall and Leon Walras were simultaneously expanding the frontiers of economic theory, there was almost no communication between the two men. Though Marshall chose partial equilibrium analysis as the appropriate method for dealing with selected markets in a complex world, he did acknowledge the correctness of Walras's general equilibrium system. Walras, on the other hand, was adamant (and sometimes rude) in his opposition to the methods that Marshall was putting forward. History has shown that both the partial and the general equilibrium approaches to economic analysis are required for understanding the functioning of the economy.

Thorstein Veblen (1857–1929)

Thorstein Veblen was born on a farm in Wisconsin to Norwegian parents. He received his Ph.D. in philosophy from Yale University, after which he returned to his father's farm because he was unable to secure an academic position. For seven years he remained there, reading voraciously on economics and other social sciences. Eventually, he took academic positions at the University of Chicago, Stanford University, the University of Missouri, and the New School for Social Research (in New York). Veblen was the founder of "institutional economics," the only uniquely North American school of economic thought.

In 1899, Veblen published *The Theory of the Leisure Class*, in which he sought to apply Charles Darwin's evolutionism to the study of modern economic life. He examined problems in the social institutions of the day, and savagely criticized Classical and Neoclassical economic analysis. Although Veblen failed to shift the path of mainstream economic analysis, he did contribute the idea of the importance of long-run institutional studies as a useful complement to short-run price theory analysis. He also reminded the profession that economics is a *social* science, and not merely a branch of mathematics.

Veblen remains most famous today for his idea of "conspicuous consumption." He observed that some commodities were consumed not for their intrinsic qualities but because they carried snob appeal. He suggested that the more expensive such a commodity became, the greater might be its ability to confer status on its purchaser.

1889–1902
South African
(Boer) War.

1896
Klondike
gold rush.

1890	1895	1900	1905

1903
The Wright Brothers'
first successful
flight.

Vilfredo Pareto (1848–1923)

Vilfredo Pareto was an Italian, born in Paris, and was trained to be an engineer. Though he actually practiced as an engineer, he would later succeed Leon Walras to the Chair of Economics in the Faculty of Law at the University of Lausanne.

Pareto built upon the system of general equilibrium that Walras had developed. In his *Cours d'économie politique* (1897) and his *Manuel d'économie politique* (1906) Pareto set forth the foundations of modern welfare economics. He showed that theories of consumer behaviour and exchange could be constructed on assumptions of ordinal utility, rather than cardinal, eliminating the need to compare one person's utility with another's. Using the indifference curve analysis developed by F. Y. Edgeworth, Pareto was able to demonstrate that total welfare could be increased by an exchange if one person could be made better off without anyone else becoming worse off. Pareto applied this analysis to consumption and exchange, as well as to production. Pareto's contributions in this area are remembered in economists' references to *Pareto optimality* and *Pareto efficiency*.

Joseph Schumpeter (1883–1950)

Joseph Schumpeter was born in Triesch, Moravia (now in the Czech Republic). He was a university professor, later a Minister of Finance in Austria, and in 1932 he emigrated to the United States to avoid the rise to power of Adolf Hitler. He spent his remaining years at Harvard University.

Schumpeter was a pioneering theorist of innovation and emphasized the role of the entrepreneur in economic development. The existence of the entrepreneur meant continuous innovation and waves of adaptation to changing technology. He is best known for his theory of "creative destruction," where the prospect of monopoly profits provides owners the incentive to finance inventions and innovations. One monopoly can replace another with superior technology or a superior product, thereby circumventing the entry barriers of a monopolized industry. He criticized mainstream economists for emphasizing the static (allocative) efficiency of perfect competition—a market structure which would, if it could ever be achieved, retard technological change and economic growth.

Schumpeter's best known works are *The Theory of Economic Development* (1911), *Business Cycles* (1939), and *Capitalism, Socialism and Democracy* (1943).

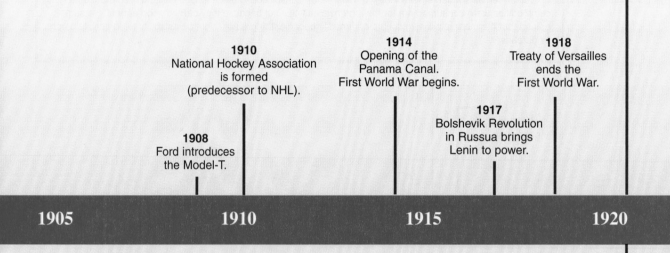

1910
National Hockey Association is formed (predecessor to NHL).

1914
Opening of the Panama Canal. First World War begins.

1918
Treaty of Versailles ends the First World War.

1917
Bolshevik Revolution in Russua brings Lenin to power.

1908
Ford introduces the Model-T.

1905 **1910** **1915** **1920**

John Maynard Keynes (1883–1946)

John Maynard Keynes was born in Cambridge, England. His parents were both intellectuals and his father, John Neville Keynes, was a famous logician and writer on economic methodology. The young Keynes was educated at Eton and then at Kings College, Cambridge, where he was a student of Alfred Marshall and Arthur Pigou. His career included appointments to the Treasury in Britain during both the First and Second World Wars, a leading role in the establishment of the International Monetary Fund (through discussions at Bretton Woods, New Hampshire, in 1944), editorship of the *Economic Journal* from 1911 to 1945, all in addition to his academic position at Kings College.

Keynes published extensively during his life but his most influential work, *The General Theory of Employment, Interest, and Money,* appeared in 1936. This book was published in the midst of the Great Depression when the output of goods and services had fallen drastically, unemployment was intolerably high and it had become clear to many that the market would not self-adjust to achieve potential output within an acceptable period of time. Fluctuations in economic activity were familiar at this point, but the failure of the economy to recover rapidly from this depression was unprecedented. Neoclassical economists held that during a downturn both wages and the interest rate would fall low enough to induce investment and employment and cause an expansion. They believed that the persistent unemployment during the 1930s was caused by inflexible wages and they recommended that workers be convinced to accept wage cuts.

Keynes believed that this policy, though perhaps correct for a single industry, was not correct for the entire economy. Widespread wage cuts would reduce the consumption portion of aggregate demand which would offset any increase in employment. Keynes argued that unemployment could only be cured by manipulating aggregate demand, whereby increased demand (through government expenditure) would increase the price level, reduce real wages, and thereby stimulate employment.

Keynes's views found acceptance after the publication of his *General Theory* and had a profound effect on government policy around the world, particularly in the 1940s, 1950s, and 1960s. As we know from this textbook, Keynes's name is attached to much of macroeconomics, from much of the basic theory to the Keynesian short-run aggregate supply curve and the Keynesian consumption function. His contributions to economics go well beyond what can be mentioned in a few paragraphs—for, in effect, he laid the foundations for modern macroeconomics.

Edward Chamberlin (1899–1967)

Edward Chamberlin was born in La Conner, Washington and received his Ph.D. from Harvard University in 1927. He became a full professor at Harvard in 1937 and stayed there until his retirement in 1966. He published *The Theory of Monopolistic Competition* in 1933.

Before Chamberlin's book (which appeared more-or-less simultaneously with Joan Robinson's *The Economics of Imperfect Competition*), the models of perfect competition and monopoly had been fairly well worked out. Though economists were aware of a middle ground between these two market structures and some analysis of duopoly (two sellers) had been presented, it was Chamberlin and Robinson that closely examined this problem of imperfect markets.

Chamberlin's main contribution was explaining the importance of product differentiation for firms in market structures between perfect competition and monopoly. Chamberlin saw that though there may be a large number of firms in the market (the competitive element), each firm created for itself a unique product or advantage that gave it some control over price (the monopoly element). Specifically, he identified items such as copyrights, trademarks, brand names, and location as monopoly elements behind a product. Though Alfred Marshall regarded price as the only variable in question, Chamberlin saw both price and the product itself as variables under control of the firm in monopolistically competitive markets.

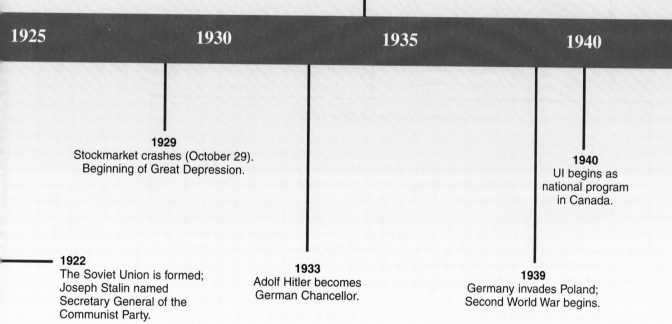

1925   1930   1935   1940

1929
Stockmarket crashes (October 29).
Beginning of Great Depression.

1940
UI begins as
national program
in Canada.

1922
The Soviet Union is formed;
Joseph Stalin named
Secretary General of the
Communist Party.

1933
Adolf Hitler becomes
German Chancellor.

1939
Germany invades Poland;
Second World War begins.

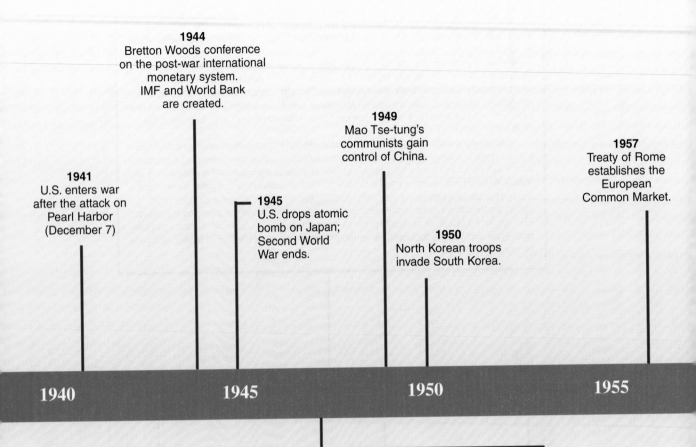

1944
Bretton Woods conference
on the post-war international
monetary system.
IMF and World Bank
are created.

1949
Mao Tse-tung's
communists gain
control of China.

1957
Treaty of Rome
establishes the
European
Common Market.

1941
U.S. enters war
after the attack on
Pearl Harbor
(December 7)

1945
U.S. drops atomic
bomb on Japan;
Second World
War ends.

1950
North Korean troops
invade South Korea.

1940   1945   1950   1955

Friedrich August von Hayek (1899–1992)

Friedrich von Hayek was born in Vienna and studied at the University of Vienna where he was trained in the Austrian tradition of economics (a school of thought originating with Carl Menger). He held academic positions at the London School of Economics and the University of Chicago. He returned to Europe in 1962 to the University of Freiburg in what was then West Germany and the University of Salzburg in Austria. He was awarded the Nobel Prize in Economics in 1974.

Hayek contributed new ideas and theories in many different areas of economics but he is perhaps best known for his general conception of economics as a "coordination problem." His observation of market economies suggested that the relative prices determined in free markets provided the signals that allowed the actions of all decision makers to mesh—even though there was no formal planning taking place to coordinate these actions. He emphasized this "spontaneous order" at work in the economy as the subject matter for economics. The role of knowledge and information in the market process became central to Hayek, an idea which has grown in importance to the economics profession over the years.

Hayek's theory of business cycles provided an example of the breakdown of this coordination. A monetary disturbance (e.g., an increase in the money supply) would distort the signals (relative prices) by artificially raising the return to certain types of economic activity. When the disturbance disappeared, the boom caused by these distorted signals would be followed by a slump. Although Hayek's business-cycle theory was eclipsed by the Keynesian revolution, his emphasis on economics as a coordination problem has had a major influence on contemporary economic thought.

Hayek was also prominent in advocating the virtues of free markets as contributing to human freedom in the broad sense as well as to economic efficiency in the narrow sense. His *The Road to Serfdom* (1944) sounded an alarm about the political and economic implications of the then-growing belief in the virtues of central planning. His *Constitution of Liberty* (1960) is a much deeper philosophical analysis of the forces, economic and otherwise, that contribute to the liberty of the individual.

1959
Fidel Castro
overthrows
Fulgencio Batista
in Cuba.

INDEX

Note: A page number followed by n indicates material found in footnotes.